Elements of Statistics

WITH APPLICATIONS TO ECONOMIC DATA

By

HAROLD T. DAVIS

Professor of Mathematics
Indiana University

and

Mathematician of the Cowles Commission
for Research in Economics

and

W. F. C. NELSON

Economist of the Cowles Commission
for Research in Economics

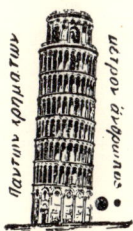

THE PRINCIPIA PRESS, INC.
Bloomington, Indiana

COPYRIGHT, 1935

BY

THE COWLES COMMISSION FOR RESEARCH IN ECONOMICS

THE DENTAN PRINTING CO.,
COLORADO SPRINGS, COLORADO

To
Alfred Cowles of Chicago
In Grateful Recognition
of His Interest in Economic Research

TABLE OF CONTENTS

CHAPTER I
PRELIMINARY ANALYSIS OF STATISTICAL DATA

		Page
1.	Introduction	1
2.	The Origins of Statistics	2
3.	Statistics in Economics	4
4.	The Scope of Statistical Science	9
5.	The Object of the Mathematical Theory of Statistics	10
6.	The Collection of Statistical Data	11
7.	Sources of Statistical Data	11
8.	The Classification of Statistical Data	14
9.	Frequency Distribution	15
10.	The Graphical Representation of Frequency Distributions	19
11.	Ogives or Cumulative Frequency Curves	23
12.	Binomial Frequencies — The Binomial Theorem	29

CHAPTER II
THE GRAPHICAL ANALYSIS OF DATA — ELEMENTARY CURVE FITTING

1.	Functions	35
2.	Correlations	38
3.	The Graphical Representation of Functions	42
4.	The Straight Line	47
5.	Fitting a Straight Line to Data	47
6.	Use of Tables in Fitting a Straight Line to Data	50
7.	The Parabola	52
8.	Fitting the Parabola to Data	54
9.	The Exponential Curve	56
10.	The Skew-Normal Probability Curve	61
11.	The Translation of Axes	63

CHAPTER III
METHODS OF AVERAGING

1.	Six Averages	66
2.	Illustrative Data	66
3.	The Arithmetic Mean	67
4.	Transforming the Arithmetic Mean from One Set of Class Marks to Another	71
5.	The Root-Mean-Square or Quadratic Mean — Standard and Mean Deviations	73
6.	Transforming the Standard Deviation from One Set of Class Marks to Another	78
7.	Moments	79
8.	Sheppard's Adjustments	81
9.	The Median	83

		Page
10.	The Mode	86
11.	The Geometric Mean	89
12.	The Harmonic Average	93
13.	Relative Magnitude of the Averages of a Series of Positive Terms	96

CHAPTER IV
INDEX NUMBERS

1.	The Unstable Dollar	100
2.	The Price Index Problem	101
3.	Price Index Formulas	105
4.	The Time Reversal Test	108
5.	The Factor Reversal Test	109
6.	Fisher's Ideal Index Number	111
7.	Types of Bases	112
8.	Some Practical Considerations Concerning the Making of Index Numbers	114
9.	Miscellaneous Applications	117

CHAPTER V
THE ANALYSIS OF TIME SERIES

1.	Historical Note	119
2.	Secular Trend	121
3.	Seasonal Variation	124
4.	Correction for Seasonal Variation and Secular Trend	129
5.	The Correlation of Time Series	132
6.	Harmonic Analysis	137

CHAPTER VI
ANALYSIS OF ARTIFICIAL DATA—PROBABILITY

1.	Definition of Probability	146
2.	Formulas from Permutations and Combinations	148
3.	Examples Illustrating the Calculation of Simple *a Priori* Probability	150
4.	The Multiplication of Probabilities	152
5.	The Addition of Probabilities	153
6.	Examples Illustrating the Multiplication and Addition of Probabilities	154
7.	The Law of Large Numbers	157
8.	Probability in Repeated Trials	159
9.	Mathematical Expectation	160
10.	Miscellaneous Examples	163

CHAPTER VII
BINOMIAL FREQUENCY DISTRIBUTIONS

1.	Binomial Frequencies	167
2.	Arithmetic Average and Standard Deviation of a Binomial Series	171
3.	The Calculation of the Mode for the Binomial Frequency Distribution	175
4.	Stirling's Formula	177
5.	Derivation of the Skew-Normal Frequency Curve	178

TABLE OF CONTENTS

		Page
6.	The Skew-Normal Curve	181
7.	Application to the Graduation of Statistical Data	183

CHAPTER VIII
THE NORMAL FREQUENCY CURVE — PROBLEMS IN SAMPLING

1.	The Meaning and Use of the Area Under the Normal Curve	187
2.	The Probable Error	190
3.	Probable Error Applied to Sampling	191
4.	Probable Errors of Various Statistical Constants	195
5.	Derivation of the Probable Error of the Mean	199
6.	A Measure of Goodness of Fit	202
7.	The Theory of Errors — Least Squares	206

CHAPTER IX
CURVE FITTING

1.	The Problem of Curve Fitting	211
2.	The Method of Least Squares	215
3.	Examples Illustrating the Method of Least Squares	218
4.	Simplification When the Curve is a Polynomial	226
5.	Fitting a Straight Line to Empirical Data	229
6.	Fitting a Parabola to Empirical Data	229
7.	The Simple Exponential	233
8.	The Method of Moments	239
9.	The Logistic Curve	240

CHAPTER X
ELEMENTS OF CORRELATION

1.	The Mathematical Theory of Drawing Conclusions	249
2.	The Correlation Coefficient	249
3.	The Correlation Table	257
4.	Calculation of the Coefficient of Correlation	263
5.	Lines of Regression	271
6.	Properties of the Correlation Coefficient	276
7.	The Correlation Surface	282
8.	Non-Linear Regression	283

CHAPTER XI
MULTIPLE AND PARTIAL CORRELATION

1.	Multiple Factors in Experience	289
2.	The Relationship Between Wheat Production, Acreage Planted, and Yield per Acre	290
3.	Partial Correlations	291
4.	Correlation Coefficients of Second Order	294
5.	Partial Regression Equations	297
6.	On the Accuracy of Estimate	300
7.	The Multiple Correlation Coefficient for Three Variables	301
8.	Multiple Correlation for Four Variables	303
9.	Appraisal of the Correlation Theory	304
10.	Extension to a Higher Number of Variables	305
11.	A Note on Linear Dependence	309

CHAPTER XII
TYPES OF STATISTICAL SERIES

	Page
1. Introduction	311
2. Excess or Kurtosis	312
3. The Lexis Ratio and the Charlier Coefficient of Disturbancy	319
4. On a Probability Classification of Distributions	322
5. Testing the Series When the Items Are Not of Uniform Size	329
6. The Poisson-Bortkewitsch "Law of Small Numbers"	331
7. Conclusion	334

APPENDIX I

BIOGRAPHICAL NOTES ON EARLY MATHEMATICAL ECONOMISTS — 336

APPENDIX II
LOGARITHMS

1. A Note on Computation	343
2. The Laws of Exponents	343
3. Logarithms	344
4. Calculation by Logarithms	348
5. The Number e — The Exponential Series	354
6. The Logarithmic Series	356

APPENDIX III
THE USE OF TABLES

1. Interpolation	359
2. Inverse Interpolation	361
3. The Calculation of Areas	362
4. References	364

TABLES

Some Useful Constants		366
Table I.	Five Place Logarithms	367
Table II.	Values of The Functions, $y = e^x$, $y = e^{-x}$	385
Table III.	Squares	387
Table IV.	Square Roots	389
Table V.	Reciprocals	395
Table VI.	The Probability Function, $y = \dfrac{1}{\sqrt{2\pi}} e^{-\frac{1}{2}t^2}$	397
Table VII.	Values of $I(t)$, The Area under the Probability Curve	398
Table VIII.	The Pearson Probability, P, (Test for Goodness of Fit)	399
Table IX.	Coefficients for Fitting a Straight Line to Data	406
Table X.	Coefficients for Fitting a Parabola to Data	408
ANSWERS TO PROBLEMS		410
INDEX OF NAMES		419
INDEX OF SUBJECTS		421

PREFACE

In 1932 the Social Science Research Council appointed a committee[1] to define the place of collegiate mathematics in the social sciences. The report of this committee urged that students of the social sciences be prepared for the study of statistics by a six to nine semester hour course covering logarithms, graphs, interpolation, equations and forms of important curves, probability, elements of differential and integral calculus, and curve fitting. The report also suggested that "illustrations from the social sciences should be used freely, and *the concepts and processes should be presented in such a manner as to make clear their application in the social sciences.*" The committee concluded that statistics courses might thus be utilized to carry the student much farther in the knowledge of statistical methods, and their possibilities and limitations.

In the development of this book, the authors have had these recommendations in mind, and have prepared a text suitable for a six semester hour course to follow such a course in mathematical analysis as that urged by the committee. While fully indorsing the recommendations of the committee, the authors realize that the instructor will in many cases be faced by the necessity of teaching classes lacking the desired preparation in mathematics. Therefore, this book has been designed for use in several ways. Algebraic processes are given in full. While the proofs do not presuppose a knowledge of the calculus, many of them are necessarily based on its principles. Therefore, for classes which have had a survey course in mathematics, or a course in calculus, the instructor may easily associate the proofs with the corresponding calculus proofs.

For those who have had preliminary training in college algebra, all parts of this text may be used, but it will probably be found necessary, in a six semester hour course, to reduce somewhat the amount of material assigned by the omission of Chapter XII, the application of Sheppard's corrections to frequency distribution

---

[1] This committee was composed of H. R. Tolley of the University of California (chairman), F. L. Griffin of Reed College, Holbrook Working of Leland Stanford University, Charles H. Titus of the University of California at Los Angeles, and Mordecai Ezekiel of the Federal Farm Board. The report of the committee was read at a joint meeting of the Econometric Society and Sections A and K of the American Association for the Advancement of Science at Syracuse, New York, June 22, 1932, and published in *Econometrica*, Vol. I, (1933), pages 197-204.

(sec. 8, Chapter III), the proof of the relative magnitude of averages (sec. 13, Chapter III), harmonic analysis (sec. 6, Chapter V), the derivation of the skew-normal probability curve from a binomial distribution (sec. 5, Chapter VII), the derivation of the probable error of the mean (sec. 5, Chapter VIII), the theory of the logistic curve (sec. 9, Chapter IX), and non-linear regression (sec. 8, Chapter X). For classes which have had no college mathematics whatever, the text may be used as an introduction to elementary statistics through the omission of Chapters IX and XI, as well as the parts indicated above for those with preliminary training in college algebra.

The illustrative materials and problems have been taken chiefly from data of economic significance. This lends, we believe, an atmosphere of coherence to the development such as is not attained when materials from a variety of disparate and unrelated disciplines are introduced in a capricious succession. The very pronounced drift in our day to a more fully quantitative science of economics would also seem to encourage such a concentration. In addition, the authors' connection with the Cowles Commission for Research in Economics afforded opportunity for access to a variety of economic materials and original research.

It need hardly be remarked, of course, that most of statistical methodology is the same, whether it is being applied to materials from economics or education or physics or astronomy. Thus, even though a student of the present volume should find his major interest in a field other than economics, by a study of this text containing economic applications he will obtain a training in statistical methodology adequate for his own field.

Some apology is perhaps necessary for the omission of a bibliography. Literature on the subject of probability and statistics has increased with bewildering rapidity in the last few years, and to give an adequate indication of this progress would outrun the scope and purpose of this volume. On the other hand, a condensed selection would do injustice by the inevitable omission of many fine works. The reader will find an extensive bibliography to 1924 in the *Handbook of Mathematical Statistics*, Boston, 1924, edited by H. L. Rietz, and a more recent one in *Studies in the History of Statistical Methods*, Baltimore, 1929, by Helen M. Walker. Contemporary developments are covered in such surveys as those of J. O. Irwin in the *Journal of the Royal Statistical Society*, Vol. 94 (1931), Vol. 95 (1932), Vol. 97 (1934); W. A. Shewhart and G. Darmois in *Econometrica*, Vol. I (1933) and II (1934); and Paul R. Rider in the *Journal of the American Statistical Association*,

Vol. XXX, No. 189 (March, 1935). Pertinent references, however, are carried in footnotes throughout the text.

The authors are under a heavy debt of gratitude to the Cowles Commission for Research in Economics and to its Director, Alfred Cowles 3rd, for having made available to them so much of the time, equipment, and conclusions, of the laboratory of the Commission. To Anne M. Lescisin and Forrest M. Danson, statisticians of the Commission, we are indebted for a multitude of helpful suggestions. Professor Charles F. Roos of Colorado College and the Cowles Commission kindly read through the manuscript and many important additions and changes are due to his criticisms. Substantial assistance has also been rendered throughout by the statistical laboratory of Indiana University, and the authors are indebted especially to Edward B. Morris, Richard E. Thompson, Harry F. Taylor and Mabel E. Inco. Responsibility for any errors which may appear is assumed by the authors alone.

HAROLD T. DAVIS,
W. F. C. NELSON.

CHAPTER I

Preliminary Analysis of Statistical Data

1. Introduction. The value of any particular course of study is enhanced if the student comprehends its scope and purpose and the relationship it bears to the rest of his training. Unless his endeavors are thus integrated into some significant pattern, each course becomes merely an isolated and irrelevant episode in a general confusion, and his efforts may be rendered futile because they lack direction. In this book it is assumed that the student's major interest is economics. What part does such a book as this play in advancing him towards his ultimate objective, which is the mastery of the processes and results of that science?

This volume seeks to set forth the mathematical theory of elementary statistics and to illustrate elementary statistical methodology through applications to data of economic significance. One is obviously concerned, therefore, with mathematics, statistics, and economics. The juxtaposition of these three disciplines is entirely natural. W. S. Jevons pointed out in 1871 (*Theory of Political Economy*, 1st. ed.) that, "It is clear that Economics, if it is to be a science at all, must be a mathematical one." Economics, he contended, must necessarily be mathematical, simply because it treats of quantities, and when the elements with which one deals are susceptible of being *greater* or *smaller*, their laws and relationships must inevitably be mathematical. In a brilliant discussion,[1] Joseph A. Schumpeter has amplified and reinforced Jevons' thesis.

"There is, however, one sense in which economics is the most quantitative, not only of 'social' or 'moral' sciences, but of all sciences, physics not excluded. For mass, velocity, current, and the like, can undoubtedly be measured, but in order to do so we must always invent a distinct process of measurement. This must be done before we can deal with these phenomena numerically. Some of the most fundamental economic facts, on the contrary, already present themselves to our observation as quantities made numerical by life itself. They carry meaning only by virtue of their nu-

---

[1] "The Common Sense of Econometrics," *Econometrica*, Vol. I (1933), pp. 5-12.

merical character. There would be movement even if we were unable to turn it into measurable quantity, but there cannot be prices independent of the numerical expression of every one of them, and of definite numerical relations among all of them. Econometrics is nothing but the explicit recognition of this rather obvious fact, and the attempt to face the consequences of it."

2. *The Origins of Statistics.* It has been only within comparatively recent times that the human race has realized the full importance of collecting and recording data relating to the phenomena of the physical and social universes. For many years the astronomers accumulated records of the motions of the heavenly bodies, and were thus enabled to make predictions about eclipses and to foretell the positions of the stars. The three laws relating to the motion of the planets, on which Sir Isaac Newton founded his theory of gravitation, were discovered by Johannes Kepler after a long study of the data collected by Tycho Brahe (1546-1601). This scientific method was adopted by men in other fields of science under the influence of Sir Francis Bacon (1561-1626), who asserted that a knowledge of nature could be obtained only by means of data collected from a study of the forms of nature. When it was observed that this method of enlarging knowledge was surprisingly fruitful in the physical sciences, men in political, social, and economic fields began to adopt a similar type of approach.

But, with the accumulation of data, need was soon felt for better methods of analyzing and interpreting the figures that had been collected. From this need the modern theory of statistics has gradually evolved over a period of more than a century.

Many definitions of the word *statistics* have been given, for example, the well known statement of G. U. Yule in his *Introduction to the Theory of Statistics*[1]: "By statistics we mean quantitative data affected to a marked extent by a multiplicity of causes. By statistical methods we mean methods specially adapted to the elucidation of quantitative data affected by a multiplicity of causes. By theory of statistics we mean the exposition of statistical method." Perhaps a good summary of the contents of the subject to be developed in the following pages may be made in the definition: "the *theory of statistics* comprises an analysis and interpretation of systematic collections of numbers relating to the enumeration of great classes."

The modern theory of statistics may be said to have been founded by the Belgian astronomer and statistician, L. A. J. Quete-

[1] 9th ed., London, 1929.

let (1796-1874). Before his time, statistical study had been carried on under the name of "political arithmetic" by Captain John Graunt of London (1620-1674), Sir William Petty (1623-1687), and J. P. Süssmilch (1707-1767), a Prussian clergyman. Quetelet advanced the theory that there existed an "average man" whose actions and ideas would "correspond to the average results obtained for society." All other men would diverge in greater or less degree from this theoretical average, and these variations could be treated by the method of errors in the theory of probability. Quetelet also emphasized the importance of the "law of large numbers" (see section 7, Chapter VI), which had been stated by Jakob Bernoulli (1654-1705) in his great work, *Ars Conjectandi*, published eight years after his death, and which had also been the subject of a paper by S. Poisson (1781-1840).

It will later be seen that the theory of statistics is highly indebted to the older theory of probability. This subject in its early history was largely an attempt to analyze the hazards of players in games of chance. G. Cardano (1501-1576), who was at the same time a mathematical genius and a gambler, wrote a treatise on games, in which he set forth rules by means of which one could protect himself against cheating. These rules were based upon the solution of problems now included in the theory of probability. After the real foundations of this subject had been laid in the work of Jakob Bernoulli and that of his nephew Daniel Bernoulli (1700-1782), who proposed the theory of "moral expectation" (see section 9, Chapter VI), Pierre Simon de Laplace (1749-1827) published in 1812 his great work on probability. It has been said that the theory of probability owes more to the work of Laplace than to that of any other man. Professor F. Y. Edgeworth, in the *Encyclopaedia Britannica* (13th ed.), remarks that, "as a comprehensive and masterly treatment of the subject as a whole, in its philosophical as well as mathematical character, there is nothing similar or second to Laplace's *Théorie analytique des probabilités*." The book is unfortunately very difficult to read, one reason being that the mathematical treatment is made to depend upon the theory of generatrix functions, a form of mathematical analysis now merged with what is called the theory of the Laplace transformation.

To enumerate all who have contributed to the subject matter of the theory of chance would be to record a majority of the prominent mathematical names of the last century. A. de Moivre (1667-1754), L. Euler (1707-1783), J. L. Lagrange (1736-1813), G. Chrystal (1851-1911), P. L. Tchebycheff (1821-1894), T. Bayes (d.

1761), I. Todhunter (1820-1884), K. F. Gauss (1777-1855), A. De Morgan (1806-1871), W. Lexis (1837-1914), H. Westergaard (b. 1853), C. Charlier (b. 1862), H. Poincaré (1854-1912), and E. Czuber (b. 1851), are particularly worthy of note.[1]

Upon the foundations laid by these men the theory of statistics was gradually constructed. In Germany, G. F. Knapp (1842-1926) and W. Lexis (1837-1914) made an exhaustive study of the statistics of mortality. Sir Francis Galton (1822-1911) was the pioneer for the epoch-making work of Karl Pearson (b. 1857) in the field of biometry. "The whole problem of evolution," to quote Pearson, "is a problem of vital statistics, —a problem of longevity, of fertility, of health, and of disease, and it is as impossible for the evolutionist to proceed without statistics as it would be for the Registrar-General to discuss the national mortality without an enumeration of the population, a classification of deaths, and a knowledge of statistical theory."

3. Statistics in Economics.[2] Statistics made its effective intrusion into the domain of economics rather late, though its primitive beginnings date from Sir William Petty's *Political Arithmetic* published in 1690. The fact that the older classical treatises on economics were comparatively destitute of statistical materials was the result of a compound of factors. The raw data were often scanty and occasionally contradictory. The dominance of the deductive method led to disinterest in the data for inductive approach, even when lip-service was paid to the value of "statistical verification." Also, there probably was some disposition (to quote Wagemann[3]) "to conceive (economic) premises in a complete vacuum .... to avoid the rude shocks which await them in the world of facts .... to shrink in terror from anything so rude and coarse as mere figures." It is difficult to assess the importance of these different considerations. The existence of a variety of statistical compilations and at least the beginnings of statistical technique in such lines as index numbers and harmonic analysis in the early nineteenth century

---

[1] For an extended account of the early history of probability, one should consult I. Todhunter, *A History of the Mathematical Theory of Probability From the Time of Pascal to That of Laplace*, Cambridge, 1865. For more recent developments, see Helen Walker, *Studies in the History of Statistical Method*, Baltimore, 1929.

[2] "Statistics and Economic Theory", by Warren M. Persons, in the *Review of Economic Statistics*, Vol. VII (1925), pp. 179-197, and Wesley C. Mitchell's *Business Cycles*, New York 1928, pp. 189-360, are comprehensive surveys of this subject, from which much of the material in this section is derived.

[3] *Economic Rhythm*, New York, 1930, p. 16.

should serve to minimize emphasis on the scarcity of materials and dearth of methodology.

On the other hand, it is not difficult to adduce verbal evidence of the place deductive writers allowed statistical evidence. J. S. Mill, for example, admitted the necessity of verification for conclusions deductively reached, indeed, "in some cases instead of deducing our conclusions from reasoning, and verifying them by observation, we begin by obtaining them provisionally from specific experience, and afterwards connect them with the principles of human nature by *a priori* reasoning." By 1871, W. S. Jevons had put the modern position forcibly. "The deductive science of economy must be verified and rendered useful by the purely inductive science of statistics. Theory must be invested with the reality and life of fact. Political economy might gradually be erected into an exact science, if only commercial statistics were far more complete and accurate than they are at present, so that the formulas could be endowed with exact meaning by the aid of numerical data." Most of any lingering hostility which some economists had borne to statistics had, by the end of the last century, been almost completely dissipated. By 1907 Alfred Marshall could write, "Disputes as to method have ceased. Qualitative analysis has done the greater part of its work . . . . . that is to say, there is general agreement as to the characters and durations of the changes which various economic forces tend to produce. Much less progress has been made towards the quantitative determination of the relative strength of different economic forces. That higher and more difficult task must wait upon the slow growth of thorough realistic statistics." In the same year Pareto wrote, "The progress of political economy in the future will depend in great part upon the investigation of empirical laws, derived from statistics, which will then be compared with known theoretical laws, or will suggest derivation from them of new laws."

Notwithstanding the fact that economists have never been uniformly unfavorable to the introduction of statistics into their science, and in the last generation have been notably friendly to the statistical approach, in running over the names of those who have contributed most to statistical theory it is not till Edgeworth is reached that an economist can be listed among those who have vitally forwarded the solution of statistical problems.

Since about 1890 two factors have combined to work a fundamental change in the position of statistics in economics. "The important developments of statistical methods—of probability, sampling, and curve-fitting; simple and partial correlation; periodicities and periodogram analysis; and index numbers—have occurred since the eighteen-eighties."[1] The improvement of statistical methods has coincided closely with the enlargement of statistical materials. The International Institute of Statistics was founded in 1885, the Census of Manufactures for the United States was greatly expanded in 1890, in 1902 the Census Bureau was made a permanent office of the government, and the first adequate investigation of American prices, a Senate Report, was issued in 1893. An expansion of data took place through those years which was not equalled till the time of the World War, which, for a variety of reasons, occasioned the publication of a wealth of fresh statistical information.

This happy conjunction of improved methods and expanded data about the close of the last century marks the real inception of statistics in economics.

For at least a hundred years, then, mathematics and statistics have occupied some place in economics. It is hardly pure coincidence that "most—and if we exclude historians, *all*—of those men whom we are justified in calling great economists invariably display a remarkably mathematical turn of mind, even when they are entirely ignorant of anything beyond the quantitative technique at the command of a school-boy; Quesnay, Ricardo, Böhm-Bawerk, are instances in point." [2]

The foundation of the Econometric Society in December 1930 was an explicit recognition of this century-old liaison among mathematics, statistics, and economics. The purpose of the Society, as officially defined, is "the advancement of economic theory in its relation to statistics and mathematics . . . . . . to promote studies that aim at a unification of the theoretical-quantitative and the empirical-quantitative approach to economic problems." The aim of econometrics is the formulation of a larger, more precise, and more realistic body of economic truth. Mathematics proves itself a useful agent in defining and refining economic concepts, and in carrying out involved processes of reasoning. It is an indispensible instrument of research. Statistics reduces general ideas to numerical conclusions, validates or destroys *a priori* notions, and often adduces unexpected conclusions which provoke fresh theoretical formulations.

In the econometric program, statistics has already played, and must continue to play, a large part. It is easily possible to envisage

---

[1] Persons, *loc. cit.*, p. 188.
[2] Schumpeter, *loc. cit.*, p. 6.

a "Statistical Theory of Econometrics." Such a study would be an exposition of economic theory in the measure that this theory has been subjected to statistical treatment. A glance at any text on economics would furnish a tentative outline. On Production, one might start with such studies as Carl Snyder's,[1] S. S. Kuznets',[2] and A. F. Burns'.[3] The literature of Cost Curves would be surveyed. Value and Price raise a host of statistical problems, chief of which is the measurement of Marginal Utility, as I. Fisher,[4] R. Frisch,[5] and F.V. Waugh,[6] for example, have attempted it. The mass of purely mathematical treatment of the problem would, of course, be outside the scope of a statistical study. Under Value and Price would be treated the literature of Demand Curves,[7] the methods used in their derivation, the conclusions reached, and the implications that rise from measurement of elasticities of demand. Money and Credit are instinct with statistics. The equation of exchange, embracing the work of I. Fisher[8] and others, would fall here. Prices, their determination, their fluctuations as measured by index numbers, the effects of these fluctuations on the level of real and dollar national income and their distribution, would all be encompassed. Under International Trade one would be concerned with such problems as the effect of production on prices as it has been treated statistically, for example, in H. Schultz's *Statistical Laws of Demand and Supply*.[9] Under Distribution appear studies of the type of Vilfredo Pareto's,[10] W. I. King's[11] and A. L. Bowley's,[12] with their appraisals of statistical formulations of income distribution. Interest raises further problems of the sort that are treated in I. Fisher's

---

[1] *Business Cycles and Business Measurements*, New York, 1927.

[2] *Secular Movements in Production and Prices*, New York, 1930.

[3] *Production Trends in the United States Since 1870*, New York, 1934.

[4] "A Statistical Method for Measuring Marginal Utility and Testing the Justice of a Progressive Income Tax," in *Economic Essays Contributed in Honor of John Bates Clark*, ed. by Jacob H. Hollander, New York, 1927.

[5] *New Methods of Measuring Marginal Utility*, Tübingen, J. C. B. Mohr, 1932.

[6] "The Marginal Utility of Money in the United States," *Econometrica*, Vol. III (1935).

[7] See the bibliography "Price Analysis", compiled by Louise O. Bercaw under the direction of Mary G. Lacy, *Econometrica*, Vol. II (1934), pp. 399-421.

[8] *The Purchasing Power of Money*, New York, 1913.

[9] Chicago, 1928.

[10] *Manuel d'économie politique* (2nd edition), Paris, 1927, pp. 384 ff.

[11] *The National Income and its Purchasing Power*, New York, 1930.

[12] "The Action of Economic Forces in Producing Frequency Distributions of Income, Prices, and Other Phenomena: A Suggestion for Study," *Econometrica*, Vol. I, 1933.

Theory of Interest.[1] These topics illustrate, but naturally do not define, the scope of such a work. Of course, a thorough evaluation of the historic work of W. S. Jevons,[2] V. Pareto,[2] H. L. Moore,[3] and others, would be involved, not to mention some appraisal of the current quantitative-theoretical contributions associated with the names of C. F. Roos,[4] J. M. Keynes,[5] G. F. Warren and F. A. Pearson,[6] Luigi Amoroso,[7] L. H. Bean,[7] Mordecai Ezekiel,[7] Jakob Marschak,[7] A. C. Pigou,[7] Hans Staehle,[7] J. Tinbergen,[7] Felice Vinci,[7] E. J. Working,[7] and others, including those previously mentioned. Such a "Statistical Theory of Econometrics" would not be merely economic statistics, and certainly not statistical methodology, but an exposition of economic theory as that theory had been developed, confirmed, challenged, or stultified, by statistical evidence or processes. The topics treated would be, for example, The Derivation of Demand Curves, The Implications of Elasticity, The Equation of Exchange, The Theory of Prices, The Measurement of Utility, The Effects of Protection, The Distribution of Income. If one compares these titles with those of this volume, Elementary Curve Fitting, Methods of Averaging, Index Numbers, Frequency Distributions, Elements of Correlation, something of the distinction between economic statistics and econometrics will be clear to him.

It does not require a violent effort of the imagination to see how statistical methods are indispensable tools in the more precise measurement and adequate interpretation of economic fact, and thus vitally forward the development of economic truth. Statistical technique bears something of the relation to econometrics that a machine tool does to an automobile. The second cannot be produced without the first. But the first derives its whole meaning from the second. It is possible to conceive of a mechanic's becoming so entranced with the beautiful and involved precision of his tool that he loved to manipulate it for its own sake, rather than to make automobiles. Statisticians are not immune from such temptation. It is important, therefore, while acquiring a mastery of statistical methodology, that one should always have his mind on

---

[1] New York, 1930.

[2] See Appendix I.

[3] e.g., *Generating Economic Cycles*, New York, 1923, and *Economic Cycles, Their Law and Cause*, New York, 1914.

[4] *Dynamic Economics*, Bloomington, Indiana, 1934.

[5] e.g., *A Treatise on Money*, New York, 1930.

[6] *Prices*, New York, 1933.

[7] See "Price Analysis," *loc. cit.*, for references.

his ultimate goal. Thus he can see the progress and direction of his efforts and probably arrive at his destination more easily and more quickly, because he knows where and why he is traveling.

In the effort to integrate mathematics and statistics with economics, the outstanding figures have been noted chiefly as mathematicians rather than as statisticians. If one may be allowed a rather crude distinction, it may be said that mathematical economics is concerned with quantities, and statistical economics with number. While, at first blush, it may seem odd to say that mathematics does not necessarily deal with numbers, on a moment's reflection one sees that this is true. It is said, and proved, that if one side of a plane triangle is greater than another, the angle opposite the greater side is greater than the angle opposite the lesser side. Here, in ordinary mathematics, is the expression of an important quantitative relationship made without any use of numbers.

Every branch of learning has its particular heroes, men who either founded their art or science, or whose genius so advanced and enriched it that they have earned a peculiar measure of veneration from all who followed them. Sir Isaac Newton (1642-1727) and James Clerk Maxwell (1831-1879) in physics, Johannes Kepler (1571-1630) and Pierre Simon de Laplace (1749-1827) in astronomy, Gregor Johann Mendel (1822-1884) and Charles Robert Darwin (1809-1882) in biology, Louis Pasteur (1822-1895) and Robert Koch (1843-1910) in bacteriology, would come within such a category. When we turn to econometrics, probably most of those familiar with the field would agree to list as its particular paragons A. A. Cournot, W. S. Jevons, M. E. L. Walras, V. Pareto, and F. Y. Edgeworth.[1]

4. The Scope of Statistical Science. The importance of a knowledge of statistics in any field of applied science is shown by the discoveries that have been made from an analysis of *empirical data,* that is to say, data derived from experience. One of the important achievements of the present century in astronomy, for example, has been the statistical analysis of stellar velocities and the discovery by J. C. Kapteyn (1851-1922) that there exist great streams of stars in our galaxy. These early researches have been greatly amplified and extended by modern astronomical statisti-

---

[1] It would seem appropriate, therefore, in a book to be studied by those who aspire to become econometricians, to give some biographical notice, however brief, of the men who first or most successfully turned the powerful apparatus of mathematics toward the solution of economic problems. This is attempted in Appendix I.

cians. The modern theory of the structure of the atom is highly indebted to the discussion by James Clerk Maxwell, an eminent English physicist, of the motion of a gas as a problem in dynamical statistics.

Modern biology, in particular as it is concerned with the subject of genetics, owes much to the theory of statistics as developed and applied in *Biometrika,* a scientific journal founded in England in 1901. Life insurance, as well as other forms of insurance, are familiar examples of the exact calculations that can be made when data associated with sufficiently large populations are collected and analyzed. It is of interest to remark that even the vagaries of such a capricious phenomenon as the weather do not lie outside the range of statistical methods.[1]

5. *The Object of the Mathematical Theory of Statistics.* It should be clearly understood by the student of statistics at the outset that there are really two points of view on the subject. On the one hand, the mathematical theory aims to set up an ideal model which will serve as a guide to the applied worker; on the other hand, the application of statistics calls for the actual manipulation of empirical or experimental data which are never exact, and often do not conform closely to the mathematical ideal. In these cases the judgment of the statistician plays an important rôle and an uninformed use of mathematical formulas may lead to serious error.

The aim of this book is to present the first point of view. Grave error often results from a lack of knowledge of the assumptions that underlie the mathematical formulas. Moreover, one's judgment in applied work is greatly aided by an appreciation of the limits of the mathematical model. All series of statistical frequencies are not normal, and yet many of the formulas used in practice are derived on the assumption that such normal frequencies are being discussed.

It is of real importance, therefore, that the student of statistics should review thoughtfully the mathematical foundations upon which the theory rests. A knowledge of the differential and integral calculus is indispensable if one wishes to acquire a thorough mastery of mathematical statistics and to appreciate the work of modern investigators. The elements of the theory, however, can

---

[1] For an instructive discussion of this problem consult: "Solar Radiation and Weather Forecasting" by C. F. Marvin and H. H. Kimball, *Journal of the Franklin Institute,* Vol. 202 (1926), pp. 273-306.

be grasped with a mathematical background of algebra, including especially logarithms,[1] the binomial theorem, a few types of series, and the elements of graphing. It is assumed that the student has a preliminary knowledge of these topics, which will be partially reviewed as need for them appears in the development of the subject.

6. *The Collection of Statistical Data.* No formal rules can be set down for the collection of statistical data, since the methods for obtaining facts about any field of knowledge depend almost wholly upon the problem that is being studied. Thus, if one is investigating the vital statistics of a community, he must turn to census reports and medical surveys; if he is studying a problem involving a city's commercial activities, he must rely upon reports furnished by impartial companies whose business it is to make such surveys.

In general, only two criteria need be applied to the data which one proposes to analyze. The data must be derived from a trustworthy source and they must be sufficiently comprehensive to give an accurate picture of the situation being studied.

The second criterion might be illustrated by means of an example. Suppose that the council of some city wishes to study the traffic problem at a busy street intersection. Would it be sufficient to employ a man to count the number of vehicles passing the corner during a single day? It is obvious that this would not supply trustworthy information, since the traffic varies with the seasons, with the days of the week, and with the hours of the day. But it is also clear that it would not be necessary to employ a man to count the number of vehicles for every hour of the day, every day, throughout an entire year. *Samples* taken judiciously at certain hours, and upon certain days, would be entirely adequate to represent the traffic population of the intersection.

7. *Sources of Statistical Data.* The collection of data thus furnishes a problem of its own. It will not be further treated in this book. It may be useful, however, to know a few general sources of relatively reliable economic data, and these are here enumerated, together with some slight indication of lines in which each is particularly helpful: [2]

---

[1] For the convenience of students, Appendix II, pages 343-358 gives a thorough discussion of logarithms.

[2] The student should consult *Source-Book of Statistical Data* (edition of 1923) prepared by the New York University Bureau of Business Research, published by Prentice-Hall, New York, for an excellent summary of economic source materials.

Bradstreet's (weekly), New York, prices and business.

Dun's Review (weekly), New York, prices and business.

Commercial and Financial Chronicle (weekly), New York, security quotations and an impressive mass of miscellaneous current statistics.

Wall Street Journal (daily), New York, security prices, corporation reports.

Journal of Commerce (daily), New York, or *New York Commercial* (daily), current banking, investment and business statistics, prices.

Survey of Current Business (monthly) and *Annual Supplement*, Department of Commerce, Washington, D. C., production, prices, trade, finance, transportation.

Monthly Summary of Foreign Commerce of the U. S. Department of Commerce, Washington, D. C., imports and exports.

Federal Reserve Bulletin (monthly), Washington, D. C., Reserve and member bank statistics, production, prices.

Annual Report of the Federal Reserve Board, Washington, D. C., currency and banking statistics.

Monthly Review of Business Conditions (Each of the twelve Federal Reserve Banks publishes a review of conditions in its district. Banking and business, in local districts).

Weather Crops and Markets (weekly), Department of Agriculture, Washington, D. C.

Monthly Labor Review, Bureau of Labor Statistics, Washington, D. C., commodity prices.

The Industrial Bulletin (monthly), Industrial Commission of State of New York, Albany, N. Y., employment and wages.

Information Bulletins, American Railway Association, Washington, D. C., car loadings, weekly.

Interstate Commerce Commission:

    (1) *Statistics of Railways in U. S.* (annual),

    (2) *Monthly Bulletins on Railway Operating Expenses and Traffic Statistics*,

    (3) *Monthly Reports on Large Telephone Companies*.

Federal Trade Commission, reports on various industries.

U. S. Census Publications:

    (1) *Decennial Census*, A treasury of information about the people of the country and American possessions.

PRELIMINARY ANALYSIS OF STATISTICAL DATA

(2) *Five Year Census of Manufactures,* Value added by manufacture, etc.

(3) Special Bulletins (e.g., Oils, Fats, and Greases).

Agricultural Year Book, Department of Agriculture, Washington, D. C., wheat, corn, cotton, production, acreage, yield, prices, etc.

Bureau of Mines, Department of Interior, various bulletins on mineral and metal products, e.g., *Monthly Refinery Statistics* (petroleum).

Geological Survey, Department of Interior, various bulletins on minerals, e.g., *Weekly Report on Coal Production,* and *Statistics of Crude Petroleum* (monthly), Washington, D. C.

Statistical Abstract of the U. S. (annual), Department of Commerce, Washington, D. C., population, production, prices, banking, etc., etc.

Trade Papers (In each trade or industry there is a leading trade journal, such as *Iron Age, Oil, Paint, and Drug Reporter, Engineering and Mining Journal,* etc.).

Standard Statistics Statistical Bulletin and Base Book, published by Standard Statistics Co., New York. Production, prices, banking, investment; both raw data and data treated for secular trend, seasonal variation, etc. Indexes of stock prices by industries. An intelligent and valuable collection.

Review of Economic Statistics (quarterly to 1931, monthly to March 1935 when it was suspended), published by Committee on Economic Research, Harvard University, Cambridge, Massachusetts. Indexes of general business conditions, manufactures, etc.

Annalist (weekly), published by the New York Times Co., weekly business and commodity price, daily stock price indexes, production, banking, etc.

Monthly Bulletin of Statistics, League of Nations, Geneva, Switzerland. General production indices, indices for separate industries, commerce and transportation, exports, imports, shipping, prices, gold reserves, interest rates, exchange rates, unemployment, etc., for all important countries in the world.

Statistical Year Book of League of Nations (annual), Geneva, Switzerland, cumulates and extends materials covered in the *Monthly Bulletin of Statistics.*

New York Stock Exchange Bulletin (monthly), stock values by industries, bond prices (foreign, domestic, and by industries), volume of trading, Stock Exchange borrowings, security offerings, loan rates, volume of short sales, etc.

For the study of any particular industry, valuable data may sometimes be secured from its Code Authority, National Recovery Administration, Washington.

8. *The Classification of Statistical Data.* The data with which one works in practical problems in statistics may usually be classified under two types:

I. Data distributed with respect to some unit of time,

II. Data distributed with respect to some physical characteristic.

The first class is conveniently referred to as a *time series,* and includes such items as daily figures on call loan rates, weekly totals of freight car loadings, monthly totals of pig iron production, national income by years, all series, in fact, which are ordered with respect to time. Most economic statistics are of this type.

The second class is known as a *frequency distribution,* where data are distributed according to class units which are suggested by the character of the subject under scrutiny. This type includes such situations as the distribution of a large number of bonds with regard to the coupon figure, or date of maturity, etc., the distribution of wheat farms according to yield per acre, the distribution of wage earners with respect to weekly wages received, and so forth.

It will be observed at once that statistical distributions such as those just mentioned can be classified under two heads. The first of these, which will be designated by the term *homograde series,* includes distributions in which all the individuals associated with a given class possess the same characteristic in the same degree. For example, in the series formed by recording the semi-annual coupon payments of a large number of industrial bonds, each item will generally fall into one of the classes: $20.00, $22.50, $25.00, $27.50, $30.00, and so forth. Though there might be, there generally are not any intermediate degrees of classification such as $20.03, or $31.53½ but, rather, definite jumps, as from $20.00 to $22.50. This condition is not true, however, of the second type of distribution, which is called a *heterograde series.* In this second type of distribution, the individuals associated with a given class do not possess the same characteristic in the same degree.

An example is found in the classification of wage-earners by income. When it is said that 100 workers have annual incomes of $1200, it is not meant that every individual draws total wages of exactly $1200, but rather that all, in varying degrees, are between the limiting values of $1150 and $1250. The difference between *homograde* and *heterograde* series may be explained by saying that one is a *discrete*, while the other is a *continuous*, distribution.[1]

9. *Frequency Distributions.* Leaving the subject of time series for later consideration, at this point the analysis that is to be applied to frequency distributions may be developed.

When some object amenable to statistical study has been measured according to some fundamental characteristic, the crude data for a frequency distribution are obtained. In order to make the analysis concrete, consider the following table of 4-6 months prime commercial paper rates, monthly, from January 1922 to December 1931:

Month	1922	1923	1924	1925	1926	1927	1928	1929	1930
Jan.	4.88	4.63	4.88	3.63	4.31	4.13	3.88	5.50	4.85
Feb.	4.88	4.69	4.78	3.65	4.19	3.88	4.00	5.56	4.63
Mar.	4.78	5.00	4.59	3.94	4.28	4.00	4.15	5.69	4.19
Apr.	4.60	5.13	4.63	3.95	4.19	4.09	4.40	5.90	3.88
May	4.25	5.13	4.23	3.88	4.00	4.13	4.55	6.00	3.72
June	4.05	4.88	3.91	3.88	3.88	4.13	4.70	6.00	3.50
July	3.94	4.94	3.53	3.93	3.97	4.06	5.13	6.00	3.13
Aug.	3.91	5.03	3.23	4.00	4.25	3.90	5.39	6.09	3.00
Sept.	4.25	5.16	3.13	4.25	4.43	3.91	5.59	6.13	3.00
Oct.	4.38	5.13	3.13	4.44	4.50	4.00	5.50	6.13	3.00
Nov.	4.63	5.09	3.28	4.38	4.43	3.94	5.38	5.41	2.97
Dec.	4.63	4.98	3.56	4.38	4.38	3.95	5.43	5.00	2.88

Since one is concerned with the *sizes* of these items, as a first step an *array* should be formed, that is, the items should be tabulated in order of magnitude, every item being included. These commercial paper rates (X) are tabulated from a mark of 2.88 to a mark of 6.13. The number of months exhibiting any one of these varying rates is given under f.

---

[1]The terms homograde and heterograde are attributed by Helen M. Walker: *Studies in the History of Statistical Method, op. cit.*, to C. V. L. Charlier, In this book one is mainly concerned with homograde series, since a proper analysis of continuous distributions requires the technique of integral calculus.

X	f	X	f	X	f	X	f	X	f	X	f	X	f	X	f
2.88	1	3.56	1	3.94	3	4.15	1	4.43	1	4.70	1	5.09	1	5.56	1
2.97	1	3.63	1	3.95	2	4.19	3	4.44	2	4.78	2	5.13	4	5.59	1
3.00	3	3.65	1	3.97	1	4.23	1	4.50	1	4.85	1	5.16	1	5.69	1
3.13	3	3.72	1	4.00	5	4.25	4	4.55	1	4.88	4	5.38	1	5.90	1
3.23	1	3.88	6	4.05	1	4.28	1	4.59	1	4.94	1	5.39	1	6.00	3
3.28	1	3.90	1	4.06	1	4.31	1	4.60	1	4.98	1	5.41	1	6.09	1
3.50	1	3.91	3	4.09	1	4.38	4	4.63	5	5.00	2	5.43	1	6.13	2
3.53	1	3.93	1	4.13	3	4.40	1	4.69	1	5.03	1	5.50	2	Σf	108

$\Sigma f = N =$ total frequency.[1]

The immediate problem is the choice of a *class interval*, the interval which sets bounds to each class of the frequency distribution. In this case it is convenient to use .50 per cent as the interval. The class limits will then be 2.50-2.99, 3.00-3.49, 3.50-3.99, 4.00-4.49, 4.50-4.99, 5.00-5.49, 5.50-5.99, 6.00-6.49. By *class mark* or *number* is meant a value (generally the arithmetic mean of the class limits) which serves to designate the class. In the example under discussion, the class marks are 2.75, 3.25, 3.75, 4.25, 4.75, 5.25, 5.75, and 6.25 per cent.

There are no fixed rules to be applied in determining the number of classes into which a frequency distribution is to be divided, except that the number should be sufficiently small so that the distribution is reasonably smooth and sufficiently large so that the concentration of frequencies at an average value such as the center of a class interval will not seriously affect the values of the statistical averages.

Some authors suggest the use of about fifteen class intervals for distributions whose total frequency is not less than a hundred. H. A. Sturges[2] has suggested the following formula for the determination of the number (m) of class intervals:

$$m = 1 + \log_{10}N/\log_{10}2 , \qquad (1/\log_{10}2 = 3.32193)$$
$$= 1 + 3.32193 \log_{10}N ,$$

where N is the total frequency.[3]

---

[1] The Greek letter Σ (capital sigma) designates summation. For a fuller explanation, see section 3, Chapter III.

[2] "The Choice of a Class Interval," *Journal of the American Statistical Association*, Vol. 21 (1926), pp. 65-66.

[3] The student who is unfamiliar with logarithms may consult Appendix II at this point.

This formula is derived from a consideration of the binomial frequency distribution based upon the problem of penny tossing, which, as will be pointed out in a later chapter, furnishes a good approach to the subject of normal frequency series. Thus, if five pennies are tossed 32 times and classified according to the number that appear heads up, in the ideal case the following distribution is to be expected:

0 Head	1 Head	2 Heads	3 Heads	4 Heads	5 Heads
1	5	10	10	5	1

Similarly, if six pennies are tossed 64 times, the ideal distribution is:

0 Head	1 Head	2 Heads	3 Heads	4 Heads	5 Heads	6 Heads
1	6	15	20	15	6	1

Thus, it is seen that for a frequency of 32 there are $1 + \log 32/\log 2 = 6$ class marks, for a frequency of 64 there are $1 + \log 64/\log 2 = 7$ class marks, etc. The generalization of this observation is expressed in the Sturges formula.

It should be observed, however, that there is no inescapable necessity for making such a choice and m (the number of class intervals) should always be selected so that it is suited to the data. The Sturges rule tends, in general, to give too great a concentration of data for large frequencies. The *American Experience Table of Mortality*, for instance, which is the basis of the great structure of life insurance, gives a very smooth curve when the data on 100,000 lives are distributed by years from 10 to 95. By applying the Sturges formula, however, one would have $m = 18$, much too small a figure, as a proper range.

In case a high concentration is desired, that is to say, if the data are to be distributed over but a few class marks, corrections should always be applied to the averages calculated from them. These corrections are discussed in section 8 of Chapter III.

Applying the Sturges formula to the data of the last table, it is found that

$$m = 1 + 3.32193 \times \log 108 = 1 + 3.32193 \times 2.03342 = 7.75 .$$

The data are very conveniently treated by using a class interval of .50 per cent, so $m = 8$ may be chosen. On the basis of this choice one arrives at the following table of frequencies:

Classes (inclusive)	Class Marks	Frequencies
2.50-2.99%	2.75%	2
3.00-3.49	3.25	8
3.50-3.99	3.75	23
4.00-4.49	4.25	30
4.50-4.99	4.75	20
5.00-5.49	5.25	13
5.50-5.99	5.75	6
6.00-6.49	6.25	6

PROBLEMS

1. The following table[1] gives women's weekly earnings (259 cases) in Stepney (London) for 1929:

Classes (inclusive)	Frequencies	Classes (inclusive)	Frequencies
Under 10s	1	35s-39s	48
10s-14s	3	40s-44s	28
15s-19s	7	45s-49s	24
20s-24s	29	50s-54s	6
25s-29s	47	55s-59s	3
30s-34s	60	60s or more	3

Does the number of intervals chosen conform to Sturges' formula? (log 259 = 2.41330).

2. The 168 figures contained in the following table give the Ratio of Investments in U. S. Government Securities to Total Investments (All Reporting Federal Reserve Member Banks), and range in magnitude from 39.7 to 63.3. Choosing a convenient unit, divide this range into a series of class intervals and construct a frequency table.

---

[1] Taken from "The Action of Economic Forces in Producing Frequency Distributions of Income, Prices, and Other Phenomena: A Suggestion for Study," by A. L. Bowley, *Econometrica*, Vol. I (1933), page 363.

PRELIMINARY ANALYSIS OF STATISTICAL DATA 19

Mo.	1919	1920	1921	1922	1923	1924	1925	1926	1927	1928	1929	1930	1931	1932
Jan.	58.0	49.8	40.9	43.4	55.9	53.8	51.3	49.5	45.4	48.5	51.1	49.1	46.7	54.8
Feb.	60.2	47.8	40.7	46.3	56.1	53.7	50.4	49.6	45.5	49.1	51.2	51.9	47.7	54.6
Mar.	62.5	45.8	40.9	45.5	56.1	53.2	50.7	49.3	46.2	48.4	51.4	50.0	49.2	54.8
Apr.	62.1	46.5	40.6	45.8	56.0	52.3	50.2	48.9	46.6	48.7	51.1	49.7	50.5	54.4
May	63.3	47.0	40.0	46.6	56.1	51.1	49.4	48.6	47.0	48.7	50.7	48.5	50.6	55.6
June	58.7	46.4	40.9	48.8	56.5	50.5	49.6	48.1	45.8	48.8	50.7	47.3	51.8	56.3
July	55.1	45.0	39.7	49.5	55.7	50.8	49.3	47.6	45.4	48.8	49.6	46.8	52.8	56.4
Aug.	56.7	44.5	40.8	51.2	55.2	50.8	49.3	47.9	45.2	49.1	49.6	46.0	52.8	58.5
Sept.	55.8	44.1	41.1	51.8	55.0	51.7	49.1	47.9	45.6	49.9	49.5	46.0	53.3	59.6
Oct.	52.9	43.0	40.4	52.0	54.8	51.5	48.9	48.0	46.2	51.0	49.1	45.7	53.7	61.1
Nov.	50.8	42.8	41.8	52.4	53.9	50.9	48.9	47.4	46.7	50.7	49.3	45.4	53.7	61.5
Dec.	50.1	42.9	42.7	53.5	53.9	51.0	49.7	46.4	47.5	50.8	48.6	46.0	54.7	61.4

Source: *Standard Statistics Base Book.*

3. The following table gives the monthly percentage deviations from trend of the Dow-Jones Industrial Averages for the pre-war period, 1897-1913. Could the data of this frequency table be advantageously spread over a smaller number of class intervals? (Use log 204 = 2.30963.)

Classes (inclusive)	Frequency	Classes (inclusive)	Frequency
60-64	1	100-104	36
65-69	4	105-109	19
70-74	10	110-114	17
75-79	8	115-119	8
80-84	9	120-124	13
85-89	20	125-129	10
90-94	22	130-134	3
95-99	24		$N = 204$

10. *The Graphical Representation of Frequency Distributions.* When the data have been collected and suitably arranged in a table, it is often useful as a next step in statistical procedure to represent them by some graphical method. Numerous devices such as pie charts, bar charts, maps, curves, etc., have been employed for this purpose. For example, see Figures 1a and 1b.

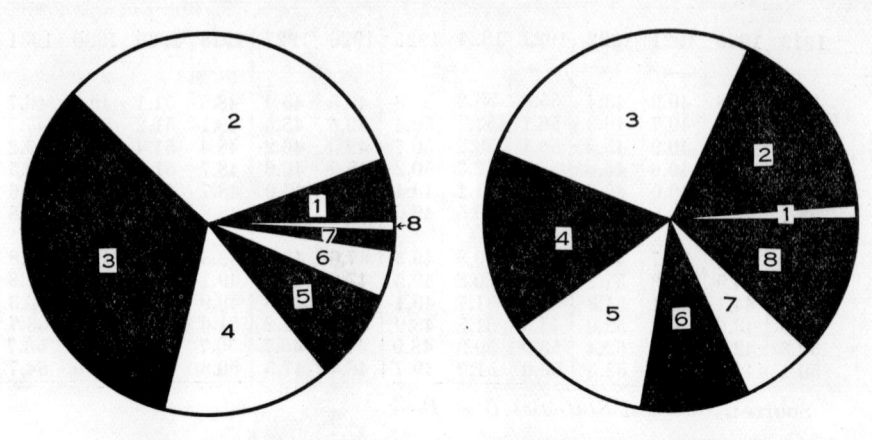

NUMBER OF PERSONS
IN EACH INCOME CLASS

AMOUNT OF TOTAL INCOME
RECEIVED BY EACH CLASS

FIGURE 1a. Pie charts comparing the number of persons in each of eight income classes with the income received by each class. The numbers refer to income ranges (1) below $500, (2) from $500-1,000, (3) $1,000-1,500, (4) $1,500-2,000, (5) $2,000-3,000, (6) $3,000-5,000, (7) $5,000-10,000, and (8) above $10,000. For the data, see the table on page 27.

PER CENT OF PERSONS
IN INCOME CLASSES

PER CENT OF TOTAL INCOME
RECEIVED BY EACH CLASS

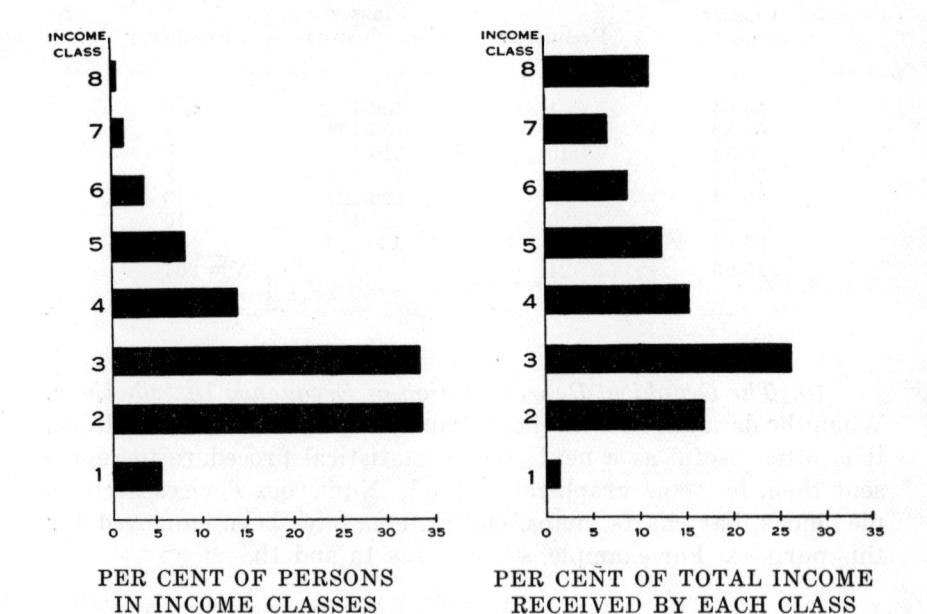

FIGURE 1b. Bar charts comparing the percentage of persons in each of eight income classes with the percentage of the total income received by each class. The numbers refer to the income ranges as stated for Figure 1a.

Helpful as these devices sometimes are, however, in the pictorial representation of statistical material, none of them is so important in the mathematical analysis of data as the ordinary method of graphing.

The most common method of graphing is that of referring the quantities involved to mutually perpendicular intersecting straight lines called *axes*, just as places on maps depicting large areas are referred to the equator and the principal meridian, or on maps of limited scope to convenient lines of latitude and longitude.

The horizontal axis is customarily referred to as the *x-axis*, the vertical axis as the *y-axis*, and their point of intersection as the *origin*. Convenient intervals are marked off on each axis.

A point is designated by the symbol (a,b), where a indicates the distance along the x-axis and b the distance along the y-axis. These values are called respectively the *abscissa* and *ordinate* of the point (a,b). The point is defined as the intersection of a line parallel to the y-axis and at a distance a from it with a line parallel to the x-axis and at a distance b from it. The abscissa a and the ordinate b are called *coordinates of the point*. They are sometimes referred to as the rectangular *Cartesian* coordinates, after René Descartes (1596-1650), who first introduced them in his famous essay on *Géométrie*.

Letting $x_1, x_2, \cdots, x_n$, denote the x values, and $y_1, y_2, \cdots, y_n$, the corresponding y values, one may record them in tabular form:

Values of y	$y_1 \quad y_2 \quad y_3 \quad \cdots\cdots\cdots\cdots \quad y_n$
Values of x	$x_1 \quad x_2 \quad x_3 \quad \cdots\cdots\cdots\cdots \quad x_n$

The number pairs (x_1,y_1), (x_2,y_2), (x_3,y_3), $\cdots$, (x_n,y_n), may then be plotted as points, and this succession of points when connected make a graph. Assuming that there exists some exact relationship between x and y, these points will not be entirely random ones, but will be found to be so arranged that a smooth curve can be drawn to approximate them.

If there is only an approximate relationship between the two variables, the points may be joined by straight lines to obtain the characteristic saw-toothed graph of statistics.[1] The method of fit-

---

[1] See, for example, Figure 10, page 46.

ting a smooth curve to the data thus plotted is treated in a later chapter under the theory of least squares.

Some variation in this procedure is to be expected in the case of frequency tables. The x-axis is then usually chosen for the representation of the class marks, and the y-axis for the representation of the frequencies. But, since each frequency is an integer and includes all the individuals within the class interval to which it applies, the frequency is customarily represented, not by a single ordinate, but by a rectangle whose base is the class interval and whose length is equal numerically to the value of the frequency. The diagram formed by these frequency rectangles is called a *histogram*.

Example: Represent graphically the data of the table on page 18.

As a preliminary simplification the original class marks are replaced by a new set composed of the numbers 0, 1, 2, 3, 4, 5, 6, 7. In this manner the origin of the axes is included in the picture, an inclusion which will often be found to be advantageous. Furthermore, as will appear later, considerable reduction in the labor of numerical calculation will result from the choice of simpler class marks.

The histogram is then constructed by forming rectangles with bases equal to unity, and altitudes equal to the successive frequencies, as shown in Figure 2.

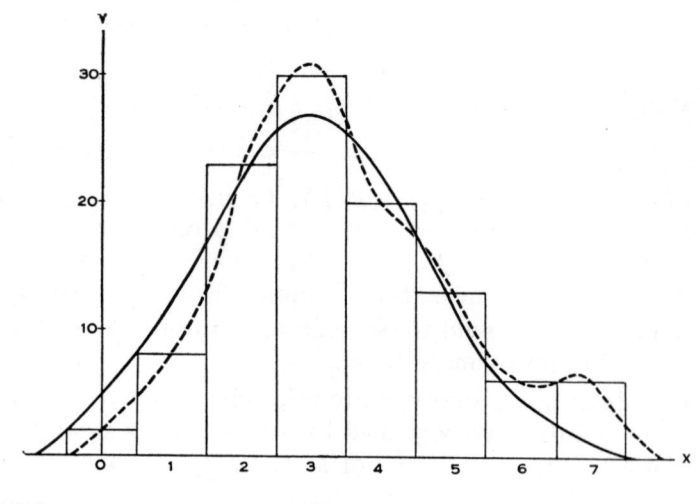

FIGURE 2

The graph is completed by drawing in a smooth curve which approximately represents the data and includes an area (almost) identical with that of the total area of the several rectangles. The computation of the ordinates of such a curve will be discussed in detail in later chapters. The values used in this example are contained in the following table:

Class marks	0	1	2	3	4	5	6	7
Frequencies	2	8	23	30	20	13	6	6

The dotted curve (process of smoothing by inspection) in the above figure represents a smoothed curve, enclosing approximately the same total area as the histogram, and so drawn through the points of the histogram that the areas gained and lost by each column are approximately equal. The top of the curve slightly overtops the highest plotted point in order to represent the probable distribution of the cases within the class of highest frequency.

11. Ogives or Cumulative Frequency Curves. One type of curve often used in the graphical representation of frequencies is the so-called *ogive* or *cumulative frequency curve.* The ordinates of such a curve are formed from a given frequency distribution by the addition of successive frequencies.

For example, the ordinates for the ogive which represents the frequency distribution given in the table on page 18 (monthly averages of 4-6 months prime commercial paper rates, January 1922 to December 1931), are the following:

Class Marks	Frequencies	Frequencies Accumulated
2.75%	2	2
3.25	8	10
3.75	23	33
4.25	30	63
4.75	20	83
5.25	13	96
5.75	6	102
6.25	6	108

The graph of the accumulated frequencies, or ogive, is given in Figure 3.

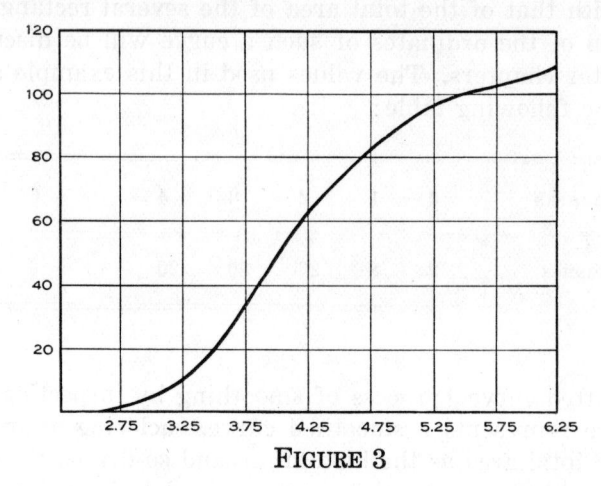

FIGURE 3

One useful application of the ogive is found in the comparison of one or more groups of data with some standard norm. To illustrate, one might be interested in comparing monthly imports and exports of the United States over a period of years, data which are contained in the following table (1912-1931, with unit as $1,000,000):

Class Intervals	Class Marks	Frequency (Imports)	Frequency (Exports)	Frequency (Composite)
Under 115	77.5	0	1	1
115-189	152.5	68	21	89
190-264	227.5	53	26	79
265-339	302.5	62	49	111
340-414	377.5	45	53	98
415-489	452.5	7	36	43
490-564	527.5	5	25	30
565-639	602.5	0	14	14
640 and over	677.5	0	15	15
Totals		240	240	480

To make the suggested comparison by means of the ogive, some norm is first selected. In the present instance it will be convenient to choose for this the composite frequency distribution obtained by adding corresponding frequencies in each group. A second table based on the one just given is then computed, reducing the cumulative frequencies to percentages of the total of the frequency column. This table is given below:

Class Intervals	Class Marks	Cumulative Frequency (Imports)	Percentage of Total	Cumulative Frequency (Exports)	Percentage of Total	Cumulative Frequency (Composite)	Percentage of Total
Under 115	77.5	0	0	1	0	1	0
115-189	152.5	68	28	22	9	90	19
190-264	227.5	121	50	48	20	169	35
265-339	302.5	183	76	97	40	280	58
340-414	377.5	228	95	150	63	378	79
415-489	452.5	235	98	186	78	421	88
490-564	527.5	240	100	211	88	451	94
565-639	602.5	240	100	225	94	465	97
640-Over	677.5	240	100	240	100	480	100

Drawing two mutually perpendicular axes, X and Y (see Figure 4), per cents from 0 to 100 are recorded as ordinates. The ruling for the X-axis is obtained as follows: At some convenient distance

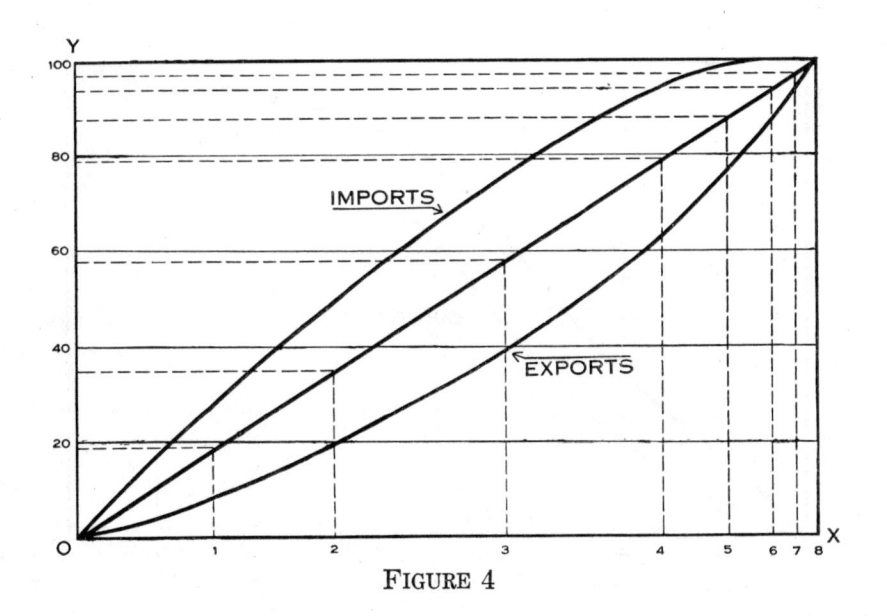

FIGURE 4

from the origin on the X-axis, a perpendicular equal in height to the range on the Y-axis is erected, i.e., the range from 0 to 100 per cent, and the origin is connected by a straight line with the extremity of this perpendicular. Then, from points on the Y-axis at the percentage values recorded in the composite column of the table, lines parallel to the X-axis are drawn until they cut the diagonal of the figure. From these points of intersection perpendiculars are dropped to the X-axis and at the extremities of these perpendiculars the class marks (substituting the simple class marks, 0, 1, 2, etc., for the original class marks 77.5, 152.5, etc.) are recorded, thus establishing a range of unequal intervals on the X-axis.

Using these new values of x, the points in the other two percentage columns of the above table are graphed. The resulting diagram gives a graphic picture of the relative value of imports and exports in the various groups, the composite or norm being represented by the straight line diagonal.

The ordinary ogives of the distribution as shown in Figure 5 may be compared with the ogives obtained by the method just described, as shown in Figure 4.

Another type of ogive curve may be formed by cumulating the variables on each axis and reducing the values thus obtained to percentages of the total. Such ogives are called Lorenz curves and are valuable statistical aids in analyzing data of certain types.

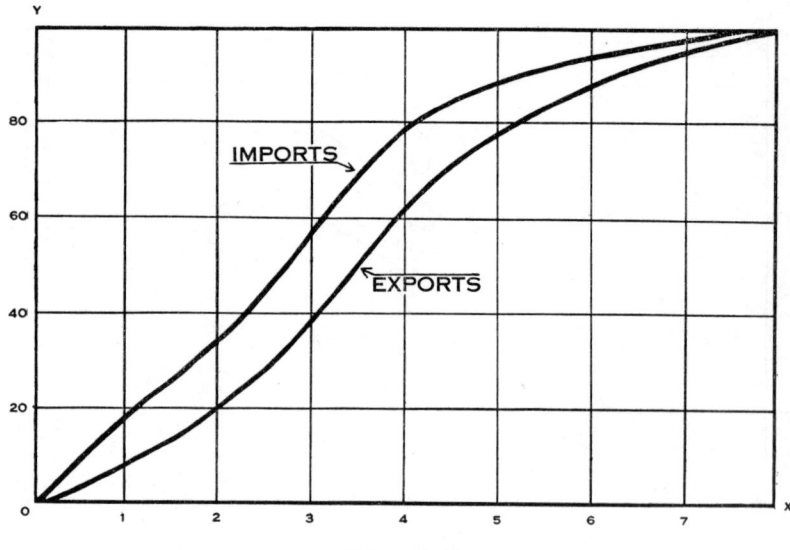

FIGURE 5

A well-known example is furnished by the figures showing the distribution of national income in the United States. The following summary (condensed) was published by the National Bureau of Economic Research in 1921 to show the amount and distribution of personal incomes in 1918:[1]

Income Class (Dollars)	Number of Persons	Amount of Income	Percentage No.	Percentage Amt.	Cumulative Distribution (Percentage) No.	Cumulative Distribution (Percentage) Amt.
Under zero	200,000	$ −125,000,000	.53	−.22	.53	−.22
000- 500	1,827,554	685,287,806	4.86	1.18	5.39	.96
500- 1,000	12,530,670	9,818,678,617	33.35	16.94	38.74	17.90
1,000- 1,500	12,498,120	15,295,790,534	33.27	26.40	72.01	44.30
1,500- 2,000	5,222,067	8,917,648,335	13.90	15.39	85.91	59.69
2,000- 3,000	3,065,024	7,314,412,994	8.16	12.62	94.07	72.31
3,000- 5,000	1,383,167	5,174,090,777	3.68	8.93	97.75	81.24
5,000- 10,000	587,824	3,937,183,313	1.57	6.79	99.32	88.03
10,000- 25,000	192,062	2,808,290,063	.51	4.85	99.83	92.88
25,000- 50,000	41,119	1,398,785,687	.11	2.41	99.94	95.29
50,000- 100,000	14,011	951,529,576	.04	1.64	99.98	96.93
100,000- 200,000	4,945	671,565,821	.01	1.16	99.99	98.09
200,000- 500,000	1,976	570,019,200	.01	.98	100.00	99.07
500,000-1,000,000	369	220,120,399	.00	.38	100.00	99.45
1,000,000-and over	152	316,319,219	.00	.55	100.00	100.00
Totals	37,569,060	57,954,722,341	100.00	100.00		

From the percentages given in the last two columns of the table, the Lorenz curve of the distribution is graphed in Figure 6:

PROBLEMS

1. Make a histogram and curve to represent the data as given in the table of problem 1, section 9, of this chapter.

2. Construct a histogram and curve for the data given in the following table, which shows the frequency distribution of the percentage deviations from

---
[1] See *Income in the United States—Its Amount and Distribution 1909-1919*, National Bureau of Economic Research, Vol. I, New York, 1923, pp. 132-3.

FIGURE 6

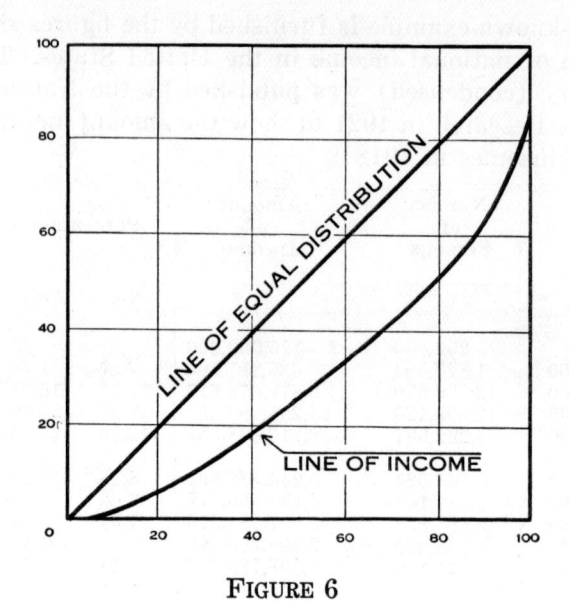

trend of Bradstreet's Commodity Prices monthly, corrected for secular trend, for the years 1897-1913:

Percentage Deviation from Trend	Class Marks	Frequency	Percentage Deviation from Trend	Class Marks	Frequency
−15 to −13	−14	3	0 to 2	1	58
−12 " −10	−11	6	3 " 5	4	39
− 9 " − 7	− 8	10	6 " 8	7	13
− 6 " − 4	− 5	31	9 " 11	10	4
− 3 " − 1	− 2	37	12 " 14	13	3

3. Draw an ogive for the data of problem 1 above.

4. Compare the ogive of problem 3 with the ogive formed from the following table:

Frequency	1	10	45	120	210	252	210	120	45	10	1
Class Marks	0	1	2	3	4	5	6	7	8	9	10

5. Compare the following frequency data by the method of this section, using the X figure as the norm:

Class Marks	0	1	2	3	4	5	6
X	1	6	15	20	15	6	1
Y	1	5	32	78	74	25	3

6. Construct a Lorenz curve for the following data taken from the U. S. census for 1920, which show the relative size and value of American farms:

Size of Farms (Acres)	Number of Farms	Percent	Value in Millions	Percent
Under 20	796,535	12.4	2,453	3.1
20-49	1,503,732	23.3	5,864	7.5
50-99	1,474,745	22.9	11,183	14.4
100-174	1,449,630	22.5	20,902	26.8
175-499	1,006,477	15.6	26,390	33.9
500-999	149,819	2.3	5,534	7.1
1000 and over	67,405	1.0	5,598	7.2
Totals	6,488,343	100.0	77,924	100.0

12. Binomial Frequencies—The Binomial Theorem. One will find as he proceeds in the analysis of frequency distributions that a considerable number of series resemble more or less closely a type whose frequencies are the successive terms of the expansion of a binomial.

The frequencies of the table on page 18 (4-6 months prime commercial paper rates, January, 1922, to December, 1931), for instance, and the successive terms of the expansion of the binomial

$$108(.55 + .45)^7$$

may be compared as follows:

Class Marks	Frequencies (Money Rates)	Terms of the Expansion
0	2	2
1	8	9
2	23	23
3	30	32
4	20	26
5	13	13
6	6	3
7	6	0

The general resemblance between the values in the table is evident. The reasons why such a resemblance is not accidental, but is to be expected in many statistical series, will be discussed at length in a later chapter. However, it may be mentioned here that such series are called *binomial frequency distributions*.

In order to prepare for a better understanding of such distributions, a few of the facts concerning the expansion of a binomial may be reviewed.

The formula representing the expansion of a binomial is called the *binomial theorem*. It has been proved in algebra that this expansion takes the following form for integral (positive whole number) values of n:

$$(a+b)^n = a^n + n\, a^{n-1} b + \frac{n(n-1)}{2!} a^{n-2} b^2$$

$$+ \frac{n(n-1)(n-2)}{3!} a^{n-3} b^3 + \cdots \qquad (1)$$

where $2!$ (read "factorial two") $= 1 \cdot 2$, and $3! = 1 \cdot 2 \cdot 3$, and, in general, $r! = 1 \cdot 2 \cdot 3 \cdots r$.

The expressions

$$n, \quad \frac{n(n-1)}{2!}, \quad \frac{n(n-1)(n-2)}{3!}, \quad \text{etc.,}$$

are called the *binomial coefficients* and are conveniently represented by the symbols, $_nC_1$, $_nC_2$, $_nC_3$, etc., which will be met later in the subject of probability.

The r-th or general, coefficient is given by the formula

$$_nC_r = \frac{n(n-1)(n-2)\cdots(n-r+1)}{r!},$$

which may be put into the following form:

$$_nC_r = \frac{n(n-1)(n-2)\cdots(n-r+1)}{r!}$$

$$\times \frac{[(n-r)(n-r-1)\cdots 3\cdot 2\cdot 1]}{[(n-r)(n-r-1)\cdots 3\cdot 2\cdot 1]} = \frac{n!}{r!(n-r)!}.$$

Since the numerical values of these constants for integral values[1] of n often occur in statistical work, a short table is given below:

TABLE OF BINOMIAL COEFFICIENTS, $_nC_r$
(Values of r)

n	0	1	2	3	4	5	6	7	8	9	10	11	12	13	14	15
1	1	1														
2	1	2	1													
3	1	3	3	1												
4	1	4	6	4	1											
5	1	5	10	10	5	1										
6	1	6	15	20	15	6	1									
7	1	7	21	35	35	21	7	1								
8	1	8	28	56	70	56	28	8	1							
9	1	9	36	84	126	126	84	36	9	1						
10	1	10	45	120	210	252	210	120	45	10	1					
11	1	11	55	165	330	462	462	330	165	55	11	1				
12	1	12	66	220	495	792	924	792	495	220	66	12	1			
13	1	13	78	286	715	1287	1716	1716	1287	715	286	78	13	1		
14	1	14	91	364	1001	2002	3003	3432	3003	2002	1001	364	91	14	1	
15	1	15	105	455	1365	3003	5005	6435	6435	5005	3003	1365	455	105	15	1

A few of the most useful values of $_nC_r$ for fractional and negative indexes are given in the following table:

---

[1]For values of n that are either negative integers or positive or negative fractions, the binomial coefficients may be computed either from formula (2) or by means of tables of the *gamma function*. By definition, the gamma function, represented by the symbol $\Gamma(x)$, is equal to $(x-1)!$. Making use of the difference relationship: $\Gamma(x+1) = x\,\Gamma(x)$, that is to say, $x! = x(x-1)!$, it is possible to define the factorial symbol for all values of x except the negative integers where $\Gamma(x)$ becomes infinite. It is interesting to note the particular value of $\Gamma(3/2) = (\frac{1}{2})! = \frac{1}{2}\sqrt{\pi}$. Elaborate tables of the gamma function have been computed (See Davis, *Tables of the Higher Mathematical Functions*, Vol. 1, Bloomington, 1933. Hence, for $_nC_r$ one may write,

$$_nC_r = \Gamma(n+1)/[\Gamma(r+1)\,\Gamma(n-r+1)].$$

If n is a negative integer, this expression may be evaluated by appropriate limiting processes, but formula (2) is easier to apply in this case.

BINOMIAL COEFFICIENTS

n	$r=$ 1	2	3	4	5
-2	-2	3	-4	5	-6
-1	-1	1	-1	1	-1
$-1/2$	$-1/2$	3/8	$-5/16$	35/128	$-63/256$
1/2	1/2	$-1/8$	1/16	$-5/128$	7/256
$-1/3$	$-1/3$	2/9	$-14/81$	35/243	$-91/729$
1/3	1/3	$-1/9$	5/81	$-10/243$	22/729
$-1/4$	$-1/4$	5/32	$-15/128$	195/2048	$-663/8192$
1/4	1/4	$-3/32$	7/128	$-77/2048$	231/8192

A simple and interesting way of arriving at a table of binomial coefficients is here shown:[1]

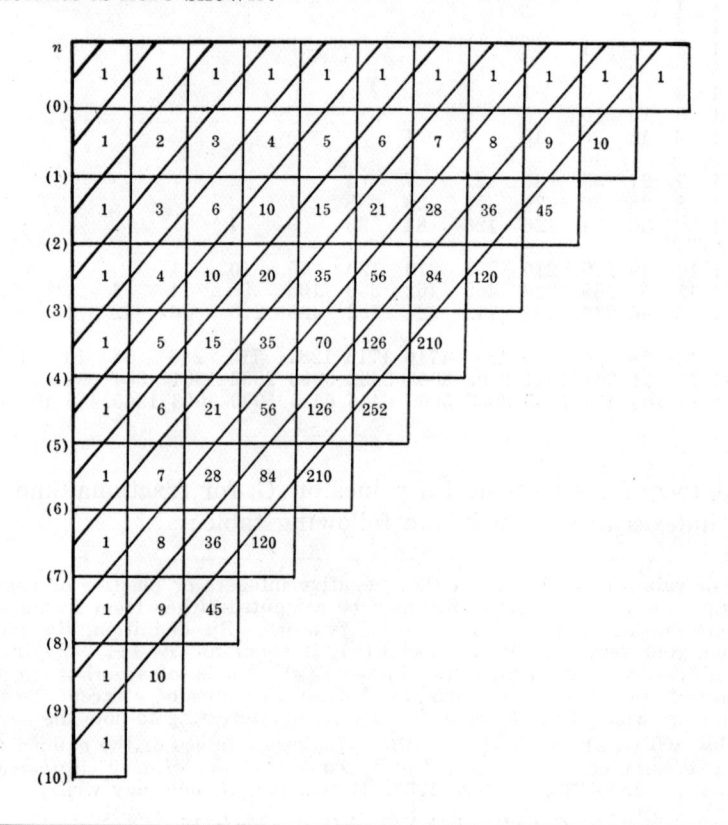

[1]This is essentially Pascal's Triangle, published by B. Pascal in 1665, although known as early as 1303 in a Chinese tract by Chu Shih-Chieh.

Given a set of squares, the top row of squares and the left column of squares are each filled with ones. Then each successive row is formed by summing the figures in the preceding row from the left, up to and including the column where the new figure is to be inserted. For example, the 2 in column two, row two, is the sum of the two 1's of the top row. Similarly, the 20 in column 4, row 4, is the sum of the 1, 3, 6, and 10, of the preceding row. When the table has been constructed in this fashion, diagonal lines are drawn through it. Reading diagonally, one has the binomial coefficients as 1, 1; 1, 2, 1; 1, 3, 3, 1; 1, 4, 6, 4, 1; etc.

The binomial series is obtained from the binomial theorem by replacing a by 1 and b by x. One thus obtains the following expansion:

$$(1+x)^n = 1 + nx + \frac{n(n-1)}{2!}x^2 + \frac{n(n-1)(n-2)}{3!}x^3 + \cdots . \qquad (2)$$

If n is an integer, this series terminates with the $(n+1)$th term. If, however, n is not an integer, the series consists of an infinite number of terms, since none of the binomial coefficients vanishes. It has been proved by methods of analysis which cannot be treated here that the series *converges*[1] for all values of n, positive or negative, provided x is a number between -1 and $+1$. By this statement is meant that if any value of x less than 1 in numerical value is substituted in the right hand side of equation (2), the sum of a finite number of terms of the series will approximately equal the value of the expression $(1+x)^n$. That this is often a useful thing to know is evident from the fact that the terms of the series are always easy to compute, whereas the value of $(1+x)^n$ is some-

---

[1] The theory of convergent and divergent series is a very extensive and important subject in mathematics and the student should have some acquaintance with it. Unfortunately the limitations of space preclude any development of this theory here. The student should consult some standard algebra or, if he has studied calculus, he should review the chapter devoted to series in any standard text. The convergence and divergence of series is illustrated by the following two examples:

$$1 + 1/2 + 1/3 + 1/4 + \cdots + 1/n + \cdots$$
$$1 + 1/4 + 1/9 + 1/16 + \cdots + 1/n^2 + \cdots$$

The first series does not converge, that is to say, as terms are added to the sum of the first n terms, the sum continues to increase without limit. Any preassigned value may be exceeded if a sufficiently large number of terms are summed. The series is said to be *divergent*. The second series does converge and has the limiting value $\pi^2/6$. As terms are added to the sum of the first n terms, the resulting sum approximates more and more closely the limiting value.

times very difficult to calculate directly, as, for example, when n equals 1/10.

Example 1. Expand $(x + 1/x)^6$.

Using the table of coefficients for $n = 6$, one has from equation (1):

$$(x + 1/x)^6 = x^6 + 6x^4 + 15x^2 + 20 + 15/x^2 + 6/x^4 + 1/x^6 .$$

Example 2. Calculate by the binomial series the value of $1/\sqrt[5]{1.05}$.

Noting that the reciprocal of the fifth root of a number is that number raised to the negative one-fifth power, one may write:

$$1/\sqrt[5]{1.05} = (1.05)^{-1/5} = (1 + .05)^{-1/5}$$

$$= 1 - (1/5)(.05) + \frac{(-1/5)(-1/5-1)}{2!}(.05)^2 + \cdots$$

$$= .9903 \text{ (approximately)}.$$

PROBLEMS

1. Make a histogram using the binomial coefficients for $n = 10$ as frequencies and the values of r for the class marks.

2. Construct an ogive curve using the binomial coefficients for $n = 7$ as frequencies and the values of r for class marks. Compare this with the ogive given in Figure 3 of this chapter.

Use the binomial series to calculate the following:

3. $\sqrt[3]{1.03}$,   4. $\sqrt[5]{1.25}$,   5. $1/\sqrt{1.02}$.

6. Form a table of the first five binomial coefficients for the values $n = 1/2, 1/3, -1, -2$.

7. When tables of logarithms are not available, binomial series can be used to calculate roots. For example,
$$\sqrt{30} = \sqrt{25 + 5} = 5\sqrt{1 + 1/5} .$$
Complete the calculation.

8. Calculate the binomial coefficients for $n = 16, n = 17$.

9. Calculate $_{18}C_8$; $_{20}C_5$.

10. Show that the sum of the binomial coefficients corresponding to an integral value of n is equal to 2^n.

11. Expand $(1 + 1/x)^4$; $-(1 - 1/x)^4$.

12. Expand $(x + 2 + 1/\sqrt{x})^3$. Hint: Consider the first two terms as representing one number.

13. Expand $(a + b + c + d)^2$.

14. Prove that the expansion of $(x_1 + x_2 + \cdots + x_n)^2$ consists of the sum of the squares of the x's plus twice the sum of their products taken two at a time.

CHAPTER II

The Graphical Analysis of Data—Elementary Curve Fitting

1. Functions. Much of the importance of the modern application of mathematics depends upon a knowledge of the properties of functions. A *function* may be defined as follows: *If two variables x and y are so related that when a value of x is given, y can be determined, then y is said to be a function of x.*

It is customary to represent a function by means of the symbol $f(x)$. For example, suppose that the function under consideration is $x^2 - 3x + 1$. Then $f(x) = x^2 - 3x + 1$, $f(1) = 1^2 - 3 + 1 = -1$, $f(2) = 2^2 - 3 \cdot 2 + 1 = -1$, $f(½) = (½)^2 - 3(½) + 1 = -¼$.

Functions sometimes cannot be represented by a mathematical expression, but may be defined by some characteristic property. For example, one might say that $y = f(x)$ is zero when x is a rational number, and y is 1 whenever x is an irrational number. Then one would have $f(½) = 0$, $f(\sqrt{2}) = 1$, $f(¼) = 0$, $f(\pi) = 1$.

Every applied field in which mathematics is used has its own particular set of functions, and one's knowledge of this field may be accurately evaluated by his familiarity with their properties. For example, the mathematical theory of finance is a study of the relationship between money and time, and this relationship is expressed by means of functions involving a rate of interest.

Example 1. Given $f(x) = \dfrac{(x-1)}{(x+1)}$, find $f(0)$, $f(\sqrt{2})$, $f(1)$.

Substituting in the explicit formula, one has

$$f(0) = \frac{(0-1)}{(0+1)} = -1 \ ;$$

$$f(\sqrt{2}) = \frac{(\sqrt{2}-1)}{(\sqrt{2}+1)} = \frac{(\sqrt{2}-1)^2}{(\sqrt{2}-1)(\sqrt{2}+1)} = 3 - 2\sqrt{2} \ ;$$

$$f(1) = \frac{(1-1)}{(1+1)} = \frac{0}{2} = 0 \ .$$

In statistics, the values of a function are usually given by a set of *empirical values*, that is, values obtained from experimental observation. One might, for example, observe the minutes of daylight for each day of the year and express these numbers as functions of the number of days from December 31. Thus, starting with December 31 as origin, one obtains for New York City the following data, tabulated for intervals of five days, which represent the number of minutes of daylight corresponding to each fifth day in the year:[1]

x	$f(x)$	x	$f(x)$	x	$f(x)$	x	$f(x)$	x	$f(x)$	x	$f(x)$
5	561	65	688	125	843	185	902	245	787	305	630
10	567	70	701	130	854	190	898	250	774	310	618
15	573	75	715	135	864	195	892	255	761	315	607
20	582	80	728	140	874	200	885	260	748	320	596
25	591	85	741	145	882	205	877	265	734	325	587
30	601	90	755	150	889	210	868	270	721	330	578
35	611	95	769	155	894	215	859	275	707	335	570
40	623	100	782	160	900	220	848	280	694	340	564
45	635	105	795	165	904	225	837	285	681	345	560
50	648	110	808	170	906	230	825	290	668	350	557
55	661	115	821	175	906	235	813	295	655	355	555
60	674	120	833	180	905	240	800	300	642	360	555

It should be observed that the functional relationship existing here is defined only for integral values of x, since it would be meaningless to ask the number of minutes of daylight corresponding to $x = 10.5$. This is characteristic of statistical theory, as was pointed out in Chapter I in the discussion of homograde frequency distributions. Some authors prefer to use the word *variate* instead of *variable* when referring to x in such functional relationships.

In order to find a value of $f(x)$ not given in the above table, it is necessary to interpolate.[2] Thus for $x = 93$, one has

$$f(93) = 755 + \frac{3}{5}(769 - 755)$$

$$= 755 + 8.4 = 763.4 .$$

An interesting fact about the function just defined is that it is *periodic*, that is to say, the values recur after a fixed interval,

---

[1] A slight variation in these figures will be found from year to year.
[2] See section 4, Appendix II. For a more extensive account of interpolation, refer to the introduction to the tables, Appendix III.

since the value for $x = 365 + 15$ is identical with the value for $x = 15$. This may be represented symbolically as follows:

$$f(x + a) = f(x) ,$$

where a is the period. In the example, $a = 365$. Time series in statistics often show this characteristic periodicity, which is called "seasonal variation."

Example 2. It has been discovered from statistical studies[1] that the *inhibition effect*, F, of foreclosures on the supply of capital available for new residential building in a large community may be adequately represented by the function

$$F = 1 - 129.6/f ,$$

where f is the number of foreclosures per year per 100,000 families.

In times of high prosperity f is approximately equal to 120 and in periods of deep depression f is around 840. Hence, one finds $F = 1 - 129.6/120 = -.08$, that is to say, approximately zero, to be the inhibition coefficient for a prosperous period and $F = 1 - 129.6/840 = 1 - .15 = .85$ to be the inhibition coefficient for a period of depression.

PROBLEMS

(If he has not already done so, the student should familiarize himself with the exponential e^x before working these exercises. See section 5, Appendix II).

1. Given $f(x) = x^2 - 3x + 1$, calculate $f(0)$, $f(2)$, $f(\sqrt{2})$, $f(-1)$, $f(5)$.

2. Is there a value of x for which $f(x) = x^2 - 3x - 5$ equals zero? Hint: Substitute various positive and negative values for x and see whether $f(x)$ changes sign. Why will this answer the question?

3. Given $f(x) = \dfrac{(x^2-1)}{(x^2+1)}$, calculate $f(0)$, $f(1)$, $f(-1)$, $f(2)$, $f(\sqrt{3})$.

4. If x is the number of days from December 31 and $f(x)$ the minutes of daylight at New York City, find $f(35)$, $f(72)$, $f(268)$, and $f(725)$.

5. The following data show the population (expressed in millions) of the United States at each census from 1790 to 1920:

Population	3.929	5.308	7.240	9.638	12.866	17.069	23.192
Year	1790	1800	1810	1820	1830	1840	1850

[1] Taken from C. F. Roos, *Dynamic Economics*, Bloomington, 1934, p. 87.

Population	31.443	38.558	50.156	62.948	75.995	91.972	105.711
Year	1860	1870	1880	1890	1900	1910	1920

Letting x be the number of years since 1780, and assuming that the population of the United States is a function of x, find $f(50)$, $f(100)$, $f(85)$. Estimate the population for 1930.

6. Assuming that for problem 5

$$f(x) = \frac{197.27}{1 + 67.32e^{-.0313x}}$$

estimate the population in 1780. Hint: Let $x = 0$.

7. If the function in problem 6 is the true law of growth for the United States, what is the limiting value for the population? Hint: Let x become very large.

8. If $f(x) = e^x$, calculate $f(0)$, $f(.1)$, $f(.2)$, $f(-1)$, $f(-1,000,000)$.

9. If $f(x) = e^x$, show that $f(x) \cdot f(y) = f(x + y)$.

10. If $f(x) = \dfrac{(x-1)}{(x+1)}$, prove that

$$f(x+1) - f(x) = \frac{2}{(x+1)(x+2)}.$$

11. If $f(x) = \log_{10} x$, calculate $f(.1)$, $f(1.63)$, $f(6.43)$.

12. Table VI gives values for the function $f(t) = \dfrac{1}{\sqrt{2\pi}} e^{-\frac{1}{2}t^2}$. Calculate $f(2.93)$ and $f(2.936)$.

13. The third binomial coefficient is $_nC_3 = \dfrac{n(n-1)(n-2)}{3!}$. Is $_nC_3$ a function of n? Calculate $_2C_3$, $_5C_3$, $_{1/2}C_3$, $_{1/4}C_3$.

2. Correlations. In illustrating the principles involved in functional relationship it is usually convenient to employ examples taken from the physical sciences because it is difficult to establish functional relationships as simple between two economic series. One cannot say, for example, that bond prices are a function of interest rates alone, because other factors complicate the relationship. There is, of course, a *tendency* toward a functional relationship between time and many economic variables, where the period is a year. Certain situations are necessarily affected by seasonal changes; the volume of shipping on the Great Lakes is an obvious instance. No periods longer than a year have been definitely and irrefutably established.

On account of the striking instances in the natural sciences, the idea of periodic functions has exercised considerable attraction over economists. W. S. Jevons, with sunspot cycles, H. L. Moore, with the transits of Venus, Sir William A. Beveridge, with rainfall cycles, have all attempted to demonstrate their existence in economic series. The attempts have been interesting but not convincing. Seasonal variation is the simplest and nearest approach to periodic functions in economic series. Egg prices are comparatively high in winter, comparatively low in summer but, due to other factors in the equation, such as inventories and the *general* price level, one is unable to say that on January 5 eggs will be exactly 40 cents a dozen with any such assurance as he can say that there will be 561 minutes of daylight in New York City on that date.

The material with which statistics deals is obtained from collections of items which do not, as a rule, have a complete functional relationship with other sets of items. The following table gives the average monthly price of eggs per dozen at New York City for the period 1923-1931:

Month	Jan. Feb. Mar. Apr. May June July Aug. Sept. Oct. Nov. Dec.
Average Price	.41 .35 .28 .27 .27 .27 .27 .30 .33 .36 .44 .44

It will be clear that egg prices are not, in the strictest sense of the word, a function of the time of year, because, if one is given any specified month, say December, he would not be justified in asserting that eggs would be selling at exactly 44 cents per dozen for, in addition to the time of year, egg prices are affected by several other variables. He could, however, assert strongly that their price will very probably be higher in December than in April. While he cannot say, then, that price is a *function* of the time of year alone, he may say that price and the time of year are *correlated*. A mathematical measure of correlation is developed later, in Chapter X.

From the very strictest point of view, it might be said that all functional relations which are derived from experiment are examples of correlation, although there are many different degrees of correlation. One may take instances from the physical sciences, where it is possible by controlled experiment to eliminate practically all extraneous possibilities that might bias the result, where the possibilities of random error may be so minimized as practically to be ignored, and where one arrives at correlations that are practically perfect and sustained through a series of tests. When the results in such cases are supported by *a priori* reasoning, one is justified in assuming he has arrived at true functional relationships. This happy situation does not often obtain in economic series. Since almost every economic variable reacts in some degree on other variables, it is difficult to distinguish the effect of different factors. It is impossible by controlled experiment to eliminate these confusing elements, for the variables the economist may be studying cannot be effectively isolated from their economic context. There is not, as there often is in the physical sciences, any possibility of minimizing the random element and reducing the relative error.[1] Take as an example the following illustration: It has already been shown in the table given in section 1 that there is a fundamental relationship between the time of year and the minutes of daylight. If the date is known, the length of day can also be known. In this case the correlation is perfect and one says that "minutes of daylight" is a function of the days from December 31. Consider, however, the case of the mean daily temperature at New York City. Is it also a function of the time of year? One sees at once that this is not the case; for instance, one cannot foretell the exact average temperature for next July 21. He is sure, however, that it will be greater than the average temperature for next December 21, and from a table of mean temperatures for July an approximate guess can be made which will probably not be far from the true value. In other words, mean daily temperature, while not an absolute function of the time of year, is closely correlated with it.

The same situation prevails among economic series also. One cannot say from the fact that it is September that pig iron production will be 2,314,700 gross tons. He can say, however, that it is very probable that pig iron production in the September of any year will be greater than in the January of that year. There is a definite association between the months of the year and pig iron production, when one considers enough cases. But the action of a multitude of effective economic elements such as cyclical phase, the construction, automotive, and railroad situations, the pressure of competitive materials, the price factor, etc., etc., prevent one from establishing any true functional relationship between the month of the year and the production of pig iron alone.

---

[1] See C. F. Roos, *Dynamic Economics*, Bloomington, Indiana, 1934, Appendix I, p. 246, for a stimulating discussion of correlation of time series.

PROBLEMS

1. The following table gives the monthly price of eggs in dollars per dozen at New York City for the five-year period 1923-1927:

Year	Jan.	Feb.	Mar.	Apr.	May	June	July	Aug.	Sept.	Oct	Nov.	Dec.
1923	.42	.37	.31	.27	.27	.24	.25	.29	.35	.39	.53	.47
1924	.42	.39	.25	.24	.25	.27	.29	.33	.39	.44	.52	.57
1925	.59	.44	.30	.29	.32	.33	.33	.33	.37	.43	.56	.51
1926	.38	.31	.29	.32	.31	.30	.29	.31	.38	.40	.50	.48
1927	.42	.32	.25	.26	.23	.23	.25	.28	.34	.40	.44	.45

Estimate the price for January, 1930; for April, 1931; for September, 1929. (The actual prices for these dates were .42, .27, and .36, respectively.)

2. The following table gives the monthly receipts of eggs (unit, 1,000 cases) at New York City for the five-year period 1923 to 1927:

Year	Jan.	Feb.	Mar.	Apr.	May	June	July	Aug.	Sept.	Oct.	Nov.	Dec.
1923	386	447	981	924	1163	796	596	528	416	377	270	272
1924	301	410	717	1082	970	789	599	429	405	361	221	259
1925	325	550	872	1115	871	838	550	490	427	328	208	320
1926	393	471	813	860	868	871	579	502	433	344	284	400
1927	458	542	863	1094	1038	716	521	441	386	355	319	315

Does a functional relationship exist between time and receipts of eggs in New York City? Does a functional relationship exist between receipts of eggs and the price of eggs as given in the table of problem 1?

3. The following table shows the ton-miles (in millions) of revenue freight for the railroads in the Eastern Division from 1890 to 1922:

Year	1890	1891	1892	1893	1894	1895	1896	1897	1898	1899	1900
Revenue Ft.	43	44	50	51	43	48	53	51	60	67	75

Year	1901	1902	1903	1904	1905	1906	1907	1908	1909	1910	1911
Revenue Ft.	76	79	87	87	94	107	118	108	106	125	131

Year	1912	1913	1914	1915	1916	1917	1918	1919	1920	1921	1922
Revenue Ft.	135	154	144	137	179	188	191	170	189	139	151

Is the amount of revenue freight hauled by railroads a function of the time? Estimate the ton-miles for 1923; for 1889; for 1930.

4. The following table gives the percentage of persons gainfully occupied in the United States, by age and sex, for the year 1930:

Age in years	Percent Gainfully Occupied Men	Percent Gainfully Occupied Women
10-13	3.3	1.5
14	9.2	4.0
15	16.3	7.6
16	32.7	17.0
17	49.9	27.5
18-19	70.7	40.5
20-24	89.9	42.4
25-29	97.0	31.0
30-34	97.6	24.4
35-39	97.7	23.1
40-44	97.6	21.9
45-49	97.2	21.0
50-54	95.7	19.7
55-59	93.0	17.3
60-64	86.8	14.7
65-69	75.7	11.4
70-74	57.5	7.6
75 and over	32.3	4.0

Is there a functional relationship between the percentage of persons gainfully occupied and age? What is the probability that a man was gainfully occupied at an age between 20 and 24? between 35 and 39? What are the corresponding probabilities for a woman? Hint: Probability is expressed as the ratio of the number of favorable cases to the total number of cases.

5. Problem 1, section 4, Chapter X, lists the dividend rates and prices of the common stocks of 200 companies listed on the New York Stock Exchange. Is there a functional relationship between dividends and prices?

3. The Graphical Representation of Functions. It is an important part of statistical procedure to represent data graphically, and to fit to these data appropriate functions which are approximate representations of them.

In the first chapter, the usual method of graphing, where points are located by referring them to mutually perpendicular intersecting straight lines, has been explained. Functional relations of all kinds are presented visually by this method.

A few examples will illustrate the essential features of the graphical representation of functions:

Example 1. Graph the function $y = 2x + 3$.

THE GRAPHICAL ANALYSIS OF DATA 43

Since only the mathematical expression for the function is given, the first task is to form a table of values convenient for use in graphing. Let arbitrary values be assigned to the variable x. Unless there is some reason to the contrary, the first values used may be —2, —1, 0, 1, 2. This choice does not represent a fixed rule, because the values to be assigned arbitrarily depend entirely upon the character of the function.

The following table of values is thus obtained:

y	—1	1	3	5	7
x	—2	—1	0	1	2

When the number pairs (—2, —1), (—1, 1), (0, 3), (1, 5), (2, 7) are plotted, as in Figure 7, they are found to lie upon a straight line, which is the graphical representation of the function.

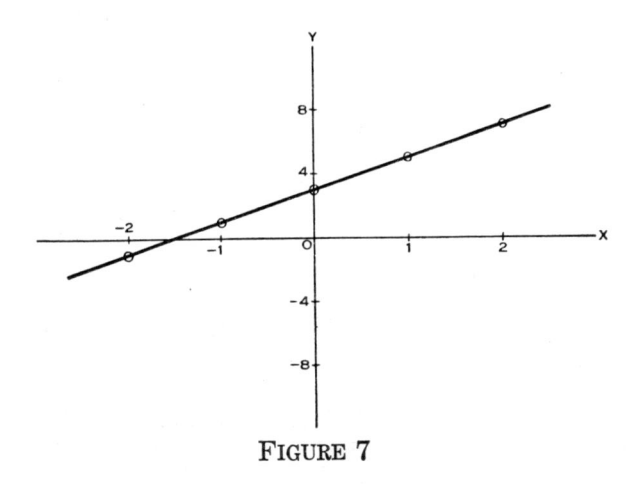

FIGURE 7

Example 2. Graph the function $y = \pm\sqrt{2x + 3}$.

Here again, one must arbitrarily assign values to the variable x in order to obtain the table used in graphing. It will also be noticed that, to each value of x, there will correspond two values of y. As before, assume the values —2, —1, 0, 1, 2. The first, it is found, must be discarded, since the corresponding values of y will be $\pm \sqrt{-1}$, which are not real numbers. The square root of a negative number is called an *imaginary*. It is also convenient to add the number $x = 3$ to the arbitrary values of the abscissa. The following table is then used to obtain the graph, which is shown in Figure 8:

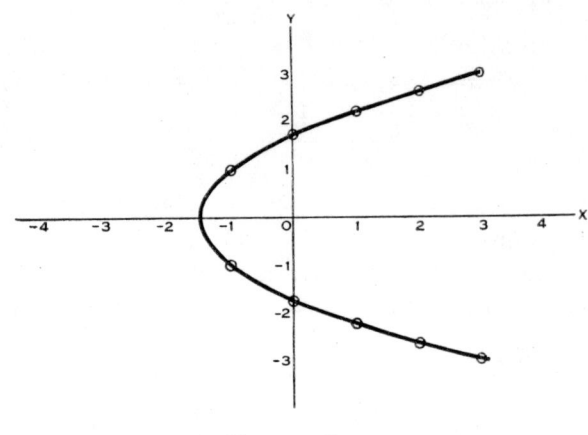

y	±1	±1.73	±2.24	±2.65	±3
x	−1	0	1	2	3

FIGURE 8

Example 3. Make a graphical representation of the data given in section 1 showing the relationship of daylight to the time of year.

The problem presented here, which is always one met with in graphing, is that of selecting proper units for the two axes. This selection should be made only after a consideration of the ranges of the two variables to be represented. In the present case, in order to show the periodicity of the function, a range of 730 days for the X-axis should be assumed. Also, since the minutes of daylight in a day at New York City are never less than 555 nor greater than 906, it will be convenient to divide the y-range into four sections of 100 units each, the origin corresponding to 500. The data are plotted in Figure 9.

The student should observe from this example that one may be required to choose different intervals on each axis, and that the lower left hand corner does not necessarily represent a zero value.

Example 4. Exhibit the following data graphically and show that the function $y = 19.40 - .07x$ is an approximate representation:

THE GRAPHICAL ANALYSIS OF DATA 45

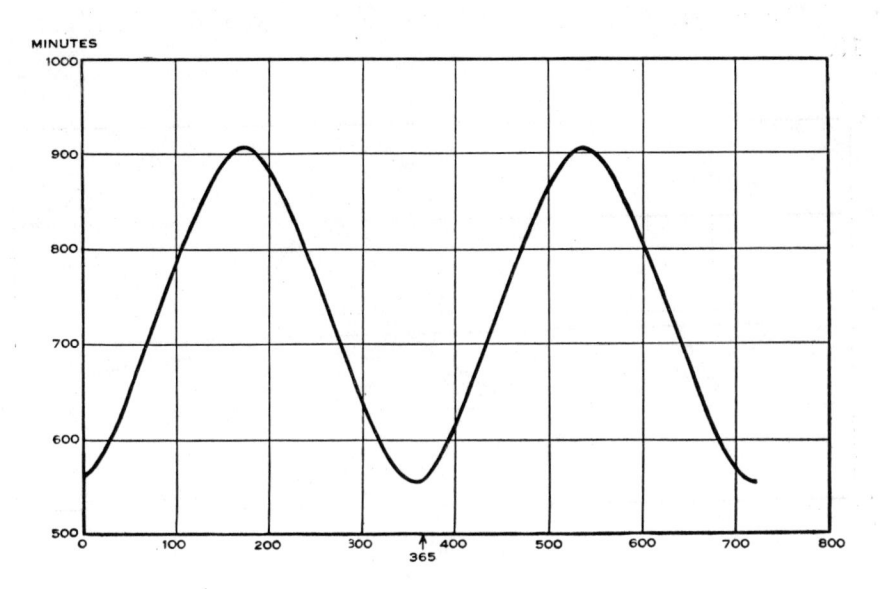

FIGURE 9

Price of Pig Iron in Dollars per Ton	19.98	15.87	22.19	19.92	15.57	17.88
Year	1900	1901	1902	1903	1904	1905
Value of x (Class Mark)	1	2	3	4	5	6

Price of Pig Iron	20.98	23.89	17.70	17.81	16.88
Year	1906	1907	1908	1909	1910
Value of x	7	8	9	10	11

Calculating values of the function $y = 19.40 - .07x$, one has

y	19.33	19.19	18.91	18.77	18.63
x	1	3	7	9	11

The graphs of the data and the function are shown in Figure 10.

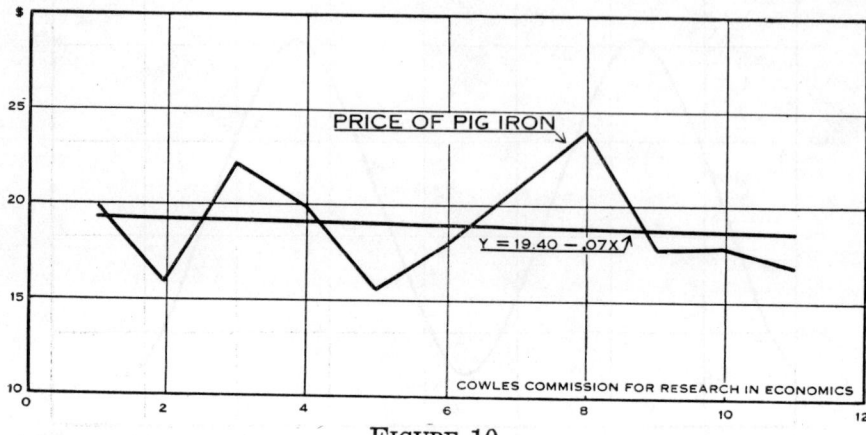

FIGURE 10

PROBLEMS

1. Graph the function $y = -\frac{1}{2}x - 3$.

2. Show that the graphs of the functions $y = 4x + 2$ and $y = -\frac{1}{4}x + 1$ are perpendicular to one another.

3. Graph $y = 4x^2$.

4. Graph $y = \frac{1}{x} + x$.

5. Show that $y = \pm\sqrt{25 - x^2}$ graphs into a circle of radius 5. Hint: Use both plus and minus values of x and notice that x cannot be greater than 5 nor smaller than -5.

6. If a box with a square base has an open top, the area A is given by the formula
$$A = a^2 + 4V/a,$$
where a is the side of the base and V the volume of the box. If V is one cubic foot, graph the value of A in terms of a and show graphically that the area is the smallest when a is equal to twice the height.

7. Graph the data of problem 1, section 2.

8. Graph the data of problem 2, section 2, for the years 1924 and 1925.

9. Graph the data of problem 4, section 2.

10. Graph the data of problem 3, section 2, Chapter V.

11. Graph the data of problem 5, section 1, and by continuing the curve estimate the population for 1930, 1940, and 1950.

12. The following table gives the values (unit, 1,000 cars) of a smooth curve fitted to automobile production (U.S. passenger cars) for the years 1913-1927:

Year	1913	1914	1915	1916	1917	1918	1919	1920
Value	33.45	42.90	54.46	68.38	84.61	103.10	123.33	144.81

Year	1921	1922	1923	1924	1925	1926	1927
Value	166.59	187.95	207.96	226.22	241.95	255.81	266.91

Represent these data graphically. In what years was automobile production growing most rapidly? (The curve obtained is known as the *logistic curve*; it approximates many forms of industrial growth.)

13. Make a graph of the "goodness of fit" curve, Table VIII (The Pearson Probability P), for $n = 3$, using χ^2 as the abscissa and the tabulated value as ordinate.

14. Make a graph of the "goodness of fit" curve, Table VIII, for $\chi^2 = 10$, using n as the abscissa and the tabulated value as ordinate.

4. *The Straight Line*. In the following sections a few typical graphs useful in statistical work are discussed. One may begin with the straight line.

The general equation of the straight line is

$$y = a + bx , \qquad (1)$$

also sometimes written as

$$y = a_1 + a_2 x ,$$

where a and b are arbitrary constants. The constant a is represented in the graph as the distance from the origin, measured along the y-axis, of a point on a straight line, namely, the distance OA in Figure 11. This distance is usually referred to as the y-intercept. The constant b is the *slope* of the straight line, and is numerically equal to the ratio BC/AB. In graphing equation (1), since it is a straight line, only three values of x and y need be used. Two of these values determine the line, and the third can be used as a check. The first example of the preceding section illustrates the problem of graphing a straight line.

5. *Fitting a Straight Line to Data*. In statistical work, one is usually more concerned with the problem inverse to that discussed in the preceding section, that is to say, with the problem of finding the equation of a straight line which approximately represents a given series of data.

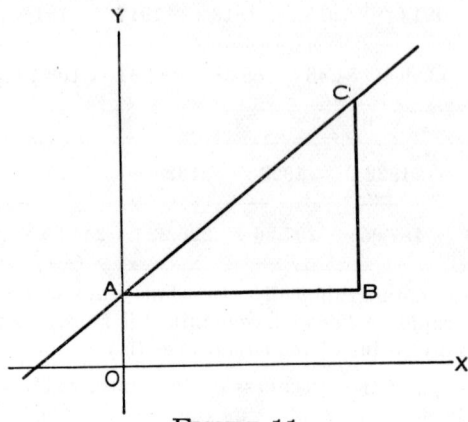

FIGURE 11

To illustrate the procedure, consider the following data:

y	2	3	4	4	5	5
x	1	2	3	4	5	6

If these points are represented graphically, they will be found to lie approximately, but not exactly, in a straight line. The problem is to calculate the coefficients a and b of the straight line $y = a + bx$, determining them in such a way that the straight line will pass as near all the given points as possible.

A method by which these coefficients may be computed is called the *method of least squares*, and is discussed more fully in Chapter IX. For our present purpose, it will be sufficient to exhibit the process by which the line is determined.

If x and y in the equation $y = a + bx$ are replaced by the values given in the table, the following set of six equations is obtained:

$$\begin{aligned} b + a &= 2, \\ 2b + a &= 3, \\ 3b + a &= 4, \\ 4b + a &= 4, \\ 5b + a &= 5, \\ 6b + a &= 5. \end{aligned}$$

It will be readily seen that no values of a and b can be obtained which will satisfy simultaneously all six equations. Hence, one must find one set of values which is *the best*[1] *approximation* to a solution of the equations.

In order to do this one may first obtain two equations called, respectively, the *first* and *second normal equations*. The first normal equation is formed by multiplying each equation by its coefficient of b and then adding together the set thus obtained. Similarly, the second normal equation is formed by multiplying each equation by the coefficient of a, (in this case by 1), and then finding the sum of the set. For the present example, this process is as follows:

$$\begin{array}{ll}
b + a = 2 & b + a = 2 \\
4b + 2a = 6 & 2b + a = 3 \\
9b + 3a = 12 & 3b + a = 4 \\
16b + 4a = 16 & 4b + a = 4 \\
25b + 5a = 25 & 5b + a = 5 \\
36b + 6a = 30 & 6b + a = 5 \\
\hline
91b + 21a = 91 & 21b + 6a = 23 \\
\text{(First Normal Equation)} & \text{(Second Normal Equation)}
\end{array}$$

The desired values of a and b are to be computed by solving the two normal equations simultaneously. To do this, divide the first equation by 91, the second by 21, and subtract the first from the second. Then

(1) $\qquad b + .2308a = 1$

(2) $\qquad b + .2857a = 1.0952$

$$\overline{\qquad .0549a = .0952}$$

Hence, one gets,

$$a = 1.73 \ .$$

Substituting this value in the first equation and solving for b, one obtains

$$b = 1 - (.2308)(1.73) = .6 \ .$$

---

[1] The word *best* is used here in a particular sense, namely, as best in the sense of *least squares*. It is not convenient at this point to amplify the definition thus implied, but a discussion of the principle will be given in section 7 of Chapter VIII. A further amplification will also be found in Chapter IX.

The least square straight line, $y = a + bx$, is then

$$y = 1.73 + .6x,$$

which is graphically represented in Figure 12.

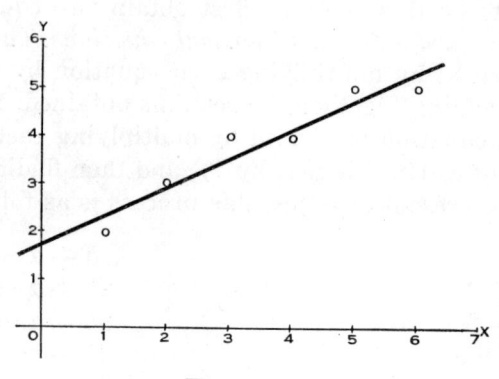

FIGURE 12.

6. Use of Tables in Fitting a Straight Line to Data. The problem of fitting a straight line to data is one so frequently met with in statistics that it is desirable to have a short cut for computing the coefficients. This can be done conveniently by means of Table IX, provided the abscissa values are the sequence 1, 2, 3, ..., p, that is to say, provided the data are given in the following form:

y	y_1	y_2	y_3	y_4	· · · · ·	y_p
x	1	2	3	4	· · · · ·	p

The derivation of the formulas from which Table IX was computed is given in section 5, Chapter IX, and will not be discussed here. The use of the table is explained in the following rule:

First calculate the values $m_0 = y_1 + y_2 + y_3 + \cdots + y_p$ *and* $m_1 = y_1 + 2y_2 + 3y_3 + \cdots + py_p$.

Then the coefficients of the straight line, $y = a + bx$, *which best fits the data, are computed from the formulas:*

$$a = Am_0 + Bm_1,$$
$$b = Bm_0 + Cm_1,$$

where $A, B, C,$ are the values in Table IX corresponding to p.

THE GRAPHICAL ANALYSIS OF DATA

Example: The coefficients a and b for the example discussed in the preceding section are thus easily obtained.

One first computes
$$m_0 = 2+3+4+4+5+5 = 23 ,$$
$$m_1 = 2+6+12+16+25+30 = 91 .$$

Using $p = 6$ (the last abscissa value), it is found from Table IX that,
$$A = .86667 , \quad B = -.20000 , \quad C = .05714 .$$

Hence,
$$a = (.86667)(23) + (-.20000)(91) = 1.73 ,$$
$$b = (-.20000)(23) + (.05714)(91) = .6 .$$

PROBLEMS

1. Graph $y = -2x + 3$.

2. Graph $2x + 3y = 6$.

3. Show that the lines $3x + 4y = 12$ and $4x - 3y = 12$ are perpendicular to one another.

4. What are the slopes of the lines $2x - 3y = 6$, $5x + y = 2$, $5x + y = 6$, and $2x + 6y = 5$?

5. Find graphically the intersection of the lines $2x + 3y = 6$ and $3x - 2y = 6$.

6. Graph the lines $4x - 6y = 1$ and $2x - 3y = 3$. From this example state the condition for parallel lines.

7. Graph the lines $x + 3y = 6$, $x - 2y = 4$, and $x + y = 6$.

8. Show that the following lines meet in a point:
$$x + 2y = 4; \quad 2y - x = 0; \quad 3x - 2y = 4.$$

9. Calculate by the method of section 5 the straight line which fits the data of example 4, section 3.

10. Calculate by means of Table IX the straight line which fits the data of example 4, section 3.

11. Obtain a straight line of the form,
$$P = a + bM ,$$
where M is the month and P is the average price, using the data given in section 2 to determine a and b. Hint: Replace the *month* class marks by the integers 1, 2, 3, ... , 12.

12. Fit a straight line to the data of problem 3, section 2, for the years from 1890-1913. Hint: Replace the years by the integers 1, 2, 3, ... , 24.

7. The Parabola. A parobla is the locus or curve determined by the equation

$$y = a_1 + a_2 x + a_3 x^2, \qquad (2)$$

where a_1, a_2, and a_3 are arbitrary constants.

Example: For the parabola

$$y = 2 + 3x - 2x^2,$$

the following table of values for x and y is determined, which, when plotted in Figure 13, give us a picture of the curve:

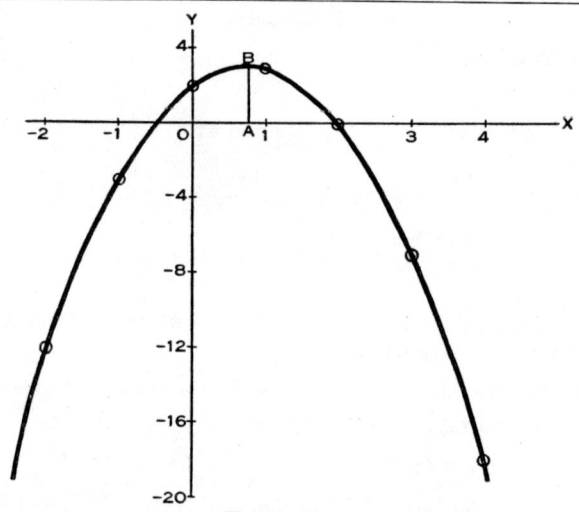

y	—12	—3	2	3	0	—7	—18
x	—2	—1	0	1	2	3	4

FIGURE 13.

A parabola, in the form in which it has been written, is characterized by the fact that it is a curve that is either concave up or concave down. In other words, it has either a *minimum*, that is, a smallest value, or a *maximum*, that is, a largest value. If a_3 is negative, the parabola is concave down, as in the example.

The value of x for which the parabola is a maximum or a minimum is

$$x = -(a_2/2a_3), \qquad (3)$$

and the maximum or minimum value for y is given by
$$y = (4a_3 a_1 - a_2^2)/4a_3 . \tag{4}$$

In the example, $a_1 = 2$, $a_2 = 3$, $a_3 = -2$. Hence, $x = -3/(-4) = .75$ and $y = \dfrac{(4)(-2)(2) - 9}{-8} = \dfrac{-25}{-8} = 3.125$. These values are represented in Figure 13 by the lines OA and AB respectively. Since the curve is concave down, AB is a maximum value.

The results (3) and (4) readily follow from the fact that equation (2) can be written in the form
$$y = \dfrac{(4a_3 a_1 - a_2^2)}{4a_3} + a_3 \left(x + \dfrac{a_2}{2a_3}\right)^2 .$$

If y is to reach its maximum or minimum value, the squared term, which is variable, must be made as small as possible, that is to say, it must equal zero. Setting it equal to zero, therefore, and solving for x, one gets (3). The remaining term is seen to be equal to the term in (4).

The parabola may cross the x-axis twice, once, or not at all. To find where the parabola crosses the x-axis, one sets $y = 0$ and thus obtains the equation
$$a_3 x^2 + a_2 x + a_1 = 0 .$$

The solution of this equation is given by the familiar quadratic formula:
$$x = \dfrac{-a_2 \pm \sqrt{a_2^2 - 4a_3 a_1}}{2a_3} .$$

From this formula it is readily seen that:

(a) if $a_2^2 - 4a_3 a_1 > 0$, the parabola crosses in two points, since x has two real values;

(b) if $a_2^2 - 4a_3 a_1 = 0$, the parabola crosses in two coincident points, since x has only one value; and

(c) if $a_2^2 - 4a_3 a_1 < 0$, the parabola crosses at no point, since x has two imaginary values.

In the example,
$$x = \dfrac{-3 \pm \sqrt{9 + 16}}{-4} ,$$

and hence one gets

$$x = 2 \text{ and } x = -1/2 \ .$$

8. Fitting the Parabola to Data. The method of fitting a straight line to data, as described in section 5, is capable of immediate generalization. In the case of the parabola

$$y = a_1 + a_2 x + a_3 x^2 \ ,$$

three normal equations instead of two may be used for the determination of the constants, a_1, a_2, and a_3.

It will be more convenient at this time, however, to postpone consideration of the general theory of curve fitting to a later chapter and to make use of Table X which is designed to simplify the problem in the case of the parabola.

The rule to be applied may be stated thus:

Let the data be given in the following form:

y	y_1	y_2	y_3	y_4	$\cdots\cdots$	y_p
x	1	2	3	4	$\cdots\cdots$	p

Then compute the values:

$$m_0 = y_1 + y_2 + y_3 + y_4 + \cdots\cdots + y_p \ ,$$
$$m_1 = y_1 + 2y_2 + 3y_3 + 4y_4 + \cdots\cdots + py_p \ ,$$
$$m_2 = y_1 + 4y_2 + 9y_3 + 16y_4 + \cdots\cdots + p^2 y_p \ .$$

From these constants determine the coefficients of the parabola by means of the formulas:

$$a_1 = Am_0 + Bm_1 + Cm_2 \ ,$$
$$a_2 = Bm_0 + Dm_1 + Em_2 \ ,$$
$$a_3 = Cm_0 + Em_1 + Fm_2 \ ,$$

where A, B, C, D, E, and F, are the values in Table X corresponding to the value p.

Example: In illustration, a parabola may be fitted to the following data:

y	−12	−3	2	3	0	−7	−18
x	−2	−1	0	1	2	3	4

(a)

Since the values of x are not the sequence of positive integers required by the rule, although successive values differ by unity, the positive integers will be chosen as new class marks and the table written thus:

y	—12	—3	2	3	0	—7	—18
x'	1	2	3	4	5	6	7

(b)

This makes it possible to use Table X and one computes:

$$m_0 = -12 - 3 + 2 + 3 + 0 - 7 - 18 = -35 ,$$
$$m_1 = -12 - 6 + 6 + 12 + 0 - 42 - 126 = -168 ,$$
$$m_2 = -12 - 12 + 18 + 48 + 0 - 252 - 882 = -1092 .$$

Referring to Table X for $p = 7$, the values for A, B, C, D, E, and F, are found to be

$$A = 2.428571 , \qquad D = .797619 ,$$
$$B = -1.285714 , \qquad E = -.0952381,$$
$$C = .142857 , \qquad F = .0119048;$$

and a_1, a_2, and a_3 are computed as follows:

$$a_1 = (-35)(2.428571) + (-168)(-1.285714)$$
$$+ (-1092)(.142857) = -25 ,$$

$$a_2 = (-35)(-1.285714) + (-168)(.797619)$$
$$+ (-1092)(-.0952381) = 15 ,$$

$$a_3 = (-35)(.142857) + (-168)(-.0952381)$$
$$+ (-1092)(.0119048) = -2 .$$

Hence, the parabola fitting the data of table (b) is

$$y = -25 + 15x' - 2(x')^2 .$$

In order to obtain the parabola fitting table (a) one observes that the class marks in (a) differ by 3 from the class marks in (b), that is to say, $x' = x + 3$. Substituting this value in the parabola just written down, one finds

$$y = -25 + 15(x+3) - 2(x+3)^2$$
$$= -25 + 15x + 45 - 2x^2 - 12x - 18$$
$$= 2 + 3x - 2x^2 .$$

This is, in fact, the parabola used in the illustrative example of section 7.

PROBLEMS

1. Graph $y = 2x^2 - 4x + 2$.
2. Graph $y = -2x^2 + 6x - 1$.
3. Which of the following parabolas cross the x-axis and which do not?
$$y = 9x^2 - 6x + 1 \; ;$$
$$y = x^2 - 2x + 4 \; ;$$
$$y = -3x^2 + 2x + 4 \, .$$
4. For what values of x do the following parabolas cross the x-axis?
$$y = 2x^2 + 3x - 5; \quad y = 9x^2 - 6x + 1 \, .$$
5. Find the lowest or highest points on the parabolas of problem 3.
6. Find the value of x for which the expression
$$3(x-2)^2 + 5(x-3)^2 + 7(x-4)^2 \, ,$$
is a minimum.
7. Fit a parabola to the following data:

y	1	2	9	22	41	66
x	1	2	3	4	5	6

8. Fit a parabola to the values in the following table:

y	1	3	7	20	42	60
x	4	5	6	7	8	9

Hint: Replace the values of x by the sequence 1, 2, 3, 4, 5, 6.

9. Fit a parabola to the population data of problem 5, section 1. In order to simplify the calculations, round off the population figures to the nearest million and replace the years by the class marks 1, 2, 3, 4, ... , 14.

9. The Exponential Curve. A curve of great importance in many branches of mathematics, and particularly in statistics, is the exponential curve, whose equation is

$$y = ae^{bx} \, , \qquad (5)$$

where a and b are given numbers. It can be conveniently graphed by referring to a table of values, such as Table II.[1]

Example: Graph $y = 3e^{x/2}$.

---

[1] If he has not already done so, the student should familiarize himself with the exponential function e^x before beginning this section. See section 5, Appendix II.

THE GRAPHICAL ANALYSIS OF DATA

Convenient values for e^t are first obtained from Table II.

e^t	.1353	.3679	.6065	1.0000	1.6487	2.7183	7.3891
t	−2	−1	−.5	0	.5	1	2

From this table the following values of y are calculated:

y	.4059	1.1037	1.8195	3.0000	4.9461	8.1549	22.1673
x	−4	−2	−1	0	1	2	4

The graph is given in Figure 14.

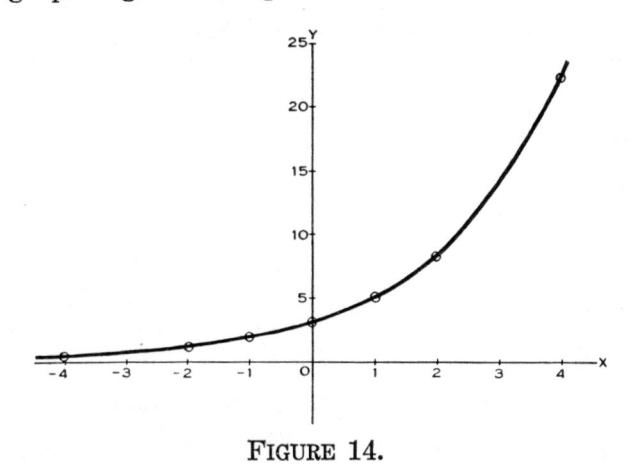

FIGURE 14.

The exponential curve is sometimes referred to as the "curve of growth," since it represents the growth of living matter under ideal conditions. It is also called "the compound interest curve," from the fact that it gives the amount to which a principal a would accumulate in time x at interest b continuously compounded.

The values a and b which occur in the general formula are to be determined from the data of the problem, namely, from given sets of values of x and y.

Thus, suppose that $y = 10$ when $x = 2$, and $y = 20$ when $x = 5$.

Taking logarithms of both sides of (5) and substituting the first set of values of x and y, one gets

$$\log 10 = \log a + 2b \log e,$$

or, since log e = .434, one then has
$$1 = \log a + .868\, b\ .$$
Also, using the second set of values, one has
$$\log 20 = \log a + 5b \log e\ ,$$
or
$$1.301 = \log a + 2.170\, b\ .$$

Eliminating log a by subtracting the first equation from the second and solving for b, one has
$$1.302\, b = .301\ ,$$
$$b = .231\ .$$

Substituting this value of b in the first equation and solving for log a, one obtains
$$\log a = 1 - .200 = .800\ ,$$
and hence
$$a = 6.31\ .$$

The desired equation is then
$$y = 6.31\, e^{.231x}\ .$$

If more than two sets of values of x and y are given for the determination of the curve, then the method of least squares explained in section 5 may be employed to advantage.

For example, suppose that the following values are given:

y	.8	2.2	3.6	6	10	19	40
x	2	3	4	5	6	7	8

and one is required to determine the "best" exponential curve that will fit them.

Taking logarithms of both sides of the equation (5), one reduces the problem to the determination of log a and b from the following expression:
$$\log a + bx \log e = \log y\ .$$

Substituting in this equation the tabulated values for x and y and remembering that log e = .434, one obtains the following set of equations:

$$\log a + (.434)(2b) = \log \ .8 ,$$
$$\log a + (.434)(3b) = \log \ 2.2 ,$$
$$\log a + (.434)(4b) = \log \ 3.6 ,$$
$$\log a + (.434)(5b) = \log \ 6 ,$$
$$\log a + (.434)(6b) = \log 10 ,$$
$$\log a + (.434)(7b) = \log 19 ,$$
$$\log a + (.434)(8b) = \log 40 .$$

Multiplying each of these equations by the coefficient of $\log a$, that is to say, by 1, and adding, one obtains the *first normal equation*. Similarly, multiplying each equation by the coefficient of b and adding, one obtains the *second normal equation*. The explicit calculations follow:

$\log a + \ \ .868\, b = -0.097$,	$.868 \log a + \ \ \ .753\, b = -.084$,
$\log a + 1.302\, b = \ \ 0.342$,	$1.302 \log a + \ \ 1.695\, b = \ \ .445$,
$\log a + 1.736\, b = \ \ 0.556$,	$1.736 \log a + \ \ 3.014\, b = \ \ .965$,
$\log a + 2.170\, b = \ \ 0.778$,	$2.170 \log a + \ \ 4.709\, b = 1.688$,
$\log a + 2.604\, b = \ \ 1.000$,	$2.604 \log a + \ \ 6.781\, b = 2.604$,
$\log a + 3.038\, b = \ \ 1.279$,	$3.038 \log a + \ \ 9.229\, b = 3.886$,
$\log a + 3.472\, b = \ \ 1.602$,	$3.472 \log a + 12.055\, b = 5.562$,

$7 \log a + 15.190\, b = 5.460$. $15.190 \log a + 38.236\, b = 15.066$.
(First Normal Equation)   (Second Normal Equation)

In order to solve these equations for b and $\log a$, one proceeds as in section 5. Dividing the first normal equation by 7 and the second by 15.190, one gets

$$\log a + 2.17000\, b = .78000$$
$$\log a + 2.51718\, b = .99184$$

Solving for b, $-.34718\, b = -.21184$,
$$b = .610 .$$

Substituting this value in the first equation above, one finds

$$\log a = .78000 - 1.32370 = -.54370 = 9.45630 - 10,$$

and hence $a = .286$.

The desired equation thus becomes
$$y = .286\, e^{.610x} .$$

Values calculated from this function are compared with the original data in the following table:

x	2	3	4	5	6	7	8
Given Values	.8	2.2	3.6	6	10	19	40
Calculated Values	1.0	1.8	3.3	6.0	11.1	20.4	37.6

PROBLEMS

Graph the following functions:

1. $y = e^{-x}$.
2. $y = 5e^{2x}$.
3. $y = e^x + e^{-x}$.
4. $y = e^x - e^{-x}$.
5. $y = e^x - e^{-2x}$.

6. Determine the exponential curve that passes through the points $(-2, 7)$ and $(4, 1)$.

7. Determine the exponential curve that passes through the points (1, 3.66), (2, 4.47), (3, 5.47), (4, 6.68), (5, 8.15).

8. Fit an exponential curve to the following data:

y	2	3	4	7	12	20
x	1.5	2	2.5	3	3.5	4

9. Fit an exponential curve to the first seven items of the population data of problem 5, section 1, replacing the years by the class marks 1, 2, 3, ... , 7. From this curve calculate the values corresponding to the next five items in the table. How do these values compare with the data? Does population growth follow the exponential law?

10. According to Raymond Pearl, the following function represents the population growth of the United States:

$$y = \frac{197.27}{1 + 67.32e^{-.0313x}},$$

where x represents the number of years since 1780. Graph this function and compare it with the actual population statistics. (See problem 5, section 1). Hint: Let x be multiples of twenty.

10. The Skew-Normal Probability Curve.

The skew-normal probability curve, which will be studied in considerable detail later, is given by the equation

$$y = \frac{N}{\sigma\sqrt{2\pi}} \, e^{[(p-q)/2\sigma^2]x} \, e^{-(1/2\sigma^2)x^2}, \qquad (6)$$

where N, p, q, and σ, are arbitrary constants whose significance will be pointed out in a subsequent chapter.

When $p = q$, the term $e^{(p-q)x/2\sigma^2}$ reduces to 1, and the curve is then called the *curve of normal probability*.

In order to graph (6), it is first written, for convenience, in the form:

$$y = \left(\frac{N}{\sigma}\right) e^{[(p-q)/2\sigma](x/\sigma)} \frac{1}{\sqrt{2\pi}} \, e^{-\frac{1}{2}(x/\sigma)^2},$$

and x is allowed to assume multiple values of σ. Values of the function $(1/\sqrt{2\pi}) e^{-t^2/2}$ have been recorded in Table VI, and this very much simplifies the calculation of values of y.

Example: Assuming the values $N = 120$, $\sigma = .6$, $p = .75$, $q = .25$, graph equation (6).

One first calculates N/σ and $(p-q)/2\sigma$, thus obtaining $N/\sigma = 200$, $(p-q)/2\sigma = .50/1.2 = .42$. Then let x take the values $-3\sigma, -2\sigma, -\sigma, -\sigma/2, 0, \sigma/2, \sigma, 2\sigma, 3\sigma$. For simplicity, the following abbreviations are made:

$$y_1 = e^{.42x/\sigma}, \qquad y_2 = \frac{1}{\sqrt{2\pi}} \, e^{-\frac{1}{2}(x/\sigma)^2}.$$

Then for $x = 2\sigma$, $y_1 = e^{.42 \times 2} = e^{.84} = 2.3164$, from Table II; and $y_2 = \frac{1}{\sqrt{2\pi}} e^{-\frac{1}{2}(2)^2} = .0540$, from Table VI. For $x = -3\sigma$, $y_1 = e^{-.42 \times 3} = e^{-1.26} = .2837$, from Table II, and $y_2 = \frac{1}{\sqrt{2\pi}} e^{-\frac{1}{2}(3)^2} = .0044$.

Calculating the values of y_1 and y_2 for each value of x, they are recorded in parallel columns together with the value of N/σ.

The products of the three numbers in each row will be the desired values of y. The following table shows the results of these calculations, and the final values are graphed in Figure 15.

$\dfrac{x}{\sigma}$	$\dfrac{N}{\sigma}$	$y_1{}^*$	$y_2{}^{**}$	$y = \dfrac{N}{\sigma} y_1 y_2$
-3	200	.2837	.0044	.25
-2	200	.4317	.0540	4.66
-1	200	.6571	.2420	31.80
$-\tfrac{1}{2}$	200	.8106	.3521	57.08
0	200	1.0000	.3989	79.78
$\tfrac{1}{2}$	200	1.2337	.3521	86.88
1	200	1.5220	.2420	73.66
2	200	2.3164	.0540	25.02
3	200	3.5254	.0044	3.10

$* \; y_1 = e^{[(p-q)/2\sigma](x/\sigma)}$

$** \; y_2 = \dfrac{1}{\sqrt{2\pi}} e^{-\tfrac{1}{2}(x/\sigma)^2}$.

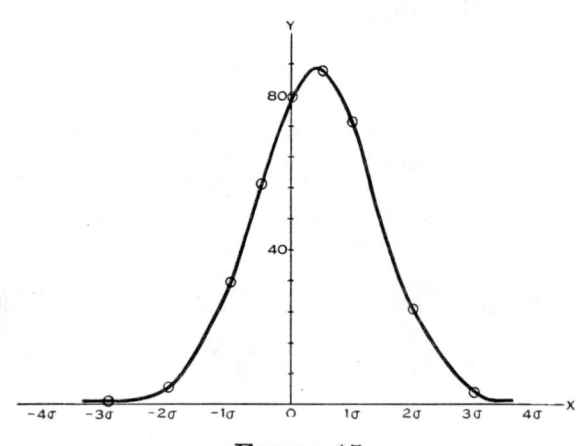

FIGURE 15

PROBLEMS

Graph equation (6) for the following values of N, σ, p, and q:

1. $N = 1024$, $\sigma = 1.58$, $p = 1/2$, $q = 1/2$.
2. $N = 59049$, $\sigma = 1.05$, $p = .33$, $q = .67$.
3. $N = 59049$, $\sigma = 1.05$, $p = .67$, $q = .33$.
4. $N = 1000$, $\sigma = 2.00$, $p = .1$, $q = .9$.
5. $N = 500$, $\sigma = 1.00$, $p = 0$, $q = 1$.
6. $N = 500$, $\sigma = 1.00$, $p = 1$, $q = 0$.

7. Calculate the binomial frequencies $_{10}C_r$ for $r = 5, 6, 7, 8, 9$, and 10; show that they are approximately equal to the ordinates of the curve of problem 1 for $x = 0, 1, 2, 3, 4, 5$.

11. The Translation of Axes. It is often convenient in the graphical representation of equations to change the origin from one point to another by moving the axes parallel to themselves. This process of *translating the axes* will often simplify the appearance of an equation of a curve although, of course, the curve itself remains unaltered. For example, if the origin of coordinates is changed to the point (—4, 3) the equation of the parabola $y = 2x^2 + 16x + 35$ reduces to the simple form $y = 2x^2$.

The method of translating axes is explained by Figure 16. Let OX and OY be the original axes and $O'X'$ and $O'Y'$ the new axes. Let (h,k) be the coordinates of the new origin O' re-

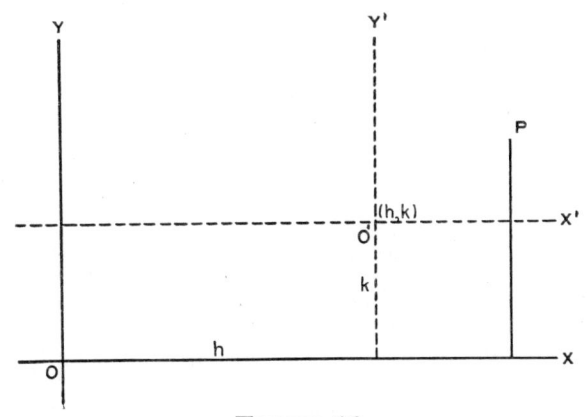

FIGURE 16

ferred to the old axes. Then, if (x,y) denotes a point with coordinates referred to OX and OY, and (x', y') the same point referred to $O'X'$ and $O'Y'$, is is clear that the coordinates x, y may be com-

puted from the coordinates x', y' by means of the following equations:
$$x = x' + h ,$$
$$y = y' + k .$$

Example: Transform the equation of the parabola $y = 2x^2 + 16x + 35$ by changing the origin from $(0, 0)$ to the point $(-4, 3)$.

In this example, $h = -4$ and $k = 3$. Therefore, if x' and y' are the new coordinates, one has
$$x = x' - 4 ,$$
$$y = y' + 3 .$$

Substituting these in the equation of the parabola, one gets
$$y' + 3 = 2(x'-4)^2 + 16(x'-4) + 35 ,$$
which reduces to
$$y' = 2x'^2 .$$

The relationship thus obtained is brought out in Figure 17.

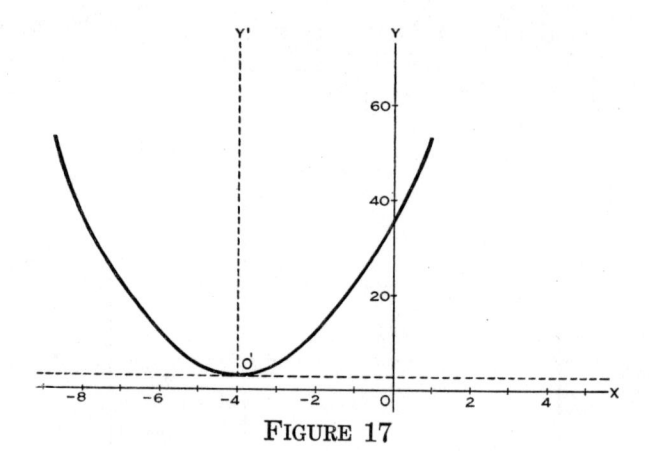

FIGURE 17

PROBLEMS

Transform each of the following equations by shifting the origin to the point indicated.

1. $3x + 4y = 3$, $(-5, 5)$.
2. $x^2 - 4x + y^2 + 6y + 9 = 0$, $(2, -3)$.

3. $y = 3x^2 - 2x + 6$, $(1,-1)$.
4. $xy + 2y + 4x - 1 = 0$, $(-2,-3)$.
5. $y = e^{-4}e^{2x} + 3$, $(2,3)$.

6. For what values of h and k will the equation $y = 3x^2 - 12x + 7$ reduce to $y' = 3x'^2$? Hint: Substitute $x = x' + h$, $y = y' + k$ in the first equation. Then set the coefficient of x and the constant term equal to zero, and solve the two equations thus obtained for h and k.

7. Reduce the equation $10x - 3y + 2 = 0$ to the form $10x' - 3y' = 0$ by a translation of axes.

8. Show that the parabola $y = a_3 x^2 + a_2 x + a_1$ may be put into the form $y' = a_3 x'^2$, if $h = -\dfrac{a_2}{2a_3}$ and $k = \dfrac{(4a_3 a_1 - a_2^2)}{4a_3}$.

CHAPTER III

METHODS OF AVERAGING

1. Six Averages. In the theory of statistics there are several averages in common use, in particular, (1) the *arithmetic mean* (A); (2) the *root-mean-square* or *quadratic mean* (R); (3) the *median* (M); (4) the *mode* (Mo); (5) the *geometric mean* (G); and (6) the *harmonic mean* (H). With so many averages to choose from, it is often very confusing to know just which one to use in the study of a particular problem. Fortunately, however, each average has its own special uses, as will appear in the ensuing discussion.

2. Illustrative Data. In order to have a common example to which the various methods of averaging may be applied for comparative purposes, the frequency distribution discussed in section 9, Chapter I, page 18, may be employed. For the sake of ready reference, Table (a) and Table (b) derived from it are repeated below:

TABLE (a) 4-6 Months Prime Commercial Paper Rates, January, 1922, to December, 1931 [1930]

x	f	x	f	x	f	x	f	x	f	x	f	x	f	x	f
2.88%	1	3.56	1	3.94	3	4.15	1	4.43	1	4.70	1	5.09	1	5.56	1
2.97	1	3.63	1	3.95	2	4.19	3	4.44	2	4.78	2	5.13	4	5.59	1
3.00	3	3.65	1	3.97	1	4.23	1	4.50	1	4.85	1	5.16	1	5.69	1
3.13	3	3.72	1	4.00	5	4.25	4	4.55	1	4.88	4	5.38	1	5.90	1
3.23	1	3.88	6	4.05	1	4.28	1	4.59	1	4.94	1	5.39	1	6.00	3
3.28	1	3.90	1	4.06	1	4.31	1	4.60	1	4.98	1	5.41	1	6.09	1
3.50	1	3.91	3	4.09	1	4.38	4	4.63	5	5.00	2	5.43	1	6.13	2
3.53	1	3.93	1	4.13	3	4.40	1	4.69	1	5.03	1	5.50	2	$N=$	108

TABLE (b) Frequency Table of 4-6 Months Prime Commercial Paper Rates, January, 1922, to December, 1931

Class Intervals	Class Marks	Frequencies
2.50-2.99%	2.75%	2
3.00-3.49	3.25	8
3.50-3.99	3.75	23
4.00-4.49	4.25	30
4.50-4.99	4.75	20
5.00-5.49	5.25	13
5.50-5.99	5.75	6
6.00-6.49	6.25	6

—66—

METHODS OF AVERAGING

3. The Arithmetic Mean. The arithmetic mean is the most commonly used average, and is generally what is referred to when speaking of the average price, average rate, average income, etc. By the arithmetic average of a set of items is meant the sum of the items divided by their number. For the following table,

Frequencies	f_1	f_2	f_3	....	f_m
Class Marks	x_1	x_2	x_3	....	x_m

the arithmetic mean is, by definition, the class mark obtained from the formula:

$$A = \frac{f_1 x_1 + f_2 x_2 + f_3 x_3 + \cdots\cdots + f_m x_m}{N},$$

where $N = f_1 + f_2 + f_3 + \cdots + f_m$.

It will frequently be convenient for us to make use of the abbreviation $\Sigma f_i x_i = f_1 x_1 + f_2 x_2 + f_3 x_3 + \cdots + f_m x_m$. The symbol Σ is the Greek letter sigma (capital) and it is used throughout all mathematics to designate summation. Often the symbol is written $\sum_{i=1}^{m} f_i x_i$, the lower value, $i = 1$, designating the beginning term and the upper value, m, the final term of the summation. Thus $\sum_{x=1}^{n} x^2 = 1^2 + 2^2 + 3^2 + \cdots + n^2$. When there exists no ambiguity, it is usually convenient to omit the limits of the summation from the symbol.

In terms of this symbol the arithmetic mean becomes

$$A = \frac{\Sigma f_i x_i}{N}.$$

Example: For frequency Table (a) one obtains:

$$A = \frac{1 \times 2.88 + 1 \times 2.97 + 3 \times 3.00 + \cdots\cdots + 2 \times 6.13}{108}$$

$$= \frac{477.36}{108} = 4.42.$$

For frequency Table (b),

$$A = \frac{2 \times 2.75 + 8 \times 3.25 + \cdots\cdots + 6 \times 6.25}{108}$$

$$= \frac{480.50}{108} = 4.45.$$

It should be noticed that the two values for the average agree very closely, as they always should if the choice of the class interval has been properly made.

An alternative form, useful in calculation, can be given to the formula for the arithmetic mean, as follows:

$$\frac{\Sigma f_i(x_i-X)}{N} = \frac{\Sigma f_i x_i}{N} - \frac{X \Sigma f_i}{N} = A - X \text{ , since } \Sigma f_i = N \text{ .}$$

Therefore,

$$A = X + \frac{\Sigma f_i(x_i-X)}{N} \text{ .}$$

By choosing for X some value close to the mean, the labor of calculation can often be materially reduced.

In calculating the arithmetic mean, it is well to follow some systematic scheme such as that given below. The value $X = 4.00$ has been chosen.

Class Mark (x_i)	Frequency (f_i)	(x_i-X)	$f_i(x_i-X)$
2.75%	2	— 1.25	— 2.50
3.25	8	— .75	— 6.00
3.75	23	— .25	— 5.75
4.25	30	.25	7.50
4.75	20	.75	15.00
5.25	13	1.25	16.25
5.75	6	1.75	10.50
6.25	6	2.25	13.50
Totals	108		48.50

$$A = 4.00 + \frac{48.50}{108} = 4.45 \text{ .}$$

PROBLEMS

1. The following table shows the distribution of the percentage deviations from trend of the Dow-Jones Industrial Averages for the pre-war period, 1897-1913:

METHODS OF AVERAGING

Class Mark (per cent)	Frequency	Class Mark (per cent)	Frequency
62	1	102	36
67	4	107	19
72	10	112	17
77	8	117	8
82	9	122	13
87	20	127	10
92	22	132	3
97	24		$N = 204$

Calculate the average percentage deviation for this distribution.

2. The following data give an ideal distribution, obtained by tossing ten pennies 1024 times and recording the number of heads that appeared on each toss. What is the average number of heads per toss?

No. of Heads	0	1	2	3	4	5	6	7	8	9	10
Frequency	1	16	42	126	199	253	209	118	53	4	3

3. Problem 2, section 11, Chapter I, gives the distribution of the percentage deviations from trend of Bradstreet's Commodity Prices, for the years 1897-1913. Calculate the average of this distribution.

4. The items in the table of problem 2, section 9, Chapter I, give the Ratio of Investments in U.S. Government Securities to Total Investments (All Reporting Federal Reserve Member Banks). Arrange these data for the five years 1924-1928 in a frequency table and calculate the average ratio of investments to total investments.

5. The following table gives the frequency distribution of the percentage weekly gains or losses of a random forecast record, divided by one-half of the corresponding stock market gain or loss, for the 230 weeks from January 1, 1928, to June 1, 1932:

Percentage Gain or Loss	Class Mark	Frequency
96.50- 97.49%	97%	1
97.50- 98.49	98	13
98.50- 99.49	99	32
99.50-100.49	100	115
100.50-101.49	101	45
101.50-102.49	102	14
102.50-103.49	103	2
103.50-104.49	104	4
104.50-105.49	105	2
105.50-106.49	106	1
106.50-107.49	107	1
Total		230

What is the average gain or loss for this distribution?

6. Find the average taxable income in 1921 in the United States from the following data[a], using the mean of the income class as the class mark:

Income Class	Number	Income Class	Number
$ 1,000- 2,000	2,440,544	$ 40,000- 50,000	6,051
2,000- 3,000	2,222,031	50,000-100,000	8,717
3,000- 4,000	702,991	100,000-150,000	1,367
4,000- 5,000	369,155	150,000-200,000	450
5,000-10,000	353,247	200,000-250,000	205
10,000-15,000	80,014	250,000-300,000	84
15,000-20,000	34,230	300,000-400,000	98
20,000-25,000	18,100	400,000-500,000	64
25,000-30,000	10,848	500,000-1000000	63
30,000-40,000	12,047	1,000,000 and over*	21

[a]This table is condensed from a summary in *Statistics of Income from Returns of Net Income for 1921*, Treasury Department Publication, Washington (1923).
*Use 1,000,000 as the class mark.

7. The following table shows the receipts and expenditures of the United States Government, expressed in per capita amounts, for the twenty-year period, 1913-1932:

Year	Per Capita Receipts	Per Capita Expenditures
1913	$ 7.50	$ 7.51
1914	7.50	7.51
1915	7.03	7.66
1916	7.77	7.29
1917	11.00	19.36
1918	35.38	122.58
1919	49.07	176.40
1920	62.91	60.91
1921	51.87	51.07
1922	37.39	34.54
1923	35.88	33.10
1924	35.28	30.83
1925	32.76	30.59
1926	33.83	30.61
1927	34.81	29.45
1928	33.68	30.36
1929	33.67	32.13
1930	34.47	32.96
1931	26.54	33.76
1932	15.81	38.96

Calculate the average receipts and average expenditures for these data.

8. The following frequency table shows the distribution of 1110 observations made on 149 commodity price series during ten business cycles:[1]

[1]Source of data: Frederick C. Mills, *The Behavior of Prices*, Ch. IV., National Bureau of Economic Research, N.Y., 1927.

Duration of Cycle (from low to ensuing low) (in months)	Class Mark	Frequency
7.50 to 12.49 months	10 months	7
12.50 to 17.49	15	27
17.50 to 22.49	20	61
22.50 to 27.49	25	115
27.50 to 32.49	30	139
32.50 to 37.49	35	186
37.50 to 42.49	40	167
42.50 to 47.49	45	124
47.50 to 52.49	50	122
52.50 to 57.49	55	67
57.50 to 62.49	60	52
62.50 to 67.49	65	15
67.50 to 72.49	70	15
72.50 to 77.49	75	8
77.50 to 82.49	80	2
82.50 to 87.49	85	2
87.50 to 92.49	90	0
92.50 to 97.49	95	1
Total		1110

Calculate the average duration of the cycle for this distribution.

4. Transforming the Arithmetic Mean from One Set of Class Marks to Another. It is frequently desirable in the study of statistical problems to be able to change from one set of class marks to another. Perhaps one wishes to change the origin or to increase or diminish the breadth of the class interval. Suppose that the old class marks, x_i, are related to the new class marks, y_i, by the formula:

$$x_i = ay_i + b . \qquad (1)$$

It can then be proved that the old average, A_x, is related to the new average, A_y, by the following formula:

$$A_x = a A_y + b .$$

By definition,

$$A_x = \frac{(\Sigma f_i x_i)}{N} .$$

Substituting the value of x_i in terms of y_i, from (1), one gets

$$A_x = \frac{\Sigma f_i(ay_i + b)}{N} = \frac{(a\Sigma f_i y_i)}{N} + \frac{b\Sigma f_i}{N}$$
$$= a A_y + b .$$

Example: Given that $A_x = 76.199$, where the average refers to the set of class marks (X), calculate the average for the following data, using the second set (Y):

Frequencies	14 41 56 85 52 21 7 5
Class Marks (X)	62 67 72 77 82 87 92 97
Class Marks (Y)	0 1 2 3 4 5 6 7

Since for $x = 62$, $y = 0$ and for $x = 97$, $y = 7$, for the determination of a and b in the transformation there are the two equations:
$$62 = 0\,a + b ,$$
$$97 = 7\,a + b .$$

Solving for a and b one gets $a = 5$, $b = 62$.

Hence $A_y = (A_x - b)/a = (76.199 - 62)/5 = 2.840$.

If, for any frequency distribution, the average for the set of class marks $0, 1, 2, \ldots, n$, where $n = m - 1$, has been calculated, this average is the *Bernoulli mean* and is designated by the symbol A_B. It will be found later to play an important rôle in normal and skew-normal frequency distributions. In the example just given, $A_B = A_y = 2.840$.

PROBLEMS

1. What is the relationship between the following sets of class marks?

X	5 10 15 20 25 30 35
Y	9 19 29 39 49 59 69

METHODS OF AVERAGING

2. Given the sets of class marks:

X	S	S + s	S + 2s	S + 3s	S + 4s	....
Y	0	1	2	3	4	......

show that the values of a and b in the formula $x_i = ay_i + b$ are $a = s$, $b = S$.

3. Given the following sets of class marks:

X	S	S + s	S + 2s	S + 3s	S + 4s	....
Y	T	T + t	T + 2t	T + 3t	T + 4t	....

calculate the values of a and b in the formula $x_i = ay_i + b$. Does the solution supply a formula for transforming from one set of class marks to another? Apply it to problem 1.

4. Calculate the Bernoulli mean for problem 5, section 3.

5. Calculate the average for the frequency table in problem 2, section 3, using the class marks 10, 9, 8, 7, 6, 5, 4, 3, 2, 1, 0.

5. The Root-Mean-Square or Quadratic Mean — Standard and Mean Deviations. Next to the arithmetic mean, the root-mean-square, or quadratic mean, plays the most important rôle in statistics because of its fundamental connection with dispersion. It may be defined as the square root of the arithmetic mean of the squares of the class marks. In symbols this definition becomes:[1]

$$R = \sqrt{\frac{(f_1 x_1^2 + f_2 x_2^2 + f_3 x_3^2 + \cdots\cdots\cdots + f_m x_m^2)}{N}}$$

$$= \sqrt{\frac{\Sigma f_i x_i^2}{N}}$$

The quadratic mean gives special weight to large class marks, since they enter into the formula as squares, and, therefore, it furnishes an effective average to use in the study of the dispersion of data.

---

[1] A generalization of the quadratic mean occasionally used is

$$R' = \sqrt[k]{\frac{(f_1 x_1^k + f_2 x_2^k + f_3 x_3^k + \cdots\cdots\cdots + f_m x_m^k)}{N}}, \qquad k > 2.$$

A *deviation* from the mean may be defined as the difference between a class mark and the arithmetic mean, i.e. $(x_i - A)$.

The *standard deviation* of a frequency distribution is the root-mean-square of the deviations of the values of the variable from their arithmetic mean. The Greek letter σ (sigma) is commonly used to denote the standard deviation. Where A is the arithmetic average as previously defined, this definition becomes in symbols

$$\sigma = \sqrt{\frac{f_1(x_1-A)^2 + f_2(x_2-A)^2 + \cdots\cdots\cdots\cdots + f_m(x_m-A)^2}{N}} \tag{2}$$

$$= \sqrt{\frac{\Sigma f_i(x_i-A)^2}{N}}.$$

In application it will usually be found simpler to use the following formula, rather than (2), where X is some conveniently chosen number:

$$\sigma_1 = \sqrt{\frac{f_1(x_1-X)^2 + f_2(x_2-X)^2 + \cdots\cdots + f_m(x_m-X)^2}{N} - (A-X)^2} \tag{3}$$

$$\sigma_1 = \sqrt{\frac{\Sigma f_i(x_i-X)^2}{N} - (A-X)^2}.$$

In applying this formula to data, it is usually desirable to let X be an integer differing as little as possible from A. It is sometimes convenient, however, to let $X = 0$.

In proving that formulas (2) and (3) are identical, one proceeds as follows:[1]

Squaring equation (2) and expanding, one obtains

$$\sigma^2 = \Sigma f_i(x_i-A)^2/N = \Sigma f_i(x_i^2 - 2Ax_i + A^2)/N$$
$$= \Sigma f_i x_i^2/N - 2A \Sigma f_i x_i/N + A^2 \Sigma f_i/N.$$

---

[1] To the student who knows differential calculus, this may be more easily proved as follows:

$$\frac{d}{dX}\sigma_1^2 = \frac{-2\Sigma f_i(x_i-X)}{N} - 2(X-A) = -2A + 2X - 2X + 2A \equiv 0.$$

Hence σ_1^2 is independent of X. To show that σ_1^2 is actually equal to σ^2, one now need merely let $X = A$ in formula (3) and compare the result with formula (2). Why is this a proof?

METHODS OF AVERAGING

Since $\Sigma f_i x_i / N = A$ and $\Sigma f_i / N = N/N = 1$, one has

$$\sigma^2 = \Sigma f_i x_i^2 / N - 2A^2 + A^2 = \Sigma f_i x_i^2 / N - A^2 .$$

In the same way, from equation (3) one finds

$$\sigma_1^2 = \Sigma f_i (x_i - X)^2 / N - (A - X)^2 = \Sigma f_i (x_i^2 - 2X x_i + X^2) / N$$
$$- (A - X)^2$$
$$= \Sigma f_i x_i^2 / N - 2AX + X^2 - A^2 + 2AX - X^2$$
$$= \Sigma f_i x_i^2 / N - A^2 .$$

Since the squares of the two expressions are identical, the equivalence of the two formulas has been proved.

Example: Calculate the standard deviations for Tables (a) and (b), section 2.

Since $A = 4.42$, for the data of Table (a), it will be convenient to let $X = 4.00$. One thus obtains

$$\sigma = \sqrt{\frac{(2.88 - 4.00)^2 + (2.97 - 4.00)^2 + \cdots + (6.13 - 4.00)^2}{108} - (.42)^2}$$

$$= \sqrt{82.85/108 - (.42)^2} = .77 .$$

As in the case of the arithmetic mean, the work of calculation should be arranged in a systematic way. Letting $X = 4.00$, the value of the standard deviation for Table (b) may be computed in the following manner:

x	f	$(x_i - X)$	$(x_i - X)^2$	$f_i (x_i - X)^2$
2.75	2	$-$ 1.25	1.56	3.12
3.25	8	$-$ .75	.56	4.48
3.75	23	$-$ .25	.06	1.38
4.25	30	.25	.06	1.80
4.75	20	.75	.56	11.20
5.25	13	1.25	1.56	20.28
5.75	6	1.75	3.06	18.36
6.25	6	2.25	5.06	30.36
Totals	108			90.98

$$\sigma = \sqrt{90.98/108 - (4.45 - 4.00)^2} = .80 .$$

The *coefficient of variability* is defined as the ratio of the standard deviation to the arithmetic mean, that is,

$$v = \sigma/A ,$$

and is used as a measure of the uniformity of data.

If one had, for example, two sets of data whose arithmetic averages were the same, but where the items of one set varied considerably in magnitude, while the items of the second set varied little in magnitude, this would be shown by the fact that the coefficient of variability in the first case was larger than in the second. By itself, the standard deviation does not give a measure of uniformity for a set of data which is directly comparable with the standard deviations of other sets of data, since the magnitudes of the original items may be very different. The standard deviation of high grade bond yields over a period might be, say, 1 per cent, and the standard deviation of national income, say, $10,000,000,000. It would be palpably absurd to say that national income varied 10,000,000,000 times as much as bond yields. Only when a standard deviation is related to the arithmetic average of the series, has one figures which are comparable measures of the uniformity of data. And this is the function of the coefficient of variability.

Example: Compare the uniformity of the following data with that of the data given in Table (b), section 2:

Frequencies	7	10	15	38	33	28	22	15
Class Marks	2.75	3.25	3.75	4.25	4.75	5.25	5.75	6.25

For this table, $A = 4.72$ and $\sigma = .91$. Hence, $v = \sigma/A = .91/4.72 = .193$. For Table (b), $v = .80/4.45 = .180$, which indicates that the variation of the second group is somewhat greater than that of the group represented by Table (b).

It occasionally happens in the study of the dispersion of data that it is not only unnecessary, but even misleading, to give too much emphasis to large deviations. In this case, the *mean or average deviation* should be used instead of the standard deviation. By the mean deviation shall be understood the arithmetic average of the absolute values, i.e., numerical values of the deviations from the mean. If the absolute value of a number m is designated by the customary symbol $|m|$, this definition may be stated as follows:

$$A.D. = \frac{\Sigma f_i |x_i - A|}{N} .$$

Example: Calculate the mean deviation for the data of Table (b), section 2, for which $A = 4.45$.

Class Mark	Frequency	$\|x_i - A\|$	$f_i\|x_i - A\|$
2.75	2	1.70	3.40
3.25	8	1.20	9.60
3.75	23	.70	16.10
4.25	30	.20	6.00
4.75	20	.30	6.00
5.25	13	.80	10.40
5.75	6	1.30	7.80
6.25	6	1.80	10.80
Totals	108		70.10

$$A.D. = 70.10/108 = .65 .$$

The mean deviation of .65 is to be compared with the standard deviation of .80, the difference being due in large part to the extra weight given in the latter to extreme items.

PROBLEMS

1. Calculate the standard and mean deviations for the data of problem 1, section 3.

2. Calculate the standard deviation for problem 2, section 3.

3. Calculate the standard deviation for the per capita receipts and expenditures of the United States Government as given in problem 7, section 3.

4. Do per capita receipts or per capita expenditures show the larger variability? (Problem 7, section 3).

5. Calculate the standard deviation for problem 5, section 3.

6. Calculate the standard and mean deviations for problem 8, section 3.

7. Two students, A and B, toss ten pennies 1024 times, recording the number of heads which appeared on each toss, with the following results:

No. of Heads	0	1	2	3	4	5	6	7	8	9	10
Frequency (A)	0	5	39	125	227	270	197	121	36	4	0
Frequency (B)	5	11	41	114	209	237	212	134	50	8	3

Which set of data shows the larger variability?

6. Transforming the Standard Deviation from One Set of Class Marks to Another. It is often important to be able to transfer from one set of class marks to another as it was in the case of the arithmetic mean.

If the old class marks, x_i, are related to the new class marks, y_i, by the formula

$$x_i = ay_i + b \; ,$$

it can be proved that the old standard deviation, σ_x, is related to the new one, σ_y, by the formula

$$\sigma_x = |a|\sigma_y \; . \tag{4}$$

By definition,

$$\sigma_x^2 = \Sigma f_i (x_i - A_x)^2 / N \; ,$$

where A_x is the average computed for the class marks x_i. In section 4, it was learned that A_x and A_y (the average in terms of the class marks y_i) are connected by the formula

$$A_x = aA_y + b \; .$$

If this value is substituted for A_x, and the value of x_i in the formula for σ_x^2, one then obtains

$$\begin{aligned}\sigma_x^2 &= \Sigma f_i (x_i - A_x)^2 / N \\ &= \Sigma f_i (ay_i + b - aA_y - b)^2 / N \\ &= a^2 \Sigma f_i (y_i - A_y)^2 / N \\ &= a^2 \sigma_y^2 \; ,\end{aligned}$$

or $\sigma_x = |a|\sigma_y$, which was to be proved.

Example: Given $\sigma_x = 7.41$, the standard deviation for the set of class marks (X), calculate σ_y using the second set (Y).

Frequencies	14	41	56	85	52	21	7	5
Class Marks (X)	62	67	72	77	82	87	92	97
Class Marks (Y)	0	1	2	3	4	5	6	7

Since the class breadth (i.e., the difference between class limits) for (X) is 5 and that for (Y) is 1, the value of a is $5/1 = 5$.

Hence, using the formula for transforming from one set to the other, one has

$$\sigma_y = \sigma_x/|a| = 7.41/5 = 1.482 \ .$$

If, for any frequency distribution, the standard deviation for the set of class marks $0, 1, 2, \cdots\cdots, n$, where $n = m-1$, has been calculated, this value is referred to as the *Bernoulli deviation* and designated by the symbol σ_B. Its importance in the theory of statistics will become apparent when normal and skew-normal frequency distributions are studied. In the example just given,

$$\sigma_B = \sigma_y = 1.482 \ .$$

7. Moments. By the rth moment of a frequency distribution is meant the sum of the products of the frequencies by the rth power of the corresponding values of the variable, i.e., $m_r = \Sigma f_i x_i^r$. Thus, for the zero-th, first, second, and third moments,[1] one has

$$m_0 = \Sigma f_i = N \ ; \qquad m_1 = \Sigma f_i x_i \ ;$$
$$m_2 = \Sigma f_i x_i^2 \ , \qquad m_3 = \Sigma f_i x_i^3 \ .$$

The arithmetic mean and the standard deviation are easily expressed in terms of the zero-th, first, and second moments, as follows:

From the definitions above, since $m_0 = \Sigma f_i = N$, and $m_1 = \Sigma f_i x_i$,

$$A = \Sigma f_i x_i / N = m_1/m_0 \ .$$

In formula (3) let $X = 0$; then

$$\sigma^2 = \frac{\Sigma f_i x_i^2}{N} - A^2 \ .$$

Since $m_2 = \Sigma f_i x_i^2$, σ^2 then becomes

$$\sigma^2 = m_2/m_0 - m_1^2/m_0^2 = (m_0 m_2 - m_1^2)/m_0^2 \ .$$

---

[1] The name moment for these sums comes from mechanics. The center of gravity of a system of masses is computed from the first moment of the masses and the radius of gyration of the system from the second moment of the masses. *Continuous moments* both of frequency distributions in statistics and of systems of masses in mechanics may be defined by replacing the sum symbols in the formulas by integrals. The history of the introduction of moments into statistics is given in *Studies in the History of Statistical Method*, by Helen M. Walker, Baltimore, 1929, Chap. 3.

By the rth moment of a frequency distribution about a number X, is meant the sum

$$N_r = \Sigma f_i(x_i - X)^r, \quad N_0 = N.$$

If one chooses $X = 0$, then $N_r = m_r = \Sigma f_i x_i^r$.

It will appear subsequently that the most important class of moments in the theory of statistics is made up of the moments taken about the arithmetic mean, i.e.,

$$M_r = \Sigma f_i(x_i - A)^r,$$

where A is the arithmetic average.

In order to obtain the relationship between M_r and N_r, it is first to be noticed that

$$N_1 = \Sigma f_i x_i - \Sigma f_i X = N(A - X).$$

Making use of the binomial theorem, the following expansion is obtained:

$$M_r = \Sigma f_i(x_i - A)^r = \Sigma f_i[(x_i - X) - (A - X)]^r$$
$$= \Sigma f_i[(x_i - X)^r - r(x_i - X)^{r-1}(A - X)$$
$$+ \frac{r(r-1)}{2!}(x_i - X)^{r-2}(A - X)^2 - \cdots\cdots$$
$$+ (-1)^r(A - X)^r]$$
$$= N_r - rN_{r-1}(A - X) + \frac{r(r-1)}{2!}N_{r-2}(A - X)^2$$
$$- \cdots + (-1)^r N_0(A - X)^r.$$

Substituting N_1/N for the value $(A - X)$ in this expression, one then obtains the formula:

$$M_r = N_r - rN_{r-1}(N_1/N) + \frac{r(r-1)}{2!}N_{r-2}(N_1/N)^2 \quad (5)$$
$$- \cdots + (-1)^r N_0(N_1/N)^r.$$

Letting $r = 1, 2, 3, 4, \cdots$, the following identities between the two sets of moments are calculated:

$$M_0 = N_0 = N,$$

$$M_1 = N_1 - N_1 = 0 ,$$
$$M_2 = N_2 - N_1^2/N ,$$
$$M_3 = N_3 - 3N_1N_2/N + 2N_1^3/N^2 ,$$
$$M_4 = N_4 - 4N_1N_3/N + 6N_1^2N_2/N^2 - 3N_1^4/N^3 .$$
(6)

Other additional relations can be readily determined by the student.[1]

PROBLEMS

1. Calculate the Bernoulli deviation for the data of problem 1, section 3.

2. Calculate the standard deviation for table (b), section 2, using the class marks .275, .325, .375, etc.

3. Calculate the Bernoulli deviation for problem 2, section 3.

4. What is the standard deviation for problem 3 if the class marks are 10, 9, 8, 7, 6, 5, 4, 3, 2, 1, 0?

5. Calculate the first, second, and third moments for problem 2, section 3. From these values calculate the first, second, and third moments about the mean.

6. Using the data obtained from problem 5, calculate the first three moments about $X = 10$. Hint: Remember that $m_1 = NA$ and that $N_1 = N(A-X)$. Then make use of the relationship between N_2 and M_2.

7. Express N_r in terms of $m_1, m_2, \ldots, m_r$.

8. *Sheppard's Adjustments.* In the case of ordinary frequency distributions, it is usually important to make an adjustment in the values of the moments to correct the error made in assuming that all the frequencies in a class interval correspond to the mean value of the interval. For example, if the rates on 90-day commercial

---

[1]There is, unfortunately, no universally adopted notation for moments. Since, however, most authors use μ_r to designate Sheppard's adjusted moments (see next section), there is a strong tendency to use ν_r, augmented by bars and primes, to represent m_r/N, M_r/N and N_r/N. In W. P. Elderton's *Frequency Curves and Correlation*, second edition, London, 1927, p. 15, the following notation is specified:

$N =$ total frequency ,
$\nu_n =$ nth unadjusted statistical moment about mean ,
$\nu_n' =$ nth unadjusted statistical moment about any other point ,
$\mu_n =$ nth moment from curve about mean ,
  $= n$th adjusted statistical moment about mean ,
$\mu_n' =$ nth moment from curve about other mean ,
  $= n$th adjusted statistical moment about other point .

These all refer to moments as defined in the text divided by N.

paper over a period of 120 months range between 2.50 and 5.00 per cent, it would be convenient to divide the range into 25 unit intervals one-tenth per cent in width. But the rates on commercial paper do not progress uniformly by increments of one-tenth per cent, so that in the interval between 2.50 and 2.60 one may find commercial paper whose rates differ by various fractions of one per cent.

By a method too intricate to give in detail here, W. F. Sheppard derived formulas to correct the moments of such *heterograde* series when each end of the frequency curve makes high contact with the x-axis, as is usually the case.[1] These corrections to the moments are often referred to as *Sheppard's adjustments*.

If one designates by $M_0, M_1, M_2, \cdots, M_r$, the various moments taken about the mean, and by $\mu_0, \mu_1, \mu_2, \cdots, \mu_r$ (μ is the Greek letter mu), the adjusted moments, the following formulas for the calculation of the latter are available:

$$\mu_0 = M_0 = N, \quad \mu_1 = 0, \quad \mu_2 = M_2 - M_0 a^2/12,$$
$$\mu_3 = M_3, \quad \mu_4 = M_4 - \tfrac{1}{2} M_2 a^2 + 7 M_0 a^4/240,$$
$$\mu_5 = M_5 - 5 M_3 a^2/6,$$
$$\mu_6 = M_6 - 5 a^2 M_4/4 + 7 M_2 a^4/16 - 31 M_0 a^6/1344,$$

where a is the breadth of the class interval.

Example: Adjust the second moment for Table (b), section 2.

Calculating the moments about the value $X = 4.00$, one finds $N = 108$, $N_1 = 48.50$, and $N_2 = 90.98$. Making use of these values, the moments about the mean are calculated to be:

$$M_0 = N = 108,$$
$$M_1 = N_1 - N_1 = 0,$$
$$M_2 = N_2 - N_1^2/N = 90.98 - 21.78 = 69.20.$$

The adjusted moments then become:

$$\mu_0 = 108,$$
$$\mu_1 = 0,$$
$$\mu_2 = 69.20 - (108)(.50)^2/12 = 66.95.$$

If, now, one computes $\sigma = \sqrt{M_2/N} = .800$ and $\sigma' = \sqrt{\mu_2/N} = .787$, it is seen that the first value is the standard deviation obtained in section 5 for Table (b) and that the second value is somewhat

---

[1] "The Calculation of the Moments of a Frequency Distribution," *Biometrika*, Vol. 5 (1906-1907), pp. 450-459.

closer to the standard deviation for Table (a), i.e., $\sigma = .769$. In other words, the distortion in σ caused by the concentration of frequencies in Table (b) has been adjusted. This illustrates the principal use of Sheppard's corrections.

PROBLEMS

1. Adjust the second moment for problem 1, section 3.
2. Express the adjusted second and third moments in terms of m_0, m_1, m_2, and m_3.
3. Calculate the adjusted second moment for problem 8, section 3.

9. The Median. Another average which is of frequent use in the theory of statistics is the *median*. By the median shall be meant the value of the class mark above and below which half the data lie. When the items of the series have been arranged in order of size, the median has the central position. Its usefulness is derived from the fact that it is easily found, since only arrangement of the data is necessary to determine it. When the median is the average used, no undue weight is given to extreme items nor, indeed, need every item in the series be explicitly known, since the position of the item in the sequence, and not its actual value, is the knowledge required.

When the items of a series are arranged by class marks in a frequency table, it is usually found to be necessary to interpolate for the value of the median, since the frequency table gives only the limits between which the median lies. This is done by means of the formula

$$M = L + \frac{C[\tfrac{1}{2}(N+1) - \Sigma f_i]}{F} \qquad (7)$$

where L is the lower limit of the median class, C is the class interval, N the total frequency, Σf_i the total number of items below L, and F the frequency of the median class.

If the class marks of the frequency distribution, the median of which is sought, are given merely as central values of the class intervals, then L and C may be determined from the formulas

$$L = x_1 + \tfrac{1}{2}(x_M - x_1)$$
$$C = \tfrac{1}{2}(x_2 - x_1) \; ,$$

where x_M is the class mark of the median class, x_1 the class mark of the class just below the median and x_2 the class mark of the class just above the median.

Example: Determine the median for the data of Table (b), section 2.

In this case the median class is 4.00-4.49. Hence, it is seen that $L = 4.00$, $C = .50$, $N = 108$, $\Sigma f_i = 33$, $F = 30$. From this

$$M = 4.00 + .50(54.5 - 33)/30 = 4.36 \ .$$

When each half of the data of a frequency table is divided into equal parts, the values representing the points of division are called the *first* and *third quartiles*.

The values which form the division between the first and second and the third and fourth quarters of a series of items arranged in a frequency table are called the *first* and *third quartiles*, respectively. If there are N items in the table, the first quartile is the value of the class mark corresponding to item $(N+1)/4$, the third quartile to item $3(N+1)/4$. In the case of eleven items, for example, the median corresponds to the sixth item and the quartiles to the third and ninth items.

The quartiles may be computed by the median formula if one replaces $(N+1)/2$ by $(N+1)/4$ and $3(N+1)/4$.

Example: Calculate the quartiles for Table (b), section 2.

Since there are 108 items, the quartiles correspond to the items 27.25 and 81.75 respectively. Using these values in place of $(N+1)/2$ in the formula for the median, and designating the quartiles by Q_1 and Q_2, it is found that

$$Q_1 = 3.50 + .50(27.25 - 10)/23 = 3.88 \ ,$$

and

$$Q_2 = 4.50 + .50(81.75 - 63)/20 = 4.97 \ .$$

In a similar way, one may define the *deciles* and *percentiles* to be the values of the class marks which divide the distribution into ten and a hundred equal parts, respectively. They are calculated in the same manner as the median and the quartiles, except that $r(N+1)/10$ and $r(N+1)/100$ are used in the median formula in place of $(N+1)/2$ for the frequencies corresponding to the rth decile and rth percentile respectively.

Example: Calculate the third decile for Table (b), section 2.

For the third decile, D_3, one has

$$D_3 = 3.50 + .50(3 \times 109/10 - 10)/23 = 3.99 \ .$$

The most striking characteristic of the median is found in the fact that the sum of the absolute values of the deviations from the median is smaller than the sum of the same deviations from any other average. This may be proved as follows:

Suppose that A, B, C, D, E, F, G, are successive points on a line. Let X be any other point. If one denotes by CX the distance, regardless of sign, between C and X, it is clear that $CX + EX$ will be smaller when X is between C and E than when it is outside this interval, and further that $CX + EX$ is constant when X lies inside the interval. The same statement holds for any other pair of points. Hence the total sum of deviations from X is smaller when as many points lie on one side of X as on the other, or, in other words, when X is the median.

The statistical importance of this statement is evident when one considers the geographical location of centers of industry. A business that lies at the geographical median of the district that it serves has its most favorable location so far as distribution is concerned.[1]

PROBLEMS

1. Calculate the median for problem 1, section 3.

2. What is the median for problem 2, section 3? What are the quartiles for this problem?

3. Calculate the median for the income data of problem 6, section 3.

4. Compute the medians for the per capita receipts and expenditures of the United States Government given in problem 7, section 3.

5. Calculate the quartiles for the data of problem 8, section 3.

6. Calculate the first, fifth, seventh, and ninth deciles for the data of problem 8, section 3.

7. A chain store dealing in a certain group of commodities has 96 branch stores in eight cities along a certain highway. Using city X with 9 branch

---

[1] If the points A, B, C, D, E, F, and G, are not on a straight line, but scattered in the plane, then the problem of finding a point, X, such that the sum of the distances from X to the given points is a minimum is one of great mathematical complexity. For a discussion of this question and its application to the center of population of the United States, the reader is referred to a paper by D. A. Scates: "Locating the Median of the Population in the United States," *Metron*, Vol. 9, No. 1 (1933), pp. 49-65. The problem for three points is treated in Goursat-Hedrick: *Mathematical Analysis*, Boston, 1904, pp. 130-131, where it is proved that the central angles formed by the lines from the points to X are all 120 degrees. If one of the angles of the triangle formed by the three points exceeds 120 degrees, then X coincides with the vertex of the obtuse angle.

stores as a reference point, the other seven cities with their branch stores are located as follows:

City	Number of Branch Stores	Distance from X (in miles)
A	10	60
B	12	33
C	5	15
D	6	— 25
E	15	— 65
F	20	— 85
G	19	—102

The company wishes to establish a main office for this group of stores and is confronted with the problem of choosing the most convenient location. What would be the most logical place for the company's main office?

8. Show graphically that the median of the values 1, 2, and 7, is the value of x for which the following function is a minimum:

$$y = |x-1| + |x-2| + |x-7| \ .$$

10. The Mode. Nearly all frequency distributions show a tendency toward the accumulation of frequencies at one or more values of the class marks. By the *mode* is meant that value of the class mark which has the largest frequency, that is to say, that value which is the most fashionable. When a distribution has but one mode, it is called uni-modal, when it has two modes, bi-modal, etc.

In order to calculate the values of the mode, it is necessary to interpolate, as was done in the case of the median. The formula for the mode is

$$Mo = L + \frac{CF}{F+f} \ , \qquad (8)$$

where L is the lower limit of the modal class, C the class interval, F the frequency of the class just above the mode, and f the frequency of the class just below the mode.

Example: Calculate the mode for Table (b), section 2.

The modal class is 4.00-4.49. Hence $L = 4.00$, $C = .50$, $F = 20$, and $f = 23$. Substituting these values in the formula above, one has

$$Mo = 4.00 + (.50)(20)/43 = 4.23 \ .$$

Frequency distributions occasionally occur where two distinct modal tendencies are apparent. These are usually indications of the existence of two separate distributions which for some reason have been mixed together.

The following is an example of bi-modal distribution formed in that manner. The table gives low prices during 1934 of 60 bonds listed on the New York Stock Exchange, 30 of the bonds being industrial and 30 railroad. When the two classes are combined, the composite distribution is distinctly bi-modal, as may be seen in Figure 18.

Class Interval $	Frequencies		
	Industrial	Railroad	Composite
under 39	1	2	3
40-49	1	2	3
50-59	2	3	5
60-69	3	8	11
70-79	4	5	9
80-89	4	5	9
90-99	9	4	13
100 and over	6	1	7
Totals	30	30	60

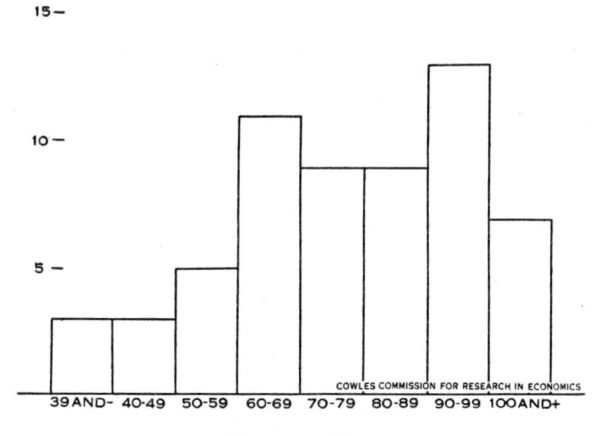

FIGURE 18

The mode is an average that is easily obtained, but obviously can be used only when the data show a strong modal tendency. It is an average that is unaffected by extremes in the data.

One important use to which the mode has been put in the theory of statistics is that of measuring the unsymmetrical character, or the *skewness*, of data. It often happens that the frequencies in a distribution will tend to pile up at one end or the other of the class range, instead of near the middle as in the so-called *normal* distribution. In other words, the mode will not correspond to the arithmetic mean, from which it may deviate in a significant manner.

As it is convenient to have some measure of this skewness, one may adopt as a more or less arbitrary definition the following ratio suggested by Karl Pearson,

$$S \text{ (Skewness)} = \frac{A - Mo}{\sigma}. \tag{9}$$

When the sign of S is negative, the skewness is to the right; when the sign is positive, the skewness is to the left. Examples are shown in Figure 19.

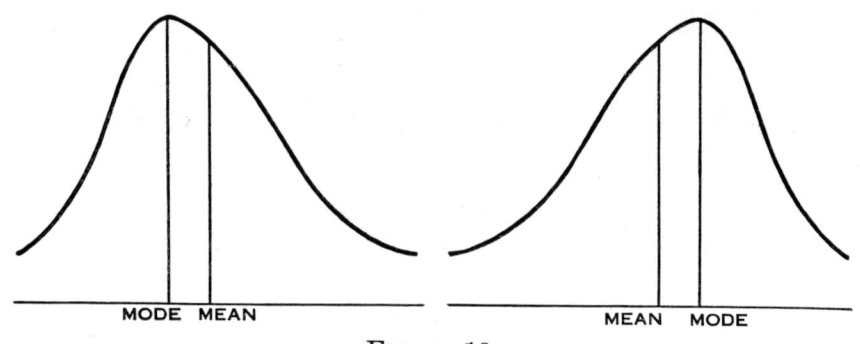

FIGURE 19.

In case the data of the statistical series under consideration are known to be skew-normal (see Chapter VII), then the following definition of skewness should be used:

$$S' \text{ (Skewness)} = \frac{1 - 2A_B/n}{2\sigma_B}, \tag{10}$$

where A_B is the Bernoulli mean, σ_B the Bernoulli deviation, and $n + 1$ is the number of class marks.[1] When the sign of S' is positive, the skewness is to the left as in the previous definition.

---

[1] The student will recall from section 6 that the *Bernoulli mean* and the *Bernoulli deviation* are computed using the class marks, $0, 1, 2, 3, \ldots n$.

When an application is made of formula (10), it will be observed that an exact determination of the value of n is sometimes difficult. A more precise definition, which is, however, essentially equivalent to (10), is found in the formula,

$$S'' \text{ (Skewness)} = \nu_3/2\sigma^3 , \qquad (11)$$

where ν_3 is the third moment about the mean divided by the total frequency, i.e., $\nu_3 = M_3/N$ (See section 7). The class marks used in this computation must be $0, 1, 2, 3 \cdots n$. A positive value of S'' indicates skewness to the right. A derivation of both formulas (10) and (11) will be given in Chapter VII.

When the data form a skew-normal distribution, the arithmetic mean and mode are theoretically equal, so that skewness calculated by the Pearson formula would be unreliable. For example, using the data of Table (b) section 2, one gets:

$$S = \frac{4.45 - 4.23}{.8} = .275 ,$$

$$S' = \frac{1 - \frac{2(3.40)}{7}}{3.2} = .0089 .$$

Since the skewness is obviously very slight (see Figure 2, section 10, Chapter I), the value of the skewness S' should be used in this case. The sign of S indicates a skewness to the left. Using formula (11) one obtains $S'' = .0380$, which again indicates a small skewness to the left.

PROBLEMS

1. Calculate the mode, the skewness S, and the skewness S', for the data of problem 5, section 3.

2. Calculate the mode for the data of problem 1, section 3.

3. Is there a modal income for the United States? (See problem 6, section 3.)

4. Calculate the mode for problem 8, section 3.

5. Calculate the skewness S and the skewness S' for the data of problem 8, section 3.

11. The Geometric Mean. The *geometric mean* of a set of N positive numbers is the Nth root of their product. In case a number is repeated one or more times, it will appear in the product as many times as it occurs in the given set. In symbols this definition becomes

$$G = \sqrt[N]{x_1^{f_1} x_2^{f_2} x_3^{f_3} x_4^{f_4} \cdots\cdots x_n^{f_n}},$$

where $f_1, f_2, \cdots, f_n$, are the frequencies of the class marks and N is the total frequency.

The use of logarithms greatly facilitates the calculation of the geometric mean. Thus, if logarithms of both sides of the above equation are taken, one has

$$\log G = \frac{f_1 \log x_1 + f_2 \log x_2 + \cdots + f_n \log x_n}{N}.$$

In other words, the logarithm of the geometric mean is the arithmetic average of the logarithms of the class marks, each multiplied by its frequency.

Example: Calculate the geometric mean of the data of Table (b), section 2.

$$G = \sqrt[108]{2.75^2 \cdot 3.25^8 \cdots\cdots 6.25^6};$$

$\log G = (2 \log 2.75 + 8 \log 3.25 + \cdots\cdots + 6 \log 6.25)/108$

$\qquad = 69.25727/108$

$\qquad = .64127;$

$G = 4.38.$

The geometric mean is useful in the averaging of ratios and rates of interest. Suppose that A held a stock which, during five successive years, increased 5 per cent, 6 per cent, 6.5 per cent, 4 per cent, and 3.5 per cent. What was the average annual increase?

The total return from unit capital on the basis of compound interest would be

$$S = (1.05)(1.06)(1.065)(1.04)(1.035).$$

Hence, it is reasonable to assume that his average rate of increase should be calculated from the equation

$$1 + r = \sqrt[5]{S}.$$

which is the geometric average of the five sums. Thus, one has

$$r = \sqrt[5]{S} - 1 = .0499,$$

or, the average return was 4.99 per cent.

One of the defects of the geometric average is the large influence exerted on the average by very small numbers. It is for this reason that the use of this mean should be largely confined to the averaging of rates which do not differ greatly, for which it is most admirably suited.

An interesting application is found in the following example: From the following data predict the total population of the United States for the 1930 census:

Year	Population
1870	38,558,000
1880	50,156,000
1890	62,948,000
1900	75,995,000
1910	91,972,000
1920	105,711,000

First, the 10-year increases are calculated by dividing each census figure by the one immediately preceding. There is thus obtained:

Ratios	Logarithms
1.3008	.11421
1.2550	.09864
1.2073	.08182
1.2102	.08286
1.1494	.06047

$$5\,)\,.43800$$
$$\log G = .08760$$
$$G = 1.2235.$$

Using this average, the population for 1930 is calculated to be $(1.2235)(105,711,000) = 129,337,000$, which is in excess of the true figure 122,775,000. What conclusion may be drawn from this?

Further application of the geometric average will be made in connection with the theory of index numbers.

PROBLEMS

1. The national income of the United States, expressed in actual dollars and in 1913 dollars, over a period of eleven years, was as follows:[1]

| | Total Income in Billion Dollars ||
Year	Actual Dollars	1913 Dollars
1921	58.3	33.6
1922	62.1	37.6
1923	69.3	42.0
1924	71.9	43.6
1925	76.6	45.2
1926	80.3	47.3
1927	82.9	49.7
1928	84.1	50.7
1929	87.5	51.2
1930	72.9	44.5
1931	57.5	38.9

What is the average rate of increase per year, in terms of actual dollars and in terms of 1913 dollars?

2. According to three census reports made five years apart, a certain city had the following population:

first report, 152,762; second report, 169,804; third report, 186,981.

A water works system large enough to supply a city of 300,000 was built at the time of the third report. In how many years may the city find it necessary to enlarge its water system?

3. Using 1926 (1926 = 100) as the comparison year, the United States Bureau of Labor Statistics Wholesale Commodity Price Index for preceding and succeeding years was as follows:

Year	Index	Year	Index
1913	70	1925	104
1919	139	1926	100
1920	154	1927	95
1921	98	1928	97
1922	97	1929	95
1923	101	1930	86
1924	98	1931	73

From this table compute the average increase in wholesale prices over this period.

---

[1] Irving Fisher, *Booms and Depressions*, New York, 1932, p. 200.

METHODS OF AVERAGING 93

4. The following table gives the monthly average of automobile production in the United States for the years 1926-1932 (unit 1,000 cars):

Year	1926	1927	1928	1929	1930	1931	1932
Production	358.4	283.4	363.2	446.5	279.7	199.1	114.2

Calculate the average per cent of change per year.

5. The automobile production for January over a seven-year period, 1926-1932, is given by the following table:

Year	1926	1927	1928	1929	1930	1931	1932
Production	309.0	238.9	231.7	401.0	273.2	171.8	119.3

Calculate the average per cent of change and compare the answer with that of the preceding problem.

6. The following data give the weekly wage rate index of union workers, also the retail price index of food, for the twelve-year period 1920-1931 (figures are relatives, with 1913 as 100):

Year	Wages Per Week	Retail Prices of Food
1920	188.5	203.4
1921	193.3	153.3
1922	183.0	141.6
1923	198.6	146.2
1924	214.3	145.9
1925	222.3	157.4
1926	233.4	160.6
1927	240.8	155.4
1928	240.6	154.3
1929	240.7	156.7
1930	243.8	147.1
1931	242.9	121.3

Calculate the average per cent increase per year for each series and compare your answers for the two.

12. The Harmonic Average. A sixth average occasionally used in statistical problems is the so-called *harmonic mean*, which is defined as the total frequency divided by the sum of the reciprocals of the class marks multiplied by their respective frequencies. In symbols this definition becomes

$$H = \frac{N}{\dfrac{f_1}{x_1} + \dfrac{f_2}{x_2} + \dfrac{f_3}{x_3} + \cdots + \dfrac{f_n}{x_n}}$$

Because of the unfamiliar nature of this average and the labor involved in its computation, it is not used so frequently as the other averages, although it is occasionally very useful in application.

The harmonic mean may be used in the averaging of rates and time. The following simple examples are illustrative of the underlying principles:

Example 1: Suppose that an aviator flies his plane for 50 minutes at the rate of 150 miles an hour and then, because of engine trouble, flies for ten minutes at 50 miles an hour. What is his average speed?

It is at once clear that his average speed is closer to 150 miles an hour than it is to 50 miles. It is, of course, equal to $150(50/60) + 50(10/60) = 133.33$ miles. Now this simple answer may be obtained in another way. One may employ the familiar formula that d (distance) equals the product of v (velocity) and t (time). Applying this to the two parts of the flight, one has

$$d_1 = v_1 t_1, \quad \text{or} \quad 125 = 150(50/60),$$
$$d_2 = v_2 t_2, \quad \text{or} \quad 8.33 = 50(10/60).$$

It is now reasonable to define the average velocity, not as the average of v_1 and v_2, but by means of the formula,

$$(d_1 + d_2) = v(t_1 + t_2),$$

where v is the desired average. Since $t_1 = d_1/v_1$ and $t_2 = d_2/v_2$, one has

$$v = \frac{d_1 + d_2}{\dfrac{d_1}{v_1} + \dfrac{d_2}{v_2}}$$

$$= \frac{125 + 8.33}{\dfrac{125}{150} + \dfrac{8.33}{50}} = 133.33.$$

A second example will show the application of the harmonic mean to the determination of time averages.

Example 2: A wholesale house has ten travelling salesmen who make trips of essentially the same length. Of these, seven make their trip in 30 days and three in 20 days. What is the average time per trip.

One can argue as was done in the first example from the equation $d = vt$, where d is the length of the trip, t, the time, and v, the speed of the salesmen. For determining the speed of the first seven salesmen, there is the equation

$$d = 30v_1 ,$$

and for the last three,

$$d = 20v_2 .$$

It is clear that a satisfactory definition of the average time per trip is obtained from the equation,

$$7d + 3d = (7v_1 + 3v_2)t ,$$

where t is the average desired. One thus gets as the answer to the problem:

$$\begin{aligned} t &= (7d + 3d)/(7v_1 + 3v_2) \\ &= 10d/(7d/30 + 3d/20) \\ &= 10/(7/30 + 3/20) = 26.09 \text{ days.} \end{aligned}$$

It will be clear that this same argument can be used to find the average time per trip when the trips are of varying length.

The harmonic mean may also be used effectively in determining the average price of commodities.

Example 3: Three items, a, b, and c, sell for $2.00, $3.00, and $5.00, respectively. What is the average price per item?

It is obvious that this problem does not have precise meaning until something is known about the volume of the sales of each item, so it will be assumed that the total return from the sale of each is the same. Consider then, the equation,

$$R = Np ,$$

where R is the total return, N, the number of articles sold, and p, the price. For a, b, and c, one then has

(a) $R = 2 \times N_1 ,$
(b) $R = 3 \times N_2 ,$
(c) $R = 5 \times N_3 .$

A reasonable basis for determining the average price is found in the equation

$$3R = (N_1 + N_2 + N_3)p .$$

96 ELEMENTS OF STATISTICS

Hence,
$$p = 3R/(N_1 + N_2 + N_3)$$
$$= 3R/(R/2 + R/3 + R/5)$$
$$= 3/(1/2 + 1/3 + 1/5) = 90/31 = \$2.90 \ .$$

An application of the harmonic average to the theory of index numbers will be made in a subsequent chapter.

PROBLEMS

1. The sales record of a certain firm showed the following items: 1,000 articles at 10 cents; 500 articles at 25 cents; 400 articles at 50 cents; 150 articles at 75 cents; 100 articles at $1.00. What was the average price per article?

2. Calculate the harmonic average for Table (b), section 2.

3. Two hundred men of a certain industry are studied with regard to their efficiency in making a certain article. They were classified into ten groups according to the time they required. From the following record calculate the average time it takes to manufacture the article:

No. of Men	Time	No. of Men	Time
5	12 Min.	37	22 Min.
12	14	25	24
17	16	19	26
20	18	14	28
42	20	9	30

4. A man travels 20 miles at 40 miles an hour, 10 miles at 30 miles an hour, and 60 miles at 50 miles an hour. What was his average velocity?

5. Compute the harmonic average of the sequence, 1, 2, 3, 4, 5, 6, 7, 8, 9, 10.

13. *Relative Magnitude of the Averages of a Series of Positive Terms.* It is occasionally of importance to know the relative magnitude of the various means. If the average of the sequence 1, 2, 3, 4, 5, 6, 7, 8, 9, and 10, is calculated by the methods developed in the preceding sections, the following results are obtained:

R (Quadratic Mean) $= 6.205$,
A (Arithmetic Mean) $= 5.5$,
G (Geometric Mean) $= 4.529$,
H (Harmonic Mean) $= 3.414$.

It is proposed to show that these relative magnitudes are not accidental, but are inherent characteristics of the four averages. The fundamental inequalities may be stated in the following theorem:

Theorem: In a series of positive terms, the quadratic mean is greater than the arithmetic mean, the arithmetic mean is greater than the geometric mean, which in turn is greater than the harmonic mean, unless the terms are all equal, in which case the values of the four are identical. Symbolically, this is expressed by the inequalities

$$R \geq A \geq G \geq H ,$$

where the equality sign prevails only when the class marks are equal.

Proof: Consider first the geometric and arithmetic means

$$G = \sqrt[n]{x_1 x_2 x_3 \cdots x_n} , \qquad A = \frac{x_1 + x_2 + x_3 + \cdots + x_n}{n} ,$$

in which at least two of the class marks are assumed different from one another. Suppose that the greatest of these class marks is x_i and the least is x_j. Now replace x_i and x_j in each average by their arithmetic mean $\frac{1}{2}(x_i + x_j)$. The effect of this is to leave the arithmetic mean unchanged but to increase the geometric mean, since

$$\tfrac{1}{4}(x_i + x_j)^2 > x_i x_j .$$

This inequality is derived as follows:

Since x_i is different from x_j, one has

$$(x_i - x_j)^2 > 0,$$
$$\text{or } x_i^2 - 2x_i x_j + x_j^2 > 0$$

When $4x_i x_j$ is added to both sides, this becomes

$$(x_i + x_j)^2 > 4x_i x_j ,$$

from which the desired inequality follows by a division by 4.

If the new class marks are still unequal, the process may be repeated again replacing the largest and the smallest by their arithmetic averages. Since this method can be continued as long as we wish, it is clear that the class marks can be made as nearly equal as we please, and G will approach A as a limiting value.

But the effect of this process has been to increase G while A has remained unchanged, so G must originally have been less than A.

In a similar way, G and the harmonic mean may be considered:

$$H = n/(1/x_1 + 1/x_2 + 1/x_3 + \cdots + 1/x_n) \ .$$

Replace the largest and smallest values of the class marks, i.e., x_i and x_j, by the value

$$2x_i x_j / (x_i + x_j) \ .$$

Now consider the inequalities:

$$(x_1 - x_j)^2 > 0 \ ,$$
$$x_i^2 + x_j^2 > 2x_i x_j \ ,$$
$$(x_i + x_j)^2 > 4x_i x_j \ ,$$
$$x_i x_j (x_i + x_j)^2 > 4x_i^2 x_j^2 \ ,$$
$$x_i x_j > 4x_i^2 x_j^2 / (x_i + x_j)^2 \ .$$

From this inequality, it is seen that the result of the substitution is to decrease the value of G while H remains unchanged, since

$$1/x_i + 1/x_j = (x_i + x_j)/x_i x_j \ .$$

By repeating this process, as before, the values of the class marks can be made to approach equality, and the value of G will approach the value of H.

But, since the effect of the process has been to reduce G while H remained unchanged, it follows that G must have been originally greater than H.

To prove that $R \geq A$, it can be shown that the following inequality is true:

$$\frac{x_1^2 + x_2^2 + x_3^2 + \cdots + x_n^2}{n} \geq \left(\frac{x_1 + x_2 + x_3 + \cdots + x_n}{n}\right)^2. \tag{1}$$

Explicitly squaring the right hand member and multiplying both sides by n^2, this inequality becomes

$$n(x_1^2 + x_2^2 + x_3^2 + \cdots + x_n^2) \geqq x_1^2 + x_2^2 + x_3^2 + \cdots$$
$$+ x_n^2 + 2x_1x_2 + 2x_1x_3 + \cdots .$$

Subtracting $x_1^2 + x_2^2 + x_3^2 + \cdots + x_n^2$ from each side of the inequality, there is obtained finally

$$(n-1)(x_1^2 + x_2^2 + x_3^2 + \cdots + x_n^2) \geqq 2x_1x_2$$
$$+ 2x_1x_3 + \cdots . \qquad (2)$$

Recalling from the previous discussion that

$$x_i^2 + x_j^2 \geqq 2x_ix_j ,$$

the following set of inequalities is formed:

$$x_1^2 + x_2^2 \geqq 2x_1x_2 ,$$
$$x_1^2 + x_3^2 \geqq 2x_1x_3 ,$$
$$\cdots\cdots\cdots\cdots\cdots$$

In the left hand array, one notices that each x_i occurs $(n-1)$ times, since it is associated once with each of the other $(n-1)$ values. Hence, if the set of inequalities be added, inequality (2) is obtained, which establishes the truth of the theorem.

It can also be proved in a somewhat similar way that R', the generalization of the quadratic mean (see section 5), is greater than R. For proof, see Chrystal's *Algebra*, Edinburgh, 1889, part 2, page 49.

PROBLEMS

1. Prove that the product of the first n odd numbers is less than n^n. Hint: Making use of the fact that $A > G$, start with the inequality
$$(1 + 3 + 5 + \ldots + 2n-1)/n > 1 \cdot 3 \cdot 5 \cdots (2n-1) .$$

2. Prove that the product of the first n numbers is less than $(1+n)^n/2^n$. For example: $4! < (1+4)^4/2^4 = 625/16 = 39 +$. Hint: make use of the fact that $A > G$ and compare the arithmetic average of the first n numbers with their geometric average.

3. Given the fact that $1 + 1/2 + 1/3 + \ldots + 1/n$ for sufficiently large values of n is approximately equal to $C + \log_e n$, where C (Euler's number) $= .5772$, show that $n! > n^n/(\log_e n + C)^n$. For example: $4! > 4^4/(\log_e 4 + .5772)^4 = 17.2$. Hint: Use the fact that $G > H$ and compare the geometric average of the first n numbers with their harmonic mean.

4. Illustrate numerically the proof of the theorem on the relative magnitudes of the four averages, using the set of class marks, 1, 3, 5, 7.

5. Show that the sum of the squares of the first n numbers is greater than $n(n+1)^2/4$. Hint: Compare the quadratic mean of the first n numbers with their arithmetic mean.

CHAPTER IV

Index Numbers

1. *The Unstable Dollar.* Under the normal operation of the gold standard, the price of gold seldom changes; the value of gold seldom ceases changing. And this second fact is possibly the most important in modern economic life. The rôle of prices is absolutely central in any consideration of the economic state. When a nation is on the gold standard, every small change in the value of gold, that is to say, in the price level, involves probably a change in, and certainly a redistribution of, the national income. Every major change in the price level is a vital factor in such world-wide upheavals as the one which began in 1929. An upward move in prices of such magnitude as took place in Germany in the post-war years may serve to eliminate all debt; a downward move of such magnitude as took place in the United States from 1929 to 1932 may serve to cripple industry and agriculture by the multiplication of debt. Curiously enough, these simple facts are not adequately appreciated. To most people a dollar is a dollar, an unvarying and immutable entity. A glance at an index of commodity prices (see Figure 22) will serve to show that a 1913 dollar was something quite different from a 1919 dollar, as the 1929 dollar was quite different from the 1932 dollar. A dollar derives its significance from its purchasing power, that is, from its capacity to command commodities in exchange for itself, and this exchange value, of course, is directly reflected in the price level. An index of prices of commodities, therefore, is an index of the fluctuations of the purchasing power of the dollar over these commodities.[1] The concern here is not with the causes of these fluctuations, but with their measurement. And this is a function of index numbers.

By an *index number* is meant a value, generally expressed as a percentage, which is designed to indicate the level at any given date of the items of a time series. Index numbers are usually thought of as applying to prices, but they may, of course, refer to any other characteristic property of a series of items. Since index

---

[1]There are, of course, fixed prices in the system. Thus, prices of commodities may change 50 per cent during a period when transportation charges remain fixed. If this occurs, the purchasing power of the dollar over transportation does not, of course, change.

numbers, however, are conveniently studied through their application to price changes, the discussion in this chapter is limited to this important problem.

Index numbers are a comparatively recent development. They were forced, so to speak, on economists by the great gold discoveries of the mid-nineteenth century with the resultant disturbances in prices. But even two hundred years ago, the question had been attacked in an elementary fashion in France, and it is interesting to note that as early as 1747 the Colony of Massachusetts initiated a crude device to stabilize the value of contractual obligations. William Stanley Jevons' publication in 1865 of a study of prices with index numbers from 1782 up to that time, entitles him, in Irving Fisher's opinion, to be considered the father of index numbers. The oldest of still current indexes is that of the *Economist* (London), which started in 1869. Sauerbeck commenced his famous index, which is still continued by the *Statist*, in 1886. Modern interest is attested by the fact that Irving Fisher lists 153 indexes being published regularly in the world in 1927. The literary landmarks of the subject are Edgeworth's two *Memoranda* for the British Association for the Advancement of Science (1889), the most thorough investigation of the question up to that time; Walsh's *Measurement of General Exchange Value* (1901), a comprehensive treatise dealing with the theory of the subject, and *The Making of Index Numbers*, by Irving Fisher (third edition revised, 1927), which must be considered the definitive work on the problem thus far.[1]

2. The Price Index Problem. The problem to be considered is that of comparing the purchasing power of a dollar in one year with its purchasing power in another. To make the problem precise, suppose that both the prices and the quantities produced of a set of n basic commodities are known for each of the two years. Employing customary notation, the price is designated by p and quantity by q, using the subscript "0" to denote the *base* or comparison year, and the subscript "1" to denote the year whose price index is desired. Thus, for the base year there may be assumed as known the following prices and quantities:

Prices for base year: $\quad p_0 \quad p_0' \quad p_0'' \quad \cdots\cdots\cdots \quad p_0^{(n-1)}$,

Quantities for base year: $\quad q_0 \quad q_0' \quad q_0'' \quad \cdots\cdots\cdots \quad q_0^{(n-1)}$.

---

[1] Special reference should also be made to the comprehensive report of W. C. Mitchell, *Index Numbers of Wholesale Prices in the United States and Foreign Countries*, U. S. Bureau of Labor Statistics, Bulletin 284 (1921) [Revision of Bulletin 173 (1915)].

Similarly, for the year whose price index is sought, the following quantities are supposed known:

Prices for second year: $p_1 \quad p_1' \quad p_1'' \quad \cdots\cdots\cdots \quad p_1^{(n-1)}$,

Quantities for second year: $q_1 \quad q_1' \quad q_1'' \quad \cdots\cdots\cdots \quad q_1^{(n-1)}$.

For simplicity in writing formulas, it is useful to employ the abbreviation

$$\Sigma pq = pq + p'q' + p''q'' + \cdots\cdots + p^{(n-1)}q^{(n-1)}.$$

To supply material for numerical examples to illustrate the theory of this chapter, two tables of price and production data for ten important agricultural products are given. Table 1 gives the prices for these products in convenient units over the twelve-year period 1920-1931. This period is a particularly interesting one to investigate because it includes the remarkable fluctuations due to post-war reactions. Table 2 contains the production figures of the ten items for the same twelve-year period.

WHOLESALE CROP PRICES[1]
Unit = $1.00

Year	Corn (bu.)	Wheat (bu.)	Oats (bu.)	Cotton (lb.)	Potatoes (bu.)	Hay (ton)	Sugar (lb.)	Tobacco (lb.)	Barley (bu.)	Rye (bu.)
1920	1.41	2.53	.80	.339	1.315	36.27	.130	.212	1.24	1.80
1921	.57	1.44	.37	.151	1.214	23.03	.048	.199	.59	1.15
1922	.62	1.15	.38	.212	.753	22.65	.047	.232	.57	.83
1923	.81	1.09	.43	.293	.946	23.90	.070	.199	.60	.70
1924	.96	1.31	.50	.287	.779	24.94	.060	.207	.76	.86
1925	1.02	1.59	.45	.235	1.834	23.53	.043	.182	.78	1.09
1926	.75	1.45	.41	.175	1.420	23.41	.043	.182	.64	.92
1927	.86	1.32	.47	.176	1.081	19.37	.047	.212	.77	1.00
1928	.97	1.18	.53	.200	.620	20.97	.042	.202	.78	1.07
1929	.94	1.21	.47	.191	1.362	20.40	.038	.185	.63	.96
1930	.84	.87	.39	.136	.904	19.89	.034	.144	.52	.61
1931	.53	.63	.27	.086	.607	17.54	.034	.127	.46	.39

TABLE 1

The simplest method of comparing one year with another is to form the price and production *relatives*. To do this, each number

---

[1] These figures are assembled from various sources as, for example, *The Daily Trade Bulletin*, U. S. Bureau of Labor Statistics, *The Grain Reporter*, U. S. Dept. of Agriculture, Bureau of Agricultural Economics, *Standard Statistics Base Book*, *Journal of Commerce*, etc. They represent yearly averages.

INDEX NUMBERS

CROP PRODUCTION
Unit = 1,000,000

Year	Corn (bu.)	Wheat (bu.)	Oats (bu.)	Cotton (lb.)	Potatoes (bu.)	Hay (ton)	Sugar (lb.)	Tobacco (lb.)	Barley (bu.)	Rye (bu.)
1920	3209	833.0	1496	6720	403.3	105.32	10,795	1582	189.3	60.49
1921	3069	814.9	1078	3977	361.7	97.77	11,101	1070	154.9	61.68
1922	2906	867.9	1216	4881	453.4	112.01	10,463	1247	182.1	103.40
1923	3054	797.4	1306	5070	416.1	106.61	10,044	1515	197.7	63.08
1924	2309	864.4	1503	6814	421.6	112.63	11,552	1251	181.6	65.47
1925	2917	676.4	1488	8052	323.5	99.42	13,527	1757	213.9	46.46
1926	2692	831.0	1247	8989	354.3	96.07	12,952	1298	184.9	40.80
1927	2763	799.3	1183	6478	402.7	123.33	12,540	1212	265.9	58.16
1928	2819	914.9	1439	7239	465.4	106.47	11,617	1375	357.5	43.37
1929	2535	812.6	1118	7413	329.1	87.30	13,830	1537	280.2	34.95
1930	2060	858.2	1278	6966	333.2	74.21	13,169	1635	304.6	45.38
1931	2557	892.3	1112	8548	376.2	72.36	9,157	1610	199.0	32.75

TABLE 2

in each column of the preceding tables is divided by the number corresponding to some base year, that is to say, the ratios p_1/p_0 and q_1/q_0 are calculated. In making index numbers for the post-war period, the base year is often chosen to be 1926. The relatives for Tables 1 and 2 referred to 1926 are given in Tables 3 and 4, respectively.

CROP PRICE RELATIVES
1926 = 100

Crops	1920	1921	1922	1923	1924	1925	1926	1927	1928	1929	1930	1931
Corn	188	76	83	108	128	136	100	115	129	125	112	71
Wheat	174	99	79	75	90	110	100	91	81	83	60	43
Oats	195	90	93	105	122	110	100	115	129	115	95	66
Cotton	194	86	121	167	164	134	100	101	114	109	78	49
Potatoes	93	85	53	67	55	129	100	76	44	96	64	43
Hay	155	98	97	102	107	101	100	83	90	87	85	75
Sugar	302	112	109	163	140	100	100	109	98	88	79	79
Tobacco	116	109	127	109	114	100	100	116	111	102	79	70
Barley	194	92	89	94	119	122	100	120	122	98	81	72
Rye	196	125	90	76	93	118	100	109	116	104	66	42

TABLE 3

CROP PRODUCTION RELATIVES
1926 = 100

Crops	1920	1921	1922	1923	1924	1925	1926	1927	1928	1929	1930	1931
Corn	119	114	108	113	86	108	100	103	105	94	77	95
Wheat	100	98	104	96	104	81	100	96	110	98	103	107
Oats	120	86	98	105	121	119	100	95	115	90	102	89
Cotton	75	44	54	56	76	90	100	72	81	82	77	95
Potatoes	114	102	128	117	119	91	100	114	131	93	94	106
Hay	110	102	117	111	117	103	100	128	111	91	77	75
Sugar	83	86	81	78	89	104	100	97	90	107	102	71
Tobacco	122	82	96	117	96	135	100	93	106	118	126	124
Barley	102	84	98	107	98	116	100	144	193	152	165	108
Rye	148	151	253	155	160	114	100	143	106	86	111	80

TABLE 4

The complex nature of the problem presented by the subject of making a price index is illustrated in the accompanying figures (Figures 20 and 21), which are formed by the composite graphing of the price and production relatives given in Tables 3 and 4. However, the price graph very distinctly shows a peak for 1920 due to the inflation of the war, with a substantial decline by 1931, although the production remained essentially uniform.

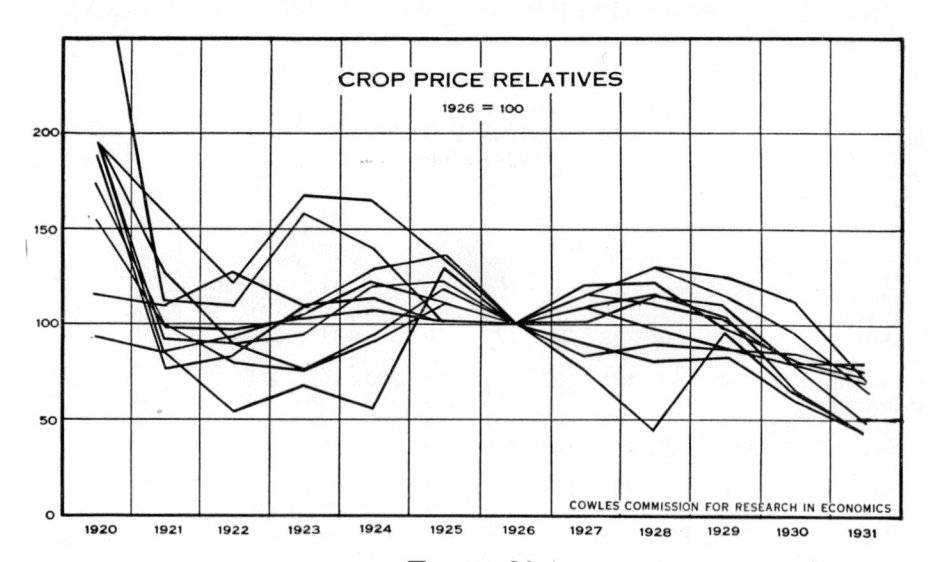

FIGURE 20

FIGURE 21

CROP PRODUCTION RELATIVES, 1926 = 100

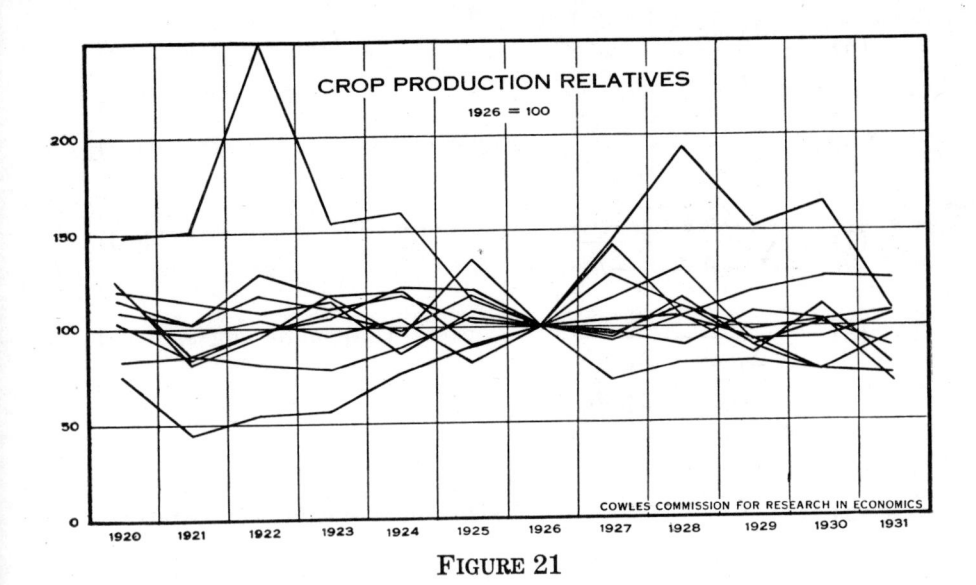

3. *Price Index Formulas.* After the data have been secured, the first problem that presents itself is to find a formula which will give an adequate index. That this is not an altogether simple matter is seen from the fact that Irving Fisher in his treatise on *The Making of Index Numbers* (1922) lists 134 formulas that have been proposed for the solution of this problem. For the sake of showing the steps by means of which he arrived at the "ideal" index number, a few of the formulas that have been proposed may be noticed. Using the notation of the preceding section, these may be written:

(1) $\dfrac{\Sigma\left(\dfrac{p_1}{p_0}\right)}{n}$, (simple arithmetic mean)

(2) $\dfrac{n}{\Sigma\left(\dfrac{p_0}{p_1}\right)}$, (simple harmonic mean)

(3) $\sqrt[n]{\dfrac{p_1}{p_0} \times \dfrac{p_1'}{p_0'} \times \dfrac{p_1''}{p_0''} \cdots}$, (simple geometric mean)

(4) $\dfrac{\Sigma p_1}{\Sigma p_0}$, (simple aggregative)

$$(5) \quad \frac{\Sigma p_1 q_0}{\Sigma p_0 q_0}, \qquad \text{(weighted aggregative)}$$

$$(6) \quad \frac{\Sigma (q_0+q_1) p_1}{\Sigma (q_0+q_1) p_0}, \qquad \text{(Edgeworth-Marshall aggregative)}$$

$$(7) \quad \sqrt{\frac{\Sigma p_1 q_0}{\Sigma p_0 q_0} \times \frac{\Sigma p_1 q_1}{\Sigma p_0 q_1}}, \qquad \text{(ideal)}$$

$$(8) \quad \frac{2}{\dfrac{\Sigma p_0 q_0}{\Sigma p_1 q_0} + \dfrac{\Sigma p_0 q_1}{\Sigma p_1 q_1}}, \qquad \text{(harmonic aggregative)}$$

$$(9) \quad \frac{\dfrac{\Sigma p_1 q_1}{\Sigma p_0 q_0}}{\dfrac{\Sigma (p_0+p_1) q_1}{\Sigma (p_0+p_1) q_0}}, \qquad \text{(Walsh's cross-weight aggregative)}$$

$$(10) \quad \sqrt{\text{(Formula 6)} \times \text{(Formula 9)}},$$
$$\text{(crossed cross-weight aggregative)}$$

These ten examples are typical of the many formulas that have been proposed. The question is how to discriminate among them and determine which index most nearly represents the true average of prices. In order to solve this problem, Irving Fisher proposed two fundamental tests, the time reversal test and the factor reversal test. These criteria will be discussed in the next two sections.

In order to make comparisons, the index numbers of the ten crop prices for the year 1930, using 1926 as base, have been calculated by several of the above formulas.

For this purpose Table 5 has been computed, the values of pq being expressed in millions of dollars.

Example 1. The index of prices for 1930 with 1926 as base, according to the simple arithmetic formula (1), is at once obtained from price relatives, Table 3:

$$I = \frac{(1.12 + .60 + .95 + \cdots\cdots + .81 + .66)}{10} = .799 \ .$$

VALUES OF pq FOR YEARS 1926 AND 1930

Crops	p_0	p_1	q_0	q_1	$p_0 q_0$	$p_1 q_1$	$p_0 q_1$	$p_1 q_0$
Corn	.75	.84	2692	2060	2019.0000	1730.4000	1545.0000	2261.2800
Wheat	1.45	.87	831.0	858.2	1204.9500	746.6340	1244.3900	722.9700
Oats	.41	.39	1247	1278	511.2700	498.4200	523.9800	486.3300
Cotton	.175	.136	8989	6966	1573.0750	947.3760	1219.0500	1222.5040
Potatoes	1.420	.904	354.3	333.2	503.1060	301.2128	473.1440	320.2872
Hay	23.41	19.89	96.07	74.21	2248.9987	1476.0369	1737.2561	1910.8323
Sugar	.043	.034	12952	13169	556.9360	447.7460	566.2670	440.3680
Tobacco	.182	.144	1298	1635	236.2360	235.4400	297.5700	186.9120
Barley	.64	.52	184.9	304.6	118.3360	158.3920	194.9440	96.1480
Rye	.92	.61	40.80	45.38	37.5360	27.6818	41.7496	24.8880
Totals					9009.4437	6569.3395	7843.3507	7672.5195

TABLE 5

Example 2. In terms of the reciprocals of the price relatives, Table 3, the index for 1930 is calculated by the simple harmonic formula (2) to be

$$I = \frac{10}{\dfrac{1}{1.12}+\dfrac{1}{.60}+\dfrac{1}{.95}+\cdots\cdots+\dfrac{1}{.81}+\dfrac{1}{.66}} = \frac{10}{12.9145} = .774 .$$

Example 3. Using formula (5), the price index for 1930 is found to be:

$$I = \frac{7672.5195}{9009.4437} = .852 .$$

Example 4. Using Fisher's ideal formula (7), one finds

$$I = \sqrt{\frac{7672.5195}{9009.4437} \times \frac{6569.3395}{7843.3507}} = \sqrt{.851609 \times .837568} = .845 .$$

PROBLEMS

In problems 1-4, calculate the price index for 1930, with 1926 as base:

1. Using formula 6.
2. By the harmonic aggregative formula.

3. Using formula 9.

4. Using formula 10. Compare this result with the value of the ideal index as given in example 4.

5. Make a price index for each of the twelve years from 1920 to 1931 using some one of the above formulas. Graph your results and compare with the general commodity price index of Figure 22. Select your own base.

4. The Time Reversal Test. It is quite obvious that with so many formulas to choose from, some reasonable test must be devised by means of which good index numbers can be detected from inadequate ones. The *time reversal test* is such a criterion, and may be defined as follows:

If I_a is the index number computed for year b with year a as base, and if I_b is the index number for year a with year b as base, then I_a and I_b should satisfy the equation

$$I_a \times I_b = 1 .$$

If the product $I_a \times I_b$ is greater than 1, then it is said that an *upward bias* exists; if the product is less than 1, the *bias* is *downward*.

It will be clear from this definition that the time reversal test reduces to a study of the product of an index number by the same number in which the subscripts "0" and "1" of p and q have been interchanged.

Example 1. Does the simple arithmetic index, formula (1), satisfy the time reversal test?

That it does not is easily proved by the following computation. The value of I for 1930, using 1926 as base, has been calculated as .799 . Changing the base to 1930 and calculating I for 1926, one has $I = 1.29$. The product of the two numbers equals 1.03, indicating an upward bias.

Consider the geometric mean of the relatives, formula (3):

$$I_G = \sqrt[n]{\frac{p_1}{p_0} \frac{p_1'}{p_0'} \frac{p_1''}{p_0''} \cdots \cdots \frac{p_1^{(n-1)}}{p_0^{(n-1)}}} .$$

It is easily seen that this index number satisfies the time reversal test, since the product of I_G by the same formula with the subscripts "0" and "1" interchanged clearly reduces to 1. But it has already been proved in section 13 of Chapter III that the arithmetic mean of a set of positive numbers always exceeds the value of the geometric mean of the same numbers. Hence, since no bias exists for I_G, the arithmetic index must always show an upward bias.

Example 2. Prove that formula (6) satisfies the time reversal test.

Changing the base by interchanging the subscripts as explained above and forming the product of the two index numbers, it is seen that

$$\frac{\Sigma(q_0+q_1)p_1}{\Sigma(q_0+q_1)p_0} \times \frac{\Sigma(q_1+q_0)p_0}{\Sigma(q_1+q_0)p_1} = 1 \ .$$

PROBLEMS

1. Explain why the time reversal test is a reasonable one to make.
2. Show that formula (2) always has a downward bias. Hint: How are the geometric and harmonic means related? Use an argument similar to the one in the first example.
3. Apply the time reversal test to formula (5).
4. Show that the "ideal" formula fulfills the time reversal test.
5. Apply the test to the harmonic aggregative.
6. Does formula (9) fulfill the test?
7. Give numerical values to p and q in formula (5) to show that it may have either an upward or a downward bias.

5. The Factor Reversal Test. A second fundamental test to which index numbers may be subjected is that to which the name of the *factor reversal test* has been given. This may be illustrated as follows: Suppose that an index of prices and an index of quantity change have been constructed. It is then reasonable to expect that the product of the two, that is, price change by quantity change, would equal the ratio of the total value — the product of price by quantity — in the second year over the total value in the base year. In order to state this algebraically, one may designate the price index by I_p and the quantity index by I_q. The factor reversal test then requires that

$$I_p \times I_q = \frac{\Sigma p_1 q_1}{\Sigma p_0 q_0} \ .$$

Since the quantity index is obtained from the price index merely by interchanging p with q, leaving the subscripts unchanged, the factor reversal test consists in showing that the product of the price index formula by the same formula in which the p's and q's have been interchanged is equal to the total value in the second year divided by the total value in the base year.

The meaning of the test is best clarified by examples.

Example 1. Apply the factor reversal test to formula (5). Making use of the data given in Table 5, one calculates the price index to be,

$$I_p = \frac{\Sigma p_1 q_0}{\Sigma p_0 q_0} = \frac{7672.5195}{9009.4437} = .852 \ .$$

Similarly, interchanging the p's and q's, the quantity index is calculated to be

$$I_q = \frac{\Sigma q_1 p_0}{\Sigma q_0 p_0} = \frac{7843.3507}{9009.4437} = .871 \ .$$

The product of these two numbers, $I_p \times I_q = .852 \times .871 = .742$, is seen to differ somewhat from the ratio

$$\frac{\Sigma p_1 q_1}{\Sigma p_0 q_0} = \frac{6569.3395}{9009.4437} = .729 \ .$$

It is also obvious algebraically from the formulas for I_p and I_q that the factor reversal test is not, in general, fulfilled.

Example 2. Prove that the "ideal" formula meets the factor reversal test.

This is proved by forming explicitly the product of I_p with I_q. It is found that

$$I_p \times I_q = \sqrt{\frac{\Sigma p_1 q_0}{\Sigma p_0 q_0} \times \frac{\Sigma p_1 q_1}{\Sigma p_0 q_1}} \cdot \sqrt{\frac{\Sigma q_1 p_0}{\Sigma q_0 p_0} \times \frac{\Sigma q_1 p_1}{\Sigma q_0 p_1}} = \frac{\Sigma p_1 q_1}{\Sigma p_0 q_0} \ .$$

PROBLEMS

1. Show by numerical examples that neither formula (1) nor formula (2) satisfies the factor reversal test.

2. Apply the factor reversal test to formula (6).

3. Show that formula (10) satisfies the factor reversal test.

4. Show that the criterion of this section is fulfilled by the index number made up of the square root of the product of the simple arithmetic index number by $\dfrac{\Sigma p_1 q_1}{\Sigma p_0 q_0} \div \dfrac{\Sigma q_1 / q_0}{n}$.

6. Fisher's Ideal Index Number.

Formula (7) has already been referred to as the "ideal" index number. This formula was obtained by Irving Fisher after an examination of 134 possible formulas, many of which had previously been used by economists and others. Fisher first applied the time reversal test to this group and from the total obtained 41 formulas which satisfied this test. From this smaller set, he then eliminated all that did not meet the factor reversal test and thus obtained 13 formulas which met both the time and factor requirements. In order to make a final choice from the field as thus limited, Fisher then examined the formulas from the practical point of view of simplicity and ease of calculation, and in this respect the "ideal" easily led the rest.

On the score of practical calculation, however, the use of formula (6) is strongly urged, since it gives results that, even in extreme cases, are very close to the results obtained by the "ideal". The following considerations will show that the discrepancy between the two formulas[1] is, in general, small.

Making use of the following abbreviations, I_6 for formula (6), I_7 for the "ideal", $\Sigma p_0 q_0 = A$, $\Sigma p_0 q_1 = B$, $\Sigma p_1 q_0 = C$, $\Sigma p_1 q_1 = D$, the following identities are obtained by straightforward algebra

$$I_6 = \frac{C+D}{A+B} = \frac{1+D/C}{1+B/A} \cdot C/A$$

$$= \frac{1+D/C}{1+B/A} \sqrt{DC/AB} \cdot \sqrt{CB/AD} =$$

$$= \frac{1+\sqrt{BD/AC}\sqrt{AD/BC}}{1+\sqrt{BD/AC}\sqrt{BC/AD}} \cdot I_7 \cdot \sqrt{CB/AD} .$$

When the further abbreviations $X^2 = AD/BC$, $Y^2 = BD/AC$, are employed, this identity reduces to the following:

$$I_6 = \frac{1+XY}{X+Y} \cdot I_7 .$$

It will be readily seen from this equation that the value of the multiplier of I_7 is less than 1, provided either of the following sets of inequalities is satisfied:

$$X < 1 < Y ,$$
$$Y < 1 < X .$$

---

[1] With variations in notation, from I. Fisher, *The Making of Index Numbers*, 1922, pp. 428-430.

Similarly, the coefficient is greater than 1 provided both X and Y are either greater than or less than 1. The two index numbers are equal when X and Y are each equal to 1.

In order to show the range of error, Fisher calculated tables of the coefficient of I_7 for values of X^2 from .90 to 1.10 and for values of Y^2 from .50 to 2.00. The maximum range of the coefficient was thus found to be from .983 to 1.016. This means that under all usual conditions formula (6) will give an answer that is within four percent of the value calculated by the "ideal" formula.

7. *Types of Bases.* In the discussion of index numbers, it has thus far been assumed that the comparison of a price level in a given year is being made with the price level in a base year. This is not always desirable and the expedient of broadening the base is often resorted to. This is done by using the arithmetic average of the prices covering m years, $(p_1 + p_2 + p_3 + \cdots\cdots + p_m)/m$, as the base, instead of referring all prices to a single year. Such a procedure often minimizes or eliminates distortions that may rise from using a single year as a base.

Another method is that of employing a moving base. In this case *chain* or *link* relatives, namely, p_1/p_0, p_2/p_1, p_3/p_2, p_4/p_3, $\cdots\cdots$, are used instead of the fixed base relatives such as were calculated in section 2. A series of index numbers, using a moving base, is called a series of *chain index numbers*. From a series of such chain index numbers, one is always able to compare the price level of one year with the price level of another by multiplication of the intervening numbers. Thus, if the index number of the second year in the chain with the first year as base is designated by I_{12}, the index number of the third year with the second year as base by I_{23}, etc., then the index number of the nth year with the first year as base is given by the product,

$$I_{1n} = I_{12} I_{23} I_{34} \cdots\cdots I_{n-1,\,n}.$$

Of course, this value will not agree exactly with the index number calculated by a direct comparison of the price level of the nth year with the price level of the first, but experience shows that it will be sufficiently near for most practical purposes.[1]

---

[1] In this connection E. E. Day in his *Statistical Analysis*, New York, 1925, has suggested that a perfect index number should meet the circular test, which he describes as follows (see p. 361): "Suppose an index number is computed by the 'ideal' formula for each successive pair of years from 1914 to 1924; thus for 1915 on the base of 1914, 1916 on the base of 1915, and so on, to the index number for 1924 on the base of 1923. Suppose these individual index numbers, first obtained as a series of year-to-year links, are welded together

Example: The following calculation is based upon the figures of Tables 1 and 2 and illustrates the method of chaining. For simplicity, price index formula (5) is used. The years 1926, 1927, 1928, and 1929, are compared. Letting p_1, p_2, p_3, p_4, represent the prices for the years 1926, 1927, 1928, and 1929, respectively, and q_1, q_2, q_3, q_4, the quantities or production for the years 1926, 1927, 1928, and 1929, respectively, one gets the following values for pq (expressed in millions of dollars).

VALUES OF pq FOR YEARS 1926, 1927, 1928, AND 1929

Crop	p_1q_1	p_2q_1	p_2q_2	p_3q_2	p_3q_3	p_4q_3	p_4q_1
Corn	2019.0000	2315.1200	2376.1800	2680.1100	2734.4300	2649.8600	2530.4800
Wheat	1204.9500	1096.9200	1055.0760	943.1740	1079.5820	1107.0290	1005.5100
Oats	511.2700	586.0900	556.0100	626.9900	762.6700	676.3300	586.0900
Cotton	1573.0750	1582.0640	1140.1280	1295.6000	1447.8000	1382.6490	1716.8990
Potatoes	503.1060	382.9983	435.3187	249.6740	288.5480	633.8748	482.5566
Hay	2248.9987	1860.8759	2388.9021	2586.2301	2232.6759	2171.9880	1959.8280
Sugar	556.9360	608.7440	589.3800	526.6800	487.9140	441.4460	492.1760
Tobacco	236.2360	275.1760	256.9440	244.8240	277.7500	254.3750	240.1300
Barley	118.3360	142.3730	204.7430	207.4020	278.8500	225.2250	116.4870
Rye	37.5360	40.8000	58.1600	62.2312	46.4059	41.6352	39.1680
Totals	9009.4437	8891.1612	9060.8418	9422.9153	9636.6259	9584.4120	9169.3246

Crop	p_1q_2	p_2q_3	p_3q_4	p_1q_4	p_4q_4	p_3q_1	p_4q_2
Corn	2072.2500	2424.3400	2458.9500	1901.2500	2382.9000	2611.2400	2597.2200
Wheat	1158.9850	1207.6680	958.8680	1178.2700	983.2460	980.5800	967.1530
Oats	485.0300	676.3300	592.5400	458.3800	525.4600	660.9100	556.0100
Cotton	1133.6500	1274.0640	1482.6000	1297.2750	1415.8830	1797.8000	1237.2980
Potatoes	571.8340	503.0974	204.0420	467.3220	448.2342	219.6660	548.4774
Hay	2887.1553	2062.3239	1830.6810	2043.6930	1780.9200	2014.5879	2515.9320
Sugar	539.2200	545.9990	580.8600	594.6900	525.5400	543.9840	476.5200
Tobacco	220.5840	291.5000	310.4740	279.7340	284.3450	262.1960	224.2200
Barley	170.1760	275.2750	218.5560	179.3280	176.5260	144.2220	167.5170
Rye	53.5072	43.3700	37.3965	32.1540	33.5520	43.6560	55.8336
Totals	9292.3915	9303.9673	8674.9675	8432.0960	8556.6062	9278.8419	9848.6834

TABLE 6

so as to make a chain for the full period of eleven years. The question may then be raised: how far is the result thus obtained for the year 1924 on the base of the year 1914 consistent with the result obtained by comparing 1924 with 1914 by direct application of the 'ideal' formula for these two years?" If the results are consistent then the formula meets the circular test. Rigorously stated the criterion would read: "Any index number meeting the circular test will give for a final year in which the data are identical with the initial year, a result identical with the index number of the initial year". The "ideal" index of Fisher does not meet this test.

Using the above data, one obtains the following chain of index numbers:

$I_{12} = 8891.1612/9009.4437 = .9869$ (index for 1927 with 1926 as base),

$I_{23} = 9422.9153/9060.8418 = 1.0400$ (index for 1928 with 1927 as base),

$I_{34} = 9584.4120/9636.6259 = .9946$ (index for 1929 with 1928 as base).

To compute the value of the index for 1929 with 1926 as base, these three numbers are multiplied together to yield

$$I_{14} = I_{12} \times I_{23} \times I_{34} = 1.0208 \ .$$

This index is seen to compare favorably with the one computed directly, namely,

$$I_{14} = 9169.3246/9009.4437 = 1.0177 \ .$$

PROBLEMS.

1. Using formula (1), calculate the price index for 1928 with the average of the preceding five years as base.

2. Using formula (5), compare the price levels for 1922 with the average of the two preceding years.

3. Make a chain of index numbers from 1926 to 1929 using the "ideal" formula. Calculate the index of 1929 with 1926 as base, by both the chain and the direct methods. Is the agreement closer using the "ideal" formula or formula (5)? Explain.

8. Some Practical Considerations Concerning the Making of Index Numbers. In the preceding sections, the making of index numbers has been considered only from the standpoint of the mathematical formula. As a matter of fact, the practical application of the theory of index numbers rests in a very fundamental way upon the actual data. For the solution of the problem of how to obtain the desired data and how many items to include, no mathematical formula, of course, exists, and, thus, this question is outside the scope of the present work.

It may be of interest, however, to note that in a comprehensive article on the subject,[1] Carl Snyder gives the following sources of

---

[1] "The Measure of the General Price Level," *Harvard Review of Economic Statistics*, Vol. 10 (1928), pp. 40-51.

material, with assumed weights, for the construction of the general price index.

1. Industrial commodity prices at wholesale, U. S. Department of Labor (Weight 10).

2. Farm prices of 30 commodities, U.S. Department of Agriculture (Weight 10).

3. Forty-three articles of food in 51 cities, U. S. Department of Labor (Weight 10).

4. Cost of housing in 32 cities, U. S. Department of Labor (Weight 5).

5. Cost in 32 cities of clothing (weight 4), fuel and light (weight 1), home furnishing goods (weight 1), miscellaneous (weights 4), U. S. Department of Labor.

6. Transportation costs, Federal Reserve Bank of New York. Railway freight rates per ton mile, U. S. Interstate Commerce Commission and U. S. Department of Commerce (Weight 5).

7. Realty values—Urban, Federal Reserve Bank of New York (weight 8), Farm, estimated value per acre, U. S. Department of Agriculture (weight 2).

8. Security prices. Preferred stocks (weight 1), common stocks (weight 4), yield on sixty high grade bonds (weight 5), Federal Reserve Bank of New York from data of the Standard Statistics Company.

9. Equipment and machinery prices: (a) Railway equipment, (b) electric car costs, (c) farm machinery, (d) telephone equipment, (e) electrical appliances, (f) electrical machinery, (g) heating appliances, Federal Reserve Bank of New York (Weight 10).

10. Hardware prices, index of National Retail Hardware Association (Weight 3).

11. Automobile prices, weighted price index of six makes of cars (Weight 2).

12. Composite wages, Federal Reserve Bank of New York (Weight 15).

The United States government in forming its general index considers the following items:

1. Commodity prices at wholesale, Bureau of Labor (Weight 20).

2. Cost of living, Bureau of Labor (Weight 35).

3. Composite wages, Federal Reserve Bank of New York (Weight 35).

4. Rents, Bureau of Labor (Weight 10).

In Figure 22 is given the index of wholesale commodity prices published by the United States Bureau of Labor Statistics.[1] In 1932 this index comprised 784 prices of different commodities, in earlier years this number was, of course, smaller. Indexes are also calculated by the Bureau of Labor Statistics for various groups of commodities such as raw materials, semi-manufactured articles, finished goods, farm products, foods, cereals, hides and leather products, textile products, metals and metal products, etc., etc.

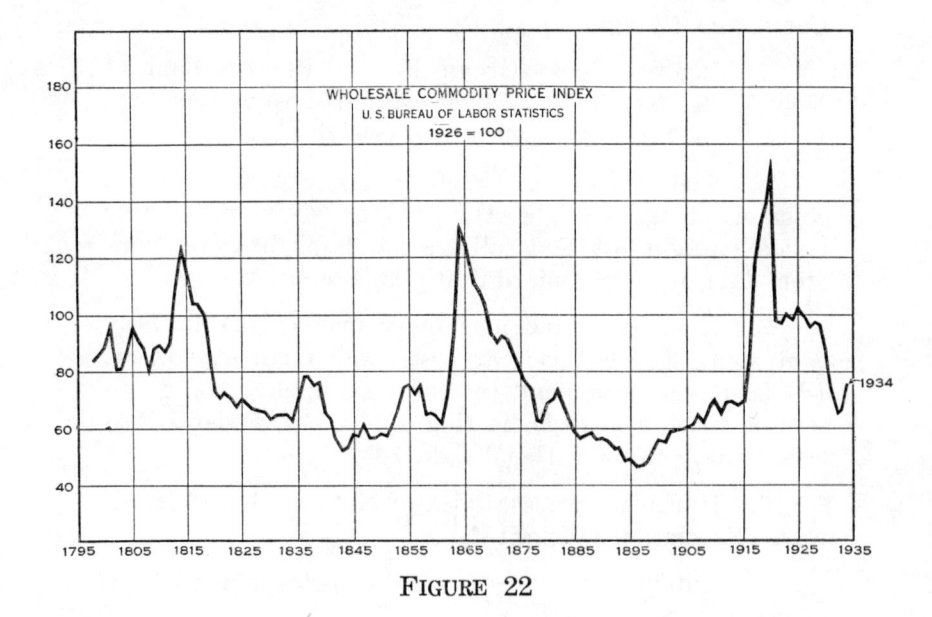

FIGURE 22

[1] Indexes for the years 1797-1889 have been prepared by Professors G. F. Warren and F. A. Pearson, of Cornell University. From 1890 to date, the indexes are by the U. S. Bureau of Labor Statistics.

INDEX NUMBERS

9. *Miscellaneous Applications.* So far the discussion has been limited to index numbers of prices. It will be clear, however, that the theory for the comparison of one section of a time series with another applies to other statistical units as well. The following problems illustrate this point.

PROBLEMS

1. Make a set of index numbers to compare the number of bank suspensions in the United States, for the various kinds of banks as well as for all banks, from 1927-1932. (The statistics of bank suspensions relate to banks closed to the public either temporarily or permanently on account of financial difficulties, by order of supervisory authorities or directors of the bank. They do not include banks closed temporarily under special or "moratorium" holidays declared by civil authorities.) The data are given in the following table:

Year	All Banks	Member Banks National	Member Banks State	Non-Member Banks	Deposits ($1,000,000) All Banks
1927	662	91	33	538	$ 193.9
1928	491	57	16	418	138.6
1929	642	64	17	561	234.5
1930	1345	161	26	1158	864.7
1931	2298	409	108	1781	1691.5
1932	1453	276	54	1123	730.5

2. Compare the bank suspensions in 1932 with the bank suspensions in 1927 using the "ideal" formula. Hint: Consider the deposit column as the product of p by q.

3. The following data give the number of wage earners in manufactures in the United States and their total yearly wages. Make an index comparing wages with 1923 as a base.

Year	Wage Earners	Total Wages
1914	6,896,190	$ 4,067,718,740
1919	9,000,059	10,461,786,869
1921	6,946,570	8,202,324,339
1923	8,778,156	11,009,297,726
1925	8,384,261	10,729,968,927
1927	8,349,755	10,848,802,532
1929	8,838,743	11,620,973,254

4. Use the "ideal" formula to compare wages in 1929 with wages in 1914. Hint: Consider total wages as the product of p by q.

5. Study the growth of the life insurance business in the United States from the following data:

Year	No. of Policies	Amount
1900	3,136,051	$ 7,093,152,380
1905	5,621,417	11,054,255,524
1910	6,954,119	13,227,213,168
1915	9,890,264	18,349,285,339
1920	16,694,561	35,091,538,279
1925	23,881,758	54,519,175,903
1930	33,498,958	79,774,840,870

CHAPTER V

THE ANALYSIS OF TIME SERIES

1. Historical Note. The analysis of time series furnishes a problem of engaging interest to the economist and statistician. Since it is only by careful study and interpretation of the past that one can hope to foretell the future, it becomes a matter of major importance to have statistical methods applicable to the analysis of conditions of the past through which some knowledge may be gained as to probable conditions in the future. The history of the development of "business cycles," a term applied to the more or less periodic alternations of business between prosperity and depression, is the story of this attempt. It is possible here to give only the briefest outline of this development.

Like many other scientific problems, a consideration of business cycles, then limited to their most spectacular phase of crisis, was forced on students by events.[1] The South Sea Bubble and Mississippi Scheme culminated in crises of the first order. The Napoleonic Wars led to grave commercial perturbations. But economists, by and large, were more interested in "the normal state", in the "conditions of equilibrium", that hypothetical Utopia of the theorist, when all parts of the economic machine function in perfect balance with faultless smoothness, than with the harsh actualities of rhythm, and perturbation, and crisis. To them crises were unwelcome and disruptive intruders on a theoretical "normal," and were treated, therefore, as mere addenda of the economic state, instead of one of its most notable characteristics. But economic heretics, notably Sismondi, raised the problem, and it has not yet been solved. The *Nouveaux Principes d'Economie Politique* of J. C. L. de Sismondi (1773-1842) was published in 1819, when the crisis of 1816, a year after Waterloo, was fresh in the minds of men. This first comprehensive explanation of crises set forth, however tentatively, many, if not most, of the theories still current in regard to the origins of crises.

Possibly Clement Juglar's *Des crises commerciales et de leur retour périodique*, which appeared in 1860, marks a turning point in cycle theory, for the reason that Juglar gave to exact observa-

---
[1] See Wesley C. Mitchell, *Business Cycles*, New York, 1928.

tion and description of the phenomena a prominence they had not hitherto had. He also raised the question of inter-crisis cycles. As early as 1833 some notice of rough periodicity in crises had been made, and by 1837 some descriptions of the phases of the cycle. These paved the way for diversion of emphasis from "crises," which were thought of as sporadic, discrete accidents, to cycles, the continuous ebb and flow of business fortune through typical patterns. Given, on the one hand, a recognition of the continuity of commercial phenomena and, on the other hand, an emphasis on precise observation and description of these phenomena, the way was paved for statistical studies.

Here again one encounters the redoubtable William Stanley Jevons, who was the most effective pioneer in this effort. Cournot had, it is true, noticed the necessity of distinguishing between secular trends and periodic variations. Although one or two papers had appeared some half dozen years before, Jevons' "On the Study of Periodic Commercial Fluctuations" (1862) marks the real beginning of work on seasonal variations. He was the father of the indispensable index number, wrote on secular trend, and analyzed British prices over a long period of years. Although William Playfair[1] justly claimed charting as his invention in 1787, Jevons first used the vertical ratio scale in his studies of trend in 1863, a practice which, despite its many advantages, did not win wide adherence till 1917. Studies made on index numbers by Jevons were not materially forwarded till Edgeworth's work. Meantime, correlation analysis was invented by Sir Francis Galton (1889) and refined by Karl Pearson.

Therefore, "by the time writers on business cycles began to make systematic use of statistics—say in the decade . . . . . . beginning in 1900—they could use many methods already developed by mathematicians, anthropometrists, biologists, and economists, and many data already collected by public and private agencies."[2]

In 1884 J. H. Poynting, in 1901 R. H. Hooker, used moving averages to determine secular trend. In 1899 G. Udney Yule, in 1901 R. H. Hooker, applied Pearson's method of correlation to economic data. In 1902 Dr. J. P. Norton in his *Statistical Studies in the New York Money Market* fitted exponential curves to his data to measure secular trend, considered the dispersions as well as the

---

[1] The student should by all means read the interesting article, "Playfair and His Charts," by H. G. Funkhouser and Helen M. Walker, in *Economic History* (A Supplement of *The Economic Journal*) Vol. III, February 1935, pp. 103-109.

[2] Mitchell, *Business Cycles*, p. 199.

averages of seasonal variations taken as percentages of his trends, and employed lines of regression and coefficients of correlation. In 1914 H. L. Moore applied harmonic analysis to time series; in 1915 Warren M. Persons made the first of his business barometers, and in 1917 began his work at Harvard on business cycles which has been so widely influential both at home and abroad.

2. Secular Trend. The first step in the analysis of time series is to obtain a homogeneous series of items, so that an item at one date is strictly comparable with an item of another date.

The second step is to determine the *secular trend* of the series, namely, that characteristic of the series which tends to extend consistently throughout the entire period. This is done by fitting a curve to the data under consideration. It is usually sufficient for this purpose to fit a straight line, but occasionally instances arise, particularly if the series is taken over a long period of time, when it may seem desirable to fit a parabola or a polynomial of higher degree to the given data, or even to fit different curves to different parts of the series. This last situation applies particularly to the analysis of business conditions before and after the World War.

MONTHLY AND ANNUAL AVERAGES OF MEAN WEEKLY FREIGHT CAR LOADINGS
(unit, 1,000 cars)

Year	Jan.	Feb.	Mar.	April	May	June	July	Aug.	Sept.	Oct.	Nov.	Dec.	Annual Av
1919	728	687	697	715	759	809	858	892	960	967	807	758	803
1920	820	776	848	731	862	860	901	968	969	1005	884	723	862
1921	705	683	692	706	757	765	751	810	841	929	761	683	757
1922	702	765	826	723	787	842	825	877	935	992	944	838	838
1923	845	842	917	941	975	1011	986	1041	1037	1078	978	826	956
1924	858	908	916	875	895	906	894	974	1037	1091	975	847	931
1925	921	905	924	941	968	989	986	1080	1074	1107	1024	888	984
1926	923	919	969	958	1037	1028	1049	1104	1148	1205	1068	904	1026
1927	946	956	1002	975	1024	999	979	1062	1097	1115	956	834	995
1928	862	897	951	935	1002	985	986	1058	1117	1175	1061	883	993
1929	893	942	962	996	1051	1052	1038	1117	1135	1169	978	835	1014
1930	837	876	883	912	914	930	895	938	931	950	798	680	879
1931	719	709	735	752	740	748	738	747	737	759	655	555	716
1932	567	561	565	557	522	491	483	525	577	634	549	485	543
Av.	809	816	849	837	878	887	884	942	971	1013	888	767	878

TABLE (a)

In order to illustrate the phenomena exhibited by a time series and to show the method of analysis, a simple example will be employed. To begin with, consider the data of the table on page 121, which shows the monthly and annual averages of mean weekly freight car loadings in the United States from January, 1919, to December, 1932. It would be difficult to say confidently *a priori* whether freight business had gained or lost over this period. The factors which would tend to increase freight business would be the increase in population and the increase in production and distribution. The major factors tending towards a decrease would be the development of pipe lines and motor truck transportation and the fact the series ends in the depths of a depression. As between this balance of forces, we should be undecided. Which judgment will the table confirm? The question is to be answered finally, of course, by determining the secular trend of the series.

In order to answer the question proposed, it will be sufficient in the present case to fit a straight line to the time series obtained by using the mean annual freight car loadings as ordinates and the years as abscissas. In general, in calculating the trend line, it is desirable to use all the data instead of annual averages but in this case, for purposes of simplicity, we shall use annual averages.

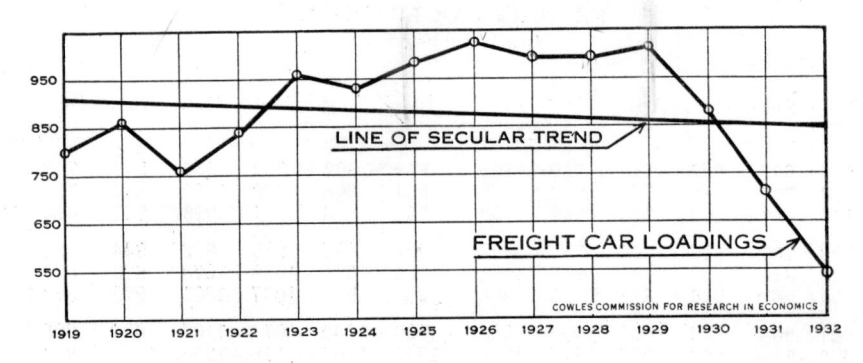

FIGURE 23

Employing the method of section 6, Chapter II, one finds that $m_0 = 12{,}297$, and $m_1 = 91{,}109$. Since there are 14 items in the series of annual averages, one refers to Table IX for $p = 14$, and finds $A = .31868$, $B = -.03297$, and $C = .004396$. The following computations are then made:

$$a_1 = Am_0 + Bm_1 = (12{,}297)(.31868) + (91{,}109)(-.03297)$$
$$= 914.94 \;,$$

$$a_2 = Bm_0 + Cm_1 = (12{,}297)(-.03297) + (91{,}109)(.004396)$$
$$= -4.92 .$$

Hence, the equation of the straight line trend is
$$y = 914.94 - 4.92x ,$$

which is graphed in Figure 23. Since the coefficient of x is small and negative, the conclusion is reached that there is indication of a slight tendency to decline in freight car loadings since 1919.

PROBLEMS

1. The following table gives the annual yield of wheat per acre for the 65 years, 1866-1930. Calculate the trend line for these data.

Year	Yield of Wheat (per acre) Bushels	Year	Yield of Wheat (per acre) Bushels	Year	Yield of Wheat (per acre) Bushels
1866	9.9	1888	11.1	1910	13.9
1867	11.6	1889	13.9	1911	12.5
1868	12.1	1890	11.1	1912	15.9
1869	13.6	1891	11.5	1913	15.2
1870	12.4	1892	13.3	1914	16.6
1871	11.6	1893	11.3	1915	17.0
1872	12.0	1894	13.1	1916	12.2
1873	12.7	1895	13.9	1917	14.1
1874	12.3	1896	12.4	1918	15.6
1875	11.1	1897	13.3	1919	12.8
1876	10.5	1898	15.1	1920	13.6
1877	13.9	1899	12.1	1921	12.8
1878	13.1	1900	11.7	1922	13.9
1879	13.0	1901	15.0	1923	13.4
1880	13.1	1902	14.6	1924	16.5
1881	10.2	1903	12.9	1925	12.9
1882	13.6	1904	12.5	1926	14.8
1883	11.6	1905	14.7	1927	14.9
1884	13.0	1906	15.8	1928	15.7
1885	10.4	1907	14.1	1929	13.2
1886	12.4	1908	14.0	1930	14.4
1887	12.1	1909	15.4		

2. Fit a trend line to the following data on electric power production (unit, mean daily output in 1,000,000 kilowatt hours):

Year	Jan.	Feb.	Mar.	Apr.	May	June	July	Aug.	Sept.	Oct.	Nov.	Dec.
1928	234.4	236.8	233.6	228.2	229.6	233.3	230.4	242.3	242.5	255.5	258.4	255.2
1929	265.8	265.3	257.7	262.7	260.8	258.9	258.5	269.5	268.7	280.9	274.8	274.5
1930	279.5	272.4	264.1	267.3	260.1	259.5	254.8	255.0	259.7	264.4	256.4	261.5
1931	256.2	255.0	253.6	255.2	245.9	250.5	249.4	246.0	251.1	250.5	246.9	250.7
1932	243.3	241.4	235.5	226.0	214.0	218.3	210.5	217.4	224.6	227.2	231.2	229.9

3. Determine from the following data whether or not the per capita income in the United States, expressed in 1913 dollars, is increasing or decreasing:[1]

Year	Per Capita Income (1913 Dollars)	Year	Per Capita Income (1913 Dollars)
1909	$322	1921	$310
1910	327	1922	342
1911	332	1923	377
1912	341	1924	384
1913	346	1925	392
1914	335	1926	403
1915	335	1927	419
1916	367	1928	423
1917	368	1929	421
1918	360	1930	365
1919	334	1931	314
1920	322	1932	228 (est.)

3. Seasonal Variation. The last section dealt only with the mean annual freight car loadings and no account was taken of the fact that in the complete data there is a typical movement having a period of one year, that is to say, the amount of freight hauled tends to conform to a certain pattern at intervals of twelve months. This phenomenon is known as *seasonal variation* and is an important characteristic of many economic series. Of course, it is seldom so well defined and regular as the seasonal variation of certain meteorological phenomena, such as temperature, but similar seasonal movements are distinctly marked in many time series encountered in the study of business and economic problems. For example, the average monthly price of a commodity such as eggs would tend to follow the seasons, being higher in winter than in summer, although relatively few price series show such a movement.

Usually the first step in the study of seasonal variation in a series is to calculate the *link relatives*,[2] that is, the ratio of each item in the series to the one just preceding. These link relatives are then arranged in order of magnitude in a table with the twelve monthly ratios as class marks, and the median value for each ratio determined. In general, the average value will serve as well as the median value, unless there are a number of exceptional ratios in the series.

For the year 1920, the link relatives for freight car loadings would be determined as follows:

---

[1] Irving Fisher, *Booms and Depressions*, New York, 1932, Appendix V.
[2] This method is given in detail because of its historic importance. The reader is warned that it is subject to considerable criticism. See, for example, H. Hotelling, *American Mathematical Monthly*, Vol. XLII, No. 3, March 1935, p. 170.

THE ANALYSIS OF TIME SERIES

$$\frac{\text{Jan.}}{\text{Dec.}} \text{ratio} = \frac{820}{758} = 1.08, \quad \frac{\text{Feb}}{\text{Jan}} \text{ratio} = .95, \quad \frac{\text{Mar.}}{\text{Feb.}} \text{ratio} = 1.09,$$

$$\frac{\text{Apr.}}{\text{Mar.}} \text{ratio} = .86, \quad \frac{\text{May}}{\text{Apr.}} \text{ratio} = 1.18, \quad \frac{\text{June}}{\text{May}} \text{ratio} = 1.00,$$

$$\frac{\text{July}}{\text{June}} \text{ratio} = 1.05, \quad \frac{\text{Aug.}}{\text{July}} \text{ratio} = 1.07, \quad \frac{\text{Sept}}{\text{Aug.}} \text{ratio} = 1.00,$$

$$\frac{\text{Oct.}}{\text{Sept.}} \text{ratio} = 1.04, \quad \frac{\text{Nov.}}{\text{Oct.}} \text{ratio} = .88, \quad \frac{\text{Dec.}}{\text{Nov.}} \text{ratio} = .82,$$

For the freight car data that are being considered, the table of link relatives, expressed as percents and arranged in order of magnitude, follows:[1]

Ratios	Jan./Dec.	Feb./Jan.	Mar./Feb.	Apr./Mar.	May/Apr.	June/May	July/June	Aug./July	Sept./Aug.	Oct./Sept.	Nov./Oct.	Dec./Nov.
	109	109	109	104	118	107	106	110	110	110	95	94
	108	106	109	103	109	107	105	109	108	110	93	90
	106	105	108	103	108	104	102	109	107	106	91	89
	105	105	106	103	107	102	100	108	106	105	90	88
	104	104	105	102	107	102	100	108	106	105	89	87
	104	100	105	102	106	101	99	107	104	104	89	87
	103	101	104	102	106	101	99	108	104	105	88	87
	103	101	102	99	105	101	99	108	103	105	87	85
	102	99	102	99	104	100	98	106	102	103	86	85
	101	99	101	98	103	100	98	106	100	103	86	85
	101	98	101	97	102	99	98	105	100	103	84	85
	100	97	101	96	100	98	98	105	99	102	84	84
	98	95	101	88	98	98	98	104	99	102	83	83
	—	94	101	86	94	94	96	101	99	101	82	82
Median	104	101	103	100	106	101	99	108	104	105	88	86
Average	103	101	104	99	105	101	100	107	103	105	88	86

From the above table, it is seen that the medians and arithmetic averages compare very closely. In the present case the medians are used as the mean values of the link relatives in each column. In order to refer these to some month as a base, set the link relative for January equal to 100 and "chain" each median to this standard. To do this, multiply the median of each link relative column by the

---

[1] It will be noticed that, if the available data begin with January, the link relatives for the Jan./Dec. ratio will be one less than the link relatives for the other ratios.

value of the median preceding it. Thus, if the medians of each of the columns, expressed as decimals, are represented by the symbols $m_1, m_2, m_3, \cdots, m_{12}$, then the chain relatives will be $c_1 = 100$, $c_2 = 100 m_2$, $c_3 = c_2 m_3, \cdots, c_{12} = c_{11} m_{12}$. For freight car loadings, these values are easily calculated to be the following:

Median		Mo.	Chain Relatives	
$m_1,$	104	Jan.	$c_1,$	100
$m_2,$	101	Feb.	$c_2,$	101
$m_3,$	103	Mar.	$c_3,$	104
$m_4,$	100	April	$c_4,$	104
$m_5,$	106	May	$c_5,$	110
$m_6,$	101	June	$c_6,$	111
$m_7,$	99	July	$c_7,$	110
$m_8,$	108	Aug.	$c_8,$	119
$m_9,$	104	Sept.	$c_9,$	124
$m_{10},$	105	Oct.	$c_{10},$	130
$m_{11},$	88	Nov.	$c_{11},$	114
$m_{12},$	86	Dec.	$c_{12},$	98

It will be noticed that these values are not entirely consistent for, if the December chain relative is multiplied by the median of the January link relative, one will not have the value with which the series started, since $c_{12} = 98$ and $c_{12} m_1 = (98)(1.04) = 102$ instead of 100. To remove this discrepancy, an adjustment is made according to the following scheme: A quantity d is calculated from the equation

$$100(1+d)^{12} = c_{12} m_1 ,$$

and the chain relative c_i is replaced by the adjusted values $c_i/(1+d)^{i-1}$. One thus derives for the new chain relatives the following values:

$$c_1, \quad \frac{c_2}{(1+d)}, \quad \frac{c_3}{(1+d)^2}, \quad \cdots\cdots, \quad \frac{c_{12}}{(1+d)^{11}} .$$

From the example,

$$100(1+d)^{12} = c_{12} m_1 = 102 .$$

Taking logarithms of both sides, it is found that

$$\log(1+d) = \frac{\log 102 - \log 100}{12} = .0007167 ,$$

from which $\quad 1+d = 1.0017$,

and, therefore, $\quad d = .0017$.

The adjusted values are easily calculated by means of logarithms. For example, to find the adjusted chain relative for c_6, the procedure is as follows:

$$\text{adjusted relative } c_6 = \frac{c_6}{(1+d)^5} ;$$

$$\log (\text{adjusted relative } c_6) = \log c_6 - 5 \log (1+d)$$
$$= \log 111 - 5 \log 1.0017$$
$$= 2.0453230 - .0035835$$
$$= 2.0417395 ;$$

adjusted relative $c_6 = 110$.

The adjusted values in the example are given in the first column of the following table:

	Adjusted Chain Relatives	Index Seasonal Variation[1]
c_1,	100	92
c_2,	101	93
c_3,	104	95
c_4,	103	94
c_5,	109	100
c_6,	110	101
c_7,	109	100
c_8,	118	108
c_9,	122	112
c_{10},	128	117
c_{11},	112	103
c_{12},	96	88
Total	1312	1203
Average	109	100

[1] S. Kuznets has prepared a very valuable book on this subject: *Seasonal Variations in Industry and Trade*, New York, 1933, in which he gives an extensive table of seasonal indexes, pp. 372-415. He gives the following figures for freight car loadings:

1918-24: 89 92 97 92   98 101 104 108 113 114 102 90
1925-29: 90 92 96 96 102 100 100 108 111 115 101 87

As a check, it will be noticed that the final adjusted value, c_{12}, multiplied by $m_1/(1+d)$, is equal to 100, within a small approximate error, that is,

$$\frac{c_{12}m_1}{(1+d)} = \frac{96 \times 104}{1.0017} = 99.67 \ .$$

As a final calculation, the adjusted chain relatives are now further adjusted by using their arithmetic average as a base and letting it be 100. The items in the new series are called the *index numbers of seasonal variation*. For the given data, the arithmetic average of the adjusted chain relatives is 109, and adjusting to this base as 100, by dividing each of the adjusted chain relatives by 109, one gets the indexes of seasonal variation. These are given in the second column of the above table. They give a clear indication of the seasonal variation of the freight car loadings data that are being studied.

PROBLEMS

1. Calculate the index numbers of seasonal variation for the electric power production data as given in problem 2, section 2, of this chapter. Also determine whether seasonal disturbance is shown.

2. The following table gives the total new orders (expressed in 1,000 short tons) of fabricated steel over a five-year period, 1927-1931. Calculate the index of seasonal variation and show the seasonal fluctuations.

	Jan.	Feb.	Mar.	Apr.	May	June	July	Aug.	Sept.	Oct.	Nov.	Dec.
1927	36	59	55	47	38	28	35	48	38	47	27	35
1928	51	64	55	56	49	40	41	51	43	59	62	52
1929	40	70	69	54	58	57	58	51	52	45	52	27
1930	57	34	46	45	38	41	38	36	41	30	33	26
1931	27	24	31	29	26	22	27	24	33	20	18	16

3. The following figures show the net earnings of public utilities over an eight-year period, 1923-1930 (Unit = $1,000,000). Is there seasonal variation in the net earnings? Calculate the index of seasonal variation.

	Jan.	Feb.	Mar.	Apr.	May	June	July	Aug.	Sept.	Oct.	Nov.	Dec.
1923	47.4	44.5	44.9	44.9	42.0	40.9	36.1	34.2	38.2	42.0	46.3	48.0
1924	51.0	48.2	47.3	45.8	43.7	41.6	36.6	36.8	42.0	46.1	50.4	56.6
1925	58.7	54.1	52.5	51.0	48.9	47.8	44.3	44.8	49.1	55.1	60.5	65.4
1926	66.9	61.6	60.7	59.5	54.9	55.7	49.2	49.9	56.9	60.9	65.8	73.0
1927	74.4	66.9	65.4	64.9	61.2	59.2	53.9	53.6	61.9	65.3	70.2	78.9
1928	79.0	74.3	72.8	68.9	67.7	67.5	62.3	61.8	68.2	73.7	81.4	91.0
1929	92.0	86.0	85.0	83.0	82.5	79.0	71.0	73.0	80.0	83.0	92.0	100.0
1930	92.0	90.0	88.0	89.5	86.0	83.0	70.6	71.5	80.8	84.1	88.3	89.0

4. Correction for Seasonal Variation and Secular Trend. In the analysis of time series, it is often desirable to eliminate seasonal variation and secular trend from the data. This is conveniently done by first calculating the deviation of each item of the series from the normal, and then representing graphically the new values thus obtained.

Any method by which this is done must, of course, be an entirely arbitrary one, but must satisfy a certain criterion dictated by common sense. If y_i represents an item in the original series, s_i the corresponding index of seasonal variation, and y the corresponding ordinate of the secular trend curve, then the relative deviation of the item from the established normal may reasonably be represented by the formula

$$D_i = \frac{y_i - s_i y}{s_i y} = \frac{y_i}{s_i y} - 1 .$$

If the values of D_i are calculated and plotted, the graph thus obtained will furnish a representation of the original data referred to a normal situation from which seasonal variation and secular trend have been eliminated. The values above and below the time axis will represent the positive and negative deviations from the normal situation of the various items of the series.

As an example, corrections for seasonal variation and secular trend may be made on freight car loadings for the 14-year period, 1919-1932. The values of y are computed from the equation of secular trend, $y = 914.94 - 4.92x$, as given in section 2. The values of the indexes of seasonal variation are given at the end of the last section and should be used as ratios in the above equation, i.e., .92, .93, .95, etc.

Combining these values with the values obtained from the table of freight car loadings, the following values for D_i are calculated:

Relative Deviations of Freight Car Loadings from Normal

	Jan.	Feb.	Mar.	Apr.	May	June	July	Aug.	Sept.	Oct.	Nov.	Dec.
1919	−.14	−.19	−.20	−.17	−.17	−.12	−.06	−.09	−.06	−.09	−.14	−.05
1920	−.02	−.08	−.02	−.14	−.05	−.06	−.01	−.01	−.05	−.05	−.05	−.09
1921	−.15	−.19	−.19	−.17	−.16	−.16	−.17	−.17	−.17	−.12	−.18	−.14
1922	−.15	−.09	−.03	−.14	−.12	−.07	−.08	−.09	−.07	−.05	.02	.06
1923	.03	.01	.08	.12	.09	.12	.10	.08	.04	.03	.07	.05
1924	.05	.10	.08	.05	.01	.01	.01	.02	.04	.05	.07	.09
1925	.13	.10	.10	.13	.10	.11	.12	.13	.09	.07	.13	.15
1926	.14	.12	.16	.16	.18	.16	.19	.16	.17	.17	.18	.17
1927	.17	.17	.21	.19	.17	.13	.12	.13	.12	.09	.07	.09
1928	.08	.11	.15	.14	.15	.12	.14	.13	.15	.16	.19	.16
1929	.12	.17	.17	.23	.22	.21	.20	.20	.18	.16	.10	.10
1930	.06	.09	.08	.13	.06	.07	.05	.01	−.03	−.05	−.10	−.10
1931	−.09	−.11	−.10	−.06	−.13	−.13	−.14	−.19	−.23	−.24	−.25	−.26
1932	−.28	−.29	−.30	−.30	−.39	−.43	−.43	−.43	−.39	−.36	−.37	−.35

These values are graphically represented in the following Figure 24. It is obvious that the graph tells a great deal more about a particular year than does the yearly average, which may have been greatly influenced by one or two unusual months although the year as a whole may have been practically normal.

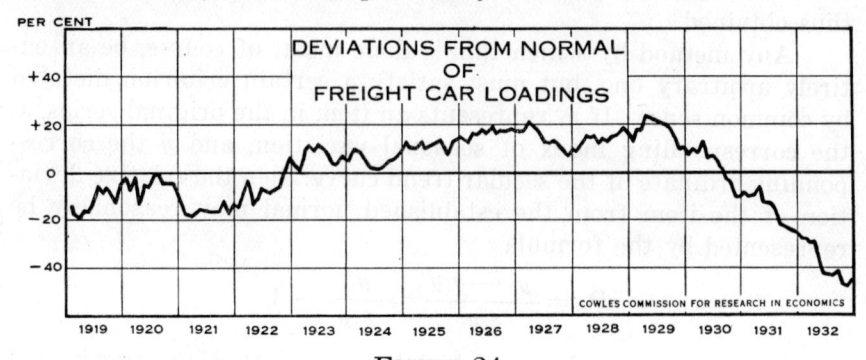

FIGURE 24

PROBLEMS

1. Correct for seasonal variation and secular trend the data of fabricated steel, as given in problem 2, section 3.

2. Among the clichés of the market place is the expression "the spring rise." From the following table of New York Times Daily Stock Price Averages determine whether there is a seasonal variation in stock prices. Logically, why would there not be such seasonal variation?

	Jan.	Feb.	Mar.	Apr.	May	June	July	Aug.	Sept.	Oct.	Nov.	Dec.
1928	183	180	194	196	201	198	192	203	207	213	229	231
1929	248	251	252	249	254	265	285	304	311	301	227	221
1930	220	228	240	245	233	229	207	204	207	186	165	161
1931	156	173	169	155	143	144	142	129	123	100	105	83
1932	80	81	79	65	52	44	47	68	72	65	62	58

3. Correct for seasonal variation and secular trend the following data, which give the average price per dozen of eggs in New York City during a nine-year period, 1923-1931:

	Jan.	Feb.	Mar.	Apr.	May	June	July	Aug.	Sept.	Oct.	Nov.	Dec.
1923	42	37	31	27	27	24	25	29	35	39	53	47
1924	42	39	25	24	25	27	29	33	39	44	52	57
1925	59	44	30	29	32	33	33	33	37	43	56	51
1926	38	31	29	32	31	30	29	31	38	40	50	48
1927	42	32	25	26	23	23	25	28	34	40	44	45
1928	45	32	29	28	30	29	30	31	33	32	37	37
1929	36	41	33	28	31	31	32	34	36	40	48	51
1930	42	35	26	27	23	24	22	25	25	26	31	29
1931	24	20	22	20	19	19	20	22	24	24	28	27

THE ANALYSIS OF TIME SERIES 131

As a check on your work, compare your results with Figure 25, which gives the original data and the line of secular trend, and Figure 26, which shows the deviations from "normal" of egg prices.

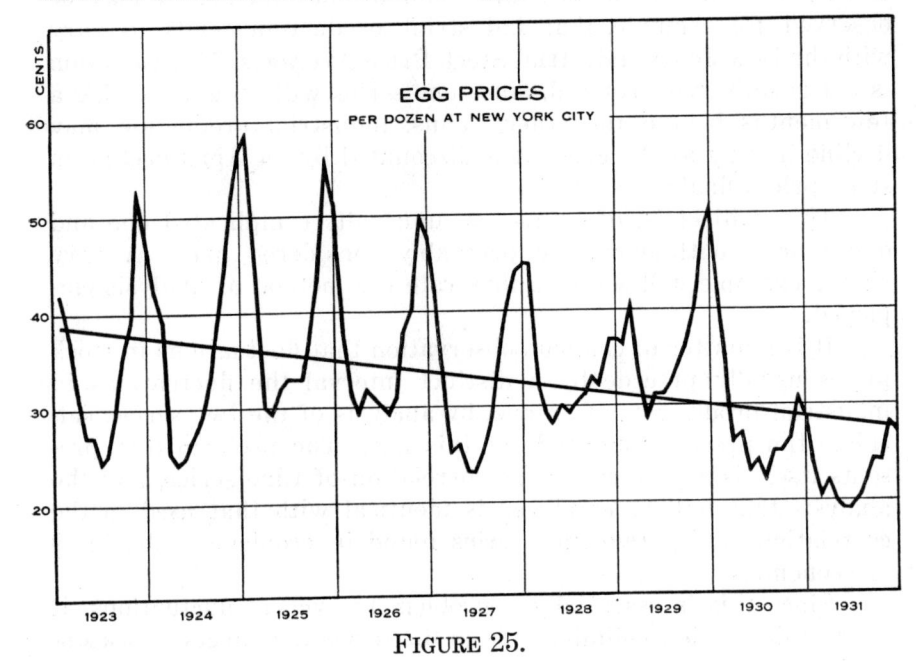

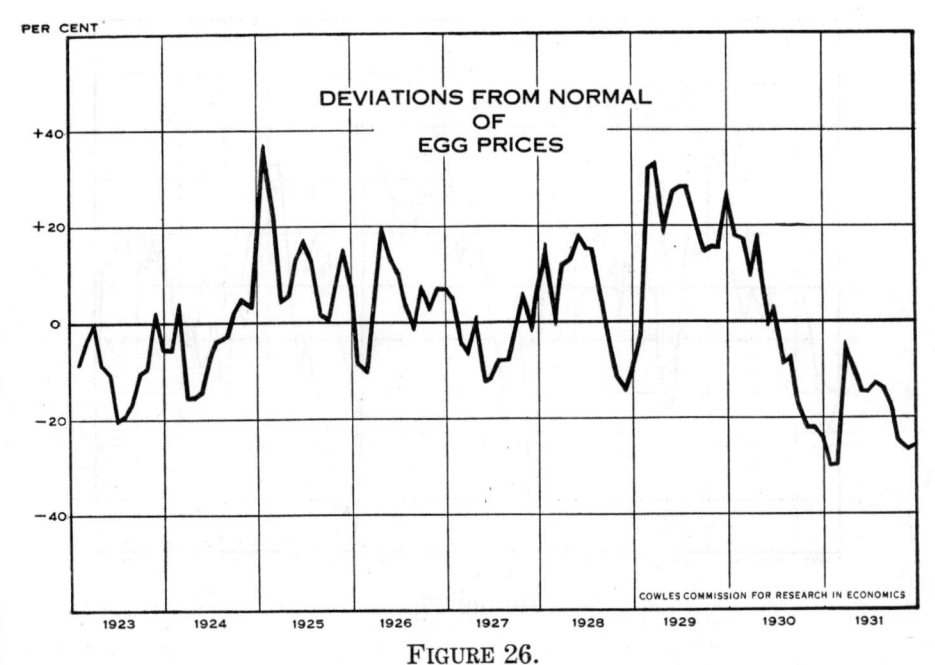

FIGURE 25.

FIGURE 26.

5. The Correlation of Time Series. An important problem connected with the study of time series is that of the *correlation* of two series which seem to exhibit similar movements. It may be observed, for example, that industrial production tends to vary with the Dow-Jones Industrial Stock Price Averages. This variation is not usually synchronized, since one series will, in general, lag a few months behind the other. Thus, industrial production may decline in July as the conditions discounted by an April decline in stock prices finally materialize.

This subject is, of course, an unusually complicated one and only a brief outline can be profitably considered here. A very simple example will serve to illustrate the method of analysis employed.

It is a matter of common observation that fluctuations in stock prices usually precede by a distinct interval the fluctuations in industrial production. Can one, by analysis of the two series, calculate the precise magnitude of this lag? The problem that presents itself is a problem in the correlation of time series, and the analysis that will be employed is identical with that used in the correlation of any two time series found in problems in business or economics.

Since this is essentially a problem in cyclical fluctuations, it is often desirable to eliminate from the series the effects of season-

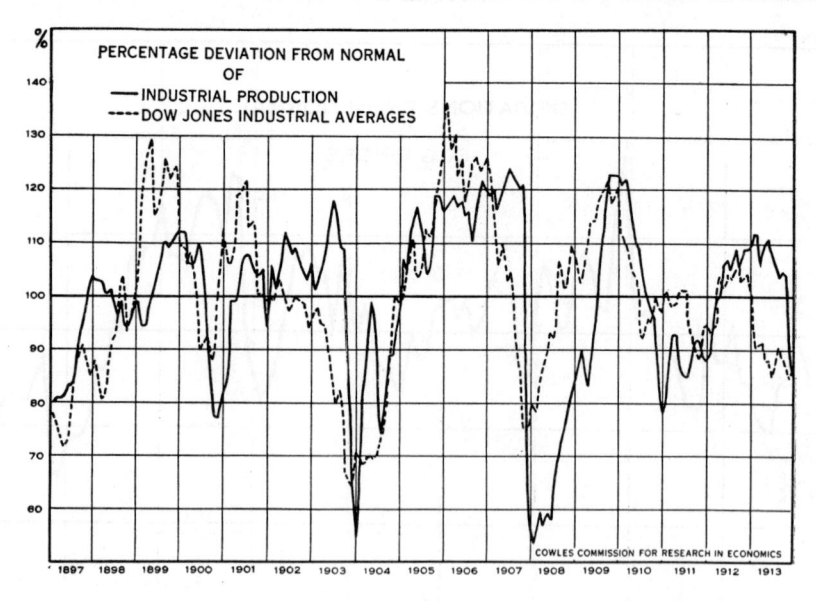

FIGURE 27.

al change and secular trend.[1] To facilitate the computations, the items of these two series may be expressed in comparable units as percentage deviations from trend; to these series the correlation process is then applied. The two series to be correlated are graphically represented in Figure 27.

At this point it is necessary to anticipate a formula which will be studied in detail in Chapter X. This formula defines a statistical constant called the *correlation coefficient*, which gives a measure of the linear relationship between two sets of class marks, namely,

$$x_1, \; x_2, \; x_3, \; \cdots \; x_N,$$

$$y_1, \; y_2, \; y_3, \; \cdots \; y_N,$$

provided such a relationship exists. By this statement, it is meant that, if the pairs of points $(x_1 \; y_1)$, $(x_2 \; y_2)$, $(x_3 \; y_3)$, $\cdots$, $(x_N \; y_N)$, when graphically represented, lie approximately along a straight line, the correlation coefficient is a measure of this approximation to linearity. If the correlation coefficient is numerically equal to one, the points all lie upon a straight line; if the correlation coefficient is zero, then no linearity exists.

The correlation coefficient is calculated from the formula

$$r = \frac{\Sigma (x_i - X)(y_i - Y)}{N \, \sigma_x \, \sigma_y},$$

or from the formula

$$r = \frac{\dfrac{\Sigma x_i y_i}{N} - X \cdot Y}{\sigma_x \sigma_y}, \qquad (1)$$

where N is the total number of items, X and σ_x the arithmetic average and standard deviation, respectively, of the x series, and Y and σ_y the same constants for the y series.

Example: As an illustration, r may be calculated for two series, industrial production (corrected for seasonal variation and secular trend) and stock prices (expressed by the Dow-Jones Industrial Averages and corrected for trend), for the pre-war period 1897-1913, where industrial production values will form the x series, and stock prices the y series.

For the industrial production series, it is found that $X = 99.4688$ and $\sigma_x = 15.9527$; for the stock price series, these

---

[1] On this point, and the problems incident to it, consult *Dynamic Economics*, by C. F. Roos, Bloomington, 1934, Appendix I.

values are $Y = 100.3229$ and $\sigma_y = 15.5350$. From the data, one has $N = 192$, and $\Sigma x_i y_i = 1{,}940{,}428$. Substituting these values in equation (1), one arrives at the value for r,

$$r = \frac{\dfrac{1{,}940{,}428}{192} - (99.4688)(100.3229)}{(15.9527)(15.5350)} = \frac{127.3973}{247.8252} = .5141 \ .$$

Since the object of this discussion is the determination of the magnitude of the lag of industrial production behind stock prices, the next step is to shift the items of the industrial production series both to the right and to the left and calculate the correlation coefficients for each combination thus obtained. By means of the maximum value of the correlation coefficient, one can then define the lag between the two series.

By making 12 shifts at intervals of one month in the industrial production series to each side of the stock price series, with the inclusion of the original data the 25 correlation coefficients tabulated are obtained. The constants used in the calculations are also shown. These coefficients may be designated by the symbols

$$r_{-12}, r_{-11}, \cdots, r_{-1}, r_0, r_1, \cdots, r_{11}, r_{12}.$$

The arithmetic average and standard deviation for each series, as well as the cross product of the two series, is, of course, slightly

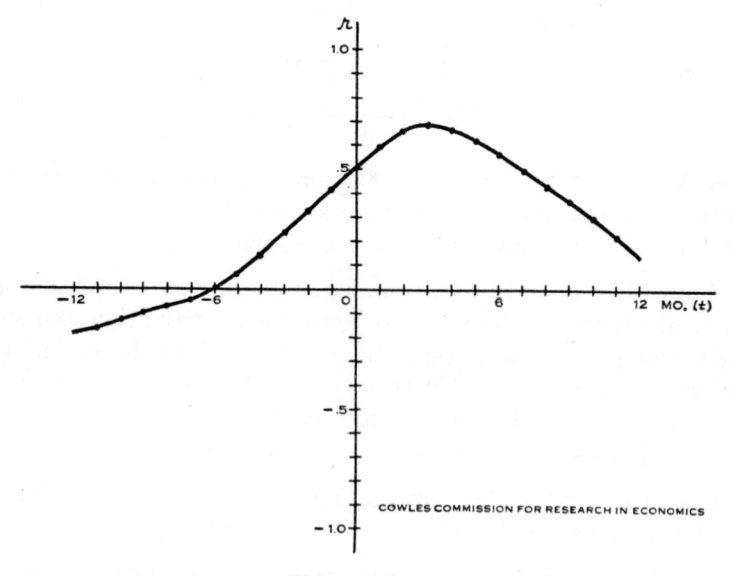

FIGURE 28.

altered by the shifting of the items, as shown in these values given in the table from which the correlation coefficient for the various lags is computed. The minus sign before the lag indicates that industrial production precedes stock prices, i.e., is ahead t months of stock prices; the plus sign indicates that industrial production follows stock prices, i.e., lags t months behind stock prices.

(t) Mo. Lag	X, Average x series	Y, Average y series	σ_x	σ_y	Σxy	Correlation Coefficient (r_t)	(t) Mo. Lag
For −12 lag	99.4688	100.7188	15.9527	15.0151	1,915,080	−.1837	−12
−11	99.4688	100.7240	15.9527	15.0105	1,916,006	−.1658	−11
−10	99.4688	100.7240	15.9527	15.0105	1,917,536	−.1325	−10
− 9	99.4688	100.7292	15.9527	15.0060	1,918,969	−.1035	− 9
− 8	99.4688	100.7396	15.9527	14.9987	1,920,243	−.0797	− 8
− 7	99.4688	100.7760	15.9527	14.9838	1,922,315	−.0502	− 7
− 6	99.4688	100.7708	15.9527	14.9888	1,924,512	−.0002	− 6
− 5	99.4688	100.7500	15.9527	15.0146	1,926,662	.0552	− 5
− 4	99.4688	100.6667	15.9527	15.1289	1,928,691	.1329	− 4
− 3	99.4688	100.5781	15.9527	15.2524	1,931,526	.2287	− 3
− 2	99.4688	100.4792	15.9527	15.3749	1,934,324	.3264	− 2
− 1	99.4688	100.4063	15.9527	15.4573	1,937,304	.4170	− 1
0	99.4688	100.3229	15.9527	15.5350	1,940,428	.5141	0
1	99.6354	100.3229	15.9160	15.5350	1,947,597	.5987	1
2	99.7969	100.3229	15.8831	15.5350	1,953,828	.6658	2
3	99.9271	100.3229	15.8306	15.5350	1,957,234	.6870	3
4	100.0781	100.3229	15.7881	15.5350	1,959,255	.6700	4
5	100.2240	100.3229	15.7586	15.5350	1,959,885	.6249	5
6	100.3542	100.3229	15.7190	15.5350	1,959,656	.5681	6
7	100.4740	100.3229	15.6814	15.5350	1,958,793	.5016	7
8	100.5573	100.3229	15.6576	15.5350	1.957,188	.4337	8
9	100.6146	100.3229	15.6536	15.5350	1,955,270	.3691	9
10	100.6510	100.3229	15.6537	15.5350	1,952,669	.2983	10
11	100.6042	100.3229	15.6626	15.5350	1,948,270	.2233	11
12	100.5104	100.3229	15.6961	15.5350	1,942,515	.1385	12

The computation of the above table can be illustrated by an example. Thus, for r_{-10}, the various values in the row for $t = -10$ months lag are used, and the following value obtained

$$r_{-10} = \frac{\frac{1,917,536}{192} - (99.4688)(100.7240)}{(15.9527)(15.0105)} = \frac{-31.7289}{239.4580} = -.1325.$$

The remaining r's are computed in a similar way.

From the above correlation coefficients it is seen that the maximum value of r is .6870 and this occurs with industrial production lagging three months behind stock prices. Figure 28 gives a picture of these correlation coefficients with a smooth curve drawn through them. Such a curve is often useful in determining the point of maximum correlation where the results are not very clearly defined.[1]

PROBLEMS

1. Graph the following indexes and test for correlation and lag:

(a) WHOLESALE PRICES
(unit, 1926 = 100)

Year	Jan.	Feb.	Mar.	Apr.	May	June	July	Aug.	Sept.	Oct.	Nov.	Dec.
1927	97	96	95	94	94	94	94	95	97	97	97	97
1928	96	96	96	97	99	98	98	99	100	98	97	97
1929	97	97	98	97	96	96	98	98	98	96	94	94
1930	93	92	91	91	89	87	84	84	84	83	80	78
1931	78	77	76	75	73	72	72	72	71	70	70	69
1932	67	66	66	66	64	64	65	65	65	64	64	63

(b) WAGE LEVEL—MANUFACTURING INDUSTRIES
(unit, monthly average, 1926 = 100)

Year	Jan.	Feb.	Mar.	Apr.	May	June	July	Aug.	Sept.	Oct.	Nov.	Dec.
1927	95	101	102	101	100	97	93	95	94	95	92	93
1928	90	94	95	94	94	94	91	94	95	99	96	98
1929	95	102	104	105	105	103	98	102	103	102	95	92
1930	88	91	91	90	88	84	76	74	74	73	68	67
1931	64	68	70	69	68	64	60	60	57	55	53	52
1932	49	50	48	45	43	39	36	36	38	40	39	38

---

[1] The subject of time series presents one of the most perplexing and controversial problems in the field of applied statistics. This is made evident by the fact that little predictive skill has been developed by students of economic time series, as has been demonstrated by Alfred Cowles III in "Can Stock Market Forecasters Forecast?", *Econometrica*, Vol. 1 (1933), pp. 309-324, where the records of professional forecasters were subjected to analysis and found to average slightly worse than forecasts based on random predictions. G. U. Yule in a paper, "Why Do we Sometimes get Nonsense-Correlations between Time Series?", *Journal of the Royal Statistical Society*, Vol. 89 (1926), pp. 1-84, has cast doubt upon the validity of correlating the residuals of time series from which trends and seasonal variations have been removed.

One of the major difficulties in dealing with time series is found in the fact that ordinary probability considerations are often submerged by the effects of current events. For example, the frequency distribution of the residuals from a straight line trend of rail stock prices in the period around the Civil War is U-shaped instead of bell-shaped as in ordinary statistical distributions.

Unfortunately, this subject is too technical to discuss in an elementary text, but the reader will find an appraisal of the problems thus presented in Appendixes I and II of C. F. Roos's *Dynamic Economics, op. cit.*

2. Correlate the following index with Table (a) of problem 1.

(c) COST OF LIVING
(unit, 1923 = 100)

Year	Jan.	Feb.	Mar.	Apr.	May	June	July	Aug.	Sept.	Oct.	Nov.	Dec.
1927	103	102	102	102	102	102	101	101	101	101	102	101
1928	101	100	100	100	100	100	100	100	101	101	101	100
1929	100	100	99	99	99	99	100	101	101	101	101	100
1930	99	99	98	98	97	97	95	95	95	95	94	93
1931	91	90	89	88	87	87	86	86	86	85	84	83
1932	81	80	80	79	77	77	77	77	77	76	76	75

3. Study the correlation between Table (c) of problem 2 and Table (b) of problem 1. Is there a lag?

4. Correlate the following index with Table (b) of problem 1. Compare your answer with the answer to problem 1. Why the similarity and why the difference?

(d) PURCHASING POWER OF THE DOLLAR
(unit, 1926 = 100)

Year	Jan.	Feb.	Mar.	Apr.	May	June	July	Aug.	Sept.	Oct.	Nov.	Dec.
1927	104	104	106	107	107	107	106	105	104	103	103	103
1928	104	104	104	103	101	103	102	101	100	102	103	103
1929	103	103	103	103	104	104	102	102	103	104	106	106
1930	107	109	110	110	112	115	119	119	119	121	124	128
1931	128	130	132	134	137	139	139	139	140	142	143	146
1932	149	151	152	153	155	157	155	153	153	155	157	160

6. *Harmonic Analysis.* In preceding sections, the problem of determining the seasonal fluctuations in time series has been discussed. This problem, as one may readily apprehend, is only one aspect, although an important one, of the study of the cyclical variation of such series, a study which is referred to in mathematical literature as the problem of harmonic analysis. By *harmonic analysis* is meant the technique of discovering the constituent periodicities which enter into the construction of a given series of data arranged in a time sequence.

This problem dates back a century and a half, one of the earliest memoirs being published in 1772 by J. L. Lagrange (1736-1813). Although it was known to L. Euler (1707-1783) that an analytic function could be represented by means of a series of sines and cosines, the full significance of this development and its application to problems in physics was not realized until the epoch-making work of J. B. J. Fourier (1768-1830). The work in which these results are incorporated is the celebrated *Théorie Analytique de la Chaleur* (1822), one of the great classics of mathematical physics. The application of the methods of harmonic analysis to statistical data may be said to begin with a series of papers published by Sir Arthur Schuster (1851-1934), who applied his method to the study of sun spots, the periodicity of earthquakes, terrestrial magnetism, etc.[1] E. T. Whittaker and G. Robinson have somewhat modified Schuster's method.[2]

Schuster's method depends upon the construction of what is known as a *periodogram*, and may be described as follows:

The equation,

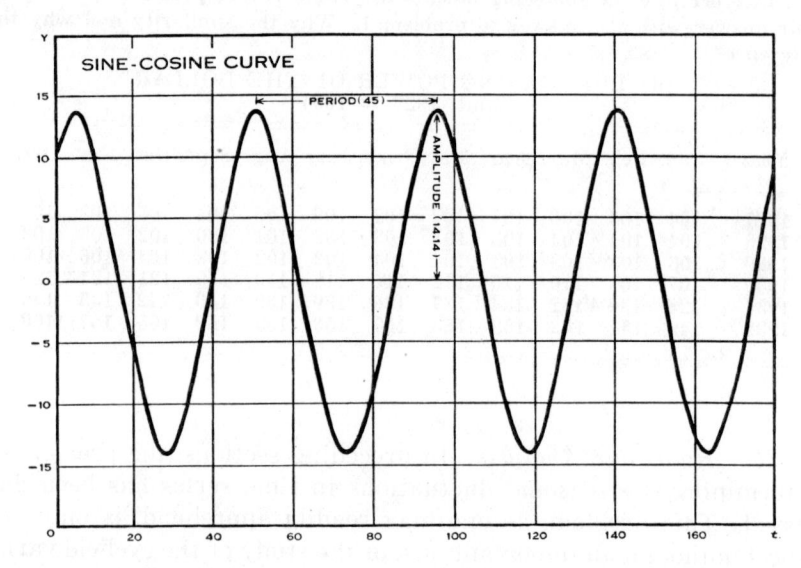

$$y = A \sin (2\pi t/T) + B \cos (2\pi t/T) , \qquad (1)$$

FIGURE 29. This is the graph of the equation

$$Y = 10 \sin \frac{2\pi t}{45} + 10 \cos \frac{2\pi t}{45} .$$

The period is thus 45 and the amplitude 14.14

---

[1] "On Interference Phenomena," *Philosophical Magazine*, Vol. 37(5) 1894, pp. 506-545. "On Lunar and Solar Periodicities of Earthquakes," *Proc. Royal Soc. of London*, Vol. 61 (A) 1897, pp. 455-465 "On the Periodicities of Sun Spots," *London Philosophical Transactions*, Vol. 206 (A) 1906, pp. 69-100.
[2] *The Calculus of Observations*, London, 1924, Chapter 13. See also *Fourier's Theorem and Harmonic Analysis*, by A. Eagle, London, 1925, Chapter 8.

when graphed as a function of t, will be found to repeat itself at intervals equal to $t = T$, and will fluctuate between the limits $y = +R$ and $y = -R$, where $R = \sqrt{A^2 + B^2}$, as shown in Figure 29. Hence T is called the *period of the function* and R the *amplitude*.

Now the object of periodogram analysis is to determine how many *components* of the kind just described are present in a statistical series. This problem Schuster undertook to solve by constructing amplitudes for all values of T which might be expected to correspond to periods in the series. The value of this amplitude function would show a significant increase in the neighborhood of a genuine period.

In order to represent the matter analytically, let the data be arranged in a set of equally spaced items:

X	X_1	X_2	X_3	X_4	......	X_N
t	t_1	t_2	t_3	t_4	......	t_N

where $t_{n+1} - t_n$ is a constant.

Then the function,

$$R(u) = \frac{2}{N} \sqrt{A^2 + B^2} , \qquad (2)$$

where one writes,

$$A(u) = \sum_{t=1}^{N} X_t \sin(2\pi t/u) ,$$
$$B(u) = \sum_{t=1}^{N} X_t \cos(2\pi t/u) , \qquad (3)$$

will reveal the presence of a period T by an increased value in the neighborhood of $u = T$, provided the data actually contain an appreciable component of the form (1).

The graph of the function,

$$y = R(u) ,$$

obtained by erecting ordinates for the values $u = 5, 6, 7, \cdots$, is called the *periodogram* associated with the series. The method as applied to statistical data is of doubtful value for periods smaller than 5.

The practical procedure is to arrange the data as follows:

$$\begin{array}{cccccc} X_1 & X_2 & X_3 & X_4 & X_5 & \cdots & X_u \\ X_{u+1} & X_{u+2} & X_{u+3} & X_{u+4} & X_{u+5} & \cdots & X_{2u} \\ X_{2u+1} & X_{2u+2} & X_{2u+3} & X_{2u+4} & X_{2u+5} & \cdots & X_{3u} \\ \cdot & \cdot & \cdot & \cdot & \cdot & & \cdot \\ X_{nu+1} & X_{nu+2} & X_{nu+3} & X_{nu+4} & X_{nu+5} & \cdots & X_{(n+1)u} \end{array}$$

Sums: $M_1 \quad M_2 \quad M_3 \quad M_4 \quad M_5 \quad \cdots \quad M_u$

where $(n+1)u$ is the largest multiple of u in the total frequency N.

The functions $A(u)$ and $B(u)$ are then computed as the sums,

$$A(u) = \sum_{t=1}^{u} M_t \sin(2\pi t/u) \; ,$$

$$B(u) = \sum_{t=1}^{u} M_t \cos(2\pi t/u) \; .$$

Whittaker and Robinson have somewhat modified Schuster's method in the following manner:

The means of the values M_i in the above table are first computed and the standard deviation, σ_M, of these averages found. Similarly, the standard deviation, σ_x, of the elements of the data is computed. The square of the correlation ratio (see Chapter X, section 8),

$$R(u) = \eta^2(u) = \frac{\sigma_M^2}{\sigma_x^2} \; ,$$

is then taken as the ordinate of the periodogram.[1] Since the significance of the periodogram is found in the variations between neighboring values of u, it is clear that the standard deviations of the sums, M_i, themselves can be used as the ordinates of the periodogram, instead of η^2. In the case of most of the series of economic data, where unnecessary refinements of technique are not profitable, it is possible to get a satisfactory idea about the variations between neighboring values of u by constructing a periodogram in which $R(u)$, as given above, is replaced by the difference between the greatest and the least values of the M_i. Much of the labor of computation, which in harmonic analysis is always large, is thus saved.

---

[1] For a justification of this technique, the reader is referred to Whittaker and Robinson, *op. cit.*, pp. 346-349.

Example: In illustration the *periodogram* difference method will be applied to the monthly averages of freight car loadings, 1919-1932, using the data as given in section 2 of this chapter.

The items in the series are first arranged in horizontal rows for each value of u, taking $u = 5, 6, 7, \cdots, 25$, and sums found for each column. Thus, for $u = 15$, one gets the following arrangement:

olumns	1	2	3	4	5	6	7	8	9	10	11	12	13	14	15
	728	687	697	715	759	809	858	892	960	967	807	758	820	776	848
	731	862	860	901	968	969	1005	884	723	705	683	692	706	757	765
	751	810	841	929	761	683	702	765	826	723	787	842	825	877	935
	992	944	838	845	842	917	941	975	1011	986	1041	1037	1078	978	826
	858	908	916	875	895	906	894	974	1037	1091	975	847	921	905	924
	941	968	989	986	1080	1074	1107	1024	888	923	919	969	958	1037	1028
	1049	1104	1148	1205	1068	904	946	956	1002	975	1024	999	979	1062	1097
	1115	956	834	862	897	951	935	1002	985	986	1058	1117	1175	1061	883
	893	942	962	996	1051	1052	1038	1117	1135	1169	978	835	837	876	883
	912	914	930	895	938	931	950	798	680	719	709	735	752	740	748
	738	747	737	759	655	555	567	561	565	557	522	491	483	525	577
ums: $\{M_i\}$	9708	9842	9752	9968	9914	9751	9943	9948	9812	9801	9503	9322	9534	9594	9514

To fill the 15 columns and 11 rows in the above table requires only 165 values of the series; the last 3 values are dropped, since there are not enough values to complete another row. In a periodogram analysis, each column must have the same number of items.

After 21 arrangements have been obtained, fashioned after the above table, for $u = 5, 6, 7, \cdots, 25$, the sums, M_i, for each u are tabulated in the manner shown in the table on pages 142 and 143. The largest value and the smallest value in each column is then noted and the difference between them is recorded at the bottom of the table. As has already been stated, however, a better though much more laborious procedure is either to compute $A(u)$ and $B(u)$ by the Schuster formula or to evaluate the standard deviations of the M_i as required by the method of Whittaker and Robinson.

Taking the differences as the ordinates and the u's as the abscissas, the periodogram shown in Figure 30 is obtained for freight car loadings.

From Figure 30, it may be seen that there is a pronounced period at 12 months and a secondary period at 6 months, which indicates that the amount of freight hauled tends to conform

PERIODOGRAM ANALYSIS, FREIGHT CAR LOADINGS, 1919-1932

M_i Column Totals	\multicolumn{9}{c}{u—Monthly Periods}
	5	6	7	8	9	10	11	12	13
1	*28962*	23695	21228	18657	16312	14430	13235	11326	10820
2	29107	24619	*21234*	18890	16031	14417	*13079*	11426	10891
3	29234	25482	*20933*	18121	*16393*	14366	13205	11887	*10651*
4	*29374*	*25893*	21171	17849	16087	14262	13256	11717	10758
5	29229	24731	20986	18557	16069	14195	13179	12293	10742
6		*23154*	20935	*19127*	16128	*14010*	13399	12415	10853
7			21087	18573	15719	14199	*13414*	12369	10972
8				*17800*	*15555*	14385	13367	13193	*11056*
9					16027	*14587*	13385	13595	10967
10						14457	13278	*14176*	10891
11							13109	12438	10760
12								*10739*	10793
13									10904
14									
15									
16									
17									
18									
19									
20									
21									
22									
23									
24									
25									
Difference (Δ)*	412	2739	301	1327	838	577	335	3437	405

*The difference is obtained by subtracting in each column the smallest value from the largest value. The figures in italics designated these values.
(See continuation of this table on page 143)

to a certain pattern every 6 and 12 months. These conclusions agree very closely with the following indexes of seasonal variation for freight car loadings:

	Jan.	Feb.	Mar.	Apr.	May	June	July	Aug.	Sept.	Oct.	Nov.	Dec.
Index of Seasonal Variation	90	92	96	96	102	100	100	108	111	*115*	101	87

as brought out by Simon Kuznetz in *Seasonal Variation in Industry and Trade,* to which reference has already been made.

The reader will observe from this brief introduction that the problem of harmonic analysis is one of great significance but of equal difficulty from both the computational and the mathematical points of view. One question which immediately challenges attention is that of determining whether a significant variation

PERIODOGRAM ANALYSIS, FREIGHT CAR LOADINGS, 1919-1932

M_i Column Totals	\multicolumn{12}{c}{u—Monthly Periods}
	14	15	16	17	18	19	20	21	22	23	24	25
1	10721	9708	9047	8022	8041	7334	7264	*7261*	6266	6587	5757	5345
2	10486	9842	9150	8191	8300	7216	7440	7075	*6215*	6465	5724	5325
3	10623	9752	8895	8245	*8731*	7206	7085	6947	6317	6246	5929	5463
4	10533	*9968*	8789	8334	8417	7388	*6816*	7033	6328	6085	6026	5666
5	10622	9914	9083	*8463*	8041	7233	7084	7019	6319	5914	6274	*5856*
6	*10759*	9751	*9398*	8242	7680	7205	7185	6927	6397	5960	6373	5768
7	10618	9943	9159	8186	7892	*7073*	7086	7080	6533	6202	6336	5603
8	10507	9948	8788	8121	8069	7245	7071	7103	6520	6268	6749	5506
9	10447	9812	9088	8254	8418	7286	7373	7060	*6548*	6500	6881	5493
10	10548	9801	9249	8230	8271	7211	*7507*	7250	6518	*6637*	7124	5257
11	10402	9503	8743	8152	7731	7256	7166	7098	6295	6624	6159	*5130*
12	*10364*	*9322*	8535	8164	7662	7307	6977	7050	6314	6519	5379	5186
13	10475	9534	8897	*7995*	7670	*7470*	7281	7249	6309	6540	5569	5391
14	10469	9594	9095	8012	8028	7413	7446	7023	6321	6325	5702	5394
15		9514	8865	8139	8448	7275	7111	6864	6367	6221	5958	5418
16			*8527*	8025	7827	7281	6825	*6798*	6295	5959	5691	5462
17				8314	*7486*	7255	7113	6974	6445	*5772*	6019	5769
18					7609	7266	7314	6804	6359	5780	6042	5780
19						7432	7214	6917	6356	5990	6033	5761
20							6950	7058	6354	6115	6444	5664
21								6984	6235	6247	6714	5442
22									6237	6419	7052	5419
23										6455	6279	5313
24											*5360*	5211
25												5245
Difference (Δ)*	395	646	871	468	1245	397	691	463	333	865	1764	726

* The difference is obtained by subtracting in each column the smallest value from the largest value. The figures in italics designate these values.

exists in $R(u)$. Answers have been given to this question both by Schuster and by R. A. Fisher.[1] Excellent summaries and examples of the problems involved in a determination of significant periods will be found in papers by E. B. Wilson[2] and B. Greenstein.[3] Unfortunately, the discussion of these tests is beyond the scope of an elementary book and must be omitted here.

It will be obvious to the reader that periods, once they have been detected, can be removed from the data by the method of link relatives previously employed in the case of seasonal variation.

---
[1] See Schuster's original papers and R. A. Fisher "Test for Significance in Harmonic Analysis," *Proc. Royal Soc. of London*, Vol. 125 (A) (1929), pp. 54-59.
[2] E. B. Wilson: The Periodogram of Business Activity. *Quarterly Journal of Economics*, Vol. 48 (1934), pp. 375-417.
[3] "Periodogram Analysis with Special Application to Business Failures," *Econometrica*, Vol. III (1935), pp. 170-198.

PERIODOGRAM OF FREIGHT CAR LOADINGS

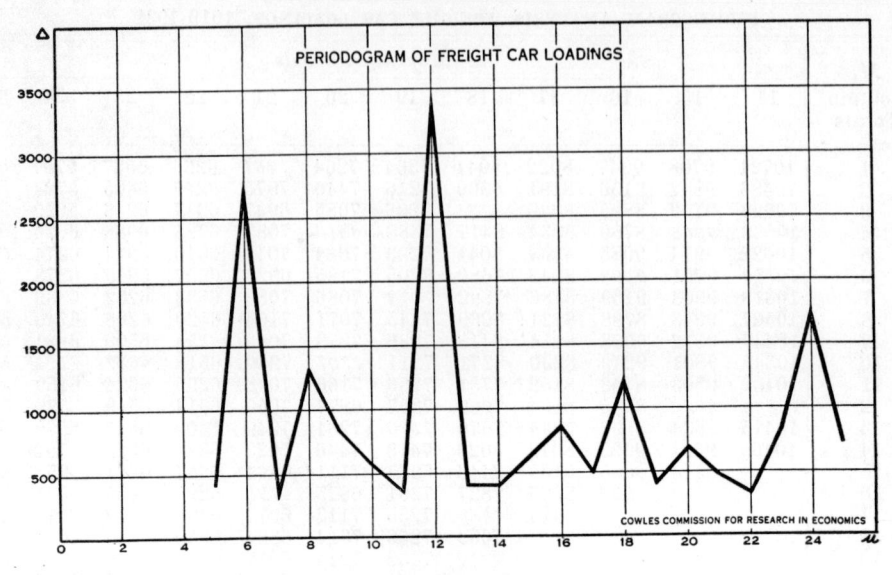

FIGURE 30

PROBLEMS

1. Carry out the computations for $u = 10$ using the data on freight car loadings given above.

2. The following values are the ordinates of the Schuster periodogram for the Dow Jones industrial stock price averages, corrected for trend, from 1897 to 1913.[1]

DOW JONES AVERAGES CORRECTED FOR TREND 1897-1913

u	R	u	R	u	R	u	R	u	R
5	.71	20	3.27	35	......	50	6.32	65	10.34
6	.44	21	3.81	36	4.93	51	5.86	66	10.51
7	.96	22	5.02	37	......	52	7.52	67	......
8	1.09	23	4.72	38	9.57	53	......	68	10.48
9	1.24	24	3.81	39	11.00	54	8.61	69	18.23
10	1.43	25	2.13	40	11.69	55	......	70	17.76
11	2.27	26	1.88	41	14.72	56	9.29	71	......
12	.11	27	......	42	14.60	57	9.73	72	17.06
13	1.17	28	1.01	43	13.97	58	10.11	73	......
14	1.33	29	2.45	44	12.93	59	......	74	16.17
15	2.62	30	4.40	45	12.06	60	10.45		
16	2.66	31	4.74	46	10.79	61	......		
17	2.27	32	......	47	......	62	10.49		
18	2.27	33	2.75	48	8.05	63	......		
19	2.13	34	1.25	49	......	64	......		

Construct the periodogram and determine the periods. Is there evidence of a seasonal movement in stock prices?

[1] See note at end of problems.

THE ANALYSIS OF TIME SERIES 145

3. The following values are the ordinates of the Whittaker-Robinson periodogram of the stock prices mentioned in problem 2. Construct the periodogram and compare with the periodogram of problem 2. Do you find the same periods?

DOW JONES AVERAGES CORRECTED FOR TREND 1897-1913

u	R	u	R	u	R	u	R
1	....	16	27.98	31	21.30	46	34.70
2	2.00	17	22.90	32	23.00	47	31.50
3	6.68	18	21.30	33	19.20	48	27.60
4	45.90	19	19.40	34	15.60	49	23.90
5	2125	20	27.30	35	24.50	50	19.90
6	12.21	21	26.80	36	22.80	51	19.90
7	21.47	22	37.70	37	29.30	52	19.70
8	30.92	23	27.70	38	35.00	53	20.10
9	23.92	24	22.40	39	42.20	54	21.30
10	23.04	25	18.80	40	44.00	55	21.70
11	28.88	26	14.10	41	45.30	56	23.20
12	17.90	27	14.60	42	44.70	57	23.60
13	17.91	28	11.70	43	48.10	58	25.80
14	17.16	29	17.90	44	40.70	59	27.30
15	26.75	30	22.60	45	38.10	60	27.30

4. The following values are the ordinates of the periodogram of the Cowles Commission Index of Investment Experience (public utility and industrial common stocks combined) from 1880 to 1897. Construct the periodogram and compare with the periodogram of problem 2. Does there appear to be a persistence of periods in these two time intervals? What conclusions would you draw?

COWLES COMMISSION INDEX OF INVESTMENT EXPERIENCE[a]
1880-1897

u	R	u	R	u	R	u	R	u	R
5	.50	20	1.51	35	....	50	2.40	65	10.80
6	.91	21	1.44	36	5.62	51	2.58	66	5.65
7	.36	22	2.46	37	....	52	3.96	67	....
8	1.06	23	2.79	38	6.27	53	....	68	5.77
9	.62	24	1.26	39	6.46	54	3.92	69	8.19
10	1.35	25	.73	40	6.21	55	....	70	....
11	.73	26	3.17	41	7.50	56	5.31	71	....
12	.31	27	....	42	7.20	57	5.83	72	8.62
13	.56	28	2.83	43	6.81	58	6.15	73	....
14	3.07	29	1.75	44	6.21	59	....	74	....
15	1.58	30	1.19	45	5.54	60	6.64		
16	1.48	31	2.91	46	4.75	61	....		
17	2.62	32	....	47	....	62	6.54		
18	.86	33	4.92	48	2.56	63	....		
19	2.00	34	5.62	49	....	64	....		

[a]NOTE: In the above tables, it will be noted that some of the values for R have not been computed. This is due to the manner in which the u's were segregated in carrying out the computations on the Hollerith tabulating machine in the laboratory of the Cowles Commission for Research in Economics. In making the periodogram, the intervals where the gap occurs should be connected by a dotted line. This procedure is often followed in actual practice to reduce the computing. The approximate location of a period usually can be detected, and then all the values in this neighborhood subsequently computed to determine the location more exactly.

CHAPTER VI

ANALYSIS OF ARTIFICIAL DATA—PROBABILITY

1. Definition of Probability. In the preceding chapters, data obtained from sources beyond our control have been studied, such as the fluctuations in prices, the distribution of income, the growth of productive activity. In this chapter, on the contrary, various types of artificial data, obtained by methods that are more or less under our control, will be discussed. These data will then be analyzed in order to study the nature of the statistical laws that produced them. These laws constitute a chapter in mathematics which is called the theory of probability.

The following definition has been generally adopted as a mathematical, or *a priori*, measure of probability:

Definition. If an event can happen in m ways and fail in n ways, *and each of these ways is equally likely,* the *probability*, or *chance*, of its happening is $p = m/(m+n)$, and that of its failing to happen is $q = n/(m+n)$. This is frequently expressed by saying that the odds are m to n that the event will happen.

For example, if a coin is tossed, the probability that it will fall a head is 1/2. If two coins are tossed, the probability that both will fall heads is 1/4. It has been argued that the answer should be 1/3, since the coins could fall in only three ways, namely, heads, tails; heads, heads; tails, tails. But the fallacy in this is seen to lie in the fact that all these events are not equally likely, since "heads, tails" can happen twice as often as either of the other two. If the student doubts this, he should verify the fact empirically by tossing two coins a number of times and making a record of the cases. *This remark applies to other statements made in this chapter, because the most convincing proof that can be offered of the reality of the theorems of probability is that of actual empirical trial.*

It is often difficult to be sure that all the events of a series are *equally likely*. Take, for example, the following case: suppose that one urn A contains 2 black balls and 3 white balls, while a second urn B contains 2 black and 7 white balls. It is required to find the probability that a blind-folded person in one draw shall obtain a white ball.

Since there are 4 black and 10 white balls in the two urns, it might seem that the probability is $10/14 = 5/7$. But the incorrectness of this reasoning becomes apparent if one considers the case where A contains 1,000 black balls and B only one white ball. On the first argument, the chance of obtaining a white ball would be 1/1001, but the real answer is seen to be 1/2, since the probability is merely that of whether A or B is chosen. The correct answer to the first case is

$$p = 1/2 \cdot 3/5 + 1/2 \cdot 7/9 = 31/45 ,$$

or approximately 2/3, since the chance of getting A, with a probability of 3/5, is 1/2, and the chance of getting B, with a probability of 7/9, is 1/2.

One can derive immediately, from the definition, the following facts:

(a) $q = 1 - p$,
(b) If success is certain, $p = 1$,
(c) If failure is certain, $p = 0$.

PROBLEMS

1. What is the probability that a letter selected at random in an English book is a vowel? Hint: Take a random page in a random English book and count the number of letters and the number of vowels.

2. What is the probability that a vowel selected at random in an English book is an e? an o? an i? an a? a u? Show that the sum of these probabilities equals 1.

3. Toss 5 coins 128 times and estimate the probabilities that in a single throw one should get: 0 Head, 1 Head, 2 Heads, 4 Heads, and 5 Heads. From these probabilities estimate the chance of getting 3 Heads in a single throw.

4. A group of scientific men reported 1705 sons and 1527 daughters. If this is a fair sample from the general population, what is the probability that a child to be born will be a boy? Do you think that this probability differs sufficiently from .5 to be significant? In order to answer this question toss 10 coins 323 times (10 × 323 is approximately equal to the total frequency 1705 + 1527) and keep a record of the total number of heads. From these data calculate the probability that a head will appear in a single throw and compare the difference between this number and .5 with the difference previously obtained.

5. Write down at random 100 pairs of numbers. Find in how many of these the numbers are prime to one another. From these data calculate the probability, P, that two numbers written down at random will be prime to one another. If you have done your work accurately, you should be able to calculate the value of $\pi = 3.1416$ to one or two decimal places, by means of the formula $\pi = \sqrt{6/P}$.

2. Formulas from Permutations and Combinations. Since formulas in the theory of permutations and combinations are often useful in calculating probabilities, some of the most important of these are recorded below. They are all derived by an application of the following fundamental principle:

If one operation can be performed in m ways and, having been performed in one of these ways, a second operation can then be performed in n ways, the number of ways of performing the two operations will be $m \cdot n$.

(a) The number of permutations or arrangements of n dissimilar things taken r at a time is

$$_nP_r = n(n-1)(n-2) \cdots (n-r+1) = n!/(n-r)!\,.$$

(b) The number of combinations or groups of n dissimilar things taken r at a time is

$$_nC_r = {_nP_r}/r! = n!/r!(n-r)!\,.$$

(c) The number of ways in which $x_1 + x_2 + \cdots + x_n$ things can be divided into n groups of $x_1, x_2, \cdots, x_n$, things, all of the x_i's being different, is

$$N = \frac{(x_1 + x_2 + \cdots + x_n)!}{x_1!x_2!\cdots x_n!}.$$

If the x's are all equal, $x_1 = x_2 \cdots = x_n = x$, this formula must be replaced by

$$N = \frac{(nx)!}{(x!)^n n!}.$$

The reason for introducing factorial n into the denominator is that there is now no way of differentiating between groups, as in the first case.

(d) The number of ways of permuting n things when x_1 are alike, x_2 are alike, $\cdots\cdots x_n$ are alike, is given by the formula

$$Q = \frac{n!}{x_1!x_2!\cdots x_n!}.$$

Example 1. How many two-digit numbers can be formed from the digits 2, 3, 5, 7?

This is a problem in permutations, since the number 23 is different from the number 32. The answer is thus

$$_4P_2 = 4!/(4-2)! = 12 .$$

Example 2. How many products of two numbers can be formed from the digits 2, 3, 5, 7?

This is a problem in combinations, since 2×3 is the same as 3×2. Hence, the answer is

$$_4C_2 = 4!/[(4-2)! 2!] = 6 .$$

Example 3. How many triangles can be formed by connecting 7 points, no three points being on the same straight line?

If one numbers the points 1, 2, 3, 4, 5, 6, 7, then it is clear that (1,2,3), (3,4,5), etc., will form triangles; but (1,3,2) and (3,2,1) will be the same as triangles (1,2,3). Hence the problem is one in combinations and the answer will be

$$_7C_3 = 7!/(3! 4!) = 35 .$$

Example 4. In how many ways can the letters in the word *combination* be arranged?

If all of the eleven letters were different, it is clear that the answer would be 11! But the two o's can be permuted with one another without altering the number of arrangements, and so also can the two i's and the two n's. Hence, the answer will be, according to principle (d),

$$11!/(2! 2! 2!) = 4,989,600 \text{ arrangements.}$$

Example 5. There are four book shelves which can hold 15, 20, 35, and 50 books, respectively. In how many ways can 120 books be allotted to the shelves?

There are four different groups to which 120 things are to be assigned. Hence, from the first formula in (c) above, there follows

$$N = 120!/(15! 20! 35! 50!) .$$

Example 6. If all of the book shelves of example 5 were identical, how many arrangements could be made?

Since there is now no way of differentiating between the groups, the answer will be, using the second formula in (c) above,

$$Q = (4 \times 30)!/[(30!)^4 4!] = 120!/[(30!)^4 4!] .$$

PROBLEMS

1. How many numbers of 4 digits can be formed from 1, 2, 3, 4, 5, and 6, allowing no repetition of digits in any one number?

2. What is the total number of numbers of three digits that can be formed from 1, 2, 3, 4, 5, if repetitions are allowed?

3. In how many ways can six people be seated in a circle in numbered chairs? Unnumbered chairs?

4. In how many ways can the letters in the word *statistics* be arranged?

5. How many committees of 5 representatives and 4 senators can be formed from 12 representatives and 10 senators?

6. In how many ways can 11 bonds be chosen from a group of 16 bonds?

7. In how many ways can four coins of different denomination be placed in one stack?

8. In how many ways can four coins of different denomination be placed on a table, attention being devoted only to the question of which side of the coin is up?

9. In how many ways can four coins of different denomination be stacked so that at least one of them has the head up?

10. In how many ways can five coins indistinguishable from each other be stacked?

11. In how many ways can 12 different objects be divided equally among four persons? In how many ways can they be put into four equal groups?

12. In how many ways may 10 different things be distributed among three persons A, B, C, so that A shall receive 5, B shall receive 3, and C shall receive 2?

13. In how many distinct ways can 4 dimes and 6 quarters be distributed among 10 persons if each person is to receive a coin?

14. How many different sums of at least three coins each can be formed from a penny a nickel, a dime, and a quarter?

15. In how many ways may 14 stocks be distributed among 4 shareholders, so that the oldest shall receive 5, the next 4, the next 3, and the youngest 2?

3. Examples Illustrating the Calculation of Simple a Priori Probability. The following examples will illustrate the application of the definition of the first section to simple problems in probability.

Example 1. What is the probability of throwing less than 6 with two dice?

There are altogether 36 ways in which the two dice can fall. Of these only the combinations (1,1), (1,2), (2,1), (1,3), (3,1),

(1,4), (4,1), (2,2), (2,3), (3,2), are less than 6. Hence, the desired probability is $10/36 = 5/18$.

Example 2. In a bag there are four white and three black balls. What is the probability that if they are drawn out one at a time, the first will be white, the second black, the third white, the fourth black, etc.?

There are altogether 7! possible arrangements of the seven balls. Of these, there will be 4! arrangements of the white balls in the odd numbered places and 3! arrangements of the black balls in the even numbered places. By the fundamental principle of permutations and combinations, there will thus be 4!×3! different arrangements of the balls. Hence the desired probability is

$$4! \times 3!/7! = 1/35.$$

Example 3. A has five shares in a lottery in which there are two prizes and ten blanks. B has two shares in a lottery in which there are five prizes and ten blanks. Which has the better chance to win a prize?

A will draw a prize unless all of his five shares are blanks. Five tickets can be chosen from the twelve in $_{12}C_5 = 12!/5!7! = 792$ ways. But, five blanks can be drawn in $_{10}C_5 = 10!/5!5! = 252$ ways. Hence, the probability that A will draw a blank is $252/792 = 7/22$, and the probability that he will draw at least one prize is $1 - 7/22 = 15/22$. Similarly, the probability that B will win a prize is $1 - {}_{10}C_2/{}_{15}C_2 = 1 - 45/105 = 4/7$. Since the first value is larger than the second, it is seen that A has a better chance than B to win a prize.

PROBLEMS

1. Three coins are tossed simultaneously. What is the probability that they will fall two heads and one tail?

2. What is the probability of throwing 8 with two dice?

3. Eight balls numbered from 1 to 8 are placed in a bag and two drawn at random. What is the probability that they are numbered 1 and 2?

4. Seven balls numbered from 1 to 7 are in a bag. Three are drawn at random. What is the probability that they are 5, 6, and 7?

5. Of ten balls in a bag, three are red. What is the probability that there will be at least one red ball in a draw of two balls? What is the probability that both will be red?

152   ELEMENTS OF STATISTICS

6. A has three shares in a lottery in which there are three prizes and five blanks. B has two shares in which there are two prizes and four blanks. Which has the better chance to win a prize?

7. In problem 6, which has the better chance of winning exactly one prize? Which of winning two prizes?

8. A bag contains four black marbles, two white marbles, and seven red marbles. What is the probability that if three marbles are drawn at random, all are red?

9. Compare the chances of throwing 4 with one die and 8 with two dice.

10. There are two works consisting of two and three volumes, respectively. If they are placed on a shelf at random, what is the probability that volumes of the same work are all together?

11. Show that the chances of throwing six with 4, 3, or 2 dice, respectively, are as 1:6:18.

12. If n people are seated at a round table, what is the probability that two named individuals will be neighbors?

13. What is the probability of receiving a hand of 13 cards all of the same suit from a deck of playing cards? What is the ratio of this probability to the probability that 12 are of one suit? 11 of one suit?

14. What is the probability that each of four people hold 13 cards of the same suit?

15. If three dice are thrown, what is the probability that the sum is 11?

4. The Multiplication of Probabilities. When two or more events can occur in connection with one another, the joint occurrence is called a *compound event*. If these events are *independent of one another*, then the following theorem is to be used in calculating this *joint probability*:

Theorem 1. If the respective probabilities of n independent events are $p_1, p_2, \cdots, p_n$, then the probability that all of them will happen is the product

$$p = p_1 \cdot p_2 \cdots p_n .$$

Considerable reflection should be given to this theorem, since errors are easily made in application. It is important always to ask oneself the question: "Are all the events independent?"

As an example, consider the problem of throwing 3, 4, with two dice. The probability that either die will come down 3 or 4 is clearly 2/6 or 1/3, but the probability sought for is not $1/3 \cdot 1/3 = 1/9$, since the second probability is affected by the first even if the events in question, the falls of the two dice, are independent of one another. Thus, if the first die shows a 3, the number on the second must be 4. The answer to the problem, is then,

$$1/3 \cdot 1/6 = 1/18 \ .$$

This answer can be verified directly by considering that two dice can fall in 36 different ways, and, of these, only two will fulfill the required conditions.

The proof of the theorem is evident from a consideration of two such events whose respective probabilities are a/A and b/B. Since, by assumption, the two events are independent, and in the first case there are A possibilities and in the second B, then by the fundamental theorem in permutations there is a total of $A \times B$ possible events. In a similar way, one sees that there are $a \times b$ favorable cases, so that the total probability is ab/AB.

5. *The Addition of Probabilities.* If a set of events is of such a character that, when one of them happens, the other cannot happen, the set is said to be *mutually exclusive*. Thus, if three runners enter a race, any events contingent upon the winning of the race are mutually exclusive, because if the first runner wins, the other two cannot. The theorem of probability connected with mutually exclusive events is the following:

Theorem 2. If the probabilities of n mutually exclusive events are $p_1, p_2, \ldots\ldots, p_n$, then the probability that some one of these events will occur is the sum

$$p = p_1 + p_2 + \cdots + p_n \ .$$

Proof: Suppose that all the probabilities have been reduced to a common denominator N, so that

$$p_1 = a_1/N \ , \ p_2 = a_2/N \ , \ p_3 = a_3/N \ , \ldots\ldots, p_n = a_n/N \ .$$

Then the event can happen a_1 times out of N in the first way, a_2 times out of N in the second way, etc. Thus, the total number of cases favorable to the event happening in any of the n ways, since they are mutually exclusive, must be

$$a_1 + a_2 + \cdots + a_n \ .$$

Hence, the probability that the event will happen in one of these ways is

$$(a_1 + a_2 + \cdots + a_n)/N = a_1/N + a_2/N + \cdots + a_n/N$$
$$= p_1 + p_2 + \cdots + p_n \ .$$

As in the case of the theorem of the preceding section, the application of this theorem is fraught with danger. The questions to be kept constantly in mind are these: "Will the occurrence of one event of the series prevent the occurrence of all of the others? Are the events *mutually exclusive?*"

An example will help to clarify the meaning of the theorem. Suppose a problem is given, and it is estimated that A's chance of solving it is 1/2, B's chance is 1/3, and C's chance is 1/4. What is the probability that the problem will be solved?

An error frequently made is that of assuming that the solving of the problem by A, B, and C, forms a set of mutually exclusive events, so that the answer would be $1/2 + 1/3 + 1/4 = 13/12$, which is greater than unity and thus absurd. The case is not like that of a race, because all three might solve the problem, while, in a race, only one could be the winner. Hence, the following mutually exclusive cases must be considered:

A, B, and C all succeed,	$p_1 = 1/2 \cdot 1/3 \cdot 1/4$	$= 1/24$
A, B succeed; C fails,	$p_2 = 1/2 \cdot 1/3 \cdot (1-1/4)$	$= 3/24$
A, C succeed; B fails,	$p_3 = 1/2 \cdot 1/4 \cdot (1-1/3)$	$= 2/24$
B, C succeed; A fails,	$p_4 = 1/3 \cdot 1/4 \cdot (1-1/2)$	$= 1/24$
A succeeds; B, C fail,	$p_5 = 1/2 \cdot (1-1/3) \cdot (1-1/4)$	$= 6/24$
B succeeds; A, B fail,	$p_6 = 1/3 \cdot (1-1/2) \cdot (1-1/4)$	$= 3/24$
C succeeds; A, B fail,	$p_7 = 1/4 \cdot (1-1/2) \cdot (1-1/3)$	$= 2/24$

$$p = 3/4$$

An easier way of getting the answer is first to calculate the probability that all three would fail to solve the problem. Then, since success in solving the problem and failure to solve the problem form a mutually exclusive system, the total probability of which is one, it follows that

$$p = 1 - q = 1 - (1-1/2) \cdot (1-1/3) \cdot (1-1/4)$$
$$= 1 - 1/4 = 3/4 \ .$$

6. Examples Illustrating the Multiplication and Addition of Probabilities. The following examples will serve as illustrations of the application of the theorems of the last two sections.

Example 1. A bag contains four red balls, five black balls, and three white balls. Three balls are drawn at random. What is the probability that they are all red?

The probability that the first is red is $4/12 = 1/3$, that the second is also red is $3/11$, and that the third is red is $2/10 = 1/5$. The desired probability is then $1/3 \cdot 3/11 \cdot 1/5 = 1/55$.

This method may be compared with the following: There are altogether $_{12}C_3 = 220$ possible drawings of three balls. Of these, there are $_4C_3 = 4$ possible drawings of three red balls. The answer is thus $4/220 = 1/55$.

Example 2. A, B, and C, in order, toss a coin. The first one who throws a head wins. What are their respective chances?

If A is to win, a head must be thrown on either the first, or fourth, or seventh, $\cdots$ toss and on no other. The sum of these probabilities is A's chance of winning. Similarly, if B is to win, a head must appear only on the second, fifth, eighth, $\cdots$ toss; and if C is to win, the head must appear on the third, sixth, ninth, $\cdots$ toss.

These respective probabilities then appear as the following geometrical progressions:

$$A: \quad 1/2 + 1/16 + 1/128 + \cdots$$
$$= \frac{1/2}{1 - 1/8} = 4/7,$$
$$B: \quad 1/4 + 1/32 + 1/256 + \cdots$$
$$= \frac{1/4}{1 - 1/8} = 2/7,$$
$$C: \quad 1/8 + 1/64 + 1/512 + \cdots$$
$$= \frac{1/8}{1 - 1/8} = 1/7.$$

Example 3. Fourteen quarters and one five-dollar gold piece are in one purse, and fifteen quarters are in another. Ten coins are taken from the first and put into the second, and then ten coins are taken from the second and put into the first. Which purse is probably the more valuable?

The purse containing the five-dollar gold piece is the more valuable, so the problem is to compare the probability that it is in the first purse with the probability that it is in the second. The probability that the gold piece was taken from the first purse and put into the second is $10/15$. Similarly, the probability that, being in the second, it was again returned to the first is 10/25. Hence the probability that the gold piece remained in the second purse is $(10/15)(1 - 10/25) = 2/5$. The conclusion is thus reached that the first purse has a larger value than the second.

PROBLEMS

1. A and B alternately throw a die. The first one to throw a six wins. Show that A's chance of winning on the third throw is 25/216.

2. Find the probability of throwing an ace at least once in two throws with a single die.

3. Two whole numbers taken at random are multiplied together. What is the probability that the last digit in the product is 1, 3, 7, or 9?

4. A bag contains 5 white, 3 red, and 6 green balls. Three balls are drawn at random. What is the probability that a white, a red, and a green ball are drawn?

5. In problem 4 enumerate the different kinds of draws of two balls that could be made and calculate the probabilities for each. Should the sum of the probabilities equal 1?

6. A and B toss a die; the first one to throw a six becomes the winner. If A throws first, what are their respective probabilities of winning?

7. A bag contains five balls. A person takes one out and replaces it. After he has done this six times, what is the probability that he has had in his hand every ball in the bag?

8. If five coins are tossed, what is the probability that at least three are heads? That exactly three are heads?

9. What is the chance of throwing 6 with a single die at least once in four trials?

10. What is the most likely throw with two dice?

11. What is the probability of throwing 7 at least twice in 3 throws with two dice?

12. How many tosses may one be allowed in order that the probability may be .90 that he gets at least one head? Hint: Consider the equation $1 - (½)^x = .90$. Use logarithms to solve for x.

13. A man throws ten coins, removes all that fall heads up, tosses the remainder, and again removes all that fall heads up, continuing the process until all of the coins are removed. How many times should he be allowed to throw in order to have an even chance of removing all of the coins? Hint: $1 - (½)^x$ is the chance that a coin falls heads at least once in x trials, and $[1 - (½)^x]^{10}$ the chance that all ten coins will have fallen heads at least once.

14. A, B, and C, in order, draw from a pack of cards, replacing their card after each draw. If the first man to draw a heart wins, what are their respective chances?

15. A man draws from an urn containing two balls, one white and one black. If he draws a white ball, he wins. If he fails to draw a white ball, the

draw is replaced, another black ball is added and he draws again. If he fails to draw a white ball in the next draw, the process is repeated. What are his respective chances of winning in 2, 3, 4, 5, 7, and 10 trials?

7. *The Law of Large Numbers.* Before proceeding to an application of the theorems of sections 4 and 5, a further word should be said in regard to the law of large numbers. The mathematical, or *a priori*, probability, p, has been defined as the ratio of the number of favorable to the total number of cases. This means that if a *large number* of trials is made, the ratio of the number of favorable to the total number of cases will be approximately p; and the larger the number of trials, the closer the approximation will be. The probability thus determined is called the *empirical*, or *a posteriori*, probability, and will be designated by p_1.

But the question remains as to the definition of *large number*. Is it 10, 100, or 1,000? In other words, would a thousand throws of a coin be sufficient to determine empirically the probability of throwing heads in one throw? The answer to this question is obviously a very important one, because it will furnish a measure of faith in statistical averages which depends upon the number of cases used. For example, would data regarding the length of life of 100,000 individuals of initial age 10 be sufficiently accurate for the establishment of a life insurance company?

A little later the idea of probable error will be introduced, which is closely associated with this question. It is possible, however, to anticipate enough at this point to obtain a good working rule for the law of large numbers. This rule may be stated as follows:

Let E be the error to be permitted in p_1, which is defined as the numerical value of the difference $p - p_1$. Then, if n trials are made in determining the empirical probability p_1, the probable error, E, of p_1 is expressed by the equation[1]

$$E = .6745 \sqrt{p_1(1-p_1)/n} ,$$

and the proportion of successes of p_1 will not be likely to fall outside the limits determined by p_1 and three times the probable error, E, that is,

$$p_1 \pm 3E .$$

---

[1] In general, if n is large, p can be substituted for p_1 in the formula without introducing an appreciable error.

Example 1. How many times must one toss a penny in order to have a 50:50 chance of calculating the *a priori* probability of throwing heads within an error of .05?

The answer is at once obtained from the formula by substituting $p = .5$, and $E = .05$ in the above equation. One thus finds

$$n = (.4550)(.25)/.0025 = 45.50 .$$

Since the error E is very rarely greater than $3(p-p_1)$, the value of n may be multiplied by 3^2, or 9, thus determining the number of trials which may be safely used to calculate p_1 with the desired accuracy. In the example chosen, $(9)(45.50) = 410$, the number of throws sufficient to calculate the desired probability within the limits of the prescribed error.

Example 2. From a mortality table it is found that out of 89,032 persons alive at age 25, 88,314 have survived to age 26. The probability of living from 25 to 26 is thus empirically equal to $88314/89032 = .99193548$. To how many decimal places is this answer correct?

In this problem, one is given $n = 89,032$ and $p_1 = .991935$, to calculate E. One thus obtains,

$$E = .6745 \sqrt{(.991935)(.008065)/89032} = .0002 .$$

It is clear from this calculation and an application of the rule stated above, that one is as likely to be right as wrong in assuming that the probability of living from 25 to 26 lies within the limits .9917 and .9921, but it is very likely that the probability lies within $.9919 \pm 3 \times .0002$.

PROBLEMS

1. How many throws of two dice would be reasonably sure to show that the probability of throwing double sixes lies between $1/36 + .01$ and $1/36 - .01$?

2. Suppose that the observed mortality rate for one year for a population of 10,000 was .0200. Calculate the error.

3. Compare the error in problem 2 with the error for a population of 100,000; of 1,000,000.

4. The *American Experience Table* states that of a population of 100,000 alive at age 10, 49,341 are alive at age 65. Calculate the probability of surviving for this period and determine the accuracy of your answer.

5. How many times would you have to throw 10 coins in order to calculate within an error of .01 the probability of getting 5 heads? to calculate within the same error the probability of getting 3 heads? ($p = 252/1024$ in the first case and $120/1024$ in the second.)

8. Probability in Repeated Trials. The following two theorems will be of important use in the discussion of the form of the normal frequency curve:

Theorem 3. The probability that an event will happen exactly r times in n trials is,

$$\frac{n(n-1)(n-2)\cdots\cdots(n-r+1)}{1\cdot 2\cdot 3\cdots r} p^r q^{n-r} = \frac{n!}{r!(n-r)!} p^r q^{n-r}$$

$$= {}_nC_r p^r q^{n-r},$$

where p is the probability that it will happen, and q the probability that it will fail to happen, in a single trial.

Proof: The probability that in r trials a series of events will happen in any given order is $p^r q^{n-r}$. But there are ${}_nC_r$ different orders, all mutually exclusive, in which the series of events could take place, so that the total probability will be ${}_nC_r p^r q^{n-r}$.

Example. What is the probability that in 5 throws with a single coin, heads will appear exactly 3 times? Using the abbreviations, H for heads, and T for tails, the favorable cases can be listed as follows:

H H H T T   H T H T H
H H T T H   T H H H T
H H T H T   T H T H H
H T H H T   T H H T H
H T T H H   T T H H H

The number of cases is seen to be identical with ${}_5C_3 = 10$, so that the desired probability is $10(1/2)^3 \cdot (1/2)^2 = 5/16$.

Theorem 4. The probability that an event will happen *at least* r times in n trials is

$$p^n + {}_nC_1 p^{n-1} q + {}_nC_2 p^{n-2} q^2 + \cdots + {}_nC_r p^r q^{n-r},$$

where p is the probability that the event will happen, and q the probability that it will fail, in a single trial.

Proof: The probability that the event will happen exactly n times in r trials is p^n; exactly $n-1$ times, is $_nC_1p^{n-1}q$; exactly r times, is $_nC_rp^rq^{n-r}$. Since all of these events are mutually exclusive, and since in any one of them the event happens *at least* r times, the desired probability must be the sum of all of these partial probabilities.

Example: What is the probability that in 5 throws with a single coin, heads will come up at least 3 times?

The cases to be considered are: (1) all heads; (2) all heads but one; (3) all heads but two. The first probability is 1/32, the second 5/32, the third 10/32; their sum, 1/2, is the desired probability.

This is an interesting answer to obtain empirically. If 5 coins are thrown 100 times and the empirical probability calculated, to how many decimal places will the answer be correct?

9. *Mathematical Expectation.* In the practical application of the theory of probability, the question of attaching a monetary value to statistical data quickly arises. For example, it may be seen from the *American Experience Table of Mortality* that the probability of a man of age 25 failing to live to age 26 is 718/89032, and one is required to find the amount, neglecting interest, that would insure him for $1,000 during the year period. The amount of this premium is taken as the *mathematical expectation,* which may be defined as the product of the probability of the occurrence of the event by the amount to be gained if the event occurs. Thus, the premium would be $1,000 $\times$ 718/89032 = $8.06.

A curious fallacy known as the *St. Petersburg problem* is very illuminating in this connection.

Suppose that A and B are playing the following game. B is to toss a coin until it falls heads. If it falls heads on the first toss, he receives a dollar; if it falls heads for the first time on the second toss, he receives two dollars; if it falls heads for the first time on the third toss four dollars and, in general, 2^{n-1} dollars if it falls heads for the first time on the nth toss. What is B's expectation?

Since all of the events are mutually exclusive, the total expectation, E, is the sum

$$E = 1 \cdot (1/2) + 2 \cdot (1/2)^2 + 2^2 \cdot (1/2)^3 + \cdots = \infty .$$

But this answer, from experience, is absurd. However, De Morgan, in his treatise *On Probabilities,* did not consider this answer to be a fallacy, quoting the experiment of Buffon as proof. The result of 2048 games, together with their calculated expectations, is tabulated below:

Toss on which Head Appeared	Frequency	Expectation
1	1061	$ 1061
2	494	988
3	232	928
4	137	1096
5	56	896
6	29	928
7	25	1600
8	8	1024
9	6	1536
Total	2048	$10,057

The average per game is calculated to be $4.91. De Morgan argued that if Buffon had tried a thousand times as many games, he not only would have made more in particular games, but the average per game would have been greater. It is not difficult to show that it is very probable that the average per game, if 2^n games are played, will be approximately $n/2$ dollars.

The conclusion to be drawn from this is not that B should pay A a very large sum of money for a particular game, which is absurd, but that A would be foolish to go into this form of gambling *as a business* for $5.00, or any other fixed sum of money per game, because, if enough customers appeared, the average cost to him can be made to exceed any pre-assigned value.

One ingenious answer to the fallacy is as follows: It may be argued that the amount of winnings A can pay is finite, so B, by a phenomenal run of luck, might win more than A's total wealth. Suppose that A's wealth is 2^p dollars, then the series E becomes

$$E = 1(1/2) + 2 \cdot (1/2)^2 + 2^2 \cdot (1/2)^3 + \cdots \cdots$$
$$+ 2^p \cdot (1/2)^{p+1} + 2^p \cdot (1/2)^{p+2} + \cdots \cdots$$
$$= \tfrac{1}{2}(p+1) + 1/4 + 1/8 + 1/16 + \cdots \cdots = \tfrac{1}{2}(p+2) .$$

Thus, if A were a millionaire, p would be equal to 20 and B's expectation would amount to $11.00.

A very different solution of the paradox was given by Daniel Bernoulli in terms of a concept which he called *moral expectation*, in contrast to *mathematical expectation*. Bernoulli argued that the pleasure a man received in adding a sum of money to his wealth depended upon his original fortune. This idea he formulated mathematically by saying that the moral expectation of a man who added b dollars to an original estate of a dollars is measured by the quantity $k \log_e (a+b)/b$, where k is a constant.

The solution to which this view leads is too intricate mathematically to be presented in an elementary text, but the values to be attached to the game on various assumptions as to B's capital do not differ materially from those obtained in the preceding solution, where the difficulty is placed upon the limitations of A's wealth. E. Czuber found, for example, that if B had $100.00, he could afford to pay $4.36 for a game; if he had $200.00, he could afford $6.00. W. A. Whitworth, in his book on *Choice and Chance*,[1] somewhat modifying the idea of moral expectation, obtained an answer of $3.80 for an initial capital of $8.00, $4.00 for a capital of $32.00, $6.00 for a capital of $1024.00.

PROBLEMS

1. A bag contains 25 quarters and one five-dollar gold piece. What is one's mathematical expectation if he has five draws from the bag?

2. A hand of five cards is dealt. If all are hearts, A is to receive $10; if four are hearts, $5; three hearts, $2; and one heart, $1. What is A's expectation?

3. A and B play the St. Petersburg game. If A has $100, what is B's expectation?

4. A is to receive $1000 if no coin in a toss of ten coins is heads. What would be an equivalent expectation for 5 heads in a toss of 10 coins?

5. A pays B $1.00 to guess the number of heads in a single toss of 4 coins. What expectation should B place on each of the possibilities: no head, one head, two heads, etc.?

6. A bag contains 5 half dollars, 7 quarters, and 8 dimes. If a person draws a single coin, what is his expectation?

7. A bag contains 15 dollars and 10 other coins of equal denomination. If one's expectation for a single draw is 80 cents, what are the other 10 coins?

8. One bag contains 5 dollars and 7 quarters, and another 6 half dollars and 4 quarters. If one coin is taken from the first bag and placed into the second, and one coin then taken from the second bag and placed into the first, what value should be assigned to the first bag?

---

[1] Cambridge, 1867, 4th edition 1886, reprinted by G. E. Stechert, 1925. See pp. 231-236.

10. *Miscellaneous Examples.* When an event is known to have happened, and it must have followed from one of several equally probable causes, the determination of the probability that it proceeded from a particular one of these causes is known as a problem in *inverse probability*. Because of the impossibility, in general, of assigning the proper probability to the primary causes, this part of the theory has recently fallen into disfavor. Its application to certain types of problems is so interesting, however, that a certain lack of rigor in obtaining answers, and a distrust of these answers when they are found, will not seriously interfere with the pleasure of the argument.

Example 1. Suppose a black ball has been drawn from one of three bags, the first containing three black balls and seven white, the second five black balls and three white, the third eight black balls and four white. What is the probability that it was drawn from the first bag?

If N drawings, with replacements each time, are made from each bag, where N is a large number, there will be approximately $3N/10$ black balls drawn from the first bag, $5N/8$ from the second, and $8N/12$ from the third. Therefore, of a total of $3N$ drawings, N from each bag, there will be approximately $3N/10 + 5N/8 + 8N/12$ black balls drawn, of which $3N/10$ came from the first bag. Hence, it is reasonable to argue that the probability that the black ball came from the first bag is

$$P = \frac{3N/10}{3N/10 + 5N/8 + 8N/12} = \frac{36}{191}.$$

The fundamental theorem in inverse probability may be stated as follows:

An event is known to have proceeded from one of n mutually exclusive causes whose probabilities are $P_1, P_2, \ldots, P_n$. Furthermore, let $p_1, p_2, \ldots, p_n$ be the respective probabilities that when one of the n causes exists, the event will then have followed. The probability that the event proceeded from the m-th cause is then

$$P = \frac{P_m p_m}{P_1 p_1 + P_2 p_2 + \cdots + P_n p_n}.$$

In the example just solved, one has $P_1 = P_2 = P_3 = 1/3$, since it is just as probable that the ball was drawn from one bag as another. (It is this assumption, based on our ignorance of the probabilities underlying the fundamental causes, that has led to the discrediting of the theory.) Also, it is known that $p_1 = 3/10$, $p_2 = 5/8$, $p_3 = 8/12$, and this leads, as before, to the answer

$$P = \frac{1/3 \cdot 3/10}{1/3 \cdot 3/10 + 1/3 \cdot 5/8 + 1/3 \cdot 8/12} = \frac{36}{191}.$$

The problem of testimony is an interesting application of the theorem just stated.

Example 2. Suppose that A is known to tell the truth in five cases out of six, and he states that a white ball was drawn from a bag containing 9 black and one white ball. What is the probability that the white ball was really drawn?

The probability that a white ball is drawn in any case is 1/10. Also, the probability that the white ball was drawn and that A told the truth is $1/10 \cdot 5/6$. Furthermore, the probability that a black ball was drawn and A told a lie about it is $9/10 \cdot 1/6$. Hence the probability that a white ball was drawn is

$$P = \frac{1/10 \cdot 5/6}{1/10 \cdot 5/6 + 9/10 \cdot 1/6} = 5/14.$$

One of the interesting historical problems in elementary probability is that known as the problem of "duration of play."

Example 3. Two players A and B having m and n counters, respectively, play a game in which their respective chances of winning are p and q, where $p + q = 1$. Each time a game is won, the winner takes a counter from the loser. What is the chance of each player of winning all of his opponent's counters?

Let u_x be the probability that A will win when he has x counters. On the next play his probability is p that he will win; and, if he wins, his chance of winning in the end is u_{x+1}. Hence, the probability that he will both win the next game and finally win all of B's counters is $p\, u_{x+1}$. Similarly, his chance of losing the game, but still ultimately winning, will be $q\, u_{x-1}$. Since these represent the only possibilities, their sum is equal to u_x, and we have the equation,

$$u_x = p u_{x+1} + q u_{x-1}.$$

One can easily verify that a solution of this equation is

$$u_x = a + b \cdot (q/p)^x,$$

where a and b are constants that can be chosen at pleasure. In order to determine a and b, notice that when A has no counters left his probability is zero; when he has $m + n$ counters, his probability is one. Thus, it is found that

$$u_0 = a + b = 0 ,$$
$$u_{m+n} = a + b \cdot (q/p)^{m+n} = 1 .$$

From these equations it results that

$$a = p^{m+n}/(p^{m+n} - q^{m+n}) ,$$
$$b = p^{m+n}/(q^{m+n} - q^{m+n}) .$$

Hence, the probability that A will win is,

$$u_m = \frac{p^{m+n}}{p^{m+n} - q^{m+n}} + \frac{p^{m+n}(q/p)^m}{q^{m+n} - p^{m+n}} ,$$

$$= \frac{p^{m+n}[1 - (q/p)^m]}{p^{m+n} - q^{m+n}} ,$$

$$= \frac{1 - (q/p)^m}{1 - (q/p)^{m+n}} .$$

If $p = q$, then $u_m = m/(m+n)$. The proof of this follows:

From elementary algebra,

$$\frac{1 - (q/p)^m}{1 - (q/p)} = 1 + (q/p) + \cdots + (q/p)^{m-2} + (q/p)^{m-1} .$$

The limits may then be calculated to be

$$\lim_{q/p = 1} \frac{1 - (q/p)^m}{1 - q/p} = 1 + 1 + \cdots + 1 \ (m \text{ terms}) = m .$$

Similarly, one has

$$\lim_{q/p = 1} \frac{1 - (q/p)^{m+n}}{1 - q/p} = m + n .$$

The student can derive the desired result from these limits.

PROBLEMS

1. A has 10 pennies and B has 5 pennies. What are the odds in favor of A if A and B match pennies?

2. A and B toss a die, the first to throw a six gaining a penny from the other. A always starts the games. If A has a dollar and B fifty cents, what is the probability that B will win all of A's money?

3. A black ball is drawn from one of two bags containing 3 white and 2 black balls and 5 white and 7 black balls respectively. What is the probability that the ball was drawn from the first bag?

4. A bag contains 5 balls which are just as likely to be white as colored. Two white balls are drawn from the bag. What is the probability that all are white? Hint: The balls may be (1) all white, (2) 4 white, (3) 3 white, (4) 2 white. The probability in the first case is 1/32, and the probability that two white balls would be drawn from such a bag is, of course, one. Hence, we have $P_1 = 1/32$, $p_1 = 1$. Find the probabilities in the other cases and apply the fundamental formula.

5. The probability that a certain event happened was 1/10, and A, who is accurate in 49 cases out of 50, said that it happened. What is the probability that it actually did occur?

6. A and B agree in stating that the event of problem 5 happened. B is accurate in 9 cases out of 10. What, now, is the probability that it happened? Hint: The probability that the event happened and both A and B told the truth is $1/10 \cdot 49/50 \cdot 9/10$.

7. If C, who is accurate in 7 cases out of 10, denies that the event of problem 6 happened, what is the probability that it happened? Hint: There are two possibilities, (1) that the event happened and that A and B told the truth while C lied, (2) that the event did not happen and that A and B lied while C told the truth.

CHAPTER VII

BINOMIAL FREQUENCY DISTRIBUTIONS

1. Binomial Frequencies. As an introduction to the general subject of frequency curves, a frequency distribution which is typical of a large and important class of such distributions met with in ordinary statistical data may now be considered. This is the so-called *binomial frequency distribution,* which is also often referred to as the *Bernoulli distribution* because of the fundamental work done in this connection by Jakob Bernoulli in his *Ars Conjectandi.*

As an example, suppose that 10 coins are thrown $2^{10} = 1024$ times, and a record kept of the number of frequencies attached to the cases: 10 heads; 9 heads, 1 tail; 8 heads, 2 tails; etc. These frequencies, as may be known from the theorems of section 8 of the preceding chapter, should be approximately equal to the terms in the expansion

$$2^{10}(1/2 + 1/2)^{10} .$$

To these various frequencies may be attached the class marks $x_0 = 0$, $x_1 = 1$, $x_2 = 2$, ..., $x_{10} = 10$, so that the following ideal statistical series is obtained:

Class Marks	Frequencies
0	1
1	10
2	45
3	120
4	210
5	252
6	210
7	120
8	45
9	10
10	1

The mode, median, and arithmetic average, are all seen to be identical and equal to 5. The standard deviation is easily computed to be

$$\sigma = \sqrt{2.5} = 1.58 .$$

If the histogram for the series is formed, it is seen that the central ordinates coincide very closely with the ordinates of the *normal frequency* curve the equation of which is

$$y = \frac{N}{\sigma\sqrt{2\pi}} e^{-\frac{1}{2}[(x-A)/\sigma]^2}, \qquad (1)$$

where one sets $N = 1024$, $A = 5$, and $\sigma = 1.58$.

The calculations involved in this *graduation* of the data, by means of the normal frequency curve, are exhibited in the following table where the abbreviation

$$y_2 = \frac{1}{\sqrt{2\pi}} e^{-\frac{1}{2}t^2}$$

is used. Values of this function will be found in Table VI.[1]

Class Marks (x_i)	Frequencies	N/σ	$t = (x_i - A)/\sigma$	y_2	Graduated Frequencies ($y_2 N/\sigma$)
0	1	648.1	−3.16	.00271	2
1	10	648.1	−2.53	.01625	11
2	45	648.1	−1.90	.06562	43
3	120	648.1	−1.27	.17810	115
4	210	648.1	−.63	.32713	212
5	252	648.1	0	.39894	259
6	210	648.1	.63	.32713	212
7	120	648.1	1.27	.17810	115
8	45	648.1	1.90	.06562	43
9	10	648.1	2.53	.01625	11
10	1	648.1	3.16	.00271	2

The values of y_2 are found by entering Table VI with the arguments in the column for t. The graduated frequencies are then obtained by multiplying y_2 by the value of N/σ. Both the histogram and the corresponding normal frequency curve have been graphed in Figure 31 with the averages as the origin of the class marks.

The importance of studying binomial frequency distributions is found in the fact that many statistical distributions are essentially of this type. The student may convince himself of this fact by turning to the list of problems in section 3, Chapter III. A casual survey of the problems shows the characteristic concentra-

---

[1] The student should consult in this connection section 10, Chapter II.

tion of frequencies about the average and the gradual diminishing of frequencies at either end of the series. What this means is that in most statistical data there is a modal class and that large deviations from this mode are rare.

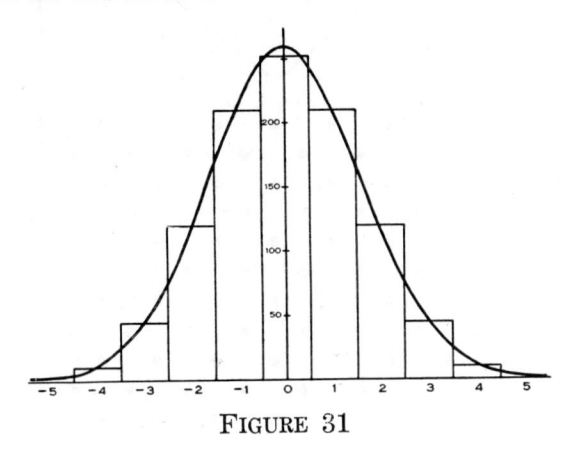

FIGURE 31

The accompanying diagram (Figure 32) shows an instructive device for forming a true normal frequency curve statistically. The apparatus is made from a shallow box, covered on one side by a piece of glass. Into the back board a large number of pegs are set in such a way that the openings between the pegs of one row are filled by the pegs of the next. Below the pegs a number of equally spaced partitions are placed so as to form a set of compartments. Now if a quantity of small shot is introduced by means of a funnel to a point midway between the compartments and above the pegs, the shot will fall between the pegs and distribute themselves in the compartments so as to form an almost perfect normal frequency histogram. This phenomenon supplies an apt illustration of the way nature and chance work to create frequency distributions. Most of the shot in falling through the pegs will be deflected as much to one side as to the other so there will be a tendency for them to accumulate in the central compartment. A few of the shot, however, by a succession of unusual collisions, will tend to move in one direction or the other and hence will fall into the outer compartments. These are the exceptions rather than the rule, however, and hence the numbers in the outer compartments are comparatively few. This device is known as the *Galton quincunx*, the word quincunx referring to the arrangement of the pegs. A description of it was first given in Sir Francis Galton's *Natural Inheritance* (1889).

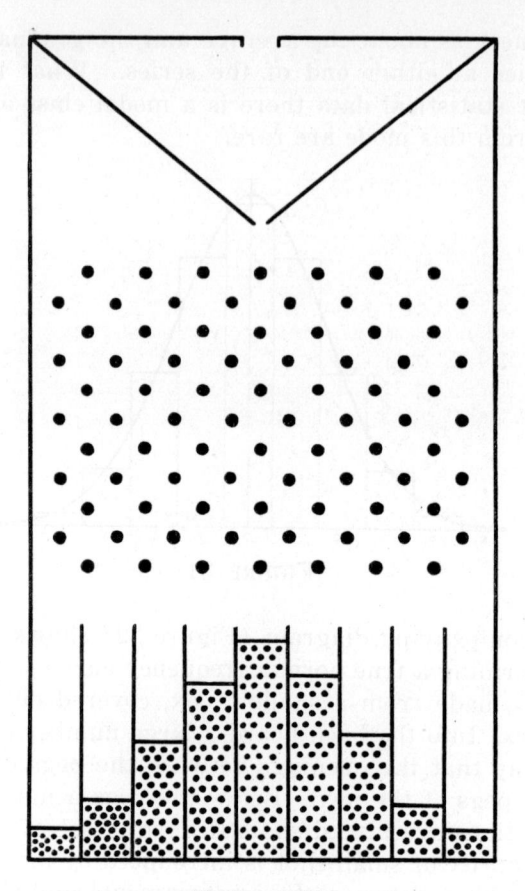

FIGURE 32

One approach to the mathematical theory of the normal and the skew normal frequency curves is through an investigation of binomial frequencies; this is the approach that is taken in this chapter. It will be seen from the numerical example that a study of the frequency table obtained from the individual terms of the binomial expansion of the expression.

$$N(q+p)^n,$$

where $p+q=1$, with which are associated the class marks 0, 1, 2, ..., n, may prove typical of the study of a large class of empirical data.

In this investigation a start may be made from the following table of frequencies, formed from the successive terms of the expansion of the binomial $N(q+p)^n$ (Section 12, Chapter I):

TABLE OF THE BINOMIAL FREQUENCY DISTRIBUTIONS

	f_0	f_1	f_2	....	f_x	...	f_n
equencies	Nq^n	$Nnq^{n-1}p$	$N\dfrac{n(n-1)}{2!}q^{n-2}p^2$	....	$N\dfrac{n!}{x!(n-x)!}q^{n-x}p^x$	...	Np^n
ass Marks	0	1	2	....	x	...	n

From this table are first calculated:

(a) the arithmetic mean,
(b) the standard deviation,
(c) the mode.

When these values have been computed, one is then in a position to derive the normal frequency curve which, as has been seen, fits approximately the histogram of the frequencies.

2. *Arithmetic Average and Standard Deviation of a Binomial Series.* The following theorem will first be proved:

Theorem 1. The arithmetic average of the binomial series, as defined in the preceding section, is equal to np.

Before proving the theorem, an example will clarify its meaning.

Example 1. Corresponding to $p = 1/3$, $q = 2/3$, $n = 5$, $N = 3^5 = 243$, one obtains the following binomial distribution:

Frequencies	$f_0 = 32$	$f_1 = 80$	$f_2 = 80$	$f_3 = 40$	$f_4 = 10$	$f_5 = 1$
Class Marks	$x_0 = 0$	$x_1 = 1$	$x_2 = 2$	$x_3 = 3$	$x_4 = 4$	$x_5 = 5$

Putting these values into the formula for the arithmetic mean (see section 3, Chapter III), one has

$$A = \frac{(30 \times 0 + 80 \times 1 + 80 \times 2 + 40 \times 3 + 10 \times 4 + 1 \times 5)}{243} = 5/3,$$

which is seen to be equal to $np = 5 \times 1/3$.

The proof of the theorem is derived from the simplification of the following sum:

$$A = \frac{(f_0 \cdot 0 + f_1 \cdot 1 + f_2 \cdot 2 + \cdots + f_n \cdot n)}{N}$$

Replacing each f by its value in the frequency table of the last section one gets

$$A = [(Nq^n \cdot 0 + Nnq^{n-1}p \cdot 1 + N\frac{n(n-1)}{2!}q^{n-2}p^2 \cdot 2 + \cdots$$

$$+ N\frac{n!}{x!(n-x)!}q^{n-x}p^x \cdot x + \cdots + Np^n \cdot n)]/N .$$

If np is factored out from each term and the N's of the numerator and denominator are cancelled, this series is seen to reduce as follows:

$$A = np\, [q^{n-1} + (n-1)q^{n-2}p + \frac{(n-1)(n-2)}{2!}q^{n-3}p^2$$

$$+ \cdots\cdots + p^{n-1}]$$

$$= np[q+p]^{n-1} .$$

Consequently, since $q + p = 1$, it follows that $A = np$, which is the statement of the theorem.

Consider next the standard deviation.

Theorem 2. The standard deviation of the binomial series is equal to $\sqrt{npq}$.

Example 2. Calculate the standard deviation for the frequency table of example 1.

Referring to formula 2, section 5, Chapter IV, and recalling that $A = 5/3$, the value for σ^2 is

$$\sigma^2 = [32(0 - 5/3)^2 + 80(1 - 5/3)^2 + 80(2 - 5/3)^2$$
$$+ 40(3 - 5/3)^2 + 10(4 - 5/3)^2 + 1(5 - 5/3)^2]/243$$
$$= 2430/(9 \times 243)$$
$$= 5 \cdot 1/3 \cdot 2/3 .$$

If the frequencies of the table in the last section are designated by $f_0, f_1, f_2, \cdots\cdots, f_n$, and one recalls that $\sigma^2 = [\Sigma f_i(x_i - A)^2]/N$,

BINOMIAL FREQUENCY DISTRIBUTION

and that $A = np$ according to theorem 1, the proof of theorem 2 consists in showing that the following series reduces to npq:

$$\sigma^2 = [f_0(0-np)^2 + f_1(1-np)^2 + f_2(2-np)^2 \\ + \cdots + f_n(n-np)^2]/N .$$

Squaring each term,

$$\sigma^2 = f_0 n^2 p^2 + f_1(n^2 p^2 - 2np + 1^2) + f_2(n^2 p^2 - 4np + 2^2) \\ + \cdots + f_n(n^2 p^2 - 2n^2 p + n^2)/N .$$

If the coefficients of n^2p^2 and np are collected, one obtains

$$\sigma^2 = n^2 p^2 (f_0 + f_1 + f_2 + \cdots + f_n) - 2np(f_1 + 2f_2 + 3f_3 \\ + \cdots + nf_n) + (1^2 f_1 + 2^2 f_2 + \cdots + n^2 f_n)/N \quad (2)$$

But it is at once seen from the explicit values of the frequencies that

$$f_0 + f_1 + f_2 \cdots + f_n = N(p+q)^n = N ,$$

and it has already been shown, in the proof of theorem 1, that

$$f_1 + 2f_2 + 3f_3 + \cdots + nf_n = NA = Npn .$$

It remains then to consider the series

$$1^2 f_1 + 2^2 f_2 + 3^2 f_3 + \cdots + n^2 f_n \\ = Nnp[q^{n-1} + (n-1)2pq^{n-2} + \frac{(n-1)(n-2)}{2!} 3p^2 q^{n-3} \\ + \cdots + np^{n-1}] , \quad (3)$$

which is obtained by replacing each frequency by its explicit value as given in the table of the first section of this chapter, and factoring out Nnp.

Next, in equation (3) replace 2 by its equivalent value $1+1$, 3 by $1+2$, 4 by $1+3, \cdots$, n by $1+(n-1)$. The above series will then break up into two parts, and the following expression is obtained:

$$Nnp\{[q^{n-1} + (n-1)pq^{n-2} + \frac{(n-1)(n-2)}{2!} p^2 q^{n-3} \\ + \cdots + p^{n-1}] + (n-1)p[q^{n-2} + (n-2)pq^{n-5} \\ + \cdots + p^{n-2}]\} \\ = Nnp[(q+p)^{n-1} + p(n-1)(q+p)^{n-2}]$$

$$= Nnp[1 + p(n-1)] = Nnp[np + (1-p)]$$
$$= N[n^2p^2 + npq] \text{ , since } q = 1-p .$$

When these values are substituted in formula (2), the following simple result is obtained:

$$\sigma^2 = n^2p^2 - 2n^2p^2 + n^2p^2 + npq = npq .$$

Corollary: For a binomial distribution, the standard deviation can be expressed in terms of the arithmetic mean as follows:

$$\sigma = \sqrt{A(1 - A/n)} ,$$

where A is the Bernoulli mean and n one less than the number of classes.

The proof of this corollary is immediate if p and q are expressed in terms of A by the relations $np = A$ and $q = 1 - p$, and these values then substituted in the formula for σ.

PROBLEMS

1. It is very unusual for a standard deviation to be in error more than $2\sigma/\sqrt{2N}$, where N is the total frequency used in the calculation of σ. Given this fact, decide whether or not the following frequency table represents a binomial distribution:

Frequencies	2	5	7	15	46	89	125	60	20	10	2
Class Marks	0	1	2	3	4	5	6	7	8	9	10

Hint: First calculate the mean and the standard deviation. Then, using the corollary, calculate the standard deviation on the assumption that the distribution is normal. Compute the difference between the two values of σ thus obtained and see by the criterion stated above whether this difference is significant.

2. Show that the following frequencies obtained from tossing 10 coins 500 times fit a normal frequency distribution:

Frequencies	0	5	33	51	94	127	110	56	20	4	0
Heads	0	1	2	3	4	5	6	7	8	9	10

3. Throw 10 coins a hundred times and compare the observed frequencies of heads and tails with those calculated.

4. A tetrahedron has its faces numbered 1, 2, 3, and 4. Five such tetrahedrons are tossed 1024 times and a count is kept of the number of times the face numbered one appears in each throw. Compute the ideal frequency table.

5. Graduate the data of problem 2 by means of the normal frequency curve.

6. Calculate the arithmetic mean and the standard deviation for the frequency table formed by calling successive terms of the expansion $(1+3)^{10}$ the frequencies corresponding to the class marks $0, 1, 2, \cdots, 10$.

7. Graduate the following data, showing the distribution of the indexes of seasonal variation for factory payrolls in 24 leading industries for the years 1923-1931, on the assumption that they form a normal distribution:

Index of Seasonal Variation	Class Marks	Frequency
Under 85	0	7
88-90	1	9
91-93	2	21
94-96	3	27
97-99	4	57
100-102	5	70
103-105	6	64
106-108	7	18
109-111	8	8
112 and over	9	7

8. Decide whether or not the above data form a binomial distribution. See hint to problem 1.

9. Show that for a binomial distribution the third moment is equal to
$$1^3 f_1 + 2^3 f_2 + 3^3 f_3 + \ldots\ldots + n^3 f_n$$
$$= Nnp \left[1 + 3(n-1)p + (n-1)(n-2)p^2 \right] .$$

3. *The Calculation of the Mode for the Binomial Frequency Distribution.* The following theorem was first proved by J. Bernoulli and contains the inequalities which define the value of the mode of the binomial series:

Theorem 3. If the probability that an event will happen is p, and the probability that it will fail to happen is q, then the most probable event in n trials is x successes and $n-x$ failures, where x is an integer defined by the inequality

$$pn - q \leq x \leq pn + p .$$

Suppose, for example, that two coins are being tossed and the probability is being considered that both will fall heads. In a single toss the probability of this event is 1/4, and the probability that it will not happen is 3/4. Suppose, then, that the two coins are tossed 10 times and one inquires what is the most probable number of times the two coins will fall heads.

The answer, x, is seen from the theorem to lie between

$$pn - q = 1\tfrac{3}{4} \quad \text{and} \quad pn + p = 2\tfrac{3}{4},$$

which means that $x = 2$.

The actual probability corresponding to this event is, of course, the third term in the expansion of $(3/4 + 1/4)^{10}$, which equals .2815. The most probable event, therefore, is not always a very probable event, on account of the fact that there are various other cases to be considered whose probabilities are relatively large.

The proof of the theorem consists in finding a value of x which will make the function

$$\bar{y}_x = N \frac{n!}{x!(n-x)!} q^{n-x} p^x \qquad (4)$$

as large as possible, since $\bar{y}_x$ is the general term in the binomial frequency table of section 1.

If such a value of x exists, it is at once seen that the values of (4) calculated at $x + 1$ and $x - 1$ must be smaller than the value of (4) calculated at the point x. This statement is expressed by means of the following inequalities:

$$\left. \begin{array}{c} \dfrac{n!}{(x+1)!(n-x-1)!} p^{x+1} q^{n-x-1} \\[2mm] \dfrac{n!}{(x-1)!(n-x+1)!} p^{x-1} q^{n-x+1} \end{array} \right\} \leq \dfrac{n!}{x!(n-x)!} p^x q^{n-x}.$$

Dividing through by each of the left-hand members and remembering that $(n-x+1)! = (n-x+1)(n-x)!$ and that $(x+1)! = (x+1)x!$, the two inequalities are simplified as follows:

$$1 \leq \frac{(x+1)}{(n-x)} \frac{q}{p},$$

$$1 \leq \frac{n-x+1}{x} \frac{p}{q}.$$

From these, multiplying by $(n-x)p$ and xq respectively, these results are derived:
$$p(n-x) \leq q(x+1) ,$$
$$qx \leq p(n-x+1) .$$

Solving the first of these inequalities for x, one has
$$pn-px \leq qx+q ,$$
$$pn-q \leq (p+q)x \leq x ,$$
and in a similar way from the second inequality,
$$x \leq pn+p .$$

Thus it is seen that the required value, x, is the integer which satisfies both of these inequalities. It should be noticed that when $pn-q$ is an integer, x may assume both the upper and lower limits of the inequality and the mode is not unique. Usually, however, this will not be the case and the mode, with a very slight error, is equal to np. It is thus seen to coincide, in general, with the value of the arithmetic mean.

4. *Stirling's Formula.* Before the equation of the normal curve can be derived from the general term of the binomial frequency table, it will be necessary to digress a little and discuss an important mathematical result known as Stirling's formula. This formula gives a very useful approximation to $n!$ which, as may readily be appreciated, is a very large number for large values of n.

Stirling's formula states that
$$n! \sim n^n \sqrt{n}\, e^{-n} \sqrt{2\pi} ,$$
where the symbol, $\sim$, means "approximates" or "is asymptotic to."

For example, by the exact formula one has
$$5! = 120 ,$$
and by Stirling's approximation
$$5! \sim 5^5 \sqrt{5}\, e^{-5} \sqrt{2\pi} = 118 + .$$

The calculations are made, of course, by means of logarithms.

It has already been seen in problems 2 and 3, section 13, Chapter III, that $n!$ is bounded by the following inequalities:
$$n^n / (\log_e n + .5772)^n < n! < (n+1)^n / 2^n = n^n (1+1/n)^n\, 2^{-n} .$$

If, then, $n!$ is written as the product $n! = f(n)n^n$, it is seen that the function $f(n)$ is limited by the following inequalities:

$$(\log_e n + .5772)^{-n} < f(n) < (1+1/n)^n 2^{-n},$$

and consequently decreases rapidly toward zero as n becomes large.

It is clear, furthermore, that

$$f(n) = n!/n^n = (1-1/n)(1-2/n)\cdots[1-(n-1)/n]. \quad (5)$$

It was A. de Moivre (1667-1754) who first succeeded in giving, in 1718, an approximate value to this function, which he determined in final form except for the unknown constant multiplier. This constant J. Stirling (1692-1770) succeeded in finding, twelve years later, and the approximation has since been called by his name.

Although many derivations of Stirling's formula have been made, none of them may be said to be entirely elementary. One of these, depending only upon algebraic processes, is given in Chrystal's *Algebra*, Edinburgh (1889), part 2, pp. 344-348. Another is found in A. Fisher's *Mathematical Theory of Probabilities*, 2nd. ed., New York, 1922, pp. 92-95. The student of calculus will find a proof in Whittaker and Watson, *Modern Analysis*, 3rd ed., Cambridge, 1920, pp. 251-255.

In this book no more will be done than to exhibit the closeness with which values of the function $\sqrt{2\pi n}\, e^{-n}$ coincide with the values of $f(n)$ calculated by means of (5). These values are recorded in the following table for a few values of n:

n	$f(n)$	$\sqrt{2\pi n}\, e^{-n}$
2	.5000	.4797
3	.2222	.1800
4	.0937	.0918
5	.0384	.0378
10	.0005	.0004

5. *Derivation of the Skew-Normal Frequency Curve.* In section 10, Chapter II, the equation of the *skew-normal* frequency curve was given as,

$$y = \frac{N}{\sigma\sqrt{2\pi}} e^{[(p-q)/2\sigma^2]x} e^{-(1/2\sigma^2)x^2}.$$

The derivation of this curve from the general term of the binomial frequency distribution is one of the elegant problems in the mathematical theory of statistics. While a knowlege of this connection between the discrete and continuous series may not add materially to one's ability to apply the theory, the thoughtful student will find the following development profitable in arriving at a knowledge of the underlying principles of the subject. An indication of another method of derivation will be found in section 8, Chapter IX.

The development begins with the general term of the binomial frequency table of section 1, which may be written

$$y_x = \frac{N\,n!}{x!(n-x)!} q^{n-x} p^x \,. \tag{6}$$

Since the maximum or modal value of this function occurs at or close to $x = np$, the origin may first be shifted to the mean by a transformation of coordinates. Referring to section 11 of Chapter II, it is seen that this is accomplished by replacing x by $np + x$. The point of departure will then be from the new function

$$y_x = \frac{N\,n!}{(np+x)!(nq-x)!} p^{np+x} q^{qn-x} \,, \tag{7}$$

which has its highest point at $x = 0$.

The connection between the discrete and continuous series is made by means of Stirling's formula. Replacing each of the factorials by its approximation—for example, replacing

$$(np + x)! \quad \text{by} \quad (np+x)^{np+x} \sqrt{np+x}\, e^{-np-x} \sqrt{2\pi} \,,$$

after cancelling common factors, one has

$$y_x \infty \frac{N\,n^n \sqrt{n}}{(np+x)^{np+x} \sqrt{np+x}\,(nq-x)^{nq-x} \sqrt{nq-x}\,\sqrt{2\pi}} p^{np+x} q^{np-x} \,. \tag{8}$$

Taking np and nq out of the parentheses and the radicals of the denominator as factors [for example, by (4) section 2, Appendix II, $(np+x)^k = (np)^k(1+x/np)^k$] equation (8) then becomes:

$$y_x \infty \frac{N\,n^n \sqrt{n}}{(np)^{np+x}(1+\dfrac{x}{np})^{np+x+\frac{1}{2}} \sqrt{np}\,(nq)^{nq-x}(1-\dfrac{x}{nq})^{nq-x+\frac{1}{2}} \sqrt{nq}\,\sqrt{2\pi}} \\ \times p^{np+x} q^{nq-x}$$

$$y_x \infty \frac{N n^n \sqrt{n}}{p^{np+x} n^{np+x} (1+\frac{x}{np})^{np+x+1/2} \sqrt{np} \; q^{nq-x} n^{nq-x} (1-\frac{x}{nq})^{nq-x+1/2} \sqrt{nq} \sqrt{2\pi}} \times p^{np+x} q^{nq-x} \; .$$

Since $np + nq = n(p+q) = n$, one can factor out $n^n \sqrt{n}$ and thus obtain

$$y_x \infty \frac{N}{\sqrt{2\pi \, npq}} \cdot (1+x/np)^{-np-x-1/2} (1-x/nq)^{-nq+x-1/2} \; .$$

If logarithms of both sides to the base e are taken, one gets

$$\log_e y_x \infty \log_e N - \tfrac{1}{2} \log_e 2\pi \, npq - (np + x + \tfrac{1}{2}) \log_e (1 + x/np)$$
$$- (nq - x + \tfrac{1}{2}) \log_e (1 - x/nq) \; .$$

Knowing from equation 9, section 6, Appendix II, that

$$\log_e (1+z) = z - z^2/2 + z^3/3 - z^4/4 + \cdots ,$$

one can expand the logarithms of the last two terms and expand the resulting series in powers of x. This leads to the further approximation,

$$\log_e y_x \infty \log_e N - \tfrac{1}{2} \log_e 2\pi npq$$
$$+ [-(np+\tfrac{1}{2})/np + (nq+\tfrac{1}{2})/nq] \, x$$
$$+ [(np+\tfrac{1}{2})/2(np)^2 + (nq+\tfrac{1}{2})/2(nq)^2 - 1/np - 1/nq] \, x^2$$
$$+ \cdots .$$

Since n was assumed to be large, terms which involve $1/n$ to the second or higher powers can be neglected. Finally, recalling that $p + q = 1$, one arrives at the approximate value

$$\log_e y_x \infty \log_e N - \tfrac{1}{2} \log_e 2\pi npq + \frac{p-q}{2npq} x - \frac{1}{2npq} x^2 \; .$$

From this, taking the anti-logarithms of both sides and calling y the approximate value of y_x, the equation is obtained,

$$y = \frac{N}{\sqrt{2npq\,\pi}} \; e^{\,[(p-q)/2npq]x} \; e^{-(1/2npq)x^2} \qquad (9)$$

BINOMIAL FREQUENCY DISTRIBUTION

6. *The Skew-Normal Curve*. The last equation of the preceding section can be put into another form by use of the results of section 2, i.e., that $p = A/n$ and $\sigma^2 = npq$. Making obvious substitutions, (9) becomes

$$y = \frac{N}{\sigma} \frac{1}{\sqrt{2\pi}} e^{-S'(x/\sigma)} e^{-\frac{1}{2}(x/\sigma)^2}, \qquad (10)$$

where S', the skewness, equals $(1 - 2A/n)/2\sigma$.[1]

It is illuminating to compare values of y_x and y for special cases.

Example 1. Let $p = q = \frac{1}{2}$, $n = 10$, $N = 1024$. One thus has, from formula (7),

$$y_x = \frac{1024 \cdot 10!}{(5+x)!(5-x)!} (\tfrac{1}{2})^{5+x} (\tfrac{1}{2})^{5-x} = \frac{10!}{(5+x)!(5-x)!},$$

and from (10),

$$y = \frac{1024}{1.58} \frac{1}{\sqrt{2\pi}} e^{-\frac{1}{2}(x/1.58)^2} .$$

Letting x take values from -5 to 5, the following table is obtained, which has already been graphically represented in Figure 31:

x	y_x	y
0	252	259
± 1	210	212
± 2	120	115
± 3	45	43
± 4	10	11
± 5	1	2

Example 2. Let

$$p = 1/3, \quad q = 2/3, \quad N = 3^9 = 19{,}683, \quad n = 9 .$$

Then

$$A = 3, \quad \sigma = \sqrt{2} = 1.4142 ,$$
$$S' = (1 - 6/9)/2.8284 = .1179 .$$

---

[1] The student should observe here that S' is also equal to $M_3/(2N\sigma^3)$ [See section 10, Chapter III]. Due to the difficulty of making an accurate determination of n in some cases, S' should be checked by comparison with $M_3/(2N\sigma^3)$.

Making the proper substitutions in the formulas for y_x and y [formulas (7) and (10), respectively], one has

$$y_x = \frac{19683 \cdot 9!}{(3+x)!(6-x)!}(1/3)^{3+x}(2/3)^{6-x} = \frac{9!}{(3+x)!(6-x)!} 2^{6-x},$$

$$y = \frac{19683}{1.4142} \frac{1}{\sqrt{2\pi}} e^{-.1179(x/1.414)} e^{-\frac{1}{2}(x/1.414)^2}.$$

If, in the last equation, $e^{-.1179(x/1.414)}$ is designated by y_1 and $e^{-\frac{1}{2}(x/1.414)^2}$ by y_2, the calculations may be tabulated as follows:

x	x/σ	N/σ	y_1	y_2	$y = (N/\sigma) \cdot y_1 y_2$	y_x
−3	−2.12	13918	1.28403	.04217	754	512
−2	−1.41	13918	1.18531	.14764	2436	2304
−1	.71	13918	1.08329	.31006	4675	4608
0	0	13918	1.00000	.39894	5552	5376
1	.71	13918	.92312	.31006	3984	4032
2	1.41	13918	.84366	.14764	1734	2016
3	2.12	13918	.77880	.04217	457	672
4	2.83	13918	.71892	.00725	73	144
5	3.54	13918	.65705	.00076	7	18
6	4.24	13918	.60653	.00005	0	1

The histogram for y_x and the graph of y are given in Figure 33:

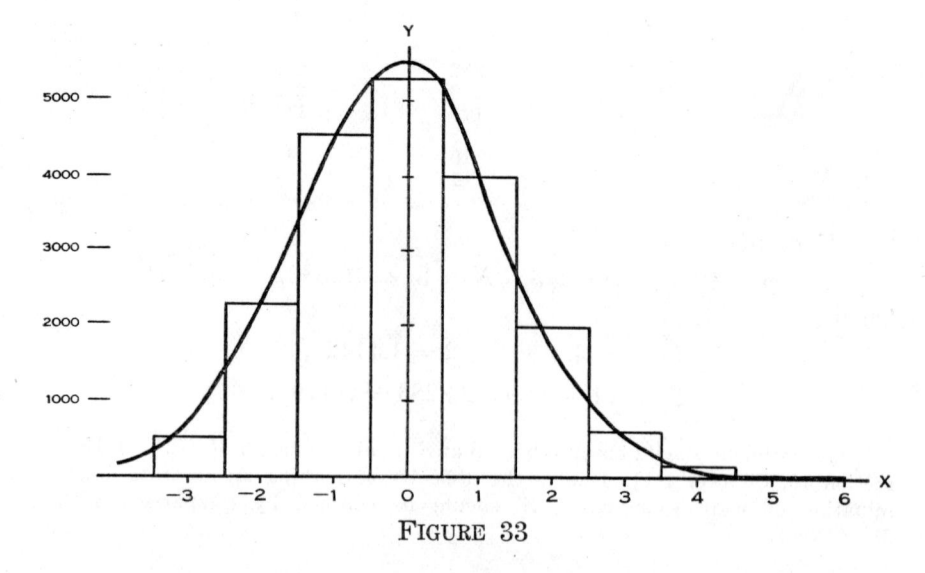

FIGURE 33

7. Application to the Graduation of Statistical Data. The problem that has just been solved is essentially one in curve fitting. Given a table of data, one is required to find a curve which will approximately fit the histogram. A great deal of work has been done in recent times in constructing a mathematical theory of curve-fitting which will apply especially to frequency histograms. Frequency distributions are usually, but not always, unimodal in character, although inherent peculiarities in the data often make it impossible to use the skew-normal curve for graduation. Two theories of curve fitting have arisen in attempts to generalize the skew-normal curve. One of these is due to Karl Pearson, the eminent English biometrician, who founded his theory upon a differential equation and developed seven types of curves, later increased to twelve types, which seemed admirably suited to the graduation of frequency distributions found in biological data.[1] The second theory is due to the Scandinavian statisticians and actuaries, Gram, Thiele, Westergaard, Charlier, Wicksell, and Jørgensen, and is well set forth in *Mathematical Theory of Probabilities* by Arne Fisher. The theory is not elementary in character, however, and depends upon a knowledge of the manipulation of series of so-called *orthogonal* functions. In this introductory treatment it is necessary to limit the discussion to the skew-normal curve, and if this will not graduate the distribution, the problem must be abandoned to higher methods. Some further account of this subject will be found in Chapter XII.

In further illustration of the principles of graduation of data, consider the following example.

Example: Fit a skew-normal curve to the data of table (b), (4-6 months prime commercial paper rates, January, 1922-December, 1931), as given in section 2, of Chapter III.

The Bernoulli mean and deviation are calculated to be 3.40 and 1.6 respectively, (see sections 4 and 6, Chapter III). The skewness, S', is then equal to $(1 - 6.80/7)/3.2 = .0089$. Keeping to the class marks 0, 1, 2, etc., one derives the skew-normal curve for these data to be (using equation 10),

$$y = \frac{108}{1.6} e^{-.0089(x-3.40)/1.60} \frac{1}{\sqrt{2\pi}} e^{-\frac{1}{2}[(x-3.40)/1.60]^2} .$$

---

[1] For a comprehensive treatment of the Pearson theory, see W. P. Elderton: *Frequency Curves and Correlation*, London, C. & E. Layton, 1906, 2nd. ed. (1927).

Designating $e^{-.0089(x-3.40)/1.60}$ and $\dfrac{1}{\sqrt{2\pi}} e^{-\frac{1}{2}[(x-3.40)/1.60]^2}$ by y_1 and y_2 respectively, the following table is calculated:

x	$(x-A)/\sigma$	N/σ	$-S'(x-A)/\sigma$	y_1	y_2	Graduates Frequencies $y = (N/\sigma) \cdot y_1 \cdot y_2$	Ungraduated Frequencies
0	−2.13	67.5	.02	1.02020	.04128	3	2
1	−1.50	67.5	.01	1.01005	.12952	9	8
2	−.88	67.5	.01	1.01005	.27086	18	23
3	−.25	67.5	.00	1.00000	.38667	26	30
4	.38	67.5	.00	1.00000	.37115	25	20
5	1.00	67.5	−.01	.99005	.24197	16	13
6	1.63	67.5	−.01	.99005	.10567	7	6
7	2.25	67.5	−.02	.98020	.03174	2	6

The histogram of the ungraduated frequencies and the graph for the graduated frequencies are given in the following Figure 34:

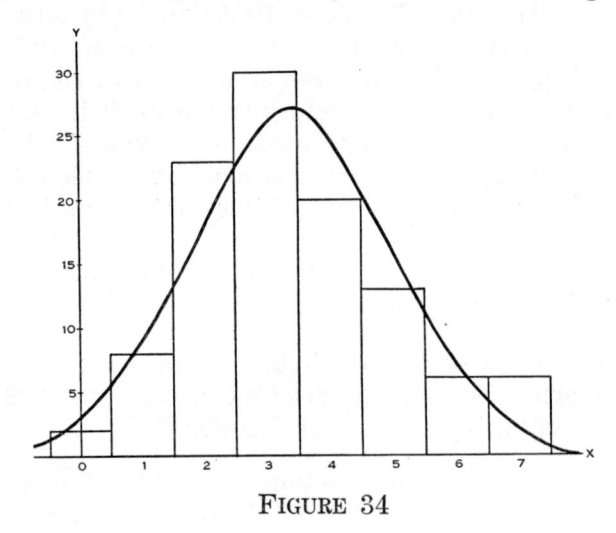

FIGURE 34

PROBLEMS

1. Calculate the mode for problem 1, section 9, Chapter I, on the assumption that it is a skew-normal distribution. How does this value compare with the value calculated by the formula for the mode given in section 10, chapter 3?

2. Compute the value of 10! and of 1000! by Stirling's formula.

BINOMIAL FREQUENCY DISTRIBUTION

3. Fit a skew-normal curve to the table obtained by using each term in the expansion of $(1+4)^5$ as a frequency.

4. Graduate the data of the following table, showing the percentage deviation from trend of Bradstreet's Index of General Prices for the pre-war period, 1897-1913:

Percentage Deviation from Trend	Class Marks	Frequency
− 15 to − 13	0	3
− 12 to − 10	1	6
− 9 to − 7	2	10
− 6 to − 4	3	31
− 3 to − 1	4	37
0 to 2	5	58
3 to 5	6	39
6 to 8	7	13
9 to 11	8	4
12 to 14	9	3

5. Graduate the following table, which shows the distribution of 1110 observations made on 149 commodity price series during ten business cycles:[1]

Duration of Cycle (from low to ensuing low) (in months)	Class Marks	Frequency
7.50-12.49	0	7
12.50-17.49	1	27
17.50-22.49	2	61
22.50-27.49	3	115
27.50-32.49	4	139
32.50-37.49	5	186
37.50-42.49	6	167
42.50-47.49	7	124
47.50-52.49	8	122
52.50-57.49	9	67
57.50-62.49	10	52
62.50-67.49	11	15
67.50-72.49	12	15
72.50-77.49	13	8
77.50-Over	14	5
Total		1110

6. The data in table (a), section 2, Chapter V, give the monthly and annual averages of mean weekly freight loadings, from January, 1919, to December, 1932. Choose proper class intervals and arrange the 168 items into a frequency distribution. Hint: Let the difference between the largest and smallest item form the range. Divide this range up into a convenient number of intervals and arrange the data into these classes. Test the distribution to see if it is either normal or skew-normal and make a table showing the graduation of the data.

---

[1] *The Behavior of Prices*, Frederick C. Mills, New York, 1927, Ch. IV.

7. Graduate the following data, which show the deviations from trend of bank clearings outside of New York City, from 1897 to 1913:

Deviations from Trend	Class Marks	Frequency
Over –17%	0	1
–16 to –14	1	1
–13 to –11	2	10
–10 to – 8	3	13
– 7 to – 5	4	15
– 4 to – 2	5	28
– 1 to 1	6	60
2 to 4	7	33
5 to 7	8	24
8 to 10	9	17
11 and Over	10	2
Total		204

8. Making use of the result of problem 9, section 2 and the expansion of M_3 as given in section 7, Chapter III, show that $M_3 = Nnpq(q-p)$. Hence show that $S' = M_3/(2N\sigma^3)$.

CHAPTER VIII

THE NORMAL FREQUENCY CURVE—PROBLEMS IN SAMPLING

1. The Meaning and Use of the Area under the Normal Curve.
In the last chapter, the formula was derived

$$y = \frac{N}{\sigma} e^{-S'x/\sigma} \frac{1}{\sqrt{2\pi}} e^{-\frac{1}{2}(x/\sigma)^2}, \qquad (1)$$

where N was the total frequency, σ the standard deviation calculated for the class marks $0, 1, 2, \ldots\ldots, n$, n one less than the number of class marks, and $S' = (1 - 2A/n)/2\sigma$, a measure of the skewness of the distribution. When $S' = 0$, the curve represents a normal symmetric distribution and is variously referred to as (a) the normal frequency curve, (b) the probability curve, (c) the Gaussian curve of error. The first two names are apparent from its derivation, the last is due to the work on it by Karl Friedrich Gauss (1777-1855), who was one of the first to point out that errors in observations could be treated by means of this curve.

It will be seen by referring to the work of the preceding chapter that the area of each rectangle of the histogram is equal numerically to the frequency which corresponds to the class mark attached to it. Thus in Figure 31 of Chapter VII, the frequency of the class mark 3 is 120. The total frequency is equal numerically to the total area of the histogram.

In a similar way, the total area under the normal curve is equal to the total frequency of the data represented by it. Hence, it is important to know the area included under the probability curve between the ordinates corresponding to $x = 0$ and $x = X$, where X is *any value*, because this area will be equal numerically to the sum of the frequencies corresponding to the class marks between 0 and X.

For convenience, the area under the curve,

$$y = \frac{1}{\sqrt{2\pi}} e^{-\frac{1}{2}t^2}, \qquad (2)$$

is tabulated for values of t from 0 to 4 in Table VII at the end of this book. To find from these tabulated values the area under the normal curve corresponding to a value of x, the following rule is used:

First, find in Table VII the area of (2) which corresponds to $t = x/\sigma$. This area will be designated by the symbol $I(t)$. The product of the value thus obtained by the total frequency N gives the desired area under the normal curve. It should be noticed from the symmetry of the function defined by (2) that the area for negative values of t is equal to the area for positive values of t, that is to say, $I(-t) = I(t)$.

Example 1. As an example, one may turn to the histogram given in Figure 31 of the preceding chapter and calculate the sum of the frequencies between the class marks $x = 0$ and $x = 2$ which correspond to the class marks $x = 5$ and $x = 7$ of the table. Since the class marks fall in the middle of the intervals, only half the initial and final frequency rectangles are to be used. The desired sum is then found to be equal to $126 + 210 + 60 = 396$. The area under the normal curve which approximates this value is calculated by finding in Table VII the area corresponding to $t = 2/\sigma = 2/1.58 = 1.266$, and multiplying the area thus found by the frequency 1024. Since t is given to three decimal places, it is necessary to interpolate in finding the value of $I(t)$. Thus, from the table, one has

$$I(1.26) = .39617$$
$$.00179 \text{ (First difference)}.$$
$$I(1.27) = .39796$$

Consequently $I(1.266) = .39617 + .6(.00179) = .39724$, and the desired frequency is this number multiplied by $N = 1024$, which gives 407 approximately.

Since the area under the normal frequency curve is exactly equal to N, and since a frequency histogram is essentially an area chart in which each frequency is represented by the area of a rectangle, the area function $I(t)$ may be used instead of the ordinate of the normal frequency curve for the graduation of data. If reference is made to Figure 31 of the preceding chapter, it is seen that the bounds of the frequency rectangle of the histogram are $-5.5, -4.5; -4.5, -3.5; -3.5, -2.5$; etc. In order to approximate the area of the rectangle between 2.5 and 3.5, for example, all that is needed is to subtract the product of N with the area function evaluated at the first station from the product of N with the area function evaluated at the second, or, in other words, to compute the difference $N I(3.5/\sigma) - N I(2.5/\sigma)$. This

THE NORMAL FREQUENCY CURVE 189

difference is easily found to be $1024\,[I(2.21) - I(1.58)] = 1024(0.48645 - 0.44295) = 44.54$, which is very close to the histogram area of 45.

The following table shows the graduation of the data of section 1, Chapter VII, where $N = 1024$ and $\sigma = 1.58$:

x	x/σ	$I(x/\sigma)$	$NI(x/\sigma)$	Graduated Frequency	Histogram Data
$-\infty$	∞	.50000	512.0		
-4.5	-2.85	.49781	509.8	2.2	1
-3.5	-2.21	.48645	498.1	11.7	10
-2.5	-1.58	.44295	453.6	44.5	45
-1.5	$-.95$	.32894	336.8	116.8	120
-0.5	$-.32$	.12552	128.5	208.3	210
0.5	.32	.12552	128.5	257.0	252
1.5	.95	.32894	336.8	208.3	210
2.5	1.58	.44295	453.6	116.8	120
3.5	2.21	.48645	498.1	44.5	45
4.5	2.85	.49781	509.8	11.7	10
∞	∞	.50000	512.0	2.2	1
Totals				1024.0	1024.0

Example 2. The skewness of the data given in the following table is not sufficient to invalidate approximate calculations based upon the assumption that a normal distribution is being dealt with:

DISTRIBUTION OF BRADSTREET'S COMMODITY PRICES (1897-1913)
(expressed as percentages of trend)

Percentage of Trend	Frequency	Percentage of Trend	Frequency
85%	1	100%	14
86	0	101	30
87	2	102	15
88	0	103	15
89	4	104	12
90	2	105	12
91	1	106	4
92	3	107	7
93	6	108	2
94	10	109	0
95	8	110	3
96	13	111	1
97	5	112	1
98	16	113	1
99	15	114	1

$N = 204,$ $\qquad A = 99.94,$ $\qquad \sigma = 4.934$.

It will be instructive to evaluate the sum of the frequencies from $x = 0$ to $x = 5$, where x is the percentage trend measured from the arithmetic mean. Since 5 is approximately equal to σ, this sum is given by

$$N I(5/\sigma) = N I(1) = 204(.34134) = 69.63 \ .$$

Since $A = 99.94$ and $\sigma = 4.934$, this frequency is equal approximately to the sum of the frequencies of the histogram from the percentage 100 to the percentage 105 on one side of the mean, and also from the percentage 100 to the percentage 95 on the other side. Since only half the frequencies of the two end values are to be included, these two sums, S_1 and S_2, are calculated to be

$$S_1 = 56.5 \ , \qquad S_2 = 80 \ ,$$
$$\tfrac{1}{2}(S_1 + S_2) = 68.25 \ .$$

2. *The Probable Error*. The *probable error* of a normal frequency distribution is a value x_0, so chosen that one half the total frequencies correspond to class marks lying between x_0 and $-x_0$.

The probable error can be readily obtained by interpolation from the table of areas, since, where x_0 is the probable error, x_0 will be equal to that value of t for which the area, $I(t) = 1/4 = .2500$. From Table VII the following values are given:

$$I(.67) = .24857$$
$$\qquad\qquad\qquad .00318 \text{ (first difference)}.$$
$$I(.68) = .25175$$

By interpolation,

$$t = .67 + \frac{.25000 - .24857}{.00318} = .6745 \ :$$

Thus, the following formula for the probable error is derived:

$$p.\ e. = .6745\sigma \ . \qquad\qquad (3)$$

Since .6745 is approximately 2/3, the probable error is often conveniently written $(2/3)\sigma$.

The significance of this formula will be clear from examples. Thus, in the data of example 2, section 1, of this chapter, the probable error is $.6745 \times 4.934 = 3.3280$. This means that any item chosen at random among the 204 has a "50-50" chance of ranging between $100 - 3 = 97$ and $100 + 3 = 103$ percent.

THE NORMAL FREQUENCY CURVE

As another example, consider the frequency distribution obtained when 9 coins are tossed 512 times and count kept of the number of times heads appeared on each toss. The probable error is calculated to be

$$p.\,e. = .6745 \times 3/2 = 1.01 \;.$$

This means that the chance is practicaly ½ that if 9 coins are tossed at random they will fall either 5 H, 4 T; or 4 H, 5 T. This probability is actually 63/128.

The probable error is one of the most important expressions in statistical study and considerable emphasis will be laid upon it in subsequent developments. Not a great deal of information is given about a distribution, for example, by stating merely the arithmetic average but considerable knowledge is derived from a statement of the arithmetic average and the probable error in combination, thus:

$$A \pm .6745\sigma \;.$$

One important fact that is easily proved is that a deviation from the mean of three times the probable error is very unlikely. Thus, if $x = 3(.6745\,\sigma) = 2.0235\,\sigma$, then $t = 2.0235$ and $2\,I(t) = 2(.47849) = .95698$. From this we derive the information that the probability is $1 - .95698 = .04302$ that a deviation will occur which is three times the probable error.

PROBLEMS

1. Calculate the values of the following: $I(1.32)$, $I(2.44)$, $I(-1.22)$, $I(0.237)$, $I(-1.268)$.

2. What is the probability that a statistical unit will lie outside of the interval $A \pm 1/2$ of its probable error? Within the interval $A \pm 3/2$ of its probable error? Outside of the interval $A \pm$ twice its probable error?

3. Using the method of areas, graduate the data of table (b), 4-6 months prime commercial paper rates, 1922-1931, as given in section 2, Chapter III. The average and standard deviation for this table are $A = 4.45$, $\sigma = .80$. Calculate the probable error.

4. From the data of problem 7, section 2, Chapter VII, compare the actual and theoretical probability of an index of seasonal variation of factory payrolls lying between the values of 97 and 105. Calculate directly from the data the probability that an index lies outside three times the probable error, and compare with the theoretical value derived above.

3. Probable Error Applied to Sampling. Any empirically derived table of frequencies may be conveniently thought of as being a *random* sample chosen from an ideal distribution, or *population*, whose total number of cases greatly exceeds that of the sample.

If one were to throw 10 coins 1024 times, for example, and record the frequencies corresponding to the number of heads thrown, the resulting table would be essentially a random sample of 1024 cases chosen from the ideal distribution which would result if the number of cases could be increased without limit.

In business, sampling is a common process used in arriving at the value of commodities. A car load of coal must be estimated with respect to size and quality by random sampling. A merchant cannot examine every bolt of cloth that is purchased, but by a proper selection of samples from the entire order he can assure himself of the average quality of the merchandise. It is not possible to go into details here about methods of sampling, because each problem has a technique of its own. The only general rule to follow is that of being sure that the sample is sufficiently large and chosen in such a way that it is perfectly random. If one bought apples by judging only from the size of those displayed, he might sometimes make a mistake, since some dealers display only the best of the lot.

The problem which can be dealt with statistically is that presented by the analysis of the sample once it has been properly chosen. With this in mind, suppose, for some ideal population of M individuals, where M is a very large number, that the frequency table is as follows:

FREQUENCY TABLE FOR AN IDEAL POPULATION

Frequencies	F_1	F_2	F_3	....	F_p
Class Marks	x_1	x_2	x_3	....	x_p

where $F_1 + F_2 + F_3 + \cdots\cdots + F_p = M$.

Next, suppose that a sample of N individuals is chosen from this population, and that the frequencies are recorded in the following table:

FREQUENCY TABLE FOR THE SAMPLE

Frequencies	f_1	f_2	f_3	....	f_p
Class Marks	x_1	x_2	x_3	....	x_p

where $f_1 + f_2 + f_3 + \cdots\cdots + f_p = N$.

THE NORMAL FREQUENCY CURVE 193

This very important problem is then considered: What is the probable error for the kth frequency, i.e., f_k, of the sample?

It is at once clear that, if a second sample of N individuals is taken from the ideal population, the kth frequency may have any one of the values from 0 to N. However, the probability is very much in favor of the value f_k, since that has already appeared in the first sample. For example, it is known that, if ten coins are tossed 1024 times, five heads will appear 252 times on the average. If some individual actually makes a toss of ten coins 1024 times, he may find that five heads appear 0 times or 1024 times. The probability is practically zero for these extreme cases, however, and the empirical figure should be close to 252. The probability in favor of 252 is high, the probabilities for 242 and 262 are lower, and the further one gets from 252, the smaller the chances become of getting that number for the frequency for 5 heads. If, then, the respective probabilities for each number between 0 and 1024 are calculated and graphed, it is evidently reasonable to assume that these probabilities will form a normal distribution about 252 as the average. The actual values of these probabilities will be, of course, the terms in the expansion of $(1/2 + 1/2)^{1024}$. Obviously, it would be foolish to attempt to calculate them. The purpose of this discussion is merely to show that one is dealing with a binomial frequency distribution to which the Bernoulli mean and the Bernoulli deviation apply.

Returning now to the general sample, it is seen that the most probable value for the frequency f_k is $M \cdot F_k/M$ and that the standard deviation of the probabilities attached to the numbers 0 to N is

$$\sigma = \sqrt{M \frac{F_k}{M}\left(1 - \frac{F_k}{M}\right)} = \sqrt{F_k\left(1 - \frac{F_k}{M}\right)} \ .$$

Thus, the highly important conclusion is reached that the probable error for an observed frequency is

$$.6745 \sqrt{F_k(1 - F_k/M)} \ .$$

In practice, of course, neither F_k nor M is known, but, if the sample is sufficiently large, F_k/M can be replaced by its approximate value f_k/N, giving

$$\sigma^2 \infty f_k(1 - f_k/N) \ . \tag{4}$$

The frequency of the kth group could then be written

$$f_k \pm .6745\sqrt{f_k(1 - f_k/N)} \ .$$

Example 1. If a student tosses 100 pennies and counts the heads, within what limits will his answer lie? In the ideal case a frequency of 50 heads would be expected. Hence, the probable error is

$$.6745\sqrt{50(1-50/100)} = 3.36 \ .$$

It is then very probable that the number of heads tossed will lie within the range $50 \pm 3(3.36)$. That is to say, it is unlikely that the student will throw more than 60 heads or fewer than 40.

Example 2. A coal dealer takes a hundred pound sample from 10 tons of coal and finds that in this sample there are 50 pounds of grade A coal worth $5.00 a ton, 30 pounds of grade B coal worth $4.00 per ton, and 20 pounds of grade C coal worth $3.00 per ton. Within what limits should the value of the coal be fixed?

Quite obviously, the true value of the coal must be somewhere between $30.00 and $50.00, since certainly all of it is neither grade A nor grade C. In order further to limit the values, one first calculates the probable errors of the samples and thus finds:

$p. e.$ for grade A $= .6745\sqrt{100 \cdot (50/100)(1-50/100)} = 3.37$,

$p. e.$ for grade B $= .6745\sqrt{100 \cdot (30/100)(1-30/100)} = 3.09$,

$p. e.$ for grade C $= .6745\sqrt{100 \cdot (20/100)(1-20/100)} = 2.70$.

Adding to and subtracting from the sample three times the probable error for each grade, the following upper and lower values for the three kinds of coal are found. These figures are expressed in percentages:

	Grade A	Grade B	Grade C
	[50±3(3.37)]	[30±3(3.09)]	[20±3(2.70)]
Upper Value:	60.11%	39.27%	28.10%
Lower Value:	39.89%	20.73%	11.90%

The highest value that can be placed upon the 10 tons of coal is that value for which grade A is the highest and C the lowest, that is,

Grade A = approximately 60%
Grade C = approximately 12%
―――――
72%

Grade B = 100% − 72% = 28% .

From the above figures, it is found that the maximum value of the coal is

$5 (60% of 10 tons) + $4 (28% of 10 tons) + $3 (12% of 10 tons)
= $30 + $11.20 + $3.60 = $44.80.

Similarly, the lowest value that can be placed on the coal is that value for which grade A is the lowest and grade C the highest, that is,

$$\text{Grade A} = \text{approximately } 40\%$$
$$\text{Grade C} = \text{approximately } 28\%$$
$$\overline{68\%}$$

Grade B = 100% — 68% = 32% .

From these figures, it is found that the minimum value of the coal is

$5 (40% of 10 tons) + $4 (32% of 10 tons) + $3 (28% of 10 tons)
= $20 + $12.80 + $8.40 = $41.20

The value of the coal can then be fixed within the limits $41.20 and $44.80.

4. Probable Errors of Various Statistical Constants. By arguments which are too long and difficult to be developed profitably in an introductory course, the probable errors of all the statistical constants can be calculated. As an example, the method of derivation of the probable error of the arithmetic mean will be given in the next section, although the theory is difficult at best and not essential for a proper understanding of the use and application of the result.

Since probable errors are of the very greatest importance in the application of the theory of statistics to practical problems, a few of them have been recorded below, together with some illustrations.

(1) p. e. of the arithmetic mean, $A_r = .6745\, \sigma/\sqrt{N}$.

(2) p. e. of the standard deviation (normal distribution), σ,
$$= .6745\, \sigma/\sqrt{2N} = .4769\, \sigma/\sqrt{N} \ .$$

(3) p. e. of the observed probability, p_1,
$$= .6745\sqrt{p_1(1-p_1)/N} \ .$$

(4) p. e. of the second moment about the mean (normal distribution), $M_2/N = .6745\ \sigma^2\sqrt{2/N} = .9539\ \sigma^2/\sqrt{N}$.

(5) p. e. of the third moment about the mean (normal distribution), $M_3/N = .6745\ \sigma^3\sqrt{6/N} = 1.6522\ \sigma^3/\sqrt{N}$.

(6) p. e. of the coefficient of variability, V,
$$= .6745\ V/\sqrt{2N}\ [1 + 2(V/100)^2]^{1/2}.$$

(7) p. e. in skewness $= .6745\ \sqrt{3/2N} = .8261/\sqrt{N}$.

(8) p. e. of the sum or difference of two independent variables x and $y = .6745\sqrt{\varepsilon_x^2 + \varepsilon_y^2}$, where ε_x and ε_y are the *standard errors*, that is to say, the *probable errors* divided by .6745.

For the probable errors associated with correlation coefficients, see (a), section 6, Chapter X; section 8, Chapter X; sections 6, 7, 8, and 9, Chapter XI.

Example 1. An industry desires to make a survey of the mean weekly wage of 10,000 of its workers. Since a study of all the workers is impossible, a representative sample of 400 workers is selected. The mean weekly wage of the 400 workers is $30.00 and the standard deviation $2.50. If additional samples were selected, by how much would the results differ from the above sample?

This can be determined by getting the probable error of the mean, which is
$$.6745(\$2.50)/\sqrt{400}) = .0843.$$

The mean weekly wage for any sample would then be given as
$$\$30.00 \pm .084.$$

Thus, one may conclude that if an additional sample of the same size were made, the chances would be even that its average wage would lie between $29.92 and $30.08.

Example 2. Calculate the probable error for the standard deviation of the above example.

Since $\sigma = 2.50$ and the number of items used in obtaining it was 400, the required probable error is
$$.4769(2.50/\sqrt{400}) = .060.$$

THE NORMAL FREQUENCY CURVE

This means that if the standard deviation for a similar group of workers is calculated it will quite probably lie within the limits: $2.50 + 3(.060) = 2.68$ and $2.50 - 3(.060) = 2.32$.

Example 3. A student tossed ten coins 1024 times and found that 5 heads appeared 260 times. What is the probability of tossing 5 heads in a single throw of ten coins?

The empirical probability is $p_1 = 260/1024 = .2539$. Consequently,

$$\text{p. e of } p_1 = .6745\sqrt{[.2539(1-.2539)]/1024} = .00917 .$$

This result can be used to calculate the probable error of the frequency, since this probable error is equal to the product of the total frequency with the probable error of the observed probability. One thus gets

$$\text{p. e. of } 260 = 1024 \times .00917 = 9.39 .$$

Since the *a priori* or expected frequency was 252, it is seen that the observed value is within the probable error, and hence is a very satisfactory number.

Example 4. The following table taken from the U. S. census for 1930 gives the number of women engaged in gainful occupation in various sections of the country. Is there a significant difference between labor conditions in New England and in the Mountain section?

	Total Female Population	Female Workers
New England	3,418,058	943,384
Middle Atlantic	10,744,622	2,643,177
E. N. Central	10,100,961	2,070,697
W. N. Central	5,267,133	948,084
S. Atlantic	6,127,071	1,476,624
E. S. Central	3,787,352	829,430
W. S. Central	4,646,581	864,264
Mountain	1,363,595	235,902
Pacific	3,307,034	767,232
Total	48,762,407	10,778,794

From the total figures it is seen that the average ratio of female workers to total female population for the United States is

$$p = 10,778,794/48,762,407 = .2210 .$$

Letting x refer to the New England and y to the Mountain section, the squares of the standard errors are calculated to be

$$\varepsilon_x^2 = pq/N_x = .2210(1 - .2210)/3{,}418{,}058 = .0000000504 \; ,$$
$$\varepsilon_y^2 = pq/N_y = .2210(1 - .2210)/1{,}363{,}595 = .0000001263 \; ,$$

Furthermore, the respective ratios in the two divisions are

$$p_x = 943{,}384/3{,}418{,}058 = .2760 \; ,$$
$$p_y = 235{,}902/1{,}363{,}595 = .1730 \; .$$

Consequently the probable error of the difference of the two ratios, i.e., .1030, is

$$.6745 \sqrt{.0000000504 + .0000001263} = .0004 \; .$$

Since the difference between the ratios of the two groups is far greater than three times the probable error, one can safely conclude that there is a marked difference in the employment status of women in these two sections of the country.

PROBLEMS

1. In tossing a hundred pennies a student gets 62 heads. Do you think that he has used sufficient care to obtain a random toss each time?

2. A life insurance company founded upon the *American Experience Table* has a thousand policies averaging $2,000 on lives at age 25. From the experience table it is found that of 89,032 alive at age 25, 88,314 are alive at age 26. Find the upper and lower values of the amount that the company will have to pay out in insurance during the year.

3. A man buys 1,000 sacks of potatoes. He finds that from 1,000 potatoes chosen from the sacks at random, 422 are of class A, worth $1.75 a sack; 252 are of class B, worth $1.50 per sack; 175 are of class C, worth $1.25 a sack; and 131 are of class D, worth $1.00 per sack. What are the upper and lower bounds for the value of the potatoes?

4. A group of scientific men reported 1,705 sons and 1,527 daughters. Do these figures conform to the hypothesis that the sex ratio is 1/2? (H. L. Reitz discusses this problem in his *Mathematical Statistics*, Chicago, 1927, p. 38. The figures are taken from the third edition of *American Men of Science*.)

5. The number of men and women in the censuses for 1920 and 1930 were found to be as follows:

	Men	Women	Total
1920	53,900,431	51,810,189	105,710,620
1930	62,137,080	60,637,966	122,775,046

Are these two samples consistent with each other? Hint: Calculate the probable error for each group. Within what limits would you place the sex ratio?

6. Are the data of problem 4 consistent with those of problem 5?

7. Within what limits is your average for problem 8, section 3, Chapter III correct?

8. What are the limits of error in the calculation of the standard deviation for example 2, section 1, of this chapter.

9. Calculate the probable error for the coefficient of variation for table (b), section 2, Chapter III.

10. What is the probable error for the second moment about the mean for the data of the distribution given in example 2, section 1, of this chapter?

5. Derivation of the Probable Error of the Mean. In a first approach to the theory of statistics, one might find it profitable to omit the derivation of the formula for the probable error of the mean, since the ideas and the mathematics that underlie it are by no means simple. However, the thoughtful student, after he has acquired a working knowledge of probable error and its application to practical problems, will wish to look deeper into the subject to see how one arrives at these formulas. It is to satisfy this very desirable curiosity that the following development is given, which is essentially a modification of a proof due to Karl Pearson.[1]

In order to derive the formula

$$\text{p. e. of the mean} = .6745\, \sigma/\sqrt{N},$$

let a second sample of N individuals be chosen from our ideal population (see the frequency tables of section 3) and its frequency table be written as follows:

FREQUENCY TABLE FOR THE SECOND SAMPLE

Frequencies	$f_1 + d_1$	$f_2 + d_2$	....	$f_p + d_p$
Class Marks	x_1	x_2	....	x_η

where $d_1, d_2, \ldots\ldots, d_p$ are deviations from the frequencies of the first sample.

The relations existing between the frequencies of the two tables must now be sought.

It will be clear that

$$d_1 + d_2 + \cdots + d_p = 0,$$

---

[1] *Biometrika*, Vol. II (1902), pp. 273-281, in particular p. 274.

because the sum of the frequencies of both samples is equal to N. This means that the sign of some of the deviations must be negative, since the gain in the frequency for one class mark must be accounted for by a deficiency in the frequency for another class mark.

If one frequency, f_j, has a positive deviation, d_j, it is reasonable to make the assumption that this error will be distributed among the other frequencies in proportion to their relative frequencies. Thus, the total frequency, exclusive of the frequency of the jth group, is $N - f_j$, so that the portion of d_j shared by the ith group will be

$$d_i = -d_j \frac{f_i}{N - f_j}.$$

From this relation the following derivation is made:

$$d_i d_j = -\frac{d_j^2}{N} \frac{f_i}{1 - (f_j/N)} = -\frac{d_j^2}{N} \frac{f_i f_j}{f_j[1 - (f_j/N)]},$$

or, since $f_j[1 - (f_j/N)] = \sigma_j^2$,

$$d_i d_j = -\frac{d_j^2}{N \sigma_j^2} f_i f_j. \qquad (5)$$

Returning now to the frequency distributions, the value of the mean for the first sample is found to be

$$A_1 = \frac{x_1 f_1 + x_2 f_2 + \cdots\cdots\cdots + x_p f_p}{N},$$

and for the second sample,

$$A_2 = \frac{x_1(f_1 + d_1) + x_2(f_2 + d_2) + \cdots\cdots + x_p(f_p + d_p)}{N}$$

$$= A_1 + \frac{x_1 d_1 + x_2 d_2 + \cdots\cdots\cdots + x_p d_p}{N}.$$

Calling the difference between the two means D_1, one has

$$D_1 = A_2 - A_1 = \frac{x_1 d_1 + x_2 d_2 + \cdots\cdots + x_p d_p}{N}.$$

Now, taking $m - 2$ new samples, so that there are m in all, the standard deviation of the different values of A, the mean, for this random set is sought. If it is assumed that the true mean does not

THE NORMAL FREQUENCY CURVE

differ greatly from the mean of the first sample, it is seen that the standard deviation for the m samples will be

$$\sigma_A^2 = \frac{D_1^2 + D_2^2 + \cdots\cdots + D_m^2}{m},$$

where D_k means the deviation of the mean of the kth sample from that of the first, i.e.,

$$D_k = A_k - A_1.$$

Denoting the deviations of the frequencies of the kth sample from the frequencies of the first by

$$d_1^{(k)}, \quad d_2^{(k)}, \quad \cdots\cdots, \quad d_p^{(k)},$$

one has

$$N^2 D_1^2 = x_1^2 d_1^2 + x_2^2 d_2^2 + \cdots + 2x_1 x_2 d_1 d_2 + 2x_1 x_3 d_1 d_3 + \cdots,$$

$$N^2 D_2^2 = [x_1 d_1^{(2)}]^2 + [x_2 d_2^{(2)}]^2 + \cdots\cdots + 2x_1 x_2 d_1^{(2)} d_2^{(2)} + 2x_1 x_3 d_1^{(2)} d_3^{(2)} + \cdots\cdots,$$

$$\cdot\quad\cdot\quad\cdot\quad\cdot\quad\cdot\quad\cdot\quad\cdot\quad\cdot\quad\cdot\quad\cdot\quad\cdot$$

$$N^2 D_m^2 = [x_1 d_1^{(m)}]^2 + [x_2 d_2^{(m)}]^2 + \cdots\cdots + 2x_1 x_2 d_1^{(m)} d_2^{(m)} + 2x_1 x_3 d_1^{(m)} d_3^{(m)} + \cdots\cdots.$$

But one has the following values:

$$\frac{d_1^2 + [d_1^{(2)}]^2 + \cdots\cdots\cdots + [d_1^{(m)}]^2}{m} = \sigma_1^2 = f_1(1 - f_1/N),$$

$$\frac{d_2^2 + [d_2^{(2)}]^2 + \cdots\cdots\cdots + [d_2^{(m)}]^2}{m} = \sigma_2^2 = f_2(1 - f_2/N),$$

etc.

It follows from formula (5) that

$$d_1 d_2 = -(d_1^2/N\,\sigma_1^2) f_1 f_2,$$
$$d_1 d_2 = -(d_2^2/N\,\sigma_2^2) f_1 f_2,$$

etc.

Substituting these values above and adding, one obtains

$$\frac{N^2(D_1^2 + D_2^2 + D_3^2 + \cdots\cdots\cdots + D_m^2)}{m} = N^2 \sigma_A^2$$

$$= x_1^2\sigma_1^2 + x_2^2\sigma_2^2 + \cdots\cdots + 2x_1x_2(-f_1f_2/N)$$
$$+ 2x_1x_3(-f_1f_3/N) + \cdots$$
$$= x_1^2f_1(1-f_1/N) + x_2^2f_2(1-f_2/N) + \cdots\cdots$$
$$+ 2x_1x_2(-f_1f_2/N) + 2x_1x_3(-f_1f_3/N) + \cdots$$
$$= x_1^2f_1 + x_2^2f_2 + \cdots\cdots + x_p^2f_p$$
$$- \frac{[x_1^2f_1^2 + x_2^2f_2^2 + \cdots + x_p^2f_p^2 + 2x_1x_2f_1f_2 + 2x_1x_3f_1f_3 + \cdots]}{N}$$
$$= x_1^2f_1 + x_2^2f_2 + \cdots\cdots + x_p^2f_p$$
$$- \frac{[x_1f_1 + x_2f_2 + \cdots + x_pf_p]^2}{N}.$$

Referring to formula (3), section 5, Chapter III, and setting $X = 0$, it is seen that the last value obtained above is identically equal to $N\sigma^2$, where σ is the standard deviation of the first sample.

Therefore, one obtains the result

$$N^2\sigma_A^2 = N\sigma^2, \text{ or } \sigma_A^2 = \frac{\sigma^2}{N}.$$

From this it follows that the probable error of the mean is equal to

$$.6745\, \sigma_A = .6745\, \frac{\sigma}{\sqrt{N}},$$

which is the desired result.

6. A Measure of Goodness of Fit. Suppose that to some frequency histogram derived from empirical data a normal frequency curve had been fitted by the method of this chapter and various statistical constants belonging to it had been calculated.

It would be very desirable to have a measure of faith in the results derived and, in particular, in the theoretical curve which had been fitted to the histogram. It would, of course, be perfectly possible in a mechanical way to fit a normal curve to any frequency table whatsoever. However, it would obviously be very foolish to try to fit a normal frequency curve to data that did not appear reasonably normal.

THE NORMAL FREQUENCY CURVE

One important contribution to modern statistical theory is the ingenious method that was devised by Karl Pearson to measure the goodness of fit between empirical and theoretical data.

Let P_p denote the probability that, in a random sample, deviations as great as, or greater than, the deviations between the empirical or observed and theoretical frequencies will occur. Such a probability, if it could be calculated, would be an excellent measure of faith in the agreement of the theoretical frequency curve with the empirical histogram to which it has been fitted. It seems appropriate to refer to P_p as the "Pearson Probability."

Let the theoretical and empirical frequencies be recorded symbolically in the following table:

Theoretical Frequencies	F_1	F_2	F_3	....	F_n
Empirical or Observed Frequencies	f_1	f_2	f_3	....	f_n
Class Marks	x_1	x_2	x_3	....	x_n

Supposing that none of the F_i's are zero, let the value of the following series be calculated.[1]

$$\chi^2 = (F_1 - f_1)^2/F_1 + (F_2 - f_2)^2/F_2 + (F_3 - f_3)^2/F_3 + \cdots + (F_n - f_n)^2/F_n \; .$$

If $\chi^2 = 0$, which means that the calculated and observed frequencies coincide exactly, one would then expect to find that $P_p = 1$ and, for χ^2 very large, that P_p was very nearly zero.

The function which Professor Pearson derived by rather elaborate means is the following:

(1) If n is even,

$$P_p = 1 - 2I(\chi)\sqrt{\frac{2}{\pi}} e^{-\chi^2/2} \left[\frac{\chi}{1} + \frac{\chi^3}{1 \cdot 3} + \frac{\chi^{n-3}}{1 \cdot 3 \cdot 5 \cdots (n-3)} \right],$$

(2) If n is odd,

$$P_p = e^{-\chi^2/2} \left[1 + \frac{\chi^2}{2} + \frac{\chi^4}{2 \cdot 4} + \cdots + \frac{\chi^{n-3}}{2 \cdot 4 \cdot 6 \cdots (n-3)} \right]$$

---

[1] The symbol χ is the Greek letter "chi," and the Pearson criterion is often referred to as the "chi square test."

where $I(\chi)$ is the value of the area function discussed in section 1 of this chapter.

As the values of this function are very tedious to calculate, they have been recorded for various values of n and χ^2 in Table VIII at the end of this book. The original table was calculated by W. P. Elderton in *Biometrika*, Vol. 1 (1902), pp. 155-163, and recomputed in 1932 by Anne M. Lescisin of the statistical laboratory of Indiana University.

It should be especially emphasized here that the theory of the "chi test" limits its application to data that are nearly normal. One should also exercise care in the handling of small frequencies, since it is in these extreme cases that the efficacy of the test seems to fail. A few examples follow:

Example 1. Test the following graduated frequencies for goodness of fit:

Theoretical	.2	.7	2.1	5.0	9.3	13.6	15.4	13.6	9.3	5.0	2.7	.7	.2
Observed	0	0	4	6	10	12	18	14	8	3	2	0	1
Class Marks	1	2	3	4	5	6	7	8	9	10	11	12	13

From these values one calculates

$$\chi^2 = (.2-0)^2/.2 + (.7-0)^2/.7 + (2.1-4)^2/2.1 \\ + \cdots + (.2-1)^2/.2 ,$$

$$= 8.63$$

and, since $n = 13$, it follows by interpolation from Table VIII that $P_p = .73337$. This means that in approximately 73 cases out of 100 a random sample will give deviations that exceed those of the observed data, which shows that the theoretical curve is a good representation of the observed data.

Example 2. The data for Table (b), section 2, Chapter III (4-6 months prime commercial paper rates), have been graduated in the illustrative example given in section 7 of the preceding chapter. The following frequencies are obtained. Does this represent a good fit?

THE NORMAL FREQUENCY CURVE

Graduated Frequencies	3	9	18	26	25	16	7	2
Observed Frequencies	2	8	23	30	20	13	6	6
Class Marks	0	1	2	3	4	5	6	7

It will be noticed that χ^2 will receive an abnormal addition if the last frequency is included, since $(6-2)^2/2 = 8$. Therefore, omitting this value, one has $\chi^2 = 4.15407$. Since $n = 7$, it is found by interpolation in Table VIII that $P_p = .65621$, which means that in 66 times out of a hundred a poorer fit than the one under discussion is to be expected.

The work of calculation can be arranged conveniently in tabular form as follows:

Class Marks	Graduated Frequencies F_i	Observed Frequencies f_i	$(F_i - f_i)$	$(F_i - f_i)^2$	$(F_i - f_i)^2/F_i$
0	3	2	1	1	.33333
1	9	8	1	1	.11111
2	18	23	-5	25	1.38889
3	26	30	-4	16	.61538
4	25	20	5	25	1.00000
5	16	13	3	9	.56250
6	7	6	1	1	.14286

$$\chi^2 = 4.15407$$

Example 3. When the data of the first table in section 1, Chapter VII were graduated by means of the ordinates of the normal curve and then by the area under the curve, it was found that slightly different results were obtained. Determine which of these graduations fits the data better.

The following frequencies have been given:

Observed Data (f)	1	10	45	120	210	252	210	120	45	10	1
First Graduation (F_1)	2	11	43	115	212	259	212	115	43	11	2
Second Graduation (F_2)	2	12	45	117	208	257	208	117	45	12	2
Class Marks	0	1	2	3	4	5	6	7	8	9	10

Calculating χ^2 for the first frequency data, one finds $\chi^2 = 3.02698$; similarly, for the second, $\chi^2 = 3.08730$. These two values for $n = 11$ lead to the Pearson probabilities, $P_p = .9805$ and $P_p = .9784$ respectively, which means that there is little to choose between the two graduations and that they are both excellent fits.

PROBLEMS

1. Ten coins are tossed 1024 times and the following frequencies observed:

No. of heads	0	1	2	3	4	5	6	7	8	9	10
Frequencies	2	10	38	106	188	257	226	128	59	7	3

How does this compare with a normal distribution?

2. Is the theoretical frequency curve which you obtained for problem 4, section 7, Chapter VII, a good fit to the observed data?

3. Test for goodness of fit the data which you have graduated for problem 7, section 7, Chapter VII.

4. Test the following data for goodness of fit (Volume of Trading on New York Stock Exchange, expressed as percentage of straight line trend, 1897-1913):

Observed Frequencies	11	35	50	48	24	15	9	7	3	1	1
Theoretical Frequencies	15	29	40	43	35	21	9	3	1	0	0
Class Marks	0	1	2	3	4	5	6	7	8	9	10

Here, $N = 204$. Is the theoretical frequency curve a good fit to the observed data?

7. The Theory of Errors—Least Squares. One important application of the normal curve has been made in the theory of errors. Suppose that, in a set of n observations, errors have occurred whose magnitudes, arranged in increasing order, may be represented by $d_1, d_2, \ldots, d_n$. If the number of observations is supposed to be very large and the errors equally likely to have occurred with either sign, then it is reasonable to assume that the frequencies $f_1, f_2, \ldots, f_n$, attached to the magnitudes $d_1, d_2, \ldots, d_n$, will form a normal distribution. It follows from this assumption that the probability that an error of magnitude d_k should have occurred in a single observation is

$$P_k = \frac{1}{\sigma\sqrt{2\pi}} e^{-d_k^2/2\sigma^2} \tag{6}$$

The thoughtful reader will not too readily accept this statement, for it may very justly be asked why errors should follow the law of normal distribution. The answer is that errors do not always follow the normal law, but that in a large number of cases, they are observed to do so. In any event, when, in ignorance as to the true distribution, some assumption must be made, this seems a reasonable one. It is pertinent, perhaps, to quote in this connection a famous remark once made by G. Lippman to H. Poincaré: "Everybody believes in the experimental law of errors; the experimenters because they believe it can be proved by mathematics, and the mathematicians because they think that it has been established by observation."[1]

The following illustration may give some experimental confidence in the assumption. W. J. Kirkham made a hundred sets of 1024 tosses of ten coins and recorded the frequencies which correspond to 0 head, 1 head, 2 heads, 3 heads, etc. For five heads the following frequencies were observed:

269; 258; 279; 225; 245; 287; 244; 260; 253; 237; 253; 231; 270; 264; 269; 240; 248; 259; 260; 251; 265; 250; 244; 261; 266; 283; 274; 262; 256; 274; 252; 251; 253; 232; 250; 266; 246; 230; 239; 264; 276; 261; 252; 265; 245; 263; 270; 260; 254; 247; 242; 268; 264; 252; 250; 273; 269; 253; 246; 249; 273; 240; 250; 258; 253; 262; 247; 232; 259; 279; 262; 254; 243; 247; 291; 254; 247; 240; 264; 246; 256; 263; 290; 280; 257; 252; 250; 268; 250; 255; 255; 253; 240; 245; 250; 253; 252; 242; 254; 259.

The expected value in every case was, of course, 252, so that the deviation from this number measures the extent of the error made. Taking as the range of error the deviations from −27 to +27, the errors can be classified in the following frequency table:

Magnitude of Error	Frequencies
Below −27	0
−27 to −22	2
−21 to −16	3
−15 to −10	8
− 9 to − 4	14
− 3 to 3	28
4 to 9	13
10 to 15	13
16 to 21	9
22 to 27	5
Above 27	5
Total	100

[1] H. Poincaré: *Calcul des probabilités*, Paris, 1896; second edition, 1912, p. 149.

It is at once seen that the mode is approximately 0 and the entire distribution is essentially normal with a slight skewness to the positive side.

Returning now to equation (6) and the distribution of errors, it may next be noticed that the probability that, in two observations, errors of magnitude d_j and d_k should both have occurred, since they are the errors of independent observations, must be

$$P_{jk} = (1/\sigma\sqrt{2\pi})\, e^{-d_j^2/2\sigma^2} (1/\sigma\sqrt{2\pi})\, e^{-d_k^2/2\sigma^2}$$
$$= (1/\sigma\sqrt{2\pi})^2 e^{-(d_j^2 + d_k^2)/2\sigma^2}$$

In general, the probability that all the n errors will occur, will be

$$P = (1/\sigma\sqrt{2\pi})^n\, e^{-(d_1^2 + d_2^2 + \cdots + d_n^2)/2\sigma^2}$$

Suppose that several individuals have made a set of independent observations and it is required to determine which of these sets is the most accurate. It is clear that the answer will be that set for which P has the largest value. This will be the set of errors which makes the exponent of e a minimum, or in other words, the values for which

$$d_1^2 + d_2^2 \cdots + d_n^2$$

has the smallest value. This is the fundamental assumption in the so-called *Method of Least Squares*, which will be applied in the theory of curve fitting in the next chapter.

One very important application immediately comes out of this assumption. Suppose that n observations have been made on an object whose true value is x and that these observations give the values $a_1, a_2, \cdots, a_n$. What is the most probable value of x?

This, by the method of least squares, is that value of x which makes the following expression a minimum:

$$d^2 = (x - a_1)^2 + (x - a_2)^2 + \cdots + (x - a_n)^2\,.$$

Squaring and collecting terms, one gets

$$d^2 = nx^2 - 2(a_1 + a_2 + \cdots + a_n)x + a_1^2 + a_2^2 + \cdots + a_n^2\,.$$

But this expression is a quadratic polynomial in x of the form

THE NORMAL FREQUENCY CURVE

$$ax^2 + bx + c, \quad a > 0,$$

which is known to assume its smallest value when x is equal to $-b/2a$.[1]

In the present case this gives us the very neat result

$$x = \frac{a_1 + a_2 + \cdots + a_n}{n},$$

or in other words;

According to the theory of least squares, the most probable value of a series of observations is the arithmetic mean of the observations.

Example: Using the first twenty-five frequencies in the coin tossing experiment recorded above, decide whether or not any bias entered, due either to irregularities in the coins used or to the method employed in tossing them.

The theoretical frequency expected was 252 and the probable error, using the methods of section 3, is easily calculated to be

$$.6745\sqrt{252(1 - 252/1024)} = 9.29.$$

But, from the result just obtained, the most probable frequency is the average, and this value, calculated from the first 25 numbers recorded, is equal to 255.52. The probable error of the mean computed from the formula p. e. $= .6745\ \sigma/\sqrt{N}$ is found for the present case to be $9.29/5 = 1.86$. Since this error is approximately half of the difference between the calculated and the theoretical value, one is justified in suspecting a slight bias in the experiment. This bias is further emphasized if the average for the entire 100 values is taken.

PROBLEMS

1. In the coin tossing experiment referred to above, the following frequencies for the case of four heads were recorded:

220; 195; 197; 206; 209; 200; 227; 201; 195; 209; 199; 217; 227; 207; 208; 233; 215; 232; 184; 220; 188; 225; 205; 200; 179; 187; 200; 212; 206; 210; 237; 221; 230; 232; 224; 217; 206; 209; 208; 205; 226; 204; 222; 239; 198; 205; 203; 226; 196; 225; 213; 206; 189; 218; 200; 198; 225; 199; 195; 211; 205; 226; 215; 219; 196; 204; 198; 186; 208; 208; 211; 213; 219; 212; 211; 210; 199; 221; 187; 209; 204; 202; 190; 172; 212; 211; 210; 200; 215; 202; 204; 203; 200; 202; 232; 212; 233; 224; 238; 216.

---

[1] See formula (3), section 7, Chapter II.

Calculate the deviations from the theoretical frequency 210 and determine whether or not they form a normal distribution. Also calculate the most probable value, and by means of the probable error of the mean decide whether or not bias existed in the experimental determination of the frequencies.

2. Three individuals measure a stick alleged to have a length of one meter (39.37) inches. Each takes five measurements. What is the most reliable set of measurements if the following are the recorded values?

A	39.37	39.38	39.40	39.36	39.35
B	39.37	39.37	39.38	39.38	39.38
C	39.35	39.38	39.39	39.36	39.37

3. What is the probable length of the stick of the above problem?

4. The following figures are the frequencies obtained in the first ten samples of the coin tossing experiment described above for the cases three heads and seven heads respectively:

Frequencies (3)	107 110 120 118 119 113 129 117 117 114
Frequencies (7)	112 132 112 131 118 101 112 115 132 134

Which set of frequencies is the most consistent? What is the most probable value for each? Do the two sets differ from one another in a significant manner?

5. Two persons, A and B, fitted a curve to the data recorded below, but their computed values did not agree. From the following results determine which one was wrong:

Data	168 17 12 18 25 29 36 43 51 63 81 117 166 239 349
A's calculation	144 59 17 4 8 21 37 49 61 71 86 111 156 233 357
B's calculation	145 55 14 4 13 30 48 63 73 81 91 111 152 229 358

For an able discussion of the problems of sampling theory and interesting applications to the control of quality of manufactured articles, see W. A. Shewhart, *Economic Control of Quality of Manufactured Product*, New York, 1931.

CHAPTER IX

CURVE FITTING

1. The Problem of Curve Fitting. The problem of *curve fitting* is the inverse of the problem of *graphing* or *curve plotting*. In the latter problem the equation of a curve is given and the geometrical figure required. In the problem of curve fitting one is given a set of points which define more or less approximately a geometrical figure and the equation of a curve is then sought which will exactly or approximately pass through these points.

The methods employed previously (See Chapters II, V, and VII) to determine a secular trend and to find a curve of normal distribution suitable for the representation of given frequency data are examples of curve fitting. It is the extension of these ideas which will be developed in this chapter. Two principal methods are in use for making the necessary calculations. The first is called *the method of least squares*, the second *the method of moments*.

To begin with, assume that a table of data has been given to which a curve of best approximation is to be fitted. These data may be represented as follows:

y	y_1	y_2	y_3	....	y_n
x	x_1	x_2	x_3	....	x_n

(1)

Unless otherwise specified, the values of x are to be regarded as equally spaced, $x_{i+1} - x_i = a$.

Obviously, the first problem that arises is that of finding the proper kind of curve to use. What geometrical figure will give a reasonable approximation to the series? Since there are many analytical formulas, graphs of which resemble one another, it is a matter of judgment and experience to decide which one to use. Sometimes the nature of the problem itself suggests the equation, but more often it is a matter of choosing the simplest formula that promises to give a reasonable approximation.

Lacking any *a priori* basis for a choice of curve, one can often find a guide in certain characteristic properties of a table of differences computed from the data.

Definition. By a *difference of the first order* of a function $f(x)$ at the point x will be meant

$$\Delta f(x) = f(x+d) - f(x) \; ;$$

by a *difference of second order*,

$$\Delta^2 f(x) = \Delta f(x+d) - \Delta f(x)$$
$$= f(x+2d) - 2f(x+d) + f(x) \; ;$$

by a *difference of n-th order*,

$$\Delta^n f(x) = \Delta^{n-1} f(x+d) - \Delta^{n-1} f(x)$$
$$= f(x+nd) - {}_nC_1 f(x+nd-d)$$
$$+ {}_nC_2 f(x+nd-2d) - \cdots + (-1)^n f(x),$$

where ${}_nC_r = \dfrac{n!}{(n-r)!\,r!}$ is the r-th binomial coefficient.

A table of differences can be conveniently represented as follows:

Argument	Tabular Value	Δ	Δ^2	Δ^3	Δ^4
....	....	....	....	....	....
$x-3d$	$f(x-3d)$		$\Delta^2 f(x-4d)$		$\Delta^4 f(x-5d)$
		$\Delta f(x-3d)$		$\Delta^3 f(x-4d)$	
$x-2d$	$f(x-2d)$		$\Delta^2 f(x-3d)$		$\Delta^4 f(x-4d)$
		$\Delta f(x-2d)$		$\Delta^3 f(x-3d)$	
$x-d$	$f(x-d)$		$\Delta^2 f(x-2d)$		$\Delta^4 f(x-3d)$
		$\Delta f(x-d)$		$\Delta^3 f(x-2d)$	
x	$f(x)$		$\Delta^2 f(x-d)$		$\Delta^4 f(x-2d)$
		$\Delta f(x)$		$\Delta^3 f(x-d)$	
$x+d$	$f(x+d)$		$\Delta^2 f(x)$		$\Delta^4 f(x-d)$
		$\Delta f(x+d)$		$\Delta^3 f(x)$	
$x+2d$	$f(x+2d)$		$\Delta^2 f(x+d)$		$\Delta^4 f(x)$
		$\Delta f(x+2d)$		$\Delta^3 f(x+d)$	
$x+3d$	$f(x+3d)$		$\Delta^2 f(x+d)$		$\Delta^4 f(x+d)$
....	....	....	....	....	....

There will now be listed a few equations which have proved useful in the application of curve fitting, together with a description of the characteristics of data to which they are applicable.

(1) The straight line,

$$y = a_1 + a_2 x \; ;$$

to be fitted to data for which the first difference is a constant.

(2) The parabola,
$$y = a_1 + a_2 x + a_3 x^2 ,$$
to be fitted to data for which the second difference is a constant.

(3) The general polynomial,
$$y = a_1 + a_2 x + a_3 x^2 + \cdots\cdots + a_{n-1} x^n .$$
When $n=1$, one has the straight line; $n=2$, the parabola; $n=3$, the cubic; $n=4$, the quartic or bi-quadratic; $n=5$, the quintic; $n=6$, the sextic; $n=7$, the septimic, etc.

The general polynomial of degree n is to be fitted to data for which the n-th difference is constant.

(4) The simple exponential curve,
$$y = ar^x , \text{ or } \log y = \log a + x \log r ,$$
to be fitted to data for which the first difference of $\log y$ is a constant.

(5) The exponential curve,
$$y = a_1 e^x + a_2 e^{-x} ,$$
to be fitted to data for which the points $\{y_{i+2}/y_i, y_{i+1}/y_i\}$ lie on a straight line. This is seen to be the case if one considers the equations
$$y_{i+2}/y_i = (e^d + e^{-d}) y_{i+1}/(y_i) - 1 ,$$
where d is the class interval.

(6) The logarithmic curve,
$$y = a_1 + a_2 \log x ,$$
to be fitted to data for which Δy tends to approach $-k/x$ as x increases, where k is a constant.

(7) The simple parabolic curve,
$$y = ax^b, \text{ or } \log y = \log a + b \log x ,$$
to be fitted to data which form a straight line on double logarithmic paper (See example 2 in section 3).

(8) The logistic curve,
$$y = k/(1 + be^{ax}) ,$$
to be fitted to data representing growth.

These various curves are illustrated in Figure 35.

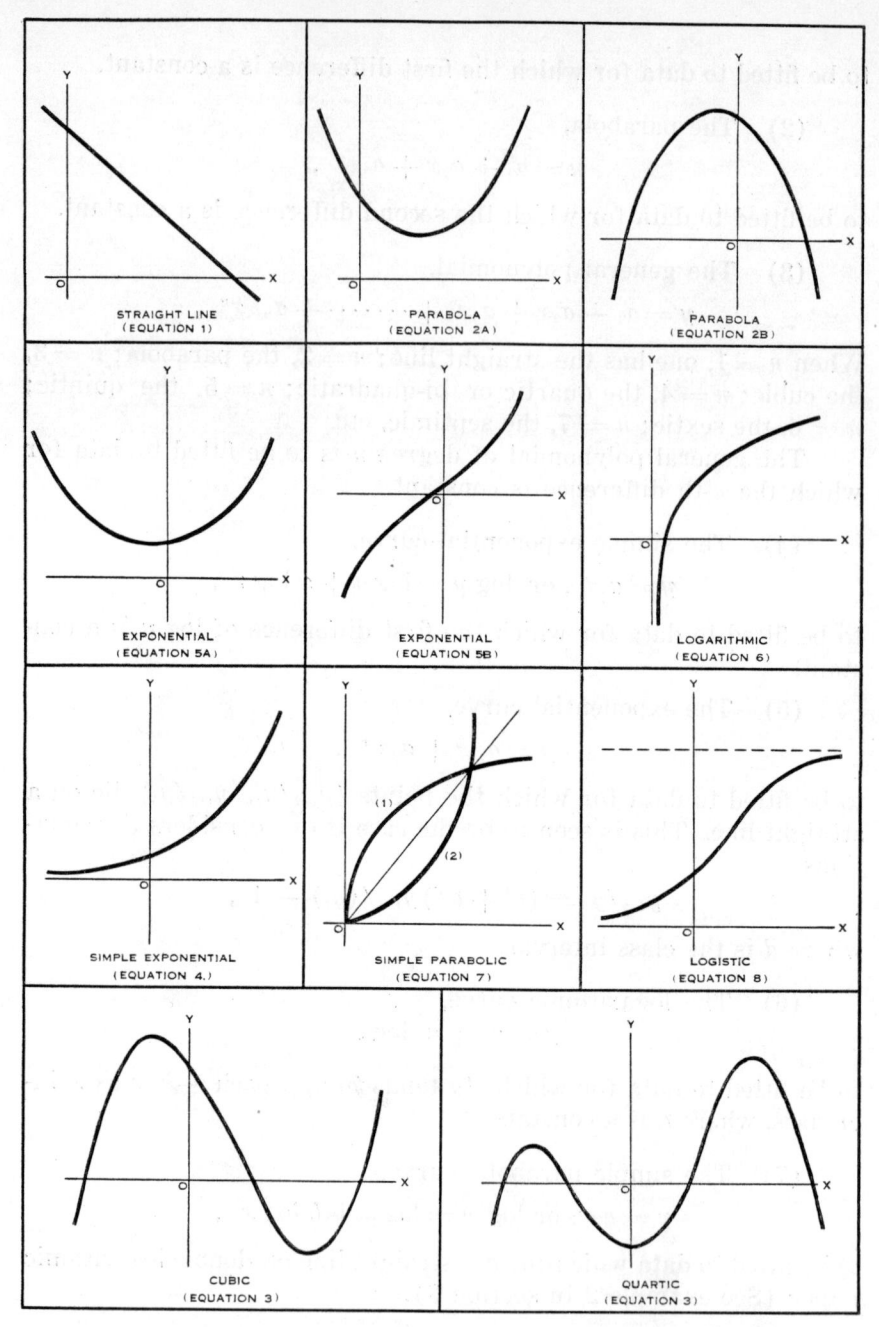

FIGURE 35. Various types of curves. For the straight line (Equation 1), a_2 is negative. In the parabola of Equation 2A, a_3 is positive, in 2B negative. In the exponential of Equation 5A, a_1 and a_2 are the same in sign, $a_1 > 0$; in 5B, a_1 and a_2 are different in sign and $a_{1'} > 0$. In the two curves of Equation 7, in (1) $b < 1$, in (2) $b > 1$.

2. The Method of Least Squares.

Suppose, now, that a choice has been made of the proper curve to fit to the data, and suppose that it contains n arbitrary constants. This can be stated symbolically by writing the equation of the curve as follows:

$$y = f(x, a_1, a_2, \cdots, a_n) \ .$$

How are the constants to be determined? One method in common use is that of least squares. *The fundamental principle of this method is that the constants are to be so determined that the sum of the squares of the deviations of the empirical values from the corresponding ordinates of the curve is to be made as small as possible* (See Chapter VIII, section 7). Referring to Figure 36, one sees that this statement means that the sum,

$$S = d_1^2 + d_2^2 + \cdots\cdots + d_p^2 \ ,$$

is to be made a minimum.

The problem of actually determining the value of the constants according to the principle of least squares is, in the general case, a very difficult one to solve. However, great simplification is introduced if the assumption is made that the constants enter *linearly*, in other words, if $y = a_1 A_1(x) + a_2 A_2(x) + \cdots + a_n A_n(x)$, where $A_1(x)$, $A_2(x)$, etc., are known functions determined upon when the choice of a curve was made. For example, if one had decided to fit a straight line to the given data, then one should have had $A_1(x) = 1$ and $A_2(x) = x$; if one had decided upon the exponential curve,

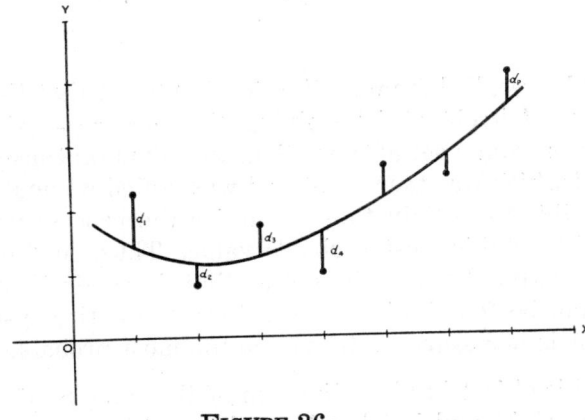

FIGURE 36.

then $A_1(x) = e^x$, and $A_2(x) = e^{-x}$; if the logarithmic curve, then $A_1(x) = 1$, and $A_2(x) = \log x$.

Before proceeding to applications, it will be desirable to have a literal solution of the problem, and for the sake of simplicity the case of two unknowns only will be considered. The general case follows without essential alteration.

The problem to be considered, then, is that of fitting a curve of the form,

$$y = a_1 A_1(x) + a_2 A_2(x),$$

to the following set of p points:

y	y_1	y_2	y_3	$\cdots$	y_p
x	x_1	x_2	x_3	$\cdots$	x_p

If, in the equation just written down, x and y are replaced successively by the values given in the table, the following set of p equations will be obtained from which the values of a_1 and a_2 are to be found;

$$y_1 = a_1 A_1(x_1) + a_2 A_2(x_2),$$
$$y_2 = a_1 A_1(x_2) + a_2 A_2(x_2),$$
$$\cdot \qquad \cdot \qquad \cdot$$
$$y_p = a_1 A_1(x_p) + a_2 A_2(x_p).$$

It will be recalled from section 5, Chapter II that the problem there presented itself of determining the *most probable value* of two constants from a set of more than two simultaneous equations. The method which was then employed was stated without proof. It is now possible to explain the reason for the process used in the determination of this most probable value. Thus, confronted by p equations in two unknowns, it is clear that, in general, values of a_1 and a_2 cannot be found which will satisfy the entire system. Consequently, it is necessary to determine the most probable values.

With this object in view, the sum of the squares of the differences of the right and left hand members of the set of equations

CURVE FITTING

are now found and the following quadratic expressions thus obtained:

$$D^2 = \{y_1 - [a_1 A_1(x_1) + a_2 A_2(x_1)]\}^2$$
$$+ \{y_2 - [a_1 A_1(x_2) + a_2 A_2(x_2)]\}^2$$
$$+ \cdots + \{y_p - [a_1 A_1(x_p) + a_2 A_2(x_p)]\}^2 \ .$$

Expanding each term of this square and collecting the coefficients of a_1, one obtains the following quadratic expression in a_1:

$$D^2 = \{A_1^2(x_1) + A_1^2(x_2) + \cdots\cdots + A_1^2(x_p)\}a_1^2$$
$$-2\{A_1(x_1)y_1 + A_1(x_2)y_2 + \cdots\cdots + A_1(x_p)y_p$$
$$+ [A_1(x_1)A_2(x_1) + A_1(x_2)A_2(x_2) + \cdots + A_1(x_p)A_2(x_p)]a_2\}a_1$$
$$+ \text{ other terms which do not contain } a_1.$$

It is now recalled from section 7, Chapter II that the minimum value of the quadratic expression,

$$y = ax^2 + bx + c \ ,$$

is obtained when $x = -b/2a$.

Applying this result to the quadratic expression above, in which a_1 is regarded as the variable quantity, one then finds as the most probable value for a_1,

$$a_1 = \{A_1(x_1)y_1 + A_1(x_2)y_2 + \cdots + A_1(x_p)y_p$$
$$+ [A_1(x_1)A_2(x_1) + A_1(x_2)A_2(x_2) + \cdots$$
$$+ A_1(x_p)A_2(x_p)]a_2\}/\{A_1^2(x_1) + A_1^2(x_2) + \cdots$$
$$+ A_1^2(x_p)\} \ . \tag{2}$$

This equation can be greatly simplified in formal appearance by use of the following customary abbreviation:

$$[A_i A_j] = A_i(x_i)A_j(x_1) + A_i(x_2)A_j(x_2) + \cdots + A_i(x_p)A_j(x_p) \ ,$$
$$[A_i y] = A_i(x_1)y_1 + A_i(x_2)y_2 + \cdots + A_i(x_p)y_p \ ,$$

where i and j may have either of the values 1 or 2. Making use of these abbreviations, equation (2), by transposition, will become,

$$[A_1 A_1]a_1 + [A_1 A_2]a_2 = [A_1 y] \ .$$

If the second constant, a_2, is treated in a like manner, a second equation is obtained which, together with the one just written down, forms a set of two linear equations from which a_1 and a_2 can be determined by the ordinary method of algebra. The name of *normal equations* has been applied to this system, which, for the special case under consideration becomes,

$$[A_1A_1]a_1 + [A_1A_2]a_2 = [A_1y] ,$$
$$[A_2A_1]a_1 + [A_2A_2]a_2 = [A_2y] . \quad (3)$$

The generalization to the case where n arbitrary constants appear in the least square curve, i.e., where

$$y = a_1A_1(x) + a_2A_2(x) + \cdots + a_nA_n(x) ,$$

is easily made, and one obtains for the normal equations in this case the following system:

$$[A_1A_1]a_1 + [A_1A_2]a_2 + \cdots + [A_1A_n]a_n = [A_1y] ,$$
$$[A_2A_1]a_1 + [A_2A_2]a_2 + \cdots + [A_2A_n]a_n = [A_2y] , \quad (4)$$
$$\cdots \cdots \cdots \cdots \cdots \cdots \cdots$$
$$[A_nA_1]a_1 + [A_nA_2]a_2 + \cdots + [A_nA_n]a_n = [A_ny] .$$

The application of the theory just developed to actual data can best be illustrated by examples, a few of which follow.

3. *Examples Illustrating the Method of Least Squares.*

Example 1. The following table gives the fire losses in the United States in millions of dollars over a period of eleven years. Fit a straight line to the data.

Fire Losses	172 258 290 259 321 448 495 507 535 549 570
Years	1915 1916 1917 1918 1919 1920 1921 1922 1923 1924 1925

Since a straight line is to be fitted to these data, the problem is that of calculating the constants a_1 and a_2 in the equation $y = a_1 + a_2x$. Hence, the functional multipliers are $A_1(x) = 1$ and $A_2(x) = x$, since these functions are the coefficients of the constants a_1 and a_2 respectively.

CURVE FITTING

When the obvious simplification is made of changing to positive integers for class marks instead of using the year numbers, the work of calculation can be tabulated as follows:

Years	Class Marks (x)	Losses (y)	$A_1(x)$	$A_2(x)$	$A_1 y$	$A_2 y$	$A_1 A_1$	$A_1 A_2$	$A_2 A_2$
1915	1	172	1	1	172	172	1	1	1
1916	2	258	1	2	258	516	1	2	4
1917	3	290	1	3	290	870	1	3	9
1918	4	259	1	4	259	1036	1	4	16
1919	5	321	1	5	321	1605	1	5	25
1920	6	448	1	6	448	2688	1	6	36
1921	7	495	1	7	495	3465	1	7	49
1922	8	507	1	8	507	4056	1	8	64
1923	9	535	1	9	535	4815	1	9	81
1924	10	549	1	10	549	5490	1	10	100
1925	11	570	1	11	570	6270	1	11	121
Totals					4404	30983	11	66	506

From the totals one obtains the values $[A_1 A_1] = 11$, $[A_1 A_2] = [A_2 A_1] = 66$, $[A_2 A_2] = 506$, and these substituted in the normal equations yield the system,

$$11a_1 + 66a_2 = 4404 ,$$
$$66a_1 + 506a_2 = 30983 .$$

Calculating a_1 and a_2, one obtains $a_1 = 151.69$ and $a_2 = 41.45$. The desired straight line thus becomes,

$$y = 151.69 + 41.45x .$$

The following table shows the closeness of agreement between the observed and calculated values. This agreement is shown graphically in Figure 37.

y (observed)	172	258	290	259	321	448	495	507	535	549	570
y (calculated)	193	235	276	317	359	400	442	483	525	566	608
x	1	2	3	4	5	6	7	8	9	10	11

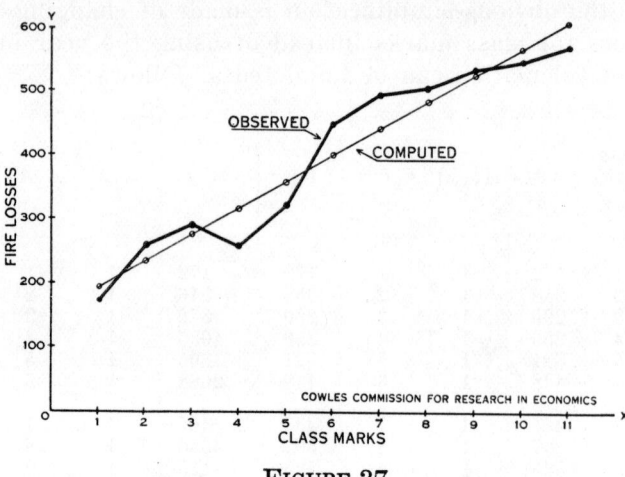

FIGURE 37

Example 2. An interesting illustration of the use of the parabolic curve $y = ax^b$, is found in the problem of the distribution of incomes. The so-called *law of Pareto,* an empirical assertion made by V. Pareto (1848-1923) in an attempt to formulate a mathematical expression which would describe the frequency distribution of incomes in all places and at all times, closely, elegantly, and, if possible, rationally, states that, if x is the size of the income and y the number of people having that income or larger, then the parabolic curve will fit the income data and b will be approximately —1.5.[1]

The following summary (condensed) is taken from the extensive study of incomes in the United States, published by the National Bureau of Economic Research in 1921, for incomes in 1919.[2]

---

[1] See Pareto, *Cours d'économie politique,* Vol. 2, pp. 306-307. A discussion of this law is given in *The Economics of Welfare,* by A. C. Pigou, London, second edition, 1924, Chap. 2, Part 4, pp. 605-613, and in *Income in the United States—Its Amount and Distribution 1909-1919,* Vol. II, National Bureau of Economic Research, New York, 1922, pp. 344-394.

[2] *Income in the United States, Its Amount and Distribution, 1909-1919,* Vol. I, *op. cit.*

Income Class	Class Mark (x)	No. of Persons (y)	Amount of Income
Under Zero	- - -	200,000	$ −125,000,000
0- 500	250	1,827,554	685,287,806
500- 1,000	750	12,530,670	9,818,678,617
1,000- 1,500	1250	12,498,120	15,295,790,534
1,500- 2,000	1750	5,222,067	8,917,648,335
2,000- 3,000	2500	3,065,024	7,314,412,994
3,000- 5,000	4000	1,383,167	5,174,090,777
5,000- 10,000	7500	587,824	3,937,183,313
10,000- 25,000	17500	192,062	2,808,290,063
25,000- 50,000	37500	41,119	1,398,785,687
50,000- 100,000	75000	14,011	951,529,576
100,000- 200,000	150000	4,945	671,565,821
200,000- 500,000	250000	1,976	570,019,200
500,000-1,000,000	750000	369	220,120,399
1,000,000 and over	- - -	152	316,319,219
Totals		37,569,060	$57,954,722,341

Class Mark (x)	Percentage No.	Percentage Amt.	Cumulative Distribution (Percentage) No.	Cumulative Distribution (Percentage) Amt.
- - -	.53	−.22	.53	−.22
250	4.86	1.18	5.39	.96
750	33.35	16.94	38.74	17.90
1250	33.27	26.40	72.01	44.30
1750	13.90	15.39	85.91	59.69
2500	8.16	12.62	94.07	72.31
4000	3.68	8.93	97.75	81.24
7500	1.57	6.79	99.32	88.03
17500	.51	4.85	99.83	92.88
37500	.11	2.41	99.94	95.29
75000	.04	1.64	99.98	96.93
150000	.01	1.16	99.99	98.09
250000	.01	.98	100.00	99.07
750000	.00	.38	100.00	99.45
- - -	.00	.55	100.00	100.00
Totals	100.00	100.00		

From these data the following table of cumulative frequencies is formed, the two lowest classes being omitted. The class mark (x) has been arbitrarily chosen as the center of the class interval.

Income x	Cumulative frequency y (unit 1000)	$\log x$	$\log y$	$(\log x) \cdot (\log y)$	$(\log x)^2$
750	35541	2.87506	4.55073	13.08362	8.26597
1250	23010	3.09691	4.36192	13.50847	9.59085
1750	10512	3.24304	4.02169	13.04250	10.51731
2500	5290	3.39794	3.72346	12.65209	11.54600
4000	2225	3.60206	3.34733	12.05728	12.97484
7500	842	3.87506	2.92531	11.33575	15.01609
17500	254	4.24304	2.40483	10.20379	18.00339
37500	62	4.57403	1.79239	8.19845	20.92175
75000	21	4.87506	1.32222	6.44590	23.76621
150000	7	5.17609	.84510	4.37431	26.79191
250000	2	5.39794	.30103	1.62494	29.13776
Totals	77766	44.35623	29.59601	106.52710	186.53208

From the totals the following normal equations are then obtained:

$$11a_1 + 44.35623 a_2 = 29.59601,$$
$$44.35623 a_1 + 186.53208 a_2 = 106.52710,$$

from which are computed,

$$a_1 = 9.42721 = \log a, \qquad a_2 = -1.67064 = b.$$

The desired curve, in logarithmic form, is thus found to be,

$$\log y = 9.42721 - 1.67064 \log x,$$

from which the following table has been computed for comparison:

Income x	y observed	y computed
750	35541	42075
1250	23010	17922
1750	10512	10216
2500	5290	5630
4000	2225	2567
7500	842	898
17500	254	218
37500	62	61
75000	21	19
150000	7	6
250000	2	3

CURVE FITTING

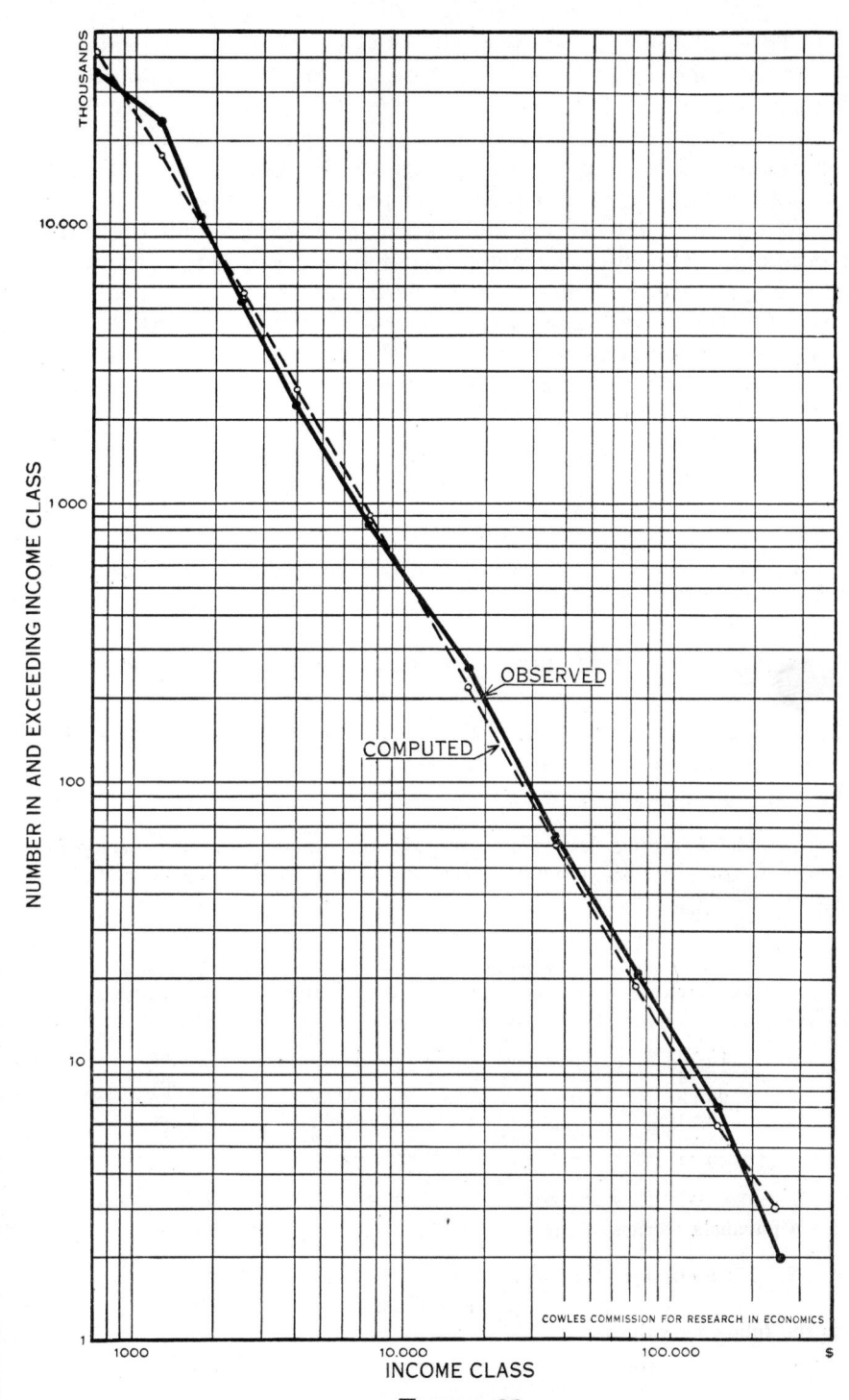

FIGURE 38

To exhibit the closeness of fit between the observed values of y and the computed values of y, these values are plotted on double logarithmic paper. By *double logarithmic paper* is meant graphing paper in which the rules on both axes are spaced according to the logarithms of the numbers. Figure 38 shows the income data graphed on this type of paper. The paper in Figure 38 has four *cycles* on the vertical axis and approximately three on the horizontal axis. The chief characteristic of such paper is that the units of one cycle are ten times as large as the units of the immediately preceding cycle. On such paper one is able to represent data in which the range is very great, as in the present example. Also, on such paper data to which the parabolic curve may be fitted are always represented by an approximately straight line.

PROBLEMS

1. The commodity price index, using 1926 as the base, i.e., 100 per cent, has been estimated as follows:

Year	1921	1922	1923	1924	1925	1926	1927	1928	1929	1930
Price Index	98	97	101	98	104	100	95	97	95	86

Fit a straight line to these data.

2. The following figures give the average annual earning capacity for five-year age intervals. (Adapted from the U.S. Bureau of Labor Statistics, Bulletin 359):

Age Group	Earning Capacity	Age Group	Earning Capacity
15-19	.56	45-49	.93
20-24	.71	50-54	.86
25-29	.84	55-59	.76
30-34	.92	60-64	.66
35-39	.97	65-69	.56
40-44	.98	70-74	.46

Fit a parabola to these figures.

3. Fit a curve of the form
$$y = a\,2^x + b\,2^{-x}$$
to the following values:

CURVE FITTING

y	4	2	1	3	5
x	-2	-1	0	1	2

4. Fit a curve of the form
$$y = a\,e^x + b\,e^{-x}$$
to the following table of values:

y	-8	-2	1	5	15
x	-2	-1	0	1	2

5. The total number of passenger automobiles and trucks produced in the United States from 1916 to 1930 was as follows:

Year	Number in millions	Year	Number in millions
1916	1.6	1924	3.7
1917	1.9	1925	4.4
1918	1.2	1926	4.5
1919	1.9	1927	3.6
1920	2.2	1928	4.6
1921	1.7	1929	5.6
1922	2.6	1930	3.5
1923	4.2		

Fit a straight line to this table and graph the observed and computed values.

6. The following data on national income in 1929 have been given by V. von Szeliski [See *Econometrica*, Vol. II (1934), pp. 215-216]:

INCOME DISTRIBUTION BY INCOME CLASSES
1929

Income Class	Number in Each Class	Cumulative	Per cent	Income in Millions	Cumulative	Per cent
Under $1,000	15,472,560	48,500,000	100.0	$9,567	$90,500	100.0
1,000- 2,000	20,117,510	33,027,440	68.1	29,487	80,933	89.4
2,000- 3,000	8,962,940	12,909,930	26.6	21,462	51,446	56.8
3,000- 4,000	1,994,920	3,946,990	8.13	6,773	29,984	33.1
4,000- 5,000	720,210	1,952,070	4.02	3,216	23,211	25.6
5,000- 10,000	770,909	1,231,860	2.54	5,339	19,995	22.1
10,000- 25,000	339,871	460,951	0.950	5,032	14,656	16.2
25,000- 50,000	77,039	121,080	0.250	2,623	9,624	10.6
50,000- 100,000	28,021	44,041	0.0909	1,908	7,001	7.73
100,000- 250,000	11,648	16,020	0.0330	1,749	5,093	5.63
250,000- 500,000	2,842	4,372	0.00891	911	3,334	3.70
500,000-1,000,000	973	1,530	0.00316	663	2,433	2.68
1,000,000 and over	557	557	0.00115	1,770	1,770	1.96

Graduate these data by the law of Pareto and estimate the accuracy of this law in its relation to these figures.

4. Simplification when the Curve is a Polynomial. Considerable simplification in the normal equations (4) can be made when the curve to be fitted is of the form:

$$y = a_1 + a_2 x + a_3 x^2 \cdots + a_n x^{n-1} ,$$

Suppose that the class marks are taken to be,

$$x_1 = 1 , \quad x_2 = 2 , \quad \cdots , \quad x_p = p ,$$

which can be done in most problems by properly choosing the unit.

Then, since

$$A_1(x) = 1 , \quad A_2(x) = x , \quad A_3(x) = x^2 , \quad \cdots ,$$
$$A_n(x) = x^{n-1} ,$$

one has

$$[A_1 A_1] = 1 + 1 + \cdots + 1 ,$$
$$[A_1 A_2] = 1 + 2 + \cdots + p ,$$
$$[A_1 A_n] = 1^{n-1} + 2^{n-1} + \cdots + p^{n-1} ,$$

and, in general,

$$[A_{i+1} A_{j+1}] = 1^i 1^j + 2^i 2^j + \cdots + p^i p^j$$
$$= 1^{i+j} + 2^{i+j} + \cdots + p^{i+j} .$$

It follows from this that if the following abbreviations are employed:

$$s^r = 1^r + 2^r + \cdots + p^r ,$$
$$[A_1 y] = y_1 + y_2 + y_3 + \cdots + y_p = m_0 ,[1]$$
$$[A_2 y] = 1 \cdot y_1 + 2 \cdot y_2 + 3 \cdot y_3 + \cdots + p \cdot y_p = m_1 , \qquad (5)$$
$$[A_3 y] = 1^2 y_1 + 2^2 y_2 + 3^2 y_3 + \cdots + p^2 y_p = m_2 ,$$
$$\cdot \qquad \cdot \qquad \cdot \qquad \cdot \qquad \cdot \qquad \cdot$$
$$[A_r y] = 1^r y_1 + 2^r y_2 + 3^r y_3 + \cdots + p^r y_p{}^r = m_r ,$$

---

[1] Recall that these values are the respective moments of the data. These are discussed in section 7, Chapter III, and applied further to curve fitting in section 8 of this chapter.

CURVE FITTING

the normal equations reduce to the following system:

$$s_0 a_1 + s_1 a_2 + \cdots + s_{n-1} a_n = m_0 ,$$
$$s_1 a_1 + s_2 a_2 + \cdots + s_n a_n = m_1 , \qquad (6)$$
$$\cdot \quad \cdot \quad \cdot \quad \cdot \quad \cdot$$
$$s_{n-1} a_1 + s_n a_2 + \cdots + s_{2n-2} a_n = m_{n-1} .$$

This leads one to enquire about the formula for the sum s_r. It is apparent that $s_0 = p$, and it is proved in elementary algebra under arithmetic progression that

$$s_1 = \tfrac{1}{2} p(p+1) .$$

The formulas for s_r, for other values of r, can be calculated from the identity,

$$(p+1)^{r+1} - 1 \equiv {}_{r+1}C_1 s_r + {}_{r+1}C_2 s_{r-1} + \cdots\cdots + {}_{r+1}C_r s_1 + s_0 ,$$

where the ${}_{r+1}C_i$ are the binomial coefficients, i.e.,

$${}_{r+1}C_1 = r+1 , \quad {}_{r+1}C_2 = \frac{(r+1)r}{2!} , \quad {}_{r+1}C_3 = \frac{(r+1)r(r-1)}{3!} , \quad \text{etc.}$$

In order to prove this, write the following identity, which is merely the binomial theorem with one member removed to the left hand side:

$$(x+1)^{r+1} - x^{r+1} \equiv {}_{r+1}C_1 x^r + {}_{r+1}C_2 x^{r-1} + \cdots\cdots + {}_{r+1}C_r x + 1 .$$

Now, let x assume successively the values 1, 2, 3, $\cdots\cdots$, p, and add the resulting identities. Noticing that all the terms except two in the left hand members of these identities cancel one another, one thus gets:

$$2^{r+1} - 1^{r+1} \equiv {}_{r+1}C_1 \, 1^r + {}_{r+1}C_2 \, 1^{r-1} + \cdots\cdots + {}_{r+1}C_r \, 1 + 1 ,$$
$$3^{r+1} - 2^{r+1} \equiv {}_{r+1}C_1 \, 2^r + {}_{r+1}C_2 \, 2^{r-1} + \cdots\cdots + {}_{r+1}C_r \, 2 + 1 ,$$
$$4^{r+1} - 3^{r+1} \equiv {}_{r+1}C_1 \, 3^r + {}_{r+1}C_2 \, 3^{r-1} + \cdots\cdots + {}_{r+1}C_r \, 3 + 1 ,$$
$$\cdot \quad \cdot \quad \cdot \quad \cdot \quad \cdot \quad \cdot \quad \cdot \qquad (7)$$
$$(p+1)^{r+1} - p^{r+1} \equiv {}_{r+1}C_1 \, p^r + {}_{r+1}C_2 \, p^{r-1} + \cdots\cdots + {}_{r+1}C_r \, p + 1 ,$$

$$\overline{(p+1)^{r+1} - 1 \equiv {}_{r+1}C_1 s_r + {}_{r+1}C_2 s_{r-1} \quad \cdots\cdots \quad \cdots\cdots + {}_{r+1}C_r s_1 + s_0 .}$$

From this identity it is possible to calculate any of the sums in terms of those which precede it.

For example,
$$(p+1)^3 - 1 = 3s_2 + 3s_1 + s_0.$$
Therefore,
$$s_2 = \frac{1}{3}[(p+1)^3 - 1 - 3s_1 - s_0]$$
$$= \frac{1}{3}[(p+1)^3 - 1 - 3 \cdot \frac{1}{2} p(p+1) - p]$$
$$= \frac{(2p^3 + 3p^2 + p)}{6} = \frac{p(p+1)(2p+1)}{6}.$$

In a similar way, the following formulas may be deduced:
$$S_3 = \{\frac{1}{2} p(p+1)\}^2,$$
$$S_4 = \frac{p(p+1)(2p+1)(3p^2+3p-1)}{30}$$
$$S_5 = \frac{p^2(p+1)^3(2p^2+2p-1)}{12}, \qquad (8)$$
$$S_6 = \frac{p(p+1)(2p+1)(3p^4+6p^3-3p+1)}{42}.$$

By means of these formulas, all the coefficients of the constants in the normal equations can be readily calculated. The labor of solving for the unknowns is still very great, however, when the value of p is large; this suggests the advisability of obtaining literal solutions for several special cases. These solutions for the straight line and the parabola are given in the next two sections.[1]

PROBLEMS

1. What is the sum of the squares of the first 100 integers?
2. Calculate the sum of the first 100 cubes.
3. Find the sum of the first hundred odd numbers.
4. Find the sum of the squares of the first hundred odd numbers. Hint: Consider the identity
$$1^2 + 2^2 + 3^2 + \ldots + (2p-1)^2 =$$
$$\{1^2 + 3^2 + 5^2 + \ldots + (2p-1)^2\} + \{2^2 + 4^2 + 6^2 + \ldots + (2p-2)^2\}.$$

---

[1] A remarkably complete treatise on the subject of polynomial curve fitting is found in *Trend Analysis of Statistics* by Max Sasuly, Washington, D. C., 1934.

CURVE FITTING

5. Fitting a Straight Line to Empirical Data. The theory given in the last section can be greatly simplified in special cases. Consider, for example, the problem of fitting a straight line, the equation of which is,

$$y = a_1 + a_2 x ,$$

to given data.

In this case the normal equations become,

$$s_0 a_1 + s_1 a_2 = m_0 ,$$
$$s_1 a_1 + s_2 a_2 = m_1 .$$

Replacing s_0, s_1, and s_2 by their explicit values and solving for a_1 and a_2, one gets

$$a_1 = \frac{(m_0 s_2 - m_1 s_1)}{(s_0 s_2 - s_1 s_1)} = \frac{2}{p(p-1)}[(2p+1)m_0 - 3m_1]$$
$$= A m_0 + B m_1 , \qquad (9)$$

$$a_2 = \frac{6}{p(p^2-1)}[-(p+1)m_0 + 2m_1]$$
$$= B m_0 + C m_1 ,$$

where $A = \dfrac{2(2p+1)}{p(p-1)}$, $B = \dfrac{-6}{p(p-1)}$, and $C = \dfrac{12}{p(p^2-1)}$. The coefficients of m_0 and m_1, namely, A, B, and C, have been computed and recorded in Table IX for values of p from 2 to 100.

An example of the application of these formulas has already been given in section 6, Chapter II, and should be restudied at this time.

6. Fitting a Parabola to Empirical Data. A similar simplification is possible in the case of the parabola

$$y = a_1 + a_2 x + a_3 x^2 .$$

In this case the normal equations become,

$$s_0 a_1 + s_1 a_2 + s_2 a_3 = m_0 ,$$
$$s_1 a_1 + s_2 a_2 + s_3 a_3 = m_1 ,$$
$$s_2 a_1 + s_3 a_2 + s_4 a_3 = m_2 .$$

After some calculation one arrives at the formulas,

$$a_1 = \frac{3}{p(p-1)(p-2)}[(3p^2+3p+2)m_0 - 6(2p+1)m_1 + 10m_2]$$

$$= Am_0 + Bm_1 + Cm_2,$$

$$a_2 = \frac{6}{p(p-1)(p-2)}[-3(2p+1)m_0 + \frac{2(2p+1)(8p+11)}{(p+1)(p+2)}m_1 - \frac{30}{p+2}m_2] \quad (10)$$

$$= Bm_0 + Dm_1 + Em_2,$$

$$a_3 = \frac{30}{p(p-1)(p-2)}[m_0 - \frac{6}{p+2}m_1 + \frac{6}{(p+1)(p+2)}m_2]$$

$$= Cm_0 + Em_1 + Fm_2,$$

where $A = \dfrac{3(3p^2+3p+2)}{p(p-1)(p-2)}$, $B = \dfrac{-18(2p+1)}{p(p-1)(p-2)}$,

$C = \dfrac{30}{p(p-1)(p-2)}$, $D = \dfrac{12(2p+1)(8p+11)}{p(p^2-1)(p^2-4)}$,

$E = \dfrac{-180}{p(p-1)(p^2-4)}$, and $F = \dfrac{180}{p(p^2-1)(p^2-4)}$.

The coefficients of m_0, m_1, and m_2, in these formulas have been evaluated and recorded as A, B, C, D, E, and F, in Table X, for values of p from 3 to 50.

Example: These formulas will be applied to determine the best parabola, in the sense of least squares, that will fit the following data, which show the average annual earning capacity for five-year age intervals, (adapted from the U.S. Bureau of Labor Statistics, Bulletin 359):

CURVE FITTING

Age Group	Class Marks (x)	Earning Capacity (y)	m_1	m_2
15-19	1	.56	.56	.56
20-24	2	.71	1.42	2.84
25-29	3	.84	2.52	7.56
30-34	4	.92	3.68	14.72
35-39	5	.97	4.85	24.25
40-44	6	.98	5.88	35.28
45-49	7	.93	6.51	45.57
50-54	8	.86	6.88	55.04
55-59	9	.76	6.84	61.56
60-64	10	.66	6.60	66.00
65-69	11	.56	6.16	67.76
70-74	12	.46	5.52	66.24
Total		9.21	57.42	447.38

It is seen at once that $p = 12$, and that the three moments are:

$m_0 = .56 + .71 + .84 + \cdots + .56 + .46 = 9.21$,

$m_1 = (1)(.56) + (2)(.71) + (3)(.84) + \cdots + (11)(.56)$
$\quad + (12)(.46) = 57.42$,

$m_2 = (1)^2(.56) + (2)^2(.71) + (3)^2(.84) + \cdots + (11)^2(.56)$
$\quad + (12)^2(.46) = 447.38$.

Referring to Table X, for $p = 12$, one finds

$A = 1.0682$, $\qquad D = .1336$,
$B = -.3409$, $\qquad E = -.009740$,
$C = .02273$, $\qquad F = .0007493$.

From these values the coefficients (10) are immediately computed.

$a_1 = (1.0682)(9.21) + (-.3409)(57.42)$
$\quad + (.02273)(447.38) = .4325$,

$a_2 = (-.3409)(9.21) + (.1336)(57.42)$
$\quad + (-.00974)(447.38) = .1741$,

$a_3 = (.02273)(9.21) + (-.00974)(57.42)$
$\quad + (.0007493)(447.38) = -.0148$.

Hence, the best fit parabola, in the sense of least squares, is

$$y = .4325 + .1741\,x - .0148\,x^2 .$$

From the above equation, the following values have been computed. These together with the observed values of y, are plotted in Figure 39. The closeness of fit is there clearly exhibited.

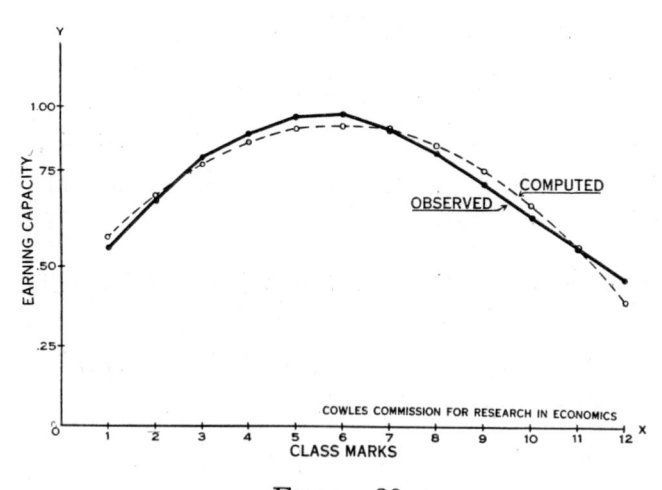

Class Marks (x)	Earning Capacity Observed (y)	Earning Capacity Calculated (y)
1	.56	.59
2	.71	.72
3	.84	.82
4	.92	.89
5	.97	.93
6	.98	.94
7	.93	.93
8	.86	.88
9	.76	.80
10	.66	.69
11	.56	.56
12	.46	.39

FIGURE 39

CURVE FITTING

PROBLEMS

1. Use the method of section 5 to fit a straight line to the data of the first illustrative example of section 3, of this chapter.

2. Fit a straight line to the data of problem 1, section 3. (Use the method of section 5).

3. Fit a parabola, by the method of section 6, to the following data:

y	8	4	2	2	4	8	14
x	1	2	3	4	5	6	7

7. The Simple Exponential. One curve that is of special importance in many statistical problems because of its frequent occurrence in natural phenomena is the simple exponential which, for convenience, will be written in the form,

$$y = a r^x .$$

It is obvious that this curve may be fitted to data by the method of least squares if logarithms of both sides are taken and a determination made of the unknown coefficients in the equation

$$\log y = a_1 + a_2 x ,$$

where $a_1 = \log a$ and $a_2 = \log r$.

The objection sometimes raised to this method is that a straight line is being fitted to the logarithms of the data instead of the exponential to the actual values of y. This objection, however, does not usually affect the fit seriously, so the method is often employed.

A second method, which is free from the difficulty just pointed out, and which has a great deal to recommend it on the score of simplicity, is the following, taken from Glover's *Tables of Applied Mathematics*, Ann Arbor, Michigan, 1923. This admirable book contains extensive tables for use in applying the method about to be described.

Suppose that the data are given in the following form:

y	y_0	y_1	y_2	y_3	....	y_{n-1}
x	0	1	2	3	....	$n-1$

Placing these values in the formula $y = ar^x$ and summing, one easily gets,

$$\Sigma y_i = m_0 = a(1 + r + r^2 + r^3 + \cdots + r^{n-1}) = a\frac{1-r^n}{1-r}.$$

Similarly, for the first moments $(\Sigma x_i y_i)$, one finds

$$\Sigma x_i y_i = m_1 = a[r + 2r^2 + 3r^3 + \cdots + (n-1)r^{n-1}]$$

$$= a\frac{nr^{n+1} - r^{n+1} - nr^n + r}{(1-r)^2} = a\frac{nr^n(r-1) - r(r^n-1)}{(1-r)^2}$$

Dividing m_1 by m_0, one gets the equation,

$$M = \frac{m_1}{m_0} = \frac{nr^n}{r^n - 1} - \frac{r}{r-1}.$$

It is clear that this equation defines r as soon as m_0 and m_1 are known, but it is equally clear that the process of finding r would usually be quite laborious. In order to simplify the calculation, the following table has been computed (most of it is an abridgement from Glover's *Tables*), from which r can be readily found by interpolation:

The function defining M is interesting in that

$$\lim_{r=1} M = \frac{(n-1)}{2},$$

$$\lim_{r=\infty} M = n - 1.$$

The proof of these statements is left to the student.

Table for $M = \dfrac{m_1}{m_0} = \dfrac{n}{(1-r^{-n})} - \dfrac{1}{(1-r^{-1})}$

r	$n=2$	$n=3$	$n=4$	$n=5$	$n=6$	$n=7$	$n=8$
1.00	.5000	1.0000	1.5000	2.0000	2.5000	3.0000	3.5000
1.01	.5025	1.0066	1.5124	2.0199	2.5290	3.0398	3.5522
1.02	.5050	1.0132	1.5248	2.0396	2.5577	3.0792	3.6039
1.03	.5074	1.0197	1.5369	2.0591	2.5862	3.1181	3.6550
1.04	.5098	1.0261	1.5490	2.0784	2.6143	3.1567	3.7056
1.05	.5122	1.0325	1.5609	2.0975	2.6421	3.1948	3.7555
1.06	.5146	1.0388	1.5728	2.1164	2.6696	3.2324	3.8048
1.07	.5169	1.0451	1.5845	2.1351	2.6968	3.2696	3.8535
1.08	.5192	1.0513	1.5960	2.1535	2.7237	3.3063	3.9015
1.09	.5215	1.0574	1.6075	2.1718	2.7502	3.3426	3.9488
1.10	.5238	1.0634	1.6188	2.1899	2.7764	3.3784	3.9955
1.20	.5455	1.1209	1.7258	2.3595	3.0212	3.7098	4.4244
1.30	.5652	1.1729	1.8217	2.5097	3.2346	3.9937	4.7844
1.40	.5833	1.2202	1.9077	2.6420	3.4189	4.2336	5.0815
1.50	.6000	1.2632	1.9846	2.7583	3.5774	4.4352	5.3248

r	$n=9$	$n=10$	$n=11$	$n=12$	$n=13$	$n=14$	$n=15$
1.00	4.0000	4.5000	5.0000	5.5000	6.0000	6.5000	7.0000
1.01	4.0663	4.5821	5.0995	5.6186	6.1393	6.6616	7.1857
1.02	4.1319	4.6633	5.1979	5.7358	6.2769	6.8214	7.3691
1.03	4.1968	4.7435	5.2951	5.8515	6.4128	6.9790	7.5500
1.04	4.2609	4.8227	5.3910	5.9657	6.5467	7.1341	7.7279
1.05	4.3242	4.9009	5.4856	6.0781	6.6785	7.2867	7.9027
1.06	4.3867	4.9780	5.5787	6.1887	6.8080	7.4365	8.0740
1.07	4.4483	5.0539	5.6704	6.2975	6.9352	7.5833	8.2417
1.08	4.5090	5.1287	5.7605	6.4043	7.0598	7.7269	8.4055
1.09	4.5688	5.2022	5.8490	6.5090	7.1818	7.8674	8.5654
1.10	4.6276	5.2745	5.9359	6.6116	7.3012	8.0045	8.7211
1.20	5.1636	5.9261	6.7107	7.5159	8.3403	9.1825	10.0412
1.30	5.6037	6.4488	7.3167	8.2048	9.1105	10.0315	10.9656
1.40	5.9578	6.8581	7.7785	8.7155	9.6659	10.6271	11.5970
1.50	6.2404	7.1765	8.1287	9.0932	10.0671	11.0481	12.0343

As soon as r is known, a can be determined from the easily derived formula,

$$a = \frac{r - (n-M)(r-1)}{n} m_0 \;. \tag{11}$$

Example: Fit an exponential to the following data, which give the average number of shares sold on the New York Stock Exchange from 1919-1930, unit 1,000,000 shares:

Year	x	Stock Sales N.Y.S.E. (y)	$x \cdot y$
1919	0	26.07	0
1920	1	18.73	18.73
1921	2	14.30	28.60
1922	3	21.73	65.19
1923	4	19.77	79.08
1924	5	23.50	117.50
1925	6	37.69	226.14
1926	7	37.42	261.94
1927	8	48.08	384.64
1928	9	76.71	690.39
1929	10	93.75	937.50
1930	11	67.55	743.05
Totals		485.30	3552.76

From the totals, one gets $m_0 = 485.30$, and $m_1 = 3{,}552.76$; so that $M = \dfrac{m_1}{m_0} = 7.3208$. Since $n = 12$, that column is entered with the value of M and r is then found by interpolation to be $r = 1.10 + .078 = 1.178$.

Substituting this value in the formula for a (formula 11), one easily computes $a = 13.956$. Hence the desired equation is,

$$y = (13.956)(1.178)^x ,$$

from which the following table has been calculated for comparison with the observed values of y:

x	Computed (y)	x	Computed (y)
0	13.96	6	37.29
1	16.44	7	43.93
2	19.36	8	51.75
3	22.80	9	60.96
4	26.87	10	71.82
5	31.65	11	84.60

CURVE FITTING

The closeness of the fit is graphically shown in the accompanying Figure 40.

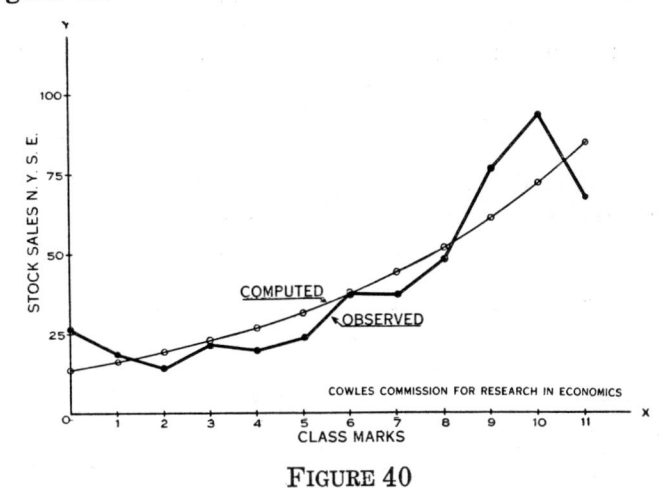

FIGURE 40

In the graphical representation of the exponential curve, it is often desirable to use *semi-logarithmic paper*, that is to say, coordinate paper in which the rulings on the y-axis are spaced according to the logarithms of the numbers. On such paper, data to which an exponential curve may be fitted lie close to a straight line. The representation of the data of the example just given and the exponential fitted to them are given in Figure 41.

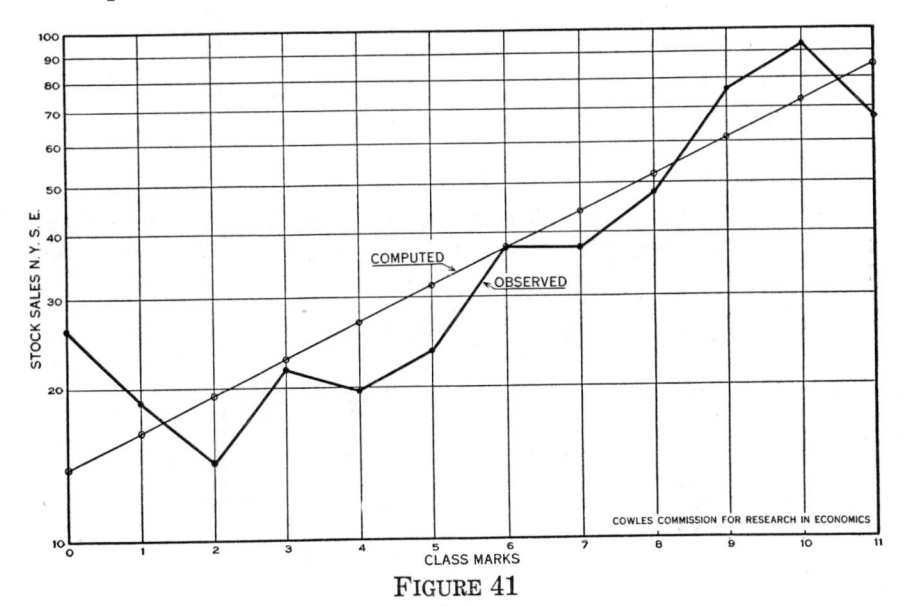

FIGURE 41

PROBLEMS

1. Fit an exponential to the following figures:

y	23	25	26	27	30	32	34	37	40	43	46
x	0	1	2	3	4	5	6	7	8	9	10

2. The following data show the number of auto trucks registered in the United States (000 omitted) from 1919 to 1930. Fit an exponential to these data.

Year	No. of Trucks	Year	No. of Trucks
1919	414	1925	2442
1920	852	1926	2764
1921	980	1927	2897
1922	1279	1928	3114
1923	1553	1929	3380
1924	2131	1930	3481

3. The following data show the population (expressed in millions) of the United States at each census since 1790:

Year	Population	Year	Population
1790	4	1860	31
1800	5	1870	39
1810	7	1880	50
1820	10	1890	63
1830	13	1900	76
1840	17	1910	92
1850	23	1920	106
		1930	123

Fit an exponential curve to these data.

4. Fit an exponential curve to the following data, which give the average bank clearings, outside of New York City, for the years 1917 to 1930 (unit, billion dollars):

Year	Bank Clearings	Year	Bank Clearings
1917	10.8	1924	17.1
1918	12.8	1925	18.9
1919	15.1	1926	19.4
1920	17.4	1927	19.0
1921	13.5	1928	19.1
1922	13.7	1929	19.8
1923	16.6	1930	16.3

8. The Method of Moments.

The method of moments is frequently employed in curve fitting where the theory of least squares leads to analytical difficulties which make that method impracticable.

Assume that the curve to be fitted to the data, y_i, $i = 1, 2, \cdots, p$, is of the form,

$$y = f(x, a_1, a_2, \cdots, a_n) . \qquad (12)$$

Then, according to the method of moments, the parameters, $a_1, a_2, \cdots, a_n$, are to be determined from a set of n equations of the form,

$$\sum_{i=1}^{p} x_i^r f(x_i, a_1, a_2, \cdots, a_n) = m_r , \quad r = 0, 1, 2, \cdots, n-1 ,$$

where $m_0 = \Sigma y_i$, $m_1 = \Sigma x_i y_i$, $m_2 = \Sigma x_i^2 y_i$, etc., the summation extending over $i = 1, 2, 3, \cdots, p$.

It is usual in curve fitting by this method, however, because of the complexities which may otherwise be introduced, to define the moments not as "moments of ordinates" but as "moments of areas" (see section 7, Chapter III). Such moments must be computed by the methods of integral calculus, a discipline which has not been assumed as a part of the equipment of the reader of this book. The method of moments, therefore, belongs to a more advanced theory of statistics. It is probably profitable to observe, however, that the graduation of frequency distributions by means of the normal frequency curve is an application of curve fitting by the method of area moments.

Thus, consider the problem of fitting the curve,

$$y = a\, e^{-c(x-b)^2} ,$$

to the data $y_1, y_2, \cdots, y_p$. Setting the first three moments of the data equal to the first three moments of the function taken over the range from $-\infty$ to $+\infty$, one obtains the following equations for the determination of the parameters a, b, c:[1]

$$a\sqrt{\pi/c} = m_0 , \quad ab\sqrt{\pi/c} = m_1 , a\sqrt{\pi/c}\left(\frac{1}{2c} + b^2\right) = m_2 .$$

---

[1] These formulas are derived in advanced books on statistics where the methods of integral calculus are employed. See, for example, E. T. Whittaker and G. Robinson, *The Calculus of Observations*, Glasgow, 1929, pp. 183-184.

Solving for a, b, and c, one gets

$$a = m_0 \sqrt{c/\pi} \ , \quad b = m_1/m_0 \ , \quad 1/2c = (m_2/m_0) - (m_1/m_0)^2 \ .$$

From the formulas:

$$N = m_0 \ , \quad A = m_1/m_0 \ , \quad \sigma^2 = (m_2/m_0) - (m_1/m_0)^2$$

(see section 7, Chapter III), the familiar values:

$$a = N/(\sqrt{2\pi}\,\sigma) \ , \quad b = A \ , \quad c = 1/(2\sigma^2)$$

are immediately derived.

Whenever the function to be fitted to the data is linear in the parameters, that is to say, when it is of the form,

$$y = a_1 A_1(x) + a_2 A_2(x) + \cdots + a_n A_n(x) \ ,$$

a better fit to the data will usually be obtained by the method of least squares than by the method of moments.

When the functions $A_1(x)$, $A_2(x)$, $\cdots$, $A_n(x)$, are powers of x, i.e., $A_1(x) = 1$, $A_2(x) = x$, $A_3(x) = x^2$, $\cdots$, $A_n(x) = x^{n-1}$, that is to say, when y is a polynomial, the method of moments becomes identical with the method of least squares.

9. The Logistic Curve. It is inevitable in any discipline which anticipates application to problems of economics that there should be a theory of growth functions. One encounters on the threshold the problem of population growth, which cannot be neglected in any attempt to anticipate the trend of primary economic series. Moreover, new industries are continually being invented in this age of scientific and industrial discovery. The automobile industry, for example, started with an insignificant production about 1908 and had reached saturation by 1929. The phenomena of growth were clearly exhibited in the production activities of the intervening years.

One of the most widely used functions in the study of growth phenomena is the *logistic curve*,[1]

---

[1] The use of this curve in population studies is to be found in the following papers by Pearl and Reed: "On the rate of growth of the population of the United States since 1790 and its mathematical representation," *Proc. Nat. Academy of Science*, Vol. 6 (1920), pp. 275-288; "On the Mathematical Theory of Population Growth," *Metron*, Vol. 3 (1923), pp. 6-19; "The Probable Error

$$y = \frac{k}{1 + b\, e^{ax}}, \qquad (13)$$

which has been extensively employed by Raymond Pearl and L. J. Reed in population studies.

If one examines attentively the graph of the curve [See Figure 35] he will see that it proceeds from an initial level to a final level which represents the maturity of the phenomenon under investigation. The two lines within which the curve lies are customarily referred to as asymptotes. Midway between the two asymptotes, the rate of growth (as distinguished from the growth itself) becomes zero, the point at which this occurs being called a *point of inflection*. It is easily proved by the methods of calculus[1] that the point of inflection is given by,

$$x = -(\log_e b)/a, \quad y = \tfrac{1}{2} k .$$

Earlier in the book (Chapter II, section 1, problem 6) the function

$$y = \frac{197.27}{1 + 67.32 e^{-.0313x}} \qquad (14)$$

was given as a representation of the population growth of the United States, x representing years since 1780. This function is due to Pearl and Reed.

---

of Certain Constants of the Population Growth Curve," *American Journal of Hygiene*, (1924). An extensive account is given in Chapter XXIV, *Studies in Human Biology*, by Raymond Pearl, Baltimore, 1924. A comprehensive article is also due to H. Hotelling, "Differential Equations Subject to Error, and Population Estimates," *Journal of the American Statistical Association*, Vol. 27, 1927, pp. 283-314.

Extensive applications of the logistic curve to economic data are to be found in *Secular Movements in Production and Prices* by S. S. Kuznets, Boston, 1930. The appendix to this book contains the numerical evaluation of the logistic curve for a number of economic series.

For a scholarly investigation of the whole problem of growth, from the *a priori* as well as from the empirical point of view, the reader is referred to A. J. Lotka, *Elements of Physical Biology*, Baltimore, 1925, in particular, to Chapters 7, 9, and 11.

[1] The student of calculus can establish this from the values of the first and second derivatives obtained directly by the differentiation of (13),

$$dy/dx = ay(y-k)/k ,$$
$$d^2y/dx^2 = a^2(2y-k)y(y-k)/k^2 .$$

The first and second derivatives both vanish at $y = 0$ and $y = k$, and the second derivative at $y = \tfrac{1}{2}k$. The value of x corresponding to this last point is $-(\log_e b)/a$.

From it one is able to calculate,

$$k = \tfrac{1}{2}(197.27) = 98.63 \text{ millions},$$

as the approximate population at the point of inflection and the corresponding time as

$$x = -(\log_e 67.32)/(-.0313)$$
$$= 134.48 .$$

That is to say, the critical period in the growth of the population of the United States, according to this curve, was in the neighborhood of the year $1780 + 134 = 1914$, when the population approximated 98.63 million people. It is certainly a curious fact, although perhaps only an interesting coincidence, that the population predicted for 1930 by this function was 122.12 million and the actual census showed 122.78 million.

The method of fitting the logistic curve to data is originally due to Pearl and Reed, who employed the method of least squares in the final adjustment of the constants which were first approximately determined as follows:

To attain this first approximation three equally spaced points are chosen which seem to be fairly characteristic of the data to which the curve is to be fitted. Designate those points by $(0, y_0)$, (x_1, y_1), $(2x_1, y_2)$.

Writing equation (13) in the form,

$$y = \frac{k}{1 + e^{c+ax}} , \quad b = e^c , \qquad (15)$$

one now solves for $c + ax$ in terms of y and k and in the resulting expression substitutes the three points given in the preceding paragraph. The following three equations are thus obtained:

$$c + a \cdot 0 = \log_e (k - y_0)/y_0 ,$$
$$c + a \cdot x_1 = \log_e (k - y_1)/y_1 ,$$
$$c + a \cdot 2x_1 = \log_e (k - y_2)/y_2 ,$$

from which k, c, and a are to be determined.

It is at once seen that a can be found from the first equation as soon as k is known, since

$$c = \log_e (k - y_0)/y_0 .$$

CURVE FITTING

In order to find k, one substitutes this value of c in the second equation and thus finds,

$$a = \frac{1}{x_1}\{\log_e(k-y_1)/y_1 - \log_e(k-y_0)/y_0\},$$

$$= \frac{1}{x_1}\{\log_e y_0(k-y_1)/y_1(k-y_0)\}.$$

Similarly, from the third equation one gets,

$$a = \frac{1}{2x_1}\log_e y_0(k-y_2)/y_2(k-y_0),$$

$$= \frac{1}{x_1}\log_e\{y_0(k-y_2)/y_2(k-y_0)\}^{1/2}.$$

Equating these two values of a and comparing the logarithms, one obtains for the determination of k the equation,

$$y_0(k-y_1)/y_1(k-y_0) = \{y_0(k-y_2)/y_2(k-y_0)\}^{1/2}.$$

Squaring both sides and collecting on the right hand side of the equation terms involving k, one gets,

$$(y_0 y_2 - y_1^2)k = 2y_0 y_1 y_2 - y_1^2(y_0 + y_2),$$

or

$$k = \{2y_0 y_1 y_2 - y_1^2(y_0 + y_2)\}/(y_0 y_2 - y_1^2).$$

The value of a is then readily found from either the second or third equation in the original system.[1]

---

[1] This same preliminary adjustment can be made for the more general equation,

$$y = \frac{k}{1+e^{a_0+a_1 x + a_2 x^2 + a_3 x^3}}.$$

Five equally spaced points, $(0, y_0)$, (x_1, y_1), $(2x_2, y_2)$, $(2x_3, y_3)$, $(4x_4, y_4)$, are first determined.

The value of k is then computed from the following equation:

$$y_1^4 y_3^4(k-y_0)(k-y_2)^6(k-y_4) = y_0 y_2^6 y_4(k-y_1)^4(k-y_3)^4,$$

and the coefficients a_0, a_1, a_2, and a_3, from the formulas,

$$a_0 = \log\frac{k-y_0}{y_0}, \quad a_1 = (18\beta_1 - 9\beta_2 + 2\beta_3)/6x_1,$$

Example: The following data give the number of automobiles produced per month in a certain state over a nine-year period. The problem proposed is to fit a trend line of the population growth type to these figures.

Jan.	2512	7324	3264	7903	11113	8830	7605	10951	9735
Feb.	4689	9292	4892	9284	13775	14072	10024	14955	15097
Mar.	6636	11236	8972	11823	17995	17841	14436	17736	21289
Apr.	6798	6343	9087	11290	16882	17980	16547	14450	22698
May	7408	9063	10028	13905	17588	15458	16537	13099	16204
June	6265	11588	12461	14155	17013	2762	16578	8504	12103
July	7141	8093	10121	11752	16184	1653	16058	8777	8853
Aug.	7868	9469	10461	13222	17564	3494	15569	13808	14949
Sept.	8543	9511	8229	11667	15902	10565	15496	12774	13805
Oct.	6384	5834	7283	10333	12401	15942	14981	9004	10255
Nov.	7104	4651	3216	9047	11315	11360	11170	7775	8449
Dec.	8430	3826	6061	7584	6308	9133	8347	6481	9923

Obviously, the problem must first be simplified. Hence, the average production per month for each year is first calculated and these values assigned to the median months. New data are thus obtained as follows:

Production (y)	6648 8019 7840 10997 14503 10758 13612 11526 13613
Month (x)	6 18 30 42 54 66 78 90 102

To these averages the foregoing theory is now applied. Because the frequency corresponding to the class mark 54 is obviously high, it is replaced by the average of the numbers corresponding to $x = 42$, $x = 54$, and $x = 66$, namely, 12,086. Hence, selecting as the three points, $(x_0, y_0) = (0, 6648)$, $(x_1, y_1) = (54, 12086)$, $(2x_1, y_2) = (108, 13613)$, one calculates,

$$a_2 = (4\beta_2 - 5\beta_1 - \beta_3)/2x_1^2 , \qquad a_3 = (\beta_3 + 3\beta_1 - 3\beta_2)/6x_1^3 ,$$

where the following abbreviations are used:

$$\beta_1 = \log_e \frac{y_0(k-y_1)}{y_1(k-y_0)} , \qquad \beta_2 = \log_e \frac{y_0(k-y_2)}{y_2(k-y_2)} ,$$

$$\beta_3 = \log_e \frac{y_0(k-y_3)}{y_3(k-y_0)} .$$

For an application of this to population data, see Raymond Pearl, *Studies in Human Biology, op. cit.*, p. 607.

CURVE FITTING

$$k = 13{,}892 \,,$$
$$c = \log_e(13{,}892 - 6{,}648)/6{,}648 = \log_e 1.0897 \,,$$
$$= 2.30259 \times .03731 = .0859 \;;$$
$$a = \frac{1}{108}\log_e .018809 = -.0368 \,.$$

The desired curve is then,

$$y = \frac{13{,}892}{1 + e^{.0859}\, e^{-.0370x}},$$

the graph of which is the dotted line in Figure 42.

It is at once clear from the method employed in its derivation that the curve just written down is only a first approximation to the curve of best fit. The method of least squares can be used to obtain a better approximation in many cases as follows:

First write equation (13) in the form,

$$y = \frac{B}{e^{-(A+h)x} + c} = \frac{B}{e^{-Ax}\, e^{-hx} + c},$$

where $A = -a$, and h, B and c are constants to be determined.

Expanding e^{-hx} one has,

$$y = \frac{B}{e^{-Ax}\left(1 - hx + \frac{h^2 x^2}{2!} - \frac{h^3 x^3}{3!} + \cdots\right) + c},$$

or, assuming that h is small, which will be true if a has been properly approximated, one gets,

$$y = \frac{B}{e^{-Ax}(1 - hx) + c}.$$

Multiplying through by the denominator of the right hand side, one obtains the new equation with linear coefficients,

$$B - Cy + hxy e^{-Ax} = y e^{-Ax}.$$

To this equation one now applies the theory of least squares as developed in the third section of this chapter, using for $A_1(x)$ the value 1, for $A_2(x)$, the value $-y$, and for $A_3(x)$, $x\, y\, e^{-Ax}$.

246 ELEMENTS OF STATISTICS

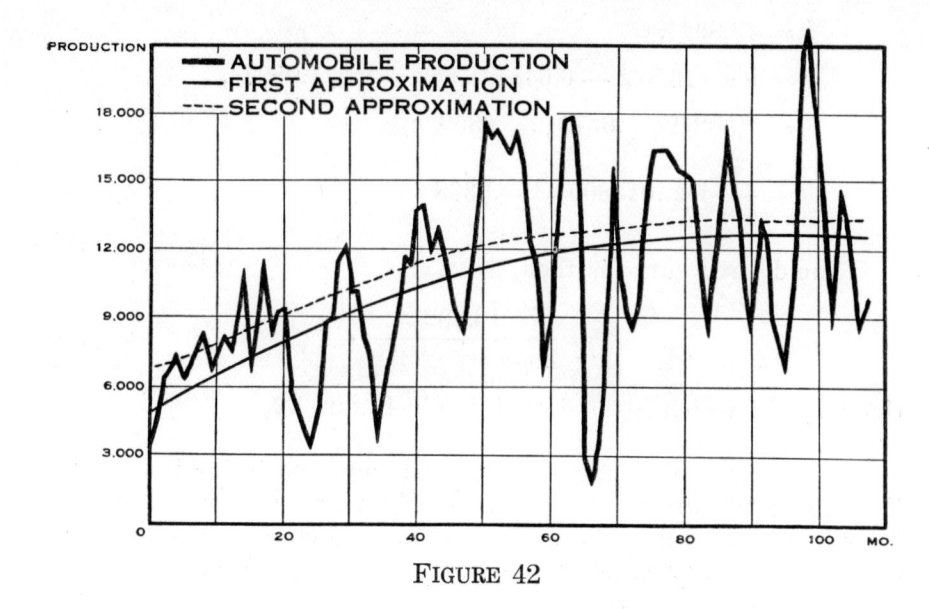

FIGURE 42

The calculations may be tabulated as follows:

COMPUTATION OF CURVE

x	y	e^{-Ax}	y^2	$xy\,e^{-Ax}$	$x\,y^2\,e^{-Ax}$
6	6,648	.80192	44,195,904	31,987	212,649,000
18	8,019	.51568	64,304,361	74,435	596,894,000
30	7,840	.33162	61,465,600	77,997	611,494,000
42	10,997	.21325	120,934,009	98,496	1,083,157,000
54	14,503	.13713	210,337,009	107,399	1,557,605,000
66	10,758	.08819	115,734,564	62,615	673,612,000
78	13,612	.05671	185,286,544	60,211	819,588,000
90	11,526	.03647	132,848,676	37,830	436,028,000
102	13,613	.02345	185,313,769	32,563	443,284,000
	97,516		1,120,420,436	583,533	6,434,311,000

$x\,y^2\,e^{-2Ax}$	$x^2\,y^2\,e^{-2Ax}$	$y\,e^{-Ax}$	$y^2\,e^{-Ax}$
170,527,000	1,023,160,000	5,331	35,441,000
307,809,000	5,540,562,000	4,135	33,161,000
202,783,000	6,083,484,000	2,600	20,383,000
230,986,000	9,701,393,000	2,345	25,789,000
213,602,000	11,534,511,000	1,989	28,845,000
59,404,000	3,920,633,000	949	10,206,000
46,479,000	3,625,332,000	772	10,508,000
15,901,000	1,431,103,000	420	4,845,000
10,396,000	1,060,368,000	319	4,346,000
1,257,887,000	43,920,546,000	18,860	173,524,000

Noting that

$$[A_1A_1] = n, \quad [A_1A_2] = \Sigma y, \quad [A_1A_3] = \Sigma xye^{-Ax},$$
$$[A_2A_2] = \Sigma y^2, \quad [A_2A_3] = \Sigma xy^2 e^{-Ax},$$
$$[A_3A_3] = \Sigma x^2 y^2 e^{-2Ax},$$
$$[A_1y] = \Sigma ye^{-Ax}, \quad [A_2y] = \Sigma y^2 e^{-Ax},$$
$$[A_3y] = \Sigma xy^2 e^{-2Ax},$$

one gets from these calculations the following set of normal equations.[1]

$$9B - 97{,}516\,C + 583{,}533\,h = 18{,}860$$
$$97{,}516\,B - 1{,}120{,}420{,}436\,C + 6{,}434{,}311{,}000\,h = 173{,}524{,}000$$
$$583{,}533\,B - 6{,}434{,}311{,}000\,C + 43{,}920{,}546{,}000\,h = 1{,}257{,}887{,}000$$

Dividing the first of these equations by 9, the second by 97,516, and the third by 583,533, one obtains the new set,

$$B - 10{,}835\,C + 64{,}837\,h = 2{,}096,$$
$$B - 11{,}490\,C + 65{,}982\,h = 1{,}779,$$
$$B - 11{,}026\,C + 75{,}267\,h = 2{,}156.$$

Eliminating B from these equations, one gets,

$$-655\,C + 1{,}145\,h = -317,$$
$$-191\,C + 10{,}430\,h = 60,$$

from which C and h are easily calculated by the same method to be,

$$C = .51037, \quad h = .01510.$$

Substituting these values in the first equation above, one finds $B = 6646$. Hence the desired curve becomes,

$$y = \frac{6646}{e^{-.0519x} + .5104} = \frac{13021}{1 + 1.9592 e^{-.0519x}}. \quad (16)$$

The closeness with which this curve fits the data[2] is graphically illustrated in Figure 42.

---

[1] The negative sign in the second terms of these equations comes from the sign of C in the original equation.
[2] This problem is furnished by the courtesy of Professor George Starr of the Bureau of Business Research of Indiana University.

PROBLEMS

1. Make a graph of equation (14) and compare with the actual census figures given in problem 5, section 1, Chapter II. What is the population predicted for the next census?

2. What was the critical year for automobile production as indicated by equation (16)?

3. On the basis of the growth curve fitted to the production of automobiles, calculate the maximum production at the saturation point. Does the fluctuation of the data make you wish to qualify your answer?

4. Obtain census reports for some city in your neighborhood and fit a population growth curve to the data thus obtained.

CHAPTER X

ELEMENTS OF CORRELATION

1. The Mathematical Theory of Drawing Conclusions. One of the most important problems that can be dealt with by means of the theory of probabilities is that of finding relations between sets of characteristics belonging to groups of phenomena. The mathematical theory by means of which these relationships are found and reduced to formula and number is called *correlation*. For example, one might plausibly suspect that great industrial activity would imply high prices for common stocks, or that a sharp rise in the cost of living would lead to a decline in highest grade (Aaa) bond prices, or that a depreciation in the dollar would, at least temporarily, stimulate export trade, but these are only guesses until they have been tested by means of the laws of averages. In other words, correlation is the mathematical theory of drawing conclusions. Some people believe that crops should be planted in the dark of the moon, and that black cats cause bad luck, but these opinions cannot be justified by mathematical theory. No real correlation exists between large crops and the light of the moon, or between black cats and bad luck, although occasional coincidences may lead to such conjectures.

Correlation may, of course, exist in various degrees. Faraday noticed that an electric current was always associated with a magnetic field, and the correlation between these two phenomena was expressed by Maxwell in absolute mathematical terms. High correlation existed between them. The economic law of diminishing returns, and Gresham's law that the less valuable element of a national currency tends to remain in circulation and the more valuable to disappear, are correlations that are less exact than those of the physical law just mentioned. Mendel's law of heredity, which states the distribution of parental characteristics in offspring, is another example of a correlation which is subject to minor fluctuations.

2. The Correlation Coefficient. In order to make the idea of correlation more exact, suppose that one has two sets of numbers which, for convenience, may be recorded in parallel rows as follows:

X data: $X_1 \quad X_2 \quad X_3 \cdots\cdots X_n$,

Y data: $Y_1 \quad Y_2 \quad Y_3 \cdots\cdots Y_n$.

It is suspected that there exists a relationship between the values of X and the values of Y, so one plots on coordinate paper the points $(X_1, Y_1), (X_2, Y_2), \cdots\cdots, (X_n, Y_n)$. If these points, when so plotted, appear to lie approximately along some curve, then one may say that the two sets of numbers are correlated. If they group themselves about a straight line, then one is concerned with the case of *linear correlation,* otherwise the correlation is said to be *non-linear.* It is with the first type that this chapter is mainly concerned. Linear correlations are much more generally used than non-linear since the calculations involved are less arduous. Very often, too, a linear correlation may be applied even when it is suspected that the relationship of the two variables is non-linear but where the departure from linearity may be so slight as to make the linear correlation a satisfactory approximation. Or, again, the range of the data treated may be sufficiently accurately dealt with by a linear approximation, even though it is logical to expect that, if data outside this range were included, only some form of curve would adequately describe the relationship between the total possible series. Thus, although a really perfect relationship may be established, the correlation coefficient, although high, may not be ± 1.0, due to a linear assumption when the relationship is really curvilinear.

In order to have some way of arriving at a numerical measure of linear correlation, the so-called *correlation coefficient* has been devised. This coefficient is given by the following formula:

$$r = \frac{(1/N)(\Sigma X_i Y_i) - \overline{X}\,\overline{Y}}{\sigma_X \sigma_Y},$$

$$= \frac{\Sigma(X_i - \overline{X})(Y_i - \overline{Y})}{N \sigma_X \sigma_Y}$$

where $\Sigma X_i Y_i$ means the sum of the products of the values of X with the corresponding values of Y, $\overline{X}$ and $\overline{Y}$ are the arithmetic averages of the two series, and σ_X and σ_Y the respective standard deviations[1].

---

[1] The discovery of the correlation coefficient is generally attributed to Sir Francis Galton, who used it early in the last quarter of the nineteenth century. Among those who contributed to the early theory of correlation, the following are especially to be noted: R. Adrian (1775-1843), P. S. Laplace (1749-1827), G. A. A. Plana (1781-1864), K. F. Gauss (1777-1855), and A. Bravais (1811-1863). An account of the history of the development of the theory of correlation will be found in Chapter V of Helen M. Walker's *Studies in the History of Statistical Method,* Baltimore, 1929.

Of the two forms in which the correlation coefficient is written above, the first is more generally used although they are, of course, equivalent to one another.

It will be proved later that r never exceeds 1 in absolute value. If r equals 0, then there exists no correlation between the two series, and if it equals 1, the correlation is perfect. If r is less than 0, the correlation is said to be *negative* or inverse.

Example: The following table gives the average annual earnings per share of the United States Steel Corporation and the price per share of its common stock. Is there any correlation between the earnings and the prices of the common stock?

Year	Earnings[1] Per Share	Price[1] of Common Stock, Per Share	Year	Earnings Per Share	Price of Common Stock, Per Share
1902	$ 7.45	$26.50	1918	$15.25	$70.25
1903	3.40	17.25	1919	6.93	70.50
1904	.68	14.25	1920	11.50	64.00
1905	5.90	23.50	1921	1.55	54.25
1906	10.00	28.75	1922	1.96	67.00
1907	10.80	25.00	1923	11.30	67.50
1908	2.80	29.25	1924	8.15	74.50
1909	7.30	47.00	1925	8.90	87.00
1910	8.48	52.50	1926	12.40	96.00
1911	4.09	45.75	1927	8.50	131.50
1912	3.95	48.00	1928	12.10	147.50
1913	7.60	41.25	1929	21.19	206.00
1914	−.24	39.75	1930	9.12	166.50
1915	6.85	44.00	1931	− 1.40	94.25
1916	33.50	72.50	1932	−11.08	37.00
1917	27.00	74.75			

[1]Corrected for the effect of a 40% stock dividend paid June 1, 1927, and for rights issued May 1, 1929. The price per share of the common stock is the average of the annual high and low prices, to the nearest quarter of a dollar.

Solution: The first series may be called X and the second series Y. One will then have $X = 8.2558$, $Y = 66.5742$, $\sigma_x = 8.1303$, $\sigma_y = 43.9487$, $\Sigma XY = 21{,}351.6075$; the correlation coefficient then is found to be

$$r = \frac{(21{,}351.6075/31) - (8.2558)(66.5742)}{(8.1303)(43.9487)} = .389$$

PROBLEMS

1. The following table gives the indexes of seasonal variation of production and shipments of pneumatic casings for the years 1923-1931.[1] Is there any correlation between these seasonal variation indexes?

Month	Jan.	Feb.	Mar.	Apr.	May	June	July	Aug.	Sept.	Oct.	Nov.	Dec.
Index - Shipments (X)	89	81	98	110	113	120	129	123	104	87	72	74
Index - Production (Y)	96	101	114	113	116	112	97	104	91	91	82	83

Shift the indexes for the production one place to the right, so that the following new series are obtained:

Shipments (X)	89	81	98	110	113	120	129	123	104	87	72	74
Production (Y)	83	96	101	114	113	116	112	97	104	91	91	82

Calculate the new correlation coefficient and call it r_1. Shift the indexes for (Y) one more place to the right and again calculate the correlation coefficient, calling it r_2. Repeat this process four more times and call the new coefficients r_3, r_4, r_5, and r_6. Now shift the original data for (Y) one unit to the left so that the following new series are obtained:

Shipments (X)	89	81	98	110	113	120	129	123	104	87	72	74
Production (Y)	101	114	113	116	112	97	104	91	91	82	83	96

Calculate the new coefficient, calling it r_1'. Repeat this process five times and calculate the coefficients r_2', r_3', r_4', r_5', and r_6'. Finally, on graph paper erect ordinates equal to r_6', r_5', r_4', r_3', r_2', r_1', r, r_1, r_2, r_3, r_4, r_5, r_6. Can a smooth curve be drawn through these points? What conclusions do you draw?

2. *A priori*, one might say that variations in long term bond prices resulted from (a) variations in the purchasing power of money, (b) variations in interest rates, and (c) variations in earnings applicable to interest charges. The following tables give annual averages for the Dow-Jones Bond Prices, an index of the cost of living, 4-6 months prime commercial paper rates, and percentage of net income to capitalization of 71 manufacturing corporations, for the years 1919-1932. Calculate the correlation coefficients between each of the last three series and the first. From this type of analysis, rate the importance of these factors on the movements of bond prices.

---

[1]Source: Simon Kuznets, *Seasonal Variations in Industry and Trade*, National Bureau of Economic Research, 1933.

Year	Dow-Jones Bond Prices (Average high and low for each month)	Index of Cost of Living	4-6 Months Prime Commercial Paper Rates	Percentage net income to capitalization of 71 manufacturing corporations
1919	$82.46	111.0	5.42	13.4
1920	76.18	119.4	7.37	8.4
1921	79.62	102.7	6.53	3.8
1922	88.23	97.3	4.43	12.1
1923	87.58	100.0	4.98	10.3
1924	89.05	101.5	3.91	10.7
1925	91.92	103.8	4.03	13.0
1926	94.63	103.8	4.24	13.3
1927	97.75	101.6	4.01	10.3
1928	97.55	100.4	4.84	11.3
1929	94.04	100.0	5.78	13.1
1930	95.27	96.2	3.56	8.3
1931	85.06	86.7	2.64	3.6
1932	77.61	77.7	2.74	.6

3. Over short periods of time one might think that the investment policies of banks exerted a considerable influence on bond prices, since the value of bonds held by banks is about 60 per cent of the value of bonds listed on the New York Stock Exchange. The following are monthly figures on investments (exclusive of U.S. Government Securities) of reporting Federal Reserve Member Banks in leading cities, and the New York Times Bond Averages (1929-1932). What is the correlation between these two series? Does it confirm the original opinion?

Year-Month	Investments Other Than U.S. Gov. Securities of Reporting Federal Reserve Member Banks (unit, billion dollars)	New York Times Average Price of 40 Bonds	Year-Month	Investments Other Than U.S. Gov. Securities of Reporting Federal Reserve Member Banks (unit, billion dollars)	New York Times Average Price of 40 Bonds
1929–Jan.	2.94	90.2	1931–Jan.	3.60	84.7
Feb.	2.93	89.7	Feb.	3.72	84.9
Mar.	2.90	88.7	Mar.	3.75	84.9
Apr.	2.89	88.0	Apr.	3.83	83.2
May	2.88	87.5	May	3.87	82.5
June	2.84	86.9	June	3.77	82.2
July	2.79	86.5	July	3.68	83.9
Aug.	2.77	86.2	Aug.	3.64	81.7
Sept.	2.75	85.8	Sept.	3.64	77.0
Oct.	2.76	85.9	Oct.	3.60	72.5
Nov.	2.85	85.5	Nov.	3.51	71.9
Dec.	2.86	86.9	Dec.	3.42	64.6
1930–Jan.	2.83	86.8	1932–Jan.	3.26	66.9
Feb.	2.77	87.2	Feb.	3.21	65.8
Mar.	2.80	88.6	Mar.	3.19	66.4
Apr.	2.90	88.5	Apr.	3.25	61.3
May	3.01	88.1	May	3.29	55.9
June	3.15	87.3	June	3.26	55.3
July	3.30	87.2	July	3.20	59.2
Aug.	3.40	88.3	Aug.	3.19	67.5
Sept.	3.44	88.8	Sept.	3.23	70.2
Oct.	3.57	86.9	Oct.	3.28	68.1
Nov.	3.71	84.6	Nov.	3.31	65.5
Dec.	3.66	82.4	Dec.	3.28	63.9

254 ELEMENTS OF STATISTICS

4. In Warren and Pearson's *Prices*, the authors contend that the general price level varies directly with the ratio existing between the supply of gold and the production of all other commodities. The following table[1] gives (a) an index of the world's stock of monetary gold, (b) an index of the world's physical volume of production, (c) the ratio of gold to production, and (d) an index of wholesale prices in gold in the United States. What is the correlation between (c) and (d)? Does this confirm the authors' contention for the period of time under consideration?

Year	Index World's Stock of Monetary Gold (1880-1914 = 100) (a)	Index World's Physical Volume of Production (1880-1914 = 100) (b)	Ratio, Gold Stock to Production (c)	Index United States Wholesale Prices (1880-1914 = 100) (d)
1900	101	106	95	94
1901	104	107	97	93
1902	108	114	95	99
1903	111	115	97	100
1904	115	115	100	100
1905	121	125	97	101
1906	125	134	93	103
1907	130	129	101	109
1908	137	129	106	105
1909	143	138	104	113
1910	147	140	105	118
1911	152	143	106	109
1912	156	156	100	116
1913	161	157	103	117
1914	168	146	115	113
1915	176	148	119	116
1916	183	142	129	143
1917	188	144	131	197
1918	194	142	137	219
1919	195	138	141	231
1920	200	156	128	259
1921	206	138	149	164
1922	208	159	131	162
1923	212	169	125	168
1924	213	171	125	164
1925	217	187	116	173
1926	222	183	121	167
1927	227	192	118	159
1928	232	202	115	162
1929	238	208	114	159
1930	243	198	123	144
1931	250	184	136	123

[1] Source: George F. Warren and Frank A. Pearson, *Prices*, New York, 1933, Ch. V, p. 79.

5. The following tables give the total national income[1] of the United States expressed in 1913 dollars, and the index of industrial production, for the years 1909-1932. What is the correlation between these two series?

Year	Total National Income in 1913 dollars (unit, billion dollars)	Index of Industrial Production 1923 = 100
1909	29.2	70.2
1910	30.2	73.8
1911	30.6	64.4
1912	32.4	78.0
1913	33.4	81.2
1914	32.8	67.1
1915	34.1	80.8
1916	36.9	101.2
1917	37.6	99.9
1918	37.2	97.0
1919	35.1	89.7
1920	34.3	94.2
1921	33.6	71.6
1922	37.6	93.1
1923	42.1	113.9
1924	43.6	104.8
1925	45.2	116.4
1926	47.3	119.9
1927	49.7	117.3
1928	50.7	120.5
1929	51.2	128.7
1930	44.5	103.7
1931	38.9	82.9
1932	28.6	62.4

6. Are the following figures correlated?

Month	Jan.	Feb.	Mar.	Apr.	May	June	July	Aug.	Sept.	Oct.	Nov.	Dec.
Egg Production, average per bird	11.71	10.87	16.11	15.85	13.92	12.46	10.87	9.84	8.19	5.50	4.63	8.91
Average Price	38.0	31.9	22.7	21.1	21.3	21.7	23.3	25.8	30.2	36.9	46.4	48.4

Can higher correlation be obtained by shifting the data as in the first problem? What conclusions do you reach?

[1] Source: Irving Fisher, *Booms and Depressions*, New York, 1932, Appendix V.

7. The following data, from Warren and Pearson's *Prices, op. cit.*, page 25, give the wholesale price indexes for all commodities and for farm products, 1850-1932. Are these figures closely correlated?

Year	Farm Products	All Commodities	Year	Farm Products	All Commodities
1850	71	84	1891	76	82
1851	71	83	1892	69	76
1852	77	89	1893	72	78
1853	83	97	1894	63	70
1854	93	108	1895	62	71
1855	98	110	1896	56	68
1856	84	105	1897	60	68
1857	95	111	1898	63	71
1858	76	93	1899	64	77
1859	82	95	1900	71	82
1860	77	93	1901	74	81
1861	75	89	1902	82	86
1862	86	104	1903	78	87
1863	113	133	1904	82	87
1864	162	193	1905	79	88
1865	148	185	1906	80	90
1866	140	174	1907	87	95
1867	133	162	1908	87	92
1868	138	158	1909	98	99
1869	128	151	1910	104	103
1870	112	135	1911	94	95
1871	102	130	1912	102	101
1872	108	136	1913	100	102
1873	103	133	1914	100	99
1874	102	126	1915	100	101
1875	99	118	1916	118	125
1876	89	110	1917	181	172
1877	89	106	1918	208	191
1878	72	91	1919	221	202
1879	72	90	1920	211	226
1880	80	100	1921	124	143
1881	89	103	1922	132	147
1882	99	108	1923	138	147
1883	87	101	1924	140	143
1884	82	93	1925	154	151
1885	72	85	1926	141	146
1886	68	82	1927	139	139
1887	71	85	1928	149	141
1888	75	86	1929	147	139
1889	67	81	1930	124	126
1890	71	82	1931	91	107
			1932	68	95

8. The law of supply and demand in economics states the reasonable proposition that when a certain commodity is scarce its price advances and *vice versa*. Test this law by obtaining the correlation between the production and the price of cotton over a certain period. It will be evident at once that some corrections must be made before a significant correlation can be ob-

tained. One of these is the correction which must be applied to the dollar whose purchasing power has fluctuated very greatly in the period under discussion. Another factor that must be taken into account is the lag of price behind production. It is reasonable to assume that the production of one year will possibly be the chief influence on the price of the succeeding year. To correct for the changing dollar, one divides the price series by the price index of the year under consideration and multiplies by 100; to take account of the lag in price, the production figures are to be shifted one year.

COTTON PRODUCTION AND PRICES
Production unit: 1,000,000 bales.
Price unit: cents per pound.

Year	Production	Price	Index-Commodity Prices, 1926=100	Year	Production	Price	Index-Commodity Prices, 1926=100
1900	10	10	56	1916	11	14	86
1901	10	9	55	1917	11	23	118
1902	11	9	59	1918	12	32	131
1903	10	11	60	1919	11	32	138
1904	14	12	61	1920	13	34	154
1905	11	9	60	1921	8	17	98
1906	14	11	62	1922	10	21	97
1907	11	12	65	1923	10	29	100
1908	14	10	63	1924	14	29	98
1909	10	12	68	1925	16	23	104
1910	12	15	70	1926	18	18	100
1911	16	13	65	1927	12	18	95
1912	14	12	69	1928	14	20	97
1913	14	13	70	1929	15	19	96
1914	16	12	68	1930	14	14	86
1915	11	10	70	1931	17	9	73
				1932	13	6	65

3. The Correlation Table. The first approach to the subject of correlation is the construction of a table which will exhibit any relationship that may exist between the frequencies of the two groups of characteristics. One might well surmise, for example, that in this Steel Age a high volume of general industrial production would be accompanied by a high volume of pig iron production. To test the validity of this conjecture, statistical data on pig iron production and general industrial production, monthly averages through the years 1897-1913, are gathered. The range of the two variates may be divided into convenient sections (for suggestions as to the choice of interval, see section 9, Chapter I). In the present case, since industrial production ranges from 54 per cent to

124 per cent, and pig iron production from 55 per cent to 125 per cent of a hypothetical "normal", it will be convenient to divide the range for both series into eight divisions of ten units each. The results of this classification can be represented by the following *correlation table* made up of 8 × 8 = 64 cells:

Industrial Production (percentage of trend) (1897-1913)									
120-129								15	15
110-119						6	34	1	41
100-109					5	51	6		62
90-99				3	33	1			37
80-89			2	24	3				29
70-79			7	2					9
60-69		2	1						3
50-59%	6	2							8
Frequencies of columns	6	4	10	29	41	58	40	16	204
	50-59%	60-69	70-79	80-89	90-99	100-109	110-119	120-129	Frequencies of rows

TABLE A   Pig Iron Production (percentage of trend), 1897-1913

One notices a pronounced tendency for the largest frequencies to group themselves about the main diagonal of the table. This tendency always indicates that a correlation exists between the variates whose frequencies have been recorded, and it is the purpose in the present chapter to see how this correlation can be expressed numerically.

As a second example, for comparison, consider the problem of determining whether or not a relationship exists between wholesale commodity prices and employment, using the United States Bureau of Labor Statistics index of wholesale commodity prices and the index of employment, from 1919-1932. Since the commodity price interval is from 104.5 to 62.6 and the employment interval from 110.9 to 55.2, nine divisions of five units were chosen for the former and twelve divisions of five units for the latter. The correlation table follows:

										Frequencies of rows
110-114								4		4
105-109							7	2		9
100-104							5	9		14
95-99						6	25	11		42
90-94						4	13			17
85-89					2	2				4
80-84				1						1
75-79			2	3	4					9
70-74			4	1						5
65-69		2	2							4
60-64		3								3
55-59	6	2								8
Frequencies of columns	6	7	8	4	5	2	12	50	26	120
	60-64	65-69	70-74	75-79	80-84	85-89	90-94	95-99	100-104	

TABLE B   Index of Commodity Prices (1919-1932)

In general, if there seems to be a tendency for the frequencies to group themselves about any line, either straight or curved, in the correlation table, then there will always be some measure of correlation existing between the two variates. As has already been stated in the preceding section, if the line about which this group-

260   ELEMENTS OF STATISTICS

ing occurs is straight, the correlation is *linear;* otherwise, *non-linear.*

As a preliminary to the study of correlation, one first erects on coordinate paper two axes along which are marked off intervals corresponding to the class marks of the two variates whose correlation is being studied. Cells, as in the correlation table, are then constructed and in these cells dots are made, as in ordinary graphing, to represent pairs of values in the frequency table. The number of dots in each cell equals the frequency with which that particular pair of values occurs. The diagram thus obtained is known as the *scatter diagram.* Figure 43 is the scatter diagram for Table A.

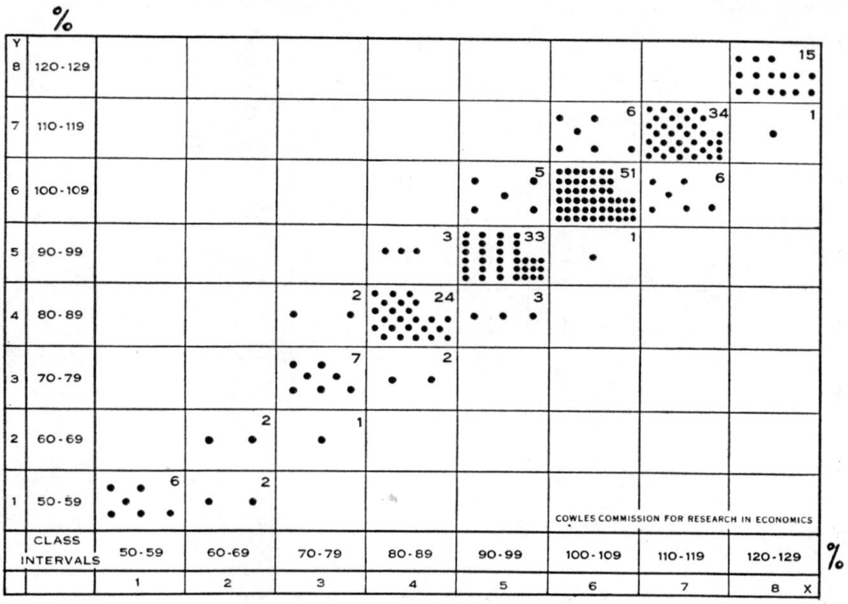

FIGURE 43

Now, if the arithmetic means of the sets of points in each column are calculated, graphed, and connected by straight lines, one obtains the so-called *regression curve of y on x,* which affords some indication as to the linear or non-linear character of the correlation. For convenience in the calculation of the means, the new class marks $y = 1, 2, 3, \ldots, n$, are used. A similar calculation of the means of the rows, using the class marks $x = 1, 2, 3, \ldots, n$, gives likewise the *regression curve of x on y.*

ELEMENTS OF CORRELATION

The two regression curves for Table A are given in the accompanying Figure 44 and indicate clearly that the correlation is essentially linear.

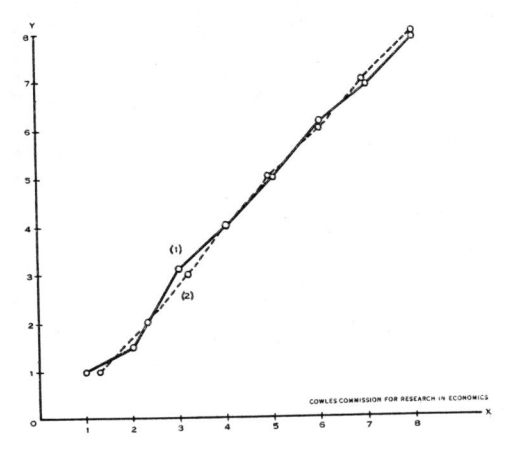

(1) Regression curve of y on x.
(2) Regression curve of x on y.

(1)		(2)	
x	y	y	x
1	1.0	1	1.3
2	1.5	2	2.3
3	3.1	3	3.2
4	4.0	4	4.0
5	5.0	5	4.9
6	6.1	6	6.0
7	6.9	7	6.9
8	7.9	8	8.0

FIGURE 44

Since it is often easier to plot a scatter diagram than to compute a correlation coefficient, and since the estimate of co-variation based on a scatter diagram is often sufficiently accurate for certain purposes, six scatter diagrams are given on page 262. Two of these diagrams exhibit high, two medium, and two low, correlations between the indicated pairs of variables. In each case the actual correlation coefficient is given. The degree of linearity is estimated from the degree of concentration of the points about a straight line. Study of these graphs in Figure 45 will enable students to approximate roughly a correlation coefficient from a scatter diagram. It should be emphasized that in practically every case it is advisable to make a scatter diagram before computing a correlation coefficient. In this way, much tedious computation is avoided while much valuable information, especially with regard to the linearity or non-linearity of relationship, is often gained.

262   ELEMENTS OF STATISTICS

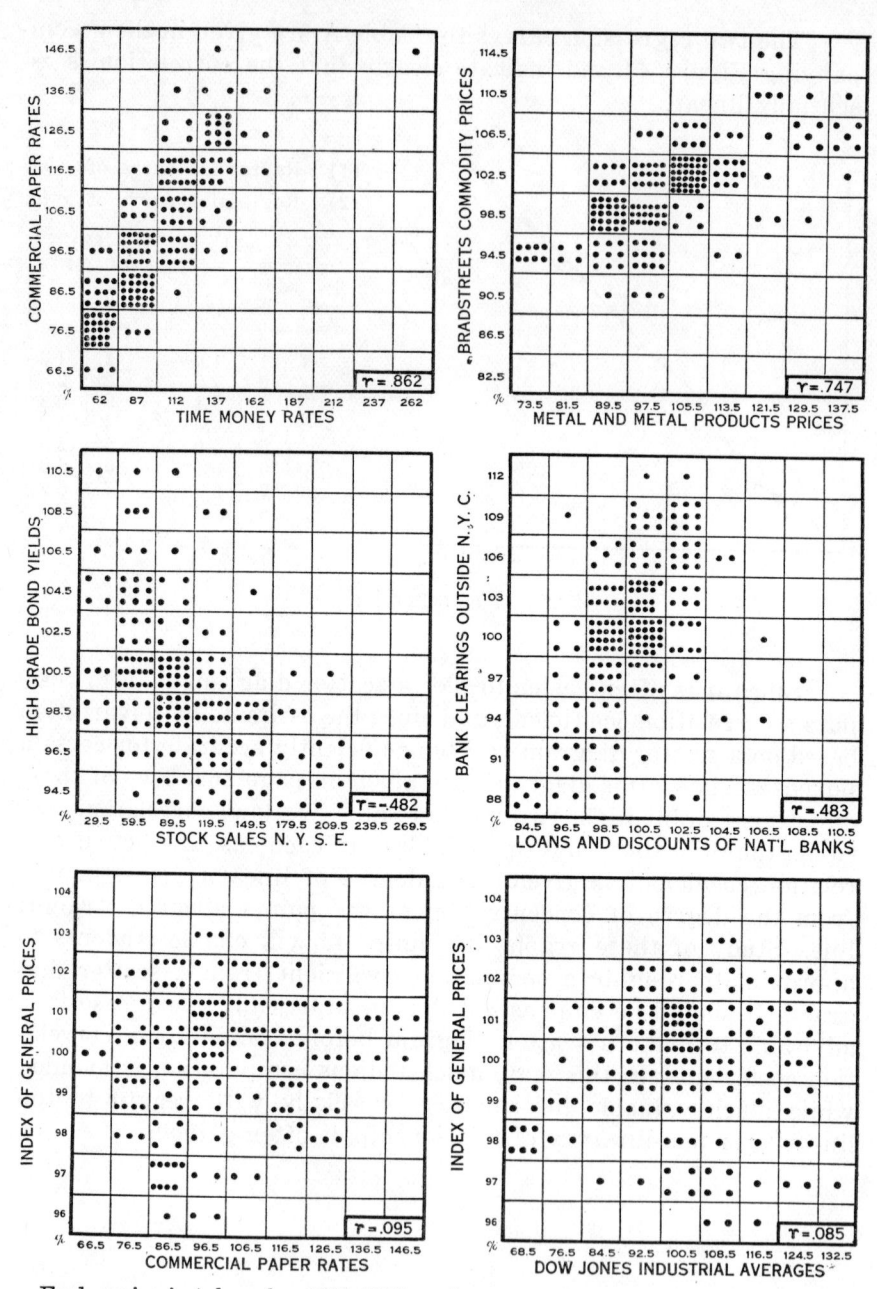

Each series is taken for 1897-1913, and expressed as percentage of trend.

FIGURE 45

ELEMENTS OF CORRELATION

4. Calculation of the Coefficient of Correlation. It is convenient to have a definite method of procedure to follow in the calculation of the coefficient of correlation from a correlation table, and the following scheme is suggested:

Class Marks (y)						Frequencies of rows	$g \cdot y$	$g \cdot y^2$	$T_i = \Sigma_j F_{ij} x_j$	$T_i \cdot y$
y_1	F_{11}	F_{12}	F_{13}	---	F_{1n}	g_1	$g_1 y_1$	$g_1 y_1^2$	T_1	$T_1 y_1$
y_2	F_{21}	F_{22}	F_{23}	---	F_{2n}	g_2	$g_2 y_2$	$g_2 y_2^2$	T_2	$T_2 y_2$
y_3	F_{31}	F_{32}	F_{33}	---	F_{3n}	g_3	$g_3 y_3$	$g_3 y_3^2$	T_3	$T_3 y_3$
y_4	F_{41}	F_{42}	F_{43}	---	F_{4n}	g_4	$g_4 y_4$	$g_4 y_4^2$	T_4	$T_4 y_4$
--	-	-	-	---	-	---	---	---	--	---
y_m	F_{m1}	F_{m2}	F_{m3}	---	F_{mn}	g_m	$g_m y_m$	$g_m y_m^2$	T_m	$T_m y_m$
Frequencies columns	f_1	f_2	f_3	---	f_n	N (Totals)	GY	GY^2	T	TY
Class Marks	x_1	x_2	x_3	---	x_n	Totals				
$f \cdot x$	$f_1 x_1$	$f_2 x_2$	$f_3 x_3$	---	$f_n x_n$	FX				
$f \cdot x^2$	$f_1 x_1^2$	$f_2 x_2^2$	$f_3 x_3^2$	---	$f_n x_n^2$	FX^2				
$= \Sigma_i F_{ij} y_i$	S_1	S_2	S_3	---	S_n	S				
$S_j \cdot x$	$S_1 x_1$	$S_2 x_2$	$S_3 x_3$	---	$S_n x_n$	SX				

$$\bar{x} = \frac{FX}{N}, \quad \bar{y} = \frac{GY}{N},$$

$$\sigma_x^2 = \frac{(FX^2)}{N} - \bar{x}^2; \quad \sigma_y^2 = \frac{(GY^2)}{N} - \bar{y}^2,$$

$$r = \frac{\frac{1}{N}\Sigma xy - \bar{x}\,\bar{y}}{\sigma_x \sigma_y} = \frac{\frac{TY}{N} - \bar{x}\,\bar{y}}{\sigma_x \sigma_y}$$

$$= \frac{N(TY) - FX \cdot GY}{\sqrt{[N(FX^2) - (FX)^2][N(GY^2) - (GY)^2]}}$$

One should note especially the computation checks: $TY = SX$, $S = GY$, $T = FX$.

The actual calculation of the two examples of the third section are given below, and the curves of regression for the first are graphed in Figure 44.

Calculation of Correlation Coefficient for Table A
Pig Iron Production (1897-1913)

Class Marks (y)								Frequencies of rows (g)	$g \cdot y$	$g \cdot y^2$	T	$T \cdot y$
7							15	15	105	735	105	735
6						6	34	1	41	246	1476	241	1446
5					5	51	6		62	310	1550	311	1555
4				3	33	1			37	148	592	146	584
3			2	24	3				29	87	261	88	264
2			7	2					9	18	36	20	40
1		2	1						3	3	3	4	4
0	6	2							8	0	0	2	0
Frequencies of columns	6	4	10	29	41	58	40	16	204	917	4653	917	4628
Class Marks (x)	0	1	2	3	4	5	6	7					
$f \cdot x$	0	4	20	87	164	290	240	112	917				
$f \cdot x^2$	0	4	40	261	656	1450	1440	784	4635				
S	0	2	21	88	166	295	234	111	917				
$S \cdot x$	0	2	42	264	664	1475	1404	777	4628				

Industrial Production (1897-1913)

Pig Iron Production (1897-1913)

$$\bar{x} = \frac{917}{204} = 4.4951, \qquad \bar{y} = \frac{917}{204} = 4.4951,$$

$$\sigma_x = \sqrt{\frac{4635}{204} - (4.4951)^2} = \sqrt{2.5147} = 1.5858,$$

$$\sigma_y = \sqrt{\frac{4653}{204} - (4.4951)^2} = \sqrt{2.6029} = 1.6134,$$

$$r = \frac{\frac{4628}{204} - (4.4951)(4.4951)}{(1.5858)(1.6134)} = \frac{2.4804}{2.5585} = .9695.$$

Note the Check: $TY = 4628 = SX$, $S = 917 = GY$, $T = 917 = FX$.

ELEMENTS OF CORRELATION

Calculation of Correlation Coefficient for Table B

Class Marks (y)									Frequencies of rows (g)	$g \cdot y$	$g \cdot y^2$	T	$T \cdot y$
6								4	4	24	144	16	96
5							7	2	9	45	225	29	145
4							5	9	14	56	224	51	204
3						6	25	11	42	126	378	131	393
2						4	13		17	34	68	47	94
1					2	2			4	4	4	6	6
0				1					1	0	0	0	0
−1			2	3	4				9	−9	9	−7	7
−2			4	1					5	−10	20	−9	18
−3		2	2						4	−12	36	−10	30
−4		3							3	−12	48	−9	36
−5	6	2							8	−40	200	−30	150
Frequencies of columns (f) Class Marks	6	7	8	4	5	2	12	50	26	120	206	1356	215	1179
(x)	−4	−3	−2	−1	0	1	2	3	4					
$f \cdot x$	−24	−21	−16	−4	0	2	24	150	104	215				
$f \cdot x^2$	96	63	32	4	0	2	48	450	416	1111				
S	−30	−28	−16	−5	−4	2	28	156	103	206				
$S \cdot x$	120	84	32	5	0	2	56	468	412	1179				

Index of Wholesale Commodity Prices (1919-1932)

$$\bar{x} = \frac{215}{120} = 1.7917 \; , \qquad \bar{y} = \frac{206}{120} = 1.7167 \; ,$$

$$\sigma_x = \sqrt{\frac{1111}{120} - (1.7917)^2} = \sqrt{6.0481} = 2.4593 \; ,$$

$$\sigma_y = \sqrt{\frac{1356}{120} - (1.7167)^2} = \sqrt{8.3529} = 2.8901 \; ,$$

$$r = \frac{\frac{1179}{120} - (1.7917)(1.7167)}{(2.4593)(2.8901)} = \frac{6.7493}{7.1076} = .9496 \; .$$

The calculations made from the correlation table are self-evident, except, perhaps, for the quantities T and S. T_i, as explained in the general table, is defined by the series

$$T_i = \Sigma_j F_{ij} x_j ,$$

that is, the frequency in each cell is multiplied by the corresponding value of x, and these products are then summed by rows.

Similarly, S is the sum of the products of the frequencies in any column by their corresponding values of y, i.e.,

$$S_j = \Sigma_i F_{ij} y_i .$$

Referring to the calculations of Table A, it is seen, for example, that
$$T_1 = 15(7) = 105 ,$$
$$T_2 = 6(5) + 34(6) + 1(7) = 241 ,$$
$$S_5 = 5(5) + 33(4) + 3(3) = 166 .$$

PROBLEMS

1. The following data give (a) the closing prices as of December 31, 1931, for 200 stocks listed on the New York Stock Exchange, and (b) the annual dividend payments per share on these stocks. Make a scatter diagram and calculate the coefficient of correlation. What do you now know of the relationship between the dividend and the price of shares? The answer to this problem is obtained by the use of the following intervals: for the dividend series, the interval range is 50-949 at units of 50, with the first interval having frequencies under 50, and the last interval having frequencies 950 and over. For the price series, the intervals range from 10 to 220 inclusive, at units of 5, with the first interval being under 10. Thus for the dividend series there will be 20 intervals, and for the price series 16 intervals.

Closing Prices as of December 31, 1931, for 200 stocks listed on the New York Stock Exchange, and Annual Dividend Payments per Share on these Stocks

No.	Dividend	Price per share	No.	Dividend	Price per share
1	1.60	16½	51	2.50	21¾
2	2.00	23	52	2.00	30
3	1.50	24¾	53	10.00	178½
4	3.00	97	54	10.00	100¼
5	.60	6½	55	3.00	34
6	.40	7¼	56	1.00	18
7	11.00	212	57	4.00	45
8	1.80	40⅛	58	1.00	7¾
9	6.00	117	59	4.00	106¼
10	3.00	60	60	1.75	21½
11	6.00	175¼	61	7.00	69⅛
12	3.00	33⅛	62	3.50	54
13	2.00	16	63	2.00	9
14	2.00	17⅞	64	2.00	11⅛
15	2.00	55	65	3.00	25
16	2.40	33	66	4.00	64⅞
17	4.00	110⅛	67	2.00	40
18	6.00	27½	68	3.00	48½
19	3.00	30	69	1.00	17
20	2.00	39¼	70	2.00	33½
21	1.00	10⅛	71	6.00	50½
22	4.20	47⅞	72	1.50	24
23	3.00	27	73	1.50	22
24	2.00	21	74	4.00	60
25	1.40	30½	75	3.00	69⅜
26	1.00	17	76	3.00	21
27	3.00	50	77	4.00	67
28	1.00	16	78	1.50	17¼
29	2.00	30¾	79	2.00	16
30	5.00	58½	80	8.00	370
31	5.00	42	81	4.00	61⅛
32	4.00	41	82	5.00	103¼
33	3.00	36¼	83	3.00	36
34	3.00	25⅞	84	1.00	14½
35	2.00	38	85	1.00	9
36	5.00	41¾	86	3.00	10⅞
37	5.00	15	87	8.00	35
38	9.00	178⅝	88	1.00	24⅛
39	5.00	105½	89	2.50	24
40	5.00	106⅛	90	4.00	42½
41	8.00	95	91	2.00	11⅝
42	3.00	60	92	3.00	35
43	2.50	30	93	3.00	58
44	1.00	22	94	2.50	39⅛
45	2.40	26½	95	1.60	17
46	1.00	13¾	96	4.00	85
47	6.00	95	97	6.00	89⅜
48	2.00	15⅛	98	3.00	27
49	1.60	21½	99	1.50	19¼
50	4.00	24	100	12.00	194

(*Continued on page 268*)

No.	Dividend	Price per share	No.	Dividend	Price per share
101	2.00	23½	151	1.00	8⅞
102	1.80	18¾	152	1.20	14⅛
103	3.00	40	153	4.00	62½
104	2.50	40⅛	154	1.00	14¾
105	4.00	34½	155	4.00	86¾
106	7.00	48¾	156	5.00	147
107	3.00	22⅞	157	1.60	13⅝
108	2.40	25¼	158	6.00	53
109	2.00	19	159	1.00	39
110	1.00	16⅜	160	5.00	50
111	3.60	36	161	5.00	37
112	.50	3⅛	162	2.40	43½
113	3.50	20	163	2.50	31¾
114	3.00	16⅜	164	3.50	65⅛
115	3.50	77	165	1.50	23⅜
116	3.00	23½	166	2.40	21¼
117	6.00	146	167	1.60	22½
118	3.00	50⅜	168	1.50	43¾
119	2.50	47¼	169	.80	6
120	1.00	21½	170	3.00	10
121	3.00	40⅛	171	2.40	22
122	2.00	34⅝	172	2.60	46
123	.75	8⅜	173	.64	6⅞
124	5.00	77	174	1.00	17¾
125	2.00	20	175	2.50	40½
126	3.00	34	176	3.00	33
127	1.00	15½	177	1.00	12⅜
128	.60	8⅛	178	2.00	42½
129	2.00	32	179	4.00	27½
130	4.00	21	180	4.00	29½
131	5.00	26¼	181	5.00	51½
132	2.00	9½	182	4.00	59½
133	4.00	84	183	3.00	24
134	1.20	7	184	5.00	33
135	2.50	48	185	1.60	43⅝
136	1.00	10½	186	3.00	49
137	.60	9¼	187	.30	4⅜
138	3.00	78	188	3.00	46½
139	2.00	30	189	3.00	35⅜
140	2.40	32¼	190	4.00	22½
141	5.00	61	191	2.50	19⅛
142	4.00	40½	192	5.00	71
143	6.00	90	193	4.00	40½
144	3.50	40	194	3.75	21½
145	.48	8¼	195	2.50	32⅛
146	9.00	136½	196	5.00	45½
147	6.00	82½	197	2.00	16
148	8.00	182½	198	1.00	20⅜
149	1.20	11⅜	199	3.00	19⅞
150	8.00	212½	200	1.00	27¾

ELEMENTS OF CORRELATION

2. The following items give (a) the closing figures of the Dow-Jones Industrial Averages for each trading day from April 20 to June 20, 1933, and (b) the franc-dollar exchange rate on each of these days. Make a scatter diagram from these data, and calculate the coefficient of correlation.

1933 Month-Day	Dow-Jones Industrial Averages Closing Price	Franc-Dollar Exchange Rate
April—20	$72.27	$.0431
21	69.78	.0420
22	72.24	.0425
24	73.69	.0436
25	72.45	.0439
26	72.64	.0436
27	71.71	.0431
28	73.10	.0436
29	77.66	.0454
May 1	77.79	.0467
2	77.29	.0462
3	77.37	.0458
4	79.16	.0463
5	79.78	.0471
6	77.61	.0461
8	77.63	.0458
9	77.23	.0457
10	80.78	.0461
11	82.48	.0464
12	82.14	.0463
13	80.85	.0463
15	79.70	.0460
16	81.29	.0459
17	82.64	.0456
18	82.57	.0454
19	81.75	.0449
20	80.21	.0450
22	79.94	.0453
23	83.06	.0456
24	84.29	.0457
25	83.73	.0457
26	86.42	.0457
27	89.61	.0466
29	90.02	.0473
31	88.11	.0466
June—1	89.10	.0466
2	92.21	.0467
3	90.02	.0468
5	91.89	.0467
6	91.90	.0470
7	92.98	.0476
8	93.52	.0477
9	94.29	.0480
10	94.42	.0483
12	96.75	.0483
13	94.79	.0476
14	94.06	.0480
15	88.87	.0467
16	89.22	.0475
17	90.23	.0473
19	95.99	.0481
20	95.23	.0484

3. The table below gives American figures for (a) area planted to wheat, (b) production of wheat, and (c) yield per acre, for the years 1894-1930. Make a scatter diagram between (a) and (b), and between (c) and (b), and calculate the correlation coefficients for these series. Do your results suggest that acreage planted, or yield per acre, is more important in wheat production?

Year	Area Planted to Wheat (1,000,000 acres)	Production of Wheat (1,000,000 bu.)	Average yield per Acre (bushels)
1894	39.4	516.5	13.1
1895	40.8	569.5	13.9
1896	43.9	544.2	12.4
1897	46.0	610.3	13.3
1898	51.0	772.2	15.1
1899	52.6	658.5	12.1
1900	51.4	602.7	11.7
1901	52.5	788.6	15.0
1902	49.6	724.8	14.6
1903	51.6	663.9	12.9
1904	47.8	596.9	12.5
1905	49.4	726.8	14.7
1906	47.8	756.8	15.8
1907	45.1	637.9	14.1
1908	45.9	644.7	14.0
1909	44.3	700.4	15.8
1910	45.7	635.1	13.9
1911	49.5	621.3	12.5
1912	45.8	730.3	15.9
1913	50.2	763.4	15.2
1914	53.5	891.0	16.6
1915	60.5	1025.8	17.0
1916	52.3	636.3	12.2
1917	45.1	636.7	14.1
1918	59.2	921.4	15.6
1919	75.7	967.9	12.8
1920	61.1	833.0	13.6
1921	63.7	814.9	12.8
1922	62.3	867.6	13.9
1923	59.7	797.4	13.4
1924	52.5	864.4	16.5
1925	52.4	676.8	12.9
1926	56.4	831.4	14.8
1927	58.8	878.4	14.9
1928	58.3	914.9	15.7
1929	61.1	806.5	13.2
1930	59.1	850.9	14.4

4. Make a scatter diagram for the following data, which give (a) monthly average dollar-yen exchange rates from June 1931-May 1933, and (b) dollar value of American imports from Japan during these same months. Cal-

culate the coefficient of correlation. What conclusion as to the effect of depreciated currencies on export trade is suggested by your answer?

Year-Month	Dollar-yen Exchange Rate	Value of Imports from Japan ($1,000,000)
1931—June	$.4937	14.99
July	.4936	16.06
Aug.	.4935	16.05
Sept.	.4934	17.26
Oct.	.4925	19.47
Nov.	.4930	20.41
Dec.	.4346	18.80
1932—Jan.	.3599	14.15
Feb.	.3432	12.72
Mar.	.3216	13.16
Apr.	.3281	11.28
May	.3197	8.81
June	.3029	8.54
July	.2745	8.58
Aug.	.2449	10.07
Sept.	.2363	12.14
Oct.	.2306	10.51
Nov.	.2062	11.73
Dec.	.2073	12.32
1933—Jan.	.2074	7.94
Feb.	.2079	5.69
Mar.	.2126	7.53
Apr.	.2209	8.06

5. Make a selection of data from some field in which you are interested and test for correlation. For example, obtain the figures for the production and price of some commodity over a period of more than fifty years and see how supply and demand are correlated. If such data are studied, two factors must be considered. First, correction must be made for increased population. This can be made by multiplying each item in the production column by $100/P$, where P is the population;[1] second, there may be a lag in the price due to the fact that the effect upon the price of an increased or a diminished supply may not be felt immediately. This can be corrected for by shifting the price figures one year.

5. *Lines of Regression.* It is natural next to inquire what are the best lines which fit the points lying on the regression curves obtained in section 3. But, upon consideration, it is seen that the values of y on the regression curve of y on x are themselves averages of the values in each column. It has seemed more desirable,

---

[1] Annual population figures, interpolated from the decennial census figures, are given in the *World Almanac* and other handbooks.

therefore, particularly since greater symmetry is gained in the resulting formulas, to fit the best line to the data by minimizing the sum of the squares of the deviations *for every value of y* instead of minimizing the sum of the squares of the deviations of *the averages of y*. The result of this is merely to replace ordinary averages by weighted averages in calculating the coefficients in the normal equations.

The line is assumed to be of the form

$$y = a_1 + a_2 x , \qquad (1)$$

and the total frequencies of the column corresponding to $x_1, x_2 \cdots \cdots x_n$ are represented by $f_1, f_2, \cdots\cdots, f_n'$; of the rows corresponding to $y_1, y_2, \cdots\cdots, y_m$ by $g_1, g_2, \cdots\cdots g_m$; and of the cells, that is, of the squares in the table corresponding to the points x_i, y_j, by F_{ji}, where, of course,

$$f_1 + f_2 + \cdots\cdots + f_n = N,$$
$$g_1 + g_2 + \cdots\cdots + g_m = N ,$$
$$F_{11} + F_{12} + \cdots\cdots + F_{mn} = N .$$

One will then have, referring to the work of the preceding chapter,

$$A_1(x) = 1 , \qquad A_2(x) = x ,$$

from which are calculated

$$[A_1 A_1] = f_1 + f_2 + \cdots\cdots + f_n = N ;$$
$$[A_1 A_2] = [A_2 A_1] = f_1 x_1 + f_2 x_2 + \cdots\cdots + f_n x_n ;$$
$$[A_2 A_2] = f_1 x_1^2 + f_2 x_2^2 + \cdots\cdots + f_n x_n^2 ;$$
$$[A_1 y] = g_1 y_1 + g_2 y_2 + \cdots\cdots + g_m y_m ;$$
$$[A_2 y] = F_{11} x_1 y_1 + F_{21} x_1 y_2 + \cdots\cdots + F_{mn} x_n y_m .$$

Solving the normal equations

$$[A_1 A_1] a_1 + [A_1 A_2] a_2 = [A_1 y] ,$$
$$[A_2 A_1] a_1 + [A_2 A_2] a_2 = [A_2 y] ,$$

one has

$$a_1 = \frac{[A_1 y][A_2 A_2] - [A_1 A_2][A_2 y]}{[A_1 A_1][A_2 A_2] - [A_2 A_1]^2} ,$$

$$a_2 = \frac{[A_1 A_1][A_2 y] - [A_2 A_1][A_2 y]}{[A_1 A_1][A_2 A_2] - [A_2 A_1]^2} .$$

As shown previously, the following expression holds:
$$[A_1A_1][A_2A_2] - [A_2A_1]^2 = N(f_1x_1^2 + f_2x_2^2 + \cdots + f_nx_n^2)$$
$$- (f_1x_1 + f_2x_2 + \cdots + f_nx_n)^2$$
$$= N^2 \sigma_x^2 .$$

If one makes the abbreviations
$$\Sigma xy = F_{11}x_1y_1 + F_{21}x_1y_2 + \cdots + F_{mn}x_ny_m ,$$
$$\bar{x} = (f_1x_1 + f_2x_2 + \cdots + f_nx_n)/N ,$$
$$\bar{y} = (g_1y_1 + g_2y_2 + \cdots + g_my_m)/N ,$$

one may then write,
$$[A_1A_1][A_2y] - [A_2A_1][A_1y] = N\Sigma xy - N^2 \bar{x}\bar{y} ,$$

and
$$[A_1y][A_2A_2] - [A_1A_2][A_2y] = N\bar{y}(f_1x_1^2 + f_2x_2^2 + \cdots + f_nx_n^2)$$
$$- N\bar{x}\Sigma xy$$
$$= N\bar{y}(N\sigma_x^2 + N\bar{x}^2) - N\bar{x}\Sigma xy = N^2\bar{y}\sigma_x^2 + \bar{x}(N^2\bar{x}\bar{y} - N\Sigma xy) .$$

Thus, for a_1 and a_2 are found the values:
$$a_1 = \frac{N\Sigma xy - N^2\bar{x}\bar{y}}{N^2\sigma_x^2} ,$$

$$a_2 = \frac{N^2\bar{y}\sigma_x^2 + \bar{x}(N^2\bar{x}\bar{y} - N\Sigma xy)}{N^2\sigma_x^2} .$$

If these values are substituted in equation (1), one obtains
$$y = \frac{N\Sigma xy - N^2\bar{x}\bar{y}}{N^2\sigma_x^2} x + \bar{y} + \frac{\bar{x}(N^2\bar{x}\bar{y} - N\Sigma xy)}{N^2\sigma_x^2} ,$$

or
$$y - \bar{y} = \frac{(1/N)\Sigma xy - \bar{x}\bar{y}}{\sigma_x^2}(x - \bar{x}) ,$$

which may be written
$$y - \bar{y} = r(\sigma_y/\sigma_x)(x - \bar{x}) , \qquad (2)$$

where

$$r = \frac{(1/N)\Sigma xy - \bar{x}\,\bar{y}}{\sigma_x \sigma_y} \,. \tag{3}$$

The quantity r, as has been stated before, is called the *coefficient of correlation*, and the line represented by (2) is called the *line of regression of y on x*. In an exactly similar way one can derive the *line of regression of x on y*,

$$x - \bar{x} = r(\sigma_x/\sigma_y)(y - \bar{y}) \,,$$

or
$$y - \bar{y} = (1/r)(\sigma_y/\sigma_x)(x - \bar{x}) \,.$$

Example: As an illustration, regression lines may be fitted to the correlation Tables A and B.

For Table A, one finds the values

$$\bar{x} = 4.4951 \,, \quad \bar{y} = 4.4951 \,, \quad \sigma_x = 1.5858 \,,$$
$$\sigma_y = 1.6134 \,, \quad r = .9695 \,.$$

Hence, the line of regression of y on x is

$$y - 4.4951 = .9695\,(1.6134/1.5858)\,(x - 4.4951) \,,$$
$$y - 4.4951 = .9864\,(x - 4.4951) \,,$$

or
$$y = .9864x + .0611 \,.$$

Similarly, the line of regression of x on y is

$$x - 4.4951 = .9695\,(1.5858/1.6134)\,(y - 4.4951) \,,$$
$$x - 4.4951 = .9529\,(y - 4.4951) \,,$$

or
$$x = .9529y + .2117 \,.$$

For Table B, one has the values

$$\bar{x} = 1.7917 \,, \quad \bar{y} = 1.7167 \,, \quad \sigma_x = 2.4593 \,,$$
$$\sigma_y = 2.8901 \,, \quad r = .9496 \,.$$

Substituting in the formulas, one obtains for the line of regression of y on x,

$$y - 1.7167 = 1.1160\,(x - 1.7917) \,,$$

ELEMENTS OF CORRELATION

or
$$y = 1.1160x - .2828 \; ;$$

and for the line of regression of x on y,

$$x - 1.7917 = .8080\,(y - 1.7167)$$

or
$$x = .8080y + .4046 \; .$$

These results are represented graphically in the accompanying Figure 46. The angles between the regression lines serve as a measure of the relative magnitude of the correlation coefficient. In the case of perfect correlation the lines coincide; in the case of zero correlation the lines are perpendicular to each other. [See section 6(d)].

(1) Line of regression of y on x,
(2) Line of regression of x on y,
- - - - Regression curve of y on x,
. . . . Regression curve of x on y.

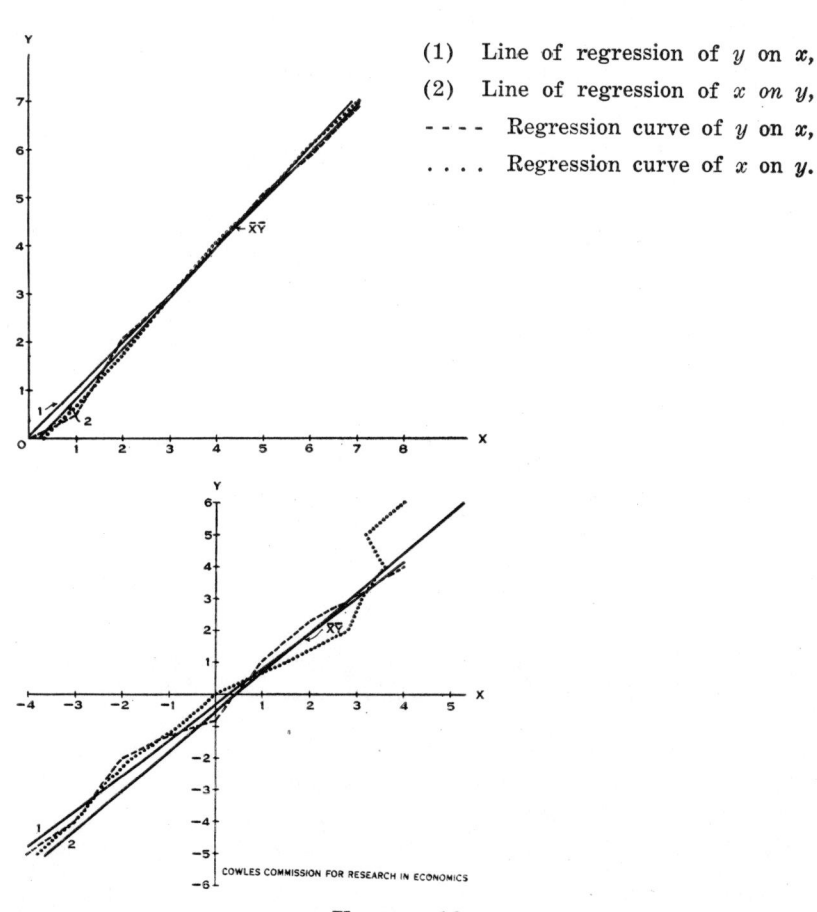

FIGURE 46

PROBLEMS

1. Calculate and graph the regression lines for the data of problem 3, section 2.

2. Fit a straight line to the data of problem 5, section 2, i.e., to National Income (x) and Index of Industrial Production (y). Compare the coefficient of x with the value $r \dfrac{\sigma_y}{\sigma_x}$; given $\sigma_y = 19.484$, $\sigma_x = 6.834$, $r = 0.9356$.

3. Fit regression lines to the correlation table of problem 2, section 4.

4. Calculate the regression lines for problem 3, section 4.

6. *Properties of the Correlation Coefficient*. The correlation coefficient, for all its importance in the theory of statistics, is rather a difficult constant to interpret. A few facts associated with it will be pointed out in this section, although, unfortunately, the mathematics involved in the proofs is usually too difficult for an elementary presentation.

(a). The probable error[1] of the correlation coefficient r, is

$$.6745[(1-r^2)/\sqrt{N}],$$

where N is the total frequency used in determining it.

Example: In Table A,

$$p.\ e.\ \text{of}\ r = .6745[1-(.9695)^2]/\sqrt{204} = .0028.$$

(b). If in the two sequences of statistical values,

X data: $X_1 \quad X_2 \quad X_3 \quad \cdots\cdots\quad X_n$,
Y data: $Y_1 \quad Y_2 \quad Y_3 \quad \cdots\cdots\quad Y_n$,

the X and Y sequences are affected by $m + n$ equally probable causes of which m are common to both, then the correlation coefficient is equal to

$$r = m/(m+n)$$

or, in other words, the correlation coefficient is the ratio of the common causes to the total number of causes.

This very beautiful interpretation of the correlation coefficient is not easily proved, so the discussion must be limited to an illustra-

---

[1] On page 161, *Statistical Methods for Research Workers*, 3rd ed., London, 1930, R. A. Fisher writes: "It is necessary to warn the student emphatically against the misleading character of the standard error of the correlation coefficient deduced from a small sample, because the principal utility of the correlation coefficient lies in its application to subjects of which little is known, and upon which the data are relatively scanty." Whenever the sample is less than 100, it is considered small.

ELEMENTS OF CORRELATION 277

tion.[1] For such an illustration, where the elements are under control, one must turn away for a moment from economic data.

Let five coins be tossed, of which three are marked so that they can be identified, and record the number of heads that appear. The value thus obtained will form one item of the X data. The two unmarked coins are picked up and thrown again, letting the three others lie as they were. The number of heads now observed in the five coins is recorded to form one item of the Y data. A series of such operations provides the X and Y data.

It will be observed that this experiment gives one the control of the underlying causes of the correlation of the two sequences and that all the forces at work are identified. It is obvious that the fundamental cause of obtaining an entry of three heads, for example, in the X sequence, is the behavior of the five coins when they are tossed. Since in each pair of items three coins are always the same, it is obvious that there are five causes of which three are common, and the correlation coefficient should equal 3/5. That this is actually the case is exhibited in the following table, which is made up of the *a priori* frequencies:

Heads on First Toss

y							g	$g \cdot y$	$g \cdot y^2$	T	$T \cdot y$
5				1	2	1	4	20	100	16	80
4			3	8	7	2	20	80	320	68	272
3		3	12	16	8	1	40	120	360	112	336
2	1	8	16	12	3		40	80	160	88	176
1	2	7	8	3			20	20	20	32	32
0	1	2	1				4	0	0	4	0
f	4	20	40	40	20	4	128	320	960		896
x	0	1	2	3	4	5					
$f \cdot x$	0	20	80	120	80	20	320				
$f \cdot x^2$	0	20	160	360	320	100	960				
S	4	32	88	112	68	16					
$S \cdot x$	0	32	176	336	272	80	896				

$$\bar{x} = \frac{320}{128} = 2.5, \qquad \bar{y} = 2.5,$$

$$\sigma_x^2 = \frac{960}{128} - (2.5)^2 = 1.25, \qquad \sigma_y^2 = 1.25.$$

$$\frac{\Sigma xy}{N} = \frac{896}{128} = 7, \qquad r = \frac{7 - 6.25}{1.25} = \frac{3}{5}.$$

[1] See D. Brunt, *The Combination of Observations*, Cambridge, 1923, pp. 169-170; also, T. L. Kelley, *Statistical Method*, New York, 1923, pp. 189-190.

One must be careful in applying this suggestive analogy to economic relationships, where the assumption of a multitude of independent random causes often cannot be made; in many instances there are common causes at work on several variables.

(c). It is also important to know that the value of the correlation coefficient lies between -1 and $+1$.

When r has the value 1, it is clear that both lines of regression coincide and the correlation is perfect; but when $r = 0$, the two lines are at right angles to one another and no correlation whatever exists. Similarly, when $r = -1$ there is perfect inverse correlation, and the regression lines again coincide. The proof of these facts follows:

Setting $y_i - \bar{y} = d_i$ and $x_j - \bar{x} = D_j$, the following identity can be formed

$$S^2 \equiv F_{11}[d_1 - r(\sigma_y/\sigma_x)D_1]^2 + F_{12}[d_1 - r(\sigma_y/\sigma_x)D_2]^2 + \cdots$$
$$F_{1n}[d_1 - r(\sigma_y/\sigma_x)D_n]^2$$
$$+ F_{21}[d_2 - r(\sigma_y/\sigma_x)D_1]^2 + F_{22}[d_2 - r(\sigma_y/\sigma_x)D_2]^2 + \cdots$$
$$+ F_{2n}[d_2 - r(\sigma_y/\sigma_x)D_n]^2 + \cdots$$
$$\cdot \quad \cdot \quad \cdot \quad \cdot \quad \cdot \quad \cdot \quad \cdot \quad \cdot \quad \cdot$$
$$+ F_{m1}[d_m - r(\sigma_y/\sigma_x)D_1]^2 + F_{m2}[d_m - r(\sigma_y/\sigma_x)D_2]^2$$
$$+ \cdots + F_{mn}[d_m - r(\sigma_y/\sigma_x)D_n]^2$$
$$= [g_1 d_1^2 + g_2 d_2^2 + \cdots + g_m d_m^2] - 2r\sigma_y/\sigma_x [F_{11}d_1 D_1 + F_{12}d_1 D_2$$
$$+ \cdots + F_{mn}d_m D_n] + r^2 \sigma_y^2/\sigma_x^2 [f_1 D_1^2 + f_2 D_2^2 + \cdots + f_n D_n^2] \;.$$

But one notices that the first term is equal to $N\sigma_y^2$, and the last term reduces to $r^2(\sigma_y^2/\sigma_x^2)N\sigma_x^2 = r^2 N\sigma_y^2$. One also has

$$F_{11}d_1 D_1 + F_{12}d_1 D_2 + \cdots + F_{mn}d_m D_n$$
$$= F_{11}(y_1 - \bar{y})(x_1 - \bar{x}) + F_{12}(y_1 - \bar{y})(x_2 - \bar{x}) + \cdots$$
$$+ F_{mn}(y_m - \bar{y})(x_n - \bar{x})$$
$$= (F_{11}y_1 x_1 + F_{12}y_1 x_2 + \cdots) - (g_1 y_1 + g_2 y_2 + \cdots)\bar{x}$$
$$- (f_1 x_1 + f_2 x_2 + \cdots)\bar{y} + N\bar{x}\bar{y}$$
$$= \Sigma xy - N\bar{y}\bar{x} - N\bar{x}\bar{y} + N\bar{x}\bar{y} = N\sigma_x \sigma_y r \;.$$

When these values are substituted in the formula for S^2, one gets
$$S^2 = N\sigma_y^2 - 2r^2\sigma_y^2 N + r^2\sigma_y^2 N$$
$$= N\sigma_y^2 (1 - r^2) \ .$$

But the left hand member is never negative, and thus it follows that r can never be greater than 1. When $r = 1$, the two regression lines are seen to be identical, which means perfect correlation, and when $r = 0$, they become

$$y = \bar{y} \ , \text{ line of regression of } y \text{ on } x,$$

and

$$x = \bar{x} \ , \text{ line of regression of } x \text{ on } y,$$

which means no correlation.

(d). From section 5, it is seen that the regression equations of y on x and x on y are

$$y - \bar{y} = r(\sigma_y/\sigma_x)(x - \bar{x}) \ ,$$
$$y - \bar{y} = (1/r)(\sigma_y/\sigma_x)(x - \bar{x}) \ .$$

Hence, from section 4, Chapter II, the slopes of the above lines are found to be $r(\sigma_y/\sigma_x)$ and $(1/r)(\sigma_y/\sigma_x)$ respectively. From analytical geometry, which says that the tangent of the angle ϑ between two lines of slopes m_1 and m_2 is given by the formula $\tan \vartheta = (m_1 - m_2)/(1 + m_1 m_2)$, the tangent of the angle between the regression lines is

$$\operatorname{Tan} \vartheta = \frac{r(\sigma_y/\sigma_x) - (1/r)(\sigma_y \sigma_x)}{1 + (\sigma_y^2/\sigma_x^2)} = \frac{\sigma_x \sigma_y}{(\sigma_x^2 + \sigma_y^2)} \cdot (r^2 - 1)/r \ .$$

Thus, it is seen that when $r = 1$, $\tan \vartheta = 0$, and the lines of regression are equal. When $r = 0$, then $\tan \vartheta = \infty$, $\vartheta = 90°$, and the lines of regression are perpendicular.

(e). A specialization of the correlation coefficient that is in common use as a method of estimating relationships is what is called the *rank correlation coefficient*.

Let the items of a set of data be ranked according to two attributes, X and Y, and let a_x and a_y be the ranks of the items with respect to X and Y respectively. It will be clear that a_x and a_y are merely the integers $1, 2, 3, \cdots, N$ in some order.

Then the correlation of the rank a_x with the rank a_y is measured by the coefficient,[1]

$$r = 1 - \frac{6 \Sigma (a_x - a_y)^2}{N(N^2 - 1)}.$$

In order to derive this formula, one will first notice that the first and second moments of both sets of rank numbers are equal respectively to

$$\sum_{n=1}^{N} n = N(N+1)/2$$

and

$$\sum_{n=1}^{N} n^2 = N(N+1)(2N+1)/6 .$$

Hence one has,

$$A_X = A_Y = (N+1)/2 , \text{ and } \sigma_x^2 = \sigma_y^2 = (N^2-1)/12 .$$

One also notes the expansion:

$$\Sigma(a_x - a_y)^2 = \Sigma(a_x^2 - 2a_x a_y + a_y^2) = -2\Sigma a_x a_y + 2 \sum_{n=1}^{N} n^2$$
$$= -2\Sigma a_x a_y + N(N+1)(2N+1)/3 .$$

Now, consider the correlation coefficient,

$$r = \frac{(1/N)\Sigma a_x a_y - A_x A_y}{\sigma_x \sigma_y} .$$

Employing the expansion of $\Sigma(a_x - a_y)^2$ to replace $\Sigma a_x a_y$, one can then write r in the form,

$$r = \frac{(N+1)(2N+1)/6 - (1/2N)\Sigma(a_x - a_y)^2 - (N+1)^2/4}{(N^2-1)/12} ,$$

which reduces to the formula given above.

---

[1] This coefficient is generally attributed to C. Spearman who published it in 1904 in the *American Journal of Psychology*, Vol. 15 (1904), pp. 72-101.

ELEMENTS OF CORRELATION

PROBLEMS

1. Calculate the probable error of the correlation coefficient given in Table B.

2. The following table gives the heads in successive tosses where 4 pennies are tossed in the second throw and 8 remain as they fell in the first throw of 12 coins. (From R. Pearl, p. 298, *Medical Biometry and Statistics*, Philadelphia, 1923, adapted from A. D. Darbishire).[1] Calculate the correlation coefficient. On the basis of the theory of this section, what should the coefficient of correlation be? Show from the probable error of r that this prediction is justified.

y													Totals
12													0
11							1						1
10						1	3	3	3				10
9				1	1	4	13	5	5	3	1		33
8				1	8	19	13	10	1				52
7			1	1	15	29	27	13	7	1			94
6			4	12	30	36	19	10	7	1			119
5			4	21	30	26	13	4					98
4		3	1	12	20	9	5	2					52
3		2	8	9	7	4							30
2		4	2	3	2								11
1													0
0													0
f	0	0	9	20	58	106	113	88	59	32	11	3	1	500
x	0	1	2	3	4	5	6	7	8	9	10	11	12	

Heads in Second Toss (row label)

Heads in First Toss.

3. Compute the angles between the regression lines of Table A, Table B.

---

[1] "Some Tables for Illustrating Statistical Correlation." *Mem. and Proc. Manchester Lit. and Phil. Soc.*, Vol. 51 (1907), 20 p.

4. Calculate the angle between the regression line for the table in (b) section 6.

5. Find the rank correlation for the two series of problem 5, section 2.

6. Compute the rank correlation for the data of problem 2, section 4.

7. *The Correlation Surface.* A very illuminating way of looking at correlation is that obtained directly from the theory of probability.

It has been shown in previous chapters that if the frequencies of two variables x and y are normal, the respective probabilities associated with class marks x and y measured from $\bar{x}$ and $\bar{y}$ as origin are

$$P_x = \frac{1}{\sigma_x \sqrt{2\pi}} e^{-\frac{x^2}{2\sigma_y^2}},$$

and

$$P_y = \frac{1}{\sigma_y \sqrt{2\pi}} e^{-\frac{y^2}{2\sigma_y^2}}.$$

If the frequencies associated with x and y are independent of one another, then the probability of a joint occurrence of x and y will be

$$P_{xy} = \frac{1}{2\pi\sigma_x\sigma_y} e^{-\frac{1}{2}\left(\frac{x^2}{\sigma_x^2} + \frac{y^2}{\sigma_y^2}\right)}. \qquad (4)$$

If straight lines, equal in length to P_{xy}, be erected at each point on the xy-plane, it is clear that the locus of these points will form a surface. This is known as the *normal frequency surface.*

Now it seems very reasonable to assume that, if the x and y frequencies are not independent; that is to say, are correlated to some extent, the probability of the joint occurrence of x and y should be represented by an equation of the form:

$$P = k\, e^{ax^2 + bxy + cy^2}.$$

The values of a, b, c, and k, should all depend upon the correlation coefficient r and be limited by the conditions (1) that P should reduce to P_{xy} for $r = 0$, and (2) that the volume included between the xy-plane and the correlation surface should be equal to unity.

The calculations[1] necessary in the determination of a, b, c, and k, depend upon integral calculus and can not be made here. The result is what should naturally be expected, i.e.,

$$P = \frac{1}{2\pi\sigma_x\sigma_y\sqrt{1-r^2}} e^{-\frac{1}{2(1-r^2)}\left(\frac{x^2}{\sigma_x^2} - \frac{2xyr}{\sigma_x\sigma_y} + \frac{y^2}{\sigma_y^2}\right)}.$$

The surface corresponding to this equation is called the *correlation* surface, and reduces to the normal frequency surface when $r = 0$. The following Figure 47 shows an ideal normal frequency surface. As the correlation increases, this surface shrinks in about the diagonal of the square, until, in perfect correlation, only a line is left.

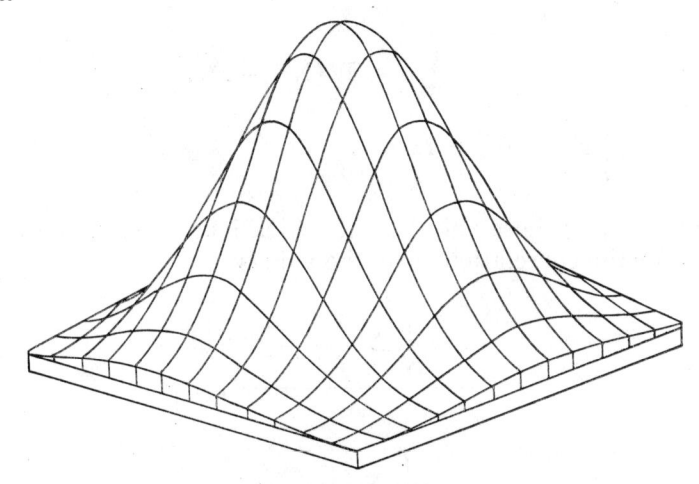

FIGURE 47

8. *Non-linear Regression.* It sometimes happens that the regression curves obtained by connecting the means of the columns (or rows) will not approximate straight lines. The correlation is then said to be non-linear and the theory is considerably more complex than in the linear case.

In order to give a measure of the correlation in this case, Karl Pearson, in 1905, introduced two new measures of correlation, η_{yx} and η_{xy}, known as the *correlation ratio* of y on x and the *correlation ratio* of x on y, respectively.[2]

---

[1] For these computations see, for example, E. T. Whittaker and G. Robinson, *The Calculus of Observations*, London and Glasgow, 1929, pp. 324-327.

[2] "On the General Theory of Skew-Correlation and Non-linear Regression," *Drapers' Company Research Memoirs, Biometric Series II*, 1905.

These ratios are defined as follows: If the symbols σ_{mx} and σ_{my} designate the standard deviations of the means of the Y arrays of X's and the X arrays of Y's respectively, then

$$\eta_{yx} = \frac{\sigma_{my}}{\sigma_y} \text{ and } \eta_{xy} = \frac{\sigma_{mx}}{\sigma_x}.$$

To put this in form for calculation, note that

$$\sigma^2{}_{my} = [\sum_i f_i(\bar{y}_i - \bar{y})^2]/N = [\sum_i f_i \bar{y}_i{}^2]/(N) - \bar{y}^2,$$

where $\bar{y}_i = [\sum_j F_{ji} y_j]/f_i = S_i/f_i$. Similarly, from symmetry, one finds $\sigma^2{}_{mx}$ to be

$$\sigma^2{}_{mx} = [\sum_i g_i \bar{x}_i{}^2]/(N) - \bar{x}^2,$$

where $\bar{x}_i = [\sum_j F_{ij} x_j]/g_i = T_i/g_i$.

Substituting these values in the equations of η_{yx} and η_{xy}, one reaches for the correlation ratio the values

$$\eta_{yx} = \frac{\sqrt{\frac{1}{N} \sum_i \frac{S_i{}^2}{f_i} - \bar{y}^2}}{\sigma_y},$$

$$\eta_{xy} = \frac{\sqrt{\frac{1}{N} \sum_i \frac{T_i{}^2}{g_i} - \bar{x}^2}}{\sigma_x}.$$

As an example, consider the following correlation table:

ELEMENTS OF CORRELATION

Class Marks (y)	1	2	3	4	5	6	7	8	9	10	Frequencies (g)	g·y	g·y²	T	T·y	T²	T²/g
1						3	5	3	2	3	16	16	16	125	125	15625	976.6
2				1	3	6	4	2	1	1	18	36	72	118	236	13924	773.6
3				1	15	17	3				36	108	324	202	606	40804	1133.4
4			2	9	16	8					35	140	560	170	680	28900	825.7
5		1	6	8	2	1					18	90	450	68	340	4624	256.9
6		3	5	1							9	54	324	25	150	625	69.4
7		4	2								6	42	294	14	98	196	32.7
8	2	2									4	32	256	6	48	36	9.0
9	3	1									4	36	324	5	45	25	6.2
10	1										1	10	100	1	10	1	1.0
Frequencies (f)	6	11	15	20	36	35	12	5	3	4	147	564	2720	734	2338		4084.5
Class Marks (x)	1	2	3	4	5	6	7	8	9	10							
f·x	6	22	45	80	180	210	84	40	27	40							
f·x²	6	44	135	320	900	1260	588	320	243	400							
S	53	76	82	87	125	103	22	7	4	5	564						
S·x	53	152	246	348	625	618	154	56	36	50	2338						
S²	2809	5776	6724	7569	15625	10609	484	49	16	25							
S²/f	468.2	525.1	448.3	378.4	434.0	303.1	40.3	9.8	5.3	6.3	2618.8						

From this table one can calculate, as in a previous section, the following values:

$$\bar{x} = 4.99, \quad \bar{y} = 3.84, \quad \sigma_x^2 = 3.75, \quad \sigma_y^2 = 3.78, \quad r = -.86,$$

$$\eta_{yx} = \frac{\sqrt{(2618.8/147) - (3.84)^2}}{\sqrt{(2720/147) - (3.84)^2}} = \frac{\sqrt{3.099}}{\sqrt{3.783}} = .90$$

$$\eta_{xy} = \frac{\sqrt{(4084.5/147) - (4.99)^2}}{\sqrt{(4212/147) - (4.99)^2}} = \frac{\sqrt{2.786}}{\sqrt{3.653}} = .87$$

It will be noticed that both of these coefficients are larger than the value for the linear correlation coefficient, r, but this fact is scarcely sufficient to give full assurance that the correlation is non-linear since the differences, $\eta^2_{yx} - r^2$, and $\eta^2_{xy} - r^2$, are not large.

The test for linearity, or non-linearity, must be made by means of some probable error formula. This question has been carefully investigated by J. Blakeman[1], but because of the intricate character of the analysis only the result can be stated here. Among the probable errors which Blakeman derives for the test of linear regression is the probable error for $\eta^2 - r^2$, i.e.,

$$\text{p. e.} = \pm .6745 \frac{2}{\sqrt{N}} \sqrt{(\eta^2 - r^2)[1 - 2(\eta^2 - r^2) + \eta^4 - r^4]} .$$

In our example, it is seen that

p. e. of $\eta^2_{yx} - r^2 = \pm .029$,

$\eta^2_{yx} - r^2 \pm$ p. e. $= .072 \pm .029$,

p. e. of $\eta^2_{xy} - r^2 = \pm .014$,

$\eta^2_{xy} - r^2 \pm$ p. e. $= .015 \pm .014$.

Since the first of these differences is almost three times its probable error while the second is just equal to its probable error, it is safe to conclude that one regression line shows a non-linear tendency but that the other is probably linear.

A second test which can be used when η and r are both small, or when $\eta^2 - r^2$ is small compared with r, is the following:

---

[1] "On Tests for Linearity of Regression," *Biometrika*, Vol. 4 (1906), pp. 332-350.

The correlation is non-linear if[1]

$$N(\eta^2 - r^2) > 11.37 .$$

In the example,

$$147(\eta^2_{yx} - r^2) = 147(.072) = 10.58$$

and

$$147(\eta^2_{xy} - r^2) = 147(.015) = 2.20 ,$$

which confirms the conclusion previously reached.

PROBLEMS

1. Calculate the correlation coefficient for the following table:

1						8	15	7	4	1		
2				1	2	10	5	8	7	6		
3				4	12	5	2	3	5	9	2	
4			2	9	6	3			2	4	3	1
5		1	2	7	5	2				1	1	2
6		3	5	5	2						1	3
7		6	3	1								2
8		2	2								1	1
Class Marks		1	2	3	4	5	6	7	8	9	10	11	12

2. Test the table of problem 1 for non-linearity. Is it more non-linear than the table used as an example in the text?

---

[1] This is derived from the formula for the probable error by assuming, first, that the p.e. may be replaced approximately by $.6745 \dfrac{2\sqrt{\eta^2 - r^2}}{\sqrt{N}}$ and assuming, second, that $\eta^2 - r^2$ is less than 2.5 times this p.e. The formula follows by solving the inequality for $N(\eta^2 - r^2)$. See *Handbook of Mathematical Statistics*, edited by H. L. Rietz, Cambridge, Mass., 1924, p. 131.

3. The following data show the relationship between Total Bills Discounted by the Federal Reserve Banks and Interest Rates on 4-6 months prime commercial paper. Calculate the correlation coefficients and determine whether this relationship is non-linear.

Total Bills Discounted by Federal Reserve Banks, (1923-1932)

Class Marks (y)										
7						1	6	6	6	
6					1	2	3	4		
5					1	3	1	2		
4				2		9	4	1		
3		1	2	1	4	9	4			
2		1		11	5	1				
1	4		2	3	3	1				
0	2	3	3	5	3					
Class Marks (x)	0	1	2	3	4	5	6	7	8	9

Interest Rates, 4-6 months Commercial Paper (1923-1932)

CHAPTER XI

MULTIPLE AND PARTIAL CORRELATION

1. *Multiple Factors in Experience.* Simple correlation is a measurement of the amount of co-variation between two series, and may indicate the degree to which one element affects another, or the degree to which the two are affected by common causes. But the most cursory thought on the situation will serve to indicate that most of the economic elements with which one deals are influenced by a variety of factors rather than by one alone. Crops, for example, are a result not only of acreage planted, but also of the yield per acre. The yield per acre, in turn, is a compound of several causal factors, the labor expended, temperature, amount of rainfall, fertilizer supplied, and perhaps irrigation. A consideration of long-term bond prices would suggest that they respond to such situations as (1) changes in the cost of living, since the public regards bonds as relatively undesirable in protracted periods of rising prices, and *vice versa,* (2) the earnings applicable to the interest charges, the bond price responding to variations in earnings which threaten or fortify the coupon payments, and (3) other interest rates, which influence the height at which bond prices will capitalize their coupon payments.

Science deals most successfully with those problems in which two or three primary causes of some phenomenon can be isolated and analyzed. In economic situations there are often obviously a multitude of factors at work. Measurements are lacking which would enable one to assess the relative importance of these factors, the primary causes are not always adequately identified, and the elements in the series cannot be controlled in order that their influences may be evaluated. This last point embraces one of the major difficulties in economic studies as compared with, say, studies in chemistry. If one wishes to determine the influences of variation in money rates on business conditions, he cannot, for purposes of experimentation, stabilize money rates for a period of years and then measure what effects ensue in commerce and industry. The elements of economics lie outside the effective control of the student of economics.

But statistical procedure has a substitute for lack of control.

Statistics allows the isolation of any one of several variables in an economic state, and a study of the influence of the remaining variables. Or it allows study of the composite influence of several variables on one variable. These ends are obtained through the techniques of partial and multiple correlation.

Unfortunately, the mathematical theory on which this subject rests is beyond the scope of an elementary treatment, but analogy with the theory of simple correlation, which has already been developed, makes possible some comprehension of the essential features.

2. *The Relationship between Wheat Production, Acreage Planted, and Yield per Acre.* The subject of partial correlation is most profitably approached by means of an example. An example may be taken in which common sense affords a solution at the beginning, so that one sees statistical technique producing results which appeal *a priori* as valid.

It is obvious that wheat production is the product of two, and only two, independent elements, the first being the acreage planted, and the second being the yield per acre. If acreage never varied, production would vary only with yield per acre; if yield never varied, only acreage would influence production.

However, one may set for himself the statistical problem of finding out how far production of wheat can be determined from a knowledge, first, of acreage planted and, second, of yield per acre.

The subscripts 1, 2, and 3, may be used to designate the annual items in production, acreage, and yield. Using the figures from 1894 through 1930, as given in problem 3, section 4, of the previous chapter, the following figures are obtained:

Wheat	Mean	Standard Deviation
1. Production	742.71 (million bu.)	124.68 ± 9.7760
2. Acreage	52.49 (million acres)	7.36 ± .5770
3. Yield	14.13 (bu. per acre)	1.40 ± .1098

The correlations among these three items are tabulated thus:

Correlation Coefficients of Zero Order

Wheat	Production	Acreage	Yield
1. Production	$r_{11} = 1.000$	$r_{12} = .782$	$r_{13} = .587$
2. Acreage	$r_{21} = .782$	$r_{22} = 1.000$	$r_{23} = .016$
3. Yield	$r_{31} = .587$	$r_{32} = .016$	$r_{33} = 1.000$

3. Partial Correlations. The table shows that there exist positive correlations among all three variables, although the coefficient as between acreage and yield is insignificant. This last is to be expected, since there exists no necessary or probable connection between the acreage which farmers plant and a yield dictated largely by the accident of weather. From the other coefficients it will be indicated that acreage planted seems to have been rather more decisive than yield per acre in influencing the production of this cereal.

A simple question, to which the approximate answer is known, may be raised. Suppose that through all these years acreage planted had been unvarying, then would not yield per acre have been much more potent in influencing production than appears from the table of coefficients of correlation given above? Or, if yield per acre had been stable through these years, would not acreage planted have been practically the sole remaining influence in dictating the level of production?

In other words, it is quite possible that the correlation between production and acreage might be materially altered if production and acreage items were correlated only for those years which had the same yield. For example, what is the correlation between production and acreage planted using only those particular years in which the yield was 15 bushels per acre?

It is often difficult to answer a question of this kind from the data at one's disposal, since the number of cases is generally too small to permit the analysis of such subdivisions of the data without greatly increasing probable errors. The answer to such a question, however, is inherent in the correlation coefficients themselves, and the elegant and powerful theory of partial correlation enables us to obtain this answer. In other words, from the theory of partial correlation, one is able to measure the relationship between two variables when one or more other variables that influence the situation are held fixed.

The following notation has become standard in this theory. Let $X_1, X_2, \ldots, X_n$, designate a set of n variables whose mutual correlations are being investigated. The correlations between them are denoted by the symbol r_{ij}, where i and j may have any of the values from 1 to n. For example, r_{12} is the correlation between X_1 and X_2; r_{34} is the correlation between X_3 and X_4, etc. These correlations are known as *coefficients of zero order*, and the subscripts are known as the *primary subscripts*. The student will, of course, recognize them as the familiar coefficients which he has studied in the previous chapter.

If one of the items, say X_k, is held fixed, and the correlation then computed for two of the other variables, for example X_i and X_j, the correlation coefficient thus obtained is designated by the symbol $r_{ij \cdot k}$, and is called the *correlation coefficient of first order*. The subscript k is called a *secondary subscript*.

Without going into its derivation, which is beyond the scope of this book, the formula for the second order correlation coefficient may be given as follows:

$$r_{ij \cdot k} = \frac{r_{ij} - r_{ik} r_{jk}}{\sqrt{(1 - r_{ik}^2)(1 - r_{jk}^2)}} \qquad (1)$$

As an example, calculate the correlation between production of wheat and acreage planted, when yield per acre has been held fixed.

Referring to the table of section 2, it is seen that one is required to find the value of $r_{12 \cdot 3}$. Making use of the values of the zero-order coefficients, one thus obtains:

$$r_{12 \cdot 3} = \frac{r_{12} - r_{13} r_{23}}{\sqrt{(1 - r_{13}^2)(1 - r_{23}^2)}} = \frac{.782 - (.587)(.016)}{\sqrt{[1 - (.587)^2][1 - (.016)^2]}}$$

$$= \frac{.782 - .009}{\sqrt{(.655)(.9997)}} = \frac{.773}{.809} = .956 \ .$$

This calculation can be made either by logarithms or from the very useful tables computed by J. R. Miner.[1]

Again, calculate the correlation between production and yield per acre when acreage planted is held fixed. From equation (1),

$$r_{13 \cdot 2} = \frac{r_{13} - r_{12} r_{32}}{\sqrt{(1 - r_{12}^2)(1 - r_{32}^2)}} = \frac{.587 - (.782)(.016)}{\sqrt{[1 - (.782)^2][1 - (.016)^2]}}$$

$$= \frac{.587 - .013}{\sqrt{(.388)(.9997)}} = \frac{.574}{.623} = .921 \ .$$

---

[1] J. R. Miner: *Tables of $\sqrt{1 - r^2}$ and $1 - r^2$ for Use in Partial Correlation and Trigonometry*, Baltimore, 1922, 49 pp.

In the third place, one may calculate the correlation between acreage planted and yield per acre when production is fixed. This involves the computation of $r_{23 \cdot 1}$ as follows:

$$r_{23 \cdot 1} = \frac{r_{23} - r_{21} r_{31}}{\sqrt{(1 - r_{21}^2)(1 - r_{31}^2)}} = \frac{.016 - (.782)(.587)}{\sqrt{[1 - (.782)^2][1 - (.587)^2]}}$$

$$= \frac{.016 - .459}{\sqrt{(.388)(.655)}} = \frac{-.443}{.504} = -.879 .$$

The following conclusions emerge. The size of the first coefficient of partial correlation indicates that in the absence of any change in yield per acre, the acreage planted practically dictates the size of the crop. The size of the second coefficient indicates that in the absence of any change in acreage planted, the yield per acre practically dictates the size of the crop. The third coefficient, which is negative, indicates that in the absence of any change in the size of the crop, acreage and yield move in almost complete inverse relationship. If crop production, for example, in two years is identical, any increase in acreage that may have occurred must have been compensated for by a decrease in yield, any increase in yield by a decrease in acreage. These conclusions, statistically reached, are, of course, entirely agreeable to common sense.

The significant thing about this conclusion is that one is able to arrive at the fundamental relationships which exist between factors without the necessity of actually studying sub-groups of data taken from the original figures. If one had actually been able to select statistics from a large number of years when production was constant, and had calculated the correlation between acreage and yield, he would have reached the same result, within sampling error.

Example: Relationships between the Dow-Jones Industrial Averages, Pig Iron Production, and Volume of Sales on the New York Stock Exchange.

The following table gives the zero-order correlation coefficients between monthly items, 1897-1913, of (1) The Dow-Jones Averages of Industrial Stock Prices, (2) Pig Iron Production, and (3) Shares of Stock Sold on the New York Stock Exchange:

	(1)	(2)	(3)
(1)	$r_{11} = 1.000$	$r_{12} = .779$	$r_{13} = .407$
(2)	$r_{21} = .779$	$r_{22} = 1.000$	$r_{23} = .074$
(3)	$r_{31} = .407$	$r_{32} = .074$	$r_{33} = 1.000$

These series were chosen for a certain analysis because two of them correlated fairly well with the third and very slightly with each other. The partial correlation coefficients of the series are

$$r_{12 \cdot 3} = .8221 ,$$
$$r_{13 \cdot 2} = .5587 ,$$
$$r_{23 \cdot 1} = -.4244 .$$

The interpretation of these coefficients is interesting. Shares Sold may be thought of as representing speculative interest, and Pig Iron Production as representing business activity. The coefficients of zero order would indicate that there is a strong tendency for stock prices to respond to business changes, and a distinct tendency for stock prices to vary with speculative interest. Curiously, there seems to be little co-variation between business and speculative interest.

When the partial correlations are considered, it appears that when changes in speculation are eliminated from the picture, business is even more heavily influential on stock prices, and that when business activity is eliminated from the picture, the importance of speculative feeling is enhanced.

PROBLEMS

1. Check the computations of the coefficients of partial correlation in the above example. What is the significance of $r_{23 \cdot 1} = -.4244$?

2. From your own knowledge of economics, select an instance where some element is presumably affected by two or three variables. Calculate the coefficients of partial correlation and interpret the answers.

4. Correlation Coefficients of Second Order. It is evident that the definition of the foregoing section can easily be generalized in case more than three variables are studied. If, for example, one is considering a problem in which four factors enter, namely, X_1, X_2, X_3, X_4, it will obviously be desirable to know the correlations which exist between any two of the factors when the other two are held fixed. The correlation coefficients in this case are designated by the symbol $r_{ij \cdot km}$, where the primary subscripts, i and j, refer to the variables whose correlation is desired, and the secondary subscripts, k and m, refer to the variables which are to be kept fixed. The correlations $r_{ij \cdot km}$ are spoken of as *coefficients of second order*, and are computed in terms of the coefficients of the first order by means of the following formula:

$$r_{ij \cdot km} = \frac{r_{ij \cdot k} - r_{im \cdot k} r_{jm \cdot k}}{\sqrt{(1 - r^2_{im \cdot k})(1 - r^2_{jm \cdot k})}} \quad . \quad (2)$$

To illustrate the calculation and use of the coefficients of second order, one may use the following data,[1] from one of the most interesting periods of American economic history — March 1, 1932 to July 1, 1933:

1. The Dow-Jones Averages of Industrial Stock Prices,
2. Franc-dollar Exchange Rate,
3. Annalist Index of Business Activity,
4. Moody's Index of Wholesale Commodity Prices.

Representing the above four series by the variables X_1, X_2, X_3, X_4, respectively, the following significant constants are calculated:

	Mean	σ
For Series X_1	64.9269	13.2692
X_2	.04042709	.00276043
X_3	69.4357	6.5587
X_4	92.0600	12.2332

Table of Correlation Coefficients

Zero Order r's	First Order r's		Second Order r's
$r_{12} = .7136$	$r_{12 \cdot 3} = .0810$	$r_{23 \cdot 1} = .7375$	$r_{12 \cdot 34} = -.4965$
$r_{13} = .7837$	$r_{12 \cdot 4} = -.2238$	$r_{23 \cdot 4} = .5953$	$r_{13 \cdot 24} = .5148$
$r_{14} = .8687$	$r_{13 \cdot 2} = .4681$	$r_{24 \cdot 1} = .7545$	$r_{14 \cdot 23} = .7437$
$r_{23} = .8801$	$r_{13 \cdot 4} = .2697$	$r_{24 \cdot 3} = .6019$	$r_{23 \cdot 14} = .6987$
$r_{24} = .8817$	$r_{14 \cdot 2} = .7247$	$r_{34 \cdot 1} = .4282$	$r_{24 \cdot 13} = .7188$
$r_{34} = .8125$	$r_{14 \cdot 3} = .6404$	$r_{34 \cdot 2} = .1629$	$r_{34 \cdot 12} = -.2896$

[1] The figures are daily except that in the case of (3), since no daily figures were available, interpolation was made on weekly data.

As examples of the calculations involved in the construction of this table, consider the following:

Example 1: Compute $r_{23 \cdot 4}$ from the coefficients of zero order. Using formula (1) with proper subscripts, one finds

$$r_{23 \cdot 4} = \frac{r_{23} - r_{24} r_{34}}{\sqrt{(1 - r^2_{24})(1 - r^2_{34})}} = \frac{.8801 - (.8817)(.8125)}{\sqrt{[1 - (.8817)^2][1 - (.8125)^2]}}$$

$$= \frac{.8801 - .7164}{\sqrt{(.2226)(.3398)}} = \frac{.1637}{.2750} = .5953 .$$

Example 2: Making use of the coefficients of first order, calculate the value of $r_{23 \cdot 14}$.

Making the proper substitution in formula (2), one finds

$$r_{23 \cdot 14} = \frac{r_{23 \cdot 1} - r_{24 \cdot 1} r_{34 \cdot 1}}{\sqrt{(1 - r^2_{24 \cdot 1})(1 - r^2_{34 \cdot 1})}}$$

$$= \frac{.7375 - (.7545)(.4282)}{\sqrt{[1 - (.7545)^2][1 - (.4282)^2]}}$$

$$= \frac{.7375 - .3231}{\sqrt{(.4307)(.8166)}} = \frac{.4144}{.5932} = .6987 .$$

It will be observed from formula (2) that in the general case of n variables there are two primary subscripts and two secondary subscripts which can be permuted among the numbers 1, 2, ······, n. It is immediately seen from the formula, however, that the coefficient $r_{ij \cdot km}$ is equal to the coefficient $r_{ji \cdot km}$, since the interchange of the subscripts i and j does not alter the quantities in the formula. One is then led to inquire whether or not this is also true for an interchange of k and m. In order to answer this question the coefficient $r_{ij \cdot km}$ is expressed in terms of the coefficients of zero order. After a straightforward algebraic simplification, one has

$$r_{ij \cdot km} = \frac{r_{ij} - r_{ik} r_{jk} - r_{im} r_{jm} + r_{ik} r_{jm} r_{mk} + r_{im} r_{jk} r_{km} - r_{ij} r^2_{km}}{\sqrt{(1 - r^2_{ik} - r^2_{im} - r^2_{km} + 2 r_{ik} r_{im} r_{km})(1 - r^2_{jk} - r^2_{jm} - r^2_{km} + 2 r_{jk} r_{jm} r_{km})}}$$

(3)

This formula remains unaltered when k and m are interchanged, and thus the conclusion is reached that

$$r_{ij \cdot km} = r_{ij \cdot mk} .$$

Since the figures used in calculating the first of these quantities are different from those used in the second, one computation may be used as a check on the other.

Since i and j make take any of the values from 1 to n in the general case, and m and k may then assume any of the remaining $n-2$ values, there will be

$$_nC_2 \cdot {}_{n-2}C_2 = \frac{n!}{(n-4)!\,4}$$

values of the second order coefficients. In the case of four variables there are thus 6 second order r's, for five variables 30 r's, etc.

Partial coefficients of higher order than two are defined in terms of the coefficients of the next lower order by a formula analogous to (2). The text will not, however, be concerned with these higher coefficients.

PROBLEMS

1. Verify by calculation two of the second order coefficients in the table in this section.

2. Calculate the values of $r_{34 \cdot 12}$ and $r_{43 \cdot 21}$ and show that they are equal.

3. Derive formula (3) by the direct substitution in formula (2) of the proper values of the first order coefficients calculated from formula (1) with proper subscripts.

5. Partial Regression Equations. In section 5 of the preceding chapter the regression line for two-variable correlation was derived, and found to be

$$y - \bar{y} = r \frac{\sigma_y}{\sigma_x} (x - \bar{x}) .$$

If the notation of the present chapter is employed, y can be replaced by X_1, x by X_2, $\bar{y}$ by M_1, $\bar{x}$ by M_2, and letting the subscripts 1 and 2 refer to the y and x variables respectively, the regression equation may be written in the following form:

$$X_1 - M_1 = r_{12} \frac{\sigma_1}{\sigma_2} (X_2 - M_2) ,$$

or

$$X_1 = r_{12} \frac{\sigma_1}{\sigma_2} X_2 + M_1 - r_{12} \frac{\sigma_1}{\sigma_2} M_2 \ .$$

This equation, it will be remembered, was obtained by fitting a straight line by the method of least squares to the correlation table. In a similar way, it is possible to derive a regression line for the case of n variables. The involved nature of the calculations does not make it desirable to present the analysis of derivation here, but the restrictions which held in the two-variable case carry over without essential modification to the general case.

For three variables one obtains as the regression line for X_i the following:

$$X_i = b_{ij \cdot k} X_j + b_{ik \cdot j} X_k + C_i \ , \tag{4}$$

where the following abbreviations have been used:

$$b_{ij \cdot k} = r_{ij \cdot k} \frac{\sigma_{i \cdot k}}{\sigma_{j \cdot k}} \ , \tag{a}$$

and

$$\sigma_{i \cdot k} = \sigma_i \sqrt{1 - r_{ik}^2} \ , \tag{b}$$

$$C_i = M_i - b_{ij \cdot k} M_j - b_{ik \cdot j} M_k \ . \tag{c}$$

The generalized standard deviation, $\sigma_{i \cdot k}$, is usually referred to as the standard deviation of first order.

Example 1: Calculate the three regression lines for the correlation problem involving the factors of Wheat Production, Acreage Planted, and Yield per Acre (section 2).

In order to solve this problem, one first calculates the first order correlation coefficients. As illustrated in section 3, these coefficients are

$$r_{12 \cdot 3} = .956 \ , \qquad r_{13 \cdot 2} = .921 \ , \qquad r_{23 \cdot 1} = -.879 \ .$$

Next, the values for the zero coefficients and the standard deviations, given in section 2 of this chapter, are substituted in the formula for $\sigma_{i \cdot k}$ (formula b), and one thus finds:

Standard Deviations of First Order ($\sigma_{i \cdot k}$)

Subscripts	$\sigma_{i \cdot k}$	Subscripts	$\sigma_{i \cdot k}$
1.2	77.7103	2.3	7.3591
1.3	100.9393	3.1	1.1334
2.1	4.5873	3.2	1.3998

From the values thus obtained, the regression coefficients (formula a) are then calculated and tabulated as follows:

Regression Coefficients ($b_{ij \cdot k}$)

Subscripts	$b_{ij \cdot k}$	Subscripts	$b_{ij \cdot k}$
12·3	13.1127	23·1	— 3.5576
13·2	51.1296	31·2	.0166
21·3	.0697	32·1	— .2172

As an example of the above computations, consider the value of $b_{12 \cdot 3}$. From formula (a), one easily gets

$$b_{12 \cdot 3} = r_{12 \cdot 3} \frac{\sigma_{1 \cdot 3}}{\sigma_{2 \cdot 3}} = .956 \frac{100.9393}{7.3591} = 13.1127 .$$

The last step is the calculation of the constant term (formula c). Substituting the values for the means (see section 2) in the formula for C_i (formula c), one obtains the following:

$$\begin{aligned}
C_1 &= M_1 - b_{12 \cdot 3} M_2 - b_{13 \cdot 2} M_3 , \\
&= 742.71 - (13.1127)(52.49) - (51.1296)(14.13) \\
&= 742.71 - 688.29 - 722.46 = -668.04; \\
C_2 &= 50.99 ; \\
C_3 &= 13.20 .
\end{aligned}$$

Using equation (4), three regression lines are at once written down from these constants:

$$\begin{aligned}
X_1 &= b_{12 \cdot 3} X_2 + b_{13 \cdot 2} X_3 + C_1 ; \\
X_1 &= 13.1127 X_2 + 51.1296 X_3 - 668.04 ; \\
X_2 &= b_{21 \cdot 3} X_1 + b_{23 \cdot 1} X_3 + C_2 ; \\
X_2 &= .0697 X_1 - 3.5576 X_3 + 50.99 ; \\
X_3 &= b_{31 \cdot 2} X_1 + b_{32 \cdot 1} X_2 + C_3 ; \\
X_3 &= .0166 X_1 - .2172 X_2 + 13.20 .
\end{aligned}$$

The meaning of these equations will be clear from analogy with the case of two variables. Consider the third equation, for example, which expresses the relationship between yield and the other two factors. Thus, for a year in which production of wheat, X_1, is 850 units (unit, 1,000,000 bushels), and area planted,

X_2, is 60 units (unit, 1,000,000 acres), the yield can be calculated as follows:

$$X_3 = (.0166)(850) - (.2172)(60) + 13.20$$
$$= 14.28 \text{ bushels per acre.}$$

This figure must not be interpreted to mean that the yield with the given production and area figures will be exactly 14.28. It means merely that 14.28 bushels per acre is a good statistical guess. In this particular case the yield is actually 14.17 bushels per acre. Further limitations will be considered in the next section.

6. On the Accuracy of Estimate. The next problem that arises is the determination of the accuracy with which one variable is expressed in terms of the others. This is done by means of the useful concept of the *probable error of estimate*.

By definition, one has

$$\text{p.e. of est. of } X_i = .6745 \, \sigma_{i \cdot jk} \,, \tag{5}$$

where

$$\sigma_{i \cdot jk} = \sigma_i \sqrt{(1 - r^2_{ij})(1 - r^2_{ik \cdot j})} \,.$$

This probable error has the same meaning as in previous chapters and gives the probable bounds of error made in calculating X_i from the regression equation.

For example, in the case of the yield of wheat, X_3, in the preceding section,

$$\text{p.e. of est. of } X_3 = .6745 \, \sigma_3 \sqrt{(1 - r^2_{31})(1 - r^2_{32 \cdot 1})}$$
$$= (.6745)(1.40) \sqrt{(.6554)(.2274)} = .3647 \,.$$

The third equation may then be written in the following form:

$$X_3 = .0166 \, X_2 - .2172 \, X_3 + 13.20 \pm .3647 \,.$$

This may be interpreted by an example. It was found in the calculation made in the last section that, with given production and area figures for wheat, the yield per acre might be expected to be 14.28 bushels per acre. The probable error of estimate would modify this statement to read that the chance is 1/2 that the yield will be somewhere between 13.92 and 14.64 bushels per acre.

For the problem of accuracy of estimate at a particular point, see Henry Schultz, "The Standard Error of a Forecast from a Curve", *Journal of The American Statistical Association*, June, 1930.

7. *The Multiple Correlation Coefficient for Three Variables.* Another important constant is the *multiple correlation coefficient*, which measures the correlation between the variable X_i and the linear combination of the other variables which makes up the right hand member of the regression equation. This coefficient, $R_{i(jk)}$, is defined by the equation

$$1 - R^2_{i(jk)} = (1 - r^2_{ij})(1 - r^2_{ik \cdot j}) \ . \tag{6}$$

The probable error of estimate for the variable X_i, as given in equation (5), may obviously be expressed in terms of this coefficient, giving

$$\text{p.e. of est. of } X_i = .6745 \, \sigma_i \sqrt{1 - R^2_{i(jk)}} \ .$$

Example: For the case of the yield of wheat, X_3, and the linear combination of the Production of Wheat, X_1, and the Area Planted, X_2, the multiple correlation coefficient $R_{3(12)}$ is found from the relation

$$1 - R^2_{3(12)} = (1 - r^2_{21})(1 - r^2_{32 \cdot 1})$$
$$= (.6554)(.2274) = .1490 \ .$$

Hence,
$$R^2_{3(12)} = .8510, \text{ and } R_{3(12)} = .9225 \ .$$

It is interesting to observe that $R_{i(jk)}$ must be larger than any of the correlation coefficients of zero or first order which involve i as a primary subscript. This is proved by noticing from equation (6) that $1 - R^2_{i(jk)}$ is smaller than either of the two factors $1 - r^2_{ij}$ and $1 - r^2_{ik \cdot j}$, since each is less than unity and hence their product is less than either separately. Consequently, $R^2_{i(jk)}$ must be larger than r^2_{ij} and $r^2_{ik \cdot j}$ and thus, since j and k can be interchanged, it must be larger than any of the coefficients having i as a primary subscript.

PROBLEMS

1. The example of section 3 of this chapter gives the zero-order correlation coefficients and the partial correlation coefficients for the three variables $X_1 =$ Dow-Jones Averages of Industrial Stock Prices, $X_2 =$ Pig Iron Production, $X_3 =$ Shares of Stock Sold on the New York Stock Exchange, monthly data, 1897-1913. The following table gives the means and standard deviations for these series:

	Mean	Standard Deviation
X_1, Dow Jones Industrial Averages	72.7746	14.7228
X_2, Pig Iron Production	55.0134	17.9565
X_3, Stock Sales, N.Y.S.E.	14.6685	6.1050

Calculate the values of the standard deviations $\sigma_{i \cdot k}$.

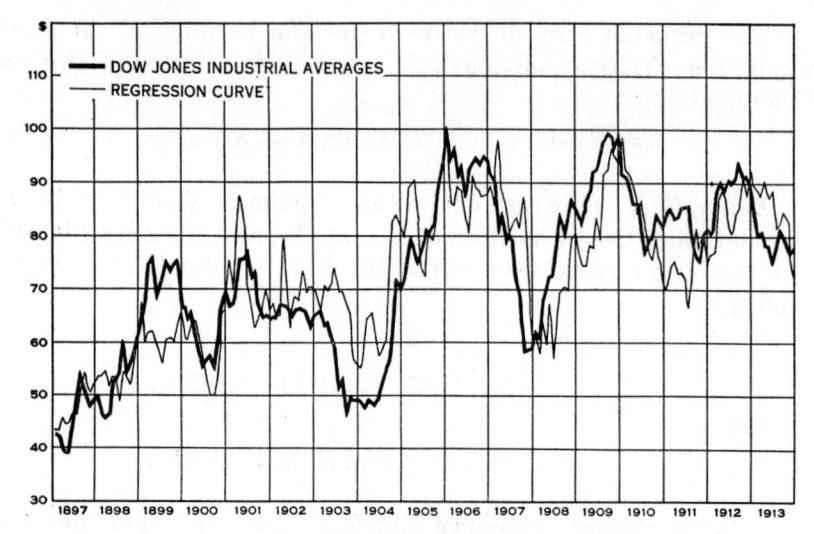

FIGURE 48. Regression of Pig Iron Production and Stock Sold on Dow Jones Industrial Averages, as discussed in problem 1, section 7.

2. Find the regression equation for the Dow-Jones Industrial Averages, X_1, in terms of the other two variables of problem 1.

3. Determine the probable error of estimate for X_1.

4. Substituting in your regression equation the latest monthly figures (end of month) for the Pig Iron Production series, X_2, and the Stock Sales[1] series, X_3, compare your value for X_2 with the actual value of the Dow-Jones Industrial Averages as given for the end of the month under consideration. Does the actual value lie within the limits determined by $X_1 \pm$ p.e. of est. of X_1?

5. Calculate the multiple correlations $R_{1(23)}$, $R_{2(13)}$, and $R_{3(12)}$ for problem 1.

6. Calculate the multiple correlations, $R_{1(23)}$ and $R_{2(13)}$, and the probable errors of estimate for the illustrative example of sections 2 and 3.

---

[1] These figures may be obtained from the Standard Statistics Company's *Statistical Bulletin*.

8. *Multiple Correlation for Four Variables.* The theory and formulas of multiple correlation apply without essential change to the case of four or more variables. Since the case of four variables is frequently met with in application, the explicit formulas are given below, and the student is referred to advanced treatises for the general statement covering any number of variables. A practical method for computing regression equations for the general case is given in section 10.

The regression line for X_i, from analogy with the work of the previous sections, is written

$$X_i = b_{ij \cdot km} X_j + b_{ik \cdot jm} X_k + b_{im \cdot jk} X_m + C_i , \qquad (7)$$

where use is made of the abbreviations

$$b_{ij \cdot km} = r_{ij \cdot km} \frac{\sigma_{i \cdot km}}{\sigma_{j \cdot km}} , \qquad (a)$$

$$\sigma_{i \cdot km} = \sigma_i \sqrt{(1 - r^2_{ik})(1 - r^2_{im \cdot k})} , \qquad (b)$$

$$C_i = M_i - b_{ij \cdot km} M_j - b_{ik \cdot jm} M_k - b_{im \cdot jk} M_m . \qquad (c)$$

Similarly, the probable error of estimate of X_i and the multiple correlation coefficient are computed from the formula,

$$\text{p.e. of est. of } X_i = .6745 \, \sigma_{i \cdot jkm} , \qquad (d)$$

$$1 - R^2_{i(jkm)} = \frac{\sigma^2_{i \cdot jkm}}{\sigma_i^2} \qquad (e)$$

where

$$\sigma_{i \cdot jkm} = \sigma_i \sqrt{(1 - r^2_{jk})(1 - r^2_{ik \cdot j})(1 - r^2_{im \cdot jk})}$$

is the standard deviation of second order.

As an example, let the regression line for the variable X_i (The Dow-Jones Averages of Industrial Stock Prices) be computed from the data given in the illustrative example of section 4.

Making the proper substitutions in formulas (b) and (a), the following values are obtained for the standard deviations and the regression coefficients:

$\sigma_{1 \cdot 24} = 6.4050$ $\qquad \sigma_{1 \cdot 23} = 8.2150 \qquad$ $b_{12 \cdot 34} = -3002.0941$
$\sigma_{1 \cdot 34} = 6.3307$ $\qquad \sigma_{4 \cdot 23} = 5.6946 \qquad$ $b_{13 \cdot 24} = 1.0733$
$\sigma_{2 \cdot 34} = .001047$ $\qquad \sigma_{3 \cdot 24} = 3.0721 \qquad$ $b_{14 \cdot 23} = 1.0729$

As an example of the calculations, consider $\sigma_{2\cdot34}$ and $b_{14\cdot23}$. Substituting in formulas (b) and (a), one obtains

$$\sigma_{2\cdot34} = \sigma_2\sqrt{(1-r^2_{23})(1-r^2_{24\cdot3})}$$
$$= .00276043\sqrt{[1-(.8801)^2][1-(.6019)^2]}$$
$$= .001047 \ ;$$

$$b_{14\cdot23} = r_{14\cdot23}\frac{\sigma_{1\cdot23}}{\sigma_{4\cdot23}} = (.7437)(1.4426) = 1.0729 \ .$$

By straightforward calculation one finds from equation (c), equation (e), and equation (d), respectively:

$$C_1 = 12.9963 \ ,$$
$$\text{p.e. of est. of } X_1 = \pm 3.7044 \ ,$$
$$R_{1(234)} = .9103 \ .$$

The regression equation may now be written down, giving

$$X_1 = -3002.0941\, X_2 + 1.0733\, X_3 + 1.0729\, X_4$$
$$+ 12.9963 \pm 3.7044 \ .$$

The meaning of this equation can be appreciated from the following example. For June 3, 1933, the franc-dollar exchange rate (X_2) was .0468; the index of business (X_3), 83.2; and the index of wholesale prices (X_4), 120.5; from the above equation the Dow-Jones Averages of Industrial Stock Prices, X_1, are calculated to be:

$$X_1 = (-3002.0941)(.0468) + (1.0733)(83.2)$$
$$+ (1.0729)(120.5) + 12.9963 \pm 3.7044$$
$$= 91.0814 \pm 3.7044 \ .$$

In other words, the chances were even that the actual average for the Dow-Jones Industrial Averages on June 3, 1933, would lie between 87.3770 and 94.7858. (The Dow-Jones Industrial Averages on June 3, 1933 were actually 90.02.)

9. *Appraisal of the Correlation Theory.* The theory of partial and multiple correlation is one of elegance and power if, in the words of Galton, it is "delicately handled" and "warily interpreted." One must first assure himself that the zero correlations are linear and that the coefficients have been calculated from a suf-

ficient number of cases. These two points can always be settled by the probable errors which were studied in Chapter VIII.

The significance of the first and second order correlation coefficients can be determined by means of their probable errors, which are given respectively by the two following formulas:

p.e. of $r_{ij \cdot k} = .6745 \dfrac{1 - r^2_{ij \cdot k}}{\sqrt{N}}$, (p.e. of first order r)

p.e. of $r_{ij \cdot km} = .6745 \dfrac{1 - r^2_{ij \cdot km}}{\sqrt{N}}$, (p.e. of second order r)

where N is the total number of cases used in the original problem.

Example: The correlations given in section 4 were calculated from 395 items. In that case

p.e. of $r_{23 \cdot 4} = .6745 \dfrac{1 - r^2_{23 \cdot 4}}{\sqrt{N}} = .6745 \dfrac{1 - (.5953)^2}{\sqrt{395}} = .0219$.

The significance of the multiple correlation of the variable X_i in terms of the others is measured by $R_{i(jkm)}$, where

p.e. of multiple correlation $R_{i(jkm)} = .6745 \dfrac{1 - R^2_{i(jkm)}}{\sqrt{N}}$,

N being again the total number of cases used in the problem.

PROBLEMS

1. Calculate the regression line for the variable X_3 in the illustrative example of section 8.

2. Compute $R_{2(134)}$ and the corresponding probable error of estimate for the example of section 8.

3. Three hundred and ninety-five items were used in calculating the constants used in the illustrative example of section 8. Calculate the probable errors of r_{12}, $r_{13 \cdot 4}$, $r_{23 \cdot 14}$, and $R_{3(124)}$.

4. Prove the formula

$$b_{ij} = \dfrac{b_{ij \cdot k} + b_{ik \cdot j} b_{kj \cdot i}}{1 - b_{ik \cdot j} b_{ki \cdot j}}.$$

10. Extension to a Higher Number of Variables. It will be obvious to the reader that the direct extension of the methods given above to the calculation of regression equations of more than four variables presents great difficulties of computation. As the number of variables is increased the number of partial correlation coefficients increases at a terrifying rate. A simple device, however, makes it possible to extend the method practically to a higher number of variables. This device may be illustrated as follows, where, for simplicity of exposition, the case will be limited to six variables. One may designate these variables by X_1, X_2, X_3, X_4, X_5, X_6, their means by M_1, M_2, M_3, M_4, M_5, M_6, and their standard deviations by σ_1, σ_2, σ_3, σ_4, σ_5, σ_6.

The array of correlation coefficients is conveniently exhibited as follows:

	X_1	X_2	X_3	X_4	X_5	X_6	
X_1	1	r_{12}	r_{13}	r_{14}	r_{15}	r_{16}	
X_2	r_{21}	1	r_{23}	r_{24}	r_{25}	r_{26}	
X_3	r_{31}	r_{32}	1	r_{34}	r_{35}	r_{36}	$(r_{ij}=r_{ji})$
X_4	r_{41}	r_{42}	r_{43}	1	r_{45}	r_{46}	
X_5	r_{51}	r_{52}	r_{53}	r_{54}	1	r_{56}	
X_6	r_{61}	r_{62}	r_{63}	r_{64}	r_{65}	1	

Selecting X_1 as the leading variable, the regression for which in terms of the other variables is desired, one then seeks for a regression equation of the following form:

$$\frac{1}{\sigma_1}(X_1-M_1) + \frac{a_1}{\sigma_2}(X_2-M_2) + \frac{b_1}{\sigma_3}(X_3-M_3) + \cdots$$

$$+ \frac{e_1}{\sigma_6}(X_6-M_6) = 0 . \qquad (8)$$

The values of the coefficients a_1, b_1, c_1, $\cdots$, e_1, are then computed as solutions of the following system of equations:

$$\begin{aligned} a_1 + r_{23}\,b_1 + r_{24}\,c_1 + r_{25}\,d_1 + r_{26}\,e_1 &= -r_{21} \\ r_{32}\,a_1 + b_1 + r_{34}\,c_1 + r_{35}\,d_1 + r_{36}\,e_1 &= -r_{31} \\ r_{42}\,a_1 + r_{43}\,b_1 + c_1 + r_{45}\,d_1 + r_{46}\,e_1 &= -r_{41} \quad (9) \\ r_{52}\,a_1 + r_{53}\,b_1 + r_{54}\,c_1 + d_1 + r_{56}\,e_1 &= -r_{51} \\ r_{62}\,a_1 + r_{63}\,b_1 + r_{64}\,c_1 + r_{65}\,d_1 + e_1 &= -r_{61} . \end{aligned}$$

The solution of these equations is most effectively accomplished by means of a computing machine. The coefficients of a_1 in the last four equations are successively divided into the coefficients of the other unknowns. The members of the resulting set are then subtracted successively from the first equation, thus eliminating the quantity a_1. This operation is again repeated on the remaining four equations, eliminating b_1. By continuing this process, the value of e_1 is finally attained, and by successive substitutions the other unknowns are then found. This method is only practical when a computing machine is available, since the divisions must be performed to a number of decimal places in order that the last quantity shall be determined to a sufficient number of places. The order of the error in the constants can be estimated by substituting them in the left hand member of one of the original equations and comparing the resulting quantity with the right hand member.

This same method, of course, can be employed to compute the regression equations in which X_2, X_3, etc. are successively selected as the leading variables. The method is also immediately generalized so as to apply to any number of variables.

Example 1. In illustration of this method, it will be illuminating to derive equation (4), section 5.

Adapting to three variables, one writes,

$$\frac{1}{\sigma_i}(X_i - M_i) + \frac{a_i}{\sigma_j}(X_j - M_j) + \frac{b_i}{\sigma_k}(X_k - M_k) = 0 \ . \tag{10}$$

Equations (9) are replaced by the simpler system,

$$a_i + r_{jk}b_i = -r_{ji} ,$$
$$r_{kj}a_i + b_i = -r_{ki} ,$$

the solution of which yields,

$$a_i = -(r_{ji} - r_{ki}r_{jk})/(1 - r^2_{jk}), \quad b_i = -(r_{ki} - r_{ji}r_{kj})/(1 - r^2_{jk}).$$

Equation (10) may then be written,

$$X_i - M_i = -\frac{\sigma_i}{\sigma_j}a_i(X_j - M_j) - \frac{\sigma_i}{\sigma_k}b_i(X_k - M_k) \ .$$

Referring now to the coefficients of equation (4), one easily computes

$$b_{ij \cdot k} = r_{ij \cdot k}\frac{\sigma_{i \cdot k}}{\sigma_{j \cdot k}} = \frac{r_{ij} - r_{ik}r_{jk}}{\sqrt{(1 - r^2_{ik})(1 - r^2_{jk})}} \cdot \frac{\sigma_i\sqrt{1 - r^2_{ik}}}{\sigma_j\sqrt{1 - r^2_{jk}}} \ .$$

Hence
$$b_{ij \cdot k} = -\frac{\sigma_i}{\sigma_j} a_i ,$$
and, similarly, $b_{ik \cdot j} = -(\sigma_i/\sigma_j) b_i$.

Hence equation (10) is identical with equation (4).

Example 2. The regression equation of the illustrative example of section 8 will be computed by the method given above.

Employing the data given in section 4, one first writes down the following system of equations:

$$a_1 + .8801 b_1 + .8817 c_1 = -.7136$$
$$.8801 a_1 + \quad\quad b_1 + .8125 c_1 = -.7837$$
$$.8817 a_1 + .8125 b_1 + \quad\quad c_1 = -.8687$$

Dividing the second and third equations by .8801 and .8817 respectively and subtracting the first from each of them, one obtains,
$$.2561345\ b_1 + .04149053 c_1 = -.17686698 ,$$
$$.04141524 b_1 + .2524726\ c_1 = -.27165574 .$$

Repeating the process, one gets,
$$5.9341405 c_1 = -5.8687945$$
and hence,
$$c_1 = -.9889881 .$$

From the first equation involving b_1 and c_1, there is computed
$$b_1 = -.53033468 ,$$
and from the third equation of the original set,
$$a_1 = .6251384 .$$

When the accuracy of these values is tested in the first equation of the system, it is found that the values are correct to six decimal places.

The regression equation is then readily obtained from (8) and found to coincide with that determined by the original computations.

11. A Note on Linear Dependence. To one familiar with the theory of determinants and linear systems of equations, it is evident that the subject of regression equations in several variables is one fraught with certain difficulties of an algebraic sort. For it might easily happen that one or more of the variables in a system is not independent of another one of the variables, or of some linear combination of several of the variables. In technical language, one says under such circumstances that the variables are *linearly dependent*.

The linear dependence of the variables in an algebraic system may always be recognized by the vanishing of the determinant formed from the array of constants (in the present instance the array of correlation coefficients given earlier in the preceding section) which multiply the variables. But, unfortunately, in statistical studies the system is not strictly algebraic, because of the probable errors of the correlation coefficients, and hence the essential vanishing of the determinant might well be masked by the magnitude of these errors.

Because of the advanced character of this important question, it is not possible to give an adequate discussion of it in an elementary book. R. Frisch in an elaborate study[1] to which the reader is referred has gone carefully into the question of linear dependence of statistical variables and has advanced empirical devices which he has used to test such dependence. H. Hotelling[2] has gone further into some phases of the problem and derives sampling distributions which enable one to test the relative importance of all the variables. It is thus possible in this book merely to call attention to the dangers lurking in a system comprising several variables, some of which may be expressible in terms of others, and to warn the reader to be on guard whenever intercorrelations between variables seem to suggest a linear dependence.

As an example, it might be required to find the regression equation for the Dow Jones Industrial Averages (X_1) in terms of Pig Iron Production (X_2) and Industrial Production (X_3). For the period from 1897 to 1913 the correlations between these three variables are $r_{12} = .515$, $r_{13} = .514$, $r_{23} = .994$. These correlations show very clearly that pig iron production and industrial production are essentially the same variable and hence any regression of X_1 with

---

[1] "Statistical Confluence Analysis by Means of Complete Regression Systems," *Nordic Statistical Journal*, Vol. 5 (1934); also issued by the Economic Institute of the University of Oslo, 1934, 192 p.

[2] "Analysis of a Complex of Statistical Variables into Principal Components," *Journal of Educational Psychology*, Vol. 24 (1933), pp. 417-441; 498-520.

X_2 and X_3 would be spurious. In the case of three variables it is obvious that the ideal regression would be one formed between variables two of which correlated highly with the other but not with one another.

CHAPTER XII

TYPES OF STATISTICAL SERIES

1. Introduction. In the earlier pages of this book, the discussion of frequency data was limited to the case of skew-normal distributions, that is to say, distributions which depended upon the assumption of a constant probability affecting equally all cases. That this assumption can only be approximately true in statistical series derived from natural phenomena, with all of their complexity of causes, is immediately apprehended. One of the best ways to be assured of the truth of this statement is to observe the frequent occurrence in practical applications of distributions which fail to correspond to normal or skew-normal patterns.

It is thus important to be able to recognize these variant frequency distributions when they appear and to know something of the probability considerations which underlie their theory.

Unfortunately, a complete mathematical description of series which do not conform to the pattern of normal or skew-normal series, as they have been developed in previous chapters, requires technical knowledge of an advanced nature. Under the leadership of Karl Pearson, the English school of statisticians has developed the theory of these higher types of distributions from the standpoint of differential equations. Twelve types have been recognized and methods devised for fitting them to numerical data. Good treatments of these types, with numerical illustrations, are to be found in W. P. Elderton's *Frequency Curves and Correlation,* second edition, London, 1927, and D. C. Jones' *A First Course in Statistics,* London, 1921. On the continent, particularly in Scandinavian countries, under the influence of J. P. Gram, T. N. Thiele, C. V. L. Charlier, and others, a method of handling these higher types of distributions has been developed in which the theory of *orthogonal functions* has been employed. The method consists essentially in a generalization of the normal frequency curve and the recognition of certain functions of the moments which characterize the distribution. These functions are customarily referred to as the *semi-invariants of Thiele.* Thiele's classical paper *The Theory of Observations,* published in London in 1903, has been reprinted in *The Annals of Mathematical Statistics,* Vol. 2 (1931), pp. 165-308, and merits careful reading by any one who wishes to get a complete understanding of the nature of frequency distributions of general type. The work of the Scandinavian school has been made the basis of Arne Fisher's *Mathematical Theory of Probabilities*, New York, 1923, and the theoretical development is accompanied by excellent numerical examples.

Since the methods of both the English and the continental schools require mathematical tools of a higher order than those assumed in this book, it will be necessary to limit the discussion to the description of general characteristics of frequency distributions which vary from the normal.

2. *Excess or Kurtosis.* In a previous chapter, skewness was defined as the ratio,
$$S' = M_3/(2N\sigma^3) ,$$
where M_3 is the third moment about the mean, σ the standard deviation, and N the total frequency. It will now be assumed that the skewness is essentially zero. Attention is then called to the following ratio,
$$\beta_2 = M_4/(N\sigma^4) ,$$
where M_4 is the fourth moment about the mean, σ the standard deviation, and N the total frequency.

By methods differing only in algebraic difficulty from those employed in Chapter VII to compute the second and third moments about the mean for binomial distributions, it can be established for a binomial distribution that,
$$M_4/N = npq(1 - 6pq + 3npq) .$$

Since one has $\sigma^2 = npq$, the following value is then readily obtained:
$$\beta_2 = (\frac{1}{npq} - \frac{6}{n} + 3) .$$

Since p and q are constant and, as a matter of fact, under the assumption of a zero skewness are both equal to ½, the first two terms approach the value zero as n becomes large. Hence one concludes that for a normal distribution,
$$\beta_2 = 3 \quad \text{(normal distribution)}.$$

By methods rather too complex to be introduced profitably here, the probable error of β_2 may be shown to equal,
$$\text{p.e. of } \beta_2 = .6745\sqrt{24/N} = 3.3044/\sqrt{N} .$$

Hence, one should not regard as normal any distribution for which $|\beta_2 - 3|$ exceeds three times the probable error just written down.

This variation of a frequency distribution from the normal is called the *excess* or *kurtosis* and it is measured by[1]

$$E = \beta_2 - 3 \ .$$

If E is positive, the distribution will show a greater cumulation about the mean than the normal curve; if E is negative, the cumulation is less than that of the normal curve, that is to say, the data tend to dispersion.

Earlier in the book, normal frequency data have been referred to as forming a *Bernoulli* distribution. In this book, distributions in which the excess is positive will be referred to as *Poisson* distributions, and those in which the excess is negative as *Lexis* distributions. The three types are also referred to as *normal*, *subnormal* and *hypernormal* respectively.

It will be instructive at this point to compute the excess for a rectangular frequency distribution, that is to say, one in which the frequency over a range from $-n$ to $+n$ is a constant, f. This type of distribution is illustrated graphically in Figure 49.

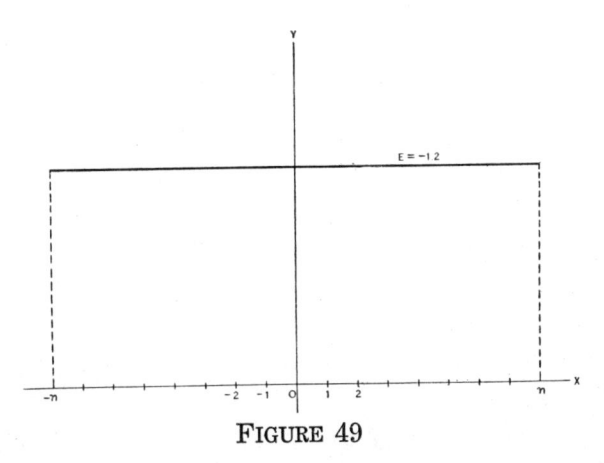

FIGURE 49

---

[1] Some authors measure kurtosis by $E/2$ or $E/8$. Karl Pearson, who originated the idea of kurtosis in *Biometrika*, Vol. 4 (1906), p. 173, says: "Given two frequency distributions which have the same variability as measured by the standard deviation, they may be relatively more or less flat-topped than the normal curve. If more flat-topped I term them *platykurtic*, if less flat-topped *leptokurtic*, and if equally flat-topped *mesokurtic*. A frequency distribution may be symmetrical, satisfying both the first two conditions for normality, but it may fail to be mesokurtic, and thus the Gaussian curve cannot describe it."

The average is obviously zero, so the square of the standard deviation is merely,[1]

$$\sigma^2 = \frac{\sum\limits_{x=-n}^{n} f x^2}{N} = \frac{f n (n+1)(2n+1)}{3N} .$$

Since $2n f = N$, this may be written,

$$\sigma^2 = (n+1)(2n+1)/6 .$$

Similarly, the average value of the fourth moment is,[1]

$$M_4/N = \frac{\sum\limits_{x=-n}^{n} f x^4}{N} = \frac{f n(n+1)(2n+1)(3n^2+3n-1)}{15N}$$

$$= (n+1)(2n+1)(3n^2+3n-1)/30 .$$

Hence, computing β_2, one finds,

$$\beta_2 = \frac{36(3n^2+3n-1)}{30(n+1)(2n+1)} .$$

If n becomes very large, β_2 approaches the limiting value,

$$\beta_2 = 1.8 .$$

Hence, since a rectangular distribution may be regarded as a bounding distribution between bell-shaped and U-shaped frequency distributions, one concludes that distributions for which $\beta_2 = 1.8$, that is to say, for which $E = -1.2$, are U-shaped. This implies a violent distortion for extreme ranges of the data.

Thus, to summarize, one may say that when

$\beta_2 = 3$, $E = 0$, the data are *normal* and belong to the *Bernoulli* type;

$\beta_2 < 3$, $E < 0$, the data are *hypernormal* and belong to the *Lexis* type;

$\beta_2 < 1.8$, $E < -1.2$, the data are U-shaped; and

$\beta_2 > 3$, $E > 0$, the data are *subnormal* and belong to the *Poisson* type.

---

[1] For these sums see Chapter IX, section 4.

These conclusions are based upon the assumption of a zero skewness in the data. Figure 50 illustrates graphically these types of distributions.

Example: In order to put the problem in concrete form, consider the following table, which gives the deaths from automobile accidents in thirty-two cities of the United States in 1930 (Data taken from the *Statistical Abstract of the U.S.*, 1931):

City	Deaths (1930) (Automobile Accidents)	Rate per 100,000	Population (1930)
Albany	35	27.7	127,412
Baltimore	198	24.8	804,874
Boston	145	18.6	781,188
Buffalo	184	32.4	573,076
Chicago	768	23.1	3,376,438
Cincinnati	150	33.5	451,160
Cleveland	312	34.9	900.429
Columbus	117	40.7	290,564
Denver	69	24.2	287,861
Indianapolis	129	35.8	364,161
Jersey City	73	23.1	316,715
Los Angeles	430	36.0	1,238,048
Milwaukee	112	19.6	578,249
Minneapolis	108	23.5	464,356
Nashville	64	41.8	153,866
Newark	126	28.6	442,337
New Haven	62	38.1	162,655
New Orleans	124	27.0	458,762
New York City	1342	19.6	6,930,446
Philadelphia	381	19.6	1,950,961
Pittsburgh	197	29.6	669,817
Providence	69	27.4	252,981
Reading	32	28.8	111,171
Rochester	58	17.8	328,132
St. Louis	172	21.0	821,960
Salt Lake City	58	41.8	140,267
San Francisco	119	19.0	634,394
Scranton	49	34.3	143,433
Toledo	106	36.8	290,718
Trenton	58	47.1	123,356
Wilmington	33	30.9	106,597
Yonkers, N.Y.	27	20.4	134,646

It appears from the above table that there is a great difference in the probability of death by automobile accident in Trenton and Rochester. Consider, then, the question of whether this difference is significant or whether the variations from city to city represent what one should normally expect. It is obvious that the *excess* will tell whether the above distribution is normal or abnormal.

FIGURE 50

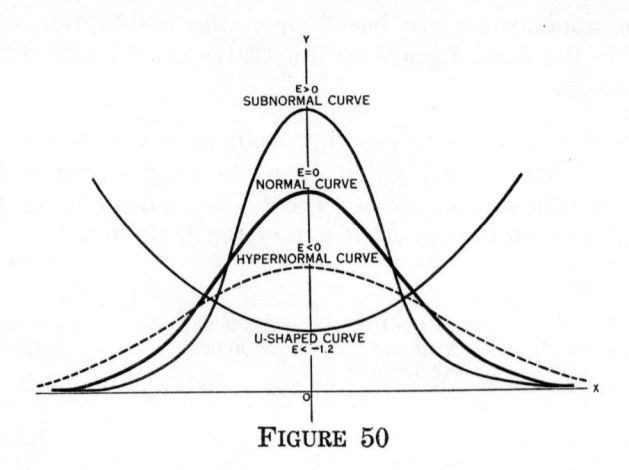

But it is at once evident that it will be necessary to derive from the data a sub-set of cities with populations which do not differ too greatly from one another. For a sub-set of cities, one has:

City	Deaths (1930) (Automobile Accidents)	Rate per 100,000	Population (1930)
Buffalo	184	32.4	573,076
Cincinnati	150	33.5	451,160
Indianapolis	129	35.8	364,161
Jersey City	73	23.1	316,715
Milwaukee	112	19.6	578,249
Minneapolis	108	23.5	464,356
Newark	126	28.6	442,337
New Orleans	124	27.0	458.762
Rochester	58	17.8	328,132
San Francisco	119	19.0	634,394
Total	1183		4,611,342

An adjustment to these figures must be made so that the deaths for each city refer to a uniform population. When the population figures agree as closely as in the present example, one may, without appreciable error, adjust the statistical items to the arithmetic average of the population as a base. This is done by multiplying the rate per 100,000 by the average population, expressed in units of 100,000, namely 4.611342. A new table is thus obtained:

City	Actual Deaths	Deaths Adjusted to an Average Population of 461,134
Buffalo	184	149
Cincinnati	150	154
Indianapolis	129	165
Jersey City	73	107
Milwaukee	112	90
Minneapolis	108	108
Newark	126	132
New Orleans	124	125
Rochester	58	82
San Francisco	119	88
Totals	1183	1200

Employing these data, one then computes the mean to be 120.1 and the second, third, and fourth moments about this value to equal,

$$M_2 = 7797, \qquad M_3 = 42325, \qquad M_4 = 9947637.$$

From these values the skewness and excess are found to be

$$S' = .194, \qquad E = -1.364.$$

Since the number of cases considered is small, the probable errors are large and conclusions correspondingly insecure. However, the implication is that there exists a significant variation in the death rates between the cities studied. In fact, the excess indicates that the distribution is essentially U-shaped.

PROBLEMS

1. From a table of sines, form a frequency distribution for the ordinates of the function $y = \sin(2\pi t/T)$, where t ranges over the values from $t = 0$ to $t = T$. Since the range is over a complete cycle, half the values will be negative and hence the average is zero. Show that σ^2 is approximately equal to .5 and that the excess is -1.5. This result is significant in business cycle theory in showing that a frequency distribution formed from the deviations from a linear trend of a series with a strong periodicity will tend to be U-shaped. Why?

2. The following table gives the frequency distribution of Rail Stock Price Averages for the period from 1859 to 1878:

Class Interval	Frequency	Class Interval	Frequency
33.0-39.9	23	75.0- 81.9	34
40.0-46.9	16	82.0- 88.9	27
47.0-53.9	12	89.0- 95.9	23
54.0-60.9	6	96.0-102.9	52
61.0-67.9	20	103.0-109.9	16
68.0-74.9	11		$N = 240$

Compute the excess for these data. The student should note that the values of the class interval can be replaced by integers without affecting the final results. Why?

3. The following table shows the frequency distribution of the deviations of Rail Stock Price Averages from the trend

$$y = \sqrt{2}\, \sigma \cos\left[(2\pi t/T) + \pi\right],$$

where σ is the standard deviation of the deviations of the actual data from a straight line:

Class Interval	Frequency	Class Interval	Frequency
−24 to −18	6	11 to 17	8
−17 to −11	31	18 to 24	9
−10 to − 4	42	25 to 31	6
− 3 to 3	90	32 to 38	1
4 to 10	47		$N = 240$

Compute the excess for these data. What do you infer about the movement of Rail Stock Prices during this period? What was the cause of the deviation from a straight line trend?

4. Compute the excess for the frequency table (b), section 2, Chapter III.

5. Make a selection of data of your own and compute the excess. What conclusions do you derive from this computation?

6. The following table gives the number of banks suspended in 1930 in ten American states having populations of approximately the same size. Calculate the excess and determine whether a significant variation exists.

State	No. of Banks Suspended (1930)	Suspensions per 100,000 population	Population (1930)
Kansas	43	22.86	1,880,999
Minnesota	22	8.58	2,563,953
Iowa	86	34.80	2,470,939
Virginia	20	8.26	2,421,851
Louisiana	9	4.28	2,101,593
Kentucky	29	11.09	2,614,589
Tennessee	28	10.70	2,616,556
Alabama	34	12.85	2,646,248
Mississippi	52	25.87	2,009,821
Oklahoma	23	9.60	2,396,040
Totals	346		23,722,589

7. Determine the excess for the following data:

State	Number of Commercial Failures (1930), x	Number of Concerns in Business (1930), y
Connecticut	592	30,974
Nebraska	202	27,622
Kansas	230	35,131
Maryland	341	30,714
Virginia	339	31,087
North Carolina	414	33,653
Georgia	387	29,737
Florida	240	27,356
Tennessee	298	31,234
Washington	622	33,524
Totals	3665	311,032

Hint: Calculate the number of failures per 1,000 concerns, by dividing x by y, and proceed from this step to compute your adjusted values.

3. The Lexis Ratio and the Charlier Coefficient of Disturbancy. Another method of detecting the disturbing influence in statistical series and thus distinguishing between the three types of distributions has been devised in what are called the *Lexis ratio* and the *Charlier coefficient of disturbancy.*

The Lexis ratio is usually denoted by L and is merely the ratio,

$$L = \sigma/\sigma_B ,$$

where σ is the standard deviation calculated directly from the data, and σ_B is the standard deviation calculated on the assumption that the given data form a normal or binomial distribution.

The Charlier coefficient of disturbancy is derived as a natural measure of variation from the fact that the squares of the standard deviations of the Poisson and Lexis series as technically defined in the next section differ from the square of the standard deviation of the Bernoulli or normal series by multiples of a common constant. [See formulas (1) and (2), section 4]. The Charlier coefficient of disturbancy, C, is defined to be,

$$C = 100 \, \frac{\sqrt{\sigma^2 - \sigma_B^2}}{A} ,$$

where A and σ are the arithmetic mean and standard deviation, respectively, of the data; σ_B is the Bernoulli deviation previously defined. When

$L = 1$, $C = 0$, the data are normal and belong to the Bernoulli type,

$L > 1$, $C > 0$, the data are hypernormal, and the distribution is of the Lexis type, and

$L < 1$, C imaginary, the data are subnormal and belong to the Poisson type.

As an example of the application of these two constants, consider the adjusted data given in the preceding section.

In computing the Bernoulli deviation, one may adopt the point of view that the population in each city is liable to death by automobile accident, and that the number of deaths constitutes a normal distribution with a number of instances equal to the average population of the ten cities, 461,134.2 in each case. Thus, to obtain the desired Bernoulli deviation $\sigma_B = \sqrt{npq}$, the probability, p, of death by automobile accident in each of the cities is computed to be

$$p = \frac{118.3}{461,134.2} = .0002565 ,$$

$$q = 1 - p = 1 - .0002565 = .9997435 ,$$

and n is taken as equal to the average population of the ten cities, that is, 461,134.2. Thus, σ_B becomes,

$$\sigma_B = \sqrt{(461{,}134.2)(.0002565)(.9997435)} = \sqrt{118.26} = 10.87 \ .$$

From the adjusted data one calculates directly,

$$\begin{aligned}\sigma^2 = [\,&(149-120.1)^2 + (154-120.1)^2 + (165-120.1)^2 \\ +\ &(107-120.1)^2 + (90-120.1)^2 + (108-120.1)^2 \\ +\ &(132-120.1)^2 + (125-120.1)^2 + (83-120.1)^2 \\ +\ &(88-120.1)^2]/N = \frac{7882.90}{10} = 788.29\ ,\end{aligned}$$

$$\sigma = \sqrt{788.29} = 28.08 \ .$$

Using these two values of the dispersion, one obtains for the Lexis ratio,

$$L = \frac{28.08}{10.87} = 2.58\ ,$$

and for the Charlier coefficient,

$$C = \frac{100\sqrt{788.29 - 118.26}}{118.3} = 21.88 \ .$$

These quantities agree with the conclusion reached in section 2 that there is a significant disturbance in the automobile deaths in the cities considered. In other words, the observed variations cannot be due merely to random sampling, but there are underlying causes which make the probability of death in automobile accidents differ in an essential manner from city to city. Such a conclusion has statistical importance in directing attention to such significant variations.

PROBLEMS

1. Compute the Lexis ratio and the Charlier coefficient for the data of problem 6, section 2.

2. Compute the Lexis ratio and the Charlier coefficient for the data of problem 7, section 2.

3. Make a selection of data of your own and determine to which of the three series the distribution belongs.

4. On a Probability Classification of Distributions.

Having now learned the technique of recognizing disturbance in frequency distributions, the reader will find it profitable to examine more closely into the probability assumptions which lead to one or the other of the variants from the normal.

In the case of the Bernoulli distribution which was studied extensively in earlier pages of this book, the assumption was made that the frequencies were derived from events subject to a constant probability. When this assumption is changed, then either a *Lexis* or a *Poisson* distribution results.

In order to form a concrete picture of the problem, consider n urns, $U_1, U_2, \cdots, U_n$, which contain white and black balls in such ratios that the probabilities of drawing a white ball from them are $p_1, p_2, \cdots, p_n$, respectively. One drawing of n balls, one from each urn, will be called a *set*. Let N sets be drawn and the frequencies in the cases where one drew *no* white ball, *one* white ball, $\cdots$, n white balls, be recorded. The following table results:

No. of white balls drawn	0	1	2	3	$\cdots$	n
Frequency	f_0	f_1	f_2	f_3	$\cdots$	f_n

where $f_0 + f_1 + f_2 + f_3 + \cdots + f_n = N$.

If the ratios of white to black balls in each urn were the same, i.e., $p_1 = p_2 = \cdots = p_n = p$, then a *Bernoulli distribution* would be formed with an arithmetic average, A_B, and a standard deviation, σ_B, equal respectively to,

$$A_B = np, \qquad \sigma_B = \sqrt{npq}.$$

If the ratios of white to black balls were different from urn to urn, then a *Poisson distribution* would result with the following arithmetic average, A_P, and square of its standard deviation σ_P:

$$A_P = np, \qquad \sigma_P^2 = npq - \sum_{i=1}^{n} (p_i - p)^2, \tag{1}$$

where $p = (p_1 + p_2 + p_3 + \cdots + p_n)/n$, $q = 1 - p$.

If the ratios of white to black balls were the same for each of m sets of drawings, but were changed for each subsequent set of m

drawings, where $m = N/r$, that is to say, if the ratios $p_1, p_2, \cdots, p_n$, were all equal to p_1 for the first m sets, to p_2 for the second m sets, and to p_r for the last m sets, then a *Lexis distribution* would result with its arithmetic averages, A_L, and the a square of its standard deviation, σ_L, equal respectively to,

$$A_L = np, \quad \sigma^2_L = npq + \frac{(n^2 - n)}{r} \sum_{i=1}^{r} (p_i - p), \quad (2)$$

where $p = (p_1 + p_2 + p_3 + \cdots + p_r)/r$, $q = 1 - p$.

From this point of view, one would then classify the three types of frequency distributions as follows:

(a) *Bernoulli, or binomial distributions, where the probability is constant through trials and sets,*

(b) *Poisson distributions, in which the probability varies from trial to trial but is constant from set to set,*

(c) *Lexis distributions, in which the probability is constant from trial to trial but varies from set to set.*

The difference between Poisson and Lexis distributions may, perhaps, be further clarified by two numerical examples.[1]

In order to construct a Poisson distribution, suppose that the drawings are to be made from three urns, U_1, U_2, U_3, in which the ratios of white to black balls are respectively 1/3, 1/2, and 2/3. For one set of drawings the following eight possibilities present themselves: *BBB; WBB, BWB, BBW; WWB, WBW, BWW; WWW.* The probabilities in these cases are respectively 1/9; 1/18, 1/9, 2/9; 1/18, 1/9, 2/9; 1/9. From these values the probability that no white ball is drawn is found to be 1/9; one white ball, 7/18; two white balls, 7/18; and three white balls, 1/9. Hence, if 72 sets are drawn, the following frequency distribution is expected in the ideal case:

No. of white balls	0	1	2	3
Frequencies	8	28	28	8

For this distribution, the arithmetic average and standard deviation squared are respectively 1/2 and 25/3, both values checking with a computation based on the formulas given in (1).

---

[1] This discussion is taken from a paper by H. T. Davis: "Elementary Derivation of the Fundamental Constants in the Poisson and Lexis Frequency Distributions," *American Math. Monthly*, Vol. 34 (1927), pp. 183-188.

For the construction of the equivalent Lexis distribution, consider the same three urns. Suppose that twenty-four drawings of three balls each, with replacements each time, are made from each of the three urns and the number of white balls recorded. The following are the probable frequencies (to the nearest integer) for each urn, since each set of 24 drawings forms a Bernoulli frequency:

No. of white balls	0	1	2	3
U_1	7	11	5	1
U_2	3	9	9	3
U_3	1	5	11	7
Totals	11	25	25	11

The arithmetic average and square of the standard deviation are found to be respectively 3/2 and 31/36, values which agree with those computed directly from formulas (2).

With these examples in mind, the reader may now proceed to the general case of n urns, $U_1, U_2, \cdots, U_n$, with respective probabilities $p_1, p_2, \cdots, p_n$.

N sets of drawings are now made to form the following *Poisson* frequency:

No. of white balls	0	1	2	$\cdots$	n
Frequencies	f_0	f_1	f_2	$\cdots$	f_n

where $f_0 + f_1 + f_2 + \cdots + f_n = N$.

It will be convenient to adopt the following abbreviations:

$$E_0 = 1 \; ; \quad E_1 = p_1 + p_2 + \cdots + p_n \; ;$$
$$E_2 = p_1 p_2 + p_1 p_3 + \cdots \; ;$$
$$E_3 = p_1 p_2 p_3 + p_1 p_2 p_4 + \cdots \; ;$$
$$E_n = p_1 p_2 p_3 \cdots p_n \; ,$$

that is to say, E_r is the sum of the products of the probabilities taken r at a time.

The following identity from algebra should also be recalled:

$$(x - p_1)(x - p_2) \cdots (x - p_n) \equiv E_0 x^n - E_1 x^{n-1} + E_2 x^{n-2} - \cdots \pm E_n .$$

Since f_0 represents the number of drawings in which no white balls are obtained, this frequency may be written,

$$f_0 = N[(1-p_1)(1-p_2) \cdots (1-p_n)]$$
$$= N[E_0 - E_1 + E_2 - \cdots \pm E_n] .$$

Similarly, one gets

$$f_1 = N[(1-p_1)(1-p_2) \cdots (1-p_{n-1}) p_n$$
$$+ (1-p_1)(1-p_2) \cdots (1-p_{n-1})(1-p_n) p_{n-1} + \cdots]$$
$$= N[E_1 - 2E_2 + 3E_3 - \cdots \pm n E_n] .$$
$$f_2 = N[(1-p_1)(1-p_2) \cdots (1-p_{n-2}) p_{n-1} p_n + \cdots] .$$

In order to express f_2 in terms of the E's, observe that there are as many terms similar to the first one given as there are combinations of the p's taken two at a time, or ${}_nC_2$. Also, for any value of r up to $n-2$, each product of the form $(1-p_1)(1-p_2) \cdots (1-p_{n-2})$ has ${}_{n-2}C_r$ terms containing r letters each. There are, for example, ${}_{n-2}C_3$ terms of the form $p_1 p_2 p_3$. Hence, in f_2 there are altogether ${}_nC_2 \cdot {}_{n-2}C_r$ terms of $r+2$ letters each. But E_{r+2}, which is the sum of the products of $r+2$ letters each, contains ${}_nC_{r+2}$ terms, so that the coefficient of E_{r+2} in f_2 is equal to ${}_nC_2 \cdot {}_{n-2}C_r / {}_nC_{r+2} = (r+2)!/(2!r!)$.

It thus follows that

$$f_2 = N[E_2 - \frac{3!}{2!1!} E_3 + \frac{4!}{2!2!} E_4 - \frac{5!}{2!3!} E_5 + \cdots$$
$$\pm \frac{n!}{2!(n-2)!} E_n] .$$

By a similar argument, the other frequencies can be expressed in terms of the E's. Thus one gets

$$f_3 = N[E_3 - \frac{4!}{3!1!} E_4 + \frac{5!}{3!2!} E_5 - \cdots \pm \frac{n!}{3!(n-3)!} E_n] ,$$

. . . .

$$f_n = N E_n .$$

From these values the arithmetic average is readily computed.
$$A_P = (f_0 \cdot 0 + f_1 \cdot 1 + f_2 \cdot 2 + \cdots + f_n \cdot n)/N ,$$
$$= E_1 + 2(1-1) E_2 + 3(1-1)^2 E_3 + \cdots + n(1-1)^{n-1} E_n ,$$
$$= (p_1 + p_2 + \cdots + p_n)/n = np .$$

Since the arithmetic average is equal to E_1, the square of the standard deviation is then computed as follows:
$$\sigma_P^2 = [f_0(E_1-0)^2 + f_1(E_1-1)^2 + \cdots + f_n(E_1-n)^2]/N$$
$$= [(f_0 + f_1 + \cdots + f_n)E_1^2 - 2E_1^2 N$$
$$\qquad + (f_0 \cdot 0^2 + f_1 \cdot 1^2 + \cdots + f_n \cdot n^2)]/N$$
$$= -E_1^2 + (f_0 \cdot 0^2 + f_1 \cdot 1^2 + \cdots + f_n \cdot n^2)/N .$$

But from the explicit values of the frequencies, one derives,
$$(f_0 \cdot 0^2 + f_1 \cdot 1^2 + \cdots + f_n \cdot n^2)/N$$
$$= E_1 - (2-4) E_2 + (3-3 \cdot 2^2 + 3^2) E_3 - \cdots .$$

It will now be seen that for $r > 2$, the coefficient of E_r is equal to
$$r \cdot 1^2 - \frac{r(r-1)}{2!} 2^2 + \frac{r(r-1)(r-2)}{3!} 3^2 - \cdots \pm \frac{r!}{r!} r^2$$
$$= r[1 - (r-1) + \frac{(r-1)(r-2)}{2!} - \cdots \pm \frac{(r-1)!}{(r-1)!}]$$
$$- r(r-1)[1 - (r-2) + \frac{(r-2)(r-3)}{2!} - \cdots \pm \frac{(r-2)!}{(r-2)!}]$$
$$= r(1-1)^{r-1} - r(r-1)(1-1)^{r-2} = 0 .$$

The square of the standard deviation thus reduces to
$$\sigma_P^2 = -E_1^2 + E_1 + 2 E_2 = np - \sum_{i=1}^{n} p_i^2 = npq - \sum_{i=1}^{n} (p_i - p)^2 .$$

The derivation of formulas (2) for the *Lexis* distribution is similarly accomplished. Consider first the following frequency distribution:

TYPES OF STATISTICAL SERIES 327

No. of white balls	0	1	2	...	n	A	σ^2
U_1	$f_0^{(1)}$	$f_1^{(1)}$	$f_2^{(1)}$	...	$f_n^{(1)}$	np_1	np_1q_1
U_2	$f_0^{(2)}$	$f_1^{(2)}$	$f_2^{(2)}$	...	$f_n^{(2)}$	np_2	np_2q_2
...	.	.	.	.	.	.	.
U_r	$f_0^{(r)}$	$f_1^{(r)}$	$f_2^{(r)}$	...	$f_n^{(r)}$	np_r	np_rq_r
Total (*Lexis* distribution)	f_0	f_1	f_2	...	f_n		

Since each group of drawings made from a single urn is a Bernoulli distribution, the arithmetic average and standard deviation squared is at once known. These are recorded above under the captions A and σ^2.

The arithmetic average of the Lexis distribution is immediately computed as follows:

$$A_L = (0 \cdot f_0 + 1 \cdot f_1 + 2 \cdot f_2 + \cdots + n \cdot f_n)/(rN)$$
$$= (A_1 + A_2 + A_3 + \cdots + A_r)/r$$
$$= n(p_1 + p_2 + p_3 + \cdots + p_r)/r = np .$$

For the calculation of the square of the standard deviation, consider the expression:

$$\sigma_L^2 = [f_0(np-0)^2 + f_1(np-1)^2 + \cdots + f_n(np-n)^2]/(rN)$$
$$= [n^2p^2(f_0 + f_1 + \cdots + f_n)/(rN)]$$
$$- [2np(0 \cdot f_0 + 1 \cdot f_1 + \cdots + n \cdot f_n)/(rN)]$$
$$+ [(0^2 f_0 + 1^2 f_1 + 2^2 f_2 + \cdots + n^2 f_n)/(rN)] ,$$
$$= -n^2p^2 + \sum_{i=1}^{r} (0^2 f_0^{(i)} + 1^2 f_1^{(i)}$$
$$+ 2^2 f_2^{(i)} + \cdots + n^2 f_n^{(i)})/(rN) .$$

From the fact that

$$\sum_{j=0}^{n} f_j^{(i)} (np-j)^2 = Nnp_iq_i ,$$

one obtains after squaring and collecting terms,

$$\sum_{i=1}^{r} [0^2 f_0^{(i)} + 1^2 f_1^{(i)} + 2^2 f_2^{(i)} + \cdots + n^2 f_n^{(i)}]$$
$$= Nnp_iq_i + N n^2 p_i^2 .$$

Hence, there is derived

$$\sum_{i=1}^{r} [0^2 f_0^{(i)} + 1^2 f_1^{(i)} + \cdots + n^2 f_n^{(i)}]/(rN) = (\sum_{i=1}^{r} np_i q_i$$

$$+ n^2 \sum_{i=1}^{r} p_i^2)/r = [n \sum_{i=1}^{r} p_i(1-p_i) + n^2 \sum_{i=1}^{r} p_i^2]/r$$

$$= np + \frac{n^2 - n}{r} \sum_{i=1}^{r} p_i^2 .$$

Substituting this above, one obtains the formula,

$$\sigma_L^2 = - n^2 p + np + \frac{n^2 - n}{r} \sum_{i=1}^{r} p_i^2 .$$

If one replaces p_i by $(p_i - p) + p$ in the last term of the above expression, he will immediately obtain the form σ_L^2 given in formula (2).

PROBLEMS

1. Make a Poisson distribution of total frequency 120 from sets drawn from four urns with probabilities 1/2, 1/3, 1/4, 1/5.

2. Make a Lexis distribution by adding the frequencies of the binomial distributions formed from the expansions of the following:

144 $(1/2 + 1/2)^3$ and 144 $(1/3 + 2/3)^3$.

3. Compute directly the arithmetic average and the standard deviation for the distribution of problem 1 and compare with the values computed from the formulas (1).

4. Compute directly the arithmetic average and the standard deviation for the distribution of problem 2 and compare with the values computed from the formulas (2).

5. The following is a Poisson distribution:

Frequency	24	44	24	4
Class marks	0	1	2	3

Noting that $f_0 = N(E_0 - E_1 + E_2 - E_3)$, $f_1 = N(E_1 - 2E_2 + 3E_3)$, $f_2 = N(E_2 - 3E_3)$, $f_3 = NE_3$, $N = 96$, compute the numerical values of the E's. Then from the fact that the probabilities which entered into the construction of the distribution satisfy the equation:

$$E_0 x^3 - E_1 x^2 + E_2 x - E_3 = 0 ,$$

compute the values of these probabilities. (Note: the cubic equation has been so devised that the roots are rational fractions. The E's should be kept in fractional form and not reduced to decimals).

5. *Testing the Series When the Items are Not of Uniform Size.* In sections 2 and 3 the disturbance in the series of automobile deaths for a set of ten cities with populations of approximately the same size was considered. It is clear, however, that most statistical series will show considerable variation in individual items, and thus the scope of the theory will be severely limited without a method for studying the variation in series the items of which are not of uniform size.

In the example of section 2, the ten cities, while of approximately the same size, varied somewhat in total population. The present theory will be applied to find corrected values for the Lexis ratio and the Charlier coefficient. When there is a wide variation in the size of the items compared, the device of adjusting the data to a fixed base cannot be employed, although in the example under discussion, where the variation is essentially small, the Lexis ratio of this section should agree closely with that obtained previously.

Arne Fisher[1] gives weighty arguments in favor of the following adjustment: Designate by s_k the number of persons or things involved in each item of the series, by m_k the number of persons or things affected by the phenomenon studied, by s some convenient base to which the items may be referred, and by N the total number of items in the series.

In the example under discussion, one means by s_k the population, by m_k the number of deaths, by s some base number such as 100,000, and by N the number of items, namely, 10.

For the calculation of the standard deviation, the following formula is then employed:

$$\sigma^2 = \frac{s}{\Sigma s_k} \Sigma \frac{s}{s_k} (m_k - s_k p)^2 ,$$

where

$$p = \frac{\Sigma m_k}{\Sigma s_k} ,$$

and the summations are taken over the N items of the series.

---

[1] *Theory of Probabilities*, New York, 1923, pp. 157-161.

For the Bernoulli deviation one has,

$$\sigma_B^2 = \frac{Ns}{\Sigma s_k} spq ,$$

and for the arithmetic mean, the value

$$A = \frac{s \Sigma m_k}{\Sigma s_k} .$$

The application of these formulas is illustrated in the following calculation based upon the data of section 2.

It is convenient to make an arbitrary choice of $s = 100,000$. The value

$$p = \frac{\Sigma m_k}{\Sigma s_k} = \frac{1183}{4,611,342} = .0002565$$

is then calculated and the following table formed:

m_k (No. of Deaths)	s_k (Population)	$s_k \cdot p$	$(m_k - s_k p)$	$(m_k - s_k p)^2$	$\dfrac{s}{s_k}$	$\dfrac{s}{s_k}(m_k - s_k p)$
184	573,076	147	37	1369	.17450	239
150	451,160	116	34	1156	.22165	256
129	364,161	93	36	1296	.27460	356
73	316,715	81	− 8	64	.31574	20
112	578,249	148	−36	1296	.17294	224
108	464,356	119	−11	121	.21535	26
126	442,337	113	13	169	.22607	38
124	458,762	118	6	36	.21798	8
58	328,132	84	−26	676	.30476	206
119	634,394	163	−44	1936	.15763	305
1183	4,611,342					1678

The two standard deviations are readily calculated to be,

$$\sigma^2 = \frac{100,000}{4,611,342}(1678) = (.021686)(1678) = 36.39 ,$$

$$\sigma = \sqrt{36.39} = 6.03 ;$$

$$\sigma_B^2 = \frac{(10)(100,000)}{4,611,342}(100,000)(.0002565)(.9997435)$$

$$\sigma_B{}^2 = \frac{25{,}643{,}400}{4{,}611{,}342} = 5.56 ,$$

$$\sigma_B = \sqrt{5.56} = 2.36 .$$

The Lexis ratio is then found to be,

$$L = \frac{6.03}{2.36} = 2.55 ,$$

which is in close agreement with the former calculation.

Using the formula for the arithmetic mean, one finds that

$$A = \frac{100{,}000}{4{,}611{,}342}(1183) = 25.65 .$$

Substituting this value and the standard deviations in the formula for the Charlier coefficient, one obtains,

$$C = \frac{100\sqrt{36.39 - 5.56}}{25.65} = \frac{555.25}{25.65} = 21.65 ,$$

which is in unusually close agreement with the previously calculated value.

PROBLEMS

1. Find the Lexis ratio and the Charlier coefficient for the complete table of automobile deaths in cities, section 2, by using the method of this section.

2. Apply the theory of this section to the data of problem 6 of section 2 and compare your result with the results reached in problem 1 of section 3.

6. The Poisson-Bortkewitsch "Law of Small Numbers." The "law of small numbers" or, as it is sometimes more properly called, "the law of small probabilities," assumes that in a group of quantitative phenomena selected without bias, a small proportion of the group will be found to deviate sharply from the characteristics of the remainder of the group, and this tendency will persist no matter how large the group may be made and irrespective of the number of samples selected. Thus, if an analysis were made of balances of savings accounts in a large number of banks located in different sections of the country, the analysis would reveal that each bank had a small number of savings accounts in which the balances were more than $10,000. Similar experiences may be found in other economic data, such, for example, as the number of days in each year in which the volume of trading on the New York Stock Exchange exceeded 5,000,000 shares, or the few large deviations from trend of some series such as the Dow Jones Industrial Averages.

The law of small numbers is applied only to events which happen rarely, that is, events in which the probability of their occurrence is very small. Small frequency distributions of this type can best be fitted by the so-called *Poisson exponential function,*

$$y = N \frac{A^x e^{-A}}{x!}, \qquad (3)$$

where N is the total frequency, x the class mark measured by integers from 0, and A the arithmetic average. Formula (3) was first derived by S. D. Poisson in 1837, but L. von Bortkewitsch pointed out its statistical importance and formulated his ideas in the "law of small numbers" in 1898.

As an example, consider the following frequency distribution in which is recorded the number of times ten tails appeared in 100 samples of 1024 tosses of ten coins:

Number of times ten tails appeared in 1024 tosses (x)	Number of samples (y)
0	35
1	36
2	19
3	7
4	2
5	1
Total	100

The average is easily found to be $A = 1.08$. Hence the Poisson exponential becomes,

$$y = 100 \frac{1.08^x e^{-1.08}}{x!}.$$

When the values of x from 0 to 5 are substituted in the above equation, the corresponding values of y are readily calculated and the graduated frequencies found to be,

Number of times ten tails appeared in 1024 tosses	Frequency (observed)	Frequency (calculated)
0	35	33.96
1	36	36.68
2	19	19.81
3	7	7.13
4	2	1.93
5	1	.43

The problem of the graduation of Lexis and Poisson series is left an open one in this book because of the mathematical difficulties that bar the way. The reader is now upon the threshold of modern mathematical statistics and the problems are both numerous and difficult.

PROBLEMS

1. In the penny tossing experiment cited in the illustrative example the following distribution was obtained for the number of times ten heads appeared in 100 samples of 1024 tosses of ten coins:

Number of times ten heads appeared	0	1	2	3	4	5
Number of samples	29	37	20	9	4	1

Graduate these data by the Poisson exponential formula.

2. Both in the illustrative example and in problem 1 the average should ideally have equalled 1. Compute the ideal graduation and compare with the observed distributions.

3. The following data give the frequency distribution of commercial paper rates in the United States which were 15% or over for the one hundred years, 1831-1930 inclusive:

Number of months in which commercial paper rates were 15% or over	0	1	2	3	4	5	6	7
Frequency in years	90	4	1	1	1	1	1	1

Graduate these data by the Poisson exponential formula.

4. Show from the sum,

$$\sum_{x=0}^{s+1} x \frac{A^x e^{-A}}{x!} = e^{-A}\left[A + A^2 + \frac{A^3}{2!} + \ldots\ldots + \frac{A^{s+1}}{s!}\right],$$

where s is a large number, that the arithmetic average of the frequency distribution equals A. Hint: Use formula 7, section 5, Appendix II.

5. Show from the summation,

$$\left\{ \sum_{x=0}^{s} x^2 \frac{A^x e^{-A}}{x!} \right\} - A^2,$$

where s is a large number, that the standard deviation for the "small number" distribution is equal to $\sqrt{A}$.

7. *Conclusion.* By way of conclusion, some words of counsel may be offered. The student is now equipped with some mastery of at least elementary statistical methodology. The danger is that he will over-estimate rather than under-estimate the value of this equipment. Statistical methodology is no magical, or even mechanical, instrument that automatically grinds out valid conclusions and allows the suspension or avoidance of personal judgment. Indeed, it may be said flatly that a statistical conclusion is no better than the judgment of the statistician who produced it. Knowing what tool to employ is just as important as knowing how to employ it. The second can be taught, but the first must be learned. The novice will tend to think that the more high-powered his methods the more cogent his analysis. This is not at all necessarily true. A scatter diagram may well yield more information than a correlation coefficient. The fact that the latter may be carried to several decimal places gives a spurious appearance of accuracy, while it may really be concealing such facts as that the relationship is curvilinear or that some of the observations are evidently grossly distorted. In such a case, the apparently crude method is really enlightening, the apparently precise method is really deceptive. Very often a free hand curve drawn through a graph will tell as much

about the trend as will ever be revealed by logistics or quintics. Again, the methods may be too refined for the data. Using a jeweller's instruments on a locomotive doesn't give the latter the precision of a chronometer. Very often the student may be misled by talk of "first and second approximations" into thinking he is attaining an accuracy he really is not getting at all. Finally, good statisticians are not made by studying textbooks but by working on statistical problems. There is a world of wisdom to be gained by wrestling with the hard figures instead of manipulating the ideal situations of the theorist. One soon learns in actual statistical work that the facts are often unyielding and intractable and the precision instruments of methodology, instead of reducing them to ideal shapes and forms, are merely blunted in the attempt. It is in wrestling with such difficulties that one becomes a statistician, for the final mastery of statistical methodology comes only from handling statistics.

APPENDIX I

Biographical Notes on Mathematical Economists

Antoine-Augustin Cournot[1] (1801-1877), was born in Gray, in Haute-Saône, France, and educated at the Lycée de Besançon and the Ecole Normale in Paris. He was successively Professor of mathematics at Lyons, Rector of the Academy at Grenoble, Inspecteur Général des Etudes, and Rector of the Academy at Dijon. Despite the existence of earlier, though much less competent, work by others, his *Recherches sur les Principes Mathématiques de la théorie des richesses,* published in 1838, may be pronounced the first notable success in the application of mathematics to economics. Of this book Edgeworth wrote: "It is still the best statement in mathematical form of some of the highest generalizations of economic science." "Cournot's genius," said Alfred Marshall, "must give a new mental activity to everyone who passes through his hands." Cournot employed mathematics, not merely as a translating device to express tersely conclusions that might as readily and adequately be expressed in words, but as an instrument of research through the use of which he might arrive at hitherto undiscovered conclusions. Briefly, he proposed to elaborate a theory of value, or of the determination of prices. He started with the case of pure monopoly, for which the solution is most easily accessible to a mathematical approach. When the cost of production is zero, monopoly price is, of course, that price which will yield the largest gross return, that is, where the product of price and quantity is a maximum. Where there are costs of production, monopoly price is that which yields the maximum net return. Cournot then expanded his analysis by the introduction first of one, then of more competitors, and by extension came, if the expression may be permitted, to an infinite number of monopolists, that is to say, to a régime of absolutely free competition. However masterly his treatment of the initial condition of monopoly, he was unable to avoid pitfalls in his expansion of his analysis. Cournot's approach was based on the law of demand, that the demand for any commodity is a continuous decreasing function of its price. The first geomet-

---

[1] See René Roy: "Cournot et l'école mathématique", *Econometrica*, Vol. I (1933), pp. 13-22.

rical figures descriptive of the demand function appeared in Cournot's epochal treatise, and he pioneered in a field which is now as intensively worked as any in economics. Unfortunately, it must be recorded of Cournot's *Recherches* that it met with a signal lack of recognition. The author was not mentioned in the bibliographies of the day, his name faded, his book passed even from libraries. A generation elapsed before the name of the first great mathematical economist was rescued from oblivion by the glowing tributes of Walras and Jevons. In a peculiar measure, the English-speaking peoples may be said to have established his fame, through Edgeworth's article in Palgrave's *Dictionary of Political Economy*, and by N. T. Bacon's English translation of his work in 1897.

William Stanley Jevons[1] (1835-1882), one of the next notable figures in econometrics, was an example of many-sided genius. He was marked from earliest youth by the sense that he would write something which, in Milton's words, "the world would not willingly let die." Born in England, before he was 19 he was assayer to the mint in Sydney, Australia. After five years of this work, which trained him to habits of scientific precision, he returned to England to continue his studies. After taking his degrees at the University of London, he taught Logic, Moral and Mental Philosophy, and Political Economy, at Owens College, Manchester, and later Political Economy at University College, London. He was an accomplished musician, built his own organ, conversed "like an early Greek philosopher, rather than a contemporary," and his work served to make him a figure of exceptional distinction, equally in logic, applied economics, pure economics, and statistics. He wrote on many subjects, including currency, bimetallism, social reform, and scientific method. His study of the Coal Question, it is said, served to reverse the government's fiscal policy, and led to an attempt to discharge the English national debt. He discovered the principle of marginal utility independently, though it had previously been set forth, unknown to him, in Gossen's work. However, the clarity and force of Jevons' exposition were such as to give the principle wide acceptance, and possibly to date the birth of pure economics. Ignoring the dictum of John Stuart Mill (1806-1873) that everything had been said about value, he set out to reconstruct economics as a calculus of satisfactions. While his contemporaries held that cost of production was the principal element in determining

---

[1] See "William Stanley Jevons", by H. Stanley and H. Winefrid Jevons, *Econometrica*, Vol. II (1933), pp. 225-237.

value, Jevons held that production took its significance entirely from consumption, that is, from the satisfactions to which it ministers, and that the significance of any special unit of production is due to the increment of satisfaction it is capable of producing. Hence, the scale of equivalence of any two commodities is determined by the scale of equivalence of the increments of satisfaction they are capable of producing and exchange value is determined by incremental efficiency as a producer of satisfactions. In other words, marginal utility governs prices. Just as the demand curves started by Cournot have been a constant and fruitful source of economic speculation and research, so has Jevons' marginal utility provoked numerous attempts at its measurement. In any consideration of the fecundity of Jevons' labors in so many fields, it should be remembered that he was drowned at the age of 47.

Marie Esprit Léon Walras[1] (1834-1910), professor at the University of Lausanne from 1870 to 1892 and founder of the "Lausanne School," first established the general conditions of economic equilibrium, and this achievement the inscription on his memorial at Lausanne cites as his peculiar claim to fame. Walras wrote on social economy and applied economics, but the definitive exposition of his pure economics is found in the fourth edition (published in 1900) of his *Elements d'économie politique pure ou théorie de la richesse sociale*. Pure economics he defined as "the theory of the determination of prices under a hypothetical system of absolutely free competition." In dealing with the exchange of two commodities, he concluded that "the equilibrium prices are equal to the ratios of 'rarity' " (i.e., the marginal utility of Jevons' work). His point of departure was his desire to apply the calculus of functions, indicated by Cournot, to a theory of exchange value set forth by his father, A. A. Walras. His work on pure economics is, therefore, really a monument of filial piety. Though his point of departure was different, he arrived at Jevons' conclusions, of which, however, he had not known. When they were called to his attention he was the first to proclaim Jevons' priority. Walras, therefore, like Gossen and Jevons, was an independent discoverer of this keystone of the economic arch. From the exchange of two commodities, as determined by their marginal utilities, he advanced to a theory of exchange of any number of commodities. His theory sets forth the conditions which the quantities of goods exchanged

[1] See "Léon Walras," by J. R. Hicks, *Econometrica*, Vol. II (1934), pp. 338-348.

in a market and the corresponding prices must satisfy to establish equilibrium. The conditions are (1) the realization of maximum satisfaction for each individual, (2) balance of receipts and expenditures for each individual, (3) equivalence between the quantities of producer services offered and asked, and (4) equality between net cost and sale price.

Walras was a particularly prolific writer, and those who conceive of mathematical economists as entirely abstracted from the actual concerns of life may note that he wrote voluminously for newspapers. He was himself for several years editor of a paper devoted to the advancement of the cooperative movement. He wrote extensively on the land question and favored nationalization as a solution of the tax problem. To solve the monetary problem, Walras advocated a gold currency supplemented by a token currency of silver, which would serve to keep prices stable. In general, he was a man of wide interest in social problems. His approach may best be indicated by a quotation. "We count today," he said, "many schools of political economy. For me, I recognize but two: the school of those who do not demonstrate, and the school —which I hope to see founded—of those who demonstrate, their conclusions."

Vilfredo Pareto (1848-1923) was a disciple of Walras and his successor in the chair of Political Economy at the University of Lausanne. His principal works bearing on pure economic theory are *Cours d'économie politique,* published in 1896 at Lausanne, *Manuale di economia politica con una introduzione alla scienza sociale,* published in Milan (1906), and *Manuel d'économie politique,* published in Paris (1909). For twenty-seven years after graduation from the Polytechnical Institute at Turin, Pareto practiced his profession as engineer. His thesis had been a study of the mathematical theory of the equilibrium of elastic bodies and his economic contribution was, in effect, an effort to expand this subject in the social sciences. Pareto proposed to treat economics from a purely scientific point of view, so that he was led to examine, in addition to a régime of free competition, the various types of monopoly, among which, of course, are the socialist régimes. Further, he strove to take as objective a position as possible, to make pure economics the first approximation in the study of concrete economic phenomena. He introduced certain fresh conceptions beyond those of Walras, which assured wider generality for his theory of economic equilibrium, while his method of analysis permitted him greater profundity, for Walras had employed no mathematics other than algebra and analytical geometry. Following Edgeworth's and Fisher's lead that the utility produced by consumption of a commodity frequently depends on the consumption of other commodities, he was led to distinguish other kinds of dependence, such as those that rise because certain things give more pleasure united than separated, because they supplement each other, or because a total of several consumptions may be influenced by their order, as a dinner served from soup to dessert presumably occasions greater satisfaction to the diner than if it started with the dessert and ended with the soup. His study of the dependence of consumption allowed Pareto to explain why bread-eating increased in famine years despite the impediment of higher prices. Malthus had explained this paradox on the assumption of the stupid obstinacy of consumers, who were determined to have bread at any price. The more reasonable solution of Pareto was that consumers are deprived of superior foods and must concentrate on bread despite its higher price. Like Marshall and others, Pareto was led to economics through mathematics. His reputation as a sociologist is certainly not inferior to his reputation as an economist.

Francis Ysidro Edgeworth[1] (1845-1926) was born in Ireland of mixed Irish-Spanish-French descent, and educated at Trinity College, Dublin and Balliol College, Oxford. After being called to the Bar, he pursued a desultory legal career for several years before becoming a lecturer in Logic, and afterwards Tooke Professor of Political Economy, at King's College, London. In 1891 he accepted the Drummond Professorship of Political Economy at Oxford and held this chair till 1922. In 1891 he also founded the *Economic Journal,* of which he was at first Editor-in-Chief, and later Joint-Editor, till his death in 1926. His views on pure economics are set forth in *Mathematical Psychics* (1881) and in the many articles published in the journal which he edited. These articles were collected in 1925 into three volumes of *Papers Relating to Political Economy.* His *Mathematical Psychics* justifies the use of mathematics in the moral sciences and applies the calculus of hedonism, the economic calculus, and the utilitarian calculus, the economic calculus having as its object the determination of conditions permitting certain individuals or groups to obtain for them-

---

[1] See "F. Y. Edgeworth", in *Essays in Biography,* by J. M. Keynes, pp. 267-293, New York, 1933; "Francis Ysidro Edgeworth", by A. L. Bowley, *Econometrica,* Vol. II (1934), pp. 113-124.

selves the maximum of utility, the utilitarian calculus relating to the realization of the greatest possible sum of utility by a community. Edgeworth introduced into pure economics certain ideas which underlie many modern works on the subject, notably the idea of dependence of consumption, where the curve of utility is replaced by a surface in the case of two goods, and by hyperspaces in the case of a great number of goods. He also set up equations similar to those of Walras, but whereas Walras had studied commercial competition only, Edgeworth added another type we may call industrial competition. In commercial competition, disutilities are necessarily equal to the utilities of the products received in exchange but, as Edgeworth showed, in industrial competition the disutility of a labor is not necessarily measured by the utility of a service rendered. This introduced new factors into the conditions of general equilibrium. When we pass, he said, to the complexities introduced by the division of labor, the problem of economic equilibrium ceases to be a simple one of algebra or geometry. Even were we in possession of the numerous data relative to the motives acting on each individual, one can hardly conceive that it would be possible to deduce *a priori* the state of equilibrium which a complicated system would reach. "I will never," said Edgeworth, "reproach mathematical economists for not having formulated the problem of industrial competition. Abstract symbols must often fail to represent reality fully." Edgeworth also took up and completed certain of the theories of Cournot. He also advanced the notion, which met with little approbation, that pleasure is measurable, that all pleasures are commensurable, and that the proper unit of measurement is the least possible assimilable quantity of pleasure. This venture of Edgeworth's into psychology met with general disfavor as tending to make economics restore long discredited metaphysical concepts. Edgeworth also wrote on probability and statistical theory, dealing especially with the law of error. "The connecting line between Edgeworth's different works," writes J. M. Keynes, "is to be found in his interest in the problem of measurement applied to the so-called moral sciences or, as he called it, 'mathematical psychics.' To him it had five branches, the measurement of utility, or ethical value; the algebraic or diagrammatic determination of economic equilibrium; the measurement of belief, or probability; the measurement of evidence, or statistics; and the measurement of economic value, or index numbers. His work on index numbers was particularly important." Again, Keynes says, "Most present day students of mathematical economics would probably consider Edgeworth the most eminent of nineteenth century pioneers in this subject."

This necessarily sketchy notice of some of the historic leaders in econometrics is given so that the student may at least be acquainted with some of the more famous names associated with the econometric movement in the past. In a textbook on statistical technique it is not amiss to emphasize that Cournot was a notable writer on probability, which underlies all statistical reasoning, and, as Edgeworth has indicated, did statistics a signal service by pointing out the application of the calculus of variations. Cournot's also was the first casual suggestion that the investigator must distinguish between secular trend and periodic fluctuations, a distinction that is now a commonplace in analysis of economic time series. Jevons' statistical work, especially on prices, was of the first order. He segregated seasonal movements, secular trends, and cycles, in the most approved modern fashion. He has been accorded the title of "the father of index numbers," and may be said to have put statistics into economics once and forever. Of Pareto's *Cours d'Economie Politique*, Irving Fisher said, "No other book contains such a compact, varied, and comprehensive collection of statistical data." Statistics was of major interest to Edgeworth and his studies of index numbers and correlations were especially notable. In speaking of the mathematical interests of these leaders of econometrics, it should not be thought that they were negligent of, or incompetent in, the statistical field.

APPENDIX II

Logarithms

1. A Note on Computation. The manipulation and analysis of statistical data must sooner or later lead to numerical calculations. In well-equipped statistical laboratories, the burden of this work has been greatly lessened by a number of mechanical devices, such as adding and multiplying machines, slide-rules, card-sorting machines, and correlation calculators.

Since these useful devices are not always available to many who must study statistical materials, it is necessary to have recourse to more easily accessible tools, such as tables of logarithms, tables of square roots, cube roots, reciprocals, and so forth. In this appendix the employment of a table of logarithms in making calculations will be explained, and also some of the properties of logarithms which are used in various parts of the book will be developed.

It will be assumed that the student is already familiar with the theory of exponents, the laws of which will merely be restated for convenience in reference.

2. The Laws of Exponents. In arithmetic, one learns that $2 \times 2 \times 2$ multiplied by 2×2 equals $2^3 \times 2^2 = 2^5$. The theory of exponents is a generalization of this simple arithmetic fact. Thus, if a is a positive number, and m and n are any numbers whatsoever, it will be assumed that the following law, called the *index law*, holds between the *base*, a, and the *exponents*, m and n:

$$a^m a^n = a^{m+n}, \qquad a > 0. \qquad (1)$$

If m and n are positive integers, this law is self-evident, but if m and n are not positive integers, the meaning of the law is not immediately clear. The student is referred to a textbook on algebra for proofs of the following three theorems derived as immediate consequences from the index law:

I. $\quad a^0 = 1,$

II. $\quad a^{-n} = 1/a^n,$

$$\text{III.} \quad a^{p/q} = \sqrt[q]{a^p} = (\sqrt[q]{a})^p,$$

where p and q are integers.

If, in the index law, n is replaced by $-n$, as may be done since n is a wholly arbitrary number, and then use is made of theorem II, another useful identity in the theory of exponents is obtained, i.e.,

$$a^m \, a^{-n} = a^m/a^n. \tag{2}$$

A third identity,

$$(a^m)^n = a^{mn}, \tag{3}$$

is readily obtained from the index law in case n is an integer, but involves an assumption whose justification is proved only in books on advanced algebra when n is not an integer.

When more than one base is employed, the following two identities are fundamental:

$$a^n \, b^n = (a\,b)^n, \tag{4}$$
$$a^n/b^n = (a/b)^n. \tag{5}$$

Example 1. Find the value of $(64/27)^{2/3} + (81/16)^{-3/4}$.

By theorems II and III, this can be written in the form

$$(64/27)^{2/3} + (16/81)^{3/4} = (\sqrt[3]{64/27})^2 + (\sqrt[4]{16/81})^3$$
$$= (4/3)^2 + (2/3)^3$$
$$= 16/9 + 8/27 = 56/27.$$

Example 2.

$$\frac{2^{-3} + 8^{1/3}}{(\tfrac{1}{2})^{-1} + (4)^{-3/2}} = \frac{1/8 + 2}{2 + 1/8} = 1.$$

Example 3.

$$[x^{1/(p-1)} \, x^{1/(p+1)}]^{(p^2-1)} \, x^{-2p} = [x^{1/(p-1) + 1/(p+1)}]^{(p^2-1)} \, x^{-2p}$$
$$= [x^{2p/(p^2-1)}]^{(p^2-1)} \, x^{-2p} = x^{2p} x^{-2p} = x^0 = 1.$$

3. Logarithms. Logarithms were invented by John Napier, (1550-1617), Baron of Merchiston in Scotland, as a calculating device. They have since appeared in many theoretical connections

APPENDIX II

and have numerous uses in applied mathematics besides that of affording a powerful aid in numerical calculations.

A logarithm is customarily defined in terms of the theory of exponents as follows: By a logarithm to the base a of a number N, is meant a number y to which power the base a must be raised in order to produce the number N. This definition is expressed in symbols thus:

$$\text{If } a^y = N, \text{ then } \log_a N = y.$$

From this definition one obtains the following theorems regarding logarithms:

    I. $\log_a 1 = 0$, since $a^0 = 1$,

    II. $\log_a xy = \log_a x + \log_a y$.

Proof: Let $\log_a x = n$ and $\log_a y = m$. From the definition of a logarithm, one has $a^n = x$ and $a^m = y$. Therefore, from the index law, $xy = a^m \cdot a^n = a^{m+n}$, and from the definition again one gets $\log_a xy = m + n = \log_a x + \log_a y$.

    III. $\log_a x/y = \log_a x - \log_a y$.

Proof: Letting $\log_a x = m$ and $\log_a y = n$, one has from the definition $a^m = x$ and $a^n = y$. Then, by (2) in the theory of exponents, $x/y = a^m/a^n = a^{m-n}$ and, consequently,

$$\log_a x/y = m - n = \log_a x - \log_a y.$$

    IV. $\log_a x^n = n \log_a x$.

Proof: If one lets $\log_a x = m$, it follows by definition that $a^m = x$. Therefore, raising both sides to the power n and referring to the theory of exponents, one has $x^n = (a^m)^n = a^{mn}$. Consequently, $\log_a x^n = mn = n \log_a x$.

Sometimes it is necessary to transfer from one base a to a second base b. For example, *common* or *Briggsian*[1] logarithms are computed to the base 10, and *natural* logarithms are computed to the base designated by the symbol e, where $e = 2.71828\cdots$. This number, often called Napier's number, is one of the most important in mathematics and it is particularly useful in statistics. Its

---

[1] Named after Henry Briggs (1556-1630), who was the first to calculate a table of logarithms to the base 10.

significance has appeared elsewhere. The following formula allows one to change from one system of logarithms to another:

$$\text{V.} \quad \log_a N = \frac{1}{\log_b a} \log_b N \ .$$

Proof: Let $\log_a N = y$; then, by the definition of a logarithm, $a^y = N$. Taking logarithms to the base b of both sides of this equation, one has

$$\log_b a^y = \log_b N \ .$$

Applying IV, it is found that

$$\log_b a^y = \log_b N \ ,$$
$$y \log_b a = \log_b N \ ;$$

substituting $y = \log_a N$, then

$$\log_a N \log_b a = \log_b N \ ,$$

and hence

$$\log_a N = \frac{1}{\log_b a} \log_b N \ .$$

It is useful to specialize this theorem for the case of common and natural logarithms. Thus, to go from the common to the natural system, one uses

$$\text{V (a).} \quad \log_e N = 2.30259 \log_{10} N \ ,$$

and from the natural to the common system,

$$\text{V (b).} \quad \log_{10} N = .43429 \log_e N \ .$$

Example 1. Calculate the value of

$$x = \log_2 \frac{8^{3/2}}{\sqrt[3]{16}\ (4)^{3/5}} \ .$$

Making use of the properties above, one finds that

$$x = \log_2 8^{3/2} - \log_2 \sqrt[3]{16} - \log_2 4^{3/5} \qquad \text{(by II and III)},$$
$$= (3/2) \log_2 8 - (1/3) \log_2 16 - (3/5) \log_2 4 \qquad \text{(by IV)},$$
$$= (3/2) \cdot 3 - (1/3) \cdot 4 - (3/5) \cdot 2 = 59/30 \ .$$

APPENDIX II

Example 2. Given $\log_{10} 2 = .301$, calculate the value of
$$x = \log_{10} 1/625 .$$

By the properties of logarithms, one has

$x = \log_{10} 1 - \log_{10} 625 ,$ \hfill (by III),

$= 0 - \log_{10} 5^4 ,$ \hfill (by I),

$= - \log_{10} (10/2)^4 = - 4 \log_{10} 10/2 ,$ \hfill (by IV),

$= -4(\log_{10} 10 - \log_{10} 2) = -4(1 - .301) = -2.796 .$

Example 3. Given $\log_{10} 2 = .301$ and $\log_{10} 6 = .778$, calculate the value of $\log_2 6$.

By V, one has
$$\log_2 6 = \frac{1}{\log_{10} 2} \log_{10} 6 = \frac{.778}{.301} = 2.585 .$$

Example 4. Calculate $\log_e 100$.

By V(a), one has

$$\log_e 100 = 2.30259 \log_{10} 100 = 2.30259 \times 2 = 4.60518 .$$

PROBLEMS

Express the following in terms of the logarithms of prime numbers:

1. $\log(\sqrt[3]{21} \cdot 15^{-2} \cdot \sqrt{35}) .$
2. $\log \sqrt[3]{49/(45)(20)} .$
3. $\log(21)(\sqrt[3]{25})(\sqrt{32}) .$
4. $\log[77^{-1/2}/(75^{2/5})(55^{-2})] .$
5. $\log[\sqrt{26}/(39^{-1/2})(52^{2/3})] .$

Using the values $\log_{10} 2 = .3010$ and $\log_{10} 3 = .4771$, calculate the following logarithms:

6. $\log_{10} \sqrt[3]{9}/\sqrt{125} .$ Hint: $\log_{10} 5 = \log_{10} 10 - \log_{10} 2 .$
7. $\log_{10} \sqrt[3]{4} \cdot \sqrt[5]{125} \cdot \sqrt{27} .$
8. $\log_{10} 625 \cdot \sqrt{8}/\sqrt{15} .$
9. $\log_{10} \sqrt{32} \cdot \sqrt{72}/\sqrt{45} .$
10. $\log_{10} 2^2 \cdot 3^0 \cdot 5^{-1} .$

11. Prove that $\log_a b = 1/\log_b a$.
12. Given $\log_{10} 3 = .4771$ and $\log_{10} 9 = .9542$, what is $\log_3 9$?
13. Given $\log_{10} 3 = .4771$ and $\log_{10} 5 = .6990$, what is $\log_3 5$?
14. Given $\log_{10} 2 = .301$ and $\log_{10} 5 = .699$, calculate the value of x for which $2^x = 5$. Hint: $x \log_{10} 2 = \log_{10} 5$.
15. From the fact that $2^1 = 2$, $2^2 = 4$, $2^3 = 8$, $2^4 = 16$, estimate $\log_2 5$ and $\log_2 10$.
16. Given $\log_{10} 2 = .301$, for what value of x does $2^x = 100$? What is the value of $\log_2 100$?
17. Given $\log_e 2 = .6931$ and $\log_e 27 = 3.2958$, for what value of x does $2^x = 27$?
18. Calculate $\log_e 125$, given $\log_{10} 2 = .30103$.
19. Calculate x where $\log_e x = 6.90776$. Hint: Convert $\log_e x$ to $\log_{10} x$.
20. Calculate $\log_{10} 65$, given $\log_e 65 = 4.1744$.

4. *Calculation by Logarithms*. Logarithms to the base 10 are adapted to numerical computation. Because of their frequent occurrence, the base need not be repeated in each symbol, but $\log x$ may stand for $\log_{10} x$. A table of common logarithms is easily constructed for special values of x. Thus one has:

$10^0 = 1$ $\log 1 = 0$
$10^1 = 10$ $\log 10 = 1$
$10^2 = 100$ $\log 100 = 2$
$10^3 = 1000$ $\log 1000 = 3$

and for negative exponents:

$10^{-1} = .1$ $\log .1 = -1$
$10^{-2} = .01$ $\log .01 = -2$
$10^{-3} = .001$ $\log .001 = -3$

It will be seen that the integral part of the logarithm of any number can be determined from the above table and its extension. Thus, $\log 643.2$ lies between 2 and 3, since 643.2 lies between 100 and 1000; similarly, $\log .06432$ lies between -1 and -2, since .06432 lies between .1 and .01. Hence, one may write

$$\log 643.2 = 2 + a,$$

$$\text{and } \log .06432 = -2 + a,$$

where a is a positive number less than one. The numbers 2 and -2 are called the *characteristics* of the logarithms and a the *mantissa*.

Definition: The integral part of a logarithm is called the *characteristic* and the decimal part, when it is written as a positive number, is called the *mantissa*.

The characteristic of a number may be found from the following rule:

The characteristic of a number greater than unity is one less than the number of digits to the left of the decimal point; the characteristic of a positive number less than unity is negative and numerically equal to the place of the first digit of the number.

For example, the characteristic of 57.6 is 1; of 8543.2 is 3; of 768 is 2; of .623 is —1; of .000243 is —4.

The mantissa of a number is found from a table of logarithms. Table I at the end of this book gives the mantissas of logarithms from 1 to 10,000, computed to five significant figures.

The following examples sufficiently illustrate how the logarithm of a given number is found and, conversely, how a number is found which corresponds to a given logarithm.

To find the logarithm of a given number.

Example 1. Find log 864.2 .

The characteristic is 2. To find the mantissa, enter the table with the first three digits 864. Then under the column headed 2 find the required mantissa, i.e., 93661. Hence log 864.2 = 2.93661.

Example 2. Find log .08642.

The characteristic in this case is —2, and the mantissa, as in the first example, is 93661. We thus have log .08642 = —2 + .93661. This logarithm may be written in either of the following ways:

$$\log .08642 = \bar{2}.93661 ,$$

$$\text{or, } \log .08642 = 8.93661 - 10 .$$

In the first case the minus sign is written above the 2 to indicate that it pertains to that number alone. The advantage of the second case lies in the fact that the logarithm is written as the difference of two positive numbers.

Example 3. Find log 86.426 .

Since the logarithm of a number of five figures cannot be looked up directly in the table, one must use *interpolation*. The mantissa corresponding to 86426 lies between the mantissas of 8642 and 8643, i.e., between 93661 and 93666. If to the former is added 6/10 of the difference between the two numbers, one will have the mantissa of 86426. Thus,

$$\text{mantissa of log } 86.43 = 93666$$
$$\text{mantissa of log } 86.42 = 93661$$

$$\text{tabular difference} = \quad 5 \ .$$

Therefore, the mantissa of log $86.426 = 93661 + (6/10) \cdot 5 = 93664$; hence, log $86.426 = 1.93664$.

To find the number corresponding to a given logarithm.

Example 1. Find x, where log $x = 2.71139$.

Entering the table of mantissas with the number 71139, one sees that this corresponds to the number 5145. Since the characteristic is 2, $x = 514.5$.

Example 2. Find x, where log $x = 8.71139 - 10$.

Since the mantissa is the same as in the first example, the problem is merely in the placing of the decimal point. Hence $x = .05145$.

Example 3. Find x, where log $x = 0.51371$.

The table of mantissas does not include the number 51371, so one must interpolate; thus, one has

mantissa of log $3264 = 51375$	mantissa of log $x \quad = 51371$
mantissa of log $3263 = 51362$	mantissa of log $3263 = 51362$
tabular difference $= \quad 13$	difference $= \quad 9$

Hence, the number corresponding to the mantissa 51371 is $3263 + 9/13 = 3263.7$. Since the characteristic of log $x =$ is 0, one finds $x = 3.2637$.

PROBLEMS

Find the logarithms of the following numbers:

1. $\pi = 3.1416$
2. 16.2715
3. $e = 2.7183$
4. 561.83
5. $1/\pi = .31831$
6. $.0081235$
7. $\log_e 10 = 2.3026$
8. $.12345$
9. $\log_{10} e = .43429$
10. $.076541$
11. C (Euler's number) $= .57722$
12. 3443.4

Find the values of x:

13. $\log x = 1.49145$
14. $\log x = 8.56317 - 10$
15. $\log x = 1.90633$
16. $\log x = \overline{6}.13542$
17. $\log x = 2.98860$
18. $\log x = 4.42412$
19. $\log x = 0.50000$
20. $\log x = 7.17244 - 10$
21. $\log x = 8.01140 - 10$
22. $\log x = 0.12174$

The use of logarithms as a calculating device depends upon the properties discussed in the preceding section. It may be remarked here that much computation, where expensive machines are not available, is greatly facilitated by the use of the slide rule, an instrument which is based, of course, on logarithms. The following examples will sufficiently illustrate the various types of problems that can be handled by logarithms:

Example 1. Find the value of $x = \dfrac{(1257)(.4277)}{2.6431}$.

Taking logarithms of both sides and applying the rules of section 3, it is found that

$$\log x = \log 1257 + \log .4277 - \log 2.6431 .$$

Considerable simplification in actual computation is obtained by making an outline of the problem first and then filling in with the values of the logarithms. The finished work should look like this:

$$\log 1257 = 3.09934$$
$$\log .4277 = 9.63114 - 10$$
$$\text{sum} \ = 2.73048$$
$$-\log 2.6431 = 0.42212$$
$$\log x = 2.30836$$
$$x = 203.40 \ .$$

Example 2. Find the value of $x = \dfrac{\sqrt[3]{62.173}\sqrt{84.19}}{\sqrt{3.429}}$.

By the rules of section 3, one has

$\log x = (1/3) \log 62.173 + (1/2) \log 84.19 - (1/2) \log 3.429$.

The actual calculation is shown below:

$$(1/3) \log 62.173 = .59787$$
$$(1/2) \log 84.19 = .96263$$

$$\text{sum} = 1.56050$$
$$-(1/2) \log 3.429 = .26758$$

$$\log x = 1.29292$$
$$x = 19.630 .$$

Example 3. Find the value of $x = \sqrt[3]{.00064172}$.

$$\log x = (1/3) \log .00064172 ,$$

$$\log .00064172 = \overline{4}.80734 = 6.80734 - 10 .$$

Since this logarithm must be divided by 3, it is obviously more convenient to write it in the equivalent form $26.80734 - 30$. One thus gets

$$(1/3) \log .00064172 = (1/3)(26.80734 - 30) ,$$
$$\log x = 8.93578 - 10 ,$$
$$x = .086254 .$$

PROBLEMS

Find the values of the following:

1. $x = \dfrac{763.12 \sqrt{863.1}}{\sqrt[3]{43414}}$

2. $x = (1.0632)^{6.5} (1.0754)^{-5.2}$.

3. $x = \sqrt[5]{62139}$.

4. $x = \dfrac{\sqrt[3]{.001234}}{\sqrt{15326}}$.

APPENDIX II

5. A formula much used in statistics is

$$y = \frac{N}{\sigma \sqrt{2\pi}} e^{-\frac{x^2}{2\sigma^2}}$$

where $\pi = 3.1416$ and $e = 2.7183$. If σ^2 (read "sigma squared") $= 2.5$, $x = 2$, $N = 1024$, calculate the value of y.

6. Find the value of the standard deviation of the binomial series, $\sigma = \sqrt{npq}$, where $n = 72$, $p = .3162$, $q = .6838$.

7. A common statistical formula is $G = \sqrt[n]{x_1 x_2 x_3 \cdots x_n}$. If $n = 5$ and the x's have the values 1.04, 1.05, 1.09, 1.11, and 1.15, calculate G.

8. The probable error of the mean is $0.6745 \, \dfrac{\sigma}{\sqrt{n}}$. If $\sigma = 56.324$ and $n = 1987$, calculate the probable error.

9. The value of factorial n, i.e., $n! = 1 \cdot 2 \cdot 3 \cdots n$, is given approximately by the expression $n^{n+1/2} e^{-n} \sqrt{2\pi}$, where $\pi = 3.1416$ and $e = 2.7183$. By how much does this approximate value of 6! differ from the true value?

10. Calculate the value of $y = 87699 (2/3)^{100} \cdot (1/3)^{50}$.

11. Calculate the value of $(1/\sqrt{2\pi}) e^{-\frac{1}{2} t^2}$, where $\pi = 3.1416$, $e = 2.7183$, and $t = 2.45$.

12. The following coefficient occurs in the theory of curve fitting:

$$\frac{12 (2p + 1)(8p + 11)}{p(p-1)(p-2)(p+1)(p+2)} m_1.$$

Calculate its value for $p = 15$, $m_1 = 15{,}328$.

13. If a frugal Roman of Augustus' time had put by one cent to compound at 6 per cent over the centuries, and his Italian descendants of today wished to convert their fortune into a gold sphere, what would the radius of the gold sphere be? (Use $n = 1932$.)

When one approaches the problem presented by the study of an economic state into which enter (1) rates of interest and (2) a fixed monetary gold standard, the following formula is relevant:

$$R(n) = .0000003548494 \, e^{.01942297 n},$$

where $R(n)$ is the radius in miles of a ball of gold equivalent to the compound amount of one cent put out at 6 per cent for n years. The formula is computed from the following values:

σ (specific gravity of gold) $= 19.27$,

ϕ (price of gold per Troy ounce) $= \$20.67183462$[1],

12 Troy ounces $= 1$ Troy pound $= .8228571429$ avoirdupois pounds,

s (weight of cubic foot of water) $= 62.5$ pounds.

---

[1] As the events of 1933 instruct us, this is not a constant but is subject to abrupt changes.

Let the student show that for $n = 1932$,
$R(1932) = 7.0309 \times 10^9$ miles = 75 times the distance from the earth to the sun.

In reflecting upon the significance of this result, one immediately speculates on whether the periodic fluctuations of financial and business phenomena do not rise from the necessity of periodically repudiating an intolerable burden of accumulated interest.

5. *The Number "e" — The Exponential Series*. In section 3, it was stated that tables of logarithms have been computed to two bases, one of these being 10, the radix of our own number system, and the other the interesting number $e = 2.71828\ldots$. Since this number plays an important part throughout statistics, it is well to acquire some familiarity with it.

The number e is most conveniently defined by means of a limiting process. With this in mind, consider the expression $(1+r)^{1/r}$, and see what values are assumed as r is given successively smaller values. For $r = 1$, one finds the value $(1+1)^1 = 2$; when $r = .5$, one has $(1+.5)^2 = 2.25$. Replacing r by still smaller values, the numbers recorded in the following table are obtained:

r	$(1+r)^{1/r}$
.1	2.5937
.05	2.6533
.01	2.7048
.005	2.7115
.001	2.7169

It appears plausible from the table that a finite limit exists for the expression: $\lim_{r=0} (1+r)^{1/r}$. This limit is, in fact, the number e. Its value to six significant figures, i.e., 2.71828, is seen to be only slightly larger than the last value in the table.

A series expansion for e^x is readily obtained from the limiting form of $(1+r)^{x/r}$ if this expression is first expanded by means of the binomial theorem and r is then set equal to zero.

Referring to equation (2) of section 12, Chapter I, one replaces x by r and n by x/r. Then

$$(1+r)^{x/r} = 1 + \frac{x}{r} r + \frac{(x/r)(x/r-1)}{2!} r^2$$

APPENDIX II

$$+ \frac{(x/r)(x/r-1)(x/r-2)}{3!} r^3 + \cdots\cdots$$

$$= 1 + x + \frac{(1-r/x)}{2!} x^2$$

$$+ \frac{(1-r/x)(1-2r/x)}{3!} x^3 + \cdots\cdots. \quad (6)$$

Letting r approach zero in the series which forms the right hand member of this equation, and recalling the definition just given for e^x, there is obtained what is called the *exponential series*:

$$\lim_{r=0} (1+r)^{x/r} = e^x = 1 + x + x^2/2! + x^3/3! + \cdots\cdots. \quad (7)$$

This series has the important property of *converging* for all values of x, that is to say, the value of e^x can be calculated by means of the series for any given x.

Values of e^x and e^{-x} are given in Table II at the end of this book.

Example 1. Calculate to four decimals the value of $e^{.2}$ and $e^{-.2}$ and show that their product equals 1.

$$e^{.2} = 1 + .2 + .04/2 + .008/6 + .0016/24 + \cdots\cdots$$
$$= 1 + .2 + .02 + .0013 + .0001 = 1.2214 \; ,$$

and

$$e^{-.2} = 1 - .2 + .02 - .0013 + .0001 = .8188 \; .$$

Multiplying these values together, one has $1.2214 \times .8188 = 1.0001$.

Example 2. From Table II calculate the values of $e^{-4.32}$ and $e^{3.43}$.

Since one has from the theory of exponents $e^{-4.32} = e^{-4} \cdot e^{-.32}$, one finds from the table

$$e^{-4.32} = e^{-4} \cdot e^{-.32} = (.01832)(.72615) = .013303 \; .$$

By logarithms,
$$\log e^{-4} = 8.26293 - 10$$
$$\log e^{-.32} = 9.86103 - 10$$

$$\log e^{-4.32} = 8.12396 - 10$$
$$e^{-4.32} = .013303 \;.$$

Similarly $e^{3.43} = e^3 \cdot e^{.43} = (20.08554)(1.53726) = 30.87670$.

By logarithms,
$$\log e^3 = 1.30288$$
$$\log e^{.43} = 0.18675$$

$$\log e^{3.43} = 1.48963$$
$$e^{3.43} = 30.8767 \;.$$

PROBLEMS

1. Compute the values of e, $e^{.1}$, and $e^{-.1}$, by substituting $x = 1$, $x = .1$, and $x = -.1$, in series (7), using enough terms to have the answer correct to four places of decimals.

2. Using Table II, calculate the values of $e^{-1.63}$ and $e^{-2.14}$.

3. Using Table II, calculate the values of $e^{1.63}$ and $e^{2.14}$.

4. Prove that the expansion of a^x is
$$a^x = 1 + x \log_e a + [x^2 (\log_e a)^2/2!] + [x^3 (\log_e a)^3/3!] + \ldots \ldots \;.$$
Hint: Write a in the form $a = e^{\log_e a}$. Explain.

5. Given $\log_e a = .5$, calculate the value of a by means of the series of problem 4. Show that the answer equals $\sqrt{2.7183}$.

6. Show that $e^{-1} = 2/3! + 4/5! + 6/7! + \ldots \ldots$.
Hint: Combine in pairs the terms in the expansion e^{-1} .

7. Show by direct multiplication that
$$(1 + x/1! + x^2/2! + x^3/3! + \ldots \ldots)(1 - x/1! + x^2/2! - x^3/3! + \ldots) = 1 \;.$$

8. Prove that $\lim\limits_{x=0} \dfrac{e^x - e^{-x}}{x} = 2$. Hint: Replace e^x and e^{-x} by their expansions and then remove the factor common to both numerator and denominator.

6. The Logarithmic Series. Another series often encountered in statistical work is the *logarithmic series*. In its derivation one may make use of the following device. Let a relationship between x and y be defined by means of the equation

$$(1 + my)^{1/m} = 1 + x \ . \tag{8}$$

From the discussion of the last section, it will be seen that
$\lim_{m=0}(1 + my)^{1/m} = \lim_{m=0}[(1 + my)^{1/my}]^y = \lim_{r=0}[(1 + r)^{1/r}]^y = e^y \ .$

Therefore, for the limiting value $m = 0$, equation (8) becomes $e^y = 1 + x$, or $y = \log_e(1+x)$. Solving for y in (8), one has

$$y = (1/m)[(1 + x)^m - 1] \ .$$

Expanding $(1+x)^m$ by the binomial series (section 12, Chapter I), one obtains

$$y = (1/m)[mx + m(m-1)x^2/2! + m(m-1)(m-2)x^3/3!$$
$$+ \cdots\cdots] \ ,$$
$$= x + (m-1)x^2/2! + (m-1)(m-2)x^3/3! + \cdots\cdots\cdots \ .$$

As m approaches zero as a limiting value, y approaches $\log_e(1+x)$, and one has the logarithmic series,

$$y = \log_e(1+x) = x - x^2/2 + x^3/3 - x^4/4 + \cdots\cdots \ . \tag{9}$$

This series is not very well adapted for calculating purposes since it converges slowly, that is to say, a comparatively large number of terms must be taken to obtain reasonable accuracy in the value of the logarithm.

Since, however, by replacing x by $-x$ one also has

$$\log_e(1-x) = -[x + x^2/2 + x^3/3 + x^4/4 + \cdots\cdots] \ ,$$

this expansion can be combined with the one for $\log_e(1+x)$, thus obtaining

$$\log_e(1+x) - \log_e(1-x) = \log_e[(1+x)/(1-x)]$$
$$= 2(x + x^3/3 + x^5/5 + \cdots\cdots) \ , \tag{10}$$

which converges much more rapidly than (9) .

Example 1. Calculate the value of $\log_e 2$.

In order to use (10), set

$$\frac{1+x}{1-x} = 2, \quad \text{or } x = 1/3 \ .$$

Hence

$$\log_e 2 = 2 \left\{ \frac{1}{3} + \frac{1}{3} \cdot \frac{1}{27} + \frac{1}{5} \cdot \frac{1}{243} + \frac{1}{7} \cdot \frac{1}{2187} \cdots \right\}$$

$$= 2(.3333 + .0123 + .0008 + .0001)$$

$$= 2(.3465) = .6930 \ .$$

Example 2. Given $\log_e 2 = .6931$, $\log_e 5 = 1.6094$, $\log_e 10 = 2.3026$, $\log_e 20 = 2.9957$, calculate the value of $C_n = 1 + 1/2 + 1/3 + \cdots + 1/n - \log_e n$.

Using the table of reciprocals, Table V, one has

$$C_2 = 1 + .5000 - .6931 = .8069 \ ,$$

$$C_5 = 1 + .5000 + .3333 + .2500 + .2000 - 1.6094$$

$$= 2.2833 - 1.6094 = .6739 \ ,$$

$$C_{10} = 2.9290 - 2.3026 = .6264 \ ,$$

$$C_{20} = 3.5977 - 2.9957 = .6020 \ .$$

The limit of C_n, as n assumes successively larger values, is called Euler's number,

$$\lim_{n=\infty} C_n = C = .5772 \ ,$$

and will be met elsewhere in the book.

PROBLEMS

1. Calculate $\log_e 1.1$ and $\log_e 1.02$ by substituting $x = .1$ and $x = .02$ in the logarithmic series.

2. Calculate $(1/m)[(1.02)^m - 1]$ for values of m equal to 1, .2, .1, .01, and compare with the value of $\log_e 1.02 = .0198$.

3. Calculate $\log_e 3$. Hint: let $(1 + x)/(1 - x) = 3$ and use series (10).

4. The following formula is used to convert logarithms from the base 10 to the base e [see formula V(a), section 3].

$$\log_e y = \log_e 10 \, \log_{10} y = 2.3026 \log_{10} y \ .$$

Calculate $\log_e 10 = 2.3026$. Hint: Since $\log_e 10 = \log_e 2 + \log_e 5$, let $(1 + x)/(1 - x) = 5$, use series (10), and make use of the calculation of the first illustrative example above.

5. Derive the series

$$\log_e \frac{a}{b} = \frac{a-b}{b} - \frac{1}{2}\left(\frac{a-b}{b}\right)^2 + \frac{1}{3}\left(\frac{a-b}{b}\right)^3 - \cdots \ .$$

6. Calculate the value of C_n for $n = 30$, given $\log_e 30 = 3.4012$.

APPENDIX III.

THE USE OF TABLES

1. Interpolation. The use of tables is greatly aided by means of interpolation formulas. An elementary form of interpolation has already been used in connection with logarithms, but the theory has an elegant and useful generalization.

Suppose that one has the tabular values of a function, $f(x)$, beginning with a and proceeding by d units of the argument. This table can be represented symbolically as follows:

Argument x	Tabular Value $f(x)$	First Difference Δ	Second Difference Δ^2	Third Difference Δ^3
a	$f(a)$			
		Δ_0		
$a+d$	$f(a+d)$		Δ_0^2	
		Δ_1		Δ_0^3
$a+2d$	$f(a+2d)$		Δ_1^2	
		Δ_2		Δ_1^3
$a+3d$	$f(a+3d)$		Δ_2^2	
		Δ_3		
$a+4d$	$f(a+4d)$			

where, by definition, $\Delta_0 = f(a+d) - f(a)$, $\Delta_1 = f(a+2d) - f(a+d)$, etc., and $\Delta_0^2 = \Delta_1 - \Delta_0$, $\Delta_0^3 = \Delta_1^2 - \Delta_0^2$ etc.

By means of Newton's formula of interpolation, $f(x)$ can be expressed in terms of these differences, as follows:

$$f(a+xd) = f(a) + x\,\Delta_0 + \frac{x(x-1)}{2!}\Delta_0^2$$
$$+ \frac{x(x-1)(x-2)}{3!}\Delta_0^3 + \cdots, \qquad (1)$$

In order to illustrate the use of this formula, consider the following examples.

—359—

Example 1. Calculate the cube of 2.4 from the following table:

x	$f(x) = x^3$	Δ	Δ^2	Δ^3
1	1			
		26		
3	27		72	
		98		48
5	125		120	
		218		48
7	343		168	
		386		48
9	729		216	
		602		
11	1331			

Since it is required to find the cube of 2.4, it is clear that one must choose $a = 1$ and use the difference $\Delta_0 = 26$, $\Delta_0^2 = 72$, $\Delta_0^3 = 48$. Moreover, it is known that $d = 2$, $xd = 1.4$, and consequently, $x = .7$.

When these values are substituted in formula (1), one obtains,

$$(2.4)^3 = 1 + .7(26) + \frac{.7(.7-1)}{2} 72 + \frac{.7(.7-1)(.7-2)}{6} 48,$$

$$= 1 + 18.2 - 7.56 + 2.184 = 13.824.$$

Example 2. Calculate the reciprocal of 1/1.56 from the table:

x	$f(x) = 1/x$	Δ	Δ^2
1.4	0.7143		
		−.0476	
1.5	0.6667		.0059
		−.0417	
1.6	0.6250		.0049
		−.0368	
1.7	0.5882		.0042
		−.0326	
1.8	0.5556		.0033
		−.0293	
1.9	0.5263		

It should be especially noticed in this example that the first differences are negative. Since it is required to find 1/1.56, one must choose $a = 1.5$, and $f(a+xd)$ becomes $f(1.5 + .06)$, from which it is seen that $xd = .06$. Since $d = .1$, $x = .6$. Substituting in formula (1), one has

$$\frac{1}{1.56} = .6667 - .6(.0417) + \frac{.6(.6-1)}{2}(.0049)$$

$$= .6667 - .0250 - .0006 = .6411.$$

2. *Inverse Interpolation.* It is sometimes important to be able to reverse the process explained in the preceding section and find the value of the argument corresponding to a given value of the function. The problem is this: Given a value, $f(a+xd)$, to calculate x.

It is at once seen that an approximate answer may be obtained by calculating x from the formula,

$$f(a+xd) = f(a) + x \Delta_0 ,$$

which is merely (1) with all terms except the first two omitted.

In order to indicate that x so obtained is merely a first approximation, it is given a subscript 1, and one calculates,

$$x_1 = \frac{f(a+xd) - f(a)}{\Delta_0} . \tag{2}$$

It will usually happen that the value x_1 is not in error by a large amount, so it may be used to obtain a second approximation. In order to do this the following formula is employed,

$$x_2 = \frac{f(a+xd) - f(a)}{\Delta_0 + \dfrac{(x_1-1)}{2!}\Delta_0^2 + \dfrac{(x_1-1)(x_1-2)}{3!}\Delta_0^3} , \tag{3}$$

which is obtained from (1) by replacing all of the x's except the first in each term by the approximate value x_1.

This value, x_2, is in turn substituted in (3) in place of x_1 to obtain a third approximation, and the process thus continued to any desired accuracy.

Example: Calculate the square root of 2.4 from the following table:

x	$f(x) = x^2$	Δ	Δ^2
1	1		
		3	
2	4		2
		5	
3	9		2
		7	
4	16		2
		9	
5	25		

Since $f(a + xd) = 2.4$, $f(a) = 1$, $x = 1$, and $\Delta_0 = 3$, one reaches as a first approximation,

$$x_1 = \frac{2.4 - 1}{3} = .4667 \ .$$

Using this value in formula (3), one finds as the second approximation,

$$x_2 = \frac{2.4 - 1}{3 + \dfrac{.4667 - 1}{2} \cdot 2} = \frac{1.4}{2.4667} = .5676 \ .$$

Similarly, using this value in (3) one reaches as the third approximation,

$$x_3 = 1.4/2.5676 = .5453 \ ,$$

and for other approximations,

$$x_4 = .5500 \ ,$$
$$x_5 = .5490 \ ,$$
$$x_6 = .5492 \ ,$$

the last being correct to four places. Hence the desired square root is equal to 1.5492.

3. The Calculation of Areas. A third problem easily solved by the use of differences is the calculation of the area under a function from a table of numerical values. In order to understand the symbols used, consider the following table:

x	$f(x)$	Δ	Δ^2
a	f_0		
		Δ_0	
$a+d$	f_1		Δ_0^2
		Δ_1	
$a+2d$	f_2		Δ_1^2
		Δ_2	
$a+3d$	f_3		
.....	...	...	Δ_{r-2}^2
.....	...	Δ_{r-1}	
$a+rd$	f_r		

In terms of this notation, the area $I(t)$ from $x = a$ to $x = t = a + rd$ is given by the formula,

$$I(t) = d\{(f_0 + f_1 + f_2 + f_3 + \cdots + f_r) - \frac{1}{2}(f_0 + f_r)$$

$$- \frac{1}{12}(\Delta_{r-1} - \Delta_0) - \frac{1}{24}(\Delta_{r-2}^2 + \Delta_0^2) + \cdots\}.$$

Example 1: Calculate the area under the parabola $y = x^2$ from $x = 0$ to $x = 5$, by means of the following table:

x	$y = x^2$	Δ	Δ^2
0	0		
		1	
1	1		2
		3	
2	4		2
		5	
3	9		2
		7	
4	16		2
		9	
5	25		

Since $d = 1$, $\Delta_0 = 1$, $\Delta^2{}_0 = 2$, $\Delta_{r-1} = 9$, and $\Delta_{r-2} = 2$, we easily calculate the area to be,

$$I = (0 + 1 + 4 + 9 + 16 + 25) - \frac{1}{2}(0 + 25) - \frac{1}{12}(9 - 1)$$

$$- \frac{1}{24}(2 + 2) = 41\frac{2}{3}.$$

Example 2: Calculate the area under the normal probability curve from $x = 0$ to $x = .4$.

From Table VI the following values are obtained:

x	y	Δ	Δ^2
0	.39894		
		−.00199	
.1	.39695		−.00392
		−.00591	
.2	.39104		−.00374
		−.00965	
.3	.38139		−.00347
		−.01312	
.4	.36827		

Since $d = .1$, one easily finds the value of the area to be,

$$I = .1\{(.39894 + .39695 + .39104 + .38139 + .36827)$$

$$- \frac{1}{2}(.39894 + .36827) - \frac{1}{12}(-.01312 + .00199)$$

$$- \frac{1}{24}(-.00347 - .00392)\}$$

$$= .1\{(1.93659 - .38361 + .00093 + .00031)\} = .15542.$$

This value is seen from Table VII to be correct to five places.

4. References. In this section only the briefest exposition of the use of tables has been possible. The reader will find the following works useful in a further exploration of this subject:

E. T. Whittaker and G. Robinson: *The Calculus of Observations*, London, 1924, 395 pp.

Karl Pearson: *On the Construction of Tables and on Interpolation.* Tracts for Computers, No. 2, London, 1920, Uni-variate Tables, 70 pp., No. 3, London 1920, Bi-variate Tables, 54 pp.

J. K. Steffenson: *Interpolation,* Baltimore, 1927, 248 pp.

H. L. Rice: *The Theory and Practice of Interpolation,* Lynn, Mass., 1899, 234 pp.

J. B. Scarborough: *Numerical Mathematical Analysis,* Baltimore 1930, 416 pp.

H. T. Davis: *Tables of the Higher Mathematical Functions,* Vol. 1, Bloomington, Ind., 1933, Part 3.

Max Sasuly: *Trend Analysis of Statistics,* Washington, D. C., 1934, 421 pp.

Milne-Thomson, L. M.: *The Calculus of Finite Differences,* London, 1933, 558 pp.

SOME USEFUL CONSTANTS

$\pi = 3.14159\,26536$ \qquad $1/\sqrt{\pi} = 0.56418\,95835$

$e = 2.71828\,18285$ \qquad $\log_{10}(1/\sqrt{\pi}) = 9.75142\,50637-10$

$\log_{10}\pi = 0.49714\,98727$ \qquad $1/\pi = 0.31830\,98862$

$M = \log_{10}e = 0.43429\,44819$ \qquad $\log_{10}(1/\pi) = 9.50285\,01273-10$

$1/M = \log_e 10 = 2.30258\,50930$ \qquad $\sqrt{2\pi} = 2.50662\,82746$

$\log_{10}M = 9.63778\,43113-10$ \qquad $\log_{10}\sqrt{2\pi} = 0.39908\,99342$

$\sqrt{\pi} = 1.77245\,38509$ \qquad $1/\sqrt{2\pi} = 0.39894\,22803$

$\log_{10}\sqrt{\pi} = 0.24857\,49363$ \qquad $\log_{10}(1/\sqrt{2\pi}) = 9.60091\,00658-10$

TABLE I
THE COMMON OR BRIGGS LOGARITHMS OF THE NATURAL NUMBERS FROM 1 TO 10,000

No.	Log.	No.	Log.	No.	Log.	No.	Log.	No.	Log.
0	———	**20**	1.30 103	**40**	1.60 206	**60**	1.77 815	**80**	1.90 309
1	0.00 000	21	1.32 222	41	1.61 278	61	1.78 533	81	1.90 849
2	0.30 103	22	1.34 242	42	1.62 325	62	1.79 239	82	1.91 381
3	0.47 712	23	1.36 173	43	1.63 347	63	1.79 934	83	1.91 908
4	0.60 206	24	1.38 021	44	1.64 345	64	1.80 618	84	1.92 428
5	0.69 897	25	1.39 794	45	1.65 321	65	1.81 291	85	1.92 942
6	0.77 815	26	1.41 497	46	1.66 276	66	1.81 954	86	1.93 450
7	0.84 510	27	1.43 136	47	1.67 210	67	1.82 607	87	1.93 952
8	0.90 309	28	1.44 716	48	1.68 124	68	1.83 251	88	1.94 448
9	0.95 424	29	1.46 240	49	1.69 020	69	1.83 885	89	1.94 939
10	1.00 000	**30**	1.47 712	**50**	1.69 897	**70**	1.84 510	**90**	1.95 424
11	1.04 139	31	1.49 136	51	1.70 757	71	1.85 126	91	1.95 904
12	1.07 918	32	1.50 515	52	1.71 600	72	1.85 733	92	1.96 379
13	1.11 394	33	1.51 851	53	1.72 428	73	1.86 332	93	1.96 848
14	1.14 613	34	1.53 148	54	1.73 239	74	1.86 923	94	1.97 313
15	1.17 609	35	1.54 407	55	1.74 036	75	1.87 506	95	1.97 772
16	1.20 412	36	1.55 630	56	1.74 819	76	1.88 081	96	1.98 227
17	1.23 045	37	1.56 820	57	1.75 587	77	1.88 649	97	1.98 677
18	1.25 527	38	1.57 978	58	1.76 343	78	1.89 209	98	1.99 123
19	1.27 875	39	1.59 106	59	1.77 085	79	1.89 763	99	1.99 564
20	1.30 103	**40**	1.60 206	**60**	1.77 815	**80**	1.90 309	**100**	2.00 000

TABLE I — LOGARITHMS

No.	0	1	2	3	4	5	6	7	8	9
100	00 000	00 043	00 087	00 130	00 173	00 217	00 260	00 303	00 346	00 389
101	00 432	00 475	00 518	00 561	00 604	00 647	00 689	00 732	00 775	00 817
102	00 860	00 903	00 945	00 988	01 030	01 072	01 115	01 157	01 199	01 242
103	01 284	01 326	01 368	01 410	01 452	01 494	01 536	01 578	01 620	01 662
104	01 703	01 745	01 787	01 828	01 870	01 912	01 953	01 995	02 036	02 078
105	02 119	02 160	02 202	02 243	02 284	02 325	02 366	02 407	02 449	02 490
106	02 531	02 572	02 612	02 653	02 694	02 735	02 776	02 816	02 857	02 898
107	02 938	02 979	03 019	03 060	03 100	03 141	03 181	03 222	03 262	03 302
108	03 342	03 383	03 423	03 463	03 503	03 543	03 583	03 623	03 663	03 703
109	03 743	03 782	03 822	03 862	03 902	03 941	03 981	04 021	04 060	04 100
110	04 139	04 179	04 218	04 258	04 297	04 336	04 376	04 415	04 454	04 493
111	04 532	04 571	04 610	04 650	04 689	04 727	04 766	04 805	04 844	04 883
112	04 922	04 961	04 999	05 038	05 077	05 115	05 154	05 192	05 231	05 269
113	05 308	05 346	05 385	05 423	05 461	05 500	05 538	05 576	05 614	05 652
114	05 690	05 729	05 767	05 805	05 843	05 881	05 918	05 956	05 994	06 032
115	06 070	06 108	06 145	06 183	06 221	06 258	06 296	06 333	06 371	06 408
116	06 446	06 483	06 521	06 558	06 595	06 633	06 670	06 707	06 744	06 781
117	06 819	06 856	06 893	06 930	06 967	07 004	07 041	07 078	07 115	07 151
118	07 188	07 225	07 262	07 298	07 335	07 372	07 408	07 445	07 482	07 518
119	07 555	07 591	07 628	07 664	07 700	07 737	07 773	07 809	07 846	07 882
120	07 918	07 954	07 990	08 027	08 063	08 099	08 135	08 171	08 207	08 243
121	08 279	08 314	08 350	08 386	08 422	08 458	08 493	08 529	08 565	08 600
122	08 636	08 672	08 707	08 743	08 778	08 814	08 849	08 884	08 920	08 955
123	08 991	09 026	09 061	09 096	09 132	09 167	09 202	09 237	09 272	09 307
124	09 342	09 377	09 412	09 447	09 482	09 517	09 552	09 587	09 621	09 656
125	09 691	09 726	09 760	09 795	09 830	09 864	09 899	09 934	09 968	10 003
126	10 037	10 072	10 106	10 140	10 175	10 209	10 243	10 278	10 312	10 346
127	10 380	10 415	10 449	10 483	10 517	10 551	10 585	10 619	10 653	10 687
128	10 721	10 755	10 789	10 823	10 857	10 890	10 924	10 958	10 992	11 025
129	11 059	11 093	11 126	11 160	11 193	11 227	11 261	11 294	11 327	11 361
130	11 394	11 428	11 461	11 494	11 528	11 561	11 594	11 628	11 661	11 694
131	11 727	11 760	11 793	11 826	11 860	11 893	11 926	11 959	11 992	12 024
132	12 057	12 090	12 123	12 156	12 189	12 222	12 254	12 287	12 320	12 352
133	12 385	12 418	12 450	12 483	12 516	12 548	12 581	12 613	12 646	12 678
134	12 710	12 743	12 775	12 808	12 840	12 872	12 905	12 937	12 969	13 001
135	13 033	13 066	13 098	13 130	13 162	13 194	13 226	13 258	13 290	13 322
136	13 354	13 386	13 418	13 450	13 481	13 513	13 545	13 577	13 609	13 640
137	13 672	13 704	13 735	13 767	13 799	13 830	13 862	13 893	13 925	13 956
138	13 988	14 019	14 051	14 082	14 114	14 145	14 176	14 208	14 239	14 270
139	14 301	14 333	14 364	14 395	14 426	14 457	14 489	14 520	14 551	14 582
140	14 613	14 644	14 675	14 706	14 737	14 768	14 799	14 829	14 860	14 891
141	14 922	14 953	14 983	15 014	15 045	15 076	15 106	15 137	15 168	15 198
142	15 229	15 259	15 290	15 320	15 351	15 381	15 412	15 442	15 473	15 503
143	15 534	15 564	15 594	15 625	15 655	15 685	15 715	15 746	15 776	15 806
144	15 836	15 866	15 897	15 927	15 957	15 987	16 017	16 047	16 077	16 107
145	16 137	16 167	16 197	16 227	16 256	16 286	16 316	16 346	16 376	16 406
146	16 435	16 465	16 495	16 524	16 554	16 584	16 613	16 643	16 673	16 702
147	16 732	16 761	16 791	16 820	16 850	16 879	16 909	16 938	16 967	16 997
148	17 026	17 056	17 085	17 114	17 143	17 173	17 202	17 231	17 260	17 289
149	17 319	17 348	17 377	17 406	17 435	17 464	17 493	17 522	17 551	17 580
No.	0	1	2	3	4	5	6	7	8	9

TABLE I — LOGARITHMS

No.	0	1	2	3	4	5	6	7	8	9
150	17 609	17 638	17 667	17 696	17 725	17 754	17 782	17 811	17 840	17 869
151	17 898	17 926	17 955	17 984	18 013	18 041	18 070	18 099	18 127	18 156
152	18 184	18 213	18 241	18 270	18 298	18 327	18 355	18 384	18 412	18 441
153	18 469	18 498	18 526	18 554	18 583	18 611	18 639	18 667	18 696	18 724
154	18 752	18 780	18 808	18 837	18 865	18 893	18 921	18 949	18 977	19 005
155	19 033	19 061	19 089	19 117	19 145	19 173	19 201	19 229	19 257	19 285
156	19 312	19 340	19 368	19 396	19 424	19 451	19 479	19 507	19 535	19 562
157	19 590	19 618	19 645	19 673	19 700	19 728	19 756	19 783	19 811	19 838
158	19 866	19 893	19 921	19 948	19 976	20 003	20 030	20 058	20 085	20 112
159	20 140	20 167	20 194	20 222	20 249	20 276	20 303	20 330	20 358	20 385
160	20 412	20 439	20 466	20 493	20 520	20 548	20 575	20 602	20 629	20 656
161	20 683	20 710	20 737	20 763	20 790	20 817	20 844	20 871	20 898	20 925
162	20 952	20 978	21 005	21 032	21 059	21 085	21 112	21 139	21 165	21 192
163	21 219	21 245	21 272	21 299	21 325	21 352	21 378	21 405	21 431	21 458
164	21 484	21 511	21 537	21 564	21 590	21 617	21 643	21 669	21 696	21 722
165	21 748	21 775	21 801	21 827	21 854	21 880	21 906	21 932	21 958	21 985
166	22 011	22 037	22 063	22 089	22 115	22 141	22 167	22 194	22 220	22 246
167	22 272	22 298	22 324	22 350	22 376	22 401	22 427	22 453	22 479	22 505
168	22 531	22 557	22 583	22 608	22 634	22 660	22 686	22 712	22 737	22 763
169	22 789	22 814	22 840	22 866	22 891	22 917	22 943	22 968	22 994	23 019
170	23 045	23 070	23 096	23 121	23 147	23 172	23 198	23 223	23 249	23 274
171	23 300	23 325	23 350	23 376	23 401	23 426	23 452	23 477	23 502	23 528
172	23 553	23 578	23 603	23 629	23 654	23 679	23 704	23 729	23 754	23 779
173	23 805	23 830	23 855	23 880	23 905	23 930	23 955	23 980	24 005	24 030
174	24 055	24 080	24 105	24 130	24 155	24 180	24 204	24 229	24 254	24 279
175	24 304	24 329	24 353	24 378	24 403	24 428	24 452	24 477	24 502	24 527
176	24 551	24 576	24 601	24 625	24 650	24 674	24 699	24 724	24 748	24 773
177	24 797	24 822	24 846	24 871	24 895	24 920	24 944	24 969	24 993	25 018
178	25 042	25 066	25 091	25 115	25 139	25 164	25 188	25 212	25 237	25 261
179	25 285	25 310	25 334	25 358	25 382	25 406	25 431	25 455	25 479	25 503
180	25 527	25 551	25 575	25 600	25 624	25 648	25 672	25 696	25 720	25 744
181	25 768	25 792	25 816	25 840	25 864	25 888	25 912	25 935	25 959	25 983
182	26 007	26 031	26 055	26 079	26 102	26 126	26 150	26 174	26 198	26 221
183	26 245	26 269	26 293	26 316	26 340	26 364	26 387	26 411	26 435	26 458
184	26 482	26 505	26 529	26 553	26 576	26 600	26 623	26 647	26 670	26 694
185	26 717	26 741	26 764	26 788	26 811	26 834	26 858	26 881	26 905	26 928
186	26 951	26 975	26 998	27 021	27 045	27 068	27 091	27 114	27 138	27 161
187	27 184	27 207	27 231	27 254	27 277	27 300	27 323	27 346	27 370	27 393
188	27 416	27 439	27 462	27 485	27 508	27 531	27 554	27 577	27 600	27 623
189	27 646	27 669	27 692	27 715	27 738	27 761	27 784	27 807	27 830	27 852
190	27 875	27 898	27 921	27 944	27 967	27 989	28 012	28 035	28 058	28 081
191	28 103	28 126	28 149	28 171	28 194	28 217	28 240	28 262	28 285	28 307
192	28 330	28 353	28 375	28 398	28 421	28 443	28 466	28 488	28 511	28 533
193	28 556	28 578	28 601	28 623	28 646	28 668	28 691	28 713	28 735	28 758
194	28 780	28 803	28 825	28 847	28 870	28 892	28 914	28 937	28 959	28 981
195	29 003	29 026	29 048	29 070	29 092	29 115	29 137	29 159	29 181	29 203
196	29 226	29 248	29 270	29 292	29 314	29 336	29 358	29 380	29 403	29 425
197	29 447	29 469	29 491	29 513	29 535	29 557	29 579	29 601	29 623	29 645
198	29 667	29 688	29 710	29 732	29 754	29 776	29 798	29 820	29 842	29 863
199	29 885	29 907	29 929	29 951	29 973	29 994	30 016	30 038	30 060	30 081
No.	0	1	2	3	4	5	6	7	8	9

TABLE I — LOGARITHMS

No.	0	1	2	3	4	5	6	7	8	9
200	30 103	30 125	30 146	30 168	30 190	30 211	30 233	30 255	30 276	30 298
201	30 320	30 341	30 363	30 384	30 406	30 428	30 449	30 471	30 492	30 514
202	30 535	30 557	30 578	30 600	30 621	30 643	30 664	30 685	30 707	30 728
203	30 750	30 771	30 792	30 814	30 835	30 856	30 878	30 899	30 920	30 942
204	30 963	30 984	31 006	31 027	31 048	31 069	31 091	31 112	31 133	31 154
205	31 175	31 197	31 218	31 239	31 260	31 281	31 302	31 323	31 345	31 366
206	31 387	31 408	31 429	31 450	31 471	31 492	31 513	31 534	31 555	31 576
207	31 597	31 618	31 639	31 660	31 681	31 702	31 723	31 744	31 765	31 785
208	31 806	31 827	31 848	31 869	31 890	31 911	31 931	31 952	31 973	31 994
209	32 015	32 035	32 056	32 077	32 098	32 118	32 139	32 160	32 181	32 201
210	32 222	32 243	32 263	32 284	32 305	32 325	32 346	32 366	32 387	32 408
211	32 428	32 449	32 469	32 490	32 510	32 531	32 552	32 572	32 593	32 613
212	32 634	32 654	32 675	32 695	32 715	32 736	32 756	32 777	32 797	32 818
213	32 838	32 858	32 879	32 899	32 919	32 940	32 960	32 980	33 001	33 021
214	33 041	33 062	33 082	33 102	33 122	33 143	33 163	33 183	33 203	33 224
215	33 244	33 264	33 284	33 304	33 325	33 345	33 365	33 385	33 405	33 425
216	33 445	33 465	33 486	33 506	33 526	33 546	33 566	33 586	33 606	33 626
217	33 646	33 666	33 686	33 706	33 726	33 746	33 766	33 786	33 806	33 826
218	33 846	33 866	33 885	33 905	33 925	33 945	33 965	33 985	34 005	34 025
219	34 044	34 064	34 084	34 104	34 124	34 143	34 163	34 183	34 203	34 223
220	34 242	34 262	34 282	34 301	34 321	34 341	34 361	34 380	34 400	34 420
221	34 439	34 459	34 479	34 498	34 518	34 537	34 557	34 577	34 596	34 616
222	34 635	34 655	34 674	34 694	34 713	34 733	34 753	34 772	34 792	34 811
223	34 830	34 850	34 869	34 889	34 908	34 928	34 947	34 967	34 986	35 005
224	35 025	35 044	35 064	35 083	35 102	35 122	35 141	35 160	35 180	35 199
225	35 218	35 238	35 257	35 276	35 295	35 315	35 334	35 353	35 372	35 392
226	35 411	35 430	35 449	35 468	35 488	35 507	35 526	35 545	35 564	35 583
227	35 603	35 622	35 641	35 660	35 679	35 698	35 717	35 736	35 755	35 774
228	35 793	35 813	35 832	35 851	35 870	35 889	35 908	35 927	35 946	35 965
229	35 984	36 003	36 021	36 040	36 059	36 078	36 097	36 116	36 135	36 154
230	36 173	36 192	36 211	36 229	36 248	36 267	36 286	36 305	36 324	36 342
231	36 361	36 380	36 399	36 418	36 436	36 455	36 474	36 493	36 511	36 530
232	36 549	36 568	36 586	36 605	36 624	36 642	36 661	36 680	36 698	36 717
233	36 736	36 754	36 773	36 791	36 810	36 829	36 847	36 866	36 884	36 903
234	36 922	36 940	36 959	36 977	36 996	37 014	37 033	37 051	37 070	37 088
235	37 107	37 125	37 144	37 162	37 181	37 199	37 218	37 236	37 254	37 273
236	37 291	37 310	37 328	37 346	37 365	37 383	37 401	37 420	37 438	37 457
237	37 475	37 493	37 511	37 530	37 548	37 566	37 585	37 603	37 621	37 639
238	37 658	37 676	37 694	37 712	37 731	37 749	37 767	37 785	37 803	37 822
239	37 840	37 858	37 876	37 894	37 912	37 931	37 949	37 967	37 985	38 003
240	38 021	38 039	38 057	38 075	38 093	38 112	38 130	38 148	38 166	38 184
241	38 202	38 220	38 238	38 256	38 274	38 292	38 310	38 328	38 346	38 364
242	38 382	38 399	38 417	38 435	38 453	38 471	38 489	38 507	38 525	38 543
243	38 561	38 578	38 596	38 614	38 632	38 650	38 668	38 686	38 703	38 721
244	38 739	38 757	38 775	38 792	38 810	38 828	38 846	38 863	38 881	38 899
245	38 917	38 934	38 952	38 970	38 987	39 005	39 023	39 041	39 058	39 076
246	39 094	39 111	39 129	39 146	39 164	39 182	39 199	39 217	39 235	39 252
247	39 270	39 287	39 305	39 322	39 340	39 358	39 375	39 393	39 410	39 428
248	39 445	39 463	39 480	39 498	39 515	39 533	39 550	39 568	39 585	39 602
249	39 620	39 637	39 655	39 672	39 690	39 707	39 724	39 742	39 759	39 777
No.	0	1	2	3	4	5	6	7	8	9

TABLE I — LOGARITHMS

No.	0	1	2	3	4	5	6	7	8	9
250	39 794	39 811	39 829	39 846	39 863	39 881	39 898	39 915	39 933	39 950
251	39 967	39 985	40 002	40 019	40 037	40 054	40 071	40 088	40 106	40 123
252	40 140	40 157	40 175	40 192	40 209	40 226	40 243	40 261	40 278	40 295
253	40 312	40 329	40 346	40 364	40 381	40 398	40 415	40 432	40 449	40 466
254	40 483	40 500	40 518	40 535	40 552	40 569	40 586	40 603	40 620	40 637
255	40 654	40 671	40 688	40 705	40 722	40 739	40 756	40 773	40 790	40 807
256	40 824	40 841	40 858	40 875	40 892	40 909	40 926	40 943	40 960	40 976
257	40 993	41 010	41 027	41 044	41 061	41 078	41 095	41 111	41 128	41 145
258	41 162	41 179	41 196	41 212	41 229	41 246	41 263	41 280	41 296	41 313
259	41 330	41 347	41 363	41 380	41 397	41 414	41 430	41 447	41 464	41 481
260	41 497	41 514	41 531	41 547	41 564	41 581	41 597	41 614	41 631	41 647
261	41 664	41 681	41 697	41 714	41 731	41 747	41 764	41 780	41 797	41 814
262	41 830	41 847	41 863	41 880	41 896	41 913	41 929	41 946	41 963	41 979
263	41 996	42 012	42 029	42 045	42 062	42 078	42 095	42 111	42 127	42 144
264	42 160	42 177	42 193	42 210	42 226	42 243	42 259	42 275	42 292	42 308
265	42 325	42 341	42 357	42 374	42 390	42 406	42 423	42 439	42 455	42 472
266	42 488	42 504	42 521	42 537	42 553	42 570	42 586	42 602	42 619	42 635
267	42 651	42 667	42 684	42 700	42 716	42 732	42 749	42 765	42 781	42 797
268	42 813	42 830	42 846	42 862	42 878	42 894	42 911	42 927	42 943	42 959
269	42 975	42 991	43 008	43 024	43 040	43 056	43 072	43 088	43 104	43 120
270	43 136	43 152	43 169	43 185	43 201	43 217	43 233	43 249	43 265	43 281
271	43 297	43 313	43 329	43 345	43 361	43 377	43 393	43 409	43 425	43 441
272	43 457	43 473	43 489	43 505	43 521	43 537	43 553	43 569	43 584	43 600
273	43 616	43 632	43 648	43 664	43 680	43 696	43 712	43 727	43 743	43 759
274	43 775	43 791	43 807	43 823	43 838	43 854	43 870	43 886	43 902	43 917
275	43 933	43 949	43 965	43 981	43 996	44 012	44 028	44 044	44 059	44 075
276	44 091	44 107	44 122	44 138	44 154	44 170	44 185	44 201	44 217	44 232
277	44 248	44 264	44 279	44 295	44 311	44 326	44 342	44 358	44 373	44 389
278	44 404	44 420	44 436	44 451	44 467	44 483	44 498	44 514	44 529	44 545
279	44 560	44 576	44 592	44 607	44 623	44 638	44 654	44 669	44 685	44 700
280	44 716	44 731	44 747	44 762	44 778	44 793	44 809	44 824	44 840	44 855
281	44 871	44 886	44 902	44 917	44 932	44 948	44 963	44 979	44 994	45 010
282	45 025	45 040	45 056	45 071	45 086	45 102	45 117	45 133	45 148	45 163
283	45 179	45 194	45 209	45 225	45 240	45 255	45 271	45 286	45 301	45 317
284	45 332	45 347	45 362	45 378	45 393	45 408	45 423	45 439	45 454	45 469
285	45 484	45 500	45 515	45 530	45 545	45 561	45 576	45 591	45 606	45 621
286	45 637	45 652	45 667	45 682	45 697	45 712	45 728	45 743	45 758	45 773
287	45 788	45 803	45 818	45 834	45 849	45 864	45 879	45 894	45 909	45 924
288	45 939	45 954	45 969	45 984	46 000	46 015	46 030	46 045	46 060	46 075
289	46 090	46 105	46 120	46 135	46 150	46 165	46 180	46 195	46 210	46 225
290	46 240	46 255	46 270	46 285	46 300	46 315	46 330	46 345	46 359	46 374
291	46 389	46 404	46 419	46 434	46 449	46 464	46 479	46 494	46 509	46 523
292	46 538	46 553	46 568	46 583	46 598	46 613	46 627	46 642	46 657	46 672
293	46 687	46 702	46 716	46 731	46 746	46 761	46 776	46 790	46 805	46 820
294	46 835	46 850	46 864	46 879	46 894	46 909	46 923	46 938	46 953	46 967
295	46 982	46 997	47 012	47 026	47 041	47 056	47 070	47 085	47 100	47 114
296	47 129	47 144	47 159	47 173	47 188	47 202	47 217	47 232	47 246	47 261
297	47 276	47 290	47 305	47 319	47 334	47 349	47 363	47 378	47 392	47 407
298	47 422	47 436	47 451	47 465	47 480	47 494	47 509	47 524	47 538	47 553
299	47 567	47 582	47 596	47 611	47 625	47 640	47 654	47 669	47 683	47 698
No.	0	1	2	3	4	5	6	7	8	9

TABLE I — LOGARITHMS

No.	0	1	2	3	4	5	6	7	8	9
300	47 712	47 727	47 741	47 756	47 770	47 784	47 799	47 813	47 828	47 842
301	47 857	47 871	47 885	47 900	47 914	47 929	47 943	47 958	47 972	47 986
302	48 001	48 015	48 029	48 044	48 058	48 073	48 087	48 101	48 116	48 130
303	48 144	48 159	48 173	48 187	48 202	48 216	48 230	48 244	48 259	48 273
304	48 287	48 302	48 316	48 330	48 344	48 359	48 373	48 387	48 401	48 416
305	48 430	48 444	48 458	48 473	48 487	48 501	48 515	48 530	48 544	48 558
306	48 572	48 586	48 601	48 615	48 629	48 643	48 657	48 671	48 686	48 700
307	48 714	48 728	48 742	48 756	48 770	48 785	48 799	48 813	48 827	48 841
308	48 855	48 869	48 883	48 897	48 911	48 926	48 940	48 954	48 968	48 982
309	48 996	49 010	49 024	49 038	49 052	49 066	49 080	49 094	49 108	49 122
310	49 136	49 150	49 164	49 178	49 192	49 206	49 220	49 234	49 248	49 262
311	49 276	49 290	49 304	49 318	49 332	49 346	49 360	49 374	49 388	49 402
312	49 415	49 429	49 443	49 457	49 471	49 485	49 499	49 513	49 527	49 541
313	49 554	49 568	49 582	49 596	49 610	49 624	49 638	49 651	49 665	49 679
314	49 693	49 707	49 721	49 734	49 748	49 762	49 776	49 790	49 803	49 817
315	49 831	49 845	49 859	49 872	49 886	49 900	49 914	49 927	49 941	49 955
316	49 969	49 982	49 996	50 010	50 024	50 037	50 051	50 065	50 079	50 092
317	50 106	50 120	50 133	50 147	50 161	50 174	50 188	50 202	50 215	50 229
318	50 243	50 256	50 270	50 284	50 297	50 311	50 325	50 338	50 352	50 365
319	50 379	50 393	50 406	50 420	50 433	50 447	50 461	50 474	50 488	50 501
320	50 515	50 529	50 542	50 556	50 569	50 583	50 596	50 610	50 623	50 637
321	50 651	50 664	50 678	50 691	50 705	50 718	50 732	50 745	50 759	50 772
322	50 786	50 799	50 813	50 826	50 840	50 853	50 866	50 880	50 893	50 907
323	50 920	50 934	50 947	50 961	50 974	50 987	51 001	51 014	51 028	51 041
324	51 055	51 068	51 081	51 095	51 108	51 121	51 135	51 148	51 162	51 175
325	51 188	51 202	51 215	51 228	51 242	51 255	51 268	51 282	51 295	51 308
326	51 322	51 335	51 348	51 362	51 375	51 388	51 402	51 415	51 428	51 441
327	51 455	51 468	51 481	51 495	51 508	51 521	51 534	51 548	51 561	51 574
328	51 587	51 601	51 614	51 627	51 640	51 654	51 667	51 680	51 693	51 706
329	51 720	51 733	51 746	51 759	51 772	51 786	51 799	51 812	51 825	51 838
330	51 851	51 865	51 878	51 891	51 904	51 917	51 930	51 943	51 957	51 970
331	51 983	51 996	52 009	52 022	52 035	52 048	52 061	52 075	52 088	52 101
332	52 114	52 127	52 140	52 153	52 166	52 179	52 192	52 205	52 218	52 231
333	52 244	52 257	52 270	52 284	52 297	52 310	52 323	52 336	52 349	52 362
334	52 375	52 388	52 401	52 414	52 427	52 440	52 453	52 466	52 479	52 492
335	52 504	52 517	52 530	52 543	52 556	52 569	52 582	52 595	52 608	52 621
336	52 634	52 647	52 660	52 673	52 686	52 699	52 711	52 724	52 737	52 750
337	52 763	52 776	52 789	52 802	52 815	52 827	52 840	52 853	52 866	52 879
338	52 892	52 905	52 917	52 930	52 943	52 956	52 969	52 982	52 994	53 007
339	53 020	53 033	53 046	53 058	53 071	53 084	53 097	53 110	53 122	53 135
340	53 148	53 161	53 173	53 186	53 199	53 212	53 224	53 237	53 250	53 263
341	53 275	53 288	53 301	53 314	53 326	53 339	53 352	53 364	53 377	53 390
342	53 403	53 415	53 428	53 441	53 453	53 466	53 479	53 491	53 504	53 517
343	53 529	53 542	53 555	53 567	53 580	53 593	53 605	53 618	53 631	53 643
344	53 656	53 668	53 681	53 694	53 706	53 719	53 732	53 744	53 757	53 769
345	53 782	53 794	53 807	53 820	53 832	53 845	53 857	53 870	53 882	53 895
346	53 908	53 920	53 933	53 945	53 958	53 970	53 983	53 995	54 008	54 020
347	54 033	54 045	54 058	54 070	54 083	54 095	54 108	54 120	54 133	54 145
348	54 158	54 170	54 183	54 195	54 208	54 220	54 233	54 245	54 258	54 270
349	54 283	54 295	54 307	54 320	54 332	54 345	54 357	54 370	54 382	54 394
No.	0	1	2	3	4	5	6	7	8	9

TABLE I — LOGARITHMS

No.	0	1	2	3	4	5	6	7	8	9
350	54 407	54 419	54 432	54 444	54 456	54 469	54 481	54 494	54 506	54 518
351	54 531	54 543	54 555	54 568	54 580	54 593	54 605	54 617	54 630	54 642
352	54 654	54 667	54 679	54 691	54 704	54 716	54 728	54 741	54 753	54 765
353	54 777	54 790	54 802	54 814	54 827	54 839	54 851	54 864	54 876	54 888
354	54 900	54 913	54 925	54 937	54 949	54 962	54 974	54 986	54 998	55 011
355	55 023	55 035	55 047	55 060	55 072	55 084	55 096	55 108	55 121	55 133
356	55 145	55 157	55 169	55 182	55 194	55 206	55 218	55 230	55 242	55 255
357	55 267	55 279	55 291	55 303	55 315	55 328	55 340	55 352	55 364	55 376
358	55 388	55 400	55 413	55 425	55 437	55 449	55 461	55 473	55 485	55 497
359	55 509	55 522	55 534	55 546	55 558	55 570	55 582	55 594	55 606	55 618
360	55 630	55 642	55 654	55 666	55 678	55 691	55 703	55 715	55 727	55 739
361	55 751	55 763	55 775	55 787	55 799	55 811	55 823	55 835	55 847	55 859
362	55 871	55 883	55 895	55 907	55 919	55 931	55 943	55 955	55 967	55 979
363	55 991	56 003	56 015	56 027	56 038	56 050	56 062	56 074	56 086	56 098
364	56 110	56 122	56 134	56 146	56 158	56 170	56 182	56 194	56 205	56 217
365	56 229	56 241	56 253	56 265	56 277	56 289	56 301	56 312	56 324	56 336
366	56 348	56 360	56 372	56 384	56 396	56 407	56 419	56 431	56 443	56 455
367	56 467	56 478	56 490	56 502	56 514	56 526	56 538	56 549	56 561	56 573
368	56 585	56 597	56 608	56 620	56 632	56 644	56 656	56 667	56 679	56 691
369	56 703	56 714	56 726	56 738	56 750	56 761	56 773	56 785	56 797	56 808
370	56 820	56 832	56 844	56 855	56 867	56 879	56 891	56 902	56 914	56 926
371	56 937	56 949	56 961	56 972	56 984	56 996	57 008	57 019	57 031	57 043
372	57 054	57 066	57 078	57 089	57 101	57 113	57 124	57 136	57 148	57 159
373	57 171	57 183	57 194	57 206	57 217	57 229	57 241	57 252	57 264	57 276
374	57 287	57 299	57 310	57 322	57 334	57 345	57 357	57 368	57 380	57 392
375	57 403	57 415	57 426	57 438	57 449	57 461	57 473	57 484	57 496	57 507
376	57 519	57 530	57 542	57 553	57 565	57 576	57 588	57 600	57 611	57 623
377	57 634	57 646	57 657	57 669	57 680	57 692	57 703	57 715	57 726	57 738
378	57 749	57 761	57 772	57 784	57 795	57 807	57 818	57 830	57 841	57 852
379	57 864	57 875	57 887	57 898	57 910	57 921	57 933	57 944	57 955	57 967
380	57 978	57 990	58 001	58 013	58 024	58 035	58 047	58 058	58 070	58 081
381	58 092	58 104	58 115	58 127	58 138	58 149	58 161	58 172	58 184	58 195
382	58 206	58 218	58 229	58 240	58 252	58 263	58 274	58 286	58 297	58 309
383	58 320	58 331	58 343	58 354	58 365	58 377	58 388	58 399	58 410	58 422
384	58 433	58 444	58 456	58 467	58 478	58 490	58 501	58 512	58 524	58 535
385	58 546	58 557	58 569	58 580	58 591	58 602	58 614	58 625	58 636	58 647
386	58 659	58 670	58 681	58 692	58 704	58 715	58 726	58 737	58 749	58 760
387	58 771	58 782	58 794	58 805	58 816	58 827	58 838	58 850	58 861	58 872
388	58 883	58 894	58 906	58 917	58 928	58 939	58 950	58 961	58 973	58 984
389	58 995	59 006	59 017	59 028	59 040	59 051	59 062	59 073	59 084	59 095
390	59 106	59 118	59 129	59 140	59 151	59 162	59 173	59 184	59 195	59 207
391	59 218	59 229	59 240	59 251	59 262	59 273	59 284	59 295	59 306	59 318
392	59 329	59 340	59 351	59 362	59 373	59 384	59 395	59 406	59 417	59 428
393	59 439	59 450	59 461	59 472	59 483	59 494	59 506	59 517	59 528	59 539
394	59 550	59 561	59 572	59 583	59 594	59 605	59 616	59 627	59 638	59 649
395	59 660	59 671	59 682	59 693	59 704	59 715	59 726	59 737	59 748	59 759
396	59 770	59 780	59 791	59 802	59 813	59 824	59 835	59 846	59 857	59 868
397	59 879	59 890	59 901	59 912	59 923	59 934	59 945	59 956	59 966	59 977
398	59 988	59 999	60 010	60 021	60 032	60 043	60 054	60 065	60 076	60 086
399	60 097	60 108	60 119	60 130	60 141	60 152	60 163	60 173	60 184	60 195
No.	0	1	2	3	4	5	6	7	8	9

TABLE I — LOGARITHMS

No.	0	1	2	3	4	5	6	7	8	9
400	60 206	60 217	60 228	60 239	60 249	60 260	60 271	60 282	60 293	60 304
401	60 314	60 325	60 336	60 347	60 358	60 369	60 379	60 390	60 401	60 412
402	60 423	60 433	60 444	60 455	60 466	60 477	60 487	60 498	60 509	60 520
403	60 531	60 541	60 552	60 563	60 574	60 584	60 595	60 606	60 617	60 627
404	60 638	60 649	60 660	60 670	60 681	60 692	60 703	60 713	60 724	60 735
405	60 746	60 756	60 767	60 778	60 788	60 799	60 810	60 821	60 831	60 842
406	60 853	60 863	60 874	60 885	60 895	60 906	60 917	60 927	60 938	60 949
407	60 959	60 970	60 981	60 991	61 002	61 013	61 023	61 034	61 045	61 055
408	61 066	61 077	61 087	61 098	61 109	61 119	61 130	61 140	61 151	61 162
409	61 172	61 183	61 194	61 204	61 215	61 225	61 236	61 247	61 257	61 268
410	61 278	61 289	61 300	61 310	61 321	61 331	61 342	61 352	61 363	61 374
411	61 384	61 395	61 405	61 416	61 426	61 437	61 448	61 458	61 469	61 479
412	61 490	61 500	61 511	61 521	61 532	61 542	61 553	61 563	61 574	61 584
413	61 595	61 606	61 616	61 627	61 637	61 648	61 658	61 669	61 679	61 690
414	61 700	61 711	61 721	61 731	61 742	61 752	61 763	61 773	61 784	61 794
415	61 805	61 815	61 826	61 836	61 847	61 857	61 868	61 878	61 888	61 899
416	61 909	61 920	61 930	61 941	61 951	61 962	61 972	61 982	61 993	62 003
417	62 014	62 024	62 034	62 045	62 055	62 066	62 076	62 086	62 097	62 107
418	62 118	62 128	62 138	62 149	62 159	62 170	62 180	62 190	62 201	62 211
419	62 221	62 232	62 242	62 252	62 263	62 273	62 284	62 294	62 304	62 315
420	62 325	62 335	62 346	62 356	62 366	62 377	62 387	62 397	62 408	62 418
421	62 428	62 439	62 449	62 459	62 469	62 480	62 490	62 500	62 511	62 521
422	62 531	62 542	62 552	62 562	62 572	62 583	62 593	62 603	62 613	62 624
423	62 634	62 644	62 655	62 665	62 675	62 685	62 696	62 706	62 716	62 726
424	62 737	62 747	62 757	62 767	62 778	62 788	62 798	62 808	62 818	62 829
425	62 839	62 849	62 859	62 870	62 880	62 890	62 900	62 910	62 921	62 931
426	62 941	62 951	62 961	62 972	62 982	62 992	63 002	63 012	63 022	63 033
427	63 043	63 053	63 063	63 073	63 083	63 094	63 104	63 114	63 124	63 134
428	63 144	63 155	63 165	63 175	63 185	63 195	63 205	63 215	63 225	63 236
429	63 246	63 256	63 266	63 276	63 286	63 296	63 306	63 317	63 327	63 337
430	63 347	63 357	63 367	63 377	63 387	63 397	63 407	63 417	63 428	63 438
431	63 448	63 458	63 468	63 478	63 488	63 498	63 508	63 518	63 528	63 538
432	63 548	63 558	63 568	63 579	63 589	63 599	63 609	63 619	63 629	63 639
433	63 649	63 659	63 669	63 679	63 689	63 699	63 709	63 719	63 729	63 739
434	63 749	63 759	63 769	63 779	63 789	63 799	63 809	63 819	63 829	63 839
435	63 849	63 859	63 869	63 879	63 889	63 899	63 909	63 919	63 929	63 939
436	63 949	63 959	63 969	63 979	63 988	63 998	64 008	64 018	64 028	64 038
437	64 048	64 058	64 068	64 078	64 088	64 098	64 108	64 118	64 128	64 137
438	64 147	64 157	64 167	64 177	64 187	64 197	64 207	64 217	64 227	64 237
439	64 246	64 256	64 266	64 276	64 286	64 296	64 306	64 316	64 326	64 335
440	64 345	64 355	64 365	64 375	64 385	64 395	64 404	64 414	64 424	64 434
441	64 444	64 454	64 464	64 473	64 483	64 493	64 503	64 513	64 523	64 532
442	64 542	64 552	64 562	64 572	64 582	64 591	64 601	64 611	64 621	64 631
443	64 640	64 650	64 660	64 670	64 680	64 689	64 699	64 709	64 719	64 729
444	64 738	64 748	64 758	64 768	64 777	64 787	64 797	64 807	64 816	64 826
445	64 836	64 846	64 856	64 865	64 875	64 885	64 895	64 904	64 914	64 924
446	64 933	64 943	64 953	64 963	64 972	64 982	64 992	65 002	65 011	65 021
447	65 031	65 040	65 050	65 060	65 070	65 079	65 089	65 099	65 108	65 118
448	65 128	65 137	65 147	65 157	65 167	65 176	65 186	65 196	65 205	65 215
449	65 225	65 234	65 244	65 254	65 263	65 273	65 283	65 292	65 302	65 312
No.	0	1	2	3	4	5	6	7	8	9

TABLE I — LOGARITHMS

No.	0	1	2	3	4	5	6	7	8	9
450	65 321	65 331	65 341	65 350	65 360	65 369	65 379	65 389	65 398	65 408
451	65 418	65 427	65 437	65 447	65 456	65 466	65 475	65 485	65 495	65 504
452	65 514	65 523	65 533	65 543	65 552	65 562	65 571	65 581	65 591	65 600
453	65 610	65 619	65 629	65 639	65 648	65 658	65 667	65 677	65 686	65 696
454	65 706	65 715	65 725	65 734	65 744	65 753	65 763	65 772	65 782	65 792
455	65 801	65 811	65 820	65 830	65 839	65 849	65 858	65 868	65 877	65 887
456	65 896	65 906	65 916	65 925	65 935	65 944	65 954	65 963	65 973	65 982
457	65 992	66 001	66 011	66 020	66 030	66 039	66 049	66 058	66 068	66 077
458	66 087	66 096	66 106	66 115	66 124	66 134	66 143	66 153	66 162	66 172
459	66 181	66 191	66 200	66 210	66 219	66 229	66 238	66 247	66 257	66 266
460	66 276	66 285	66 295	66 304	66 314	66 323	66 332	66 342	66 351	66 361
461	66 370	66 380	66 389	66 398	66 408	66 417	66 427	66 436	66 445	66 455
462	66 464	66 474	66 483	66 492	66 502	66 511	66 521	66 530	66 539	66 549
463	66 558	66 567	66 577	66 586	66 596	66 605	66 614	66 624	66 633	66 642
464	66 652	66 661	66 671	66 680	66 689	66 699	66 708	66 717	66 727	66 736
465	66 745	66 755	66 764	66 773	66 783	66 792	66 801	66 811	66 820	66 829
466	66 839	66 848	66 857	66 867	66 876	66 885	66 894	66 904	66 913	66 922
467	66 932	66 941	66 950	66 960	66 969	66 978	66 987	66 997	67 006	67 015
468	67 025	67 034	67 043	67 052	67 062	67 071	67 080	67 089	67 099	67 108
469	67 117	67 127	67 136	67 145	67 154	67 164	67 173	67 182	67 191	67 201
470	67 210	67 219	67 228	67 237	67 247	67 256	67 265	67 274	67 284	67 293
471	67 302	67 311	67 321	67 330	67 339	67 348	67 357	67 367	67 376	67 385
472	67 394	67 403	67 413	67 422	67 431	67 440	67 449	67 459	67 468	67 477
473	67 486	67 495	67 504	67 514	67 523	67 532	67 541	67 550	67 560	67 569
474	67 578	67 587	67 596	67 605	67 614	67 624	67 633	67 642	67 651	67 660
475	67 669	67 679	67 688	67 697	67 706	67 715	67 724	67 733	67 742	67 752
476	67 761	67 770	67 779	67 788	67 797	67 806	67 815	67 825	67 834	67 843
477	67 852	67 861	67 870	67 879	67 888	67 897	67 906	67 916	67 925	67 934
478	67 943	67 952	67 961	67 970	67 979	67 988	67 997	68 006	68 015	68 024
479	68 034	68 043	68 052	68 061	68 070	68 079	68 088	68 097	68 106	68 115
480	68 124	68 133	68 142	68 151	68 160	68 169	68 178	68 187	68 196	68 205
481	68 215	68 224	68 233	68 242	68 251	68 260	68 269	68 278	68 287	68 296
482	68 305	68 314	68 323	68 332	68 341	68 350	68 359	68 368	68 377	68 386
483	68 395	68 404	68 413	68 422	68 431	68 440	68 449	68 458	68 467	68 476
484	68 485	68 494	68 502	68 511	68 520	68 529	68 538	68 547	68 556	68 565
485	68 574	68 583	68 592	68 601	68 610	68 619	68 628	68 637	68 646	68 655
486	68 664	68 673	68 681	68 690	68 699	68 708	68 717	68 726	68 735	68 744
487	68 753	68 762	68 771	68 780	68 789	68 797	68 806	68 815	68 824	68 833
488	68 842	68 851	68 860	68 869	68 878	68 886	68 895	68 904	68 913	68 922
489	68 931	68 940	68 949	68 958	68 966	68 975	68 984	68 993	69 002	69 011
490	69 020	69 028	69 037	69 046	69 055	69 064	69 073	69 082	69 090	69 099
491	69 108	69 117	69 126	69 135	69 144	69 152	69 161	69 170	69 179	69 188
492	69 197	69 205	69 214	69 223	69 232	69 241	69 249	69 258	69 267	69 276
493	69 285	69 294	69 302	69 311	69 320	69 329	69 338	69 346	69 355	69 364
494	69 373	69 381	69 390	69 399	69 408	69 417	69 425	69 434	69 443	69 452
495	69 461	69 469	69 478	69 487	69 496	69 504	69 513	69 522	69 531	69 539
496	69 548	69 557	69 566	69 574	69 583	69 592	69 601	69 609	69 618	69 627
497	69 636	69 644	69 653	69 662	69 671	69 679	69 688	69 697	69 705	69 714
498	69 723	69 732	69 740	69 749	69 758	69 767	69 775	69 784	69 793	69 801
499	69 810	69 819	69 827	69 836	69 845	69 854	69 862	69 871	69 880	69 888
No.	0	1	2	3	4	5	6	7	8	9

TABLE I — LOGARITHMS

No.	0	1	2	3	4	5	6	7	8	9
500	69 897	69 906	69 914	69 923	69 932	69 940	69 949	69 958	69 966	69 975
501	69 984	69 992	70 001	70 010	70 018	70 027	70 036	70 044	70 053	70 062
502	70 070	70 079	70 088	70 096	70 105	70 114	70 122	70 131	70 140	70 148
503	70 157	70 165	70 174	70 183	70 191	70 200	70 209	70 217	70 226	70 234
504	70 243	70 252	70 260	70 269	70 278	70 286	70 295	70 303	70 312	70 321
505	70 329	70 338	70 346	70 355	70 364	70 372	70 381	70 389	70 398	70 406
506	70 415	70 424	70 432	70 441	70 449	70 458	70 467	70 475	70 484	70 492
507	70 501	70 509	70 518	70 526	70 535	70 544	70 552	70 561	70 569	70 578
508	70 586	70 595	70 603	70 612	70 621	70 629	70 638	70 646	70 655	70 663
509	70 672	70 680	70 689	70 697	70 706	70 714	70 723	70 731	70 740	70 749
510	70 757	70 766	70 774	70 783	70 791	70 800	70 808	70 817	70 825	70 834
511	70 842	70 851	70 859	70 868	70 876	70 885	70 893	70 902	70 910	70 919
512	70 927	70 935	70 944	70 952	70 961	70 969	70 978	70 986	70 995	71 003
513	71 012	71 020	71 029	71 037	71 046	71 054	71 063	71 071	71 079	71 088
514	71 096	71 105	71 113	71 122	71 130	71 139	71 147	71 155	71 164	71 172
515	71 181	71 189	71 198	71 206	71 214	71 223	71 231	71 240	71 248	71 257
516	71 265	71 273	71 282	71 290	71 299	71 307	71 315	71 324	71 332	71 341
517	71 349	71 357	71 366	71 374	71 383	71 391	71 399	71 408	71 416	71 425
518	71 433	71 441	71 450	71 458	71 466	71 475	71 483	71 492	71 500	71 508
519	71 517	71 525	71 533	71 542	71 550	71 559	71 567	71 575	71 584	71 592
520	71 600	71 609	71 617	71 625	71 634	71 642	71 650	71 659	71 667	71 675
521	71 684	71 692	71 700	71 709	71 717	71 725	71 734	71 742	71 750	71 759
522	71 767	71 775	71 784	71 792	71 800	71 809	71 817	71 825	71 834	71 842
523	71 850	71 858	71 867	71 875	71 883	71 892	71 900	71 908	71 917	71 925
524	71 933	71 941	71 950	71 958	71 966	71 975	71 983	71 991	71 999	72 008
525	72 016	72 024	72 032	72 041	72 049	72 057	72 066	72 074	72 082	72 090
526	72 099	72 107	72 115	72 123	72 132	72 140	72 148	72 156	72 165	72 173
527	72 181	72 189	72 198	72 206	72 214	72 222	72 230	72 239	72 247	72 255
528	72 263	72 272	72 280	72 288	72 296	72 304	72 313	72 321	72 329	72 337
529	72 346	72 354	72 362	72 370	72 378	72 387	72 395	72 403	72 411	72 419
530	72 428	72 436	72 444	72 452	72 460	72 469	72 477	72 485	72 493	72 501
531	72 509	72 518	72 526	72 534	72 542	72 550	72 558	72 567	72 575	72 583
532	72 591	72 599	72 607	72 616	72 624	72 632	72 640	72 648	72 656	72 665
533	72 673	72 681	72 689	72 697	72 705	72 713	72 722	72 730	72 738	72 746
534	72 754	72 762	72 770	72 779	72 787	72 795	72 803	72 811	72 819	72 827
535	72 835	72 843	72 852	72 860	72 868	72 876	72 884	72 892	72 900	72 908
536	72 916	72 925	72 933	72 941	72 949	72 957	72 965	72 973	72 981	72 989
537	72 997	73 006	73 014	73 022	73 030	73 038	73 046	73 054	73 062	73 070
538	73 078	73 086	73 094	73 102	73 111	73 119	73 127	73 135	73 143	73 151
539	73 159	73 167	73 175	73 183	73 191	73 199	73 207	73 215	73 223	73 231
540	73 239	73 247	73 255	73 263	73 272	73 280	73 288	73 296	73 304	73 312
541	73 320	73 328	73 336	73 344	73 352	73 360	73 368	73 376	73 384	73 392
542	73 400	73 408	73 416	73 424	73 432	73 440	73 448	73 456	73 464	73 472
543	73 480	73 488	73 496	73 504	73 512	73 520	73 528	73 536	73 544	73 552
544	73 560	73 568	73 576	73 584	73 592	73 600	73 608	73 616	73 624	73 632
545	73 640	73 648	73 656	73 664	73 672	73 679	73 687	73 695	73 703	73 711
546	73 719	73 727	73 735	73 743	73 751	73 759	73 767	73 775	73 783	73 791
547	73 799	73 807	73 815	73 823	73 830	73 838	73 846	73 854	73 862	73 870
548	73 878	73 886	73 894	73 902	73 910	73 918	73 926	73 933	73 941	73 949
549	73 957	73 965	73 973	73 981	73 989	73 997	74 005	74 013	74 020	74 028
No.	0	1	2	3	4	5	6	7	8	9

TABLE I — LOGARITHMS

No.	0	1	2	3	4	5	6	7	8	9
550	74 036	74 044	74 052	74 060	74 068	74 076	74 084	74 092	74 099	74 107
551	74 115	74 123	74 131	74 139	74 147	74 155	74 162	74 170	74 178	74 186
552	74 194	74 202	74 210	74 218	74 225	74 233	74 241	74 249	74 257	74 265
553	74 273	74 280	74 288	74 296	74 304	74 312	74 320	74 327	74 335	74 343
554	74 351	74 359	74 367	74 374	74 382	74 390	74 398	74 406	74 414	74 421
555	74 429	74 437	74 445	74 453	74 461	74 468	74 476	74 484	74 492	74 500
556	74 507	74 515	74 523	74 531	74 539	74 547	74 554	74 562	74 570	74 578
557	74 586	74 593	74 601	74 609	74 617	74 624	74 632	74 640	74 648	74 656
558	74 663	74 671	74 679	74 687	74 695	74 702	74 710	74 718	74 726	74 733
559	74 741	74 749	74 757	74 764	74 772	74 780	74 788	74 796	74 803	74 811
560	74 819	74 827	74 834	74 842	74 850	74 858	74 865	74 873	74 881	74 889
561	74 896	74 904	74 912	74 920	74 927	74 935	74 943	74 950	74 958	74 966
562	74 974	74 981	74 989	74 997	75 005	75 012	75 020	75 028	75 035	75 043
563	75 051	75 059	75 066	75 074	75 082	75 089	75 097	75 105	75 113	75 120
564	75 128	75 136	75 143	75 151	75 159	75 166	75 174	75 182	75 189	75 197
565	75 205	75 213	75 220	75 228	75 236	75 243	75 251	75 259	75 266	75 274
566	75 282	75 289	75 297	75 305	75 312	75 320	75 328	75 335	75 343	75 351
567	75 358	75 366	75 374	75 381	75 389	75 397	75 404	75 412	75 420	75 427
568	75 435	75 442	75 450	75 458	75 465	75 473	75 481	75 488	75 496	75 504
569	75 511	75 519	75 526	75 534	75 542	75 549	75 557	75 565	75 572	75 580
570	75 587	75 595	75 603	75 610	75 618	75 626	75 633	75 641	75 648	75 656
571	75 664	75 671	75 679	75 686	75 694	75 702	75 709	75 717	75 724	75 732
572	75 740	75 747	75 755	75 762	75 770	75 778	75 785	75 793	75 800	75 808
573	75 815	75 823	75 831	75 838	75 846	75 853	75 861	75 868	75 876	75 884
574	75 891	75 899	75 906	75 914	75 921	75 929	75 937	75 944	75 952	75 959
575	75 967	75 974	75 982	75 989	75 997	76 005	76 012	76 020	76 027	76 035
576	76 042	76 050	76 057	76 065	76 072	76 080	76 087	76 095	76 103	76 110
577	76 118	76 125	76 133	76 140	76 148	76 155	76 163	76 170	76 178	76 185
578	76 193	76 200	76 208	76 215	76 223	76 230	76 238	76 245	76 253	76 260
579	76 268	76 275	76 283	76 290	76 298	76 305	76 313	76 320	76 328	76 335
580	76 343	76 350	76 358	76 365	76 373	76 380	76 388	76 395	76 403	76 410
581	76 418	76 425	76 433	76 440	76 448	76 455	76 462	76 470	76 477	76 485
582	76 492	76 500	76 507	76 515	76 522	76 530	76 537	76 545	76 552	76 559
583	76 567	76 574	76 582	76 589	76 597	76 604	76 612	76 619	76 626	76 634
584	76 641	76 649	76 656	76 664	76 671	76 678	76 686	76 693	76 701	76 708
585	76 716	76 723	76 730	76 738	76 745	76 753	76 760	76 768	76 775	76 782
586	76 790	76 797	76 805	76 812	76 819	76 827	76 834	76 842	76 849	76 856
587	76 864	76 871	76 879	76 886	76 893	76 901	76 908	76 916	76 923	76 930
588	76 938	76 945	76 953	76 960	76 967	76 975	76 982	76 989	76 997	77 004
589	77 012	77 019	77 026	77 034	77 041	77 048	77 056	77 063	77 070	77 078
590	77 085	77 093	77 100	77 107	77 115	77 122	77 129	77 137	77 144	77 151
591	77 159	77 166	77 173	77 181	77 188	77 195	77 203	77 210	77 217	77 225
592	77 232	77 240	77 247	77 254	77 262	77 269	77 276	77 283	77 291	77 298
593	77 305	77 313	77 320	77 327	77 335	77 342	77 349	77 357	77 364	77 371
594	77 379	77 386	77 393	77 401	77 408	77 415	77 422	77 430	77 437	77 444
595	77 452	77 459	77 466	77 474	77 481	77 488	77 495	77 503	77 510	77 517
596	77 525	77 532	77 539	77 546	77 554	77 561	77 568	77 576	77 583	77 590
597	77 597	77 605	77 612	77 619	77 627	77 634	77 641	77 648	77 656	77 663
598	77 670	77 677	77 685	77 692	77 699	77 706	77 714	77 721	77 728	77 735
599	77 743	77 750	77 757	77 764	77 772	77 779	77 786	77 793	77 801	77 808
No.	0	1	2	3	4	5	6	7	8	9

TABLE I — LOGARITHMS

No.	0	1	2	3	4	5	6	7	8	9
600	77 815	77 822	77 830	77 837	77 844	77 851	77 859	77 866	77 873	77 880
601	77 887	77 895	77 902	77 909	77 916	77 924	77 931	77 938	77 945	77 952
602	77 960	77 967	77 974	77 981	77 988	77 996	78 003	78 010	78 017	78 025
603	78 032	78 039	78 046	78 053	78 061	78 068	78 075	78 082	78 089	78 097
604	78 104	78 111	78 118	78 125	78 132	78 140	78 147	78 154	78 161	78 168
605	78 176	78 183	78 190	78 197	78 204	78 211	78 219	78 226	78 233	78 240
606	78 247	78 254	78 262	78 269	78 276	78 283	78 290	78 297	78 305	78 312
607	78 319	78 326	78 333	78 340	78 347	78 355	78 362	78 369	78 376	78 383
608	78 390	78 398	78 405	78 412	78 419	78 426	78 433	78 440	78 447	78 455
609	78 462	78 469	78 476	78 483	78 490	78 497	78 504	78 512	78 519	78 526
610	78 533	78 540	78 547	78 554	78 561	78 569	78 576	78 583	78 590	78 597
611	78 604	78 611	78 618	78 625	78 633	78 640	78 647	78 654	78 661	78 668
612	78 675	78 682	78 689	78 696	78 704	78 711	78 718	78 725	78 732	78 739
613	78 746	78 753	78 760	78 767	78 774	78 781	78 789	78 796	78 803	78 810
614	78 817	78 824	78 831	78 838	78 845	78 852	78 859	78 866	78 873	78 880
615	78 888	78 895	78 902	78 909	78 916	78 923	78 930	78 937	78 944	78 951
616	78 958	78 965	78 972	78 979	78 986	78 993	79 000	79 007	79 014	79 021
617	79 029	79 036	79 043	79 050	79 057	79 064	79 071	79 078	79 085	79 092
618	79 099	79 106	79 113	79 120	79 127	79 134	79 141	79 148	79 155	79 162
619	79 169	79 176	79 183	79 190	79 197	79 204	79 211	79 218	79 225	79 232
620	79 239	79 246	79 253	79 260	79 267	79 274	79 281	79 288	79 295	79 302
621	79 309	79 316	79 323	79 330	79 337	79 344	79 351	79 358	79 365	79 372
622	79 379	79 386	79 393	79 400	79 407	79 414	79 421	79 428	79 435	79 442
623	79 449	79 456	79 463	79 470	79 477	79 484	79 491	79 498	79 505	79 511
624	79 518	79 525	79 532	79 539	79 546	79 553	79 560	79 567	79 574	79 581
625	79 588	79 595	79 602	79 609	79 616	79 623	79 630	79 637	79 644	79 650
626	79 657	79 664	79 671	79 678	79 685	79 692	79 699	79 706	79 713	79 720
627	79 727	79 734	79 741	79 748	79 754	79 761	79 768	79 775	79 782	79 789
628	79 796	79 803	79 810	79 817	79 824	79 831	79 837	79 844	79 851	79 858
629	79 865	79 872	79 879	79 886	79 893	79 900	79 906	79 913	79 920	79 927
630	79 934	79 941	79 948	79 955	79 962	79 969	79 975	79 982	79 989	79 996
631	80 003	80 010	80 017	80 024	80 030	80 037	80 044	80 051	80 058	80 065
632	80 072	80 079	80 085	80 092	80 099	80 106	80 113	80 120	80 127	80 134
633	80 140	80 147	80 154	80 161	80 168	80 175	80 182	80 188	80 195	80 202
634	80 209	80 216	80 223	80 229	80 236	80 243	80 250	80 257	80 264	80 271
635	80 277	80 284	80 291	80 298	80 305	80 312	80 318	80 325	80 332	80 339
636	80 346	80 353	80 359	80 366	80 373	80 380	80 387	80 393	80 400	80 407
637	80 414	80 421	80 428	80 434	80 441	80 448	80 455	80 462	80 468	80 475
638	80 482	80 489	80 496	80 502	80 509	80 516	80 523	80 530	80 536	80 543
639	80 550	80 557	80 564	80 570	80 577	80 584	80 591	80 598	80 604	80 611
640	80 618	80 625	80 632	80 638	80 645	80 652	80 659	80 665	80 672	80 679
641	80 686	80 693	80 699	80 706	80 713	80 720	80 726	80 733	80 740	80 747
642	80 754	80 760	80 767	80 774	80 781	80 787	80 794	80 801	80 808	80 814
643	80 821	80 828	80 835	80 841	80 848	80 855	80 862	80 868	80 875	80 882
644	80 889	80 895	80 902	80 909	80 916	80 922	80 929	80 936	80 943	80 949
645	80 956	80 963	80 969	80 976	80 983	80 990	80 996	81 003	81 010	81 017
646	81 023	81 030	81 037	81 043	81 050	81 057	81 064	81 070	81 077	81 084
647	81 090	81 097	81 104	81 111	81 117	81 124	81 131	81 137	81 144	81 151
648	81 158	81 164	81 171	81 178	81 184	81 191	81 198	81 204	81 211	81 218
649	81 224	81 231	81 238	81 245	81 251	81 258	81 265	81 271	81 278	81 285
No.	0	1	2	3	4	5	6	7	8	9

TABLE I — LOGARITHMS

No.	0	1	2	3	4	5	6	7	8	9
650	81 291	81 298	81 305	81 311	81 318	81 325	81 331	81 338	81 345	81 351
651	81 358	81 365	81 371	81 378	81 385	81 391	81 398	81 405	81 411	81 418
652	81 425	81 431	81 438	81 445	81 451	81 458	81 465	81 471	81 478	81 485
653	81 491	81 498	81 505	81 511	81 518	81 525	81 531	81 538	81 544	81 551
654	81 558	81 564	81 571	81 578	81 584	81 591	81 598	81 604	81 611	81 617
655	81 624	81 631	81 637	81 644	81 651	81 657	81 664	81 671	81 677	81 684
656	81 690	81 697	81 704	81 710	81 717	81 723	81 730	81 737	81 743	81 750
657	81 757	81 763	81 770	81 776	81 783	81 790	81 796	81 803	81 809	81 816
658	81 823	81 829	81 836	81 842	81 849	81 856	81 862	81 869	81 875	81 882
659	81 889	81 895	81 902	81 908	81 915	81 921	81 928	81 935	81 941	81 948
660	81 954	81 961	81 968	81 974	81 981	81 987	81 994	82 000	82 007	82 014
661	82 020	82 027	82 033	82 040	82 046	82 053	82 060	82 066	82 073	82 079
662	82 086	82 092	82 099	82 105	82 112	82 119	82 125	82 132	82 138	82 145
663	82 151	82 158	82 164	82 171	82 178	82 184	82 191	82 197	82 204	82 210
664	82 217	82 223	82 230	82 236	82 243	82 249	82 256	82 263	82 269	82 276
665	82 282	82 289	82 295	82 302	82 308	82 315	82 321	82 328	82 334	82 341
666	82 347	82 354	82 360	82 367	82 373	82 380	82 387	82 393	82 400	82 406
667	82 413	82 419	82 426	82 432	82 439	82 445	82 452	82 458	82 465	82 471
668	82 478	82 484	82 491	82 497	82 504	82 510	82 517	82 523	82 530	82 536
669	82 543	82 549	82 556	82 562	82 569	82 575	82 582	82 588	82 595	82 601
670	82 607	82 614	82 620	82 627	82 633	82 640	82 646	82 653	82 659	82 666
671	82 672	82 679	82 685	82 692	82 698	82 705	82 711	82 718	82 724	82 730
672	82 737	82 743	82 750	82 756	82 763	82 769	82 776	82 782	82 789	82 795
673	82 802	82 808	82 814	82 821	82 827	82 834	82 840	82 847	82 853	82 860
674	82 866	82 872	82 879	82 885	82 892	82 898	82 905	82 911	82 918	82 924
675	82 930	82 937	82 943	82 950	82 956	82 963	82 969	82 975	82 982	82 988
676	82 995	83 001	83 008	83 014	83 020	83 027	83 033	83 040	83 046	83 052
677	83 059	83 065	83 072	83 078	83 085	83 091	83 097	83 104	83 110	83 117
678	83 123	83 129	83 136	83 142	83 149	83 155	83 161	83 168	83 174	83 181
679	83 187	83 193	83 200	83 206	83 213	83 219	83 225	83 232	83 238	83 245
680	83 251	83 257	83 264	83 270	83 276	83 283	83 289	83 296	83 302	83 308
681	83 315	83 321	83 327	83 334	83 340	83 347	83 353	83 359	83 366	83 372
682	83 378	83 385	83 391	83 398	83 404	83 410	83 417	83 423	83 429	83 436
683	83 442	83 448	83 455	83 461	83 467	83 474	83 480	83 487	83 493	83 499
684	83 506	83 512	83 518	83 525	83 531	83 537	83 544	83 550	83 556	83 563
685	83 569	83 575	83 582	83 588	83 594	83 601	83 607	83 613	83 620	83 626
686	83 632	83 639	83 645	83 651	83 658	83 664	83 670	83 677	83 683	83 689
687	83 696	83 702	83 708	83 715	83 721	83 727	83 734	83 740	83 746	83 753
688	83 759	83 765	83 771	83 778	83 784	83 790	83 797	83 803	83 809	83 816
689	83 822	83 828	83 835	83 841	83 847	83 853	83 860	83 866	83 872	83 879
690	83 885	83 891	83 897	83 904	83 910	83 916	83 923	83 929	83 935	83 942
691	83 948	83 954	83 960	83 967	83 973	83 979	83 985	83 992	83 998	84 004
692	84 011	84 017	84 023	84 029	84 036	84 042	84 048	84 055	84 061	84 067
693	84 073	84 080	84 086	84 092	84 098	84 105	84 111	84 117	84 123	84 130
694	84 136	84 142	84 148	84 155	84 161	84 167	84 173	84 180	84 186	84 192
695	84 198	84 205	84 211	84 217	84 223	84 230	84 236	84 242	84 248	84 255
696	84 261	84 267	84 273	84 280	84 286	84 292	84 298	84 305	84 311	84 317
697	84 323	84 330	84 336	84 342	84 348	84 354	84 361	84 367	84 373	84 379
698	84 386	84 392	84 398	84 404	84 410	84 417	84 423	84 429	84 435	84 442
699	84 448	84 454	84 460	84 466	84 473	84 479	84 485	84 491	84 497	84 504
No.	0	1	2	3	4	5	6	7	8	9

TABLE I — LOGARITHMS

No.	0	1	2	3	4	5	6	7	8	9
700	84 510	84 516	84 522	84 528	84 535	84 541	84 547	84 553	84 559	84 566
701	84 572	84 578	84 584	84 590	84 597	84 603	84 609	84 615	84 621	84 628
702	84 634	84 640	84 646	84 652	84 658	84 665	84 671	84 677	84 683	84 689
703	84 696	84 702	84 708	84 714	84 720	84 726	84 733	84 739	84 745	84 751
704	84 757	84 763	84 770	84 776	84 782	84 788	84 794	84 800	84 807	84 813
705	84 819	84 825	84 831	84 837	84 844	84 850	84 856	84 862	84 868	84 874
706	84 880	84 887	84 893	84 899	84 905	84 911	84 917	84 924	84 930	84 936
707	84 942	84 948	84 954	84 960	84 967	84 973	84 979	84 985	84 991	84 997
708	85 003	85 009	85 016	85 022	85 028	85 034	85 040	85 046	85 052	85 058
709	85 065	85 071	85 077	85 083	85 089	85 095	85 101	85 107	85 114	85 120
710	85 126	85 132	85 138	85 144	85 150	85 156	85 163	85 169	85 175	85 181
711	85 187	85 193	85 199	85 205	85 211	85 217	85 224	85 230	85 236	85 242
712	85 248	85 254	85 260	85 266	85 272	85 278	85 285	85 291	85 297	85 303
713	85 309	85 315	85 321	85 327	85 333	85 339	85 345	85 352	85 358	85 364
714	85 370	85 376	85 382	85 388	85 394	85 400	85 406	85 412	85 418	85 425
715	85 431	85 437	85 443	85 449	85 455	85 461	85 467	85 473	85 479	85 485
716	85 491	85 497	85 503	85 509	85 516	85 522	85 528	85 534	85 540	85 546
717	85 552	85 558	85 564	85 570	85 576	85 582	85 588	85 594	85 600	85 606
718	85 612	85 618	85 625	85 631	85 637	85 643	85 649	85 655	85 661	85 667
719	85 673	85 679	85 685	85 691	85 697	85 703	85 709	85 715	85 721	85 727
720	85 733	85 739	85 745	85 751	85 757	85 763	85 769	85 775	85 781	85 788
721	85 794	85 800	85 806	85 812	85 818	85 824	85 830	85 836	85 842	85 848
722	85 854	85 860	85 866	85 872	85 878	85 884	85 890	85 896	85 902	85 908
723	85 914	85 920	85 926	85 932	85 938	85 944	85 950	85 956	85 962	85 968
724	85 974	85 980	85 986	85 992	85 998	86 004	86 010	86 016	86 022	86 028
725	86 034	86 040	86 046	86 052	86 058	86 064	86 070	86 076	86 082	86 088
726	86 094	86 100	86 106	86 112	86 118	86 124	86 130	86 136	86 141	86 147
727	86 153	86 159	86 165	86 171	86 177	86 183	86 189	86 195	86 201	86 207
728	86 213	86 219	86 225	86 231	86 237	86 243	86 249	86 255	86 261	86 267
729	86 273	86 279	86 285	86 291	86 297	86 303	86 308	86 314	86 320	86 326
730	86 332	86 338	86 344	86 350	86 356	86 362	86 368	86 374	86 380	86 386
731	86 392	86 398	86 404	86 410	86 415	86 421	86 427	86 433	86 439	86 445
732	86 451	86 457	86 463	86 469	86 475	86 481	86 487	86 493	86 499	86 504
733	86 510	86 516	86 522	86 528	86 534	86 540	86 546	86 552	86 558	86 564
734	86 570	86 576	86 581	86 587	86 593	86 599	86 605	86 611	86 617	86 623
735	86 629	86 635	86 641	86 646	86 652	86 658	86 664	86 670	86 676	86 682
736	86 688	86 694	86 700	86 705	86 711	86 717	86 723	86 729	86 735	86 741
737	86 747	86 753	86 759	86 764	86 770	86 776	86 782	86 788	86 794	86 800
738	86 806	86 812	86 817	86 823	86 829	86 835	86 841	86 847	86 853	86 859
739	86 864	86 870	86 876	86 882	86 888	86 894	86 900	86 906	86 911	86 917
740	86 923	86 929	86 935	86 941	86 947	86 953	86 958	86 964	86 970	86 976
741	86 982	86 988	86 994	86 999	87 005	87 011	87 017	87 023	87 029	87 035
742	87 040	87 046	87 052	87 058	87 064	87 070	87 075	87 081	87 087	87 093
743	87 099	87 105	87 111	87 116	87 122	87 128	87 134	87 140	87 146	87 151
744	87 157	87 163	87 169	87 175	87 181	87 186	87 192	87 198	87 204	87 210
745	87 216	87 221	87 227	87 233	87 239	87 245	87 251	87 256	87 262	87 268
746	87 274	87 280	87 286	87 291	87 297	87 303	87 309	87 315	87 320	87 326
747	87 332	87 338	87 344	87 349	87 355	87 361	87 367	87 373	87 379	87 384
748	87 390	87 396	87 402	87 408	87 413	87 419	87 425	87 431	87 437	87 442
749	87 448	87 454	87 460	87 466	87 471	87 477	87 483	87 489	87 495	87 500
No.	0	1	2	3	4	5	6	7	8	9

TABLE I — LOGARITHMS

No.	0	1	2	3	4	5	6	7	8	9
750	87 506	87 512	87 518	87 523	87 529	87 535	87 541	87 547	87 552	87 558
751	87 564	87 570	87 576	87 581	87 587	87 593	87 599	87 604	87 610	87 616
752	87 622	87 628	87 633	87 639	87 645	87 651	87 656	87 662	87 668	87 674
753	87 679	87 685	87 691	87 697	87 703	87 708	87 714	87 720	87 726	87 731
754	87 737	87 743	87 749	87 754	87 760	87 766	87 772	87 777	87 783	87 789
755	87 795	87 800	87 806	87 812	87 818	87 823	87 829	87 835	87 841	87 846
756	87 852	87 858	87 864	87 869	87 875	87 881	87 887	87 892	87 898	87 904
757	87 910	87 915	87 921	87 927	87 933	87 938	87 944	87 950	87 955	87 961
758	87 967	87 973	87 978	87 984	87 990	87 996	88 001	88 007	88 013	88 018
759	88 024	88 030	88 036	88 041	88 047	88 053	88 058	88 064	88 070	88 076
760	88 081	88 087	88 093	88 098	88 104	88 110	88 116	88 121	88 127	88 133
761	88 138	88 144	88 150	88 156	88 161	88 167	88 173	88 178	88 184	88 190
762	88 195	88 201	88 207	88 213	88 218	88 224	88 230	88 235	88 241	88 247
763	88 252	88 258	88 264	88 270	88 275	88 281	88 287	88 292	88 298	88 304
764	88 309	88 315	88 321	88 326	88 332	88 338	88 343	88 349	88 355	88 360
765	88 366	88 372	88 377	88 383	88 389	88 395	88 400	88 406	88 412	88 417
766	88 423	88 429	88 434	88 440	88 446	88 451	88 457	88 463	88 468	88 474
767	88 480	88 485	88 491	88 497	88 502	88 508	88 513	88 519	88 525	88 530
768	88 536	88 542	88 547	88 553	88 559	88 564	88 570	88 576	88 581	88 587
769	88 593	88 598	88 604	88 610	88 615	88 621	88 627	88 632	88 638	88 643
770	88 649	88 655	88 660	88 666	88 672	88 677	88 683	88 689	88 694	88 700
771	88 705	88 711	88 717	88 722	88 728	88 734	88 739	88 745	88 750	88 756
772	88 762	88 767	88 773	88 779	88 784	88 790	88 795	88 801	88 807	88 812
773	88 818	88 824	88 829	88 835	88 840	88 846	88 852	88 857	88 863	88 868
774	88 874	88 880	88 885	88 891	88 897	88 902	88 908	88 913	88 919	88 925
775	88 930	88 936	88 941	88 947	88 953	88 958	88 964	88 969	88 975	88 981
776	88 986	88 992	88 997	88 003	89 009	89 014	89 020	89 025	89 031	89 037
777	89 042	89 048	89 053	89 059	89 064	89 070	89 076	89 081	89 087	89 092
778	89 098	89 104	89 109	89 115	89 120	89 126	89 131	89 137	89 143	89 148
779	89 154	89 159	89 165	89 170	89 176	89 182	89 187	89 193	89 198	89 204
780	89 209	89 215	89 221	89 226	89 232	89 237	89 243	89 248	89 254	89 260
781	89 265	89 271	89 276	89 282	89 287	89 293	89 298	89 304	89 310	89 315
782	89 321	89 326	89 332	89 337	89 343	89 348	89 354	89 360	89 365	89 371
783	89 376	89 382	89 387	89 393	89 398	89 404	89 409	89 415	89 421	89 426
784	89 432	89 437	89 443	89 448	89 454	89 459	89 465	89 470	89 476	89 481
785	89 487	89 492	89 498	89 504	89 509	89 515	89 520	89 526	89 531	89 537
786	89 542	89 548	89 553	89 559	89 564	89 570	89 575	89 581	89 586	89 592
787	89 597	89 603	89 609	89 614	89 620	89 625	89 631	89 636	89 642	89 647
788	89 653	89 658	89 664	89 669	89 675	89 680	89 686	89 691	89 697	89 702
789	89 708	89 713	89 719	89 724	89 730	89 735	89 741	89 746	89 752	89 757
790	89 763	89 768	89 774	89 779	89 785	89 790	89 796	89 801	89 807	89 812
791	89 818	89 823	89 829	89 834	89 840	89 845	89 851	89 856	89 862	89 867
792	89 873	89 878	89 883	89 889	89 894	89 900	89 905	89 811	89 916	89 922
793	89 927	89 933	89 938	89 944	89 949	89 955	89 960	89 966	89 971	89 977
794	89 982	89 988	89 993	89 998	90 004	90 009	90 015	90 020	90 026	90 031
795	90 037	90 042	90 048	90 053	90 059	90 064	90 069	90 075	90 080	90 086
796	90 091	90 097	90 102	90 108	90 113	90 119	90 124	90 129	90 135	90 140
797	90 146	90 151	90 157	90 162	90 168	90 173	90 179	90 184	90 189	90 195
798	90 200	90 206	90 211	90 217	90 222	90 227	90 233	90 238	90 244	90 249
799	90 255	90 260	90 266	90 271	90 276	90 282	90 287	90 293	90 298	90 304
No.	0	1	2	3	4	5	6	7	8	9

TABLE I — LOGARITHMS

No.	0	1	2	3	4	5	6	7	8	9
800	90 309	90 314	90 320	90 325	90 331	90 336	90 342	90 347	90 352	90 358
801	90 363	90 369	90 374	90 380	90 385	90 390	90 396	90 401	90 407	90 412
802	90 417	90 423	90 428	90 434	90 439	90 445	90 450	90 455	90 461	90 466
803	90 472	90 477	90 482	90 488	90 493	90 499	90 504	90 509	90 515	90 520
804	90 526	90 531	90 536	90 542	90 547	90 553	90 558	90 563	90 569	90 574
805	90 580	90 585	90 590	90 596	90 601	90 607	90 612	90 617	90 623	90 628
806	90 634	90 639	90 644	90 650	90 655	90 660	90 666	90 671	90 677	90 685
807	90 687	90 693	90 698	90 703	90 709	90 714	90 720	90 725	90 730	90 736
808	90 741	90 747	90 752	90 757	90 763	90 768	90 773	90 779	90 784	90 789
809	90 795	90 800	90 806	90 811	90 816	90 822	90 827	90 832	90 838	90 843
810	90 849	90 854	90 859	90 865	90 870	90 875	90 881	90 886	90 891	90 897
811	90 902	90 907	90 913	90 918	90 924	90 929	90 934	90 940	90 945	90 950
812	90 956	90 961	90 966	90 972	90 977	90 982	90 988	90 993	90 998	91 004
813	91 009	91 014	91 020	91 025	91 030	91 036	91 041	91 046	91 052	91 057
814	91 062	91 068	91 073	91 078	91 084	91 089	91 094	91 100	91 105	91 110
815	91 116	91 121	91 126	91 132	91 137	91 142	91 148	91 153	91 158	91 164
816	91 169	91 174	91 180	91 185	91 190	91 196	91 201	91 206	91 212	91 217
817	91 222	91 228	91 233	91 238	91 243	91 249	91 254	91 259	91 265	91 270
818	91 275	91 281	91 286	91 291	91 297	91 302	91 307	91 312	91 318	91 323
819	91 328	91 334	91 339	91 344	91 350	91 355	91 360	91 365	91 371	91 376
820	91 381	91 387	91 392	91 397	91 403	91 408	91 413	91 418	91 424	91 429
821	91 434	91 440	91 445	91 450	91 455	91 461	91 466	91 471	91 477	91 482
822	91 487	91 492	91 498	91 503	91 508	91 514	91 519	91 524	91 529	91 535
823	91 540	91 545	91 551	91 556	91 561	91 566	91 572	91 577	91 582	91 587
824	91 593	91 598	91 603	91 609	91 614	91 619	91 624	91 630	91 635	91 640
825	91 645	91 651	91 656	91 661	91 666	91 672	91 677	91 682	91 687	91 693
826	91 698	91 703	91 709	91 714	91 719	91 724	91 730	91 735	91 740	91 745
827	91 751	91 756	91 761	91 766	91 772	91 777	91 782	91 787	91 793	91 798
828	91 803	91 808	91 814	91 819	91 824	91 829	91 834	91 840	91 845	91 850
829	91 855	91 861	91 866	91 871	91 876	91 882	91 887	91 892	91 897	91 903
830	91 908	91 913	91 918	91 924	91 929	91 934	91 939	91 944	91 950	91 955
831	91 960	91 965	91 971	91 976	91 981	91 986	91 991	91 997	92 002	92 007
832	92 012	92 018	92 023	92 028	92 033	92 038	92 044	92 049	92 054	92 059
833	92 065	92 070	92 075	92 080	92 085	92 091	92 096	92 101	92 106	92 111
834	92 117	92 122	92 127	92 132	92 137	92 143	92 148	92 153	92 158	92 163
835	92 169	92 174	92 179	92 184	92 189	92 195	92 200	92 205	92 210	92 215
836	92 221	92 226	92 231	92 236	92 241	92 247	92 252	92 257	92 262	92 267
837	92 273	92 278	92 283	92 288	92 293	92 298	92 304	92 309	92 314	92 319
838	92 324	92 330	92 335	92 340	92 345	92 350	92 355	92 361	92 366	92 371
839	92 376	92 381	92 387	92 392	92 397	92 402	92 407	92 412	92 418	92 423
840	92 428	92 433	92 438	92 443	92 449	92 454	92 459	92 464	92 469	92 474
841	92 480	92 485	92 490	92 495	92 500	92 505	92 511	92 516	92 521	92 526
842	92 531	92 536	92 542	92 547	92 552	92 557	92 562	92 567	92 572	92 578
843	92 583	92 588	92 593	92 598	92 603	92 609	92 614	92 619	92 624	92 629
844	92 634	92 639	92 645	92 650	92 655	92 660	92 665	92 670	92 675	92 681
845	92 686	92 691	92 696	92 701	92 706	92 711	92 716	92 722	92 727	92 732
846	92 737	92 742	92 747	92 752	92 758	92 763	92 768	92 773	92 778	92 783
847	92 788	92 793	92 799	92 804	92 809	92 814	92 819	92 824	92 829	92 834
848	92 840	92 845	92 850	92 855	92 860	92 865	92 870	92 875	92 881	92 886
849	92 891	92 896	92 901	92 906	92 911	92 916	92 921	92 927	92 932	92 937
No.	0	1	2	3	4	5	6	7	8	9

TABLE I — LOGARITHMS

No.	0	1	2	3	4	5	6	7	8	9
850	92 942	92 947	92 952	92 957	92 962	92 967	92 973	92 978	92 983	92 988
851	92 993	92 998	93 003	93 008	93 013	93 018	93 024	93 029	93 034	93 039
852	93 044	93 049	93 054	93 059	93 064	93 069	93 075	93 080	93 085	93 090
853	93 095	93 100	93 105	93 110	93 115	93 120	93 125	93 131	93 136	93 141
854	93 146	93 151	93 156	93 161	93 166	93 171	93 176	93 181	93 186	93 192
855	93 197	93 202	93 207	93 212	93 217	93 222	93 227	93 232	93 237	93 242
856	93 247	93 252	93 258	93 263	93 268	93 273	93 278	93 283	93 288	93 293
857	93 298	93 303	93 308	93 313	93 318	93 323	93 328	93 334	93 339	93 344
858	93 349	93 354	93 359	93 364	93 369	93 374	93 379	93 384	93 389	93 394
859	93 399	93 404	93 409	93 414	93 420	93 425	93 430	93 435	93 440	93 445
860	93 450	93 455	93 460	93 465	93 470	93 475	93 480	93 485	93 490	93 495
861	93 500	93 505	93 510	93 515	93 520	93 526	93 531	93 536	93 541	93 546
862	93 551	93 556	93 561	93 566	93 571	93 576	93 581	93 586	93 591	93 596
863	93 601	93 606	93 611	93 616	93 621	93 626	93 631	93 636	93 641	93 646
864	93 651	93 656	93 661	93 666	93 671	93 676	93 682	93 687	93 692	93 697
865	93 702	93 707	93 712	93 717	93 722	93 727	93 732	93 737	93 742	93 747
866	93 752	93 757	93 762	93 767	93 772	93 777	93 782	93 787	93 792	93 797
867	93 802	93 807	93 812	93 817	93 822	93 827	93 832	93 837	93 842	93 847
868	93 852	93 857	93 862	93 867	93 872	93 877	93 882	93 887	93 892	93 897
869	93 902	93 907	93 912	93 917	93 922	93 927	93 932	93 937	93 942	93 947
870	93 952	93 957	93 962	93 967	93 972	93 977	93 982	93 987	93 992	93 997
871	94 002	94 007	94 012	94 017	94 022	94 027	94 032	94 037	94 042	94 047
872	94 052	94 057	94 062	94 067	94 072	94 077	94 082	94 086	94 091	94 096
873	94 101	94 106	94 111	94 116	94 121	94 126	94 131	94 136	94 141	94 146
874	94 151	94 156	94 161	94 166	94 171	94 176	94 181	94 186	94 191	94 196
875	94 201	94 206	94 211	94 216	94 221	94 226	94 231	94 236	94 240	94 245
876	94 250	94 255	94 260	94 265	94 270	94 275	94 280	94 285	94 290	94 295
877	94 300	94 305	94 310	94 315	94 320	94 325	94 330	94 335	94 340	94 345
878	94 349	94 354	94 359	94 364	94 369	94 374	94 379	94 384	94 389	94 394
879	94 399	94 404	94 409	94 414	94 419	94 424	94 429	94 433	94 438	94 443
880	94 448	94 453	94 458	94 463	94 468	94 473	94 478	94 483	94 488	94 493
881	94 498	94 503	94 507	94 512	94 517	94 522	94 527	94 532	94 537	94 542
882	94 547	94 552	94 557	94 562	94 567	94 571	94 576	94 581	94 586	94 591
883	94 596	94 601	94 606	94 611	94 616	94 621	94 626	94 630	94 635	94 640
884	94 645	94 650	94 655	94 660	94 665	94 670	94 675	94 680	94 685	94 689
885	94 694	94 699	94 704	94 709	94 714	94 719	94 724	94 729	94 734	94 738
886	94 743	94 748	94 753	94 758	94 763	94 768	94 773	94 778	94 783	94 787
887	94 792	94 797	94 802	94 807	94 812	94 817	94 822	94 827	94 832	94 836
888	94 841	94 846	94 851	94 856	94 861	94 866	94 871	94 876	94 880	94 885
889	94 890	94 895	94 900	94 905	94 910	94 915	94 919	94 924	94 929	94 934
890	94 939	94 944	94 949	94 954	94 959	94 963	94 968	94 973	94 978	94 983
891	94 988	94 993	94 998	95 002	95 007	95 012	95 017	95 022	95 027	95 032
892	95 036	95 041	95 046	95 051	95 056	95 061	95 066	95 071	95 075	95 080
893	95 085	95 090	95 095	95 100	95 105	95 109	95 114	95 119	95 124	95 129
894	95 134	95 139	95 143	95 148	95 153	95 158	95 163	95 168	95 173	95 177
895	95 182	95 187	95 192	95 197	95 202	95 207	95 211	95 216	95 221	95 226
896	95 231	95 236	95 240	95 245	95 250	95 255	95 260	95 265	95 270	95 274
897	95 279	95 284	95 289	95 294	95 299	95 303	95 308	95 313	95 318	95 323
898	95 328	95 332	95 337	95 342	95 347	95 352	95 357	95 361	95 366	95 371
899	95 376	95 381	95 386	95 390	95 395	95 400	95 405	95 410	95 415	95 419
No.	0	1	2	3	4	5	6	7	8	9

TABLE I — LOGARITHMS

No.	0	1	2	3	4	5	6	7	8	9
900	95 424	95 429	95 434	95 439	95 444	95 448	95 453	95 458	95 463	95 468
901	95 472	95 477	95 482	95 487	95 492	95 497	95 501	95 506	95 511	95 516
902	95 521	95 525	95 530	95 535	95 540	95 545	95 550	95 554	95 559	95 564
903	95 569	95 574	95 578	95 583	95 588	95 593	95 598	95 602	95 607	95 612
904	95 617	95 622	95 626	95 631	95 636	95 641	95 646	95 650	95 655	95 660
905	95 665	95 670	95 674	95 679	95 684	95 689	95 694	95 698	95 703	95 708
906	95 713	95 718	95 722	95 727	95 732	95 737	95 742	95 746	95 751	95 756
907	95 761	95 766	95 770	95 775	95 780	95 785	95 789	95 794	95 799	95 804
908	95 809	95 813	95 818	95 823	95 828	95 832	95 837	95 842	95 847	95 852
909	95 856	95 861	95 866	95 871	95 875	95 880	95 885	95 890	95 895	95 899
910	95 904	95 909	95 914	95 918	95 923	95 928	95 933	95 938	95 942	95 947
911	95 952	95 957	95 961	95 966	95 971	95 976	95 980	95 985	95 990	95 995
912	95 999	96 004	96 009	96 014	96 019	96 023	96 028	96 033	96 038	96 042
913	96 047	96 052	96 057	96 061	96 066	96 071	96 076	96 080	96 085	96 090
914	96 095	96 099	96 104	96 109	96 114	96 118	96 123	96 128	96 133	96 137
915	96 142	96 147	96 152	96 156	96 161	96 166	96 171	96 175	96 180	96 185
916	96 190	96 194	96 199	96 204	96 209	96 213	96 218	96 223	96 227	96 232
917	96 237	96 242	96 246	96 251	96 256	96 261	96 265	96 270	96 275	96 280
918	96 284	96 289	96 294	96 298	96 303	96 308	96 313	96 317	96 322	96 327
919	96 332	96 336	96 341	96 346	96 350	96 355	96 360	96 365	96 369	96 374
920	96 379	96 384	96 388	96 393	96 398	96 402	96 407	96 412	96 417	96 421
921	96 426	96 431	96 435	96 440	96 445	96 450	96 454	96 459	96 464	96 468
922	96 473	96 478	96 483	96 487	96 492	96 497	96 501	96 506	96 511	96 515
923	96 520	96 525	96 530	96 534	96 539	96 544	96 548	96 553	96 558	96 562
924	96 567	96 572	96 577	96 581	96 586	96 591	96 595	96 600	96 605	96 609
925	96 614	96 619	96 624	96 628	96 633	96 638	96 642	96 647	96 652	96 656
926	96 661	96 666	96 670	96 675	96 680	96 685	96 689	96 694	96 699	96 703
927	96 708	96 713	96 717	96 722	96 727	96 731	96 736	96 741	96 745	96 750
928	96 755	96 759	96 764	96 769	96 774	96 778	96 783	96 788	96 792	96 797
929	96 802	96 806	96 811	96 816	96 820	96 825	96 830	96 834	96 839	96 844
930	96 848	96 853	96 858	96 862	96 867	96 872	96 876	96 881	96 886	96 890
931	96 895	96 900	96 904	96 909	96 914	96 918	96 923	96 928	96 932	96 937
932	96 942	96 946	96 951	96 956	96 960	96 965	96 970	96 974	96 979	96 984
933	96 988	96 993	96 997	97 002	97 007	97 011	97 016	97 021	97 025	97 030
934	97 035	97 039	97 044	97 049	97 053	97 058	97 063	97 067	97 072	97 077
935	97 081	97 086	97 090	97 095	97 100	97 104	97 109	97 114	97 118	97 123
936	97 128	97 132	97 137	97 142	97 146	97 151	97 155	97 160	97 165	97 169
937	97 174	97 179	97 183	97 188	97 192	97 197	97 202	97 206	97 211	97 216
938	97 220	97 225	97 230	97 234	97 239	97 243	97 248	97 253	97 257	97 262
939	97 267	97 271	97 276	97 280	97 285	97 290	97 294	97 299	97 304	97 308
940	97 313	97 317	97 322	97 327	97 331	97 336	97 340	97 345	97 350	97 354
941	97 359	97 364	97 368	97 373	97 377	97 382	97 387	97 391	97 396	97 400
942	97 405	97 410	97 414	97 419	97 424	97 428	97 433	97 437	97 442	97 447
943	97 451	97 456	97 460	97 465	97 470	97 474	97 479	97 483	97 488	97 493
944	97 497	97 502	97 506	97 511	97 516	97 520	97 525	97 529	97 534	97 539
945	97 543	97 548	97 552	97 557	97 562	97 566	97 571	97 575	97 580	97 585
946	97 589	97 594	97 598	97 603	97 607	97 612	97 617	97 621	97 626	97 630
947	97 635	97 640	97 644	97 649	97 653	97 658	97 663	97 667	97 672	97 676
948	97 681	97 685	97 690	97 695	97 699	97 704	97 708	97 713	97 717	97 722
949	97 727	97 731	97 736	97 740	97 745	97 749	97 754	97 759	97 763	97 768
No.	0	1	2	3	4	5	6	7	8	9

TABLE I — LOGARITHMS

No.	0	1	2	3	4	5	6	7	8	9
950	97 772	97 777	97 782	97 786	97 791	97 795	97 800	97 804	97 809	97 813
951	97 818	97 823	97 827	97 832	97 836	97 841	97 845	97 850	97 855	97 859
952	97 864	97 868	97 873	97 877	97 882	97 886	97 891	97 896	97 900	97 905
953	97 907	97 914	97 918	97 923	97 928	97 932	97 937	97 941	97 946	97 950
954	97 955	97 959	97 964	97 968	97 973	97 978	97 982	97 987	97 991	97 996
955	98 000	98 005	98 009	98 014	98 019	98 023	98 028	98 032	98 037	98 041
956	98 046	98 050	98 055	98 059	98 064	98 068	98 073	98 078	98 082	98 087
957	98 091	98 096	98 100	98 105	98 109	98 114	98 118	98 123	98 127	98 132
958	98 137	98 141	98 146	98 150	98 155	98 159	98 164	98 168	98 173	98 177
959	98 182	98 186	98 191	98 195	98 200	98 204	98 209	98 214	98 218	98 223
960	98 227	98 232	98 236	98 241	98 245	98 250	98 254	98 259	98 263	98 268
961	98 272	98 277	98 281	98 286	98 290	98 295	98 299	98 304	98 308	98 313
962	98 318	98 322	98 327	98 331	98 336	98 340	98 345	98 349	98 354	98 358
963	98 363	98 367	98 372	98 376	98 381	98 385	98 390	98 394	98 399	98 403
964	98 408	98 412	98 417	98 421	98 426	98 430	98 435	98 439	98 444	98 448
965	98 453	98 457	98 462	98 466	98 471	98 475	98 480	98 484	98 489	98 493
966	98 498	98 502	98 507	98 511	98 516	98 520	98 525	98 529	98 534	98 538
967	98 543	98 547	98 552	98 556	98 561	98 565	98 570	98 574	98 579	98 583
968	98 588	98 592	98 597	98 601	98 605	98 610	98 614	98 619	98 623	98 628
969	98 632	98 637	98 641	98 646	98 650	98 655	98 659	98 664	98 668	98 673
970	98 677	98 682	98 686	98 691	98 695	98 700	98 704	98 709	98 713	98 717
971	98 722	98 726	98 731	98 735	98 740	98 744	98 749	98 753	98 758	98 762
972	98 767	98 771	98 776	98 780	98 784	98 789	98 793	98 798	98 802	98 807
973	98 811	98 816	98 820	98 825	98 829	98 834	98 838	98 843	98 847	98 851
974	98 856	98 860	98 865	98 869	98 874	98 878	98 883	98 887	98 892	98 896
975	98 900	98 905	98 909	98 914	98 918	98 923	98 927	98 932	98 936	98 941
976	98 945	98 949	98 954	98 958	98 963	98 967	98 972	98 976	98 981	98 985
977	98 989	98 994	98 998	99 003	99 007	99 012	99 016	99 021	99 025	99 029
978	99 034	99 038	99 043	99 047	99 052	99 056	99 061	99 065	99 069	99 074
979	99 078	99 083	99 087	99 092	99 096	99 100	99 105	99 109	99 114	99 118
980	99 123	99 127	99 131	99 136	99 140	99 145	99 149	99 154	99 158	99 162
981	99 167	99 171	99 176	99 180	99 185	99 189	99 193	99 198	99 202	99 207
982	99 211	99 216	99 220	99 224	99 229	99 233	99 238	99 242	99 247	99 251
983	99 255	99 260	99 264	99 269	99 273	99 277	99 282	99 286	99 291	99 295
984	99 300	99 304	99 308	99 313	99 317	99 322	99 326	99 330	99 335	99 339
985	99 344	99 348	99 352	99 357	99 361	99 366	99 370	99 374	99 379	99 383
986	99 388	99 392	99 396	99 401	99 405	99 410	99 414	99 419	99 423	99 427
987	99 432	99 436	99 441	99 445	99 449	99 454	99 458	99 463	99 467	99 471
988	99 476	99 480	99 484	99 489	99 493	99 498	99 502	99 506	99 511	99 515
989	99 520	99 524	99 528	99 533	99 537	99 542	99 546	99 550	99 555	99 559
990	99 564	99 568	99 572	99 577	99 581	99 585	99 590	99 594	99 599	99 603
991	99 607	99 612	99 616	99 621	99 625	99 629	99 634	99 638	99 642	99 647
992	99 651	99 656	99 660	99 664	99 669	99 673	99 677	99 682	99 686	99 691
993	99 695	99 699	99 704	99 708	99 712	99 717	99 721	99 726	99 730	99 734
994	99 739	99 743	99 747	99 752	99 756	99 760	99 765	99 769	99 774	99 778
995	99 782	99 787	99 791	99 795	99 800	99 804	99 808	99 813	99 817	99 822
996	99 826	99 830	99 835	99 839	99 843	99 848	99 852	99 856	99 861	99 865
997	99 870	99 874	99 878	99 883	99 887	99 891	99 896	99 900	99 904	99 909
998	99 913	99 917	99 922	99 926	99 930	99 935	99 939	99 944	99 948	99 952
999	99 957	99 961	99 965	99 970	99 974	99 978	99 983	99 987	99 991	99 996
1000	00 000	00 004	00 009	00 013	00 017	00 022	00 026	00 030	00 035	00 039
No.	0	1	2	3	4	5	6	7	8	9

TABLE II — VALUES OF THE FUNCTION $y = e^x$

x	0	1	2	3	4	5	6	7	8	9
0.0	1.00000	01005	02020	03045	04081	05127	06184	07251	08329	09417
0.1	1.10517	11628	12750	13883	15027	16183	17351	18530	19722	20925
0.2	1.22140	23368	24608	25860	27125	28403	29693	30996	32313	33643
0.3	1.34986	36343	37713	39097	40495	41907	43333	44773	46228	47698
0.4	1.49182	50682	52196	53726	55271	56831	58407	59999	61607	63232
0.5	1.64872	66529	68203	69893	71601	73325	75067	76827	78604	80399
0.6	1.82212	84043	85893	87761	89648	91554	93479	95424	97388	99372
0.7	2.01375	03399	05443	07508	09594	11700	13828	15977	18147	20340
0.8	2.22554	24791	27050	29332	31637	33965	36316	38691	41090	43513
0.9	2.45960	48432	50929	53451	55998	58571	61170	63794	66446	69123
1.0	2.71828	74560	77319	80107	82922	85765	88637	91538	94468	97427
1.1	3.00417	03436	06485	09566	12677	15819	18993	22199	25437	28708
1.2	3.32012	35348	38719	42123	45561	49034	52542	56085	59664	63279
1.3	3.66930	70617	74342	78104	81904	85743	89619	93535	97490	*01485
1.4	4.05520	09596	13712	17870	22070	26311	30596	34924	39295	43710
1.5	4.48169	52673	57223	61818	66459	71147	75882	80665	85496	90375
1.6	4.95303	*00281	*05309	*10387	*15517	*20698	*25931	*31217	*36556	*41948
1.7	5.47395	52896	58453	64065	69734	75460	81244	87085	92986	98945
1.8	6.04965	11045	17186	23389	29654	35982	42374	48830	55350	61937
1.9	6.68589	75309	82096	88951	95875	*02869	*09933	*17068	*24274	*31553
2.0	7.38906	46332	53832	61409	69061	76790	84597	92482	*00447	*08492
2.1	8.16617	24824	33114	41487	49944	58486	67114	75828	84631	93521
2.2	9.02501	11572	20733	29987	39333	48774	58309	67940	77668	87494
2.3	9.97418	10.07442	17567	27794	38124	48557	59095	69739	80490	91349
2.4	11.02318	13396	24586	35888	47304	58835	70481	82245	94126	*06128
2.5	12.18249	30493	42860	55351	67967	80710	93582	*06582	*19714	*32977
2.6	13.46374	59905	73572	87377	*01320	*15404	*29629	*43997	*58509	*73168
2.7	14.87973	15.02928	18032	33289	48699	64263	79984	95863	*11902	*28102
2.8	16.44465	60992	77685	94546	17.11577	28778	46153	63702	81427	99331
2.9	18.17415	35680	54129	72763	91585	19.10595	29797	49192	68782	88568

x	e^x	x	e^x
1.	2.71828	6.	403.42879
2.	7.38906	7.	1096.63316
3.	20.08554	8.	2980.95799
4.	54.59815	9.	8103.08393
5.	148.41316	10.	22026.4658

TABLE II — VALUES OF THE FUNCTION $y = e^{-x}$

x	0	1	2	3	4	5	6	7	8	9
0.0	1.00000	*99005	*98020	*97045	*96079	*95123	*94176	*93239	*92312	*91393
0.1	0.90484	89583	88692	87810	86936	86071	85214	84366	83527	82696
0.2	0.81873	81058	80252	79453	78663	77880	77105	76338	75578	74826
0.3	0.74082	73345	72615	71892	71177	70469	69768	69073	68386	67706
0.4	0.67032	66365	65705	65051	64404	63763	63128	62500	61878	61263
0.5	0.60653	60050	59452	58860	58275	57695	57121	56553	55990	55433
0.6	0.54881	54335	53794	53259	52729	52205	51685	51171	50662	50158
0.7	0.49659	49164	48675	48191	47711	47237	46767	46301	45841	45384
0.8	0.44933	44486	44043	43605	43171	42741	42316	41895	41478	41066
0.9	0.40657	40252	39852	39455	39063	38674	38289	37908	37531	37158
1.0	0.36788	36422	36059	35701	35345	34994	34646	34301	33960	33622
1.1	0.33287	32956	32628	32303	31982	31664	31349	31037	30728	30422
1.2	0.30119	29820	29523	29229	28938	28650	28365	28083	27804	27527
1.3	0.27253	26982	26714	26448	26185	25924	25666	25411	25158	24908
1.4	0.24660	24414	24171	23931	23693	23457	23224	22993	22764	22537
1.5	0.22313	22091	21871	21654	21438	21225	21014	20805	20598	20393
1.6	0.20190	19989	19790	19593	19398	19205	19014	18825	18637	18452
1.7	0.18268	18087	17907	17728	17552	17377	17204	17033	16864	16696
1.8	0.16530	16365	16203	16041	15882	15724	15567	15412	15259	15107
1.9	0.14957	14808	14661	14515	14370	14227	14086	13946	13807	13670
2.0	0.13534	13399	13266	13134	13003	12873	12745	12619	12493	12369
2.1	0.12246	12124	12003	11884	11765	11648	11533	11418	11304	11192
2.2	0.11080	10970	10861	10753	10646	10540	10435	10331	10228	10127
2.3	0.10026	09926	09827	09730	09633	09537	09442	09348	09255	09163
2.4	0.09072	08982	08892	08804	08716	08629	08543	08458	08374	08291
2.5	0.08208	08127	08046	07966	07887	07808	07730	07654	07577	07502
2.6	0.07427	07353	07280	07208	07136	07065	06995	06925	06856	06788
2.7	0.06721	06654	06587	06522	06457	06393	06329	06266	06204	06142
2.8	0.06081	06020	05961	05901	05843	05784	05727	05670	05613	05558
2.9	0.05502	05448	05393	05340	05287	05234	05182	05130	05079	05029

x	e^{-x}	x	e^{-x}
1	0.36788	6	0.00248
2	0.13534	7	0.00091
3	0.04979	8	0.00034
4	0.01832	9	0.00012
5	0.00674	10	0.00005

TABLE III — SQUARES

	0	1	2	3	4	5	6	7	8	9
0	0	1	4	9	16	25	36	49	64	81
1	100	121	144	169	196	225	256	289	324	361
2	400	441	484	529	576	625	676	729	784	841
3	900	961	1024	1089	1156	1225	1296	1369	1444	1521
4	1600	1681	1764	1849	1936	2025	2116	2209	2304	2401
5	2500	2601	2704	2809	2916	3025	3136	3249	3364	3481
6	3600	3721	3844	3969	4096	4225	4356	4489	4624	4761
7	4900	5041	5184	5329	5476	5625	5776	5929	6084	6241
8	6400	6561	6724	6889	7056	7225	7396	7569	7744	7921
9	8100	8281	8464	8649	8836	9025	9216	9409	9604	9801
10	10000	10201	10404	10609	10816	11025	11236	11449	11664	11881
11	12100	12321	12544	12769	12996	13225	13456	13689	13924	14161
12	14400	14641	14884	15129	15376	15625	15876	16129	16384	16641
13	16900	17161	17424	17689	17956	18225	18496	18769	19044	19321
14	19600	19881	20164	20449	20736	21025	21316	21609	21904	22201
15	22500	22801	23104	23409	23716	24025	24336	24649	24964	25281
16	25600	25921	26244	26569	26896	27225	27556	27889	28224	28561
17	28900	29241	29584	29929	30276	30625	30976	31329	31684	32041
18	32400	32761	33124	33489	33856	34225	34596	34969	35344	35721
19	36100	36481	36864	37249	37636	38025	38416	38809	39204	39601
20	40000	40401	40804	41209	41616	42025	42436	42849	43264	43681
21	44100	44521	44944	45369	45796	46225	46656	47089	47524	47961
22	48400	48841	49284	49729	50176	50625	51076	51529	51984	52441
23	52900	53361	53824	54289	54756	55225	55696	56169	56644	57121
24	57600	58081	58564	59049	59536	60025	60516	61009	61504	62001
25	62500	63001	63504	64009	64516	65025	65536	66049	66564	67081
26	67600	68121	68644	69169	69696	70225	70756	71289	71824	72361
27	72900	73441	73984	74529	75076	75625	76176	76729	77284	77841
28	78400	78961	79524	80089	80656	81225	81796	82369	82944	83521
29	84100	84681	85264	85849	86436	87025	87616	88209	88804	89401
30	90000	90601	91204	91809	92416	93025	93636	94249	94864	95481
31	96100	96721	97344	97969	98596	99225	99856	100489	101124	101761
32	102400	103041	103684	104329	104976	105625	106276	106929	107584	108241
33	108900	109561	110224	110889	111556	112225	112896	113569	114244	114921
34	115600	116281	116964	117649	118336	119025	119716	120409	121104	121801
35	122500	123201	123904	124609	125316	126025	126736	127449	128164	128881
36	129600	130321	131044	131769	132496	133225	133956	134689	135424	136161
37	136900	137641	138384	139129	139876	140625	141376	142129	142884	143641
38	144400	145161	145924	146689	147456	148225	148996	149769	150544	151321
39	152100	152881	153664	154449	155236	156025	156816	157609	158404	159201
40	160000	160801	161604	162409	163216	164025	164836	165649	166464	167281
41	168100	168921	169744	170569	171396	172225	173056	173889	174724	175561
42	176400	177241	178084	178929	179776	180625	181476	182329	183184	184041
43	184900	185761	186624	187489	188356	189225	190096	190969	191844	192721
44	193600	194481	195364	196249	197136	198025	198916	199809	200704	201601
45	202500	203401	204304	205209	206116	207025	207936	208849	209764	210681
46	211600	212521	213444	214369	215296	216225	217156	218089	219024	219961
47	220900	221841	222784	223729	224676	225625	226576	227529	228484	229441
48	230400	231361	232324	233289	234256	235225	236196	237169	238144	239121
49	240100	241081	242064	243049	244036	245025	246016	247009	248004	249001

TABLE III — SQUARES

	0	1	2	3	4	5	6	7	8	9
50	250000	251001	252004	253009	254016	255025	256036	257049	258064	259081
51	260100	261121	262144	263169	264196	265225	266256	267289	268324	269361
52	270400	271441	272484	273529	274576	275625	276676	277729	278784	279841
53	280900	281961	283024	284089	285156	286225	287296	288369	289444	290521
54	291600	292681	293764	294849	295936	297025	298116	299209	300304	301401
55	302500	303601	304704	305809	306916	308025	309136	310249	311364	312481
56	313600	314721	315844	316969	318096	319225	320356	321489	322624	323761
57	324900	326041	327184	328329	329476	330625	331776	332929	334084	335241
58	336400	337561	338724	339889	341056	342225	343396	344569	345744	346921
59	348100	349281	350464	351649	352836	354025	355216	356409	357604	358801
60	360000	361201	362404	363609	364816	366025	367236	368449	369664	370881
61	372100	373321	374544	375769	376996	378225	379456	380689	381924	383161
62	384400	385641	386884	388129	389376	390625	391876	393129	394384	395641
63	396900	398161	399424	400689	401956	403225	404496	405769	407044	408321
64	409600	410881	412164	413449	414736	416025	417316	418609	419904	421201
65	422500	423801	425104	426409	427716	429025	430336	431649	432964	434281
66	435600	436921	438244	439569	440896	442225	443556	444889	446224	447561
67	448900	450241	451584	452929	454276	455625	456976	458329	459684	461041
68	462400	463761	465124	466489	467856	469225	470596	471969	473344	474721
69	476100	477481	478864	480249	481636	483025	484416	485809	487204	488601
70	490000	491401	492804	494209	495616	497025	498436	499849	501264	502681
71	504100	505521	506944	508369	509796	511225	512656	514089	515524	516961
72	518400	519841	521284	522729	524176	525625	527076	528529	529984	531441
73	532900	534361	535824	537289	538756	540225	541696	543169	544644	546121
74	547600	549081	550564	552049	553536	555025	556516	558009	559504	561001
75	562500	564001	565504	567009	568516	570025	571536	573049	574564	576081
76	577600	579121	580644	582169	583696	585225	586756	588289	589824	591361
77	592900	594441	595984	597529	599076	600625	602176	603729	605284	606841
78	608400	609961	611524	613089	614656	616225	617796	619369	620944	622521
79	624100	625681	627264	628849	630436	632025	633616	635209	636804	638401
80	640000	641601	643204	644809	646416	648025	649636	651249	652864	654481
81	656100	657721	659344	660969	662596	664225	665856	667489	669124	670761
82	672400	674041	675684	677329	678976	680625	682276	683929	685584	687241
83	688900	690561	692224	693889	695556	697225	698896	700569	702244	703921
84	705600	707281	708964	710649	712336	714025	715716	717409	719104	720801
85	722500	724201	725904	727609	729316	731025	732736	734449	736164	737881
86	739600	741321	743044	744769	746496	748225	749956	751689	753424	755161
87	756900	758641	760384	762129	763876	765625	767376	769129	770884	772641
88	774400	776161	777924	779689	781456	783225	784996	786769	788544	790321
89	792100	793881	795664	797449	799236	801025	802816	804609	806404	808201
90	810000	811801	813604	815409	817216	819025	820836	822649	824464	826281
91	828100	829921	831744	833569	835396	837225	839056	840889	842724	844561
92	846400	848241	850084	851929	853776	855625	857476	859329	861184	863041
93	864900	866761	868624	870489	872356	874225	876096	877969	879844	881721
94	883600	885481	887364	889249	891136	893025	894916	896809	898704	900601
95	902500	904401	906304	908209	910116	912025	913936	915849	917764	919681
96	921600	923521	925444	927369	929296	931225	933156	935089	937024	938961
97	940900	942841	944784	946729	948676	950625	952576	954529	956484	958441
98	960400	962361	964324	966289	968256	970225	972196	974169	976144	978121
99	980100	982081	984064	986049	988036	990025	992016	994009	996004	998001

TABLE IV — SQUARE ROOTS

n	$\sqrt{n}$	$\sqrt{10n}$	n	$\sqrt{n}$	$\sqrt{10n}$	n	$\sqrt{n}$	$\sqrt{10n}$
1.00	1.00000	3.16228	1.50	1.22474	3.87298	2.00	1.41421	4.47214
1.01	1.00499	3.17805	1.51	1.22882	3.88587	2.01	1.41774	4.48330
1.02	1.00995	3.19374	1.52	1.23288	3.89872	2.02	1.42127	4.49444
1.03	1.01489	3.20936	1.53	1.23693	3.91152	2.03	1.42478	4.50555
1.04	1.01980	3.22490	1.54	1.24097	3.92428	2.04	1.42829	4.51664
1.05	1.02470	3.24037	1.55	1.24499	3.93700	2.05	1.43178	4.52769
1.06	1.02956	3.25576	1.56	1.24900	3.94968	2.06	1.43527	4.53872
1.07	1.03441	3.27109	1.57	1.25300	3.96232	2.07	1.43875	4.54973
1.08	1.03923	3.28634	1.58	1.25698	3.97492	2.08	1.44222	4.56070
1.09	1.04403	3.30151	1.59	1.26095	3.98748	2.09	1.44568	4.57165
1.10	1.04881	3.31662	1.60	1.26491	4.00000	2.10	1.44914	4.58258
1.11	1.05357	3.33167	1.61	1.26886	4.01248	2.11	1.45258	4.59347
1.12	1.05830	3.34664	1.62	1.27279	4.02492	2.12	1.45602	4.60435
1.13	1.06301	3.36155	1.63	1.27671	4.03733	2.13	1.45945	4.61519
1.14	1.06771	3.37639	1.64	1.28062	4.04969	2.14	1.46287	4.62601
1.15	1.07238	3.39116	1.65	1.28452	4.06202	2.15	1.46629	4.63681
1.16	1.07703	3.40588	1.66	1.28841	4.07431	2.16	1.46969	4.64758
1.17	1.08167	3.42053	1.67	1.29228	4.08656	2.17	1.47309	4.65833
1.18	1.08628	3.43511	1.68	1.29615	4.09878	2.18	1.47648	4.66905
1.19	1.09087	3.44964	1.69	1.30000	4.11096	2.19	1.47986	4.67974
1.20	1.09545	3.46410	1.70	1.30384	4.12311	2.20	1.48324	4.69042
1.21	1.10000	3.47851	1.71	1.30767	4.13521	2.21	1.48661	4.70106
1.22	1.10454	3.49285	1.72	1.31149	4.14729	2.22	1.48997	4.71169
1.23	1.10905	3.50714	1.73	1.31529	4.15933	2.23	1.49332	4.72229
1.24	1.11355	3.52136	1.74	1.31909	4.17133	2.24	1.49666	4.73286
1.25	1.11803	3.53553	1.75	1.32288	4.18330	2.25	1.50000	4.74342
1.26	1.12250	3.54965	1.76	1.32665	4.19524	2.26	1.50333	4.75395
1.27	1.12694	3.56371	1.77	1.33041	4.20714	2.27	1.50665	4.76445
1.28	1.13137	3.57771	1.78	1.33417	4.21900	2.28	1.50997	4.77493
1.29	1.13578	3.59166	1.79	1.33791	4.23084	2.29	1.51327	4.78539
1.30	1.14018	3.60555	1.80	1.34164	4.24264	2.30	1.51658	4.79583
1.31	1.14455	3.61939	1.81	1.34536	4.25441	2.31	1.51987	4.80625
1.32	1.14891	3.63318	1.82	1.34907	4.26615	2.32	1.52315	4.81664
1.33	1.15326	3.64692	1.83	1.35277	4.27785	2.33	1.52643	4.82701
1.34	1.15758	3.66060	1.84	1.35647	4.28952	2.34	1.52971	4.83735
1.35	1.16190	3.67423	1.85	1.36015	4.30116	2.35	1.53297	4.84768
1.36	1.16619	3.68782	1.86	1.36382	4.31277	2.36	1.53623	4.85798
1.37	1.17047	3.70135	1.87	1.36748	4.32435	2.37	1.53948	4.86826
1.38	1.17473	3.71484	1.88	1.37113	4.33590	2.38	1.54272	4.87852
1.39	1.17898	3.72827	1.89	1.37477	4.34741	2.39	1.54596	4.88876
1.40	1.18322	3.74166	1.90	1.37840	4.35890	2.40	1.54919	4.89898
1.41	1.18743	3.75500	1.91	1.38203	4.37035	2.41	1.55242	4.90918
1.42	1.19164	3.76829	1.92	1.38564	4.38178	2.42	1.55563	4.91935
1.43	1.19583	3.78153	1.93	1.38924	4.39318	2.43	1.55885	4.92950
1.44	1.20000	3.79473	1.94	1.39284	4.40454	2.44	1.56205	4.93964
1.45	1.20416	3.80789	1.95	1.39642	4.41588	2.45	1.56525	4.94975
1.46	1.20830	3.82099	1.96	1.40000	4.42719	2.46	1.56844	4.95984
1.47	1.21244	3.83406	1.97	1.40357	4.43847	2.47	1.57162	4.96991
1.48	1.21655	3.84708	1.98	1.40712	4.44972	2.48	1.57480	4.97996
1.49	1.22066	3.86005	1.99	1.41067	4.46094	2.49	1.57797	4.98999

TABLE IV — SQUARE ROOTS

n	$\sqrt{n}$	$\sqrt{10n}$	n	$\sqrt{n}$	$\sqrt{10n}$	n	$\sqrt{n}$	$\sqrt{10n}$
2.50	1.58114	5.00000	3.00	1.73205	5.47723	3.50	1.87083	5.91608
2.51	1.58430	5.00999	3.01	1.73494	5.48635	3.51	1.87350	5.92453
2.52	1.58745	5.01996	3.02	1.73781	5.49545	3.52	1.87617	5.93296
2.53	1.59060	5.02991	3.03	1.74069	5.50454	3.53	1.87883	5.94138
2.54	1.59374	5.03984	3.04	1.74356	5.51362	3.54	1.88149	5.94979
2.55	1.59687	5.04975	3.05	1.74642	5.52268	3.55	1.88414	5.95819
2.56	1.60000	5.05964	3.06	1.74929	5.53173	3.56	1.88680	5.96657
2.57	1.60312	5.06952	3.07	1.75214	5.54076	3.57	1.88944	5.97495
2.58	1.60624	5.07937	3.08	1.75499	5.54977	3.58	1.89209	5.98331
2.59	1.60935	5.08920	3.09	1.75784	5.55878	3.59	1.89473	5.99166
2.60	1.61245	5.09902	3.10	1.76068	5.56776	3.60	1.89737	6.00000
2.61	1.61555	5.10882	3.11	1.76352	5.57674	3.61	1.90000	6.00833
2.62	1.61864	5.11859	3.12	1.76635	5.58570	3.62	1.90263	6.01664
2.63	1.62173	5.12835	3.13	1.76918	5.59464	3.63	1.90526	6.02495
2.64	1.62481	5.13809	3.14	1.77200	5.60357	3.64	1.90788	6.03324
2.65	1.62788	5.14782	3.15	1.77482	5.61249	3.65	1.91050	6.04152
2.66	1.63095	5.15752	3.16	1.77764	5.62139	3.66	1.91311	6.04979
2.67	1.63401	5.16720	3.17	1.78045	5.63028	3.67	1.91572	6.05805
2.68	1.63707	5.17687	3.18	1.78326	5.63915	3.68	1.91833	6.06630
2.69	1.64012	5.18652	3.19	1.78606	5.64801	3.69	1.92094	6.07454
2.70	1.64317	5.19615	3.20	1.78885	5.65685	3.70	1.92354	6.08276
2.71	1.64621	5.20577	3.21	1.79165	5.66569	3.71	1.92614	6.09098
2.72	1.64924	5.21536	3.22	1.79444	5.67450	3.72	1.92873	6.09918
2.73	1.65227	5.22494	3.23	1.79722	5.68331	3.73	1.93132	6.10737
2.74	1.65529	5.23450	3.24	1.80000	5.69210	3.74	1.93391	6.11555
2.75	1.65831	5.24404	3.25	1.80278	5.70088	3.75	1.93649	6.12372
2.76	1.66132	5.25357	3.26	1.80555	5.70964	3.76	1.93907	6.13188
2.77	1.66433	5.26308	3.27	1.80831	5.71839	3.77	1.94165	6.14003
2.78	1.66733	5.27257	3.28	1.81108	5.72713	3.78	1.94422	6.14817
2.79	1.67033	5.28205	3.29	1.81384	5.73585	3.79	1.94679	6.15630
2.80	1.67332	5.29150	3.30	1.81659	5.74456	3.80	1.94936	6.16441
2.81	1.67631	5.30094	3.31	1.81934	5.75326	3.81	1.95192	6.17252
2.82	1.67929	5.31037	3.32	1.82209	5.76194	3.82	1.95448	6.18061
2.83	1.68226	5.31977	3.33	1.82483	5.77062	3.83	1.95704	6.18870
2.84	1.68523	5.32917	3.34	1.82757	5.77927	3.84	1.95959	6.19677
2.85	1.68819	5.33854	3.35	1.83030	5.78792	3.85	1.96214	6.20484
2.86	1.69115	5.34790	3.36	1.83303	5.79655	3.86	1.96469	6.21289
2.87	1.69411	5.35724	3.37	1.83576	5.80517	3.87	1.96723	6.22093
2.88	1.69706	5.36656	3.38	1.83848	5.81378	3.88	1.96977	6.22896
2.89	1.70000	5.37587	3.39	1.84120	5.82237	3.89	1.97231	6.23699
2.90	1.70294	5.38516	3.40	1.84391	5.83095	3.90	1.97484	6.24500
2.91	1.70587	5.39444	3.41	1.84662	5.83952	3.91	1.97737	6.25300
2.92	1.70880	5.40370	3.42	1.84932	5.84808	3.92	1.97990	6.26099
2.93	1.71172	5.41295	3.43	1.85203	5.85662	3.93	1.98242	6.26897
2.94	1.71464	5.42218	3.44	1.85472	5.86515	3.94	1.98494	6.27694
2.95	1.71756	5.43139	3.45	1.85742	5.87367	3.95	1.98746	6.28490
2.96	1.72047	5.44059	3.46	1.86011	5.88218	3.96	1.98997	6.29285
2.97	1.72337	5.44977	3.47	1.86279	5.89067	3.97	1.99249	6.30079
2.98	1.72627	5.45894	3.48	1.86548	5.89915	3.98	1.99499	6.30872
2.99	1.72916	5.46809	3.49	1.86815	5.90762	3.99	1.99750	6.31664

TABLE IV — SQUARE ROOTS

n	$\sqrt{n}$	$\sqrt{10n}$	n	$\sqrt{n}$	$\sqrt{10n}$	n	$\sqrt{n}$	$\sqrt{10n}$
4.00	2.00000	6.32456	4.50	2.12132	6.70820	5.00	2.23607	7.07107
4.01	2.00250	6.33246	4.51	2.12368	6.71565	5.01	2.23830	7.07814
4.02	2.00499	6.34035	4.52	2.12603	6.72309	5.02	2.24054	7.08520
4.03	2.00749	6.34823	4.53	2.12838	6.73053	5.03	2.24277	7.09225
4.04	2.00998	6.35610	4.54	2.13073	6.73795	5.04	2.24499	7.09930
4.05	2.01246	6.36396	4.55	2.13307	6.74537	5.05	2.24722	7.10634
4.06	2.01494	6.37181	4.56	2.13542	6.75278	5.06	2.24944	7.11337
4.07	2.01742	6.37966	4.57	2.13776	6.76018	5.07	2.25167	7.12039
4.08	2.01990	6.38749	4.58	2.14009	6.76757	5.08	2.25389	7.12741
4.09	2.02237	6.39531	4.59	2.14243	6.77495	5.09	2.25610	7.13442
4.10	2.02485	6.40312	4.60	2.14476	6.78233	5.10	2.25832	7.14143
4.11	2.02731	6.41093	4.61	2.14709	6.78970	5.11	2.26053	7.14843
4.12	2.02978	6.41872	4.62	2.14942	6.79706	5.12	2.26274	7.15542
4.13	2.03224	6.42651	4.63	2.15174	6.80441	5.13	2.26495	7.16240
4.14	2.03470	6.43428	4.64	2.15407	6.81175	5.14	2.26716	7.16938
4.15	2.03715	6.44205	4.65	2.15639	6.81909	5.15	2.26936	7.17635
4.16	2.03961	6.44981	4.66	2.15870	6.82642	5.16	2.27156	7.18331
4.17	2.04206	6.45755	4.67	2.16102	6.83374	5.17	2.27376	7.19027
4.18	2.04450	6.46529	4.68	2.16333	6.84105	5.18	2.27596	7.19722
4.19	2.04695	6.47302	4.69	2.16564	6.84836	5.19	2.27816	7.20417
4.20	2.04939	6.48074	4.70	2.16795	6.85565	5.20	2.28035	7.21110
4.21	2.05183	6.48845	4.71	2.17025	6.86294	5.21	2.28254	7.21803
4.22	2.05426	6.49615	4.72	2.17256	6.87023	5.22	2.28473	7.22496
4.23	2.05670	6.50384	4.73	2.17486	6.87750	5.23	2.28692	7.23187
4.24	2.05913	6.51153	4.74	2.17715	6.88477	5.24	2.28910	7.23878
4.25	2.06155	6.51920	4.75	2.17945	6.89202	5.25	2.29129	7.24569
4.26	2.06398	6.52687	4.76	2.18174	6.89928	5.26	2.29347	7.25259
4.27	2.06640	6.53452	4.77	2.18403	6.90652	5.27	2.29565	7.25948
4.28	2.06882	6.54217	4.78	2.18632	6.91375	5.28	2.29783	7.26636
4.29	2.07123	6.54981	4.79	2.18861	6.92098	5.29	2.30000	7.27324
4.30	2.07364	6.55744	4.80	2.19089	6.92820	5.30	2.30217	7.28011
4.31	2.07605	6.56506	4.81	2.19317	6.93542	5.31	2.30434	7.28697
4.32	2.07846	6.57267	4.82	2.19545	6.94262	5.32	2.30651	7.29383
4.33	2.08087	6.58027	4.83	2.19773	6.94982	5.33	2.30868	7.30068
4.34	2.08327	6.58787	4.84	2.20000	6.95701	5.34	2.31084	7.30753
4.35	2.08567	6.59545	4.85	2.20227	6.96419	5.35	2.31301	7.31437
4.36	2.08806	6.60303	4.86	2.20454	6.97137	5.36	2.31517	7.32120
4.37	2.09045	6.61060	4.87	2.20681	6.97854	5.37	2.31733	7.32803
4.38	2.09284	6.61816	4.88	2.20907	6.98570	5.38	2.31948	7.33485
4.39	2.09523	6.62571	4.89	2.21133	6.99285	5.39	2.32164	7.34166
4.40	2.09762	6.63325	4.90	2.21359	7.00000	5.40	2.32379	7.34847
4.41	2.10000	6.64078	4.91	2.21585	7.00714	5.41	2.32594	7.35527
4.42	2.10238	6.64831	4.92	2.21811	7.01427	5.42	2.32809	7.36206
4.43	2.10476	6.65582	4.93	2.22036	7.02140	5.43	2.33024	7.36885
4.44	2.10713	6.66333	4.94	2.22261	7.02851	5.44	2.33238	7.37564
4.45	2.10950	6.67083	4.95	2.22486	7.03562	5.45	2.33452	7.38241
4.46	2.11187	6.67832	4.96	2.22711	7.04273	5.46	2.33666	7.38918
4.47	2.11424	6.68581	4.97	2.22935	7.04982	5.47	2.33880	7.39594
4.48	2.11660	6.69328	4.98	2.23159	7.05691	5.48	2.34094	7.40270
4.49	2.11896	6.70075	4.99	2.23383	7.06399	5.49	2.34307	7.40945

TABLE IV — SQUARE ROOTS

n	$\sqrt{n}$	$\sqrt{10n}$	n	$\sqrt{n}$	$\sqrt{10n}$	n	$\sqrt{n}$	$\sqrt{10n}$
5.50	2.34521	7.41620	6.00	2.44949	7.74597	6.50	2.54951	8.06226
5.51	2.34734	7.42294	6.01	2.45153	7.75242	6.51	2.55147	8.06846
5.52	2.34947	7.42967	6.02	2.45357	7.75887	6.52	2.55343	8.07465
5.53	2.35160	7.43640	6.03	2.45561	7.76531	6.53	2.55539	8.08084
5.54	2.35372	7.44312	6.04	2.45764	7.77174	6.54	2.55734	8.08703
5.55	2.35584	7.44983	6.05	2.45967	7.77817	6.55	2.55930	8.09321
5.56	2.35797	7.45654	6.06	2.46171	7.78460	6.56	2.56125	8.09938
5.57	2.36008	7.46324	6.07	2.46374	7.79102	6.57	2.56320	8.10555
5.58	2.36220	7.46994	6.08	2.46577	7.79744	6.58	2.56515	8.11172
5.59	2.36432	7.47663	6.09	2.46779	7.80385	6.59	2.56710	8.11788
5.60	2.36643	7.48331	6.10	2.46982	7.81025	6.60	2.56905	8.12404
5.61	2.36854	7.48999	6.11	2.47184	7.81665	6.61	2.57099	8.13019
5.62	2.37065	7.49667	6.12	2.47386	7.82304	6.62	2.57294	8.13634
5.63	2.37276	7.50333	6.13	2.47588	7.82943	6.63	2.57488	8.14248
5.64	2.37487	7.50999	6.14	2.47790	7.83582	6.64	2.57682	8.14862
5.65	2.37697	7.51665	6.15	2.47992	7.84219	6.65	2.57876	8.15475
5.66	2.37908	7.52330	6.16	2.48193	7.84857	6.66	2.58070	8.16088
5.67	2.38118	7.52994	6.17	2.48395	7.85493	6.67	2.58263	8.16701
5.68	2.38328	7.53658	6.18	2.48596	7.86130	6.68	2.58457	8.17313
5.69	2.38537	7.54321	6.19	2.48797	7.86766	6.69	2.58650	8.17924
5.70	2.38747	7.54983	6.20	2.48998	7.87401	6.70	2.58844	8.18535
5.71	2.38956	7.55645	6.21	2.49199	7.88036	6.71	2.59037	8.19146
5.72	2.39165	7.56307	6.22	2.49399	7.88670	6.72	2.59230	8.19756
5.73	2.39374	7.56968	6.23	2.49600	7.89303	6.73	2.59422	8.20366
5.74	2.39583	7.57628	6.24	2.49800	7.89937	6.74	2.59615	8.20975
5.75	2.39792	7.58288	6.25	2.50000	7.90569	6.75	2.59808	8.21584
5.76	2.40000	7.58947	6.26	2.50200	7.91202	6.76	2.60000	8.22192
5.77	2.40208	7.59605	6.27	2.50400	7.91833	6.77	2.60192	8.22800
5.78	2.40416	7.60263	6.28	2.50599	7.92465	6.78	2.60384	8.23408
5.79	2.40624	7.60920	6.29	2.50799	7.93095	6.79	2.60576	8.24015
5.80	2.40832	7.61577	6.30	2.50998	7.93725	6.80	2.60768	8.24621
5.81	2.41039	7.62234	6.31	2.51197	7.94355	6.81	2.60960	8.25227
5.82	2.41247	7.62889	6.32	2.51396	7.94984	6.82	2.61151	8.25833
5.83	2.41454	7.63544	6.33	2.51595	7.95613	6.83	2.61343	8.26438
5.84	2.41661	7.64199	6.34	2.51794	7.96241	6.84	2.61534	8.27043
5.85	2.41868	7.64853	6.35	2.51992	7.96869	6.85	2.61725	8.27647
5.86	2.42074	7.65506	6.36	2.52190	7.97496	6.86	2.61916	8.28251
5.87	2.42281	7.66159	6.37	2.52389	7.98123	6.87	2.62107	8.28855
5.88	2.42487	7.66812	6.38	2.52587	7.98749	6.88	2.62298	8.29458
5.89	2.42693	7.67463	6.39	2.52784	7.99375	6.89	2.62488	8.30060
5.90	2.42899	7.68115	6.40	2.52982	8.00000	6.90	2.62679	8.30662
5.91	2.43105	7.68765	6.41	2.53180	8.00625	6.91	2.62869	8.31264
5.92	2.43311	7.69415	6.42	2.53377	8.01249	6.92	2.63059	8.31865
5.93	2.43516	7.70065	6.43	2.53574	8.01873	6.93	2.63249	8.32466
5.94	2.43721	7.70714	6.44	2.53772	8.02496	6.94	2.63439	8.33067
5.95	2.43926	7.71362	6.45	2.53969	8.03119	6.95	2.63629	8.33667
5.96	2.44131	7.72010	6.46	2.54165	8.03741	6.96	2.63818	8.34266
5.97	2.44336	7.72658	6.47	2.54362	8.04363	6.97	2.64008	8.34865
5.98	2.44540	7.73305	6.48	2.54558	8.04984	6.98	2.64197	8.35464
5.99	2.44745	7.73951	6.49	2.54755	8.05605	6.99	2.64386	8.36062

TABLE IV — SQUARE ROOTS

n	$\sqrt{n}$	$\sqrt{10n}$	n	$\sqrt{n}$	$\sqrt{10n}$	n	$\sqrt{n}$	$\sqrt{10n}$
7.00	2.64575	8.36660	7.50	2.73861	8.66025	8.00	2.82843	8.94427
7.01	2.64764	8.37257	7.51	2.74044	8.66603	8.01	2.83019	8.94986
7.02	2.64953	8.37854	7.52	2.74226	8.67179	8.02	2.83196	8.95545
7.03	2.65141	8.38451	7.53	2.74408	8.67756	8.03	2.83373	8.96103
7.04	2.65330	8.39047	7.54	2.74591	8.68332	8.04	2.83549	8.96660
7.05	2.65518	8.39643	7.55	2.74773	8.68907	8.05	2.83725	8.97218
7.06	2.65707	8.40238	7.56	2.74955	8.69483	8.06	2.83901	8.97775
7.07	2.65895	8.40833	7.57	2.75136	8.70057	8.07	2.84077	8.98332
7.08	2.66083	8.41427	7.58	2.75318	8.70632	8.08	2.84253	8.98888
7.09	2.66271	8.42021	7.59	2.75500	8.71206	8.09	2.84429	8.99444
7.10	2.66458	8.42615	7.60	2.75681	8.71780	8.10	2.84605	9.00000
7.11	2.66646	8.43208	7.61	2.75862	8.72353	8.11	2.84781	9.00555
7.12	2.66833	8.43801	7.62	2.76043	8.72926	8.12	2.84956	9.01110
7.13	2.67021	8.44393	7.63	2.76225	8.73499	8.13	2.85132	9.01665
7.14	2.67208	8.44985	7.64	2.76405	8.74071	8.14	2.85307	9.02219
7.15	2.67395	8.45577	7.65	2.76586	8.74643	8.15	2.85482	9.02774
7.16	2.67582	8.46168	7.66	2.76767	8.75214	8.16	2.85657	9.03327
7.17	2.67769	8.46759	7.67	2.76948	8.75785	8.17	2.85832	9.03881
7.18	2.67955	8.47349	7.68	2.77128	8.76356	8.18	2.86007	9.04434
7.19	2.68142	8.47939	7.69	2.77308	8.76926	8.19	2.86182	9.04986
7.20	2.68328	8.48528	7.70	2.77489	8.77496	8.20	2.86356	9.05539
7.21	2.68514	8.49117	7.71	2.77669	8.78066	8.21	2.86531	9.06091
7.22	2.68701	8.49706	7.72	2.77849	8.78635	8.22	2.86705	9.06642
7.23	2.68887	8.50294	7.73	2.78029	8.79204	8.23	2.86880	9.07193
7.24	2.69072	8.50882	7.74	2.78209	8.79773	8.24	2.87054	9.07744
7.25	2.69258	8.51469	7.75	2.78388	8.80341	8.25	2.87228	9.08295
7.26	2.69444	8.52056	7.76	2.78568	8.80909	8.26	2.87402	9.08845
7.27	2.69629	8.52643	7.77	2.78747	8.81476	8.27	2.87576	9.09395
7.28	2.69815	8.53229	7.78	2.78927	8.82043	8.28	2.87750	9.09945
7.29	2.70000	8.53815	7.79	2.79106	8.82610	8.29	2.87924	9.10494
7.30	2.70185	8.54400	7.80	2.79285	8.83176	8.30	2.88097	9.11043
7.31	2.70370	8.54985	7.81	2.79464	8.83742	8.31	2.88271	9.11592
7.32	2.70555	8.55570	7.82	2.79643	8.84308	8.32	2.88444	9.12140
7.33	2.70740	8.56154	7.83	2.79821	8.84873	8.33	2.88617	9.12688
7.34	2.70924	8.56738	7.84	2.80000	8.85438	8.34	2.88791	9.13236
7.35	2.71109	8.57321	7.85	2.80179	8.86002	8.35	2.88964	9.13783
7.36	2.71293	8.57904	7.86	2.80357	8.86566	8.36	2.89137	9.14330
7.37	2.71477	8.58487	7.87	2.80535	8.87130	8.37	2.89310	9.14877
7.38	2.71662	8.59069	7.88	2.80713	8.87694	8.38	2.89482	9.15423
7.39	2.71846	8.59651	7.89	2.80891	8.88257	8.39	2.89655	9.15969
7.40	2.72029	8.60233	7.90	2.81069	8.88819	8.40	2.89828	9.16515
7.41	2.72213	8.60814	7.91	2.81247	8.89382	8.41	2.90000	9.17061
7.42	2.72397	8.61394	7.92	2.81425	8.89944	8.42	2.90172	9.17606
7.43	2.72580	8.61974	7.93	2.81603	8.90505	8.43	2.90345	9.18150
7.44	2.72764	8.62554	7.94	2.81780	8.91067	8.44	2.90517	9.18695
7.45	2.72947	8.63134	7.95	2.81957	8.91628	8.45	2.90689	9.19239
7.46	2.73130	8.63713	7.96	2.82135	8.92188	8.46	2.90861	9.19783
7.47	2.73313	8.64292	7.97	2.82312	8.92749	8.47	2.91033	9.20326
7.48	2.73496	8.64870	7.98	2.82489	8.93308	8.48	2.91204	9.20869
7.49	2.73679	8.65448	7.99	2.82666	8.93868	8.49	2.91376	9.21412

TABLE IV — SQUARE ROOTS

n	$\sqrt{n}$	$\sqrt{10n}$	n	$\sqrt{n}$	$\sqrt{10n}$	n	$\sqrt{n}$	$\sqrt{10n}$
8.50	2.91548	9.21954	9.00	3.00000	9.48683	9.50	3.08221	9.74679
8.51	2.91719	9.22497	9.01	3.00167	9.49210	9.51	3.08383	9.75192
8.52	2.91890	9.23038	9.02	3.00333	9.49737	9.52	3.08545	9.75705
8.53	2.92062	9.23580	9.03	3.00500	9.50263	9.53	3.08707	9.76217
8.54	2.92233	9.24121	9.04	3.00666	9.50789	9.54	3.08869	9.76729
8.55	2.92404	9.24662	9.05	3.00832	9.51315	9.55	3.09031	9.77241
8.56	2.92575	9.25203	9.06	3.00998	9.51840	9.56	3.09192	9.77753
8.57	2.92746	9.25743	9.07	3.01164	9.52365	9.57	3.09354	9.78264
8.58	2.92916	9.26283	9.08	3.01330	9.52890	9.58	3.09516	9.78775
8.59	2.93087	9.26823	9.09	3.01496	9.53415	9.59	3.09677	9.79285
8.60	2.93258	9.27362	9.10	3.01662	9.53939	9.60	3.09839	9.79796
8.61	2.93428	9.27901	9.11	3.01828	9.54463	9.61	3.10000	9.80306
8.62	2.93598	9.28440	9.12	3.01993	9.54987	9.62	3.10161	9.80816
8.63	2.93769	9.28978	9.13	3.02159	9.55510	9.63	3.10322	9.81326
8.64	2.93939	9.29516	9.14	3.02324	9.56033	9.64	3.10483	9.81835
8.65	2.94109	9.30054	9.15	3.02490	9.56556	9.65	3.10644	9.82344
8.66	2.94279	9.30591	9.16	3.02655	9.57079	9.66	3.10805	9.82853
8.67	2.94449	9.31128	9.17	3.02820	9.57601	9.67	3.10966	9.83362
8.68	2.94618	9.31665	9.18	3.02985	9.58123	9.68	3.11127	9.83870
8.69	2.94788	9.32202	9.19	3.03150	9.58645	9.69	3.11288	9.84378
8.70	2.94958	9.32738	9.20	3.03315	9.59166	9.70	3.11448	9.84886
8.71	2.95127	9.33274	9.21	3.03480	9.59687	9.71	3.11609	9.85393
8.72	2.95296	9.33809	9.22	3.03645	9.60208	9.72	3.11769	9.85901
8.73	2.95466	9.34345	9.23	3.03809	9.60729	9.73	3.11929	9.86408
8.74	2.95635	9.34880	9.24	3.03974	9.61249	9.74	3.12090	9.86914
8.75	2.95804	9.35414	9.25	3.04138	9.61769	9.75	3.12250	9.87421
8.76	2.95973	9.35949	9.26	3.04302	9.62289	9.76	3.12410	9.87927
8.77	2.96142	9.36483	9.27	3.04467	9.62808	9.77	3.12570	9.88433
8.78	2.96311	9.37017	9.28	3.04631	9.63328	9.78	3.12730	9.88939
8.79	2.96479	9.37550	9.29	3.04795	9.63846	9.79	3.12890	9.89444
8.80	2.96648	9.38083	9.30	3.04959	9.64365	9.80	3.13050	9.89949
8.81	2.96816	9.38616	9.31	3.05123	9.64883	9.81	3.13209	9.90454
8.82	2.96985	9.39149	9.32	3.05287	9.65401	9.82	3.13369	9.90959
8.83	2.97153	9.39681	9.33	3.05450	9.65919	9.83	3.13528	9.91464
8.84	2.97321	9.40213	9.34	3.05614	9.66437	9.84	3.13688	9.91968
8.85	2.97489	9.40744	9.35	3.05778	9.66954	9.85	3.13847	9.92472
8.86	2.97658	9.41276	9.36	3.05941	9.67471	9.86	3.14006	9.92975
8.87	2.97825	9.41807	9.37	3.06105	9.67988	9.87	3.14166	9.93479
8.88	2.97993	9.42338	9.38	3.06268	9.68504	9.88	3.14325	9.93982
8.89	2.98161	9.42868	9.39	3.06431	9.69020	9.89	3.14484	9.94485
8.90	2.98329	9.43398	9.40	3.06594	9.69536	9.90	3.14643	9.94987
8.91	2.98496	9.43928	9.41	3.06757	9.70052	9.91	3.14802	9.95490
8.92	2.98664	9.44458	9.42	3.06920	9.70567	9.92	3.14960	9.95992
8.93	2.98831	9.44987	9.43	3.07083	9.71082	9.93	3.15119	9.96494
8.94	2.98998	9.45516	9.44	3.07246	9.71597	9.94	3.15278	9.96995
8.95	2.99166	9.46044	9.45	3.07409	9.72111	9.95	3.15436	9.97497
8.96	2.99333	9.46573	9.46	3.07571	9.72625	9.96	3.15595	9.97998
8.97	2.99500	9.47101	9.47	3.07734	9.73139	9.97	3.15753	9.98499
8.98	2.99666	9.47629	9.48	3.07896	9.73653	9.98	3.15911	9.98999
8.99	2.99833	9.48156	9.49	3.08058	9.74166	9.99	3.16070	9.99500

TABLE V — RECIPROCALS, $1/n$

n	0	1	2	3	4	5	6	7	8	9
.0	········	100.0	50.00	33.33	25.00	20.00	16.67	14.29	12.50	11.11
.1	10.0000	9.091	8.333	7.692	7.143	6.667	6.250	5.882	5.556	5.263
.2	5.0000	4.762	4.545	4.348	4.167	4.000	3.846	3.704	3.571	3.448
.3	3.3333	3.226	3.125	3.030	2.941	2.857	2.778	2.703	2.632	2.564
.4	2.5000	2.439	2.381	2.326	2.273	2.222	2.174	2.128	2.083	2.041
.5	2.0000	*9608	*9231	*8868	*8519	*8182	*7857	*7544	*7241	*6949
.6	1.6667	6393	6129	5873	5625	5385	5152	4925	4706	4493
.7	1.4286	4085	3889	3699	3514	3333	3158	2987	2821	2658
.8	1.2500	2346	2195	2048	1905	1765	1628	1494	1364	1236
.9	1.1111	0989	0870	0753	0638	0526	0417	0309	0204	0101
1.0	1.0000	*9901	*9804	*9709	*9615	*9524	*9434	*9346	*9259	*9174
1.1	0.9091	9009	8929	8850	8772	8696	8621	8547	8475	8403
1.2	0.8333	8264	8197	8130	8065	8000	7937	7874	7813	7752
1.3	0.7692	7634	7576	7519	7463	7407	7353	7299	7246	7194
1.4	0.7143	7092	7042	6993	6944	6897	6849	6803	6757	6711
1.5	0.6667	6623	6579	6536	6494	6452	6410	6369	6329	6289
1.6	0.6250	6211	6173	6135	6098	6061	6024	5988	5952	5917
1.7	0.5882	5848	5814	5780	5747	5714	5682	5650	5618	5587
1.8	0.5556	5525	5495	5464	5435	5405	5376	5348	5319	5291
1.9	0.5263	5236	5208	5181	5155	5128	5102	5076	5051	5025
2.0	0.5000	4975	4950	4926	4902	4878	4854	4831	4808	4785
2.1	0.4762	4739	4717	4695	4673	4651	4630	4608	4587	4566
2.2	0.4545	4525	4505	4484	4464	4444	4425	4405	4386	4367
2.3	0.4348	4329	4310	4292	4274	4255	4237	4219	4202	4184
2.4	0.4167	4149	4132	4115	4098	4082	4065	4049	4032	4016
2.5	0.4000	3984	3968	3953	3937	3922	3906	3891	3876	3861
2.6	0.3846	3831	3817	3802	3788	3774	3759	3745	3731	3717
2.7	0.3704	3690	3676	3663	3650	3636	3623	3610	3597	3584
2.8	0.3571	3559	3546	3534	3521	3509	3497	3484	3472	3460
2.9	0.3448	3436	3425	3413	3401	3390	3378	3367	3356	3344
3.0	0.3333	3322	3311	3300	3289	3279	3268	3257	3247	3236
3.1	0.3226	3215	3205	3195	3185	3175	3165	3155	3145	3135
3.2	0.3125	3115	3106	3096	3086	3077	3067	3058	3049	3040
3.3	0.3030	3021	3012	3003	2994	2985	2976	2967	2959	2950
3.4	0.2941	2933	2924	2915	2907	2899	2890	2882	2874	2865
3.5	0.2857	2849	2841	2833	2825	2817	2809	2801	2793	2786
3.6	0.2778	2770	2762	2755	2747	2740	2732	2725	2717	2710
3.7	0.2703	2695	2688	2681	2674	2667	2660	2653	2646	2639
3.8	0.2632	2625	2618	2611	2604	2597	2591	2584	2577	2571
3.9	0.2564	2558	2551	2545	2538	2532	2525	2519	2513	2506
4.0	0.2500	2494	2488	2481	2475	2469	2463	2457	2451	2445
4.1	0.2439	2433	2427	2421	2415	2410	2404	2398	2392	2387
4.2	0.2381	2375	2370	2364	2358	2353	2347	2342	2336	2331
4.3	0.2326	2320	2315	2309	2304	2299	2294	2288	2283	2278
4.4	0.2273	2268	2262	2257	2252	2247	2242	2237	2232	2227
4.5	0.2222	2217	2212	2208	2203	2198	2193	2188	2183	2179
4.6	0.2174	2169	2165	2160	2155	2151	2146	2141	2137	2132
4.7	0.2128	2123	2119	2114	2110	2105	2101	2096	2092	2088
4.8	0.2083	2079	2075	2070	2066	2062	2058	2053	2049	2045
4.9	0.2041	2037	2033	2028	2024	2020	2016	2012	2008	2004
5.0	0.2000	1996	1992	1988	1984	1980	1976	1972	1969	1965

TABLE V — RECIPROCALS, $1/n$

n	0	1	2	3	4	5	6	7	8	9
5.0	0.2000	1996	1992	1988	1984	1980	1976	1972	1969	1965
5.1	0.1961	1957	1953	1949	1946	1942	1938	1934	1931	1927
5.2	0.1923	1919	1916	1912	1908	1905	1901	1898	1894	1890
5.3	0.1887	1883	1880	1876	1873	1869	1866	1862	1859	1855
5.4	0.1852	1848	1845	1842	1838	1835	1832	1828	1825	1821
5.5	0.1818	1815	1812	1808	1805	1802	1799	1795	1792	1789
5.6	0.1786	1783	1779	1776	1773	1770	1767	1764	1761	1757
5.7	0.1754	1751	1748	1745	1742	1739	1736	1733	1730	1727
5.8	0.1724	1721	1718	1715	1712	1709	1706	1704	1701	1698
5.9	0.1695	1692	1689	1686	1684	1681	1678	1675	1672	1669
6.0	0.1667	1664	1661	1658	1656	1653	1650	1647	1645	1642
6.1	0.1639	1637	1634	1631	1629	1626	1623	1621	1618	1616
6.2	0.1613	1610	1608	1605	1603	1600	1597	1595	1592	1590
6.3	0.1587	1585	1582	1580	1577	1575	1572	1570	1567	1565
6.4	0.1563	1560	1558	1555	1553	1550	1548	1546	1543	1541
6.5	0.1538	1536	1534	1531	1529	1527	1524	1522	1520	1517
6.6	0.1515	1513	1511	1508	1506	1504	1502	1499	1497	1495
6.7	0.1493	1490	1488	1486	1484	1481	1479	1477	1475	1473
6.8	0.1471	1468	1466	1464	1462	1460	1458	1456	1453	1451
6.9	0.1449	1447	1445	1443	1441	1439	1437	1435	1433	1431
7.0	0.1429	1427	1425	1422	1420	1418	1416	1414	1412	1410
7.1	0.1408	1406	1404	1403	1401	1399	1397	1395	1393	1391
7.2	0.1389	1387	1385	1383	1381	1379	1377	1376	1374	1372
7.3	0.1370	1368	1366	1364	1362	1361	1359	1357	1355	1353
7.4	0.1351	1350	1348	1346	1344	1342	1340	1339	1337	1335
7.5	0.1333	1332	1330	1328	1326	1325	1323	1321	1319	1318
7.6	0.1316	1314	1312	1311	1309	1307	1305	1304	1302	1300
7.7	0.1299	1297	1295	1294	1292	1290	1289	1287	1285	1284
7.8	0.1282	1280	1279	1277	1276	1274	1272	1271	1269	1267
7.9	0.1266	1264	1263	1261	1259	1258	1256	1255	1253	1252
8.0	0.1250	1248	1247	1245	1244	1242	1241	1239	1238	1236
8.1	0.1235	1233	1232	1230	1229	1227	1225	1224	1222	1221
8.2	0.1220	1218	1217	1215	1214	1212	1211	1209	1208	1206
8.3	0.1205	1203	1202	1200	1199	1198	1196	1195	1193	1192
8.4	0.1190	1189	1188	1186	1185	1183	1182	1181	1179	1178
8.5	0.1176	1175	1174	1172	1171	1170	1168	1167	1166	1164
8.6	0.1163	1161	1160	1159	1157	1156	1155	1153	1152	1151
8.7	0.1149	1148	1147	1145	1144	1143	1142	1140	1139	1138
8.8	0.1136	1135	1134	1133	1131	1130	1129	1127	1126	1125
8.9	0.1124	1122	1121	1120	1119	1117	1116	1115	1114	1112
9.0	0.1111	1110	1109	1107	1106	1105	1104	1103	1101	1100
9.1	0.1099	1098	1096	1095	1094	1093	1092	1091	1089	1088
9.2	0.1087	1086	1085	1083	1082	1081	1080	1079	1078	1076
9.3	0.1075	1074	1073	1072	1071	1070	1068	1067	1066	1065
9.4	0.1064	1063	1062	1060	1059	1058	1057	1056	1055	1054
9.5	0.1053	1052	1050	1049	1048	1047	1046	1045	1044	1043
9.6	0.1042	1041	1040	1038	1037	1036	1035	1034	1033	1032
9.7	0.1031	1030	1029	1028	1027	1026	1025	1024	1022	1021
9.8	0.1020	1019	1018	1017	1016	1015	1014	1013	1012	1011
9.9	0.1010	1009	1008	1007	1006	1005	1004	1003	1002	1001

TABLE VI

VALUES OF THE FUNCTION $y = \dfrac{1}{\sqrt{2\pi}} e^{-\frac{1}{2}t^2}$

t	0	1	2	3	4	5	6	7	8	9
0.0	0.39894	39892	39886	39876	39862	39844	39822	39797	39767	39733
0.1	0.39695	39654	39608	39559	39505	39448	39387	39322	39253	39181
0.2	0.39104	39024	38940	38853	38762	38667	38568	38466	38361	38251
0.3	0.38139	38023	37903	37780	37654	37524	37391	37255	37115	36973
0.4	0.36827	36678	36526	36371	36213	36053	35889	35723	35553	35381
0.5	0.35207	35029	34849	34667	34482	34294	34105	33912	33718	33521
0.6	0.33322	33121	32918	32713	32506	32297	32086	31874	31659	31443
0.7	0.31225	31006	30785	30563	30339	30114	29887	29659	29431	29200
0.8	0.28969	28737	28504	28269	28034	27798	27562	27324	27086	26848
0.9	0.26609	26369	26129	25888	25647	25406	25164	24923	24681	24439
1.0	0.24197	23955	23713	23471	23230	22988	22747	22506	22265	22025
1.1	0.21785	21546	21307	21069	20831	20594	20357	20121	19886	19652
1.2	0.19419	19186	18954	18724	18494	18265	18037	17810	17585	17360
1.3	0.17137	16915	16694	16474	16256	16038	15822	15608	15395	15183
1.4	0.14973	14764	14556	14350	14146	13943	13742	13542	13344	13147
1.5	0.12952	12758	12566	12376	12188	12001	11816	11632	11450	11270
1.6	0.11092	10915	10741	10567	10396	10226	10059	09893	09728	09566
1.7	0.09405	09246	09089	08933	08780	08628	08478	08329	08183	08038
1.8	0.07895	07754	07614	07477	07341	07206	07074	06943	06814	06687
1.9	0.06562	06438	06316	06195	06077	05959	05844	05730	05618	05508
2.0	0.05399	05292	05186	05082	04980	04879	04780	04682	04586	04491
2.1	0.04398	04307	04217	04128	04041	03955	03871	03788	03706	03626
2.2	0.03547	03470	03394	03319	03246	03174	03103	03034	02965	02898
2.3	0.02833	02768	02705	02643	02582	02522	02463	02406	02349	02294
2.4	0.02239	02186	02134	02083	02033	01984	01936	01889	01842	01797
2.5	0.01753	01709	01667	01625	01585	01545	01506	01468	01431	01394
2.6	0.01358	01323	01289	01256	01223	01191	01160	01130	01100	01071
2.7	0.01042	01014	00987	00961	00935	00909	00885	00861	00837	00814
2.8	0.00792	00770	00748	00727	00707	00687	00668	00649	00631	00613
2.9	0.00595	00578	00562	00545	00530	00514	00499	00485	00471	00457
3.0	0.00443	00430	00417	00405	00393	00381	00370	00358	00348	00337
3.1	0.00327	00317	00307	00298	00288	00279	00271	00262	00254	00246
3.2	0.00238	00231	00224	00216	00210	00203	00196	00190	00184	00178
3.3	0.00172	00167	00161	00156	00151	00146	00141	00136	00132	00127
3.4	0.00123	00119	00115	00111	00107	00104	00100	00097	00094	00090
3.5	0.00087	00084	00081	00079	00076	00073	00071	00068	00066	00063
3.6	0.00061	00059	00057	00055	00053	00051	00049	00047	00046	00044
3.7	0.00042	00041	00039	00038	00037	00035	00034	00033	00031	00030
3.8	0.00029	00028	00027	00026	00025	00024	00023	00022	00021	00021
3.9	0.00020	00019	00018	00018	00017	00016	00016	00015	00014	00014

TABLE VII

VALUES OF $I(t)$, AREA UNDER NORMAL PROBABILITY CURVE

t	0	1	2	3	4	5	6	7	8	9
0.0	0.00000	00399	00798	01197	01595	01994	02392	02790	03188	03586
0.1	0.03983	04380	04776	05172	05567	05962	06356	06749	07142	07535
0.2	0.07926	08317	08706	09095	09483	09871	10257	10642	11026	11409
0.3	0.11791	12172	12552	12930	13307	13683	14058	14431	14803	15173
0.4	0.15542	15910	16276	16640	17003	17364	17724	18082	18439	18793
0.5	0.19146	19497	19847	20194	20540	20884	21226	21566	21904	22240
0.6	0.22575	22907	23237	23565	23891	24215	24537	24857	25175	25490
0.7	0.25804	26115	26424	26730	27035	27337	27637	27935	28230	28524
0.8	0.28814	29103	29389	29673	29955	30234	30511	30785	31057	31327
0.9	0.31594	31859	32121	32381	32639	32894	33147	33398	33646	33891
1.0	0.34134	34375	34614	34850	35083	35314	35543	35769	35993	36214
1.1	0.36433	36650	36864	37076	37286	37493	37698	37900	38100	38298
1.2	0.38493	38686	38877	39065	39251	39435	39617	39796	39973	40147
1.3	0.40320	40490	40658	40824	40988	41149	41309	41466	41621	41774
1.4	0.41924	42073	42220	42364	42507	42647	42786	42922	43056	43189
1.5	0.43319	43448	43574	43699	43822	43943	44062	44179	44295	44408
1.6	0.44520	44630	44738	44845	44950	45053	45154	45254	45352	45449
1.7	0.45543	45637	45728	45818	45907	45994	46080	46164	46246	46327
1.8	0.46407	46485	46562	46638	46712	46784	46856	46926	46995	47062
1.9	0.47128	47193	47257	47320	47381	47441	47500	47558	47615	47670
2.0	0.47725	47778	47831	47882	47932	47982	48030	48077	48124	48169
2.1	0.48214	48257	48300	48341	48382	48422	48461	48500	48537	48574
2.2	0.48610	48645	48679	48713	48745	48778	48809	48840	48870	48899
2.3	0.48928	48956	48983	49010	49036	49061	49086	49111	49134	49158
2.4	0.49180	49202	49224	49245	49266	49286	49305	49324	49343	49361
2.5	0.49379	49396	49413	49430	49446	49461	49477	49492	49506	49520
2.6	0.49534	49547	49560	49573	49585	49598	49609	49621	49632	49643
2.7	0.49653	49664	49674	49683	49693	49702	49711	49720	49728	49736
2.8	0.49744	49752	49760	49767	49774	49781	49788	49795	49801	49807
2.9	0.49813	49819	49825	49831	49836	49841	49846	49851	49856	49861
3.0	0.49865	49869	49874	49878	49882	49886	49889	49893	49897	49900
3.1	0.49903	49906	49910	49913	49916	49918	49921	49924	49926	49929
3.2	0.49931	49934	49936	49938	49940	49942	49944	49946	49948	49950
3.3	0.49952	49953	49955	49957	49958	49960	49961	49962	49964	49965
3.4	0.49966	49968	49969	49970	49971	49972	49973	49974	49975	49976
3.5	0.49977	49978	49978	49979	49980	49981	49981	49982	49983	49983
3.6	0.49984	49985	49985	49986	49986	49987	49987	49988	49988	49989
3.7	0.49989	49990	49990	49990	49991	49991	49992	49992	49992	49992
3.8	0.49993	49993	49993	49994	49994	49994	49994	49995	49995	49995
3.9	0.49995	49995	49996	49996	49996	49996	49996	49996	49997	49997

TABLE VIII

TEST FOR GOODNESS OF FIT
VALUES OF THE PEARSON PROBABILITY, P

χ^2	$n=3$	$n=4$	$n=5$	$n=6$
1	.60653 06597	.80125 195(69)	.90979 598(96)	.96256 577(32)
2	.36787 94412	.57240 670(44)	.73575 888(23)	.84914 503(60)
3	.22313 01601	.39162 517(63)	.55782 540(04)	.69998 583(59)
4	.13533 52832	.26146 412(99)	.40600 584(97)	.54941 595(12)
5	.08208 49986	.17179 714(43)	.28729 749(52)	.41588 018(72)
6	.04978 70684	.11161 022(51)	.19914 827(35)	.30621 891(86)
7	.03019 73834	.07189 777(25)	.13588 822(54)	.22064 030(80)
8	.01831 56389	.04601 170(57)	.09157 819(44)	.15623 562(76)
9	.01110 89965	.02929 088(65)	.06109 948(10)	.10906 415(79)
10	.00673 79470	.01856 612(57)	.04042 768(20)	.07523 523(64)
11	.00408 67714	.01172 587(55)	.02656 401(44)	.05137 998(34)
12	.00247 87522	.00738 316(05)	.01735 126(52)	.03478 778(05)
13	.00150 34392	.00463 660(55)	.01127 579(39)	.02337 876(81)
14	.00091 18820	.00290 515(28)	.00729 505(57)	.01560 941(61)
15	.00055 30844	.00181 664(90)	.00470 121(71)	.01036 233(79)
16	.00033 54626	.00113 398(42)	.00301 916(37)	.00684 407(35)
17	.00020 34684	.00070 674(24)	.00193 294(95)	.00449 979(70)
18	.00012 34098	.00043 984(97)	.00123 409(80)	.00294 640(46)
19	.00007 48518	.00027 339(89)	.00078 594(42)	.00192 213(68)
20	.00004 53999	.00016 974(16)	.00049 939(92)	.00124 972(97)
21	.00002 75364	.00010 527(62)	.00031 666(92)	.00081 005(96)
22	.00001 67017	.00006 523(11)	.00020 042(04)	.00052 359(83)
23	.00001 01301	.00004 038(30)	.00012 662(62)	.00033 756(61)
24	.00000 61442	.00002 498(00)	.00007 987(48)	.00021 711(29)
25	.00000 37267	.00001 544(05)	.00005 030(98)	.00013 933(73)
26	.00000 22603	.00000 953(74)	.00003 164(46)	.00008 923(60)
27	.00000 13710	.00000 600(96)	.00001 987(89)	.00005 716(47)
28	.00000 08315	.00000 361(89)	.00001 247(29)	.00003 638(57)
29	.00000 05043	.00000 223(94)	.00000 781(74)	.00002 318(76)
30	.00000 03059	.00000 137(09)	.00000 489(44)	.00001 473(95)
40	.00000 00021	.00000 001(07)	.00000 004(12)	.00000 014(93)
50	.00000 00000	.00000 000(00)	.00000 000(03)	.00000 000(13)
60	.00000 00000	.00000 000(00)	.00000 000(00)	.00000 000(00)
70	.00000 00000	.00000 000(00)	.00000 000(00)	.00000 000(00)

TABLE VIII

VALUES OF THE PEARSON PROBABILITY, P

χ^2	$n=7$	$n=8$	$n=9$	$n=10$
1	.98561 232(20)	.99482 853(65)	.99824 837(74)	.99943 750(26)
2	.91969 860(29)	.95984 036(87)	.98101 184(31)	.99146 760(65)
3	.80884 683(05)	.88500 223(17)	.93435 754(56)	.96429 497(27)
4	.67667 641(62)	.77977 740(84)	.85712 346(05)	.91141 252(67)
5	.54381 311(59)	.65996 323(00)	.75757 613(31)	.83430 826(07)
6	.42319 008(11)	.53974 935(08)	.64723 188(88)	.73991 829(27)
7	.32084 719(89)	.42887 985(77)	.53663 266(80)	.63711 940(74)
8	.23810 330(56)	.33259 390(26)	.43347 012(03)	.53414 621(68)
9	.17357 807(09)	.25265 604(65)	.34229 595(58)	.43727 418(87)
10	.12465 201(95)	.18857 345(78)	.26502 591(53)	.35048 520(26)
11	.08837 643(24)	.13861 902(08)	.20169 919(87)	.27570 893(67)
12	.06196 880(44)	.10055 886(85)	.15120 388(28)	.21330 930(51)
13	.04303 594(69)	.07210 839(10)	.11184 961(16)	.16260 626(22)
14	.02963 616(39)	.05118 135(34)	.08176 541(63)	.12232 522(80)
15	.02025 671(51)	.03599 940(48)	.05914 545(98)	.09093 597(66)
16	.01375 396(77)	.02511 635(89)	.04238 011(41)	.06688 158(26)
17	.00928 324(43)	.01739 618(25)	.03010 907(97)	.04871 597(63)
18	.00623 219(51)	.01197 000(23)	.02122 648(63)	.03517 353(94)
19	.00416 363(30)	.00818 734(10)	.01485 964(77)	.02519 289(50)
20	.00276 939(57)	.00556 968(23)	.01033 605(07)	.01791 240(37)
21	.00183 461(59)	.00377 015(01)	.00714 742(96)	.01265 042(13)
22	.00121 087(33)	.00254 041(40)	.00491 586(73)	.00887 897(75)
23	.00079 647(86)	.00170 458(70)	.00336 424(63)	.00619 629(64)
24	.00052 225(81)	.00113 935(12)	.00229 179(12)	.00430 131(09)
25	.00034 145(46)	.00075 880(38)	.00155 455(79)	.00297 118(41)
26	.00022 264(24)	.00050 366(86)	.00105 029(97)	.00204 298(97)
27	.00014 480(76)	.00033 340(23)	.00070 698(65)	.00139 889(00)
28	.00009 396(27)	.00021 987(94)	.00047 424(85)	.00095 385(41)
29	.00006 083(69)	.00014 468(69)	.00031 709(81)	.00064 804(12)
30	.00003 930(84)	.00009 495(06)	.00021 137(85)	.00043 871(26)
40	.00000 045(34)	.00000 125(87)	.00000 320(16)	..00000 759(84)
50	.00000 000(47)	.00000 001(44)	.00000 004(09)	.00000 010(77)
60	.00000 000(00)	.00000 000(02)	.00000 000(05)	.00000 000(13)
70	.00000 000(00)	.00000 000(00)	.00000 000(00)	.00000 000(00)

TABLE VIII

VALUES OF THE PEARSON PROBABILITY, P

χ^2	$n=11$	$n=12$	$n=13$	$n=14$
1	.99982 788(44)	.99994 961(00)	.99998 583(51)	.99999 616(52)
2	.99634 015(31)	.99849 588(16)	.99940 581(51)	.99977 374(98)
3	.98142 406(38)	.99072 588(63)	.99554 401(93)	.99793 431(73)
4	.94734 698(27)	.96991 702(37)	.98343 639(15)	.99119 138(63)
5	.89117 801(89)	.93116 661(10)	.95797 896(18)	.97519 313(39)
6	.81526 324(46)	.87336 425(39)	.91608 205(80)	.94615 296(01)
7	.72544 495(35)	.79908 350(16)	.85761 355(34)	.90215 156(16)
8	.62883 693(51)	.71330 382(93)	.78513 038(69)	.84360 027(48)
9	.53210 357(63)	.62189 233(10)	.70293 043(47)	.77294 353(83)
10	.44049 328(51)	.53038 714(13)	.61596 065(48)	.69393 435(82)
11	.35751 800(24)	.44326 327(82)	.52891 868(64)	.61081 761(97)
12	.28505 650(03)	.36364 322(05)	.44567 964(13)	.52764 385(54)
13	.22367 181(68)	.29332 540(93)	.36904 068(36)	.44781 167(41)
14	.17299 160(79)	.23299 347(74)'	.30070 827(62)	.37384 397(66)
15	.13206 185(63)	.18249 692(96)	.24143 645(10)	.30735 277(37)
16	.09963 240(69)	.14113 086(91)	.19123 607(53)	.24912 983(01)
17	.07436 397(98)	.10787 558(68)	.14959 731(00)	.19930 407(58)
18	.05496 364(15)	.08158 061(36)	.11569 052(09)	.15751 946(23)
19	.04026 268(23)	.06109 350(92)	.08852 844(83)	.12310 366(09)
20	.02925 268(81)	.04534 067(37)	.06708 596(29)	.09521 025(54)
21	.02109 356(56)	.03337 105(44)	.05038 045(10)	.07292 862(65)
22	.01510 460(07)	.02437 324(38)	.03751 981(41)	.05536 177(64)
23	.01074 657(84)	.01767 510(94)	.02772 594(22)	.04167 626(37)
24	.00760 039(07)	.01273 320(34)	.02034 102(96)	.03113 005(98)
25	.00534 550(55)	.00911 668(47)	.01482 287(47)	.02308 373(18)
26	.00374 018(59)	.00648 991(72)	.01073 388(99)	.01700 083(68)
27	.00260 434(03)	.00459 532(06)	.00772 719(57)	.01244 118(45)
28	.00180 524(88)	.00323 733(11)	.00553 204(96)	.00904 981(79)
29	.00124 604(48)	.00226 996(07)	.00393 999(04)	.00654 593(03)
30	.00085 664(12)	.00158 458(60)	.00279 242(92)	.00470 969(53)
40	.00001 694(26)	.00003 577(50)	.00007 190(68)	.00013 823(54)
50	.00000 026(69)	.00000 062(59)	.00000 139(71)	.00000 298(14)
60	.00000 000(36)	.00000 000(93)	.00000 002(26)	.00000 005(25)
70	.00000 000(00)	.00000 000(01)	.00000 000(03)	.00000 000(08)

TABLE VIII

VALUES OF THE PEARSON PROBABILITY, P

χ^2	$n = 15$	$n = 16$	$n = 17$	$n = 18$
1	.99999 899(76)	.99999 974(64)	.99999 993(78)	.99999 998(51)
2	.99991 675(88)	.99997 034(49)	.99998 975(08)	.99999 655(76)
3	.99907 400(81)	.99959 780(14)	.99983 043(43)	.99993 049(82)
4	.99546 619(45)	.99773 734(40)	.99890 328(10)	.99948 293(27)
5	.98581 268(80)	.99212 641(19)	.99575 330(45)	.99777 083(79)
6	.96649 146(48)	.97974 774(76)	.98809 549(63)	.99318 566(26)
7	.93471 190(33)	.95764 974(76)	.97326 107(83)	.98354 890(12)
8	.88932 602(14)	.92378 270(28)	.94886 638(40)	.96654 676(94)
9	.83105 057(86)	.87751 745(11)	.91341 352(82)	.94026 179(87)
10	.76218 346(30)	.81973 990(96)	.86662 832(59)	.90361 027(73)
11	.68603 598(02)	.75259 437(02)	.80948 528(25)	.85656 398(72)
12	.60630 278(23)	.67902 905(67)	.74397 976(03)	.80013 721(78)
13	.52652 362(26)	.60229 793(88)	.67275 778(02)	.73618 603(49)
14	.44971 105(59)	.52552 912(95)	.59871 383(57)	.66710 193(89)
15	.37815 469(44)	.45141 720(81)	.52463 852(65)	.59548 164(24)
16	.31337 429(98)	.38205 162(82)	.45296 084(21)	.52383 487(84)
17	.25617 786(12)	.31886 440(74)	.38559 710(17)	.45436 611(65)
18	.20678 083(99)	.26266 556(05)	.32389 696(44)	.38884 087(72)
19	.16494 924(43)	.21373 388(26)	.26866 318(18)	.32853 216(35)
20	.13014 142(10)	.17193 268(88)	.22022 064(68)	.27422 926(67)
21	.10163 250(05)	.13682 931(99)	.17851 057(49)	.22629 029(06)
22	.07861 437(21)	.10780 390(86)	.14319 153(47)	.18471 903(57)
23	.06026 972(28)	.08413 984(45)	.11373 450(53)	.14925 066(84)
24	.04582 230(72)	.06509 348(69)	.08950 449(75)	.11943 497(03)
25	.03456 739(39)	.04994 343(75)	.06982 546(38)	.09470 961(38)
26	.02588 691(53)	.03802 267(61)	.05402 824(82)	.07446 053(08)
27	.01925 362(03)	.02873 644(02)	.04148 315(34)	.05806 790(06)
28	.01422 795(80)	.02156 902(04)	.03161 977(49)	.04493 819(83)
29	.01045 035(87)	.01608 463(15)	.02393 612(18)	.03452 612(06)
30	.00763 189(92)	.01192 148(60)	.01800 219(20)	.02634 506(73)
40	.00025 512(04)	.00045 339(40)	.00077 858(80)	.00129 409(44)
50	.00000 610(63)	.00001 204(12)	.00002 292(48)	.00004 224(03)
60	.00000 018(95)	.00000 025(22)	.00000 059(55)	.00000 105(09)
70	.00000 000(19)	.00000 000(37)	.00000 001(00)	.00000 002(16)

TABLE VIII

VALUES OF THE PEARSON PROBABILITY, P

χ^2	$n = 19$	$n = 20$	$n = 21$	$n = 22$
1	.99999 999(66)	.99999 999(92)	.99999 999(98)	.99999 999(99)
2	.99999 887(48)	.99999 964(15)	.99999 988(85)	.99999 996(61)
3	.99997 226(42)	.99998 920(94)	.99999 590(25)	.99999 847(96)
4	.99976 255(27)	.99989 365(95)	.99995 350(19)	.99998 012(83)
5	.99885 974(71)	.99943 096(32)	.99972 264(79)	.99986 783(83)
6	.99619 700(81)	.99792 845(61)	.99889 751(20)	.99942 618(03)
7	.99012 634(23)	.99421 325(85)	.99668 505(61)	.99814 223(22)
8	.97863 656(53)	.98667 098(89)	.99186 775(69)	.99514 434(45)
9	.95974 268(74)	.97347 939(45)	.98290 726(70)	.98921 404(51)
10	.93190 636(53)	.95294 578(77)	.96817 194(28)	.97891 184(58)
11	.89435 667(78)	.92383 844(53)	.94622 253(05)	.96278 681(57)
12	.84723 749(38)	.88562 533(15)	.91607 598(28)	.93961 782(44)
13	.79157 303(33)	.83857 104(69)	.87738 404(94)	.90862 395(00)
14	.72909 126(79)	.78369 131(12)	.83049 593(74)	.86959 927(03)
15	.66196 711(92)	.72259 731(97)	.77640 761(31)	.82295 180(17)
16	.59254 738(44)	.65727 793(65)	.71662 431(09)	.76965 103(81)
17	.52310 504(49)	.58986 782(45)	.65297 365(78)	.71110 620(38)
18	.45565 260(45)	.52243 827(24)	.58740 824(45)	.64900 422(58)
19	.39182 348(26)	.45683 612(43)	.52182 602(24)	.58514 008(51)
20	.33281 967(91)	.39457 818(17)	.45792 971(48)	.52126 125(02)
21	.27941 304(74)	.33680 090(00)	.39713 259(87)	.45894 420(52)
22	.23198 513(32)	.28425 625(90)	.34051 068(25)	.39950 988(60)
23	.19059 013(01)	.23734 178(30)	.28879 453(95)	.34397 839(55)
24	.15502 778(29)	.19615 235(87)	.24239 216(34)	.29305 853(34)
25	.12491 619(79)	.16054 222(60)	.20143 110(65)	.24716 408(41)
26	.09975 791(41)	.13018 901(46)	.16581 187(60)	.20644 904(49)
27	.07899 549(06)	.10465 316(12)	.13526 399(63)	.17085 326(84)
28	.06205 545(45)	.08342 860(90)	.10939 984(50)	.14015 131(95)
29	.04837 906(72)	.06598 513(15)	.08775 938(83)	.11400 151(65)
30	.03744 649(10)	.05179 844(62)	.06985 365(61)	.09198 799(17)
40	.00208 725(70)	.00327 221(30)	.00499 541(03)	.00743 667(32)
50	.00007 548(26)	.00013 106(12)	.00022 147(66)	.00036 480(05)
60	.00000 211(82)	.00000 386(98)	.00000 719(39)	.00001 277(17)
70	.00000 004(52)	.00000 009(19)	.00000 018(21)	.00000 035(14)

TABLE VIII

VALUES OF THE PEARSON PROBABILITY, P

χ^2	$n = 23$	$n = 24$	$n = 25$	$n = 26$
1	.99999 999(99)	.99999 999(99)	.99999 999(99)	.99999 999(99)
2	.99999 998(99)	.99999 999(70)	.99999 999(91)	.99999 999(97)
3	.99999 944(83)	.99999 980(39)	.99999 993(18)	.99999 997(66)
4	.99999 169(18)	.99999 659(85)	.99999 863(54)	.99999 946(29)
5	.99993 837(31)	.99997 185(62)	.99998 740(15)	.99999 446(87)
6	.99970 766(32)	.99985 410(16)	.99992 861(35)	.99996 573(32)
7	.99898 060(60)	.99945 189(02)	.99971 100(82)	.99985 048(17)
8	.99716 023(36)	.99837 228(95)	.99908 477(06)	.99949 505(30)
9	.99333 132(78)	.99595 746(68)	.99759 571(63)	.99859 619(71)
10	.98630 473(15)	.99127 663(54)	.99454 690(82)	.99665 263(08)
11	.97474 874(95)	.98318 834(31)	.98901 185(90)	.99294 559(53)
12	.95737 907(62)	.97047 067(75)	.97990 803(63)	.98656 781(82)
13	.93316 120(99)	.95199 003(28)	.96612 044(11)	.97650 129(70)
14	.90147 920(61)	.92687 124(27)	.94665 037(70)	.96173 244(31)
15	.86223 798(36)	.89463 357(45)	.92075 869(07)	.94138 255(68)
16	.81588 585(21)	.85526 863(92)	.88807 606(39)	.91482 870(95)
17	.76336 197(88)	.80925 155(83)	.84866 204(50)	.88179 377(69)
18	.70598 832(06)	.75748 932(86)	.80300 838(29)	.84239 071(34)
19	.64532 843(52)	.70122 462(06)	.75198 960(99)	.79712 054(12)
20	.58303 975(06)	.64191 179(15)	.69677 614(68)	.74682 530(56)
21	.52073 812(75)	.58108 751(03)	.63872 522(33)	.69260 965(84)
22	.45988 878(67)	.52025 178(10)	.57926 689(09)	.63574 402(83)
23	.40172 961(04)	.46077 087(57)	.51979 809(34)	.57756 335(59)
24	.34722 942(00)	.40380 844(65)	.46159 733(63)	.51937 357(32)
25	.29707 473(13)	.35028 534(37)	.40576 068(10)	.46237 366(94)
26	.25168 202(65)	.30086 622(54)	.35316 493(16)	.40759 869(02)
27	.21122 647(90)	.25596 769(19)	.30445 316(24)	.35588 462(38)
28	.17568 199(16)	.21578 160(01)	.26004 108(74)	.30785 324(61)
29	.14486 085(38)	.18030 985(77)	.22013 096(75)	.26391 602(70)
30	.11846 440(38)	.14940 162(81)	.18475 178(70)	.22428 897(99)
40	.01081 171(68)	.01536 897(83)	.02138 681(95)	.02916 429(15)
50	.00058 646(16)	.00092 132(26)	.00141 597(28)	.00213 115(34)
60	.00002 242(10)	.00003 820(56)	.00006 394(92)	.00010 455(49)
70	.00000 066(14)	.00000 121(61)	.00000 218(65)	.00000 384(79)

TABLE VIII

VALUES OF THE PEARSON PROBABILITY, P

χ^2	$n=27$	$n=28$	$n=29$	$n=30$
1	.99999 999(99)	.99999 999(99)	.99999 999(99)	.99999 999(99)
2	.99999 999(99)	.99999 999(99)	.99999 999(99)	.99999 999(99)
3	.99999 999(22)	.99999 999(74)	.99999 999(92)	.99999 999(97)
4	.99999 979(27)	.99999 992(12)	.99999 997(07)	.99999 998(91)
5	.99999 771(58)	.99999 899(13)	.99999 968(01)	.99999 982(88)
6	.99998 385(11)	.99999 252(42)	.99999 659(82)	.99999 847(85)
7	.99992 404(22)	.99996 208(73)	.99998 139(75)	.99999 102(21)
8	.99972 628(29)	.99985 433(73)	.99992 367(13)	.99996 079(19)
9	.99919 486(20)	.99954 613(99)	.99974 841(25)	.99986 278(76)
10	.99798 114(85)	.99880 302(90)	.99930 201(01)	.99959 947(28)
11	.99554 911(75)	.99723 878(63)	.99831 488(07)	.99898 786(41)
12	.99117 251(63)	.99429 444(57)	.99637 150(71)	.99772 850(24)
13	.98397 335(80)	.98924 715(43)	.99289 981(64)	.99538 404(86)
14	.97300 022(67)	.98125 471(54)	.98718 860(74)	.99137 737(52)
15	.95733 413(26)	.96943 194(61)	.97843 534(91)	.98501 494(02)
16	.93620 287(18)	.95294 715(46)	.96581 936(89)	.97553 586(27)
17	.90908 299(53)	.93112 248(54)	.94858 895(54)	.96218 130(19)
18	.87577 342(96)	.90351 971(04)	.92614 923(12)	.94427 237(51)
19	.83642 970(66)	.87000 144(09)	.89813 593(12)	.92128 799(99)
20	.79155 647(69)	.83075 611(69)	.86446 442(32)	.89292 708(80)
21	.74196 393(21)	78628 826(28)	.82534 904(31)	.85914 939(95)
22	.68869 681(98)	.73737 720(58)	.78129 137(50)	.82018 942(45)
23	.63294 705(64)	.68501 243(77)	.73304 036(98)	.77654 313(69)
24	.57596 525(26)	.63031 609(48)	.68153 563(69)	.72893 166(96)
25	.51897 521(19)	.57446 199(50)	.62783 533(79)	.67824 748(16)
26	.46310 474(55)	.51860 045(36)	.57304 455(93)	.62549 104(05)
27	.40933 318(11)	.46379 491(03)	.51824 704(67)	.57170 519(67)
28	.35846 003(25)	.41097 348(97)	.46444 966(56)	.51791 300(14)
29	.31108 235(48)	.36089 918(32)	.41252 813(30)	.46506 627(69)
30	.26761 101(60)	.31415 380(21)	.36321 781(87)	.41400 360(46)
40	.03901 199(08)	.05123 679(26)	.06612 763(88)	.08393 679(44)
50	.00314 412(10)	.00455 081(48)	.00646 748(31)	.00903 166(94)
60	.00016 776(98)	.00026 379(32)	.00040 735(59)	.00061 765(60)
70	.00000 663(45)	.00001 121(69)	.00001 861(00)	.00003 032(18)

TABLE IX

COEFFICIENTS FOR FITTING STRAIGHT LINES TO DATA

(The numbers in parentheses denote the number of ciphers between the decimal point and the first significant figure.)

p	A	B	C
2	5.000 0000 000	− 3.000 0000 009	2.000 0000 000
3	2.333 3333 333	− 1.000 0000 000	.500 0000 000
4	1.500 0000 000	− .5000 0000 000	.200 0000 000
5	1.100 0000 000	− .300 0000 000	.100 0000 000
6	.866 6666 667	− .200 0000 000	
7	.714 2857 143	− .142 8571 429	.(1) 571 4285 714
8	.607 1428 571	− .107 1428 571	.(1) 357 1428 571
9	.527 7777 778	−.(1) 833 3333 333	.(1) 238 0952 381
10	.466 6666 667	−.(1) 666 6666 667	.(1) 166 6666 667
			.(1) 121 2121 212
11	.418 1818 182	−.(1) 545 4545 455	.(2) 909 0909 091
12	.378 7878 788	−.(1) 454 5454 545	.(2) 699 3006 993
13	.346 1538 462	−.(1) 384 6153 846	.(2) 549 4505 495
14	.318 6813 187	−.(1) 329 6703 297	.(2) 439 5604 396
15	.295 2380 952	−.(1) 285 7142 857	.(2) 357 1428 571
16	.275 0000 000	−.(1) 250 0000 000	.(2) 294 1176 471
17	.257 3529 412	−.(1) 220 5882 353	.(2) 245 0980 392
18	.241 8300 654	−.(1) 196 0784 314	.(2) 206 3983 488
19	.228 0701 754	−.(1) 175 4385 965	.(2) 175 4385 965
20	.215 7894 737	−.(1) 157 8947 368	.(2) 150 3759 398
21	.204 7619 048	−.(1) 142 8571 429	.(2) 129 8701 299
22	.194 8051 948	−.(1) 129 8701 299	.(2) 112 9305 477
23	.185 7707 510	−.(1) 118 5770 751	.(3) 988 1422 925
24	.177 5362 319	−.(1) 108 6956 522	.(3) 869 5652 174
25	.170 0000 000	−.(1) 100 0000 000	.(3) 769 2307 692
26	.163 0769 231	−.(2) 923 0769 231	.(3) 683 7606 838
27	.156 6951 567	−.(2) 854 7008 547	.(3) 610 5006 105
28	.150 7936 508	−.(2) 793 6507 937	.(3) 547 3453 749
29	.145 3201 970	−.(2) 738 9162 562	.(3) 492 6108 374
30	.140 2298 851	−.(2) 689 6551 724	.(3) 444 9388 209
31	.135 4838 710	−.(2) 645 1612 903	.(3) 403 2258 065
32	.131 0483 871	−.(2) 604 8387 097	.(3) 366 5689 150
33	.126 8939 394	−.(2) 568 1818 182	.(3) 334 2245 989
34	.122 9946 524	−.(2) 534 7593 583	.(3) 305 5767 762
35	.119 3277 311	−.(2) 504 2016 807	.(3) 280 1120 448
36	.115 8730 159	−.(2) 476 1904 762	.(3) 257 4002 574
37	.112 6126 126	−.(2) 450 4504 505	.(3) 237 0791 844
38	.109 5305 832	−.(2) 426 7425 320	.(3) 218 8423 241
39	.106 6126 856	−.(2) 404 8582 996	.(3) 202 4291 498
40	.103 8461 538	−.(2) 384 6153 846	.(3) 187 6172 608
41	.101 2195 122	−.(2) 365 8536 585	.(3) 174 2160 279
42	.(1) 987 2241 580	−.(2) 348 4320 557	.(3) 162 0614 213
43	.(1) 963 4551 495	−.(2) 332 2259 136	.(3) 151 0117 789
44	.(1) 940 8033 827	−.(2) 317 1247 357	.(3) 140 9443 270
45	.(1) 919 1919 192	−.(2) 303 0303 030	.(3) 131 7523 057
46	.(1) 898 5507 246	−.(2) 289 8550 725	.(3) 123 3425 840
47	.(1) 878 8159 112	−.(2) 277 5208 141	.(3) 115 6336 725
48	.(1) 859 9290 780	−.(2) 265 9574 468	.(3) 108 5540 599
49	.(1) 841 8367 347	−.(2) 255 1020 408	.(3) 102 0408 163
50	.(1) 824 4897 959	−.(2) 244 8979 592	.(4) 960 3841 537

TABLE IX

COEFFICIENTS FOR FITTING STRAIGHT LINES TO DATA

(The numbers in parentheses denote the number of ciphers between the decimal point and the first significant figure.)

p	A	B	C
51	.(1) 807 8431 373	−.(2) 235 2941 176	.(4) 904 9773 756
52	.(1) 791 8552 036	−.(2) 226 2443 439	.(4) 853 7522 411
53	.(1) 776 4876 633	−.(2) 217 7068 215	.(4) 806 3215 610
54	.(1) 761 7051 013	−.(2) 209 6436 059	.(4) 762 3403 843
55	.(1) 747 4747 475	−.(2) 202 0202 020	.(4) 721 5007 215
56	.(1) 733 7662 338	−.(2) 194 8051 948	.(4) 683 5269 993
57	.(1) 720 5513 784	−.(2) 187 9699 248	.(4) 648 1721 545
58	.(1) 707 8039 927	−.(2) 181 4882 033	.(4) 615 2142 484
59	.(1) 695 4997 078	−.(2) 175 3360 608	.(4) 584 4535 359
60	.(1) 683 6158 192	−.(2) 169 4915 254	.(4) 555 7099 194
61	.(1) 672 1311 475	−.(2) 163 9344 262	.(4) 528 8207 298
62	.(1) 661 0259 122	−.(2) 158 6462 189	.(4) 503 6387 903
63	.(1) 650 2816 180	−.(2) 153 6098 310	.(4) 480 0307 220
64	.(1) 639 8809 524	−.(2) 148 8095 238	.(4) 457 8754 579
65	.(1) 629 8076 923	−.(2) 144 2307 692	.(4) 437 0629 371
66	.(1) 620 0466 200	−.(2) 139 8601 399	.(4) 417 4929 548
67	.(1) 610 5834 464	−.(2) 135 6852 103	.(4) 399 0741 480
68	.(1) 601 4047 410	−.(2) 131 6944 688	.(4) 381 7230 981
69	.(1) 592 4978 687	−.(2) 127 8772 379	.(4) 365 3635 367
70	.(1) 583 8509 317	−.(2) 124 2236 025	.(4) 349 9256 408
71	.(1) 575 4527 163	−.(2) 120 7243 461	.(4) 335 3454 058
72	.(1) 567 2926 448	−.(2) 117 3708 920	.(4) 321 5640 877
73	.(1) 559 3607 306	−.(2) 114 1552 511	.(4) 308 5277 058
74	.(1) 551 6475 379	−.(2) 111 0699 741	.(4) 296 1865 976
75	.(1) 544 1441 441	−.(2) 108 1081 081	.(4) 284 4950 213
76	.(1) 536 8421 053	−.(2) 105 2631 579	.(4) 273 4107 997
77	.(1) 529 7334 245	−.(2) 102 5290 499	.(4) 262 8949 997
78	.(1) 522 8105 228	−.(3) 999 0009 990	.(4) 252 9116 453
79	.(1) 516 0662 123	−.(3) 973 7098 345	.(4) 243 4274 586
80	.(1) 509 4936 709	−.(3) 949 3670 886	.(4) 234 4116 268
81	.(1) 503 0864 198	−.(3) 925 9259 259	.(4) 225 8355 917
82	.(1) 496 8383 017	−.(3) 903 3423 668	.(4) 217 6728 595
83	.(1) 490 7434 617	−.(3) 881 5750 808	.(4) 209 8988 288
84	.(1) 484 7963 282	−.(3) 860 5851 979	.(4) 202 4906 348
85	.(1) 478 9915 966	−.(3) 840 3361 345	.(4) 195 4270 080
86	.(1) 473 3242 134	−.(3) 820 7934 337	.(4) 188 6881 457
87	.(1) 467 7893 611	−.(3) 801 9246 191	.(4) 182 2555 952
88	.(1) 462 3824 451	−.(3) 783 6990 596	.(4) 176 1121 482
89	.(1) 457 0990 807	−.(3) 766 0878 447	.(4) 170 2417 433
90	.(1) 451 9350 811	−.(3) 749 0636 704	.(4) 164 6293 781
91	.(1) 446 8864 469	−.(3) 732 6007 326	.(4) 159 2610 288
92	.(1) 441 9493 550	−.(3) 716 6746 297	.(4) 154 1235 763
93	.(1) 437 1201 496	−.(3) 701 2622 721	.(4) 149 2047 387
94	.(1) 432 3953 329	−.(3) 686 3417 982	.(4) 144 4930 102
95	.(1) 427 7715 566	−.(3) 671 8924 972	.(4) 139 9776 036
96	.(1) 423 2456 140	−.(3) 657 8947 368	.(4) 135 6483 993
97	.(1) 418 8144 330	−.(3) 644 3298 969	.(4) 131 4958 973
98	.(1) 414 4750 681	−.(3) 631 1803 072	.(4) 127 5111 732
99	.(1) 410 2246 959	−.(3) 618 4291 899	.(4) 123 6858 380
100	.(1) 406 0606 061	−.(3) 606 0606 061	.(4) 120 0120 012

TABLE X

COEFFICIENTS FOR FITTING PARABOLAS TO DATA

(The numbers in parentheses denote the number of ciphers between the decimal point and the first significant figure.)

p	A	B	C
3	19.000 0000 00	− 21.000 0000 000	5.000 0000 000
4	7.750 0000 00	− 6.750 0000 000	1.250 0000 000
5	4.600 0000 00	− 3.300 0000 000	.500 0000 000
6	3.200 0000 00	− 1.950 0000 000	.250 0000 000
7	2.428 5714 29	− 1.285 7142 860	.142 8571 429
8	1.946 4285 71	− .910 7142 857	.(1) 892 8571 429
9	1.619 0476 19	− .678 5714 286	.(1) 595 2380 952
10	1.383 3333 33	− .525 0000 000	.(1) 416 6666 667
11	1.206 0606 061	− .418 1818 182	.(1) 303 0303 030
12	1.068 1818 182	− .340 9090 909	.(1) 227 2727 273
13	.958 0419 580	− .283 2167 832	.(1) 174 8251 748
14	.868 1318 681	− .239 0109 890	.(1) 137 3626 374
15	.793 4065 934	− .204 3956 044	.(1) 109 8901 099
16	.730 3571 429	− .176 7857 143	.(2) 892 8571 429
17	.676 4705 882	− .154 4117 647	.(2) 735 2941 176
18	.629 9019 608	− .136 0294 118	.(2) 612 7450 980
19	.589 2672 859	− .120 7430 341	.(2) 515 9958 720
20	.553 5087 719	− .107 8947 368	.(2) 438 5964 912
21	.521 8045 113	−.(1) 969 9248 120	.(2) 375 9398 496
22	.493 5064 935	−.(1) 876 6233 766	.(2) 324 6753 247
23	.468 0971 203	−.(1) 796 1603 614	.(2) 282 3263 693
24	.445 1581 028	−.(1) 726 2845 850	.(2) 247 0355 731
25	.424 3478 261	−.(1) 665 2173 913	.(2) 217 3913 043
26	.405 3846 154	−.(1) 611 5384 615	.(2) 192 3076 923
27	.388 0341 880	−.(1) 564 1025 641	.(2) 170 9401 709
28	.372 1001 221	−.(1) 521 9780 220	.(2) 152 6251 526
29	.357 4165 298	−.(1) 484 4006 568	.(2) 136 8363 437
30	.343 8423 645	−.(1) 450 7389 163	.(2) 123 1527 094
31	.331 2569 522	−.(1) 420 4671 857	.(2) 111 2347 052
32	.319 5564 516	−.(1) 393 1451 613	.(2) 100 8064 516
33	.308 6510 264	−.(1) 368 4017 595	.(3) 916 4222 874
34	.298 4625 668	−.(1) 345 9224 599	.(3) 835 5614 973
35	.288 9228 419	−.(1) 325 4392 666	.(3) 763 9419 404
36	.279 9719 888	−.(1) 306 7226 891	.(3) 700 2801 120
37	.271 5572 716	−.(1) 289 5752 896	.(3) 643 5006 435
38	.263 6320 531	−.(1) 273 8264 580	.(3) 592 6979 611
39	.256 1549 404	−.(1) 259 3281 541	.(3) 547 1058 103
40	.249 0890 688	−.(1) 245 9514 170	.(3) 506 0728 745
41	.242 4015 009	−.(1) 233 5834 897	.(3) 469 0431 520
42	.236 0627 178	−.(1) 222 1254 355	.(3) 435 5400 697
43	.230 0461 874	−.(1) 211 4901 548	.(3) 405 1535 532
44	.224 3279 976	−.(1) 201 6007 248	.(3) 377 5294 473
45	.218 8865 398	−.(1) 192 3890 063	.(3) 352 3608 175
46	.213 7022 398	−.(1) 183 7944 664	.(3) 329 3807 642
47	.208 7573 235	−.(1) 175 7631 822	.(3) 308 3564 601
48	.204 0356 152	−.(1) 168 2469 935	.(3) 289 0841 813
49	.199 5223 621	−.(1) 161 2027 790	.(3) 271 3851 498
50	.195 2040 816	−.(1) 154 5918 367	.(3) 255 1020 408

TABLE X

COEFFICIENTS FOR FITTING PARABOLAS TO DATA

(The numbers in parentheses denote the number of ciphers between the decimal point and the first significant figure.)

p	D	E	F
3	24.500 0000 000	− 6.000 0000 000	1.500 0000 000
4	6.450 0000 000	− 1.250 0000 000	.250 0000 000
5	2.671 4285 710	− .428 5714 286	.(1)714 2857 143
6	1.369 6428 570	− .187 5000 000	.(1)267 8571 429
7	.797 6190 476	−.(1)952 3809 524	.(1)119 0476 190
8	.505 9523 810	−.(1)535 7142 857	.(2)595 2380 952
9	.341 3419 913	−.(1)324 6753 247	.(2)324 6753 247
10	.241 2878 788	−.(1)208 3333 333	.(2)189 3939 394
11	.176 9230 769	−.(1)139 8601 399	.(2)116 5501 166
12	.133 6163 836	−.(2)974 0259 740	.(3)749 2507 493
13	.103 3966 034	−.(2)699 3006 993	.(3)499 5004 995
14	.(1)816 6208 791	−.(2)515 1098 901	.(3)343 4065 934
15	.(1)656 2702 004	−.(2)387 8474 467	.(3)242 4046 542
16	.(1)535 3641 457	−.(2)297 6190 476	.(3)175 0700 280
17	.(1)442 4664 603	−.(2)232 1981 424	.(3)128 9989 680
18	.(1)369 9045 408	−.(2)183 8235 294	.(4)967 4922 601
19	.(1)312 3986 437	−.(2)147 4273 920	.(4)737 1369 600
20	.(1)266 2337 662	−.(2)119 6172 249	.(4)569 6058 328
21	.(1)228 7437 962	−.(3)980 7126 512	.(4)445 7784 778
22	.(1)197 9813 665	−.(3)811 6883 117	.(4)352 9079 616
23	.(1)172 5014 116	−.(3)677 5832 863	.(4)282 3263 693
24	.(1)151 2161 751	−.(3)570 0820 918	.(4)228 0328 367
25	.(1)133 2961 724	−.(3)483 0917 874	.(4)185 8045 336
26	.(1)118 1013 431	−.(3)412 0879 121	.(4)152 6251 526
27	.(1)105 1324 155	−.(3)353 6693 192	.(4)126 3104 711
28	.(2)939 9604 227	−.(3)305 2503 053	.(4)105 2587 260
29	.(2)843 7946 925	−.(3)264 8445 363	.(5)882 8151 209
30	.(2)760 3190 052	−.(3)230 9113 301	.(5)744 8752 582
31	.(2)687 5063 202	−.(3)202 2449 186	.(5)632 0153 706
32	.(2)623 7062 274	−.(3)177 8937 381	.(5)539 0719 338
33	.(2)567 5657 360	−.(3)157 1009 636	.(5)462 0616 575
34	.(2)517 9685 511	−.(3)139 2602 496	.(5)397 8864 273
35	.(2)473 9881 210	−.(3)123 8824 768	.(5)344 1179 912
36	.(2)434 8510 386	−.(3)110 5705 440	.(5)298 8393 081
37	.(2)399 9082 946	−.(4)990 0009 900	.(5)260 5265 763
38	.(2)368 6125 397	−.(4)889 0469 417	.(5)227 9607 543
39	.(2)340 4999 746	−.(4)800 6426 492	.(5)200 1606 623
40	.(2)315 1758 383	−.(4)722 9612 493	.(5)176 3320 120
41	.(2)292 3027 058	−.(4)654 4788 167	.(5)155 8282 897
42	.(2)271 5910 012	−.(4)593 9182 768	.(5)138 1205 295
43	.(2)252 7912 624	−.(4)540 2047 376	.(5)122 7738 040
44	.(2)235 6878 040	−.(4)492 4297 139	.(5)109 4288 253
45	.(2)220 0934 979	−.(4)449 8223 202	.(6)977 8746 091
46	.(2)205 8454 573	−.(4)411 7259 552	.(6)876 0126 706
47	.(2)192 8014 499	−.(4)377 5793 389	.(6)786 6236 226
48	.(2)180 8369 046	−.(4)346 9010 176	.(6)707 9612 604
49	.(2)169 8424 050	−.(4)319 2766 468	.(6)638 5532 937
50	.(2)159 7215 809	−.(4)294 3485 086	.(6)577 1539 385

ANSWERS TO PROBLEMS

(In using these answers the student is advised to remember that a different order of approximation used in computation will lead in general to slightly different results from those given here.)

CHAPTER I

Page 18; Section 9.

1. $m = 9$; **2.** $m = 8$; **3.** $m = 9$.

Page 34; Section 12.

3. 1.0099; **4.** 1.0456; **5.** .99015; **6.** See table, page 32; **7.** 5.4772; **8.** For $n = 16$; 1, 16, 120, 560, 1820, 4368, 8008, 11440, 12870, 11440, 8008, 4368, 1820, 560, 120, 16, 1; For $n = 17$; 1, 17, 136, 680, 2380, 6188, 12376, 19448, 24310, 24310, 19448, 12376, 6188, 2380, 680, 136, 17, 1; **9.** $_{18}C_8 = 43758$; $_{20}C_5 = 15504$; **10.** Expand $(1+1)^n$, which is equivalent to 2^n; **11.** $(1 + 1/x)^4 = 1 + 4/x + 6/x^2 + 4/x^3 + 1/x^4$; $-(1 - 1/x)^4 = -1 + 4/x - 6/x^2 + 4/x^3 - 1/x^4$; **12.** $x^3 + 6x^2 + 12x + 11 + 3x\sqrt{x} + 12\sqrt{x} + 12/\sqrt{x} + 6/x + 1/(x\sqrt{x})$; **13.** $a^2 + b^2 + c^2 + d^2 + 2ab + 2ac + 2ad + 2bc + 2bd + 2cd$.

CHAPTER II

Page 37; Section 1.

1. 1, -1, $3(1 - \sqrt{2})$, 5, 11; **2.** Yes, for $4 < x < 5$ and $-2 < x < -1$; **3.** -1, 0, 0, 3/5, 1/2; **4.** 611, 706.6, 726.2, 555; **5.** 12.866, 50.156, 35.000, 119.450 million; **6.** 2.89 million; **7.** 197.27 million; **8.** 1, 1.10517, 1.22140, .36788, 0; **11.** -1, .21219, .80821; **12.** .00545, .00536; **13.** 0, 10, 1/6, 7/128.

Page 41; Section 2.

1. 44.6c, 27.6c, 36.6c; **2.** 177, 42, 143 (These are only suggestive estimates since various methods used to determine these values will lead to different answers); **4.** .90, .98, .42, .23.

Page 46; Section 6.

4. 2/3, -5, -5, $-1/3$; **9.** $y = 19.40 - .07x$; **10.** $y = 19.40 - .07x$; **11.** $P = .2851 + .0072 M$; **12.** $y = 25.48 + 4.61x$.

Page 56; Section 8.

4. -2.5 and 1, 1/3; **5.** (1/3, 0), (1, 3), (1/3, 13/3); **6.** 49/15; **7.** $y = 6 - 8x + 3x^2$; **8.** $y = 50 - 23.14x + 2.714x^2$; **9.** $y = 7.23 - 2.43x + .680x^2$.

Page 60; Section 9.

6. $y = 3.67\, e^{-.325x}$; **7.** $y = 2.993\, e^{.201x}$; **8.** $y = .455\, e^{.93x}$; **9.** $y = 2.945\, e^{.295x}$; 31.190, 41.893, 56.267, 75.573, 101.505.

—410—

ANSWERS TO PROBLEMS 411

Page 63; Section 10.

7. 252, 210, 120, 45, 10, 1; these values are to be compared with 259, 212. 115, 43, 11, 2.

Page 64; Section 11.

1. $3x' + 4y' = -2$; **2.** $x'^2 + y'^2 = 4$; **3.** $y' = 3x'^2 + 4x' + 8$; **4.** $x'(y' + 1) = 9$; **5.** $y' = e^{2x}$; **6.** $h = 2, k = -5$; **7.** $h = 0, k = 2/3$ is one set of values. Any set which satisfies the equation $10h - 3k + 2 = 0$ will reduce the equation to the desired form.

CHAPTER III

Page 68, Section 3.

1. 99.48%; **2.** 5 heads per toss; **3.** $-.16$ of one per cent; **4.** 49.07; **5.** 100.25%; **6.** $3,209.00; **7.** Av. receipts = $29.71; Av. expenditures = $40.88; **8.** 39.158 months.

Page 72; Section 4.

1. $a = 1/2, b = 1/2$; **3.** $a = s/t, b = (St - Ts)/t$; **4.** 3.25; **5.** 5.

Page 77, Section 5.

1. $\sigma = 15.38$, $A.D. = 12.28$; **2.** 1.6; **3.** $\sigma(\text{receipts}) = 15.44$, $\sigma(\text{expenditures}) = 39.57$; **4.** $v(\text{receipts}) = .52$, $v(\text{expenditures}) = .97$; **5.** 1.31; **6.** $\sigma = 12.92$ months, $A.D. = 10.27$; **7.** $\sigma_{(A)} = 1.47$, $\sigma_{(B)} = 1.62$, $v_{(A)} = .297$, $v_{(B)} = .321$.

Page 81, Section 7.

1. 3.08; **2.** .08; **3.** 1.6; **4.** 1.6; **5.** $m_1 = 5109$, $m_2 = 28149$, $m_3 = 166785$, $M_1 = 0$, $M_2 = 2659$, $M_3 = -189$; **6.** $N_1 = -5131$, $N_2 = 28369$, $N_3 = -168985$; **7.** $N_r = m_r - rm_{r-1}X + r\dfrac{(r-1)}{2}m_{r-2}X^2 - \ldots\ldots + (-1)^r m_0 X^r$.

Page 83; Section 8.

1. $\mu_2 = 47799.88$, $\sigma = 15.375$;

2. $\mu_2 = \dfrac{m_0 m_2 - m_1^2}{m_0} - \dfrac{a^2 m_0}{12}$, $\mu_3 = m_3 - \dfrac{3m_1 m_2}{m_0} + \dfrac{2m_1^3}{m_0^2}$;

3. $\mu_2 = 183,024.91$.

Page 85; Section 9.

1. 100.13; **2.** $M = 5$; $Q_1 = 4$, $Q_2 = 6$; **3.** $M = 2310.36$; **4.** $M(\text{receipts}) = 33.76$, $M(\text{expenditures}) = 31.48$; **5.** $Q_1 = 29.94$, $Q_2 = 47.80$; **6.** $D_1 = 23.20$, $D_5 = 38.11$, $D_7 = 45.55$, $D_9 = 56.37$; **7.** The best location is E.

Page 89, Section 10.

1. $Mo = 100.08$, $S = .13$, $S' = .13$; **2.** $Mo = 104.21$; **4.** $Mo = 35.23$; **5.** $S = .30$, $S' = .60$.

Page 92, Section 11.

1. (a) decrease of .14 of one per cent.; (b) increase of 1.47%; **2.** 23.4 years; **3.** .33 of one per cent; **4.** —17.36%; **5.** —14.7%; **6.** (a) 2.31% increase; (b) 4.59% decrease.

Page 96; Section 12.

1. 29.65 cents; **2.** 4.31; **3.** 21.35; **4.** 44.3; **5.** 3.414.

CHAPTER IV

Page 107; Section 3.

1. .8451; **2.** .8445; **3.** .8440; **4.** .8445.

Page 114; Section 7.

1. .9533; **2.** .6920; **3.** $I_{12} = .9810$, $I_{23} = 1.0379$, $I_{34} = .9905$; $I_{14} = 1.0163$ $I = I_{12} \times I_{23} \times I_{34} = 1.0083$.

Page 117; Section 9.

2. (By ideal formula) 1.7165; **4.** 2.229.

CHAPTER V

Page 123, Section 2.

1. $y = 11.52 + .0522x$ (Class marks 1, 2, 3, etc.); **2.** $y = 259.56 - .334x$ (Class marks, 1, 2, 3, etc.); **3.** $y = 336.59 + 1.30x$.

Page 128, Section 3.

1. 100, 100, 98, 99, 96, 98, 97, 99, 101, 103, 102, 102; **2.** 90, 116, 118, 114, 104, 91, 97, 95, 100, 90, 97, 84; **3.** 116, 108, 106, 102, 97, 93, 83, 83, 92, 99, 106, 116.

Page 130, Section 4.

1. The trend is: $y = 54.42 - .41x$.

CHAPTER VI.

Page 147; Section 1.

4. $p = .528$ that child will be a boy.

Page 150; Section 2.

1. 360; **2.** 125; **3.** (a) 720, (b) 120; **4.** 50,400; **5.** 166,320; **6.** 4,368; **7.** 384; **8.** 16; **9.** 360; **10.** 32; **11.** 369,600; 15,400; **12.** 2,520; **13.** 210; **14.** 5; **15.** 2,522,520.

Page 151; Section 3.

1. 3/8; **2.** 5/36; **3.** 1/28; **4.** 1/35; **5.** 8/15; 1/15; **6.** A has best chance; **7.** A has best chance in both cases; **8.** 35/286; **9.** 1/6 is to be compared with 5/36; **10.** 1/5; **12.** $2/(n-1)$; **13.** 4/635,013,559,600, 1:507:57798; **14.** $(13!)^4/52! = 1/53644737765488792839237440000$; **15.** 1/8.

ANSWERS TO PROBLEMS

Page 156; Section 6.

2. 11/36; **3.** 4/25; **4.** 45/182; **6.** A:6/11, B:5/11; **7.** 72/625; **8.** 1/2 ,5/16; **9.** 671/1296; **10.** 7; **11.** 1/54; **12.** 4; **13.** 4; **14.** 16/37, 12/37, 9/37; **15.** 2/3, 3/4, 4/5, 5/6, 7/8 and 10/11.

Page 158; Section 7.

1. 1106; **2.** $E = .0009$; **3.** The errors are .0003 and .00009 respectively; **4.** $p = .4934, E = .0016$; **5.** 844, 471.

Page 162; Section 9.

1. $2.16; **2.** 63 cents; **3.** $4.28; **4.** $3.97; **5.** $.0625; $.25, $.375; $.25, $.0625; **6.** 25¼ cents; **7.** Half dollars; **8.** $6.60.

Page 166; Section 10.

1. 10:5; **2.** .000000012; **3.** 24/59; **4.** 1/8; **5.** 49/58; **6.** 49/50; **7.** 21/22.

CHAPTER VII

Page 174; Section 2.

1. $A = 5.60$, $\sigma = 1.55$, $\sigma' = \sqrt{A(1-A/n)} = 1.57$, $2\sigma/\sqrt{2N} = 0.11$. Since $\sigma' - \sigma = .02$, the frequency is a binomial distribution.

2. $A = 4.97$, $\sigma = 1.58$, $\sigma' = \sqrt{A(1-A/n)} = 1.58$, $2\sigma/\sqrt{2N} = 0.11$. The frequency is a binomial distribution.

4.

No. of ones	Frequencies
0	243
1	405
2	270
3	90
4	15
5	1
	1024

5.

x	y	x	y
0	0.92	6	101.81
1	5.46	7	55.19
2	21.77	8	20.07
3	58.27	9	4.90
4	104.62	10	0.80
5	126.00		499.81

6. $A = 7.5$, $\sigma = 1.37$.

8. $A = 4.68$, $\sigma = 1.83$, $\sigma' = \sqrt{A(1-A/n)} = 1.56$, $2\sigma/\sqrt{2N} = 0.15$, $\sigma - \sigma' = 0.27$. The distribution shows too great a dispersion for normal frequency data.

7.

x	y	x	y
0	2.39	5	61.86
1	8.32	6	48.37
2	21.52	7	28.04
3	41.26	8	12.05
4	58.67	9	3.84

Page 184; Section 7.

1. By formula of chapter 3, $Mo = 32$; by methods of this chapter, $Mo = 33$.

2. $10! = 3,628,800$; by Stirling's formula, $10! \sim 3,598,696$; $\log 1000! \sim 2567.6046$. From Duarte's, *Nouvelles Tables de log n!* Paris (1927), $\log 1000! = 2567.60464422$.

414 ELEMENTS OF STATISTICS

3. $A = 4$, $\sigma = .8944$;

x	Graduated	Exact
0	0.0	1
1	1.6	20
2	54.1	160
3	512.8	640
4	1393.9	1280
5	1085.6	1024

4. $A = 4.6127$, $\sigma = 1.6663$;

x	Frequency	x	Frequency
0	1.25	5	46.87
1	5.31	6	32.82
2	15.72	7	16.03
3	32.44	8	5.46
4	46.68	9	1.30

5. $A = 5.8270$, $\sigma = 2.6925$;

x	Frequency	x	Frequency	x	Frequency	x	Frequency	x	Frequency
0	16.9	3	97.9	6	163.8	9	79.2	12	11.1
1	33.0	4	133.4	7	147.6	10	47.2	13	4.4
2	62.6	5	158.4	8	115.8	11	24.5	14	1.5

6.

Class Intervals	x	Data	Graduated Values
481-560	0	8	2.29
561-640	1	5	6.72
641-720	2	13	15.05
721-800	3	22	25.75
801-880	4	26	33.65
881-960	5	39	33.56
961-1040	6	32	25.63
1041-1120	7	18	14.93
1121-1200	8	4	6.65
1201-1280	9	1	2.26

$A = 4.4940$, $\sigma = 1.9272$, $S' = 0.0003$, $\sigma' = \sqrt{A(1 - A/n)} = 1.50$, $2\sigma/\sqrt{2N} = .2103$.

7. $A = 5.9608$, $\sigma = 1.9042$, $S' = -0.0505$.

x	Graduated values	x	Graduated values
0	0.27	6	42.77
1	1.26	7	37.86
2	4.42	8	25.43
3	11.80	9	12.96
4	23.87	10	5.02
5	36.68		202.34

ANSWERS TO PROBLEMS

CHAPTER VIII

Page 191, Section 2.

1. 0.40658, 0.49266, 0.38877, 0.09367, 0.39760; **2.** 0.7359, 0.3117, 0.1773; **3.** p. e. $= 0.5396$; graduating by deviations from the average one has,

x	Frequencies
Below −1.45	3.78
−1.45	8.92
−0.95	18.28
−0.45	25.71
0.05	24.75
0.55	16.33
1.05	7.39
1.55	2.84
Above 1.55	0.00
	108.00

4. The actual probability is 0.66319. To get the theoretical probability, note that 97 corresponds to $x = 3.667$ and 105 to $x = 6.333$. Hence computing $I(\frac{x-A}{\sigma})$ for both values of x and subtracting, one obtains 0.52530 for the theoretical probability.

For second part of problem, $p = 0.0799$ as compared with 0.04305.

Page 198, Section 4.

1. No; **2.** $p = 0.00806 \pm 0.00191$. Hence the expected number of deaths is 8 ± 2. The upper and lower values of the amount that the company will have to pay out are $4000 and $28,000; **3.** Between $1476.44 and $1526.07. **4.** No; **5.** $p_1 = 0.50988662 \pm 0.00003280$, $p_2 = 0.50610511 \pm 0.00003043$. The probable error of the difference is 0.00004474, which is much less than the actual difference; **6.** The probable error of the difference between the probabilities of the data of problem 4 and of the two sets of data of problem 5 is .0059. The differences are 0.0176 and 0.0214 respectively. Hence the samples are not consistent, the probability of inconsistency being greater in the second case. **7.** $A = 39.158 \pm 0.262$; **8.** $\sigma = 4.934 \pm 0.165$; **9.** $v = 0.180 \pm 0.084$; **10.** 1.626.

Page 206, Section 6.

1. $P_p = 0.0470$; **2.** $P_p = 0.0644$; if the first item is omitted, $P_p = 0.308$; **3.** $P_p = 0.0027$; **4.** $P_p = 0.0187$.

Page 209, Section 7.

1. Taking the range from 178 to 242 by intervals of 4, one obtains the frequencies 2, 4, 3, 6, 16, 15, 19, 8, 8, 10, 4, 3, 2. From this one finds, $A = 209.4 \pm .91$, $\sigma = 13.16$. The distribution of errors is not quite normal.

2. B's set; **3.** 39.373; **4.** First set; 116.4, 119.9; the sets differ significantly; **5.** B was wrong.

CHAPTER IX

Page 224; Section 3.

1. $y = 102.27 - 0.94x$ (Years replaced by class marks 1, 2, 3, $\cdots$, 10); $y = 0.43 + 0.175x - 0.0148x^2$ (Age Group replaced by class marks, 1, 2,

3, ⋯ , 12); **3.** $y = (1.192)\ 2^x + (0.910)\ 2^{-x}$; **4.** $y = 2.045e^x - 1.107e^{-x}$; **5.** $y = 1.07 + 0.26x$; **6.** $\log y = 11.91 - 1.48 \log x$.

Page 228; Section 4.

1. 338,350; **2.** 25,502,500; **3.** 10,000; **4.** 1,333,300; **5.** $s_3 = [\tfrac{1}{2}p(p+1)]^2 = s_1^2$.

Page 233; Section 6.

1. $y = 151.69 + 41.45x$; **3.** $y = 14 - 7x + x^2$.

Page 238; Section 7.

1. $y = 22.63\ (1.073)^x$; **2.** $y = 809.29\ (1.160)^x$ (Years replaced by class marks 0, 1, 2, ⋯ , 11); using the formula, one gets a slightly different result: $y = 837.52\ (1.157)^x$; **3.** $y = 5.18\ (1.258)^x$ (Years replaced by class marks 0, 1, 2, ⋯ , 14); **4.** $y = 13.16\ (1.033)^x$ (Years replaced by the class marks, 0, 1, 2, ⋯ , 13).

Page 248; Section 9.

2. About the 13th month. **3.** 13021.

CHAPTER X.

Page 252; Section 2.

1. The lag correlation coefficients from r_6' to r_6 are respectively: —0.6444, —0.8538, —0.9060, —0.6666, —0.1966, 0.2492, 0.6257, 0.7873, 0.8344, 0.6549, 0.2714, —0.1553, —0.6444. One concludes that shipments lag two months behind production. **2.** Referring to the four series by the numbers 1, 2, 3, and 4 in the order Dow Jones, Index of Living, Paper Rates, Percentage Net Income, the correlations are $r_{12} = -0.0108$, $r_{13} = -0.2977$, $r_{14} = 0.5882$. The largest influence on bond price is thus the percentage-net income to capitalization. **3.** $r = -0.2183$; **4.** $r = 0.7688$; **5.** $r = 0.9356$; **6.** $r = -0.7324$, $r' = -0.9226$. Conclusion: prices lag behind production; **7.** $r = 0.9552$; **8.** $r = -0.4839$.

Page 266; Section 4.

1. $r = 0.7884$; **2.** $r = 0.8760$. Based on a division of the ranges into 15 and 13 intervals; $r = 0.8807$ by direct computation. **3.** $r_{ab} = 0.782$, $r_{bc} = 0.587$; **4.** $r = 0.8551$.

Page 276; Section 5.

1. $y = -6.597x + 100.82$, $y = -138.4x + 528.3$; **2.** $y = 2.667x - 8.850$.

Page 281; Section 6.

1. 0.0060; **2.** $r = 0.6755 \pm 0.0168$, a priori value = 0.6667; **3.** $\theta = 1°\ 46'\ 30''$, $\theta = 2°\ 55'\ 30''$; **4.** $\theta = 33°\ 41'\ 30''$; **5.** 0.9452; **6.** 0.8538.

ANSWERS TO PROBLEMS

Page 287; Section 8.

1. $r = -.4115$; **2.** $\eta_{yx} = -.8805$, $\eta_{xy} = -.6111$; $204(\eta^2 - r^2) = 115.22$ and 41.64; **3.** $r = 0.8140$, $\eta_{yx} = 0.8516$, $\eta_{xy} = 0.8352$; $120(\eta^2 - r^2) = 7.52$ and 4.19.

CHAPTER XI.

Page 297; Section 4.

2. $-.2896$.

Page 301; Section 7.

1. $\sigma_{1\cdot 2} = 9.2312$, $\sigma_{1\cdot 3} = 13.4419$, $\sigma_{2\cdot 3} = 17.9026$, $\sigma_{2\cdot 1} = 11.2587$, $\sigma_{3\cdot 1} = 5.5739$, $\sigma_{3\cdot 2} = 6.0867$; **2.** $X_1 = .6173 X_2 + .8471 X_3 + 26.3891$; **3.** P.E. of est. of $X_1 = \pm 5.1642$; **5.** $R_{1(23)} = .8541$, $R_{2(13)} = .8232$, $R_{3(12)} = .5620$; **6.** $R_{1(23)} = .9701$, P. E. of est. of $X_1 = \pm 20.4108$; $R_{2(13)} = .9548$, P. E. of est. of $X_2 = \pm 1.4754$.

Page 305; Section 9.

1. $X_3 = .2470 X_1 + 2026.7233 X_2 - .0200 X_4 - 26.6880$; **2.** $R_{2(134)} = .9444$, P. E. of est. of $X_2 = \pm .0006$; **3.** .0167, .0315, .0174, .0021.

CHAPTER XII

Page 317; Section 2.

2. $E = -.958$; **3.** $E = .930$; **4.** $E = -.213$; **6.** $E = -.268$; **7.** $E = -.583$.

Page 321; Section 3.

1. $L = 3.71$, $C = 60.76$; **2.** $L = 6.74$, $C = 34.6$.

Page 328; Section 4.

1. 24, 50, 35, 10, 1; **2.** 23, 86, 118, 61; **3.** $A = 1.283$, $\sigma^2 = .8197$; **4.** $A = 1.75 +$, $\sigma^2 = .770$; **5.** $E_0 = 1$, $E_1 = 13/12$, $E_2 = 3/8$, $E_3 = 1/24$; $x_1 = 1/2$, $x_2 = 1/3$, $x_3 = 1/4$.

Page 331; Section 5.

1. $L = 3.61$, $C = 25.50$; **2.** $L = 3.65$. $C = 59.67$.

APPENDIX II

Page 347; Section 3.

1. $-5/3 \log 3 - 3/2 \log 5 - 5/6 \log 7$; **2.** $-2/3 (\log 2 + \log 3 + \log 5 - \log 7)$; **3.** $5/2 \log 2 + \log 3 + 2/3 \log 5 + \log 7$; **4.** $-2/5 \log 3 + 5/6 \log 5 - 1/2 \log 7 + 3/2 \log 11$; **5.** $-5/6 \log 2 - 1/2 \log 3 - 2/3 \log 13$; **6.** $-.7304$; **7.** 1.3358; **8.** 2.6594; **9.** .8546; **10.** $-.0970$; **12.** 2; **13.** 1.4651; **14.** 2.3223; **15.** 2.25, 3.25; **16.** 6.645; **17.** 4.755; **18.** 4.82831; **19.** 1,000; **20.** 1.8129.

Page 351; Section 4.

1. 0.49715; **2.** 1.21143; **3.** 0.43429; **4.** 2.74960; **5.** 9.50285 — 10; **6.** 7.90974 — 10; **7.** 0.36222; **8.** 9.09149 — 10; **9.** 9.63778 — 10; **10.** 8.88389 — 10; **11.** 9.76134 — 10; **12.** 3.53699; **13.** 31.006; **14.** .03657; **15.** .80599; **16.** .0000013659; **17.** 974.09; **18.** 26553.4; **19.** 3.1623; **20.** .0014874; **21.** .010266; **22.** 1.3235.

Page 353; Section 4.

1. 637.89; **2.** 1.0205; **3.** 9.0923; **4.** .00028375; **5.** 116.10— **6.** 3.9456; **7.** 1.0873; **8.** .85227; **9.** 9.95; **10.** .(36 zeros)3005; **11.** .019837; **12.** 1005.9.

Page 356; Section 5.

1. 2.7183, 1.1052, .9048; **2.** .1959, .1177; **3.** 5.1039, 8.4994.

Page 358; Section 6.

1. .0953, .0198; **2.** .02, .01984, .01982, .019802; **3.** 1.0958; **6.** .5938.

INDEX OF NAMES

Adrian, R., 250n.
Amoroso, Luigi, 8.

Bacon, N. T., 337.
Bacon, Sir Francis, 2.
Bayes, T., 3.
Bean, L. H., 8.
Bercaw, Louise O., 7n.
Bernoulli, Daniel, 3, 163.
Bernoulli, Jakob, 3, 167.
Beveridge, Sir William, 39.
Blakeman, J., 286.
Bowley, A. L., 7, 18n.
Brahe, Tycho, 2.
Bravais, A., 250n.
Briggs, Henry, 345n.
Brunt, D., 276n.
Burns, A. F., 7.

Cardano, G., 3.
Charlier, C. V. L., 4, 15n, 183, 311.
Chrystal, G., 3, 99, 178.
Cowles, Alfred III, 136n.
Cournot, A. A., 9, Appendix I (336)
Czuber, E., 4, 162.

Darwin, Charles Robert, 9.
Davis, H. T., 31n, 323.
Day, E. E., 112n.
Darbishire, A. D., 281.
De Moivre, A., 3, 178.
De Morgan, A., 4, 160.
Descartes, René, 20.

Edgeworth, F. Y., 3, 5, 9, 101, 120.
Elderton, W. P., 81n, 204, 311.
Euler, L., 3, 137.
Ezekiel, Mordecai, 8.

Fisher, Arne, 178, 183, 312, 329.
Fisher, I., 7, 92n, 101, 111n, 124n, 255n, 340.
Fisher, R. A., 143, 276n.
Fourier, J. B. J., 138.
Frisch, R., 7, 309.
Funkhouser, H. G., 120n.

Galton, Sir Francis, 4, 120, 169, 250n.
Gauss, K. F., 4, 187, 250n.
Glover, J. W., 233, 234.
Goursat, E., 85n.
Gram, J. P., 183, 311.
Graunt, Captain John, 3.

Hollander, Jacob H., 7n.
Hedrick, E. R., 85n.
Hicks, J. R., 338.

Hotelling, H., 124n, 241n, 309.

Jevons, H. Stanley, 337n.
Jevons, H. Winefrid, 337n.
Jevons, W. S., 1, 5, 8, 9, 39, 101, 120, Appendix I (337).
Jones, D. C., 311.
Juglar, Clement, 119.

Kapteyn, J. C., 9.
Kelley, T. L., 276n.
Kepler, Johannes, 2, 9.
Keynes, J. M., 8, 340n, 341.
Kimball, H. H., 10n.
King, W. I., 7.
Kirkham, W. J., 207.
Koch, Robert, 9.
Kuznets, S. S., 7, 127n, 142, 241n, 252.

Lacy, Mary G., 7n.
Lagrange, J. L., 3, 137n.
Laplace, Pierre Simon de, 3, 9, 250n.
Lescisin, Anne M., 204.
Lexis, W., 4.
Lotka, A. J., 241n.

Malthus, T. R., 340.
Marschak, Jakob, 8.
Marshall, Alfred, 5, 336.
Marvin, C. F., 10n.
Maxwell, James Clerk, 9, 10, 249.
Mendel, Gregor Johann, 9.
Mill, John Stuart, 5, 337.
Mills, Frederick C., 71n, 185n.
Milne-Thomson, L. M., 365.
Miner, J. R., 292, 292n.
Mitchell, Wesley C., 4n, 101n, 119n, 120n.
Moore, H. L., 8, 39, 121.

Napier, John, 344.
Newton, Sir Isaac, 2, 9.
Norton, J. P., 120.

Pareto, Vilfredo, 5, 7, 8, 9, 220n, Appendix III (339).
Pascal, B., 32n.
Pasteur, Louis, 9.
Pearl, Raymond, 60, 240n, 241, 241n, 242, 244, 281.
Pearson, F. A., 8, 254, 254n, 256.
Pearson, Karl, 4, 88, 120, 183, 203, 283, 311, 313n.
Persons, Warren M., 4n, 6n, 121.
Petty, Sir William, 3, 4.
Pigou, A. C., 8, 220.

Plana, G. A. A., 250n.
Playfair, William, 120
Poincaré, H., 4.
Poisson, S. D., 3, 332.
Poynting, J. H., 120.
Quesnay, 6.
Quetelet, L. A. J., 2, 3.

Reed, L. J., 240n, 241, 241n, 242.
Rider, P. R., x.
Rietz, H. L., x, 198, 287n.
Ricardo, D., 6.
Robinson, G., 138, 140, 140n, 239n, 283n.
Roos, C. F., 8, 37n, 40n, 133n, 136n.
Roy, René, 336.

Sasuly, Max, 228n, 365.
Scates, D. A., 85n.
Schultz, H., 7, 300.
Schuster, Sir Arthur, 138, 140, 143, 143n.
Schumpeter, Joseph A., 1, 6n.
Sheppard, W. F., 82.
Shewhart, W. A., x, 210.
Sismondi, J. C. L. de, 119.
Snyder, Carl, 7.
Spearman, C., 280n.
Staehle, Hans, 8.

Starr, George, 247n.
Stirling, J., 178.
Sturges, H. A., 17.
Süssmilch, J. P., 3.
Tchebycheff, P. L., 3.
Thiele, T. N., 183, 311.
Tinbergen, J., 8.
Todhunter, I., 4, 4n.

Vinci, Felice, 8.
von Bortkewitsch, L., 332.
von Szeliski, Victor, 225.

Wagemann, E., 4.
Walker, Helen, 4n, 15n, 120n, 250n.
Walras, A. A., 338.
Walras, M. E. L., 9, Appendix III (337).
Walsh, C. M., 101.
Warren, G. F., 8, 254, 254n, 256.
Waugh, F. V., 7.
Westergaard, H., 4, 183.
Whittaker, E. T., 138, 140, 140n, 178, 239n, 283n.
Whitworth, W. A., 162.
Wicksell, K., 183.
Wilson, E. B., 143n.
Working, E. J., 8.
Yule, G. U., 2, 136n.

INDEX OF SUBJECTS

Abscissa, definition of, 21.
Accuracy of estimate, 300.
Addition of probabilities, 153.
Areas, calculation of, 362.
Arithmetic mean, 66, 67-73, 97; transformation of, 71; of binomial distribution, 171-172; Bernoulli, 72, 193; probable error of, 195; in theory of errors, 209.
Automobile, production, 47, 93, 225, 244-247; registration, 238; accidents, 315-316, 330.
Averages, Chap. III.

Bank clearings, 262; deviations from trend of, 186; average, 238.
Bank suspensions, 117, 319.
Bernoulli deviation, Chap. VII, 79, 193.
Bernoulli frequency distribution, (See binomial frequencies).
Bernoulli mean, Chap. VII, 72, 193.
Bonds, prices of, 253; yields of, 262.
Bias, definition of, 108.
Bills discounted, 288.
Bi-modal distributions, 87.
Binomial coefficients, 30-32; tables of, 31, 32.
Binomial (or Bernoulli) frequencies, Chap. VII, 29-30, 313-314, 320, 322-329.
Binomial series, 33.
Binomial theorem, 29-34.
Bi-quadratic curve, 213-214.
Briggsian logarithms, 345.
Business cycles, Chap. V; history of, 119-121; of commodity prices, 70-71, 185.

Capitalization, ratio of net income to, 253.
Cartesian coordinates, 21.
Chain index numbers, 112.
Characteristic, 348; definition of, 349.
Charlier coefficient of disturbancy, 319-321.
Chi squared function, 202-206.
Circular test for index numbers, 112-113.
Classification of statistical data, 14.
Class interval, 16; determination of size of, 16-17.
Class mark, 16.
Coefficient of variability, 76; probable error of, 196.
Coin tossing, frequencies in, 207, 209.

Combinations, 148-150.
Commercial failures, 319.
Commercial paper rates, 15, 18, 66, 204-205, 253, 262, 288, 333.
Commodity prices, 28, 70-71, 92, 93, 185, 189, 224, 259, 262.
Common logarithms, 345.
Compound interest curve, 57.
Convergence of series, 33.
Correction for seasonal variation, 129-132.
Correction for secular trend, 129-132.
Correlation, Chaps. X and XI, 38-42; of time series, 132-137; coefficient of, 133, 250, 263-266, 276-281; coefficients of first order, 292-294; of second order, 294-297; of multiple correlation, 301-304; lag, 134-135; linear, 250, 260; non-linear, 250, 260, 283-288; negative, 250; rank, 279-280; surface of, 282-283; ratio, 283-288; multiple and partial, 289-310; multiple for three variables, 301-302; for four variables, 303-304; in general, 305-308.
Correlation coefficient, 133, 250; calculation of, 263-266; properties of, 276-281; probable error of, 276; relation to common causes, 276-278; magnitude of, 278-279; of rank correlation, 279-280; of multiple correlation for three variables, 301-302; for four variables, 303-304.
Correlation ratio, 283-288; probable error test of, 286-287.
Correlation surface, 282, 283.
Correlation table, 257-262.
Cost of living, index of, 137, 253.
Cotton, production and prices of, 257.
Cowles Commission index of investment experience, 145.
Crop prices, index numbers of, 102.
Crop production, index numbers of, 103.
Crossed cross-weight aggregative index number, 106.
Cubic curve, 213-214.
Cumulative frequency curves, (See ogives).
Curve fitting, Chap. IX; problem of, 211; Gram-Charlier theory of, 183; Pearson method of, 183.
Curve of error, (See normal probability function), 187.
Curve of growth, 57.

—421—

Deciles, 84.
Dependence, linear, 309-310.
Deviation, definition of, 74; mean or average, 76.
Differences, definition of, 212.
Disturbancy, Charlier coefficient of, 319-321.
Divergence of series, 33.
Dow-Jones stock price averages, 19, 68-69, 132, 133-135, 262, 269, 293, 302; periodogram of, 144-145.
Duration of play, problem of, 164.

Earning capacity, 224, 230-231.
Edgeworth-Marshall aggregative index number, 106.
Eggs, data on price of, 39, 41, 130-131; receipt of, 41.
Electric power production, 123.
Employment, 42, 259, 265; of women, 197-198.
Errors, theory of, 206-210; curve of, (See normal probability function).
Estimate, accuracy of, 300; probable error of, 300, 301, 303.
Euler's number, 99, 358.
Excess, 312-319.
Exchange rate, franc-dollar, 269; dollar-yen, 271.
Exponential curve, 56-60, 213-214; fitting to date of, 58-60, 233-338.
Exponential function, 56-60, Table II; of Poisson, 332.
Exponents, laws of, 343-344.
Exports, national, 24-25.

Factor reversal test, 109.
Farm products, price index of, 256.
Farms, size of, 29.
Fisher's ideal index number, (See ideal index number).
Forecasting, problem of, 136; random, 69.
Freight car loadings, data of, 121; trend of, 122; seasonal index numbers of, 127; corrected for seasonal variation and secular trend, 129-130; periodogram of, 141-144.
Freight, revenue, 41.
Frequency distributions, Chaps. VII and VIII, 14, 15-19; graphical representation of, 19-29; homograde, 14-15; heterograde, 14-15; ogives of, 23-27; binomial (or Bernoulli), 29-30, 313-314, 320, 322-329; bimodal, 87; Poisson, 313-314, 320, 322-329; Lexis, 313-314, 320, 322-329; subnormal, 313-314, 320, 322-329; hypernormal, 313-314, 320, 322-329; of non-uniform items, 329-331.
Function, definition of, 35; periodic, 36; gamma, 31; graphical representation of, 42-47; linear, 47-51; parabolic, 52-56; exponential, 56-60, 355-356, Table II; skew-normal probability, 61-63; normal probability, Chaps. VII and VIII, 168, Tables VI and VII; chi squared, 203-206, Table VIII; logarithmic, 356-358, Table I; squares, Table III; square roots, Table IV; reciprocals, Table V.

Galton quincunx, 169-170.
Gamma function, 31; Sterling's approximation for, 177-178.
Gaussian curve of error, (See normal probability function).
Geometric mean, 66, 89-93, 97.
Gold, index of world's stock, 254; ratio to production, 254.
Goodness of fit, 202-205.
Government expenditures, 70.
Government receipts, 70.
Gram-Charlier method of curve fitting, 183, 311.

Harmonic aggregative index number, 106.
Harmonic analysis, 137-145; significance of, 143.
Harmonic mean, 66, 93-96, 97.
Heterograde distributions, definition of, 14-15; Sheppard's adjustments of moments of, 82.
Histogram, 22.
Homograde distributions, definition of, 14-15.
Hypernormal frequency distributions, 313-314, 320, 322-329.

Ideal index number, 106, 109, 110, 111, 113.
Imaginary number, definition of, 43.
Imports, national, 24-25, 271.
Income, national, 20, 27, 70, 92, 124, 221-223, 225, 255.
Independent events, probability of, 152; examples illustrating, 154-157.
Index law, 343.
Index numbers, Chap. IV, (See price index numbers), history of, 100-101, time reversal test for, 108; factor reversal test for, 109; chain of, 112; circular test for, 112-113; bases for, 112-114; weighting systems for, 115-116.
Industrial production, 133-135, 255, 258, 264.
Inhibition effect in building, 37.
Interpolation, Appendix III, 36, 188, 350; inverse, 361.
Inverse interpolation, 361.
Inverse probability, 163-165.

INDEX OF SUBJECTS

Investment experience, Cowles Commission index of, 145; other than U. S. securities, 253.
Kurtosis, 312-319.

Lag correlation, 134-135.
Large numbers, law of, 157-159.
Law of large numbers, 157-159.
Law of small numbers, 331-333.
Least squares, method of, 48, 206-210; in curve fitting, 211, 215-225.
Lexis distributions, 313-314, 320, 322-329.
Lexis ratio, 319-321.
Life insurance, growth of, 118.
Linear correlation, (See correlation).
Linear dependence, 309-310.
Logarithmic curve, 213-214.
Logarithmic paper, 223, 237.
Logarithms, Appendix II; definition of, 343; common (Briggsian), 345; natural, 345; laws of, 345-346; change of base of, 346; calculation by, 348-353; characteristic of, 348-349; mantissa of, 348-349, Table I.
Logistic curve, 213-214; fitting to data of, 240-248.
Loans and discounts, 262.
Lorenz curves, 26-28.

Mantissa, 348; definition of, 349.
Mathematical expectation, 160-162.
Median, 66, 83-86.
Metal and metal products, prices of, 262.
Minutes of daylight, 36.
Mode, 66, 86-89; of binomial distribution, 175-177.
Moments, 79-83; continuous, 79; Sheppard's adjustments of, 81-83; probable errors of second and third, 196; in curve fitting, 211, 239-240.
Moral expectation, 161-162.
Multiple correlation, Chap. XI; for three variables, 301-302; for four variables, 303-304; in general, 305-308.
Multiplication of probabilities, 152.
Mutually exclusive events, probability of, 153; examples illustrating, 154-157.

Napier's number, 345.
National exports and imports, 24-25, 271.
National income, 20, 27, 70, 92, 124, 221-223, 225.
Natural logarithms, 345.
Non-linear correlation, 250, 260, 283-288.
Non-linear regression, 283-288.
Normal equations, 49, 218.

Normal probability function, Chaps. VII and VIII, 61-63, 168; area under, 188-191.

Ogives, 23-27.
Ordinate, definition of, 21.
Orthogonal functions, 183.

Parabola, 52-56, 213-214; maximum and minimum of, 52-53; x-intercepts of, 53; fitting to data of, 54-55, 229-232.
Parabolic curve, 213-214; fitting to data of, 220-224; law of Pareto as, 220.
Pareto, law of, 220-225.
Partial correlation, Chap. XI, 291-294.
Partial correlation coefficients of first order, 292-294; of second order, 294-297.
Partial regression equations, 297-300.
Pascal's triangle, 32.
Pearson chi test, 202-206.
Pearson method of curve fitting, 183, 311.
Pearson probability, 203.
Percentiles, 84.
Periodogram, 138-139.
Permutations, 148-150.
Pig Iron, price of, 45-46; production of, 258, 264, 293-302.
Pneumatic casings, production and shipping of, 252.
Point of inflection, 241.
Poisson-Bortkewitsch law of small numbers, 331-333.
Poisson distributions, 313-314, 320, 322-329.
Poisson's exponential function, 332.
Polynomials, general, 213-214; curve fitting of, 226-228.
Population, growth of, 37-38, 60, 91, 238, 241-242; sex ratio in, 198.
Price index numbers, problem of, 101-105; formulas for, 105-106; time reversal test for, 108; factor reversal test for, 109; chain of, 112; circular test for, 112-113; wholesale commodity, 116.
Prices, retail food, 93; commodity, 28, 92, 116, 185, 189, 224, 259, 262; egg, 39, 41, 130-131; wholesale, 136, 254, 256, 265; of crops, 102; of pig iron, 45-46; Bradstreets index of general, 185; of bonds, 253; of farm products, 256; of cotton, 257; of metal and metal products, 262; general, 262.
Probability, Chap. VI; definition of, 146; joint, 152; of independent events, 152; of mutually exclusive

events, 153; in repeated trials, 159; inverse, 163-165; probable error of, 195; Pearson, 203.
Probable error, Chap. VIII; definition of, 190; applied to sampling, 191-199; of various constants, 195-196; examples of use of, 196-198; derivation for the mean, 199-202; of correlation coefficient, 276; in testing correlation ratio, 286-287; of estimate, 300, 301, 303; of partial correlation coefficients, 305.
Production, index of world's, 254.
Public utilities, net earnings of, 128.
Purchasing power of the dollar, 137.

Quadratic mean, (See root-mean-square).
Quartic curve, 213-214.
Quartiles, 84.
Quintic curve, 213.

Railroad bonds, 87.
Rail stock prices, 315-316.
Rank correlation, 279-280.
Ratio of investments, 18-19.
Reciprocals, Table V.
Regression curves, 260-261; non-linear, 283; partial, 297-300.
Regression lines, 271-276.
Relative magnitude of averages, 96-99.
Root-mean-square, 66, 73-78, 97.

St. Petersburg paradox, 160-161.
Sampling, the problem of, Chap. VIII, 11.
Scatter diagram, 260.
Seasonal variation, 37, 124-128; index numbers of, 128; correction for, 129-132.
Secular trend, 121-124; correction for, 129-132.
Semi-invariants of Thiele, 311.
Septimic curve, 213.
Series, binomial, 33; convergence of, 33; divergence of, 33; exponential, 355; logarithmic, 356-357; types of statistical, Chap. XII.
Sextic curve, 213.
Sheppard's adjustments of moments, 81-83.
Simple aggregative index number, 105.
Skewness, 88-89, 181; probable error of, 196, 312.
Skew-normal probability curve, 61-63; derivation of, 178-180; application of, 181-184.
Sources of statistical data, 11-14.
Square roots, Table IV.
Squares, Table III.
Standard deviation, 74; transformation of, 78; of binomial distribution, 172-174; Bernoulli, 79, 193; probable error of, 195.
Statistical data, sources of, 11-14; classification of, 14.
Statistical series, types of, Chap. XII.
Statistics, origins of, 2-4; definition of, 2; in economics, 4-9; scope of, 9-10; mathematical theory of, 10-11; types of series in, Chap. XII.
Stirling's formula, 177-178.
Steel, new orders of fabricated, 128; earnings per share, 251.
Stock dividends, 267-268.
Stock earnings, 251.
Stock price averages, 19, 68-69, 130, 132, 133-135, 262, 267-268, 269, 317-318.
Stock sales, 236-237, 262, 293, 302.
Straight line, 47-51, 212-214; fitting to data of, 218-220, 229; 47-51; slope of, 47.
Subnormal frequency distributions, 313-314, 320, 322-329.

Testimony, problem of, 164.
Time money rates, 262.
Time reversal test, 108.
Time series, Chap. V; secular trend of, 121-124; seasonal variation of, 124-128; correlation of, 132-137; harmonic analysis of, 137-145.
Transformation of arithmetic mean, 71; of standard deviation, 78.
Translation of axes, 63-65.

Variability, coefficient of, 76; probable error of, 196.

Wage earners, 117.
Wage level, manufacturing industries, 136.
Wages, 93; of women, 16.
Walsh's cross-weight aggregative index number, 106.
Weighted aggregative index number, 106.
Wheat, yield of, 123, 270, 290; area planted, 270, 290.
Wholesale prices, 136, 254, 265; of crops, 102; of commodities, 92, 116.